Until the Last Man Comes Home

Until the Last Man Comes Home

POWS, MIAS, AND THE

UNENDING VIETNAM WAR

Michael J. Allen

THE UNIVERSITY OF

NORTH CAROLINA PRESS

Chapel Hill

© 2009

THE UNIVERSITY OF NORTH CAROLINA PRESS

ALL RIGHTS RESERVED

Portions of chapter 1 originally appeared in "'Help Us Tell the Truth about Vietnam': POW/MIA Politics and the End of the American War," in *Making Sense of the Vietnam Wars: Local, National, and Transnational Perspectives*, ed. by Mark Philip Bradley and Marilyn B. Young (New York: Oxford University Press, 2008). Reprinted with permission.

Designed by Courtney Leigh Baker

Set in Whitman by Tseng Information Systems, Inc.

Manufactured in the United States of America

The paper in this book meets the guidelines for permanence and durability of the Committee on Production Guidelines for Book Longevity of the Council on Library Resources.

The University of North Carolina Press has been a member of the Green Press Initiative since 2003.

Library of Congress Cataloging-in-Publication Data

Allen, Michael J. (Michael Joe), 1974–

Until the last man comes home : POWs, MIAs, and the unending Vietnam War / Michael J. Allen.

  p. cm.

Includes bibliographical references and index.

ISBN 978-0-8078-3261-5 (cloth : alk. paper)

1. Vietnam War, 1961–1975—Prisoners and prisons, North Vietnamese. 2. Prisoners of war—United States. 3. Political activists—United States. 4. Vietnam War, 1961–1975—Missing in action—United States. 5. Vietnam War, 1961–1975—Influence. 6. Vietnam War, 1961–1975—Political aspects. 7. United States—Relations—Vietnam. 8. Vietnam—Relations—United States. 9. United States—Politics and government—1945–1989. 10. United States—Politics and government—1989– I. Title.

  DS559.4.A44 2009

  959.704'37—dc22

  2009002894

13 12 11 10 09   5 4 3 2 1

For Julie Ann

But if the cause be not good, the king himself hath a heavy reckoning to make, when all those legs and arms and heads, chopped off in battle, shall join together at the latter day and cry all, "We died at such a place."—SHAKESPEARE, *HENRY V*

CONTENTS

Abbreviations xi

INTRODUCTION. *The Politics of Loss* 1

1. GO PUBLIC
The Construction of Loss 13

2. FOR US THE WAR STILL GOES ON
The Limits of Homecoming 63

3. AS IT HAS IN THE PAST
A Short History of Oblivion 101

4. FULLEST POSSIBLE ACCOUNTING
The Persistence of the Past 137

5. THE WILDERNESS YEARS
Life after Death 179

6. HIGHEST NATIONAL PRIORITY
Resurrection and Retribution 215

7. NOT TO CLOSE THE DOOR, BUT TO OPEN IT

The Ambiguity of Recovery 250

CONCLUSION. *This Thing Has Consumed*
American Politics for Years 291

Notes 307

Bibliography 393

Acknowledgments 411

Index 413

ILLUSTRATIONS

North Vietnamese stamp commemorating
the capture of American POWs   23

President Richard Nixon welcomes League
wives and mothers to the White House   36

VFW magazine cover warning of POW abandonment   51

Life magazine cover featuring antiwar
POW wife Valerie Kushner   56

Homecoming POWs welcomed at
Camp Pendleton, California   65

Arthur Burer and Nancy Burer embrace
after seven years apart   73

President Richard Nixon greets
returning POW John McCain   82

Bodies of Confederate dead gathered for burial   109

An unburied Confederate lies next to the
marked grave of a Union soldier   114

Crowd observes the burial of the
Unknown Soldier from World War I   122

A bugler blows taps at Margraten
Military Cemetery in World War II 126

John Fischetti cartoon depicting a Chinese soldier
atop the grave of a missing American 133

Douglas Borgstedt cartoon suggesting that missing
Americans prevent closure after Vietnam 147

League chairman E. C. Mills places a POW/MIA
lapel pin on President Gerald Ford 161

American remains return to Travis Air Force Base in 1977 185

Iran hostage crisis imagery recalls
American captivity in Vietnam 204

Senate Select Committee graph illustrates
the growth in "unaccounted for" Americans in 1980 210

President Ronald Reagan addresses the League
on the tenth anniversary of the Paris agreement 216

Soldier of Fortune magazine devotes an
entire issue to the POW/MIA issue in 1983 224

Ann Mills Griffiths briefs President Ronald Reagan
and his national security advisers 235

President Ronald Reagan presides over the burial
of an Unknown Soldier from the Vietnam War 240

Bamboo Connection cartoon shows American POWs left behind 245

President Bill Clinton observes a crash site excavation 251

Vietnamese officials present Senator John Kerry
with Senator John McCain's flight helmet 276

President George Bush confronts League critics 280

President Bill Clinton normalizes relations with Vietnam 288

ABBREVIATIONS

The following abbreviations appear in the text.

CILHI	Central Identification Laboratory — Hawaii
COLIAFAM	Committee of Liaison with Families of Servicemen Detained in North Vietnam
DIA	Defense Intelligence Agency
DPMO	Defense Prisoner of War/ Missing in Action Office
DRV	Democratic Republic of Vietnam
IAG	Interagency Group on POW/MIAs
ICRC	International Committee of the Red Cross
JCRC	Joint Casualty Resolution Center
JPRC	Joint Personnel Recovery Center
JTF-FA	Joint Task Force — Full Accounting
KIA/BNR	Killed In Action/Body Not Recovered
NLF	National Liberation Front
NSC	National Security Council
PRG	Provisional Revolutionary Government
RVN	Republic of Vietnam
SOP	Support Our POW/MIAs
UN	United Nations
USSDP	Uniformed Services Savings Deposit Program

VFW   Veterans of Foreign Wars

VIVA   Victory in Vietnam Association/
Voices in Vital America

VVAW   Vietnam Veterans against the War

Until the Last Man Comes Home

Introduction

The Politics of Loss

On 22 September 1992, former secretary of state Henry Kissinger appeared before the Senate Select Committee on POW/MIA Affairs to rebut charges that he and President Richard Nixon had abandoned American captives at the end of the Vietnam War. "That allegation is a flat-out lie," Kissinger objected. "What has happened to this country that a congressional committee could be asked to inquire whether any American official of whatever administration would fail to move heaven and earth to fight for the release of American POWs and for an accounting of the missing? Can anyone seriously believe that any honorable public official would neglect America's servicemen, and especially those who had suffered so much for their country, or, even worse, arrange for a conspiracy to obscure the fate of the prisoners left behind?"[1]

These questions warrant more sober consideration than scholars have yet shown them. For despite Kissinger's attempt to dismiss such ideas as absurd, this book will show that belief in POW/MIA abandonment was so serious and widespread as to alter U.S. politics and foreign policy over four decades. Kissinger was, after all, appearing before some of the Senate's leading policymakers and savviest politicians to dispute claims that Americans were left behind in Vietnam. And the ferocity of his response, as he accused committee chairman John Kerry of "unforgivable libel" and charged Kerry and other antiwar activists with having tied his hands as he negotiated the release of American captives, showed how seriously Kissinger took such claims, as did Kerry's curt reply. "Look, I didn't ask for this job. I'm here because twenty years later this question confounds America."[2]

Had he wished, Kerry could have cited polling data to substantiate his claim. A 1991 *Wall Street Journal*/NBC News poll showed that 69 percent of Americans believed that their countrymen were being held against their will in Indochina, and over half believed that their government was doing too little to rescue them.[3] He could have pointed to President George Bush's July 1992 address to the National League of Families of American Prisoners and Missing in Southeast Asia, which disintegrated into a shouting match after audience members interrupted his remarks with chants of "No more lies! Tell the truth!"[4] He could have discussed dozens of congressional hearings on POWs and MIAs dating to 1969, or efforts of the House Select Committee on Missing Persons in Southeast Asia in 1975–76 and the 1977 Presidential Commission on Americans Missing and Unaccounted for in Southeast Asia (widely known as the Woodcock Commision), all of which failed to resolve questions about the fate of the missing.[5] He could have brought up the diplomatic and economic embargo that Kissinger imposed on Vietnam in 1975 for its alleged failure to account for missing Americans, policies still in place when Kissinger came before the Select Committee seventeen years later, ostensibly for the same reason.

He could have mentioned all this and more, but there was no need. Despite Kissinger's rhetorical naiveté, he knew as well as anyone how politically charged the issue was from his long and bitter history with the POW/MIA lobby. Still, there were legitimate reasons for Kissinger's bewilderment. The degree of concern expressed over imprisoned and missing Americans during and after the Vietnam War was unprecedented, despite the fact that their numbers were modest by historical standards. The 2,500 Americans who failed to return from the war, less than 5 percent of all Americans killed in the conflict, paled in comparison to the 170,000 Union troops, nearly half of all Union dead, left unrecovered or unidentified in the Civil War. One-fifth of all Americans killed in World War II — over 78,000 — were never found and 8,500 more were never identified. More than 8,000 Americans are still missing from the Korean War, nearly a quarter of American losses.[6] Even relatively brief American military engagements in the Mexican War and the First World War left greater numbers missing than America's longest war, particularly when measured against smaller populations.[7]

And while each of these wars was followed by attempts to find, identify, and bury the dead, nothing so extensive as the post-Vietnam accounting effort had ever been attempted in the history of warfare. When Kissinger came before the Kerry committee, that effort was entering its third decade, involved hundreds of Department of Defense personnel, and consumed over $100 million annually.[8] Presidents Ronald Reagan and George Bush had declared "the fullest possible accounting" for missing Americans to be "the highest national priority," a commitment Bill Clinton reiterated when he became president, and the fate of these men had defined U.S.-Vietnam relations since the war's end. "There is no military mission more relentless than the United States' hunt for its missing soldiers in Indochina," observed the *New York Times* in a 2002 article that described one site in Laos excavated repeatedly over many years and at great expense in order to recover a single tooth denture.[9] Today that hunt continues, though in recent years it has come to include missing casualties from earlier conflicts, as the search for the Vietnam missing has renewed interest in their long-neglected forebears.[10]

If fewer Americans were missing after the Vietnam War than after earlier wars, and the U.S. government went to greater lengths than ever to recover them, how was it that Kissinger and dozens of other senior government officials were being called before Congress to answer charges that they had abandoned American servicemen in Southeast Asia? What caused so many Americans to suspect that their leaders had betrayed these men and to allege an ongoing conspiracy to conceal that fact? Where did these ideas come from, why did they persist, and how did they shape U.S. politics and policy after the Vietnam War?

"Because in Vietnam we lost!" answered MIA activist Donna Long.[11] Her response is the starting point for addressing these questions. As this book will show, the ordeal of captivity during the war and the inability to recover missing Americans at its end became the dominant means through which millions of Americans addressed their nation's defeat in Vietnam. Because most captive and missing Americans were well-educated, white, middle-class airmen that civilians came to know more intimately than other populations fighting in Vietnam, their loss came particularly hard to Americans, many of whom lacked more direct connections to the war. And because the circumstances of their loss — most were shot down or crashed over enemy territory, often in forbidding environments at high rates of speed — made their survival uncertain and their recovery difficult, efforts to retrieve these men often proved futile. After the release of 591 American prisoners following the Paris Agreement in 1973, only one American — Robert Garwood — returned from Vietnam alive, and his 1979 homecoming was decidedly dispiriting, occurring independently of U.S. accounting efforts and resulting in his court-martial conviction for collaborating with the enemy and striking a fellow POW.[12] Despite the unrelenting search, just over 900 Americans have been accounted for through the recovery and identification of remains, roughly one-third of the total missing at war's end.[13]

For many Americans, the inability to recover these men was proof not of their demise but of their betrayal. This conviction had less to do with the facts of their disappearance than with wartime activism that made them and their families the foremost victims or beneficiaries of the nation's military commitment in Vietnam. From its start, opponents of the war publicized their plight to encourage an end to that commitment while its promoters insisted that any lessening of resolve would abandon them to the enemy. As chapter 1 shows, these arguments and those who made them played an important, if complicated, part in the erosion of public support for the war, and in the pace and timing of U.S. withdrawal from Vietnam. But once withdrawal was completed and the last American captives were returned, the idea that those still missing were forsaken persisted as a way to establish the war's costs and assign responsibility for its failures. Talk about lost warriors became a way to talk about a lost war, and the effort to account for them was as much a means to establish accountability for their loss as it was a search for their remains. "We family members are not here beating on your doors because we believe our loved ones are alive," the chairman of the Minnesota League of POW/MIA Families testified before the Senate Select Committee; "we are here because we know the government is lying about them." "You are going to have to account for those men," otherwise "we will always pursue you."[14]

As his admonition suggests, it was the families of the missing, particularly those active in the National League of Families of American Prisoners and Missing in Southeast Asia, who were responsible for the stubborn persistence of the postwar accounting effort. By insisting on a full accounting and refusing to accept anything short of this elastic standard, they exerted intense pressure on U.S. government officials and their Vietnamese counterparts to continue the search indefinitely. Never numbering more than a few thousand members, the League was among the most formidable interest groups in wartime and postwar Washington. Its influence, like that of the POW/MIA population, was a function of symbolism, not size. The League's exclusivity gave it a cultural coherence that a larger group would have lacked, enhancing its appeal to millions of Americans who sympathized with its wounded nationalism and middle-class respectability. As a group dominated by the wives, mothers, siblings, and children of missing men, with its top leadership posts typically occupied by women, the League's power was rooted in gender conventions and popular concerns about the family. By presenting the nation's failure in Vietnam as a private trauma, League families illustrated the costs of defeat in terms that were easily grasped and difficult to refute, giving them unrivaled authority in debates about the war.[15]

Initially, MIA families and their supporters directed their demands and their ire at the Vietnamese. As we will see, Vietnamese communists used American POWs to great effect in their wartime diplomacy. In accusing the enemy of torturing American prisoners during the war and withholding them afterward, League members voiced their sense of injury at the other side's triumph and tried to reverse communist successes through economic sanctions and diplomatic isolation. Unable to disprove League accusations, the Vietnamese were denied billions of dollars in promised reconstruction aid. But as in the war's combat phase, the Vietnamese were more than passive victims, insisting on economic assistance in return for their cooperation in returning American remains. Vietnam never gained the billions Nixon pledged in the Paris agreement, but by the late 1980s its leaders had persuaded U.S. officials to pay steep fees in order to search for remains, including humanitarian aid for victims of the American war. Only after this recognition of each side's war wounds did the former adversaries move toward normalized relations.

For most MIA activists, though, punishing Vietnam was less important than punishing those Americans they blamed for their loss. With mounting ferocity as the war receded in time, the MIA lobby reserved its full fury for domestic opponents. Kissinger and Kerry were near the top of its enemies list, with Kissinger representing the political elites who sent Americans to war only to abandon them, and Kerry representing the antiwar activists alleged to have stabbed them in the back. But they were only symbols of larger populations deemed insufficiently supportive of U.S. forces in Vietnam, and anyone could join their ranks by breaking with League positions. One irony of the POW/MIA issue is that while public officials often seized on it as a means to shape public attitudes toward the war, in so doing they empowered a movement that invariably turned against them. For if the League would not have attained such influence without official support, by war's end its members were profoundly hostile toward the national state and those who served it. Turning the official accounting effort to their own ends, they insisted that the war was not over "until the last man comes home."[16]

Since most missing Americans would never be found, this was less a formula for ultimate victory than a prescription for persistent ideological warfare about the past. Rather than a road to redemption, the accounting effort served as an ever-present reminder of loss, a ritual that focused attention on a small and unrepresentative band of missing Americans and made them into victims rather than perpetrators of the war in Vietnam. Through the search for the missing, families and activists elevated exceptional American casualties over wholesale Vietnamese suffering, and implicated Vietnamese communists, antiwar activists, and U.S. officials in their disappearance. Its utility in asserting their grievances made activists ambivalent about its progress yet reluctant to see it end. U.S. search teams "go to the field and run around," League executive director Ann Mills Griffiths charged in 1993, and return with "a lot of ash and trash."[17] "The bone fragments are crap," the stepmother of one missing man declared. "He could live without these bones."[18] Such views were not universal among MIA families, most of whom welcomed information that resolved the fate of their loved ones, but they were characteristic of those who insisted that the accounting effort continue even as they challenged its legitimacy and turned its limits into a new source of injury.

As the effort to retrieve POWs and MIAs taught some Americans to see themselves as victims of the Vietnam War, it turned other Americans into the guilty parties who victimized them. For it was not the perils of war that threatened captive and missing Americans, according to their advocates, or even a racial and ideological enemy thought to be especially cruel. Such risks were inherent to the nation's Cold War mission and were bearable with proper leadership and resolve. The real threat that endangered the white middle-class volunteers who made up the POW/MIA population came from a feckless government and a faithless citizenry, or so their surrogates claimed. And it was through efforts to liberate these men and to recover their missing comrades that the treachery of their domestic enemies would be revealed and punished. These ideas were not at all obvious, nor easily substantiated by the historical record, and they did not go unchallenged. But through years of repetition and elaboration by League families, backed by a chorus of public officials, media propagandists, and returned POWs, such claims achieved currency in American politics. What proof was required came from the accounting effort. Always ongoing but forever unable to resurrect the proverbial last man, the search for the missing offered inexhaustible evidence of the nation's betrayal of its martyred warriors.

The guilty parties were seldom named with precision. The accounting effort endured because it lent itself to all sorts of Americans aggrieved by the war, including politicians from both parties who sought to capitalize on widespread unhappiness with the war by associating themselves with the POW/MIA cause. Among the surprises of this study is the degree to which opponents of the war engaged in POW/MIA activism, and the extent to which that activism was a vehicle for dissent against the war among populations presumed to support it. Still, POW/MIA politics privileged some Americans over others, granting the families of missing Americans a platform to condemn those they blamed for their loss. If they rarely named names, their contempt for antiwar activists, for government bureaucrats, and for the Vietnamese was unmistakable. And in more subtle ways, the League's insistence on drawing distinctions between those who served and those who did not, and its dramatization of the deadly stakes of that decision, reinforced the notion that white warriors were more deserving than other citizens at the very moment those ideas were being challenged by various reform movements. To those who claimed that martial values, racial arrogance, or patriotic orthodoxy had led the nation astray in Vietnam, POW and MIA families argued the opposite: that decadent and disloyal domestic elements were responsible for the debacle in Vietnam, and accountable for the men lost there.

Such an argument cast critics of the war as enemies within who must be silenced or purged before the nation could return to its proper foundations. One goal of MIA activism was to effect such a result, as when the League insisted that draft evaders not be allowed reentry to the United States until all MIAs were returned. Yet even as it disdained dissent, League rhetoric emphasized, even enhanced, a pained recognition of the war's failures, and trafficked in the darkest doubts about the nation and its leaders. Aside from assertions of the nobility of American servicemen, the League rank and file had no patience for uplifting visions of the Vietnam War, whether they came in the form of healing, forgiveness, and closure or talk of a noble cause. They focused relentlessly on what they had lost and who was to blame, rejecting official entreaties to relinquish their wartime antagonisms. In this they were not so different from liberal activists who spent considerable energy exposing government lies and abuses of power in the postwar period. Both revealed deep dissatisfaction with the war and sought to harness that discontent to a broader critique of the status quo.[19] But whereas those on the left usually moved on to other things once the fighting stopped in South Vietnam, activists in the League nourished conspiracy theories and revenge fantasies that reflected public indignation over the war and directed it against enemies at home and abroad.

Their contempt for the federal government and disdain for the antiwar left, along with their commitment to the Cold War struggle, contributed to Richard Nixon's ascendancy in the late 1960s and helped fuel the conservative resurgence that culminated in Ronald Reagan's presidency in the 1980s. By lionizing patriotic white fliers lost in Vietnam while denigrating the civilian authorities and hand-wringing liberals who were unable to save them, League activists blamed the voices of domestic reform and foreign policy moderation for the nation's failure in Vietnam, even as they held out hope for the restoration of an earlier order through the return of American warriors and military values. Conservative elites made similar arguments throughout the 1970s and 1980s, but the League's unique ability to illustrate the costs of national weakness in personal terms lent it disproportionate influence, influence it used to promote tough-talking Republicans and revanchist policies meant to avenge American defeat. Through a close examination of the League, this study reveals the inner workings of a key component of the conservative movement, and in so doing establishes the degree to which popular outrage over the Vietnam War spurred conservative gains after 1968.

But as this book will also show, the bitter memories propagated by MIA activists made it difficult for conservative leaders to resurrect prewar visions of national unity or to wield military power with the ease and assurance of an earlier generation of Cold Warriors. MIA activists were more interested in fighting the still unfinished Vietnam War than in waging new wars, preferring to attack old foes rather than join them in new military crusades. Time and again activists broke ranks with presidents who first expressed sympathy for their loss only to later assert more anodyne narratives of the war. The break was particularly wrenching with Republicans, who seemed to forgo vows of accountability for past wrongs in favor of national reunion once they took office. That presidents often cited their progress in recovering the remains of the missing as they sought to forge national unity only enflamed the MIA lobby further. When the triumphalism of the Cold War's end threatened to displace memories of defeat in Vietnam, activists made the body recovery process into a new source of victimization, this time at the hands of the Reagan and Bush administrations.

POW and MIA activists were driven not by party politics but by the politics of loss. Rather than seek to define this term in overly precise ways, or to apply partisan labels to its practitioners, this study charts its varied forms and provides examples of its influence on U.S. politics and policy. That influence can be measured in partisan terms, but its greater influence was on popular attitudes toward the American nation. By the end of the Vietnam War, Americans had come to rethink the relationship between the war dead and the nation-state. That relationship emerged during the Civil War and persisted for more than a century, but became strained under the intense and unequal demands of near-constant Cold War conflict. Where once the state's commitment to the war dead gave institutional form and ideological substance to the national community, justifying an expansion of government powers and war-making authority, after Vietnam the state's obligations to and responsibility for the war dead were made an indictment of a government grown too powerful for the good of its people. This was the big idea behind the politics of loss, promoted and popularized through the perpetual search for the missing.

HISTORIANS HAVE YET to recognize the full importance of the POW/MIA issue and have largely overlooked the postwar accounting effort, despite an exhaustive scholarly literature on the Vietnam War. Given their interest in origins and causes, and their reliance on archival records that are slow to open, most historians have focused on the war's roots and early years over its outcome and legacies. With few historians ready to venture into the post-Vietnam era, the study of the war's aftermath has been dominated by journalists and cultural studies scholars accustomed to working without archives.[20] Such work is excellent at revealing the cultural shifts the war unleashed, but much of it remains tangential to historical studies of the Vietnam War, which are dominated by political, military, and diplomatic concerns and tend to focus on high politics and state diplomacy. When cultural studies of the war are referenced in histories of the war it is usually in passing, without grappling with the implications of such work for the subject at hand.

Similarly, cultural studies of the war's legacy have been largely overlooked by political historians, who have done a fine job tracing the decline of midcentury liberalism and revealing the roots of the conservative movement in the 1960s, but too often skip over the Vietnam War and its residues in their rush to reach the Reagan culmination.[21] While numerous scholars have argued that breaking down barriers between cultural approaches to the past and political and diplomatic history is essential to understanding the post-Vietnam era, such an approach has yet to appear with regard to the one issue that dominated all others in the 1970s and 1980s: the Vietnam War.[22]

Despite its insights, much of the current literature leans too heavily on discursive analysis and dips too sparingly into archival evidence to satisfy most historians, much less students and readers curious about flesh-and-blood historical actors. This is not to discount ideas nor to fetishize experience, but only to recognize the limits of focusing on one to the exclusion of the other, an approach that fails to bridge the gap between culture and policy just as surely as more traditional approaches focused on national security elites. Relying on popular culture, public monuments, and political speech for evidence of American responses to the war, the existing literature has too readily assumed that the nation's leaders successfully replaced the war's troubling realities with more pleasing fantasies. Without more attention to textual reception, resistance, and reinvention by more humble historical actors, this approach reduces memory to a function of power rather than something contingent.[23] As a result, cultural studies of post-Vietnam memory often evince a hostility toward the few people who appear in their pages, which prevents a deeper investigation of their motives and mental universe. Anger that the "war lost abroad was subsequently won at home," that the "verdict of history" was reversed "to find the innocent guilty and the guilty innocent," courses through this work, with too many authors excoriating change rather than explaining it.[24]

By drawing on government records, unpublished sources from MIA activist groups, popular reporting, and published scholarship, this study transcends the documentary limits and disciplinary boundaries of earlier work. It reveals the complicated interplay between national leaders and grassroots activists that made the search for missing airmen the dominant means through which Americans recalled and responded to the Vietnam War. At the heart of this interchange was the MIA accounting process, which is similarly at the heart of this book. The search for the missing, particularly the effort to recover their remains, was the one arena where American leaders, MIA activists, and Vietnamese officials consistently came together to struggle over the meaning and memory of the war, a struggle that defined U.S.-Vietnam relations for many years and redefined U.S. politics. In tracing that struggle, I show that neither American elites generally nor conservative nationalists specifically erased harrowing memories of the war. Instead, MIA activists used the search for the missing to focus attention on their own victimization, fostering hostility toward Vietnam and distrust of their own government.

My emphasis on those who actually did the work of remembrance, and my attempt to elucidate their motivations and the consequences of their actions, is meant to contribute to a rethinking of the study of memory and its utility for historians. While memory studies have proliferated in recent years, they have yielded few surprises, usually concluding that what is remembered about the past was constructed by powerful elites in the service of their interests. This study presents a more participatory process in which seemingly marginal figures played leading roles. I consider an emphasis on those who engaged in public remembrance essential to any attempt to employ memory as a useful category of historical analysis. Memory is not "the property of dominant forces in the state," as historians Jay

Winter and Emmanuel Sivan have written, nor "some facet of the mental furniture of a population." It is "constructed through the actions of groups and individuals in the light of day."[25] Their memory work occurs in conversation with other, competing constructions, and those conversations can only be understood through research that attends to as many voices as possible, drawing on the full range of available evidence.[26]

Using memory to highlight not just power but agency, contingency, and multivocality, I seek to better integrate the war's legacy into the changing historiographies of the Vietnam War and recent American politics. Scholarship on the war has undergone dramatic shifts over the last decade as historians have moved beyond their traditional focus on American leaders to include international perspectives and to incorporate internal differences among Americans and among Vietnamese.[27] Likewise, historians have begun supplementing well-established treatments of liberal infighting after World War II with new studies of grassroots conservatism in order to explain conservative dominance since 1968.[28] My treatment of the local, national, and transnational dimensions of POW/MIA activism promises not only to complement the new international history of the war and emerging histories of grassroots conservatism but to integrate them.

By focusing on the central site where Americans debated and defined the meaning of the nation's defeat, this study seeks both depth and breadth. With the exception of chapter 3, which tracks the handling of the war dead from early American history to the brink of the Vietnam War in search of historical perspective and theoretical insight on the Vietnam accounting effort, it is organized chronologically, with each chapter treating high politics, cultural politics, and foreign relations to reveal the legacy of American defeat in Vietnam. The story told here is strange, as readers will soon learn, but for most readers it will also prove instantly familiar. For the politics of loss is still present in American life (perhaps it was always there in more muted forms), and given that the United States is again embroiled in a war with unequal sacrifices and uncertain prospects, it appears likely to endure.

—— . ——

Go Public

The Construction of Loss

On 27 November 1965 the National Liberation Front (NLF) announced the release of Sergeants George Smith and Claude McClure in "response to the friendly sentiments of the American people against the war in South Vietnam," specifically the March on Washington for Peace in Vietnam scheduled for later that day. "With sympathy and support of all strata of American people and progressive people the world over," NLF chairman Nguyen Huu Tho proclaimed in the radio announcement of their release, "we are sure to realize our just goal and win complete victory." With high hopes for the "brilliant success" of the March for Peace, Tho sent Smith and McClure across the border and into Cambodia, ending their two-year ordeal as prisoners of war. Upon reaching the Cambodian capital of Phnom Penh, the returnees were greeted by a cable from the antiwar group Students for a Democratic Society (SDS) telling them "millions of Americans support you. Help us tell the truth about Vietnam."[1]

"I want to tell people the truth about Vietnam," echoed Smith at the pair's first press conference three days later. Asked "how will you do that?" he replied, "I will join the peace movement." "I didn't have any idea what the peace movement really was," he later admitted, "but they had somehow influenced my release, so they sure as hell weren't the bad guys." Neither, he and McClure made clear, were their former captors. "The Vietcong treated us very well," McClure insisted, before adding that "the United States has nothing to gain from the war in Vietnam." "I have known both sides," agreed Smith, "and the war in Vietnam is of no interest to the United States." Military officials dismissed their words as evidence of "brainwashing," a charge McClure denied, before quietly releasing the returnees with less than honorable general discharges. While a repentant McClure eventually returned to the army, though not to Vietnam, Smith denounced the war until the last Americans were withdrawn, publishing his antiwar memoir in 1971.[2]

Front-page news at the time, this episode is now largely forgotten, obscured by the striking outpouring of concern for imprisoned and missing Americans in the war's final years and its aftermath.[3] American POWs and MIAs dominated public discussion of the Vietnam War after 1968 and played a central role in political debates and international diplomacy concerning the war's end. "The wounded, the dying, and the dead went virtually unnoticed," Jonathan Schell recalled in his 1975 history of the war's end, as "attention was focused on the prisoners of war." Along with their missing-in-action counterparts, captive Americans "became the objects of a virtual cult" as "many people were persuaded that the United States was fighting in Vietnam in order to get its prisoners back." According to Schell, and most other observers at the time and since, this preoccupation could be attributed above all to President Richard Nixon. "With the encouragement of the White House," he reported, "a remarkable movement began to grow up around the issue of the prisoners of war." "Following the president's lead, people began to speak as though the North Vietnamese had kidnapped four hundred Americans and the United States had gone to war to retrieve them."[4]

Schell presented no real proof for this analysis; none was needed. After Watergate, Americans were inclined to believe that the disgraced former president was capable of anything. Well before Schell's *The Time of Illusion* appeared, consensus had emerged that Nixon deserved the credit or blame for virtually every significant development in American life between his 1968 election and his 1974 resignation, particularly anything that featured or intensified outrage, enmity, and fear as the POW issue did. Since early in Nixon's first term, supporters had credited him with publicizing the plight of POWs while detractors accused him of exaggerating their numbers and misery in order to prolong the war.

The balance between these camps shifted toward greater cynicism once Nixon resigned, but the tendency to ascribe public concern for POWs to the former president only intensified as the conviction that he was a liar and a cheat was borne out by the archival record. H. Bruce Franklin was the first to use official sources to examine the origins of the POW/MIA issue in his landmark study *M.I.A. or Mythmaking in America*, which argued that "the fate of American prisoners did not become a major public issue until the spring of 1969" when "the incoming Nixon administration decided to make the American prisoners and missing a major issue" to serve "as an indispensable device for continuing the war." Neil Sheehan popularized this idea in a 1993 piece for the *New Yorker*. "To buy time and divert attention from the fact that instead of ending the war he was trying to win it," he wrote, "Nixon launched a campaign to focus public hatred on the Vietnamese for holding American prisoners." By dint of repetition, this interpretation became conventional wisdom. "Having inherited an unpopular and frustrating war," Arnold Isaacs reiterated, Nixon "decided that recovering American prisoners of war was one policy goal that might sustain public sympathy and support." "As a public relations strategy, the POW campaign was ultimately successful," Jeffrey Kimball concluded, as "the demand for a quick release of POWs deflected attention from the real purposes of Nixon's strategy while creating 'deep emotional support' for the war." Robert Schulzinger called POWs "Nixon's trump card in the domestic political debate over Vietnam." More recently, Edwin Martini argued that "conservative forces in American society conspired with the incoming Nixon administration to conjure up an issue that would provide justification for Nixon's escalation of the war," while Natasha Zaretsky characterized "the POW publicity campaign" as a "manic and defensive attempt on the part of the Nixon administration to deflect attention away from revelations about American war conduct." [5]

Scholars have emphasized Nixon for good reason. The archival record makes clear how hard Nixon and his staff worked to turn concern for POWs to their own ends. Yet current scholarship cannot explain or even accommodate the release of Smith and McClure, when Vietnamese communists, American peace activists, and antiwar POWs used American captivity to seek an end to the war, not its continuation, years before Nixon took office. Nor can it account for the dozens more American captives the Vietnamese released before the 1973 Paris peace agreement, over half of whom were freed before Nixon's inauguration, often directly into the hands of the antiwar movement. [6] Its disregard for Vietnamese and local grassroots actors with diverse, often competing agendas leads to an unnecessarily cramped view of POW/MIA politics and its place in the Vietnam War and after.

Rather than invent public concern for POWs and MIAs, Nixon tried to thwart a campaign initiated elsewhere which used that concern to undermine support for the war. Vietnamese communists, antiwar activists, POW and MIA families, even POWs themselves publicized the plight of American prisoners before Nixon, and each redoubled their efforts once he entered the fray. Their motives varied and changed over time, but many who participated in POW/MIA activism did so to end the war and mitigate its violence. Opponents of the war used POW imprisonment and the uncertainty surrounding MIAs, along with the anguish of their families, to press for the one thing that could end their suffering—U.S. withdrawal. Nixon's intervention muddied this message, but it did not unite Americans behind his policies. To the contrary, it generated mounting pressure to trade withdrawal for the prisoners' return. That pressure did not end the war, but it frustrated Nixon's ambitions and revealed deep disillusionment with the war among its presumed supporters.

Overemphasizing Nixon's role, scholars have confused support for POWs with support for Nixon, just as he hoped when he seized on the POW issue. Such a view flies in the face of evidence that concern over American captives intensified as support for the war declined. This chapter reexamines the "massive and sustained outpouring of sympathetic concern, protest, and entreaty" that emerged on behalf of American POWs and MIAs during the war.[7] I argue that this outpouring was a way for Americans to voice their concerns about the war without condemning those who fought it. Recognizing concern for POWs as a form of indirect protest against the war suggests the complicated ways in which doubts about the war manifested themselves in domestic politics and in diplomatic negotiations to end the war. It also prompts, even necessitates, a reassessment of the postwar POW/MIA issue that is the subject of later chapters.

GO PUBLIC

Most accounts trace the origins of public concern for POWs and MIAs to a May 1969 news conference where Defense Secretary Melvin Laird complained that although "the North Vietnamese have claimed that they are treating our men humanely," there was "clear evidence that this is not the case." The enemy had "never identified the names of all the U.S. prisoners whom they hold," Laird insisted, nor allowed the "free exchange of mail between the prisoners and their families." He closed with a call for "the prompt release of all American prisoners," which soon became a staple at the Paris Peace Talks.[8]

The news conference marked the beginning of the Go Public campaign, which officials hoped would "marshal public opinion" in support of POWs and their advocates in the new Nixon administration.[9] But Laird's briefing garnered "less attention than its authors hoped," according to the Pentagon's official history of POW/MIA policy.[10] The *Chicago Tribune*, for instance, buried its coverage on page fifteen, where it noted "renewed demands" that "the United States long has sought." "As far back as 1966," it reminded readers, elder statesman "W. Averell Harriman publicly threatened American retaliation if the prisoners were mistreated."[11]

In fact, the history of American prisoners in Southeast Asia dated back to World War II, when the League for the Independence of Vietnam, or Viet Minh, rescued Allied pilots shot down over Vietnam and returned them to U.S. authorities in China. Viet Minh leader Ho Chi Minh repatriated the pilots to curry favor with U.S. officials while his lieutenants publicized such initiatives. The February 1945 edition of *Vietnam Independence* promised that "whoever saves American pilots will be generously rewarded by the Viet Minh," and dramatic reenactments spread the word throughout the region. Though the fate of these fliers was hardly foremost on the minds of most Americans amid the bloody world war, U.S. officials rewarded their return by making Ho Chi Minh an OSS agent and supplying his forces with arms and equipment.[12]

A decade later, with the Viet Minh on the verge of winning national independence, Vietnamese forces captured five Americans sent to assist the French in their doomed bid to retain Indochina. Seized while swimming near Danang in June 1954, the Americans spent ten weeks in Viet Minh custody while the Geneva Accords that ended the first Indochina War were finalized. Upon their release, their captors broadcast their confession over the radio. "Since our capture we slowly came to realize American intervention in the Indochina war was against peoples fighting resolutely for independence," they professed in language that was likely written for them. "Had we realized the truth beforehand, we would not have agreed to come to this country."[13] Their repudiation of U.S. involvement in Vietnam was the first of many such statements American prisoners would make — voluntarily and involuntarily — over the next two decades.

These early instances of American captivity in Indochina reveal a Vietnamese leadership attuned to the political dynamics of imprisonment. President Ho Chi Minh, Premier Pham Van Dong, Defense Minister Vo Nguyen Giap, Secretary General Truong Chinh, Secretary General Le Duan, Foreign Minister Xuan Thuy, Foreign Minister Nguyen Thi Binh, politburo member Le Duc Tho, NLF chairman Nguyen Huu Tho, and nearly every other high-ranking official who led the fight for Vietnamese independence spent time in colonial prisons, an experience central to their radicalization and organization.[14] Having experienced prison's power, these former victims of imprisonment became its masters as U.S. escalation in Vietnam led to growing numbers of American POWs. Three dozen Americans were captured in Vietnam and Laos by the end of 1964. By the end of 1965 that number exceeded 100. Over 100 more Americans were captured in 1966, and another 350 were added in 1967 and 1968. President Lyndon Johnson's partial bombing halt over North Vietnam in March 1968, extended to a full stop in October, reduced the numbers captured between 1969 and 1971 to fewer than 100. But when Nixon resumed bombing North Vietnam in 1972 the number of new captives soared, with over 100 Americans captured in the war's final year. All told, over 700 Americans spent some time in enemy prisons, and as their numbers grew their captors gained a potent propaganda tool that they put to use quickly, frequently, and sometimes brutally.[15]

On 25 June 1965 communist guerrillas announced the execution of Sergeant Harold Bennett in reprisal for the South Vietnamese government's execution of Tran Van Dong three days prior. Accused of a plot to destroy an American barracks, Dong was shot to death in Saigon's central market as part of the Nguyen Cao Ky regime's "campaign against terror."[16] Three months later, after Saigon executed three more communists for organizing an anti-government demonstration, NLF Radio announced the deaths of Captain Humbert Versace and Sergeant Kenneth Roraback in retaliation. Subsequent testimony from escaped and released prisoners suggests these Americans may have been killed for insubordination or simply succumbed to the hardships of war, but by linking their deaths to Saigon's executions, the NLF drove a wedge between the United States and its Saigon ally.[17] Alarmed, U.S. officials demanded an end to Saigon's public executions while calling on the International Committee of the Red Cross (ICRC) to condemn communist actions, which it did in October. Rather than take sides, though, the ICRC urged "all authorities" to abide by the Geneva Convention, which gave Saigon's prisoners the same protections afforded Americans.[18]

Having halted public executions, the NLF may have hoped to offset resultant adverse publicity with the November release of Smith and Mc-Clure. Or its abrupt reversal may have reflected uncertainty over how to respond to the rapid influx of American forces.[19] Just as likely, the NLF made a virtue of necessity in releasing Smith and McClure. Due to the furtive nature of its operations and unrelenting American bombardment, the NLF struggled to keep its prisoners alive and concealed, not to mention preventing their escape. Twenty percent of American prisoners held in the South died, compared to five percent in the North, and ten percent escaped. With Smith and McClure ready to oppose the war, it made sense to release them in hopes of achieving a propaganda coup rather than watch them die or escape.[20]

Similarly in the North, the Democratic Republic of Vietnam (DRV) used POWs to pressure U.S. policymakers. North Vietnam captured its first American in August 1964 during the Gulf of Tonkin reprisal attacks. From then on, the DRV captured more Americans than the NLF, since the airmen shot down over North Vietnam were harder for U.S. forces to retrieve than lost or wounded foot soldiers in the south. And since these aviators were engaged in what DRV officials deemed an illegal war of aggression, North Vietnam threatened to prosecute them. When the DRV signed the Geneva Convention, it did so with the express reservation that its provisions did not extend to "prisoners of war prosecuted for and convicted of war crimes." In early 1966 its Ministry of Foreign Affairs made the case against the Americans with a seventy-seven-page pamphlet entitled *US War Crimes in North Vietnam*, which detailed the devastation wrought by the air war carried out by American prisoners.[21]

Fearing that the pamphlet was the first step in criminal prosecutions, New York senator Robert F. Kennedy wrote to Secretary of State Dean Rusk in April urging "that efforts to free [the prisoners] go forward with all possible speed." Later that month Rusk announced the formation of the Interdepartmental Prisoner of War Committee and assigned senior statesman Averell Harriman "general supervision of Department actions concerning prisoners held by both sides in the conflict in Viet-Nam."[22] But neither Johnson nor his advisers were dissuaded from waging air war on North Vietnam, which promised more POWs. When Johnson attacked oil depots near Hanoi and Haiphong in June, DRV officials retaliated by marching American POWs through the streets of Hanoi, where they were mobbed by crowds chanting, "Death to you who have massacred our dear ones."[23] Since many of these men reported upon homecoming that Vietnamese soldiers had once saved them from angry civilians when they were shot down, the march seemed intended to threaten Americans in Washington more than those in Hanoi. No doubt it was also meant to appease an angry populace suffering under American bombs, as commentators on both the left and right suggested at the time.[24]

Still, this performance and the publication of the DRV's war crimes case against the POWs in the Hanoi newspaper *Nhan Dan* rattled Washington. Harriman embarked on "a major diplomatic campaign to warn the DRV of the inadvisability of holding war crimes trials."[25] He asked the Soviet Union and Poland to intercede with Ho Chi Minh and met with neutral parties such as Sweden, India, the Red Cross, and the Vatican that might sway Hanoi.[26] Meanwhile in Washington, Rusk warned that a trial would be regarded as "a very, very grave development."[27] At the administration's behest, eighteen senators who had criticized the war, including William

Fulbright, Eugene McCarthy, and George McGovern, released a statement urging North Vietnam to "refrain from any act of vengeance" lest it incite "public demand for retaliation swift and sure, inflicting new levels of suffering and sorrow."[28] Senate Armed Services Committee chairman Richard Russell backed up this threat with a promise to "make a desert of their country" should North Vietnam execute American airmen.[29] Johnson capped off this flurry of words with a press conference where he vowed to "react accordingly" should Americans be tried and convicted.[30]

By then, Ho Chi Minh had backed away from the idea of prosecuting American POWs. But in doing so, he responded to his friends, not his foes. On the day of Johnson's news conference, Ho cabled the National Committee for a Sane Nuclear Policy and American socialist leader Norman Thomas that "the policy of the Government with regard to the enemies captured in war is a humanitarian policy."[31] Four days later he told CBS News that there was "no trial in view."[32]

Harriman's special assistant Frank Sieverts, who would become the only high-ranking official to handle POW matters in both the Johnson and Nixon administrations, later cited this crisis as "an earlier example of how it was possible to use what I guess nowadays is called 'public diplomacy'" on behalf of POWs.[33] From his institutional vantage point, he saw more continuity than difference between this little-known episode and the later Go Public campaign. Much like Nixon, Johnson used the threat to POWs to compel his critics and opponents to close ranks behind his leadership without altering the policies that imperiled them. But for a president unable to win the war and unwilling to end it, the passions these men inspired posed problems. Without hope of bringing them home, Johnson had little to gain and much to lose by drawing attention to their plight.[34]

But putting the POW genie back in the bottle proved impossible. In the POWs, the war's supporters found a cause that might inspire Americans to pursue victory — or vengeance — at all costs. As the *Nation* observed, those like Senator Russell behaved "as if they *wanted* the men to be put to death, so that their hawkish passions would be justified."[35] Conversely, critics of the war saw in the POWs a cost that might dissuade Americans from continuing their open-ended commitment in Vietnam. The war's advocates always minimized the war's costs in favor of the dire consequences they predicted would follow defeat. But the plight of the POWs illustrated the war's toll in ways Americans found difficult to ignore. By calling attention to their captivity, the war's opponents could question its value while avoiding charges of being un-American.

Above all, though, Vietnamese communists publicized the plight of

American POWs. Unlike Johnson, Nixon, Congress, or the American people, they controlled the fate of American captives. In a kind of good-cop bad-cop routine, they threatened and absolved these men to turn public opinion against U.S. intervention in Vietnam. The early release of co-operative POWs to antiwar activists was a key part of that strategy. After Ho lifted the threat of war crimes trials, the NLF and DRV regularly released Americans to foster good will and encourage negotiation. In February 1967 the NLF placed Sergeant Sammie Womack and Private Charles Crafts on a civilian bus to freedom.[36] In November it released Sergeants Edward Johnson, Daniel Pitzer, and James Jackson Jr. to SDS leader Tom Hayden. And in January 1968, it freed Private Luis Ortiz-Rivera and Lance Corporal Jose Agosto-Santos in return for six communist prisoners. At the same time, the DRV invited to Hanoi David Dellinger of the National Mobilization Committee to End the War in Vietnam, popularly known as "the Mobe," to receive the first POWs released from the North. Dellinger asked antiwar activists Daniel Berrigan and Howard Zinn to go in his stead, and in the midst of the Tet offensive they took custody of Major Norris Overly, Captain Jon Black, and Lieutenant David Matheny. Talks between the NLF and the United States surrounding these releases left some in Saigon concerned that the Americans were seeking a coalition government or negotiated settlement, leading some historians to speculate that the releases were intended as "diversions or propaganda enhancements" to maximize Tet's effect.[37]

If the precise aims of the prisoner program can only be guessed, the broader goals are clear. POW propaganda was meant to win friends and demoralize foes in Vietnam, the United States, and the wider world. Produced first and foremost for internal consumption, images and accounts of "lightly armed (and diminutive) soldiers guarding giant American prisoners came to represent a new iconography of triumph" for the Vietnamese people.[38] Depictions of captured airmen circulated widely inside North Vietnam and were exported across the communist bloc as DRV officials worked to instill confidence among supporters and allies. Throughout the war, and especially in its early years, most reporting on the POW situation simply repackaged such enemy propaganda — without ICRC monitoring of Vietnamese prisons, it was the only reliable source of information. *Life* magazine's October 1967 cover story on "U.S. Prisoners in North Vietnam," for instance, reprinted eleven pages of images and text supplied by East German sources showing well-treated but submissive American captives. Depictions of unsmiling POWs robotically engaged in compulsory "exercise therapy" at prisons described as "hotels for unasked guests" probably angered most Americans—Harriman called the East German depiction a "travesty"—but communist propagandists produced such material as a form of psychological warfare.[39] Their aims were made plain by the party newspaper *Nhan Dan*, which instructed its readers to make every effort to capture downed pilots since "to lose one of these 'precious sons'" created "anxiety over losing someone whose worth cannot be calculated in terms of money, such as military secrets which he possesses and the loss of morale by his friends."[40]

Like the fighting-while-talking strategy of which it was a part, the capture and release of American POWs used coercive diplomacy to encourage U.S. withdrawal. If the loss of these men and their frequent appearances in enemy propaganda showed Americans the costs of U.S. involvement in Vietnamese affairs, their release indicated that the enemy could give Americans something they dearly wanted in return for their withdrawal. In a 1966 conversation at Hoa Lo prison, communist intellectual Nguyen Khac Vien told Commander James Stockdale that he and his fellow captives would be used to help end the war, leaving Stockdale convinced that "we were a major factor in the strategy of the Vietnamese. We would be, sort of, a branch of the American antiwar movement."[41] Indeed, a small "Peace Committee" formed inside Vietnamese prisons, and a number of Americans granted early release spoke favorably of their captors.[42] Not all those released condemned the war, and some who did later recanted, but men who acknowledged U.S. aggression were more likely to be released than those who refused, and enlisted men and racial minorities were favored over the more intransigent, predominantly white officer aviators.[43] Through careful selection, the communists did what they could to reinforce the appeals for peace that invariably accompanied early releases.

Since their rescue of American pilots in World War II, the Vietnamese had returned POWs to solicit American support, and they never deviated from that course, even when half a million Americans invaded their country. Instead, they reoriented their POW outreach toward the antiwar movement. As that movement grew, communist officials relied on its leaders to inspect prison camps, to carry mail to and from prisoners, and to repatriate prisoners. Nearly half of the three dozen Americans freed after the September 1967 international conference against the war in Bratislava, Czechoslovakia, were released to antiwar activists, including all twelve repatriates from North Vietnam.[44] By releasing POWs to activists, party officials enlisted their support in convincing Americans that the only thing standing in the way of a general prisoner release was U.S. government intransi-

This 1967 North Vietnamese stamp commemorating the "2000th U.S. Aircraft Brought Down over North Viet Nam" depicts Nguyen Thi Kim Lai escorting air force sergeant William Robinson, captured when his helicopter was shot down in Ha Tinh province. It illustrates what Tom Engelhardt called an "iconography of triumph," which made American prisoners of war submitting to Vietnamese guards representative of ultimate Vietnamese victory.

gence. Robert Sheer, who participated in the August 1968 release of three air force pilots, proclaimed that "those who are working for peace have better success in negotiating than the State Department and the Pentagon . . . because the Government is not willing to make concessions."[45] "The obvious solution to the POW problem is to end the war," reasoned an antiwar pamphlet published by the Joe Hill Collective.[46] Until that happened, Senator George McGovern told Vietnamese delegates to the Paris talks in 1971, POW releases "unquestionably strengthened the efforts of those of us in this country who are working for a complete U.S. withdrawal."[47]

McGovern's crushing defeat in the 1972 presidential election suggests that POW diplomacy was not such an unalloyed benefit for the antiwar left. The heavy-handedness of POW propaganda, involving prisoners in coercive press conferences and parades and making them props for visiting peace delegations, outraged many Americans and made pariahs of most who participated in such spectacles. American POWs resulted from combat, and the purposes the Vietnamese made them serve were more combative and less humanitarian than the peace movement was willing to recognize, just as their pre-capture combat missions were more destructive than their American apologists cared to admit.

But if the effect of POW propaganda on American audiences was complicated, it is clear that the Vietnamese were the first to publicize American POWs and that they did so for reasons of their own. Subsequent steps by American citizens and government officials were *reactions* to Vietnamese actions. The failure of American commentators to recognize this reflects a long-standing reluctance to see the Vietnamese as meaningful participants in their own history, a blindness rooted in the war that historians have only recently begun to recognize and correct. Upon entering the war Americans assumed "that if you just kept hitting the enemy hard enough he would quit," as General Douglas Kinnard put it. They imagined that they held the initiative and could dictate the war's terms. But as Kinnard eventually realized, "the assumption was totally wrong." "The problem was," Kinnard explained, that "while we had the power, it turned out they had the will."[48] Through the capture, coercion, and release of Americans, the communists demonstrated their will in ways that were impossible to ignore.

THE LEAGUE OF WIVES

The urge to respond to enemy POW initiatives began not with the Nixon administration but with POW wives. The National League of Families of American Prisoners and Missing in Southeast Asia began to take shape in April 1966 after Sybil Stockdale received two letters from her husband Jim. With this confirmation that Jim had survived shootdown eight months earlier, Stockdale sprang into action, inviting naval intelligence officers to her Coronado Island home to interpret coded elements in Jim's letters. That meeting led to others, and in May Stockdale flew to Washington at government expense to meet Pentagon officials who proposed converting her correspondence with Jim into a covert communications channel, an arrangement she agreed to during a return trip in July when she met Admiral David McDonald, the Chief of Naval Operations, and Ambassador Harriman, who had just assumed responsibility for POW affairs.

From the start, Stockdale was driven by a desire to respond to communist propaganda. Angry over North Vietnam's handling of American prisoners, she told McDonald that the navy should "launch its own anti–North Vietnamese propaganda campaign." Failing that, she at least hoped to "send a newsletter to other wives in my circumstances" to counter enemy claims with official information. Lacking their names and addresses, Stockdale asked the navy to forward her letter. When its personnel chief demurred, she sought them out on her own.[49]

Because many prisoners were aviators deployed out of California's naval and air bases, the women she was looking for were close at hand. Unlike enlisted men, who were usually unmarried and, married or not, left homes and families scattered across the country during year-long tours, aviators tended to be older career officers with wives and children who lived where they were based.[50] Inviting POW and MIA wives she knew in the San Diego area to a luncheon in October, Stockdale began to assemble what one early member called a "sorority." By 1967 she had organized thirty-three women as the League of Wives of American Prisoners in Vietnam, which later became the National League of Families.[51]

As officers' wives, these women were immersed in a military culture that reinforced their geographic proximity. Sharing their husbands' regimented lives, they attended many of the same functions, served on the same boards, shopped in the same post exchanges, sent their children to the same schools, and were otherwise integrated into the routines of military life. Sociability was a professional requirement and a practical necessity, as every officer's wife understood. It not only ameliorated the hardships of frequent moves, extended deployments, and imminent dangers that went with military life, it was essential to the business of advancing careers.[52] Though most military wives found compulsory socializing onerous at times, it provided those whose husbands were shot down over Vietnam with the makings of a support group. Customs of duty, rank, and command along with commonalities of race, class, and political outlook laid the basis for their organization. "Navy tradition dictated that, as the wife of the commanding officer of a fighter squadron, I should guide and help the younger wives," Stockdale explained, and having "been a Navy Relief volunteer for years and an officer in numerous wives organization," she knew she "liked being president best."[53]

However tight-knit, military communities had no room for the wives of prisoners and the missing. Because their membership in the community depended on their husbands' place in the military, Stockdale and her cohort found themselves isolated when their husbands disappeared. As reminders of war's risks, they soon learned that "other squadron wives don't feel comfortable with us around."[54] Senior officers often sought to exclude them from base housing because of "the emotional impact they might have on the community of wives waiting their husbands return."[55] Stripped of their accustomed place in the military, these women created new communities on its margins. In San Diego, Virginia Beach, Omaha, and other centers of military aviation they forged new bonds based on but distinct from their old world.[56]

They did so despite and because of the pressures and constraints that made public life so difficult for women in the mid-1960s. The vast majority of these women had children, often in multiples characteristic of the baby boom.[57] Stockdale was typical, with four sons who ranged in age from three to fifteen when Jim was shot down.[58] Her Virginia Beach counterpart Louise Mulligan raised six sons while organizing wives in the mid-Atlantic after her husband was shot down in 1966.[59] Many of these women had shouldered the burdens of single parenting before, but once their husbands were lost their situation became semi-permanent and oppressive, leaving little time or energy for activism.

At the same time, the impossibility of their situation compelled some women to seek escape. For some, drugs or alcohol did the trick — over half reported using tranquilizers and one-quarter said that their alcohol consumption increased. Others sought companionship through dating or cohabitation. Twenty-three percent worried that their spouse would disapprove of their dating during separation and one-third of POW couples divorced within twelve months of repatriation. Most women found more morally sanctioned outlets for their energies. Half returned to school and one-third took full- or part-time jobs. Nearly half reported engaging in civic or religious activism.[60] Not surprisingly, many focused on POW/MIA activism and viewed their political involvement as a temporary reaction to their predicament — "I know perfectly well that all of my activity is a substitute for sex," POW wife Valerie Kushner explained. But as extraordinary as their situation was, their entry into public life fit a larger pattern of women's political mobilization.[61] For all their seeming peculiarity, POW/MIA wives were similar to the white middle-class married women from the suburban South and Southwest whom historians Lisa McGirr and David Lassiter, among others, have revealed as key players in the burgeoning conservative movement.[62]

Like so many similarly situated women, POW/MIA wives "took advantage of their time and flexible schedules to do political work" that addressed perceived threats to their families and communities.[63] Ironically, activities undertaken to preserve their families irrevocably changed them. As the Center for Prisoner of War Studies found in its analysis of 215 POW/MIA wives, circumstances compelled these women "to assert themselves, gain control of the family, and establish themselves as the rightful and legal representatives of their absent husband and the family." As they did so, they "gained self-confidence, and developed a style of life for a family without a husband or father" just as "the movement toward women's liberation appeared to legitimate and support the wives and their development in this direction." Of all their concerns, what most worried POW/MIA wives in the war's waning days was how their husbands would react to their newfound independence and the social changes that independence reflected and advanced.[64]

Nothing did more to foster confidence among them than their POW/MIA activism. "The last generation of hat-and-glove military wives," they seemed unlikely activists.[65] But despite their feminine mystique, most were well-educated, well-connected, and well-versed in military politics, which rewarded playing by the rules. They knew or soon learned how to pressure the Pentagon and politicians into providing them with information and services. As they interacted with powerful men over matters of war and peace, they became important public figures in their own right, engaging in national and international politics to a degree none had dared when their husbands were around. Their husbands' absence gave them freedom to participate in public life. By necessity "the active, masculine role vacated by the POWs was assumed, to a degree, by their families."[66]

Here, too, Stockdale was extraordinary but instructive. A woman of prodigious energy and talent, she earned a master's degree in education from Stanford University in 1959 with two boys and a third on the way, and taught school once her fourth and youngest son started kindergarten. Teaching full-time and raising four kids, she still found time to organize the League, engage in espionage, and lobby national leaders. Like many activist wives, she recognized that her status as a devoted wife and mother gave her influence—"my first job is to help Jim and try to take care of our boys," she typically told reporters.[67] But she could modulate those roles—"I had to be careful not to become shrill or too emotional or I'd be written off as an unbalanced female," she recalled of her first meeting with Admiral Thomas Moorer soon after he became Chief of Naval Operations in August 1967.[68] Not all POW/MIA wives were as accomplished or self-possessed, but most knew how to use gender conventions to their own and their husbands' advantage.

That Stockdale could command an appointment with Moorer two weeks after he became the navy's senior-ranking officer suggested her growing clout. Visits with Harriman and Senate minority leader Everett Dirksen during the same swing through Washington confirmed it. As public support for the war plunged below fifty percent that summer, Stockdale's distress over her situation became perilous for the Johnson administration.[69] Being privy to Jim's secret communications overlaid in invisible ink atop his letters, Stockdale was uniquely aware of the hardships he faced.[70] Her knowledge of his suffering imparted an urgency to her efforts that government officials seldom shared, and it gave her leverage to make demands. In a four-page statement she read to Moorer at their luncheon she complained that "the enemy's flagrant violations of the Geneva Conventions were totally ignored," and expressed "dismay at the U.S. government letting the North Vietnamese fill our media with propaganda and never responding." "Up to now I'd had faith that my government would do the right thing," she told him, but "now my faith wavered, and one had only to examine the record of events to know why."[71]

Stockdale's frustration with the Johnson administration stemmed above all from its inability to counter POW propaganda. Knowing that her husband had been abused for his refusal to denounce the war, it angered her that his captors rewarded prisoners and peace activists who willingly did so through early releases. When Hanoi followed its initial release of Overly, Black, and Matheny in February 1968 with the release of Majors James Low and Fred Thompson and Captain Joe Carpenter to the Mobe's Rennie Davis in August, Stockdale fired off a cable to Harriman and Secretary of Defense Clark Clifford: "What steps are being taken to prevent these present and future violations" of the Code of Conduct, which prohibited "oral or written statements disloyal to my country" and forbade "special favors from the enemy"? Harriman replied that the releases were "a gesture of good will" that would hopefully lead to "further releases," prompting Stockdale to seek an interview with the *San Diego Union*.[72] Appearing days before the election, the front-page feature detailed Stockdale's three-year ordeal and outlined her efforts to organize the League, whose "main purpose" was "to help the men in any way we can, by writing letters to congressmen, by trying to bring pressure on Hanoi." Expressing frustration over unanswered enemy propaganda, Stockdale appealed to U.S. officials to "help us with the anti-propaganda campaign against Hanoi's propaganda campaign" and urged "the public to join in the letter-writing campaign."[73]

"Nixon had to win," she recalled feeling at the time. Without his "fresh approach to this quagmire we'd gotten ourselves into," "the future was bleak and hopeless."[74] It is impossible to know whether her interview contributed in any significant way to Nixon's 367,000-vote plurality in California, which proved the decisive margin in a surprisingly close election. Clearly, though, POW/MIA wives concentrated around California's military bases resembled the many well-educated, middle-class migrants employed in the state's massive defense industries who were the heart and soul of the nascent conservative movement. California had twice as many POW/MIA relatives as any other state, followed by Texas and Florida, all hotbeds of an emerging grassroots conservative activism. Conservative activists had vaulted Ronald Reagan to California's governor's office in 1966 and delivered the state's electoral votes to Nixon in 1968. Many must have identified with the technocratic POW pilots and their long-suffering wives who remained committed Cold Warriors in the face of growing doubts about the war.[75]

When Nixon won, Stockdale called on this grassroots network to generate 2,000 telegrams to the new president in his first week in office, urging him to make POWs a top priority. He replied to each one, and so began his bid to turn POWs to his advantage. When Nixon joined her cause, Stockdale believed "that the organizational efforts of us wives and families on a national level had been influential in forcing our government to join us in speaking out publicly."[76] Some POW/MIA families later claimed that their early efforts convinced the incoming administration that "they'd best facilitate and try to work with the families lest it get completely out of control."[77] Such language of compulsion overstates the case. Instead of fearing the nascent League, Nixon and his staff recognized it as a potential ally that could help him seize control of an issue that had been dominated by his enemies. Still, if Stockdale and her successors overestimated their influence, subsequent observers have overlooked the League's early history and its implications.[78] Though hardly the juggernaut it became in the early 1970s, the League and its concerns preceded (and survived) Nixon's presidency. Its members welcomed Nixon's attention and shared his compulsion to lash out at their rivals, but few felt beholden to him. "Sure there's been a calculated campaign," League chairman Carol North admitted when her group was later accused of acting as an administration mouthpiece, "but it's our calculated campaign, not theirs."[79]

GO FOR BROKE

What brought Nixon and the League together was a shared desire to seize the initiative in Vietnam and regain the moral high-ground from the war's critics. Nixon took office vowing that "I'm not going to end up like LBJ, holed up in the White House afraid to show my face on the street," determined to end the war in Vietnam on his terms.[80] Adopting the word "GO" as his mantra, Nixon ordered himself and his staff to "get going, take risks, be exciting. . . . Now is the time to go. . . . Go for broke." His pursuit of the "big play" led him to Go Public on the abuse of American prisoners in order to throw his opponents on the defensive.[81] But as so often happened in his presidency, Nixon's instincts played into the hands of his enemies. As Heyward Isham, the principal American staffer at the Paris Peace Talks, told the Senate Select Committee on POW/MIA Affairs in 1992, the Vietnamese fought the war "like jujitsu, where you use the superior power of the enemy to force him to tumble over himself. You let him lunge at you then you just trip him."[82] In that sense, publicizing POWs represented less a shrewd gambit than another desperate lunge that, like all the others, resulted in a further loss of leverage and control.

Befitting Nixon's secretive style, Go Public began in private, first with Nixon's personal replies to the 2,000 telegrams Stockdale had organized, then with a series of unpublicized meetings with families of imprisoned and missing men meant to build a larger, more active League of Wives. Beginning with a visit to the League in March, State Department and Pentagon officials conducted a cross-country tour that briefed an estimated 1,400 POW and MIA relatives over the next six months, knitting together scattered cells and isolated individuals into a national organization.[83] The transcript of one such meeting indicates how novel the idea of organizing was for some families. When Ambassador Henry Cabot Lodge told them that "to maintain this organization the way you are doing is very good," a confused audience member objected, "This group doesn't have an organization. I think it is responding to the invitation of the Air Force to meet here today." "Oh, I see," replied Lodge.[84] Looking back on his handiwork, Deputy Assistant Secretary of Defense for Public Affairs Dick Capen, who organized these meetings, took credit for bringing the families "together for the first time." Joseph Lelyveld's 1971 assessment for the *New York Times Magazine* came closer to the truth. "The Administration did not start—and probably could not have prevented—the campaign by the wives to bring the plight of their husbands into the open. But there is no doubt that it helped orchestrate their efforts."[85]

In addition to helping make the League a truly national organization, Capen and his State Department equivalent Frank Sieverts helped generate "publicity for the wives and families of our captured and missing men." Thanks to their efforts, each television network scheduled specials on the story that summer and "the Air Force and Navy are providing the names and addresses of wives to take part in such programs."[86] Shortly thereafter, Stockdale appeared on the CBS Morning News and was featured in a full-page story in the *New York Times*. In the meantime she and a dozen other POW/MIA relatives received a private briefing "about President Nixon's plans for 'Vietnamization'" from Secretary of Defense Laird. "I thought it was a pretty weak plan," Stockdale confessed. "But I couldn't help liking

Secretary Laird. He'd ended the 'keep-quiet' policy and had the guts to talk about the truth of the prisoners' treatment in public."[87]

The Go Public program seemed to work to perfection, increasing public concern about missing and imprisoned Americans and enlisting their families as administration allies. But as Stockdale's reaction to Vietnamization hints, problems lurked beneath the surface. Vietnamization, which proposed gradually replacing U.S. forces with beefed-up South Vietnamese forces, raised more starkly than ever before the specter of war without end. Under Johnson "the feeling was that the war could well, and should, be over soon, and then we can resolve the prisoners quickly and easily," Frank Sieverts explained. But with Vietnamization, Sieverts realized, the war could go on forever.[88] Thinking the enemy incapable of expelling them, Nixon and his National Security Adviser Henry Kissinger believed they "could credibly threaten to hold on in South Vietnam indefinitely."[89] For Stockdale, who wrote Laird in March with the "SUPER QUESTION: HOW MUCH LONGER?" such a prospect was bound to disappoint.[90] Anxious to see the war end, her rapidly growing legions of supporters would be equally dismayed. Nixon tried to tamp down impatience with the war through troop withdrawals and reduced draft calls, and he tried to redirect blame for the war through Go Public, among other things. But even if he withdrew all ground forces and cut draft calls to zero, Nixon could not recover the prisoners and missing without communist cooperation. The prisoners were the one problem Vietnamization could never solve and Go Public could only amplify.

Observers were slow to grasp this conundrum in the early days of Go Public. But the diplomatic and dialectic response it encouraged drove home the realities of the situation. After releasing ten Americans in 1968, communist forces freed eighteen more in 1969, the largest totals of the war.[91] As much as anything the administration did, these releases raised the profile of the POW/MIA issue. The July 1969 announcement that Hanoi would release three more men to antiwar activists, in particular, prompted mass media coverage and heated public debate. As it had eighteen months earlier, the DRV asked David Dellinger to coordinate the release, inviting him to Paris to discuss the arrangements. Recently indicted for his involvement in antiwar demonstrations at the 1968 Democratic National Convention in Chicago, Dellinger was prohibited from traveling abroad. By inviting him to Paris, then inviting his indicted co-conspirator Rennie Davis to Hanoi to receive Captain Wesley Rumble, Lieutenant Robert Frishman, and Seaman Douglas Hegdahl, DRV officials put the administration in an untenable position. Either it could permit Dellinger and Davis to participate, angering hawks in the League and elsewhere who resented their involvement, or it could refuse and risk scuttling the release, upsetting the League and its supporters even more. Reluctantly, the Justice Department lifted the travel restrictions. "We have no alternative if we want our men back," Under Secretary of State Elliot Richardson told Vice President Spiro Agnew when he objected. Agnew admitted "humanitarian considerations probably outweigh the obvious propaganda advantages conceded to the enemy," but fumed that such acts "undermine confidence in the strength and will of the government and people of the United States." North Vietnam was seeking to embarrass the administration, Laird echoed, calling it "vital that we cease giving official sanction to negotiations by people such as Davis and Dellinger."[92]

It was around this time that Nixon decided to go for broke. After a honeymoon period in which Americans waited anxiously for the new president to end the war, it was clear Nixon's plans were not "working out right," as Chief of Staff H. R. Haldeman put it in June.[93] The war raged unabated, with only a modest 25,000 troop reduction; the NLF's unyielding Ten-Point Program for Peace announced in May, along with the DRV's provocative POW moves in July and August, showed that the enemy remained resolute; and opposition to the war continued, with the Vietnam Moratorium scheduled for mid-October and the Mobilization Against the War to follow in mid-November.[94] Frustration mounting, Nixon exhorted his staff "to *do something.*" "Power of the United States must be used more effectively at home and abroad or we go down the drain."[95]

Casting about for a counter-offensive, Nixon settled on a series of public relations initiatives, since it was in the realm of words where the president possessed the greatest freedom of movement and his staff the most expertise.[96] Two days before the October Moratorium he announced that he would make a major address to the nation on 3 November. On that evening, he offered no new diplomatic or military initiatives. Instead, in the most important speech of his presidency, he called to life "the great silent majority." Describing the war as a conflict between a "vocal minority" and "silent majority," Nixon recast the war as a fight between Americans. "North Vietnam cannot defeat or humiliate the United States," he insisted; "only Americans can do that."[97] Though untrue, Nixon's formulation of the soon-to-be commonplace "stabbed-in-the-back" thesis enhanced the sense among Americans that they were at war with one another more than with the Vietnamese, and that unless they fought to defend their own guiding vision of American society they would suffer humiliation and defeat. The speech did nothing to end the war, but by framing the war in terms of words it intensified the struggle over its meaning that would one day become a fight for its memory. "It was a speech that seemed to be designed not to persuade the opposition but to overwhelm it," James Reston wrote in his analysis for the *New York Times*, "and the chances are that this will merely divide and polarize the debaters in the United States, without bringing the enemy into serious negotiations."[98]

While Nixon applauded taciturn Americans, he knew that "in a war of words, a 'silent majority,' no matter how large, would be ineffective."[99] In the months leading up to the speech, the White House developed a "game plan for follow-up" that would "make the November speech the occasion for the birth of a movement." They hoped to "give ordinary people who need to expend energy on 'helping to end the war' something to be *for*"; something "simple and reasonable and something everyone can understand"; "something to do," like "join a committee," "sign a petition," "hold a rally," "march in a parade," and "picket the UN."[100] "We need bumper stickers," White House adviser Lyn Nofziger declared.[101]

Fifty million POW/MIA bumper stickers were sold over the next four years, along with 135 million POW/MIA postage stamps.[102] Nixon hand-picked handsome captives and their attractive wives as the heroes of his silent majority. On 23 September Haldeman informed Kissinger, Press Secretary Ron Ziegler, and Communications Director Herb Klein that Nixon had noted a news story on "the wives of the captive pilots" and "feels this is the sort of propaganda offensive that we need to keep generating."[103] Haldeman proposed bringing in "one or two of the wives" to see the president with "proper game plan follow up."[104] The idea was put on hold when Kissinger warned that "government linkage with these women at this time could be used as a basis by Hanoi for refusal to give the wives the names of their loved ones," and would lend credence to "those who claim this is the President's war." "The wives might ultimately resent White House interference," he cautioned.[105] Though prescient, Kissinger's warnings were dismissed by the rest of the White House staff. "A White House visit by some POW wives would be a big plus," adviser Harry Dent told Haldeman in October; "these ladies have the sympathy of just about everybody these days."[106] Eager to proceed, Nixon asked his appointments secretary, Dwight Chapin, "to check with Henry each week in regard to his visiting with the prisoner of war wives."[107] By November the notoriously insecure Kissinger had relented. "A meeting between the President and a group of wives of American POW's in Vietnam would be a good idea now that the President has delivered his address on Vietnam," he wrote Chapin.[108] Preparations to bring Stockdale and two dozen other wives to the White House began immediately.

In the meantime, the administration moved forward with a flurry of POW activities. On 2 September, Laird presided over a news conference at Bethesda Naval Hospital where recently released POWs Hegdahl and Frishman reported on "barbaric" conditions inside North Vietnam's prisons. Though the details were vague (and the few specifics were later recanted under direct questioning), officials published their story in *Air Force/Space Digest* to make the public "aware of the facts." It was then reprinted by *Reader's Digest* alongside a request for readers to write DRV Foreign Minister Xuan Thuy on the prisoners' behalf. "The United States is speaking out" and "citizens must join the attack," the *Digest* implored. The Pentagon arranged for the two men to testify before the House Armed Services Committee, sent them on a speaking tour to address POW/MIA families, and supplied transcripts of their Bethesda briefing to all POW/MIA next of kin with the winking reassurance that "we are certain that you will not become unduly concerned over the briefing if you keep in mind the purpose for which it was tailored."[109] The State Department did its part by asking POW/MIA wives to "send messages to the organizers of the Vietnam 'Moratorium' appealing for humane treatment of our prisoners of war," then "release the telegrams themselves to the press and wire services."[110] In the two weeks between the "silent majority" speech and the Mobilization Against the War, full-page advertisements entitled "The Majority Speaks: Release the Prisoners" and "The Majority Speaks: Vietnam" ran in newspapers across the country soliciting support for the president. Ghostwritten by presidential speechwriter William Safire and paid for by Texas millionaire H. Ross Perot, the ads urged Nixon supporters to sign petitions that were organized by congressional district and turned over to the White House, where the president was photographed reading huge bags of mail.[111] Defense contractors Fairchild Hiller and North American Rockwell contributed their own letter drives, and Fairchild Hiller paid for Stockdale and other wives to travel to Paris for widely publicized meetings with communist officials.[112] The American Red Cross also stepped up its involvement in POW/MIA matters, encouraging newspaper editors to join "our efforts to have the public understand this question, and to do something about it, even to the point of communicating directly with North Vietnam."[113] Though much of this activity appeared spontaneous, Stockdale was right to believe "the government was quietly helping us accomplish our objectives."[114] A December memo for the president detailed these "POW Campaign Activities," promising to generate further "private sector interest" in "a massive campaign to bring pressure to bear on the Hanoi government."[115]

The cynicism behind the White House campaign can be seen in preparations for Nixon's December visit with POW/MIA wives and mothers. Days before the visit, White House aide Alexander Butterfield wrote to Nixon's military assistant criticizing the "demographic spread" of the guest list—there were too many officers' families and too few families of enlisted men from the "Deep South or Rocky Mountain–North Central Plains," making them poor representatives of Middle America. Butterfield also announced that "a final decision has been made that there will be no fathers among those invited" in order to intensify their pathos. He indicated that Stockdale would act as spokeswoman, though he "would prefer that none of the women speak . . . that they merely stand by the President while he speaks." Steve Bull, the White House aide charged with "staging for this appointment," even directed the physically awkward Nixon to position "yourself in front of the fireplace before the microphone, and flanked by two women on each side."[116] The visiting women would serve as props—stand-ins for the silent majority, with the emphasis on silent. Though some in the White House talked of making "a movement" out of the silent majority, the importance they placed on the women standing still while Nixon spoke suggests they were more interested in manufacturing consent. By 1969 the war was so unpopular that public opinion had to be "mobilized," as Tom Engelhardt has written, just "to remain inert."[117]

The fall escalation of Go Public generated "mountains" of mail, with more than 50,000 telegrams and 118,000 letters sent to the White House by early 1970.[118] The mail was supposed to "tell it to Hanoi," but its real audience was Congress and the American people. Whether or not Hanoi was listening, the antiwar movement got the message.[119] An editorial cartoon on the front page of the *Chicago Tribune* showed "critics of Nixon's peace program" buried under a "Deluge of Mail Supporting Nixon."[120] Even though some suspected Republican operatives were behind this "groundswell," the scale of the response seemed to prove Nixon's claim that he enjoyed the support of most Americans.[121] At its zenith, the antiwar movement appeared outnumbered. On the heels of the two largest peace demonstrations in U.S. history, *Time* magazine named "Middle Americans," first cousins to the silent majority, its "Man of the Year." "We've got those liberal bastards on the run now!" Nixon exulted. "While you've got the power, you have to move quickly," he told Haldeman; "when we're up,

President Richard Nixon meets with wives and mothers of American POWs and MIAs at the White House on 12 December 1969. The women depicted, from left, are Carole Hanson, Louise Mulligan, Sybil Stockdale, Andrea Rander, and Mary Mearns. White House aide Alexander Butterfield stands at the right edge of the frame. (Courtesy National Archives, Nixon Presidential Materials)

build a mythology." Noting an item from his news summary on how "North Vietnam is showing itself to be acutely sensitive to charges that it has ill-treated U.S. POWs," he ordered his chief of staff to "get a massive campaign going on this."[122]

BACK AND FORTH

In view of these machinations, it is easy to become mesmerized by Nixon's Machiavellian instincts. But even when he was most active in the Go Public campaign, Nixon never controlled the POW/MIA issue. His enemies parried his moves with additional early releases to disprove his depiction of them as inhumane. South Vietnamese guerrillas followed the August release of Rumble, Frishman, and Hegdahl with the release of an additional six Americans in three separate incidents over the last three months of 1969. The releases were part of a campaign to gain recognition for the newly formed Provisional Revolutionary Government (PRG) as it sought legitimacy as an independent party to the Paris talks.[123] The fall releases also signaled solidarity with antiwar Americans, helping to counteract Nixon's POW politicking. On the same day the *Chicago Tribune* ran Perot's full-page pro-Nixon ad, for instance, newly freed American GIs praised their former captors on the paper's front page.[124]

POW initiatives took on a back-and-forth quality in late 1969 as each side jockeyed for position. Joining Nixon's offensive, forty U.S. senators greeted the Rumble, Frishman, and Hegdahl release by condemning North Vietnam's refusal to identify the prisoners it held.[125] In an obvious attempt to offset the Mobilization Against the War, the House Subcommittee on National Security Policy, chaired by the hawkish Democrat Clement Zablocki of Wisconsin, held hearings in November to consider twenty-one resolutions expressing concern for POWs. Zablocki's opening remarks — "Regardless of how they may feel about the Vietnam war, all Americans are united in their hopes and prayers for our captured servicemen" — previewed Nixon's language at his December meeting with League women.[126] "We all know there is disagreement in this country about the war in Vietnam," he admitted, but "on this issue, the treatment of prisoners of war, there can be and there should be no disagreement."[127] The House substantiated such claims when it unanimously approved Concurrent Resolution 454 three days later, declaring that "the Congress strongly protests the treatment of United States servicemen held prisoner by North Vietnam and the National Liberation Front." The Senate unanimously concurred in February.[128]

But widespread sympathy for POWs did not translate into universal support for the war, as the massive fall demonstrations against the war and its shrinking support in opinion polls made clear. When proponents of the war tried to equate the two, they faced stiff opposition. On the day before Thanksgiving, Dellinger and Davis produced a list of fifty-nine American POWs in North Vietnam supplied to them by the DRV delegation to the Paris talks. The list included five men previously listed as MIA, giving it significance and credibility.[129] Internally, the Defense Intelligence Agency recognized it as "valid," but in public the Pentagon suggested otherwise.[130] Despite internal distinctions between Americans known to be in captivity — POWs — and the larger number missing without evidence of capture — MIAs — the Pentagon's public affairs chief recommended "that we establish for future public release purposes a single category of 'Missing in Action or Captured,'" in order to make North Vietnam accountable for all 1,406 Americans then missing in Indochina.[131]

Communist officials did not back down. Presented with a complete list of U.S. missing personnel at the Paris talks, they denounced it as a "perfidious maneuver to camouflage the fact that the United States is pursuing the war, committing crimes against the Vietnamese people and misleading public opinion."[132] When League delegations visited Paris to pressure DRV officials, those officials patiently insisted that the best way to help the prisoners was to end the war.[133] To show their readiness to return the prisoners when peace prevailed, the DRV provided prisoner mail to Cora Weiss of Women Strike for Peace, who was then in Hanoi. Weiss returned on Christmas Eve 1969 carrying the names and letters of 132 American captives. Shortly thereafter she founded the Committee of Liaison with Families of Servicemen Detained in North Vietnam (COLIAFAM). Led by Weiss and Dellinger, COLIAFAM demonstrated immediate results, including an updated list of 156 POWs in January 1970, followed by a more complete list of 335 names in April, and it tripled the volume of prisoner mail over its 1969 level.[134] Until war's end, its members traveled to Hanoi every month to deliver and retrieve prisoner mail.[135] As it passed mail and information to POW families, COLIAFAM reminded them that "the safe return of U.S. servicemen . . . can only come with a decision on the part of the U.S. government to completely withdraw from Vietnam," turning concern for POWs into another reason to end the war.[136]

Facing unexpected opposition, Nixon and his allies redoubled their efforts. Enraged by COLIAFAM's "cynical exploitation of the POW's," Congressman Bob Wilson of San Diego demanded the group be registered under the Foreign Agents Registration Act.[137] The Pentagon, too desperate for the information the group provided to stand in its way, helped defeat a House provision that criminalized private intercessions in POW affairs.[138] Such impotence heightened the need to lash out. Angered by a large counterdemonstration outside a small POW rally at Constitution Hall in February, Nixon ally Senator Bob Dole of Kansas demanded a do-over, vowing to fill the 3,811-seat hall with "good, decent American people" on 1 May in an "Appeal for International Justice." Naming Stockdale and Perot co-chairs, Dole lined up a prestigious group of co-sponsors, including leading Senate doves Edmund Muskie and Majority Leader Mike Mansfield and their bellicose rivals John Stennis and Barry Goldwater. To "bring attention to the bipartisan, congressionally sponsored rally," Zablocki convened a second set of POW hearings on 29 April, inviting Dole, Stockdale, and Perot to testify.[139] And to make sure the event was well attended, the Air National Guard airlifted 700 POW/MIA relatives to Washington at federal expense.[140]

Dole promised a "nonpartisan and nonideological" event. "We are not there to discuss whether we should escalate or deescalate," he explained, only "to demonstrate that Americans care." In practice this meant that debate was forbidden but contempt for the war's critics was not, as speaker after speaker attacked those protesting the Cambodian invasion announced the night before. Railing that "there's a pack of idiots just a few miles north of here burning down an ROTC headquarters" and "I don't think America wants to win this war!" earned Goldwater "one of the evening's biggest ovations."[141] Dole complained that POW/MIA families who "make the sacrifices day after day" were not given the attention "that they would if they were here to burn the flag or storm the Pentagon."[142] Agnew and Laird also spoke, and a letter from Nixon graced the program—the president spent the evening watching the film *Patton* rather than attending in person—while Mansfield and Muskie were conspicuously missing.[143] Also notably absent was any mention of the COLIAFAM prisoner list released the day before, though the group came in for criticism at the Zablocki hearings earlier in the week.[144] Both speakers and audience made clear that they shared Nixon's contempt for protestors, whom he had called "bums" earlier in the day.[145] They seemed to say that only those who could not or would not speak against the war—like the POWs and MIAs—had the right to do so.

Underwritten by defense contractors, the Constitution Hall rally was a coming-out party for the League. With Dole, Agnew, Laird, Goldwater, Stennis, and House Armed Services Committee chairman Olin Teague all in attendance, along with four of the five Joint Chiefs of Staff, the guest list was a Who's Who of the defense establishment. For the families of career officers, the sight of so much military brass was a reminder of happier times and a promise of better days ahead. "For every two or three family members, there was a military officer in dress uniform," MIA wife Barbara Mullen observed. "It had been a long time since these women had had such attention."[146]

The next day, the assembled families met with Charles Havens III to formally incorporate their association before returning home aboard military aircraft reserved for their use. Havens, then among the top Pentagon experts on POW/MIA affairs, counseled League leaders to declare their group nonpartisan in order to obtain tax-exempt status.[147] But the largesse lavished on the League belied its apolitical stance. The Reserve Officers Association supplied its office space, the White House provided a WATS long-distance line, the vice president donated $10,000 in proceeds from the sale of Spiro Agnew watches, and Pentagon casualty assistance officers mailed every POW/MIA family a League membership application. This last bit of assistance was crucial in building the League's mailing list, which soon became its most prized possession.[148] Though the League had a long history by 1970, its ability to communicate directly with a far-flung network of POW/MIA families made it a truly national organization for the first time.

Critics charged that such lucre corrupted the League. They argued that League efforts like "Operation 100 tons," which delivered sixteen million letters to DRV officials on behalf of POWs, addressed the war's prisoners in "perfect abstraction from other facts about the war."[149] For journalist Seymour Hersh, the reason for this avoidance of war's realities was clear: the "Pentagon directs efforts by wives," as Hersh's five-part exposé on the League put it.[150] There is ample evidence to support this view. An Agnew aide conceived of Operation 100 tons and the White House facilitated it, though it was advertised as a "non-partisan and non-political" campaign.[151]

Yet we should not assume that all 1,600 League families or the 16 million Americans who generated 100 tons of mail on their behalf agreed with the administration or its policies. Officials hid behind a group that was ostensibly nonpartisan because to do otherwise, to reveal their involvement and avow their motives, would drive too many people away. Americans supported imprisoned and missing Americans and their families, not the war that held them hostage. Captive to a war without end, these men and their families became stand-ins for the countless Americans who had lost faith in the war but could not escape it. Nixon mobilized this constituency at his peril.

ALL OUR SONS IN VIETNAM ARE POWS

"The truth of the matter is that all our sons in Vietnam are POWs," POW mother Jane Dudley wrote in an Another Mother for Peace pamphlet put out in February 1971. Accusing the White House of using POWs "to create public sympathy so that it can justify continuing this horrible, unpopular war," Dudley sought to turn the tables. "There can only be an 'exchange of prisoners' when a war *ends*!" Until then, "we cannot for one moment forget the danger and deprivation which the rest of our 337,900 sons in Vietnam face daily."[152] Her antiwar argument showed the plasticity of POW/MIA politics. By collapsing debate over the war into concern for POWs and their families, Go Public encouraged emotional attachments to strikingly homogenous pro-military men and women whom Nixon believed he could count on to support the war. At the same time, this identification with families who could only be reunited at war's end intensified impatience with Nixon's slow-motion withdrawal.

Despite Dudley's suggestions to the contrary, POWs and MIAs were far different from most men who fought in Indochina. In a war fought disproportionately by very young, poorly educated, working-class conscripts who skulked through the jungle with little sense of purpose, POWs and MIAs were "proud, patriotic, and largely white career military officers" who soared through the air.[153] With no fixed battle lines and few protracted battles, the ground war produced relatively few unrecovered casualties since dead and wounded soldiers were usually recovered. Pilots shot down over enemy territory were harder to retrieve and captured in larger numbers.[154] At war's end, 84 percent of American POWs were airmen.[155] With such a large number of pilots, 88 percent of returned POWs were officers, as were three-quarters of MIAs.[156] The army was the only service where officers did not dominate its prisoner ranks.[157]

The top-heavy nature of the POW/MIA population made it a near perfect inversion of the Vietnam-era military. While "non-white, working-class, less-well-educated men were far more likely to serve and see combat" in Vietnam, the opposite was true of those likely to become prisoners. Only sixteen black POWs returned at the end of the conflict, despite the fact that African Americans represented nearly 14 percent of the war's casualties.[158] The number of black repatriates was low in part because the NLF released black prisoners to show "solidarity and support for the just struggle of U.S. Negroes."[159] But beyond that, there were few black prisoners because there were few black pilots—so few that navy lieutenant Porter Halyburton was initially "suspicious" of his black cellmate, air force major Fred Cherry, because he "did not know that the Air Force had black pilots."[160]

Overwhelmingly white, most POWs also possessed college degrees when just 13 percent of Vietnam veterans exiting the armed forces between 1966 and 1971 had attended college and a mere 7 percent graduated.[161] Prisoners were also older than most troops. Seventeen had served in World War II and thirty had fought in Korea.[162] Navy prisoners averaged thirty years of age at the time of capture.[163] After spending four to six years in prison on average, depending on branch of service, the POWs left Vietnam far older than most men who served year-long tours in the field.[164] Most had already settled into family life: 64 percent were married and there were more than 1,000 children of POWs in 1972, with the war's third highest annual rate of capture still ahead.[165] Collectively, their ranks looked less like the Oakland Induction Center that funneled so many young infantrymen into Vietnam than a class reunion at the military service academies so many had attended.

The class consciousness of the prisoners and the missing is hard to measure, but the pay and allowances for a married captain with three children was $13,000 in 1966 and reached $22,300 by 1970, more than double the national median family income.[166] POW/MIA deposits in the Uniformed Services Savings Deposit Program grew so large that Congress waived the $10,000 limit for these men. With a 10 percent annual rate of return, these accounts averaged almost $20,000 apiece by 1972, with the largest valued at $120,000. The waiver was one of many financial rewards given POWs and MIAs in the Nixon years. Congress doubled compensation for internment under the War Claims Act to five dollars per day on top of base pay and hazardous duty pay, terminated limits on the accrual of leave, extended flight pay and incentive pay for one year after repatriation, and exempted all income received while in POW or MIA status from federal income taxes. Given their skills and prolonged captivity or violent deaths, these men were hardly overcompensated. But as some in the Pentagon grumbled, their pay and benefits exceeded that of "at least two larger groups whose sacrifices were far greater, those who were killed and those who were maimed."[167]

The prisoners and the missing were the military's best, carefully chosen for the most demanding and glamorous work it had to offer. They could have been cast by Hollywood, so perfectly did they embody the warrior ideal. Shortly before he was shot down, air force colonel Robinson "Robbie" Risner appeared on the cover of *Time* "as the classic example of the kind of dedicated military professional who was leading the American effort in Vietnam."[168] Strangely, those words became more true over the seven years he spent in Hanoi, as POWs became central to the American war effort and Risner became one of their celebrated leaders. In fact, the war's extraordinary length contributed to the prisoners' mystique. Since men shot down over South Vietnam and Laos were easier to recover than those lost over North Vietnam, most POWs and MIAs were shot down before the 1968 bombing halt over North Vietnam.[169] This prolonged their captivity and produced unusually distinguished prisoners, as the war's early shootdowns included many senior officers seeking combat experience to propel them up the ranks after a decade-long hiatus since Korea. Twenty-four achieved flag rank before retiring. Eight received the Congressional Medal of Honor. And one, Colonel George "Bud" Day, counts himself among the most highly decorated officers in the twentieth century.[170] After working with these men and their families over two decades, Frank Sieverts called them "the top levels of their culture and society. They had about them an air of invulnerability, of almost magic."[171] As a similar sense of national invulnerability disappeared in Vietnam, these Cold War icons were reminders of all that was lost.

As much as who they were, it was their role in the war that distinguished downed pilots. If the war's critics reserved their harshest scorn for the volunteers who fought the air war, most Americans saw them as more comfortably removed from the war's moral ambiguities since the devastating effects of aerial bombardment were seldom reported by the American press.[172] The more illogical and ineffective the war of attrition on the ground became, the more attractive air war appeared, producing fewer American casualties, fewer documented atrocities, and fewer complaints from the field. The career professionals who carried it out were unlikely to risk their advancement with dissent. Instead, they were likely to celebrate their skills and exaggerate their success. Once shot down, pilots became even more sympathetic. For some they were victims of the enemy, for others victims of government policy, for others victims of antiwar activists, but always victims.[173] "The POW hero could have it both ways," literary critic Elliot Gruner argued; "he could prosecute the war as daredevil pilot at the same time that he could transfer any deep responsibility for his activities to the political superstructure he served."[174]

Who the prisoners were shaped how Americans responded to them. Their middle-class respectability allowed Middle Americans to share the conceit "that all our sons in Vietnam are POWs" even though few white middle-class men fought there, while their stoic suffering rallied the working Americans who supplied the bulk of U.S. forces in Vietnam to their side. As the army disintegrated into chaos and veterans grew alienated from the mainstream, POWs were obedient ciphers.[175] In place of a pluralistic society divided by war, they and their relatives substituted seemingly tight-knit families. As Christian Appy and David Farber have observed, the families of those fighting in Vietnam were unlikely to protest the war or condone those who did. By encouraging familiarity with captive and missing Americans, Nixon supporters sought to foster a similar silence across society. Yet, Appy and Farber also suggest, support for the war was lowest among those who sacrificed the most in Vietnam.[176] If POWs and their families were more familiar than soldiers and veterans, their unending sacrifice was only more disturbing as a result. By asking Americans to imagine "that all our sons in Vietnam are POWs," Nixon's critics invited those comfortably removed from the war to feel its ongoing burdens.

In either case, the moral authority of the family was essential to the desired identification, making the League of Families, not Nixon, the central player in debates about the prisoners. Americans were only dimly aware of the sociological characteristics of the POW population. The fact that most captives were pilots was widely reported, but the ramifications were unclear to most civilians. What everyone understood, though—what every news story and speech made clear—was that these were family men. And it was their families, particularly their wives, who were the focus and agents of public concern.

POW/MIA wives were as distinctive as their husbands. Helpmeets of the aviator corps, they represented a High Cold War feminine ideal. Attending her first League meeting in 1969, Barbara Mullen recalled that "we were identical except for size and hair color: A-line dresses, just short enough but not mini, closed-toed shoes, and hair in various stages of teased and sprayed perfection."[177] Asked to describe them, one man compared them to another staple of jet set sex appeal, calling them "pretty—like airline stewardesses." With most in their mid-twenties to mid-thirties, these women cut striking figures in a national debate over the war dominated by wealthy, powerful men and college-age youths. Unlike other participants in that debate, they were middle-class women whose arguments hinged on personal experience rather than political theory. "Bright, attractive, with that clean tanned outdoor look of so many young American women," they appealed to the broad middle in a polarized political culture. "Slender, gracious and attractive," the POW/MIA wives around Oceana Naval Base "have children and live in tasteful homes with well-manicured lawns," Judy Klemesrud reported for the *New York Times*, but behind closed doors they were "going through a personal kind of hell, an agony that only those in the same situations can really understand."[178]

The spectacle of these beautiful young women living in a state of suspended animation, often with children in tow, gave the wives unmistakable pathos. Some writers went out of their way to infantilize these accomplished, worldly women, seeking out atypical young wives like Patty Zuhoski who "probably didn't even realize there was a Viet Nam War" when she married in 1967. Only twenty years old at the time, Zuhoski spent just ten days with her husband before he deployed, soon after which he was shot down. Unable to hold down her job, she returned to live with her parents, where she did "volunteer Red Cross work, audited college courses, played bridge, read a good deal." Though her circumstances were unusual, her lonely isolation became the emotional archetype associated with the wives. "What am I supposed to do?" she asked *Time*. "I can't go out and date. But I can only put up with these wives once or twice a week. . . . It's a very lonely existence. You're married but you're not married. You're not divorced or widowed. Where does that put you?" This lament came up again and again. "It's hard," Eileen Cormier told *Life*; "we're not divorced, not widowed, and we're not really married either." Limbo was a common trope, lending its name to a serial novel about POW wives that ran in *Mc-Call's* before becoming a B-movie of the same name. Married for two weeks when her husband left for Vietnam, *Limbo's* protagonist endured six years before she saw him again. "The lack of definition is what bothered her the most . . . she was neither wife nor widow . . . nothing to look forward to, nor anything to mourn . . . and no end to this emotional wasteland was in sight."[179]

The nightmare of war without end gave these stories resonance. Just as POW wives wed themselves to war in marrying their husbands, Americans felt trapped in a commitment they had not anticipated and could not honorably escape. This view ignored U.S. responsibility for the war and obscured American aggression—Americans may have been misled about the war in Vietnam, but by the time POWs dominated public discourse only the willfully ignorant could persist in the idea that they were its passive victims. "There's a good deal of sentiment and dreamy invention attached to the American prisoners of war," Grace Paley wrote in a 1972 opinion piece for the *New York Times*. "Politicians and newsmen often talk as though these pilots had been kidnapped from a farm in Iowa or out of a canoe paddling the waterways of Minnesota. In reality, they were fliers shot down out of the North Vietnamese sky where they had no business to be; out of that blueness they were dumping death." Politicians, reporters, and their audiences romanticized prisoners because they typically encountered them through their families, whose memories gravitated toward Iowa farms and Minnesota waterways. Knowing this, Paley ended her article by recounting a conversation with an MIA wife: "I told her about the villagers living in wet dark tunnels for years, shattered by pellets—seared by napalm—I told her only what my own eyes had seen, the miles of maniac craters." "Oh, Mrs. Paley," exclaimed the unnamed woman. "My husband wouldn't do that!"[180]

Critics like Paley charged such women and their supporters with ignoring war's realities in favor of fantasies. Yet not all wives were blind to the war's brutality and not all who reported on them emphasized innocence. The same story that profiled Patty Zuhoski also featured Lynn Glenn, who acknowledged that her husband may have "bombed schools, maimed women, killed children." "I was a twenty-year-old teeny-bopper," Glenn said of the woman she was when her husband went to war. Five years later, her poem "War Waste" made clear that she had changed. "Where are the big brave warriors now?" it asked. "His silver, supersonic soarer. His bomb-blowing, truck-finding Sea-swooping carrier, Where is it? Him, the educated engineer, architect, Geologist, economist, turned Bon vivant aviator, Where is he? . . . He was proud. Mom, apple pie and the red, white and blue were with him. Now he is in a cell. He wears pajamas, sleeps on a mat . . . and waits." Such jaundiced depictions were rare among POW families, but so were ringing endorsements of the war. War-weariness was more common. "I never knew what war was," Zuhoski told *Time*. "I know now."[181]

Like most Americans, the families shared the antiwar movement's doubts about the war. But like most Americans, they distrusted the movement's motives. Stockdale "felt strongly that these antiwar activists were spreading enemy propaganda in the United States." COLIAFAM made a "pretense of being helpful," but in her view its members "serve[d] Hanoi's propaganda purposes." "If they hadn't kept shouting in the media that the poor innocent North Vietnamese were the victims of United States imperialists, our own population would have been more inclined to support our forces." More than anything, this reversal of their preferred victimology convinced League leaders that war protestors were disloyal. Seeing themselves "as living, breathing proof that the North Vietnamese are inhumane barbarians rather than the warmhearted, innocent loving humanitarians some of the press preferred to believe," few could fathom how "anyone with a sense of honor" could sympathize with the enemy.[182]

This is not to say that antiwar activists antagonized the families. There were those like Paley who insisted that "the man in the sky is a killer" and instances when wives were told "your husband is a murderer!" but the movement took pains to show concern for POWs and their families, and its members did more than most Americans, including those in the Nixon administration, to improve their lot.[183] Suggestions to the contrary were meant to alienate the war's vocal opponents from the millions who quietly agreed with them.[184] But women whose interests and identities were densely interwoven with the military establishment found it difficult to separate criticism of the war from criticism of its warriors.

Paula Woods illustrates how heavily some were invested in military power. Writing to an NSC staffer on "Mrs. Brian D. Woods" stationery, she confessed that if she "demonstrate[d] against our country . . . Brian would divorce me."[185] She might also have been disowned by her father and father-in-law, both retired admirals.[186] Such military ties were common in the shadow of World War II. "America in the fifties was a strangely militarized land," Tom Engelhardt recalled of his boyhood trips to West Point with his veteran father.[187] For League women it remained so well afterward. When Patty Zuhoski returned to her girlhood home, "talks with her father, a retired Air Force colonel, and a friend who had been a World War II p.o.w., at least reduced the unknown terrors."[188] Stockdale called on her best friend, Doyen Salsig, whose father was an admiral and husband a captain, for advice and support.[189] "My husband is a career officer," Kathleen Risner told reporters. "I don't think he'd like me to feel very anti-this or anti-that, and until he comes back and tells me it wasn't worth it, I'm not going to let myself feel that way."[190] "The men are still up for promotion while they're prisoners, and we live off their rank in a lot of ways," another wife confessed. "There's a temptation to politick for promotion by trying to please the Pentagon."[191]

However much their ties to the military left the League disinclined to side with antiwar activists, though, those ties did not guarantee perpetual support for the war. As she listened to Nixon explain how "he would try to separate the prisoner issue out from the war" in December 1969, Stockdale thought to herself that "that didn't make any sense to me. How could you separate one from the other when one was an integral part of the other?"[192] Stockdale wrote to Nixon's military aide in January that "just because publicly we, the wives and families, still say that we think our government is doing everything possible to help our men, we do NOT really believe this is the case." "Time is running out for our patience. . . . Seeing another year come up on that calendar and being trapped in this untenable situation tests a person's loyalty beyond the limits of endurance." "It seems perfectly reasonable to me and many others," she closed, to expect "everyone out and properly accounted for by Christmas." Here was the authentic voice of the silent majority—silent not in support of the war but in terror "at the alternatives I am being forced to consider."[193] Having declared these women the leaders of this vaporous constituency, Nixon could ill afford their defection.

HANOI MAY USE PRISONERS TO SQUEEZE US

"The PW situation is not good," Frank Sieverts confessed in a June 1970 memo to Elliot Richardson. "There are virtually no signs of progress toward the release of our PW's" and "even the superficials are wearing thin." To get things moving he suggested tying troop withdrawals to prisoner releases, despite "concern on Kissinger's staff that Hanoi may use prisoners explicitly to try to squeeze a timetable out of us." "Such a possibility is always there," Sieverts conceded, "but we might as well capitalize on it. . . . If nothing else, this will ease the feelings of the families, many of whom see our gradual troop withdrawals and Vietnamization as an eroding process in which the prisoners are the forgotten factor."[194]

Pinned between the League's impatience and stasis at the bargaining table, his superiors preferred to play for time. In August Nixon dispatched astronaut Frank Borman on a twelve-nation tour as a presidential emissary on prisoners of war. Borman returned to report no "major breakthroughs or significant change in the position of the North Vietnamese Government."[195] The breakthrough came two weeks later when PRG Foreign Minister Madam Nguyen Thi Binh put forth an eight-point plan at the Paris talks that offered to "engage at once in discussions" concerning the release of American POWs in return for a pledge to withdraw all U.S. forces from Vietnam by 30 June 1971 and the formation of a neutral coalition government in Saigon. The first time the other side had proposed negotiating over POWs prior to war's end, the proposal seemed like a serious concession.[196] In fact, it was the beginning of the squeeze Kissinger feared. Rather than concede to the groundswell of support for POWs, Binh used it to force Nixon from Vietnam. By making him choose between POWs and South Vietnamese leader Nguyen Van Thieu, party strategists exposed "an uncomfortable contradiction in the Nixon camp." "If Nixon refused to respond," Robert Brigham has written, "doves in the United States Congress and antiwar forces would make it difficult for Washington to manage the domestic crisis."[197]

Nixon was less worried about doves than hawks. "I came into office without the support of all the people who oppose me today," he told his staff, "and I can get reelected without their support."[198] "We've got the Left where we want it," he told Kissinger. "All they've got to argue for is a bug-out." For Nixon, the danger of Binh's plan came from the right — "when the Right starts wanting to get out, for whatever reason, that's *our* problem."[199] With a prisoner release on the table, POW families might break with the White House, taking millions of Nixon voters with them. To dramatize the threat, a letter from Mrs. T. E. Collins III in Mississippi landed on the president's desk days after Binh's proposal: "I can no longer remain silent . . . while you and our leaders in Washington play God and politics with the life of my wonderful husband and hundreds of other brave Americans rotting in enemy 'hell-holes.'" This woman was no member of the antiwar left. "These primitive and barbaric people understand only one thing — FORCE!" she said of the Vietnamese. But that expression of hatred for the enemy was buried in four pages of vitriol directed at Nixon. "I am all out of *answers*, Mr. President," but "I am now through with flag waving!" "My voice is small crying out in the darkness of my distress, but I tell you it will soon be joined by others in their plight, and rest assured we will be heard."[200]

To forestall such defections from the silent majority, Nixon offered his own five-point plan in October, proposing "the immediate and unconditional release of all prisoners of war held by both sides" along with a cease-fire in place.[201] The communists refused to relinquish their POW bargaining chip, but the plan provided "temporary relief from public pressures" while Nixon plotted his next move—a dramatic raid on an empty prison in Son Tay, North Vietnam, on 21 November. At 2:00 A.M. that morning roughly five dozen Special Forces raided the prison twenty-three miles west of Hanoi only to find it empty. Meanwhile, 200 American aircraft carried out "protective reaction" strikes against Hanoi, Haiphong, and the Ho Chi Minh trail, continuing the bombardment over two days though the raid lasted less than an hour. Kissinger blamed an "egregious failure of intelligence" for the absence of prisoners at Son Tay, but DIA informed Laird and the Joint Chiefs that the camp was likely empty days before the raid.[202] Still, if the raid failed, it gave Nixon an excuse to violate the bombing halt, showed the communists that he could use the POWs to escalate the war as easily as end it, and threw red meat to his base. When the chairman of the Joint Chiefs telephoned Stockdale for her reaction, she told him it "was a real shot in the arm."[203] In an op-ed piece for the *New York Times*, MIA sister Barbara Ondarisk pronounced herself "delighted" that "after all these agonizing years, somebody was doing something."[204]

Nixon's critics were less impressed. Calling the raid "very provocative," Senator Fulbright refused to allow a resolution commending it out of the Foreign Relations Committee, charging that "officials knew there were no prisoners there and that the mission had other purposes."[205] Editorialists at the *St. Louis Post-Dispatch* blasted it as a "blunder of the first magnitude," while those at the *New York Times* called it "an abortive exercise in military theatrics." "The Pentagon has established such a reputation for mendacity," the *Post-Dispatch* chided, "that all explanations of such actions must be viewed skeptically."[206] Some POW/MIA shared such suspicions, with one contending that "they went into an empty camp deliberately" and another dismissing the raid as a "grandstand play."[207] Cora Weiss accused Nixon of "deceiving the American public about the P.O.W. issue" "to gain support for a win-the-war policy."[208]

Having run out of other compelling reasons to wage war, Nixon increasingly emphasized the prisoners as his justification. "As long as the North Vietnamese have any Americans," he vowed in February 1971, "there will be Americans in South Vietnam and enough Americans to give them an incentive to release the prisoners."[209] At the same time, he grossly inflated the number in captivity, claiming "there are 1,600 Americans in North Vietnam jails" when the DRV reported just 339 American captives and the Pentagon listed only 460 men in POW status. By suggesting some 1,200 MIAs were alive when all evidence suggested otherwise, Nixon created a Catch-22 formula for endless war.[210] "As long as there is one American being held prisoner by North Vietnam," he told newspaper editors in April, "we are going to retain that force," adding that "I think it will work in the end."[211]

He was wrong. In the end, his attempt to use the prisoners to prolong the war backfired. By focusing on POWs, Nixon only increased their value and raised more questions as to why he did not withdraw in order to win their return. Madame Binh, Xuan Thuy, and Le Duc Tho exploited the flaws in Nixon's logic by repeating earlier offers to exchange the POWs for peace. In July Tho promised that "all American prisoners may promptly return to their homes" with the "withdrawal of all American forces from Vietnam."[212] Outplayed, Kissinger seethed that "we will not settle the war just for prisoners" at their next secret meeting.[213] But he could hardly say this publicly. Unwilling to admit that they valued Thieu's survival over that of American prisoners, administration officials could only complain, as Agnew did, that "North Vietnam thinks that by holding our men hostages, they can compel the President to cave in to their demands — demands for a United States pullout, abandonment of the present elected government of South Vietnam, an end to all military activity."[214]

Most Americans no longer saw an alternative. Opinion polls found that 70 percent of Americans favored withdrawal from Vietnam by the end of the year even if it meant South Vietnam's collapse.[215] The White House countered with its own numbers showing that 75 percent opposed disengagement "that threatens the lives or safety of American prisoners of war," essentially confirming *New Yorker* correspondent Richard Rovere's claim that prisoner welfare was "the only remaining war aim of any respectability."[216] But as the president leaned more heavily on POWs to shore up his support, a growing number of their families broke ranks. After meeting with League leaders in January, Deputy National Security Adviser Alexander Haig alerted Kissinger that "they are on the verge of launching a major attack against the Administration." "The wives appear especially anguished at the prospect of what Vietnamization means in terms of U.S. leverage to obtain a release of their loved ones," Haig told his boss, and "equally concerned at the high level of fog content and phony assurance that they have received." Advising Kissinger to see them soon, Haig concluded glumly

MAY • 1971

V ★ F ★ W

VETERANS OF FOREIGN WARS MAGAZINE

P.O.W.

"I Hope Those Withdrawal Plans Include Us"

As demands for U.S. withdrawal gained momentum, White House officials warned that such a step risked POW abandonment. This VFW cover suggesting such a danger circulated widely inside the White House. (Courtesy Jan Erdmann and VFW *Magazine*)

51

— • —

that "it would be difficult, if not impossible, to ameliorate their fundamental concerns which are legitimate and understandable."[217]

At a hastily arranged meeting with Kissinger thirty-six hours later, Stockdale and Louise Mulligan, the League's West and East coast founders, informed him that "since there would be withdrawal and no Allied victory in Vietnam," they were ready to support anyone "who sounded confident on trading a withdrawal date and other concessions for the possibility of POW exchanges."[218] Angry letters from the League rank and file backed up their threat. "I am fed up (to say the least) with the way the Missing and Prisoner of War situation is being handled," one MIA wife wrote in March. "I demand a *complete troop withdrawal NOW!*"[219] In April, 123 dissidents calling themselves POW/MIA Families for Immediate Release placed an ad in the *Washington Post* demanding a timetable for withdrawal. By October the group had grown to 350 members despite the Pentagon's refusal to mail its application materials to POW/MIA families on the grounds that "your organization's efforts focus to some extent on the political/military issues involving a settlement of the conflict in Southeast Asia."[220] In May, another group of comparable size called the Ad Hoc Committee for POWs and MIAs placed an ad in the *Post* advocating withdrawal within 150 days of a commitment to release all POWs on both sides. Dismissing other war aims, the ad shrugged: "Let Hanoi stand before the tribunal of world opinion if this war continues."[221] When the marines sent Families for Immediate Release co-founder Barbara Mullen a stern reminder that "your efforts should be void of reference to political or military issues," she responded, "Bullshit!"[222]

"It shook me up when the administration made it appear we were there because of the POWs," one wife told the *Wall Street Journal*. "I resent using the POWs as an excuse to stay in Vietnam."[223] Asking if "the 'residual force' was to be left in South Vietnam for the sake of the prisoners, or whether the prisoners were to be left in North Vietnam for the sake of the 'residual force,'" these relatives grasped the logic of the antiwar position for the first time.[224] "The cruel deception in President Nixon's policy of Vietnamization is the assertion that American troops will remain in South Vietnam as long as there are any American prisoners of war in North Vietnam," the *Virginian-Pilot* told its large military readership around Norfolk, when "the effect is just the reverse: the American POWs will stay in North Vietnam as long as American forces are maintained in the South."[225] "The pledge of President Nixon to maintain a residual force of troops within South Vietnam gives no real hope for the release of our men," Valerie Kushner of Families for Immediate Release fumed; "it creates a situation in which the prisoners have become political hostages."[226] "When I see how we have been used to gain support for the war, I wish I had never put up that billboard or urged anyone to write to Hanoi," another POW wife seethed. "I would like to put up a new billboard now—one which reads: 'President Nixon, end the war so the prisoners can come home.'"[227]

The wives' revolt alarmed the White House. At an April meeting with the president, Senator Dole, the Republican National Committee chairman, warned that "there is a real danger of great numbers of POW wives reversing their support of the President."[228] His words left Nixon "with great concern that the families of the POW/MIA are about to defect spontaneously and in large numbers."[229] With thousands of Vietnam veterans gathered in Washington to protest the war that spring, Haldeman instructed his staff: "We've got to be doubly sure we are keeping the POW wives in line."[230] Chiming in from Defense, Laird added that "the families have become increasingly impatient, frustrated and susceptible to any scheme that holds promise of securing the release of their men." "If the families should turn against the Administration," he predicted, "we believe that general public support would also."[231]

To avoid this fate, Nixon ordered his military aide General James Hughes to put together "a fairly major move for cosmetic purposes."[232] Hughes promised him "a dramatic, innovative move—perhaps only of cosmetic nature."[233] But he told Haldeman that "the frustration which the families feel is sufficiently deep to preclude being satisfied or allayed by an Administration PR or 'cosmetic' effort. I believe it will have to be something substantive in the area of policy affecting the conduct of the war or the Paris talks."[234] Nonetheless, Hughes returned with a PR-intensive package "devoted to keeping the families on the reservation." Devised with input from special counsel Charles Colson, the plan included daily phone calls to the League from senior administration officials, frequent meetings with Kissinger, a $150 million Ad Council campaign, and appearances by Nixon and Laird at the League's second annual convention in September designed to offset an appearance by antiwar senator Edward Kennedy.[235] With Dole's help, Hughes also arranged to share the RNC donor list with the League, along with detailed fundraising instructions.[236]

Back from briefing the families on a twenty-one-stop tour in June, Roger Shields reported that "only a very small minority," which he estimated at 5 percent on the left and 5 percent on the right, was "ready to openly dissociate themselves from the Administration." But he found as few as "twenty percent of attending families supports completely Administration policy," with most "discouraged because of the duration of the problem."[237] The validity of his assessment is difficult to judge since League leaders refused to allow dissidents to poll its membership. Louise Mulligan, the League's East Coast organizer, quit the group in May over its refusal to poll, maintaining that its leadership was "no longer representative of the wishes of the members."[238] But Shields may have been right that dissenters were no more representative. Many high-profile POW wives were ready to end the war at all costs, but MIA families were more reluctant. "The MIA wives tended to be more hawkish," Taylor Branch reported, "perhaps because they felt sure they had already made their sacrifice and wanted it to count for something." Financial incentives were also at work since MIA families continued to draw the missing man's salary as long as the war continued. "When the war ends and my husband is presumed dead," one MIA wife confessed, "I start living off his pension. It's less than half as much." Unable to replace a lost loved one through remarriage, MIA parents and siblings were more bellicose still.[239] With so many internal divisions, it is impossible to measure the precise state of family sentiment on the war, but assuming the 1,076 family members who attended the Pentagon's June briefings can be taken as a rough estimate of active POW/MIA relatives, the 350 members of Families for Immediate Release and 150 co-signers of the Ad Hoc Committee's advertisement represented a sizable percentage of all active relatives, including many of the most prominent POW wives.[240]

Like other Americans, POW/MIA families were divided and confused, but above all sick of the war. Encountering "seething unrest" at the League's September meeting, Stockdale told Kissinger "that revolution against the administration was brewing within our organization." Though she was unwilling to break with Nixon, she approved the formation of a political lobby within the League and reasoned that "it didn't do any harm at all to have a radical fringe group as part of our organization" in order to bring "pressure to bear on the administration."[241] Following its September meeting the League formally petitioned Congress "to undertake immediate and vigorous action to resolve the conflict in Southeast Asia and to assure the prompt return of all prisoners and an accounting of the missing in all areas in Southeast Asia."[242]

Visible dissent among the families gave legitimacy to those who advocated peaceful solutions to the POW problem. In January, twenty-three congressmen sponsored a bipartisan plan for "proportional repatriation" linking troop withdrawals to POW releases on a percentage basis. Seizing on the plan as "a vehicle to show . . . how mistaken is the view that the families are in accord with the Administration," Louise Mulligan embraced it.[243] "My initial instincts are very much opposed to it," Republican congressman Wendell Wyatt of Oregon wrote Kissinger; "however, the pressures for such a proposition are building enormously."[244] After listening to one POW wife call for "total withdrawal," his Democratic colleague, Charles Bennett of Florida, told Nixon that "we have now gone so far in the direction of ending our participation in the war that it makes more sense to me to remove ourselves entirely as promptly as we can from South Vietnam in a way in which we can secure the prisoners of war."[245]

Hardly Nixon's trump card in domestic political debate, POWs were increasingly cited as a rationale to end the war. While historians are right to note that legislation cutting off funds for the war included escape clauses to ensure POW release, these measures were meant to attract supporters to end the war initiatives, not repel them.[246] One week before the vote on the McGovern-Hatfield amendment requiring withdrawal of all U.S. forces by the end of the year, Xuan Thuy assured Americans that "the question of the release of prisoners is related only to the military question," while former defense secretary Clark Clifford told an antiwar group that talks with the DRV had convinced him that all Americans would be released within thirty days of an agreement to withdraw.[247] Rather than using the prisoners to head off the amendment, Secretary of State William Rogers called a news conference on the eve of the vote to announce that "although we have tremendous concern for the safety of the prisoners, we can't lose sight of our national purposes and we can't absolutely abandon our national objectives to pay ransom."[248]

After his amendment was narrowly defeated, McGovern flew to Paris to extract Thuy's promise that the prisoners would be released with an American withdrawal. He told Thuy such a step would "greatly strengthen my political ability" to "bring an end of the war." Thuy refused without a commitment to replace Thieu as head of state, showing he had distorted his bargaining position in order to increase pressure on Nixon.[249] He recognized that the POWs were "the only remaining major incentive for the United States to negotiate seriously on a political settlement," and would not give them up solely for military withdrawal when his party's ultimate goal was to put an end to the U.S.-backed government of South Vietnam.[250] McGovern emerged from the meeting with only a sound bite — "President Nixon holds the key to the jail cells in Hanoi" — albeit one that placed additional pressure on Nixon to pull out.

In truth the communists held the keys and were jangling them loudly. The splintering of POW/MIA families freed Nixon's opponents to turn up the volume. "The clamor will rise for a straight deal of fixed withdrawals for release of prisoners," Kissinger predicted.[251] Increasingly, Democratic presidential aspirants like McGovern sought to make POWs "the issue that cuts most deeply against the incumbent administration"; "I just think the administration is so vulnerable on this issue," Edward Kennedy told reporters after appearing at the League's 1971 convention.[252] So did McGovern, which is why he asked POW wife Valerie Kushner to second his nomination at the 1972 Democratic National Convention, and ran ads in the days before the election accusing Nixon of "dooming our prisoners of war to remain locked in their cells indefinitely."[253] So did the Vietnamese, who tried to tip the outcome in McGovern's favor by releasing three Americans to COLIAFAM and antiwar POW families six weeks before the election. By then even the White House knew the issue worked against it. "We may be sure that the upcoming release of three U.S. POWs will be exploited to the hilt by the anti-war activists," Haig wrote to Agnew on the eve of the 1972 release. "We strongly feel that our best tactic at present is to avoid drawing attention to the role played by anti-war activists in the release of the POWs."[254]

Haig's reversal of the Go Public strategy illustrates how badly the Nixon administration was outmaneuvered on the POW/MIA issue. Though the POW/MIA issue failed to swing the election in McGovern's favor, the plight

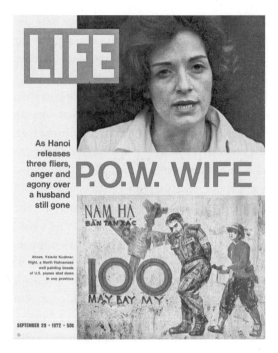

As Hanoi releases three fliers, anger and agony over a husband still gone

P.O.W. WIFE

Above, Valerie Kushner. Right, a North Vietnamese wall painting boasts of U.S. planes shot down in one province

SEPTEMBER 29 · 1972 · 50¢

This *Life* magazine cover, featuring antiwar activist Valerie Kushner and Vietnamese POW propaganda, was characteristic of late war reporting on the POWs. (Top photo and LIFE® used by permission of Life Inc.; bottom photo © Marc Riboud/Magnum Photos)

of the POWs only added to the list of reasons to end the war. It strengthened the hand of those who held them captive and highlighted the efforts of the antiwar movement working to bring them home. Though Go Public began a counteroffensive to POW/MIA initiatives already underway from those quarters, enlisting millions of Americans in POW/MIA activism, there is little evidence to suggest that such activism translated into support for the war. Though POW posturing gave Nixon political cover for extending the war, its unintended consequences also created the conditions for bringing about its end. When Nixon reversed preelection claims that peace was at hand by resuming bombardment over Hanoi, the DRV's first countermeasure was to threaten to withhold the repatriation of American POWs until all political prisoners were released from South Vietnam. Combined with its success in downing fifteen B-52s and capturing another thirty-one airmen, such threats helped bring Nixon back to the bargaining table, while the sixty-day prisoner repatriation prevented him from breaking the peace agreement that was finally signed there on 27 January 1973.[255]

ONE WAY TO SHOW THEIR FRUSTRATION

Eighteen months after he helped orchestrate the League's Constitution Hall debut, Bob Dole told CBS News that "we don't want to get out just for the prisoners. They're very important, but they represent less than one half of one percent of the Americans who've died in South Vietnam."[256] Dole's observation not only illustrates the reversals of POW/MIA politics in the war's last years, but also raises an important question: Why did Americans care so much about POWs when they represented a fraction of the war's costs? The answer can be found in the phenomenal sales of copper and nickel ID bracelets bearing the names of individual missing and imprisoned Americans. Unveiled by a Los Angeles group named VIVA in May 1970, POW/MIA bracelets adorned the wrists of over four million Americans by early 1973. Particularly popular among young people, the bracelets were also worn by Ronald Reagan, George McGovern, George Wallace, General William Westmoreland, General Creighton Abrams, Charlton Heston, Sonny and Cher, Miss America, and Princess Grace of Monaco. Their enormous appeal—sales peaked at 60,000 bracelets per day in 1972—provides insight into the intentions of the millions of Americans who signed petitions, wrote letters, and bought bracelets on behalf of POWs and MIAs.[257]

The motives of the bracelet's inventors were clear enough. An acronym for Victory in Vietnam Association, VIVA was incorporated in 1967 to "support and encourage our American government and our American servicemen wherever they might be involved in a struggle against aggression, most specifically at this time in Vietnam."[258] Before its bracelets brought it fame and fortune, VIVA achieved notoriety in conservative circles when one of its leaders removed barricades set up by striking students at Los Angeles City College, earning an appreciative phone call from Nixon.[259] VIVA intended the bracelets to be "a symbol of cooperation between the concerned businessman, responsible students, and the P.O.W. families" in support of the Vietnam War.[260]

Like their Young Americans for Freedom peers, VIVA preferred "the lectern and the party caucus"—not to mention the cocktail party—to the picket line, so it was appropriate that the group only became fully formed once five of its members met Los Angeles socialite Gloria Coppin at a dinner party in 1966 and made her their chairwoman.[261] As Sybil Stockdale would do for the League, Coppin made VIVA a prominent voice in the national conversation about the war. Coppin had much in common with Stockdale and other League wives. Like them, she was a Sunbelt mother of three married to a man with a career in military aviation, though her husband's position with the aerospace giant Hydro-Mills, the company her father founded, was safer and far better paying.[262] A "housewife who can afford household help," Coppin used her wealth, connections, and leisure time to make VIVA a serious player in California politics.[263] Under her direction, it attracted conservative luminaries such as Ronald Reagan, Los Angeles mayor Samuel Yorty, Nebraska senator Carl Curtis, General Curtis LeMay, Ross Perot, Bob Hope, and Pat Boone to its annual Salute to the Armed Forces ball, where guests thrilled to the grand cavalcade of admirals and generals in attendance, set to spotlights and trumpet fanfare by famed Hollywood choreographer Leroy Prinz.[264] It also moved off campus onto Westwood Boulevard, where Stephen Frank and Carol Bates quit college to become its salaried "student" leaders.[265]

With support for the war plummeting, in 1969 VIVA changed the meaning of its name from Victory in Vietnam Association to Voices in Vital America. "I wondered whether or not somebody might think we were one of those 'Let's Bomb Hanoi' groups," Coppin worried. "The word 'victory,'" she proposed, was never intended "to mean military conquest. Rather, it meant support."[266] Coppin's repositioning of VIVA's views reflected a larger effort in conservative circles to redefine support for the unpopular war as support for its troops and prisoners, an effort eventually coordinated from the White House, but which began at the grassroots and depended on private initiatives. Inspired but unsatisfied by Nixon's "silent majority" speech, VIVA sought to give this inert constituency a voice. "Once a substantial portion of the so called 'silent majority' is unified by something other than silence," its 1970 prospectus theorized, "it can easily be directed to act as a deterrent to destructive groups."[267]

In the POW/MIA bracelet, unveiled in the same prospectus, VIVA found its cause. Both Coppin and Bates take credit for conceiving of the bracelet after meeting radio host and future right-wing congressman Bob Dornan, who wore a wristband he received from a Montagnard tribesman. Thinking such a memento would make an excellent reminder "of the suffering of POWs," Coppin hired a metal shop in Santa Monica to produce the initial run of 1,200 metal bands using metals donated by Hydro-Mills. Stamped with the name of an individual POW or MIA and his date of loss, the bracelet was meant to "stimulate personal involvement and awareness throughout the nation on the plight of Americans who are missing in action or prisoners of war of the communists in Asia" and reduce "the antagonism of young people toward our military" as "rapport was built between a student and the family of a P.O.W." The idea was not only "timely, necessary, and worthwhile but it will also generate much needed revenue," Stephen Frank explained in an appeal to corporate donors for advertising funds.[268]

With production costs of thirty cents per piece for bracelets that sold for $2.50 to $3.00 each, the bracelet was the goose that laid a golden egg.

In 1972 VIVA took in $3.7 million; in 1973 its income rose to $7.4 million. In addition to lavish executive compensation, it spent its millions on a massive POW/MIA public awareness campaign that included newspaper ads and billboards, tens of millions of buttons, brochures, bumper-stickers, and matchbooks, and direct mail and monthly newsletters sent to a mailing list of over 150,000.[269] "There wasn't a day that there weren't three or four POW/MIA events going on somewhere in the nation," Coppin later recalled.[270] Presented as charitable rather than promotional, such programs fueled bracelet sales while protecting the proceeds from taxation.

Newsweek dismissed the bracelets as a "fad," the first in a decade-long series of pet rocks and other inert objects invested with undue significance. But VIVA's mail convinced it that the bracelets were powerful totems for the millions who wore them. "It is not a fad," executive director Robert Treese responded in a letter to the editor, "it's a deep concern. It's a movement. It's compassion. It's love. It's Americanism."[271] Empty as his words may seem, the bracelet was some or all of these things to its owners.

"When you wear this bracelet, the war isn't far away," explained the head of a New York modeling agency.[272] A columnist for the Record in Cedar Falls, Iowa, wrote that the man on her bracelet "became part of my life, and I part of his." She imagined him as her "brother," who "speaks directly to me every hour." "Please, for God's sake, somebody help me," he implored through her "bracelet of unspeakable despair."[273] "It's almost as if I've adopted him," another young woman told VIVA. "I'm only 21, so that probably sounds silly, but I don't know how else to say it."[274] Some buyers heightened their sense of connection by requesting a man from their state or a particular branch of service; others requested the name of an enlisted man. VIVA kept a list of black POWs and MIAs to satisfy orders from African Americans.[275] Many wearers sought information about the man on their wrist. The bulk of VIVA's mail consisted of letters asking, "Can I write a letter of support to his family?" or requests for advice, such as "What should be written to his family?" since "I find it very difficult to relay my feelings to a family that must be living in such despair."[276]

These letters indicate that the bracelets reduced antagonism between the wearer and the soldier named on the bracelet, as VIVA intended. But this sentiment can hardly be equated to "Victory in Vietnam"–style jingoism. Some buyers embraced the brand of national unity VIVA promoted. "I think this country needed an issue like this to occur," one wrote, "so that it would unite people." But at a time when most Americans considered the war a mistake, their remorse was only intensified by a sense of connection with one of its victims.[277] "I've gone to bed many nights and just stayed awake thinking of what Mr. Dodge is like and hating to even imagine what awful things happened to him in Vietnam," wrote one. "I know there are hundreds of thousands of other Americans who were killed or captured, and I cringe every time I think how unnecessary it was."[278] One sailor on the USS *Kansas City* off the coast of Vietnam sent $130 of combat pay to VIVA with instructions to "see to it that the money aids those P.O.W.'s and persons missing in action in the atrocity we refer to as the Vietnam War."[279] His money was undoubtedly spent on purposes other than he intended, but his gesture reveals the range of meanings the bracelets held for the millions who wore them and the sense of loss at the heart of POW/MIA activism. An adviser to the "Interhigh Student Council Association" in Nashville, where half of all students were thought to wear VIVA bracelets, surmised that most who wore them were "from more or less middle-class homes where they are expected to honor their country. They didn't want to feel antiwar, but they couldn't feel in favor of the war." "The bracelets were one way to show their frustration."[280]

CRITICS OF THE POW/MIA issue have charged that it used "simulated images of American POWs in the savage hands of Asian Communists" to transform "America's vision of the war," replacing the war's real Vietnamese victims with fabricated American ones.[281] They contend that Nixon originated this shift, and that later presidents continued it in order to reconstruct American national identity in the aftermath of defeat. For work meant to challenge the historical revisionism and national revanchism that began with Nixon and intensified once he left office, such scholarship is strangely indebted to Nixon's Manichean worldview. Its concern with national leaders and relative disinterest in grassroots and international actors suggests that even scholars who reject the narcissism of Nixon's "silent majority" speech too often make powerful Americans the object of analysis, subordinating everyone else to their will. Caught up in the war of words Nixon helped inspire, thrown on the defensive by his rhetorical assaults, contemporary critics and subsequent scholars assumed that Nixon's plots worked as planned and set out to discount, disprove, or deconstruct the POW/MIA issue without pausing to consider its complexities.

Clearly, Nixon helped focus attention on POWs and MIAs. Yet the real puzzle is why these men and their families mobilized public opinion so powerfully. All presidents, after all, seek to shape public opinion, particularly in wartime, and while such schemes obsessed Nixon, they should not surprise historians. Over three decades five American presidents offered a litany of reasons for U.S. involvement in Vietnam, but few caught the American imagination like POWs and MIAs, and none were seized on by such a wide variety of historical actors for such a host of political, diplomatic, and ideological ends. What ultimately gave the issue such currency and purchase was its accessibility to people outside the White House, beginning with the Vietnamese who first publicized the POWs as a way to pressure the Johnson administration and who continued to do so throughout Nixon's counterattacks. "All kinds of people have been trying to justify their causes in the name of the POW families," Valerie Kushner complained in 1971.[282] "Our husbands were used to fight the war, and we have been used as a reason to keep fighting," another POW wife echoed. "Now we are being used as a reason to get out of the war, but the men are still there."[283] All the while the communists made them constant reminders of the price of war while promising their release in return for withdrawal. Caught in the middle of a war without end, these men and their families became stand-ins for millions of Americans who had lost faith in the war but were unable to escape it.

The idea that Vietnamese communists, antiwar activists, and POW/MIA families played a leading part in POW/MIA politics and diplomacy complicates a received narrative that presents these groups as victims of Nixon's wars. Some may claim that such an analysis ignores power imbalances that make Nixon more culpable than his opponents. But as the new international history on the Vietnam War has shown, placing U.S. policymakers within an expanded field not only allows for an enriched understanding of the war's origins, course, and outcome, it reiterates the degree to which American leaders were ultimately responsible for the war and its losses.[284] While many groups used captive and missing Americans, only one — the Nixon administration — consistently used them to prolong the war.

Other Americans were drawn to these men out of anger, ambivalence, and despair. Their anguish supplemented rather than supplanted negative views of the war and reinforced preexisting grievances. For conservatives they were long-suffering victims of the hated Vietnamese and their cursed allies in the antiwar movement. For antiwar activists, they represented the war's heavy costs, which the war's supporters were loath to admit. For both groups and for those in the middle, their appeal stemmed from the fact that they had been used by their government and abused by their enemy, yet clung loyally to a country and code that had changed irrevocably in their absence. From Puritans to pioneers to POWs, captivity narratives have helped Americans lacking traditional bonds to imagine their community.[285] For Americans living through the social, cultural, and political upheavals of the late 1960s and early 1970s, POWs simultaneously affirmed enduring values and suggested their peril in powerful ways.

In a sense, the massive outpouring of public concern for POWs and MIAs after 1969 represented the final repudiation of the Vietnam War. A war that was entered into, explained, justified, measured, and contested with arguments of Byzantine complexity was reduced to a hostage situation and all that still mattered was getting the prisoners home and recovering the dead. The thought of these men and their families suffering so much for so long for so little purpose moved people to act in ways small and large. Their actions were often wasted energy aimed at Hanoi, or bitterly divisive, blaming Americans for prolonging the prisoners' captivity, or so sodden with sentiment that they became empty gestures. But together they added up to the conviction that the war was not worth the price. Johnson hoped to avoid discussion of the POWs in order to prevent reflection on the terrible cost of the war. Nixon encouraged what he deemed a distraction to accomplish the same end. By the time his advisers recognized, as Al Haig put it to H. R. Haldeman, that "it is self-defeating to beat our breasts about the dilemma of the POWs in a way which contributes to public frustration about our involvement in the war," it was too late to reverse "the overall U.S. attitude of war weariness and frustration with respect to the conflict itself."[286] By encouraging a fixation on seemingly permanent, idealized victims of the war, the POW/MIA issue served as a constant reminder that the war was not over, and that its price in lives destroyed was still to be measured.

For Us the War Still Goes On

The Limits of Homecoming

"For the first time in twelve years, no American military forces are in Vietnam," President Richard Nixon announced in a televised address on 29 March 1973. "All of our American POWs are on their way home." "We can be proud tonight," he told viewers, "that we have achieved our goal of obtaining peace with honor in Vietnam."[1] The return of 591 American prisoners of war was the best evidence he could offer to substantiate his claims of an honorable peace. "The nation's longest battle had ended in nothing like glory," *Time* magazine reported, but the return of the POWs brought "something that the war had always denied—the sense of men redeemed, the satisfaction of something retrieved from the tragedy."[2] Americans who took no pride in the war now hoped "that these impressive men who had become the symbols of American sacrifice in Indochina might help the country heal the lingering wounds of war." As the prisoners returned to a heroes' welcome, "it was almost possible for a moment," *Newsweek* rhapsodized, "to forget the 45,943 other Americans who had lost their lives in Vietnam and 1,334 more who are still listed as missing and unaccounted for."[3]

If it ever existed, that amnesiac moment was fleeting. The day the first returnees touched down on American soil, Tom Wicker wondered in the *New York Times*, "in what way are these relatively few P.O.W.'s greater heroes than the 50,000 dead boys who came home in body bags?"[4] However heroic, the POWs were vastly outnumbered by the number killed in Vietnam, outnumbered too by the roughly 1,400 missing in action in Southeast Asia and the 1,100 dead for whom a body was never recovered.[5] However heartfelt, the goodwill lavished on the returnees could not erase the deep distrust

Americans had developed toward their government during the war. To use *Time*'s calculus, 591 men redeemed far too little from the Vietnam War.

Suggestions to the contrary only antagonized the war's anguished survivors and angry critics, particularly those still missing a loved one after the last POWs returned.[6] MIA families did not hesitate to voice suspicion that Nixon's "peace with honor" had come at their expense. "We find it increasingly more difficult at this point to conceal our bitterness," the head of the New York chapter of the National League of Families wrote to former defense secretary Melvin Laird in July 1973. "We are convinced that our son and the other 1300 MIAs are being written off by the U.S. Government—literally abandoned!"[7] "When the prisoners of war came home, everyone said the war was over," another MIA mother raged at a protest on Capitol Hill in November. "But when you abandon 1,300 men there is no peace with honor."[8] "I am sure there are many other people in our country that feel the same as I do," another MIA relative warned. "For us the war still goes on."[9]

After years of fighting, many Americans were unwilling to walk away from the war. To those who had lost friends or loved ones, something irreplaceable had vanished in Vietnam for reasons unclear and for ends never realized. Before those mobilized through wartime POW/MIA activism would accept the administration's claims of peace with honor, they insisted upon "the fullest possible accounting" for the missing. But the slim prospects of recovering American MIAs reinforced the impossibility of returning to prewar certainties or arrangements, no matter how fervently some wished to do so. The longer they remained missing, the more they stood in the way of national reunion and peaceful relations with the former enemy.

Just as expressions of concern on behalf of POWs allowed Americans holding diverse views on the war to voice concerns about its costs, questions about the MIAs became a way for defeated Americans to identify and address the war's failures. And though immediate postwar queries about the missing attracted less attention than wartime POW advocacy, MIA families and their supporters retained an extraordinary influence over public policy and public perceptions of the Vietnam War. As the war receded into the past, the ceaseless search for the missing reinforced its irresolution.

WE NOW HAVE SOME HEROES IN THIS WAR

After years of activism aimed at winning their release, the return of American POWs was eagerly anticipated by their families, the Nixon administration, and the American people. Their sixty-day homecoming domi-

Homecoming POWs received a warm welcome from groups like this gathering at Camp Pendleton, California, where various symbols and slogans suggest the mixed sentiments that greeted returning prisoners. (Courtesy National Archives, Still Picture Branch)

nated the news in February and March, generating the most positive press the administration received in its embattled second term. Reporters raved that the prisoners "emerged from their years of torment with a strength and spirit that surpassed even the wildest expectations of their families, the military, and the nation," while crowds greeted them with signs and painted bed sheets reading, "We Love You" and "Welcome Home Beautiful Men."[10] Returnees were showered with gifts, including free travel and admission to Disneyland, a gold-plated lifetime pass to all Major League Baseball games, and free use of a new Ford for a year to go along with the sizable leave and pay packages accrued over years in captivity.[11] Hometowns hosted parades and ceremonies to show their pride and gratitude. And flags lowered to half-staff to mark Lyndon Johnson's death in January were returned to full height by Executive Order.[12]

As warm as the welcome was, it was uncomfortable, even painful for some. Residents of Scituate, Massachusetts, refused to raise the town's flag for the prisoners, having lowered it to protest the war.[13] Others refused to become sentimental over "professional fighting men [who] were trained in the calculated destruction of property and human life."[14] Still others, like veteran Sam Bunge, experienced "churlish resentment about the solicitous attention the returning p.o.w.'s are receiving," contrasting it with the disinterest that greeted "draftees who faced the war 24 hours a day on the ground."[15] Even among those who greeted the POWs in person there was a feeling articulated by William Lavelle at Travis Air Force Base: "I think it's about time. It's really just a bummer."[16]

Astute observers sensed something artificial in the pageantry of the prisoners' return. "If it was a war without heroes," *Time* assessed, "many Americans were intent upon making the prisoners fill the role."[17] Nixon headed the list. "We now have some heroes in this war," he told General Andrew Goodpaster on the day the first POWs returned.[18] An hour later he told his new secretary of defense, Elliot Richardson, and the Joint Chiefs of Staff that "we now have an invaluable opportunity to revise the history of this war." Richardson assured him the program was already underway—"the returning POWs have dramatically launched what DOD is trying to do to restore the military to its proper position"—and asked, "What more should be done?" "They should be returned to the Service with an appropriate promotion, or found a job," answered Nixon.[19] Still later he elaborated on his plans with Chief of Staff Haldeman. "I want them to get a ribbon—and a star for each year they were in prison. I want jobs—for those who don't stay in the Service. Each one of these men will get a job."[20] The POWs "could have a great impact on the destiny of this country," but "they must be used effectively."[21]

Defense officials hardly needed Nixon's reminders; they had planned the return for years. In 1967 the Pentagon established a POW Policy Committee under Assistant Secretary of Defense for International Security Affairs Paul Warnke to develop policy regarding early releases. In taking such a step, the Pentagon showed its sensitivity to the propaganda potential and pitfalls of the POWs, and sought to avoid mistakes made after the Korean War, when officials provoked controversy by accusing returnees of having succumbed to communist "brainwashing," sparking fears that the United States was losing the ideological struggle against communism.[22] After Go Public began, homecoming preparations grew more elaborate. In early 1971 Laird established the PW/MIA Task Group to handle POW matters and to plan for repatriation. Roger Shields, a young economist and former student of Warnke's replacement at the Pentagon, headed up the group, which spent much of its time seeking to strike a balance between censoring released prisoners and capitalizing on their celebrity.[23]

Still, knowing that most homecoming men were commissioned officers who had proven loyal through years in captivity, authorities shifted toward greater openness as the war went on. In place of early plans for a postwar quarantine, officials developed less formal means of control. Returnees were advised that their "answers to news media questions should be limited to very brief statements about such things as feelings about being on the way home and your anticipated reunion with your family and friends." To ensure that this guidance was followed, each returnee was assigned his own public affairs officer to "provide protection against inadvertent disclosure of classified information," and these chaperones were ordered to keep their "observations and conversations to themselves."[24]

Such preparations proved largely unnecessary as the POWs returned in better health than expected, and even better spirits. Before the men left Hanoi, Captain Galand Kramer unfurled a sign reading, "God Bless America & Nixon."[25] As the first plane arrived at Clark Air Force Base in the Philippines, Captain Jeremiah Denton exited, saluted, then turned to the waiting television cameras to intone: "We are honored to have the opportunity to serve our country under difficult circumstances. We are profoundly grateful to our Commander in Chief and to our nation for this day. God bless America!"[26] Minutes later Robbie Risner called Nixon at his San Clemente home, the "Western White House," "to convey to you, Mr. President, that it would be the greatest personal honor and pleasure to shake your hand and tell you personally how proud we are to have you as our President."[27] By the time Nixon had his staff compile the "best 'one liners' on support of country, flag and President" in mid-March, the list ran to seven single-spaced pages. "A loving President preserved my honor and with honor I return," read one entry; "it's time we start raising flags instead of burning them," read another. Nixon cited as his favorite "Glad we came back on our feet rather than our knees."[28]

Those who regarded the POW issue as propaganda saw their suspicions confirmed in "Operation Homecoming," the military's official name of the repatriation. The *New York Times* derided the event as "a succession of hand salutes, stiffly prepared statements, medical bulletins and canned handouts concerning the joys of steak and ice cream."[29] With little to report except the prodigious amounts of food prisoners wolfed down, James Sterba noted that "although the men were in excellent health and able to shop, see movies, drink beer, and talk with people on base, and were not unwilling to talk with newsmen, reporters were not being allowed to observe or talk to them."[30] Such complaints flowed into a larger set of concerns about the prisoners' patriotism. How was it, the *Washington Post* asked, that "paeans to 'honorable peace' . . . happened to be among the first to pop out of the mouths of men in captivity for such long periods of time" unless Operation Homecoming was a "military-managed event down to the last 'God-bless America?'"[31]

Official manipulation of the prisoners was real but misunderstood. The White House and Pentagon were eager to "get a lot of people out selling our line," but most returnees were eager to play the heroic roles assigned to them.[32] Suppression of free speech was reserved for a handful of prisoners, mostly infantrymen held in South Vietnam, with critical views on the war.[33] But the number of antiwar POWs was always low, especially among the senior officers who dominated the first release, and the communists concentrated prowar sentiment among the 1973 returnees by granting antiwar prisoners early release. "The simple fact of the matter is the returnees, who are a tightly knit and highly disciplined group, had long planned their own arrival," the assistant secretary of defense for public affairs assured Secretary Richardson, when asked about official interference. "They decided themselves the manner in which they would embark, including the smart salutes, and what would be said."[34]

Prisoner memoirs confirm this claim. Mindful that the Code of Conduct was adopted in response to the performance of Korean War POWs, and determined to avoid the suspicions that greeted their predecessors, the scrupulous aviators held in Hanoi rehearsed their release under the Nixonian motto "Return With Honor," going so far as to form toastmaster clubs where they gave patriotic speeches and answered barbed questions from mock reporters.[35] Like so much of their behavior, these rehearsals reflected an instinct for self-promotion harnessed to a deep faith in American institutions. The more aggressively their captors pressed them to relinquish that faith, the more tightly most clung to it. As one reporter recognized, "the words God, flag and country" that spilled forth from these men upon their return were "not slogans but the linchpins of their prison existence which enabled them to endure the long, often hopeless months and years."[36]

Still, with the White House worried that "there would be some bad actors among the POWs," the administration did all it could to control the production.[37] At a meeting with Roger Shields in the Oval Office in April, Nixon blasted complaints "that it's all been fixed and staged," but then proceeded to liken Shields's role to that of "a producer putting on a great play or a great movie — you had a helluva bunch of stars on this one — it's an all-star cast." Shields haltingly confirmed his sense by recounting his conversation with Denton while en route to Clark Air Force Base.

I, ah, sat down with Captain Denton. You were concerned at the time about, we knew that there were, ah, some problems, a few problems with regard to misconduct. And you wanted to be sure that was channeled through, ah, through, ah, the right, ah, the right, ah, conduit. Ah, the Captain [Denton] said, "what should, ah, what should I say?" And I suggested that, ah, he not talk about casualty information . . . but otherwise the way he, ah, he felt. And, ah, he wrote down some words and he got on the PA, ah, system of the aircraft and talked to the men and said, "I now represent you and here is what I, I plan on saying. Is this an adequate expression of your feelings?" And they all gave those thumbs up.[38]

69

"You can't equal this," Nixon told Shields. "These guys have been great for this country." "They must be used in an effective way," he continued. "They have thought deeply about themselves and their country and we should benefit by it."[39]

As Craig Howes, Elliot Gruner, and others have shown, returning POWs hoped to achieve much the same thing. After their years in the wilderness, they hoped to spread their sustaining faiths in duty, honor, country, and their commander-in-chief to a nation they felt had grown self-indulgent in their absence. "I'm told that the prisoner issue is one of the few things in recent years on which the entire country was united," Colonel Armand Myers told the crowd at Lackland Air Force Base upon his return. "I think that we POWs, through some sort of transference, have become a symbol of that unity we would like to see in America once more," he continued; "the unity we had before this war precipitated so many diverging view points on what the role of America should be."[40] But returnees who hoped to serve as agents of national reunion and moral regeneration were soon caught up in the very divisions they claimed to deplore. "For the past four years, the prisoners of war have played a leading role in the bitter national debate over Vietnam," Steven Roberts wrote in the *New York Times* two days after Myers's return. "And as they return from captivity, they remain the focus of deep and angry divisions that have not been obliterated by their homecoming."[41]

HAS HE COME BACK TO THE SAME COUNTRY?

Like Washington Irving's Rip Van Winkle, who awoke from twenty years of sleep to find his world transformed by the American Revolution, POWs returned to a society far different from the one they left. "It's as though he walked back into the world after walking out of it a long time ago," one mother said upon seeing her son for the first time since 1965.[42] For those who were gone for so long, "there would be a Rip Van Winkle effect," *Time* magazine wrote, "the dislocating experience of time travel to a startlingly changed American culture." Essayist Stefan Kanfer imagined them as "a new breed of Van Winkle," confronting "the remnants of a great tidal wave of protest" under "the perennial banners of militancy, each inscribed with the device, Liberation. Over it are the words Gay, Black, Women's, Chicano and People's."[43] "Exposed to all of this after years of isolation," David Brinkley mused, a returnee "might wonder if he has come back to the same country."[44]

The idea that POWs were encountering social revolutions for the first time was not true—they learned a great deal about domestic upheavals from their captors, antiwar activists who visited them, pilots shot down in the last year of the war, and their mail. But this notion of novelty served as a way to address ordinary Americans' anxieties over wartime change. The prisoners reminded Americans of the dramatic changes they had lived through in recent years and "restored continuity with a pre–Vietnam War America many ached to recover."[45] Their first encounters with "the new America" prompted one magazine reader "to wonder what and where 'home' really is in this country" and "jolted" another "into a conviction that it is they who are whole and the rest of us are the ones who are fragmented."[46]

Questions about "how would these men react to the turmoil and anguish of a society that telescopes a half century of change into a single decade" were often explored in stories about encounters with their wives and other women.[47] Since Odysseus reclaimed Penelope from her suitors, warrior homecoming has involved contests to reestablish patriarchal authority, and stories about returning veterans have been useful in illustrating and intervening in that process. As twentieth-century warfare deployed ever larger armies at ever greater physical and psychological remove from the home front, warrior homecoming became a liminal moment when neither prewar nor wartime rules applied and multiple claims of authority and obligation vied for supremacy. In her study of interwar France, Mary Louise Roberts found that "debate concerning gender identity became a primary way to embrace, resist, or reconcile oneself to changes associated with the war." Susan Jeffords, Jerry Lembcke, and others have identified a similar process after the Vietnam War. These authors have shown that political conservatives and moral traditionalists presented the restoration of veterans to positions of leadership in their homes and in society as pivotal to the reestablishment of order.[48] Without mass demobilization after the war due to yearlong tours of duty and the slow pace of withdrawal, Operation Homecoming was the one moment when the confrontation between returning veterans and a feminized home front played out in dramatic fashion.

Reporters and returnees made women key markers of what had changed in American life and understood gender as a crucial site for addressing those changes. Without question, the most commonly reported theme from Operation Homecoming concerned POW encounters with liberated women. Weeks prior to release, Peter Arnett reported that "if the nurses at Clark Air Base Hospital have their way, the American prisoners of war scheduled to make their first stop here on their journey home from Hanoi will get a sweet taste of femininity and fun," adding that doctors were "collecting stacks of Playboy magazines and other male literature for the men to read."[49] Such stories frequently made the reintroduction to Playboy, which began publishing full-frontal nudes in 1971, symbolic of the POWs' first exposure to the sexual revolution. One widely circulated anecdote from the first forty-eight hours was that returnees were "taken aback by Playboy's famous nudes, having seen nothing akin to that in a long, long time."[50] Suggestions that the men looked "stricken" seem dubious given that peace activists had brought them copies of Playboy while they were still in prison that featured film stills of the white actress Raquel Welch having sex with the African American football star Jim Brown. Prisoners passed the magazine around remarking, "Wait 'til you see what's changed," the intended message of such reporting all along.[51]

NBC reported that the "miniskirt was a central—and favorable—impression on return."[52] Favorable for some, but disconcerting for Ted Guy, who experienced "culture shock" upon seeing "women wearing see-through blouses and miniskirts."[53] While returnees often responded to changing styles in a light-hearted way—"Say honey, it's me," one joked in his first phone call home; "I hope you haven't burned all your brassieres!"—many felt real anxiety over these changes.[54] "I find it a little disconcerting to find women wearing pants and men wearing women's hair styles," Harry Jenkins admitted, while Jim Thompson wondered, "What is this country coming to?" after he noticed that some women had stopped wearing bras during his nine years in captivity.[55]

Americans who shared such concerns hoped the prisoners would set things right. In what quickly became the iconic image of Operation Homecoming, uniformed returnees were shown sweeping women off their feet in a joyous embrace. Recalling Alfred Eisenstaedt's famous photograph of the exuberant sailor kissing a nurse in Times Square on V-J Day, such scenes transformed the war's most visible victims into symbols of individual transcendence and national deliverance. *Washington Post* ombudsman Robert Maynard singled out one such "spontaneous photographed instant" depicting Arthur Burer lifting his wife, Nancy, "literally off the ground in exhilaration," as the one thing "we can take away from this story as belonging to ordinary people, not to the managers."[56] Even Nixon knew better than to profane such displays, rejecting suggestions that he fly to Hawaii to deliver "Nixon's Gettysburg Address" to "50 ambulatory-type" returnees. "When you get back to see your wife for the first time in a year and a half you don't want a lot of cameras, you don't want a VIP there," he told reporters, "you just want to see your wife."[57]

If matrimonial reunions seemed heartwarmingly sincere compared to flag salutes and patriotic sermons, they sent a subtle political message. Like Eisenstaedt's photo, such scenes reassured those anxious over wartime license that returning warriors would bend liberated women to their will. After running a four-frame sequence of the Burer reunion, *Time* reported that "the couple decided to take their marriage vows over again." "I'd often thought of what I'd say to her when I first saw her again," Burer confessed after seven years away. "But she solved it all when she came sprinting out and leaped into my arms. That assured me that everything would be all right and any problems could be solved." Later in the same story, "P.O.W.s: A Needed Tonic for America," Robert Shumaker avowed that his wife, Lorraine, looked "exactly as I remembered her . . . like a high school cheerleader," despite his eight years in captivity. The eight-year old son he had never met was another matter. "After someone remarked that his daughter must be glad to have him home," Shumaker ordered the boy's hair cut.[58] Similarly, *Newsweek* showcased the Burer reunion—"she leapt into his waiting arms, and he lifted her up in a bear-hug embrace and gleefully whirled her around"—while devoting three pages to photos of POWs embracing their wives. Its cover depicted a returnee in service dress khaki with close-cropped hair smiling serenely as he wrapped his arm around his wife, who returned his embrace in Jackie-era white gloves. Redolent with patriotic and patriarchal ideals, the image and its antifeminist caption "Lt. Comdr. Paul Galanti and Wife" evoked a bygone era.[59]

Rather than bewildered Rip Van Winkles, returnees might restore the prewar order, such coverage implied. "How sharp a contrast there is between the appearance, self discipline, and visible sense of responsibility among the returning POWs and the opposite characteristics of those who . . . refused to answer the call of their country," thundered the *San Diego Union*.

This photo of air force major Arthur Burer and his wife, Nancy Burer, embracing after seven years apart became the iconic image of Operation Homecoming. The *Washington Post* ombudsman declared it the one thing "that we can take away from this story as belonging to ordinary people, not the managers." (Arnold Sachs/Hulton Archive/Getty Images)

"Their love for their families and their country is truly inspiring to their fellow Americans who have so frequently been told in recent years that flag, honor, patriotism, and our many other blessings are outmoded."[60]

Virtually everyone recognized this subtext, but not all embraced it. "Without a doubt," one reader wrote *Newsweek*, the Galanti photo was "the most wonderful cover I have ever seen!" Felicia Lincoln was less impressed, blasting the "all-dressed-for-the-party photograph" as a "Pentagon 'pin-up' picture, conveying a subtle message that war, for all its suffering and sacrifice, can be beautiful." "Let us not forget," another chimed in, "that these professional fighting men were trained in the calculated destruction of property and human life." Even the cover girl Phyllis Galanti challenged the notion that she would revert to prewar norms. "I've become pretty aggressive," the League chairwoman told the press.[61]

While *Time* celebrated the prisoners' return with a cover photo of Joan Abbott and her seven children with a "Welcome home, Daddy!" sign, its sister publication *Life* predicted that divergent experiences would make it hard for prisoners and their families to pick up where they left off. Despite Joan Abbott's proclamation that "my principal function is to be a woman to my man," *Life* forecast that most wives were "unlikely to be content to change back into the major's sweet wife who is docile at home," and that "difficulties may arise from the new, necessary independence of many prisoners' wives." "The first time he opposes a decision I've made, it won't sit well," Eileen Cormier professed. "I think he will suffer a great deal of disillusionment. He'll think the world has noticed what he's done, when it's pretty much gone about its own business." "I'm afraid of Daddy," seven-year-old Lauren Borling told her mother of the father she had never met. "I'm afraid of Daddy too," her mother answered.[62]

Having lived with idealized images of those they left behind, returnees often found their reintroduction to their families equally frightful. "For the majority of married ex-prisoners," the Center for Prisoner of War Studies found, "the biggest readjustment they faced upon return was to the vast changes which had occurred in their wives." Some, like John McCain, found women they no longer recognized. McCain's wife, Carol, a swimsuit model when he deployed, survived a horrible car crash during his incarceration that required two dozen reconstructive surgeries that left her four inches shorter than her prewar height. Their marriage soon foundered and McCain divorced her to marry the much younger heiress Cindy Hensley in early 1980.[63] For others the changes were more subtle, but still striking. As soon as he saw her, Don MacPhail knew "everything was different" about his wife — her "hairstyle, the way she carried herself. She didn't look bad, just different. She had an air about her. Very independent." Rejoining women who had carried on without them, returnees asked, "'What is my role?' and 'am I really needed?'"[64]

Wives agonized over whether and how to accommodate their husbands into their new lives. Nearly 10 percent "planned to obtain a divorce or separation."[65] A handful had already done so, most famously Tangee Alvarez, who divorced Everett Alvarez in 1971, making the longest-held Hanoi POW a poster-boy for female abandonment given that his mother and sister were also outspoken critics of the war.[66] Civilian captive Ernest Brace recalled that he and returnee Steve Long "could not remember crying through all the years of beatings and persecution until they were informed at the processing center that their wives had left them."[67] For most, though, the split came after they exited the media spotlight. "At Balboa Naval Hospital," Gail Meyer recalled, "it was like the Spanish Inquisition. Everyone asked how the wives had behaved. I could hear beatings in some rooms."[68]

Some couples tried to close the gulf that developed during their years apart by renewing their marriage vows, taking a second honeymoon, or attending religious retreats.[69] Ned Shuman took his wife and children on a three-month cruise to get reacquainted with the family he had not seen in five years. But the distance between them was too great. "It was horrible," Shuman admitted. "We ended up getting divorced and it was pretty miserable on the kids."[70] His story was not unique. One-third of POW marriages ended in divorce within the year. Half were over within five years, nearly 60 percent within twenty years. These rates were far higher than the average among Vietnam vets and for civilian men of their age group. POWs also showed a greater propensity to second and third divorces.[71] "Seventy-five percent or more of us got divorced," Ted Guy estimated. "And it wasn't that we didn't love our wives anymore. But the changes were so dramatic."[72] After seven years in captivity, Edward Brudno took his own life when, according to his rabbi, he found the wife "he had known in her youth and immaturity had developed into a very strong person . . . and he couldn't stand it."[73]

The longest-held POW in American history, Jim Thompson faced similar problems with his wife, Alyce. Shot down in early 1964, Thompson endured 3,275 days in captivity, most of them in the central highlands of South Vietnam. When he returned in 1973, Alyce found "the sight of him turned my stomach. I hate to say that. But he looked so bad." Likewise, Jim found Alyce, who greeted him in "a red minidress with white polka dots and white boots," a changed woman. "What's happened to you?" he asked? "You're not the Alyce I left." "No, I'm not," she snapped. "I had to learn to fight my own battles and be my own woman." When he insisted that "I want what I left," she told him, "Well, you ain't going to get it." Her independence was one of many things that ruined any hope of their reconciliation. Jim was angry that Alyce had been living with another man for eight of his nine years in prison, that she had lived on his pay despite her infidelity, that she refused VIVA's request to inscribe his name on POW/MIA bracelets, and that she asked the army not to publicize his longest-held status for fear it would call attention to her extramarital affair. Alyce was disgusted when Jim asked her to accompany him to X-rated movies, abused their children in alcoholic rages, and began frequenting gay bars. Within a year Alyce had left him, telling friends, "Jim and I are a statistic."[74] "Absence does little for an unfond heart," Life explained, recalling that "Rip Van Winkle was relieved, after his twenty-year nap, to find that his hen-pecking wife had died."[75]

The irony of homecoming was that the struggle to bring POWs home had empowered their wives in ways that were jeopardized by their husbands' actual return. Whereas captivity deprived POWs of freedom and homecoming restored it, captivity meant greater freedom for their wives and homecoming threatened to take it away.[76] Through the networks they had built up during the war, POW wives knew that they were all being told that "if you would only change and be like you were everything would be all right."[77] But few were willing to revert to prewar norms.[78] For every POW wife like Dorothy McDaniel, who burned her League papers "to celebrate 'the end of Mom's public life,'" there were those like Gail Meyer who were unwilling to "return to the little women of the fifties and sixties."[79]

WE WALKED OUT OF HANOI AS WINNERS

If "the United States emerged from Vietnam with only two aspects of its war story intact: victimhood/underdog-ness and captivity," as Tom Engelhardt has argued, then POW hardships ultimately may have resonated with the public in ways that their triumphs did not.[80] While the White House applauded the prisoners' testimonials to duty, honor, country, and Nixon, others found their struggles more compelling. Tiring of their rehearsed statements, news outlets soon reported on divisions in their ranks and diluted their words with those of disgruntled veterans, like the 25,000 paraplegics Newsweek declared "permanent war prisoners."[81] "Prisoner or not," the New York Times remarked, Vietnam veterans faced "difficulties of identity and adjustment beyond all those experienced by the veterans of America's other twentieth-century wars."[82]

The senior officers who dominated discussion of the POW experience rejected such talk. They, more than anyone, emphasized their suffering, but unlike those who saw it as a waste, they imbued it with heroic meaning. "I've been broken," James Mulligan conceded. "Everyone here has been broken."[83] Still, "I want you all to remember we walked out of Hanoi as winners."[84] "The V's got nothing," he insisted. "They tortured people but they got nothing." "I kept faith in what I believed in — my God, my country, and my family."[85]

Evincing what antiwar psychologist Robert Jay Lifton called "a survivor's need to feel that their ordeal was significant," these men presented their captivity as an ideological struggle.[86] As soon as the last American prisoners were released, returnees began to recount torture by their captors. Though some antiwar activists and a handful of antiwar prisoners challenged their claims, or contextualized their abuse as a regrettable practice on all sides, their accounts "reinforced the idea that the United States had been fighting an unscrupulous and inhumane enemy who deserved any treatment he got."[87] Few knew enough about enemy prisons to contradict their claims and most were predisposed to believe them as a result of wartime rhetoric and a centuries-old tradition of captivity narratives in which dark-skinned savages tortured and killed white innocents.[88]

What distinguished Vietnam captivity narratives from earlier iterations, however, was that POWs claimed the active role for themselves rather than serving as passive victims whose violation warranted vengeance. "Everybody says we had nothing to do," one returnee told reporters, "but we did have something to do . . . to resist the North Vietnamese attempts to exploit us." In the "battle of Hanoi," as one called it, "the only weapons we had were our bodies and our pain."[89] "We forced them to be brutal to us," Jeremiah Denton explained. "And this policy was successful in that the consequent exposure to their brutality ultimately caused United States public and official pressure to bear so heavily on our captors."[90] Ordering their men that they "were required to take torture, forcing the Vietnamese to impose significant pain" before acceding to their captors' demands, senior officers waged ideological war in North Vietnam's prisons. Not all prisoners lived by these rules — those who cooperated with camp authorities were generally well treated and often granted early release — and even the hardcore broke under abuse that left Denton "like a crippled roach."[91] But despite setbacks, senior prisoners insisted that their resistance demonstrated their moral superiority and spiritual fortitude in the face of communist aggression, producing a propaganda victory.

At its heart, "the battle of Hanoi" was a contest over the nature, meaning, and memory of the war. For all concerned—Vietnamese communists, American prisoners, and activists of all stripes—it was a fight to fix responsibility for the war, to claim the moral high ground, and to establish the nature of national character and the extent of national power. Proving American aggression and their ability to overcome it was so important to communist authorities that they resorted to force to compel war crimes confessions. Likewise, notions of American innocence were so vital to their captives that men like Stockdale endured torture, even attempted suicide, to conceal what he had seen with his own eyes: that the alleged attack on U.S. destroyers in the Tonkin Gulf that was used to justify U.S. combat operations in Vietnam never happened.[92] This same contest for moral supremacy attracted millions of Americans to POW/MIA activism during and after the war.

The importance that all sides attached to these men who had so little material bearing on the terms of battle reminds us of the extent to which the Vietnam War was always an ideological struggle. Establishing its legitimacy as the sole rightful leader of the Vietnamese people was the Communist Party's central war aim, and propaganda wrested from POWs helped it achieve that goal on the national and world stage. What Americans hoped to achieve in Vietnam is less clear. But accepting the historiographical mainstay that the U.S. commitment in Vietnam grew out of a desire to make its far-flung security commitments credible, it follows that among the war's main goals was to project an image of toughness and resolve to audiences at home and abroad. Since the ultimate deterrent to communist expansion was self-destructive nuclear war, "a nation that wished to have its way in international affairs was obliged, in a sense, to make demonstrations of indifference to its own survival," as Jonathan Schell observed.[93] In that sense, the prisoners' disregard for their own well-being, their willingness to suffer to prove their indomitable will, was the ultimate expression of American credibility. It is little wonder, then, that these men became the ultimate heroes of the American war in Vietnam or that Stockdale became the first warrior in history to receive the Congressional Medal of Honor for attempted suicide. According to his 1976 citation, Stockdale "resolved to make himself a symbol of resistance regardless of personal sacrifice. He deliberately inflicted a near-mortal wound to his person in order to convince his captors of his willingness to give up his life rather than capitulate."[94] Lyndon Johnson and Richard Nixon could surely relate.

What made these men heroic in their own eyes and in the eyes of their countrymen was their fidelity. "The communists spent upwards of four, five, six, seven, eight, nine years trying to turn us against our country, against our way of life, against America," recalled Ronald Webb; "the natural reaction on the part of ninety-nine percent of us was to build our patriotism even stronger." Yet for all their professed love of country, POWs harbored deep resentments toward their countrymen. Having experienced the war not as a test of arms but a contest of wills, many of these men, like their commander-in-chief, had come to see irresolute Americans as a greater threat than their communist foes. Within days of their return, senior prisoners condemned peace activists who "shamed our nation in the eyes of the enemy."[95] "It was very evident to all of us that the Communists' spirit or morale went up and down along with the amount of demonstrations, protests, and antiwar movement back in the States," Risner asserted. "I feel beyond any doubt that those people kept us in prison an extra year or two."[96] "I would personally like to see every member of [COLIAFAM] tried and convicted and sentenced for what they did to me and my friends in Hanoi," Mulligan fumed. "They manipulated the mail, tried to use my family against my country, and tried to deprive me of my legal rights."[97] For POW hardliners, antiwar activists were but a symptom of a larger national enervation. "We're not as tough as we used to be," growled Harry Jenkins.[98]

If POW militants came home embittered by efforts to enlist them in the antiwar cause, they still hoped to return the nation to its prewar footing. "I have pride in America's past and hope for her future," Denton wrote to the White House two weeks after his return. But "too many of her citizens may have developed, through soft environment, a blurred awareness of fundamentals such as a recognition of the rights and needs of authority." "So many Americans have expressed to me the hope that God will use us returning POWs to arouse our citizens to some new awarenesses," he concluded. "I intend to tackle this task as opportunity permits."[99] Upon his retirement as commandant of the Armed Forces Staff College four years later, Denton founded the Coalition for Decency to restore "the traditional values of the country" via consumer boycotts of objectionable media. This helped launch Denton's successful 1980 bid for a U.S. Senate seat from Alabama, making him the first Republican senator from the state in 112 years.[100]

Denton was not alone in his determination to turn back the clock, nor was he the first to seek public office in order to do so. Three returnees ran for Congress in 1974, most notably Leo Thorsness, who declared his intention to challenge Senator George McGovern from the moment he set foot on U.S. soil. A Minnesota native returning from Hanoi with no political experience, Thorsness made an unlikely challenger to the South

Dakota senator who was the Democratic nominee for president in 1972. But his wife's relocation to Sioux Falls while he was in prison qualified him to run, and his POW laurels won the support of the White House and RNC chairman George H. W. Bush. Republicans recruited several returning prisoners to run for office in 1974, with White House Counsel Harry Dent promoting J. Quincy Collins as a contender for South Carolina's Senate seat: "The basic conviction he has is that America is turning too soft, and down here that hits better than anything."[101] Four returnees won primaries, but each lost the general election. Thorsness might have prevailed without the anti-Republican headwind Watergate inspired—he also campaigned for the House in 1978 only to lose to future Senate Democratic leader Tom Daschle by a mere 105 votes—but even some Republicans considered returnees poorly suited for public office.[102] One dismissed Thorsness as "not really a candidate at all, but simply an angry man fighting a personal war with another man."[103]

In time, other returnees succeeded where Thorsness failed, beginning with Denton in 1980. John McCain was elected to Congress in 1982, winning election to the Senate in 1986, the same year that Denton was defeated by a razor-thin margin in his reelection bid. Sam Johnson and Pete Peterson were elected to Congress in the early 1990s. Peterson served his Florida panhandle district for three terms before relinquishing his seat to become the first U.S. Ambassador to Vietnam in 1997, and Johnson won his tenth term in north Texas in 2008. Jim Stockdale served as Ross Perot's running mate in Perot's failed presidential bid in 1992, and McCain was a serious presidential contender in 2000 and the Republican presidential nominee in 2008. In each case these men entered politics in the Sunbelt, and in all but Peterson's they did so as conservatives committed to military rearmament as a means of moral redemption. Along with dozens of returnees who penned patriotic memoirs, they crafted a post-Vietnam version of what George Mosse called "The Myth of the War Experience" to "direct human memory from the horrors to the meaningfulness and glory of war."[104]

Yet for all their success, prominent POWs struggled to transcend their past. With the exception of McCain, none wielded the power and influence achieved by Vietnam veterans less scarred by their experience, such as Colin Powell, Al Gore, and John Kerry, or scaled the heights attained by Bill Clinton, George W. Bush, and Dick Cheney, their generational counterparts who avoided the war. And even McCain has often been at odds with other lawmakers for his bellicose stands on military matters that many veterans on Capitol Hill attribute to his isolation from the war's messy realities in the ideological hothouse of Hanoi's prisons.[105] As a group, the returnees proved too troubled by their experience and angry at those they deemed responsible to ever fully escape its shadow.[106]

Writing in 1973, Richard Slotkin explained that the author of the Puritan captivity narrative simultaneously sought "to ingratiate himself with his society by portraying himself as its symbolic martyr" while venting "hostility and contempt for his society and its smug ignorance of its true plight."[107] Returnees evinced the same mix of emotions.[108] But unlike seventeenth-century captives who represented "the whole, chastened body of Puritan society," POWs were unrepresentative of a diverse and divided home front.[109] They talked and looked like the past, and the people who identified with them most strongly were those who longed to return to the world they represented.

Others were more wary or dismissive. "The POWs have been assigned the role of heroes in a war that has no heroes," Dr. Herbert Kelman wrote in an editorial for the American Psychological Association, "to create the illusion of victory and to arouse a sense of patriotic fervor."[110] Calling the POWs "war criminals," Rev. Philip Berrigan asked, "What else would you expect from the Government but to distort the true nature of the men?" "What's disturbing is the image being created of simple, old-fashioned American military virtue," Robert Jay Lifton stated flatly, "as though nothing had happened in Vietnam, and as though the understandable emotion around these men can wipe away ten years of an ugly unjust war."[111]

Women and racial minorities had particular difficulty relating to the militant white men who returned from Hanoi. Historian and director of the Vietnam Resource Center Ngo Vinh Long complained that the effusive welcome given prisoners "served to cover up and justify the inhumane policies of the United States against the Indochinese people—the gooks, the dinks, the slant-eyes" and "lays the groundwork for the attacks that are to come" against the left.[112] "I have seen only high ranking officers being released in the POW exchange," Charles Evers, the mayor of Fayette, Mississippi, and brother of slain civil rights leader Medgar Evers, cabled Nixon. "What happened to the foot soldiers, the marines and especially the black and Mexican-American GI's?"[113] "It seems as if the high ranking officers in all branches of services are all white," Mrs. William E. Steward noted in a letter to the Pentagon. "I thought in this day and time things should have changed."[114]

Of course things had changed—if not as much as some would have

President Richard Nixon greets Lieutenant Commander John McCain at the White House Correspondents' Association's dinner at the Washington Hilton on 14 April 1973. (Courtesy National Archives, Nixon Presidential Materials)

liked, then more than others wanted. Among other, more long-term developments, the Watergate scandal engulfed the Nixon White House just as the last POWs returned to the United States. Nixon's top advisers H. R. Haldeman and John Ehrlichman were forced to resign on 30 April, along with Attorney General Richard Kleindienst and White House Counsel John Dean. On 17 May the Senate Select Committee on Presidential Campaign Activities began televised hearings into who knew what and when about the Watergate break-in the previous June. The next day attorney general–designate Elliot Richardson, who departed the Pentagon after only four months as secretary of defense, named Archibald Cox as special prosecutor and Nixon's approval rating dropped below 50 percent.[115]

Besieged, Nixon called on the POWs once more. On 24 May, he airlifted over 600 former prisoners and their wives, girlfriends, and, in one case, a *Playboy* playmate to Washington for the largest state dinner in White House history. Before dining on seafood Neptune, hearts of palm, and roast sirloin beneath an enormous orange and yellow circus tent on the South Lawn, the POWs heard Nixon insist that without his trademark "secrecy that allowed for the kind of exchange that is essential, you men would still be in Hanoi." His voice rising and hands slashing, he exploded that "it is time to quit making national heroes out of those who steal secrets and publish them in the newspapers," provoking a minute-long standing ovation from men who had endured torture rather than admit wrongdoing.[116] At the gala that evening, returnees presented a plaque to "Our leader, Our comrade, Richard the Lionhearted" for "fortitude and perseverance under fire."[117]

"Looking toward the balance of the second four years, let me say I feel better," the beleaguered president told the men and their dates, "because out in this room, I think I have some allies, and I will appreciate your help," setting off another standing ovation.[118] The event buoyed his spirits but did nothing to reverse his flagging fortunes. Less than fifteen months later, facing impeachment, conviction, and removal from office, Nixon resigned with an approval rating of 24 percent.[119]

THEY'VE GOT TO FIGURE WE ARE
DOING EVERYTHING WE CAN

As the headline "'Greatest Mission': POWs on Way" sprawled across the front page of the *Washington Post* on 12 February 1973, page A7 was dominated by darker themes. "HAVE YOU FORGOTTEN HIM?" asked big, block letters above a grainy photograph of a bandaged American surrounded by stern Vietnamese guards. According to the full-page advertisement, which ran in major and mid-market newspapers nationwide, the man in the photo, identified as navy lieutenant Ron Dodge, was "one of the many men of whom there is proof of capture, whose name does not appear living or dead on the list" of prisoners provided by North Vietnam. "DON'T TAKE OFF YOUR BRACELET!" the VIVA ad implored. "THERE IS MORE YOU MUST DO!" "Public opinion must be mustered, as never before in history, to demand that the terms of the Peace Treaty are complied with and that all our Prisoners of War are returned."[120]

The White House staff took note.[121] When Brent Scowcroft briefed Nixon for his April meeting with Pentagon POW/MIA man Roger Shields, over half of his talking points dealt with the missing, and the MIAs dominated Nixon's subsequent meeting with Shields. "These bastards probably aren't going to come out with anything," Nixon told Shields.

> The main thing is certainty. Ah, and I am in a mood on that to say, look, it's over now, it's over, we can't find them, but if those that, that, let's continue our search but without you see, that is a delicate thing. They've got to figure we are doing everything we can to be sure that we have found everybody. But on the other hand we must not destroy the certainty that they have. It is better of them to be certain, the man is gone, than it is to be uncertain and continue to have . . . we, we, we, of course, you know, will carry out our obligations to the POWs and those who returned but we have an equal obligation to the missing in action, ah, to, to, doing everything we possibly can, leaving no stone

unturned, to uh, to uh, see uh, the return of, anybody else can be found, ah, more remains . . . but, anyway, you know how to do it.[122]

Certainty may have been the main thing, but Nixon's tortured syntax suggested he had no idea how to answer questions about American MIAs. In the two years before the fall of Saigon, the U.S. government's accounting efforts were as confused and ineffectual as the orders its chief executive gave to its top POW/MIA official. The overarching aim of those efforts, though, was to resolve the MIA problem in a way that would prevent rather than provoke further criticism of the war in Vietnam—to create certainty from uncertainty.

Like Nixon's rambling discourse, that effort ultimately focused on the retrieval and identification of MIA remains. "The identified body," political theorist Thomas Hawley has noted, "is presented as the only means of resolving the deep-rooted uncertainty generated by missing soldiers specifically and loss of the Vietnam War generally." Beyond resolving the questions of an MIA family, "the movement from unaccounted for to identified permits the materiality of the repatriated body to serve as an unambiguous indicator of success," fashioning, as Hawley puts it, "a sort of victory from the remains of the war."[123] But while Hawley suggests the symbolic power of MIA remains, he often overlooks their limits—limits readily apparent in Nixon's wretched oration and the accounting effort it launched.

The day after his Oval Office visit, Shields called a press conference at the Pentagon to announce that "we have no indications at this time that there are any Americans alive in Indochina." With Nixon's "you know how to do it" endorsement still ringing in his ears, Shields pledged to continue "accounting for the missing" through the Joint Casualty Resolution Center (JCRC) in Thailand. Established on 23 January, the JCRC would carry out Article 8(b) of the Paris peace agreement, which specified: "The parties shall help each other to get information about those military personnel and foreign civilians of the parties missing in action, to determine the location and take care of the graves of the dead so as to facilitate the exhumation and repatriation of the remains, and to take any such other measures as may be required to get information about those still considered missing in action."[124] The JCRC's mission—to "resolve the status of United States missing/body not recovered personnel through the conduct of operations to locate and investigate crash/grave sites and recover remains"—distinguished it from its predecessor, the Joint Personnel Recovery Center (JPRC), which focused on recovering live Americans before they fell into enemy hands. As the name change made clear, the JCRC's "emphasis was on those dead rather than those alive." Under the command of General Robert Kingston, the 160-man unit began work in February, sifting through JPRC files to determine where to find missing American remains.[125]

The JCRC soon learned that the overwhelming majority of missing Americans were lost in areas to which it had no access. "Ninety-five percent of the sites we know about are in disputed or enemy territory," Kingston estimated.[126] Most were missing in the first place because they disappeared in areas where search-and-rescue operations could not safely recover them. Over half of the missing were lost in North Vietnam, Laos, Cambodia, or southern China. Even in South Vietnam, "most unresolved situations were related to portions of the country under the effective control of the PRG."[127] As many as 400 missing Americans were lost over water and were also beyond the reach of U.S. authorities given the technologies of the day.[128]

Under the provisions of the peace agreement, the four sides to the conflict were obliged to help each other recover enemy personnel. But when the ceasefire was immediately violated, its other stipulations, including Article 8(b), were caught up in the fight.[129] By the time the Four-Part Joint Military Team (FPJMT) first met in April to discuss how to implement 8(b), any hope of JCRC recovery operations in communist territory had vanished. When Americans presented case files for 104 MIAs they thought the communists could account for, their communist counterparts warned that allegations of torture from returned American POWs threatened to halt all accounting efforts.[130] Future Four-Party meetings were consumed by similar recriminations. Without permission to search in enemy territory, JCRC teams were restricted to areas "deemed to be under the control of the RVN [Republic of Vietnam]." And "since there was no clear delineation of these areas," they risked coming under fire whenever they ventured outside Saigon.[131]

The difficulties of JCRC operations were clear from the start. On its first field activity, the JCRC's South Vietnamese military escort detonated a landmine that killed one Vietnamese soldier and wounded another. The search, an excavation of a helicopter crash site, failed to yield any remains. Locating such sites was difficult since most incidents happened years earlier over rugged terrain in a fast-growing and often heavily cultivated tropical environment. Finding remains was virtually impossible without the help of locals, since downed aircraft were usually raided for valuables and the bodies of the crew were often moved. When villagers refused to cooperate, as they usually did, the JCRC could spend weeks sifting soil and still find nothing. When remains were found, they often turned out to be

Vietnamese or were too fragmentary to be identified.[132] As one retired officer who led a search and rescue unit during the war wrote to *Newsweek* in May, "The mission of the Joint Casualty Resolution Center, if not too little, is definitely too late. Anyone who thinks that he is going to find anyone or anything at a crash site in the jungle doesn't know the country or the people."[133]

Handcuffed by physical and political realities, the JCRC was "largely unemployed" by December 1973.[134] In its eight months of field operations, the unit had conducted roughly "a dozen search and recovery activities" resulting in the recovery of eleven American remains.[135] But what it lacked in the field, the JCRC made up for in Washington, where officials depended on it to demonstrate that they were doing everything possible to account for MIAs. Despite its lack of work, Shields assured Congress that "we are continuing our efforts within the military services and the Defense Department and anticipate we will renew those efforts, and, if anything augment them."[136]

No doubt, the JCRC would have continued operations with further limited results had it not been for the worsening security situation in Vietnam. On 15 December three JCRC helicopters came under attack as they touched down twenty kilometers southwest of Saigon. Team leader Captain Richard Rees and a Vietnamese crewman were killed in the ambush, and four Americans and three Vietnamese were wounded. Although justification for the attack was unclear, "the PRG and DRV had voiced their objections over the JCRC activities" in the past, claiming that its work was a ruse to spy and move troops through communist-controlled areas.[137] Such suspicions may have been well founded. Soon after the attack, an employee at the U.S. Communication Center in Saigon claimed to have handled orders authorizing JCRC espionage. U.S. officials denied the charges, but the JCRC's freedom of movement and its reliance on South Vietnamese military escorts lent itself to such dual uses. U.S. delegates to the Four-Party talks similarly claimed that DRV accounting efforts were a front for communist infiltration, and each side may have used the process to its advantage in the ongoing war since neither honored the ceasefire.[138]

Whatever the cause, the attack ended the American-led recovery effort. By late 1974, even South Vietnamese efforts ground to a halt as every available South Vietnamese soldier was thrown into a desperate struggle for survival. Only five additional American remains were found before communist forces seized Saigon on 30 April 1975, bringing the postwar accounting total to a paltry sixteen sets of remains.[139] The DRV outpaced two years of JCRC efforts in a single day in March 1974 when it repatriated twenty-three American remains in return for the release of political prisoners held in South Vietnam.[140]

Despite high costs, minimal results, and dim prospects for success in
a country now completely controlled by the communists, the JCRC soldiered on. Reduced to a staff of eighty in 1975, then to nineteen in 1976,
it gathered information from refugees, hoping that their testimony would
shed light on the fate of American MIAs.[141] While the JCRC shrank in size,
officials refused to shutter it lest their professed commitment to MIA accounting be called into question.

ARTICLE 8 AND ARTICLE 21

The Paris Peace Accords gave the two principal combatants something both wanted: U.S. withdrawal. To achieve this goal each side offered
concessions, but in the end U.S. withdrawal was the only stipulation either
scrupulously adhered to. Still, ancillary agreements were needed to bring
about the American departure, and once U.S. withdrawal was complete,
two articles crucial to bringing the two sides into agreement became the
source of endless conflict.

For Americans, Article 8(a) providing for "the return of captured military personnel and foreign civilians of the parties" to "be carried out simultaneously with and completed not later than the same day as the troop
withdrawal" was the most important condition in the agreement. Though
the Nixon administration refused to sign any agreement that terminated
Nguyen Van Thieu's leadership of South Vietnam, it could not possibly end
the war without an agreement to repatriate American prisoners. While
Nixon and Kissinger fought for Thieu, they negotiated for POWs, and
Nixon signaled that their return was the price of withdrawal by threatening to halt the pullout if their return was impeded. On 26 February he
suspended troop withdrawals and minesweeping operations when North
Vietnam withheld a list of Americans to be released the next day as an
act of protest against Saigon's refusal to release communist captives. The
Americans were freed as scheduled. A month later, when North Vietnam
claimed that it had no control over Americans captured in Laos, the chairman of the Joint Chiefs again halted troop withdrawals until the "U.S. has
been provided with a complete list of all U.S. PW's including those held by
the Pathet Lao, as well as the time and place of release," an order he rescinded only after assurances that the Laos captives would be released.[142]

Such threats worked both ways. Nixon could halt U.S. withdrawal if
North Vietnam violated 8(a), but the communists could stop prisoner re-

patriation if he did so. Their custody of POWs gave the communists the ability to enforce U.S. withdrawal, constraining Nixon's ability to remilitarize the conflict, which he all but promised to do in order to win Thieu's signature on the agreement. "The major use of the agreement to you," Kissinger told South Vietnamese Ambassador Tran Kim Phuong, "is it links us legally to you on a long-term basis for an indefinite period." "With a settlement the United States people will support the need to enforce it," White House Chief of Staff Alexander Haig told Thai strongman Thanom Kittikachorn. "We will keep the agreement if it serves us," Nixon told the Joint Chiefs. In making such promises, Nixon was not only "deceiving the public but perhaps also himself," as Larry Berman has written.[143]

Throughout the winter and spring of 1973, Nixon entertained thoughts of bombing North Vietnam in reprisal for ceasefire violations. Yet he was unable to pull the trigger. Watergate has typically been cited as the reason for his restraint. Following Kissinger's self-exculpatory lead, the Senate Select Committee on POW/MIA Affairs called Watergate a "highly important factor inhibiting President Nixon's ability to respond forcefully to DRV violations," a claim Nixon biographers have accepted and few historians of the Vietnam War have questioned.[144] Chronology lends credence to this view, as the Watergate crisis exploded shortly after the peace agreement was signed.

Yet even without Watergate, the logic of POW diplomacy tied Nixon's hands. When Kissinger proposed two to three days of "prompt and violent response" to "North Vietnamese infiltration and logistics activity in the South" after the 16 March prisoner release, Nixon refused until the final group of POWs returned two weeks later, by which time Watergate had grown far more debilitating. Having promoted POWs as his principal war aim and having cited their return as the best evidence of peace with honor, he could not endanger their repatriation with renewed bombing. Nor could he easily resume bombing once they were back lest he create more American prisoners. As columnist James Reston asked in March, "once the withdrawal of American prisoners and troops is complete . . . what legal authority would the President then have to order American men and bombers back into battle?"[145] Bob Dole offered a possibility in May when he tried to amend legislation to cut off funding for the war with a provision that allowed bombing if "North Vietnam is not making an accounting, to the best of its ability, of missing in action personnel." But renewed bombing promised "casualties, and maybe, worst of all, American POWs," as Congressman Les Aspin warned, and the amendment was defeated. The spending deadline took effect in August.[146] "Speaking as a dyed-in-the-wool, moss-backed administration Republican," Senator Norris Cotton declared in explaining his opposition to further funding for military operations, "I have just been a dove since we got our prisoners back."[147] Caught in a Catch-22—if he bombed before the POWs were home, he jeopardized their return, but once they were free, there was nothing to justify bombing—Nixon had no way to enforce the ceasefire or fulfill the secret concessions he had made to gain the agreement.

Though Nixon and Kissinger liked to pretend that they had bombed Hanoi back to the bargaining table, Kissinger's aide John Negroponte came closer to the truth when he quipped, "We bombed them into accepting our concessions."[148] Foremost among those concessions was their secret pledge to provide the communists billions of dollars in reconstruction aid. Article 21 of the Paris agreement specified, "The United States will contribute to healing the wounds of war and to postwar reconstruction of the Democratic Republic of Viet-Nam." This commitment was hardly secret— none of the agreement's provisions generated such anger among the president's supporters or won more praise from his detractors—but its details were not learned until December 1975, long after the ceasefire agreement had been shot full of holes and Nixon had resigned. By then the communist victory in Vietnam had rendered the Paris agreement a dead letter in the eyes of most Americans and few paid much attention to yet another broken promise in the war's long litany of lies. To this day, Article 21 languishes in obscurity in most diplomatic histories of the war, though it achieved popular notoriety after the 1985 movie *Rambo: First Blood Part II* made its unmet commitments the motive for Vietnam's alleged failure to free American captives. "We were supposed to pay the Cong $4.5 billion in war reparations," Rambo's commander tells a treacherous CIA agent. "We reneged. They kept the POWs."[149]

This linkage, with its dubious origins and implicit racial demonology, must strike most historians as absurd. Yet the history of Article 21 and the handling of the secret communiqué spelling out its terms make clear that reconstruction aid was always linked to Article 8(a) by the governments in question. As Pierre Asselin has shown, in the final round of negotiations over the agreement in mid-January, Kissinger promised Le Duc Tho "that the White House would give Hanoi a note pledging $3 billion in postwar aid in exchange for an accounting of Americans held in Laos."[150] The secret codicil that followed specified that "the United States contribution to postwar reconstruction will fall in the range of $3.25 billion of grant aid over five years," with additional aid "in the range of $1 billion to $1.5 billion, depending on food and other commodity needs." Two days prior to its delivery, the U.S. delegation informed its DRV counterparts that Nixon had prepared such a letter to be delivered once North Vietnam provided a list of American POWs in Laos. A similar message was sent directly to Tho the following day. On 1 February the letter was exchanged for a list of ten American prisoners then in Laos. Despite Kissinger's insistence that the "greatest caution should be against any inference that we are paying ransom to get the prisoners out," the fact that the envelopes traded hands simultaneously indicates that both sides saw reconstruction aid as a quid pro quo for American POWs.

On 2 February Nixon cabled Pham Van Dong that it was "inconceivable that only ten of these men would be held prisoner in Laos."[151] Given that the Defense Intelligence Agency (DIA) listed only thirteen Americans as prisoners in Laos at the time, including four who were already accounted for through earlier DRV and PRG lists, and considering that only two to six of these men met the military services' more rigorous criteria for classification as prisoners of war, the Laos list actually exceeded expectations. "We don't know what we will get from Laos," one Pentagon official admitted to Kissinger on 29 January, making Nixon's overnight denunciation of the list less a statement of fact than a thinly veiled threat to rescind his offer.[152] In April he suspended Joint Economic Commission meetings that were to implement the aid program to protest Hanoi's alleged failure to account for American MIAs, and though they resumed in June they soon broke off again. By then it was clear that Congress had no intention of financing reconstruction aid, as it made clear when it prohibited any funds to North Vietnam until it provided a full accounting of U.S. personnel.[153]

Because a one-paragraph addendum to Nixon's letter specified that reconstruction aid would "be implemented by each member in accordance with its own constitutional provisions," Nixon and Kissinger later claimed that the codicil provided mere estimates of aid that remained subject to congressional approval, despite its promise of aid "without any political conditions." But congressional fiat could not undo the linkage between Article 8 and Article 21. And by citing Vietnam's alleged MIA accounting failure as grounds for withholding aid, Nixon and Congress reinforced this linkage. For the next quarter-century, Vietnam would insist on the reconstruction aid promised in Article 21 as the price for their cooperation in accounting for missing Americans. Though it must be stressed that there is no evidence that Vietnamese leaders ever sought to ransom American captives for reparations, as is widely believed within the POW/MIA movement, Vietnamese officials regularly protested that Americans could not expect an accounting under Article 8 without honoring Article 21. As one

DRV representative assigned to the Four-Part Joint Military team set up to implement the accords told his American counterpart, "Of course we have information on many of your MIA personnel, and in some cases even the remains of your pilots." "But why should we give them to you for nothing?" he asked. "Your government has done so much damage to our people and our land that it must pay. That is your obligation, and even your president committed himself to this."[154]

When MIA activists learned of Nixon's promises, many convinced themselves he had knowingly abandoned captive Americans to escape his obligations. Yet, as later chapters show, this conviction led few MIA activists to advocate payment of Article 21 commitments. The news only reinforced their determination to deny Vietnam reconstruction aid lest it reward their alleged hostage-taking. Article 21 remains controversial not only because of its secret promises but because of its implicit admission of U.S. war guilt and its recognition of communist dominance of the peace process. By highlighting the hurtfulness but ultimate impotence of American power in Vietnam, Article 21 provoked an equally impotent, though hurtful, vindictiveness on the part of many Americans that masqueraded as concern for MIAs. One VIVA advertisement from February 1973 urged voters to tell Congress that "not one penny of your taxpayers money be spent on rebuilding North Vietnam unless they return all our prisoners."[155]

AFLOAT IN FIGURES, UTTERLY
PRECISE YET FANTASTIC

Anger and distrust among MIA families was unavoidable once Operation Homecoming ended and the hybridized "POW/MIA issue" was wrenched into distinct categories of the living and the dead. Wartime rhetoric that enemy prisoner lists failed to include known captives and references to "1,600 Americans in North Vietnam jails" erased distinctions between POWs and MIAs, at least in the eyes of their families.[156] With the White House and Pentagon "saying there are more prisoners and that the ruthless enemy is concealing some," wrote one reporter, "it is nearly irresistible for each MIA wife to believe that *her* husband might be a concealed prisoner."[157] "Since there was no reality," Barbara Mullen explained, "I believed anything I wanted."[158] Painful reality returned with the 591 POWs who came home in Operation Homecoming, leaving more than 1,300 MIAs and another 1,100 additional unrecovered dead.

Though the loss of a loved one would be wrenching under any circumstance, the shock and betrayal MIA families experienced in 1973 was exacerbated by misleading information provided by administration officials. Throughout the war's last three years, Pentagon experts rejected enemy prisoner lists as unreliable while privately admitting that they were in rough agreement with U.S. intelligence estimates. After North Vietnam supplied a prisoner list with 368 names to Senators Edward Kennedy and William Fulbright in December 1970, pw Policy Committee chairman Dr. G. Warren Nutter advised his superiors that "I believe, and State concurs, that this list reflects the true status of the men listed, and that we should accept this list as an official notification." The list failed to account for twenty-six men thought to be prisoners, but given the limits of U.S. intelligence, Nutter concluded, "the information is not inconsistent with what we know." The air force and army agreed, and Nutter believed the navy could be persuaded.[159] But the Pentagon's Public Affairs staff dissented, advising Secretary Laird to reject the list in order "to maintain our public posture . . . that North Vietnam owes us a full accounting for all the men missing in Indochina."[160]

Public Affairs carried the day. Insisting that his office had "reason to believe that the North Vietnamese hold more men than the 339 listed," Pentagon spokesman General Daniel "Chappie" James sought to discredit the list without offering any contradictory evidence. "To let them know that we know that they've got what we think they have got, then it could endanger the safety or the lives of the people that they have that we still don't know about," he asserted.[161] Roger Shields, brought in to oversee pow/mia policy shortly thereafter, later admitted that "we carried a small number of people captive that were not on those lists," but the discrepancies were so few that had he presumed "the North Vietnamese were honest . . . [the list] tells you that our intelligence system was amazingly accurate." "The problem with accepting a list like that," Shields explained, was not its inaccuracy but "that you give the North Vietnamese latitude to give us a list, adding a few more dead to it every time."[162]

By insisting that the communists identify those they held, then refuting that information in the interest of "public posture," the Nixon administration encouraged mia families and their supporters to believe the Vietnamese were holding men its own experts suspected were dead. Contrary to Nixon's allusions to 1,600 American pows, the armed services carried just 591 servicemen in pow status when the Paris agreement was signed. Using a lower threshold of proof, dia arrived at a slightly higher number, listing 626 military personnel and forty-one civilians as pows at war's end. Far more were mia: 1,306 military and civilian according to the dia, 1,338 according to the military services.[163] Another 1,113 Americans were listed as "killed in action/body not recovered" or KIA/BNR, though these men were not considered unaccounted for by either the military or, at that point, by the National League of Families, VIVA, or any other Americans.

Through years of war, intelligence estimates of survivability were honed using prisoner mail, prisoner appearances in enemy propaganda, enemy prisoner lists, and the testimony of escaped and released POWs. "There were people," Frank Sieverts recollected, "whose full-time job was . . . to draw up elaborate tables to show that different names appeared on this list and that list, this list, that list," to the point where he created a file entitled "Lists" to hold them all. Such lists were part of a war "afloat in figures, utterly precise, yet fantastic"; an example of the many optimistic statistics the military produced in order to manipulate a more stubborn reality on the ground.[164] They represented a bid for control in a war fought largely on the enemy's terms, as if manufacturing data could substitute for strategic dominance. "A colonel and I sat up one whole night with a bottle of Scotch, not changing the figures but moving them around and labeling them so it would turn out we were winning," an American adviser to the South Vietnamese Army recalled, illuminating the impulse that motivated the production of precise lists of POWs and MIAs and their deliberate confusion into the single misleading category of POW/MIA for public consumption.[165]

Whatever the lists indicated, in the end "there either is a real, live, breathing human being or there isn't," as Sieverts told the Senate Select Committee. "The number of people that came out were very close to the numbers that I expected," he recalled. "There were a couple of surprises of additional people who came out that we didn't expect, and there were a number who we had hoped for . . . who didn't come out," but such cases were less common than official rhetoric at the time suggested.[166] When Kissinger asked the Joint Chiefs if there were "any surprises in the list of POWs from North Vietnam" on 29 January, they assured him that "the information they have given us about prisoners in North Vietnam is quite accurate" and "pretty close to what we expected."[167] That so few MIA activists recognized this, or were willing to accept it, reflected their long exposure to deliberately misleading official statements that suggested a large cache of hidden captives. Even with the war over and peace with honor the official line, administration officials were unwilling to endorse the return of American POWs as accurate and complete since such an admission would make clear their earlier deceit. Instead they tried to finesse the issue, hinting that the enemy accounting effort was dishonest while simultaneously claiming to "have no indications at this time that there are any Americans alive in Indochina." This evasion—"that live POWs *might* exist while avoiding the position that they *do* exist," as H. Bruce Franklin put it—has been the stated position of the U.S. government ever since, encouraging a perpetual search for proof of postwar survival on the part of MIA activists.[168]

From the start, that search has focused on so-called "discrepancy cases" in which an American thought to be in captivity failed to return. Such cases have fueled MIA activism since VIVA first advertised the alleged disappearance of Ron Dodge on Operation Homecoming's opening day. Extraordinary efforts have been made to quantify these cases, to little avail since even intelligence experts disagreed in the most difficult cases whether a downed pilot or lost soldier should be classified as a POW or MIA, and regularly revised their estimates before, during, and after prisoner repatriation. Still, using the 591 servicemen the military services listed as POWs on 27 January 1973 when the Paris agreement was signed, it is possible to establish how closely Operation Homecoming corresponded to official expectations.[169]

Five hundred and sixty-six military personnel and 25 civilian detainees returned in Operation Homecoming. Of the military returnees, the services carried 513 as POWs and 53 as MIAs. Since the services carried a total of 591 servicemen as POWs at the signing of the agreement, the return of 513 military personnel left 78 soldiers, sailors, airmen, and marines unaccounted for that were believed to be in captivity. Debriefs of homecoming POWs, however, indicated "the possible death of 46 Americans who had been listed as POW," meaning that the return of American servicemen or their direct testimony explained the fate of 559 of the 591 Americans classified as POWs, leaving 32 cases in which an American serviceman thought to be in captivity failed to return without explanation.[170] In addition, the DRV, the PRG, and Laos provided notification that 63 Americans had died in captivity, including 27 who were counted among the estimated 591 POWs, confirming over half the reports of death from returning POWs and shedding light on others.[171] An additional 12 civilians listed as POWs by DIA failed to return without a report of death.[172] Relying solely on U.S. intelligence, fewer than 50 discrepancy cases existed at the conclusion of Operation Homecoming, and far fewer if the communists' reliable reporting is considered.

If some Americans who were expected to return failed to do so, 53 Americans not known to be in captivity came home, including one man thought to be KIA/BNR.[173] Thirty-six of these unanticipated returnees were shot down during the 1972 Christmas bombings and were not in captivity long enough to be reported by Vietnamese officials. Whatever the reason for their absence from enemy lists, these unexpected returnees exceeded those thought to be alive who failed to return.[174] If the 63 prisoners who the communists reported to have died in captivity are included with unanticipated returnees, then the other side "returned or otherwise accounted for 621, which is 28 *more* military prisoners than the Pentagon believed they held," as H. Bruce Franklin has pointed out. "With mathematics like these," he contends, Americans are "in no position to charge the other side with 'discrepancies,'" especially in light of the staggering number of Vietnamese, typically estimated at 300,000, left missing after the war.[175] Indeed, from a historical perspective what is remarkable about the American war in Vietnam is not how many but how few Americans were missing at war's end, as the next chapter shows.

But however useful such computations may be in demonstrating the reasonableness of DRV and PRG accounting, they do little to explain how ordinary Americans who participated in POW/MIA activism understood the gap between their high hopes for survival and the grim realities of wartime loss. If one conclusion to be drawn from measuring wartime POW lists against the numbers that returned at war's end was that "the information that had come out from people who were released and the information we had on shootdowns and disappearance in the field and so forth was amazingly accurate," another view was that the large numbers still missing "simply stresses the fact of how little we did know." In fact, Roger Shields, the self-professed "repository for all the information" available on POWs, made both these statements within the space of three paragraphs in his 1992 deposition before the Senate Select Committee.[176]

What Shields was trying to say was that he had fairly precise knowledge of Americans in captivity, but that the MIA category was an informational black hole. "MIA's are either dead or in enemy hands from the day they disappear — except this information is not available to their country," Douglas Clarke wrote in his unflinching analysis of the status determination process. Clarke, who flew 300 combat missions over three tours of duty during the Vietnam War and spent eighteen months in the office of the Special Assistant for Prisoner of War Matters to the Chief of Naval Personnel before writing his 1979 study, concluded that commanders displayed a "tendency towards optimistic findings" when a pilot was lost, avoiding "a KIA finding in the absence of *prima facie* evidence of death."[177] Pilots who ejected from their aircraft, popped their parachute, or activated their emergency beacon were invariably listed as MIA, even POW, though none of these steps guaranteed their survival, much less their captivity, in a combat environment. Pilots were often shot, injured, or killed before, during, or after ejection, and communist forces were known to activate their radio beacons to attract rescue craft that they could then attempt to bring down. After investigating three dozen unresolved POW cases, the House Select Committee on Missing Persons in Southeast Asia concluded that at least nine "should have been classified as MIA rather than POW, because of the hazards of landing and surviving in a hostile environment and lack of positive information that the missing man had been captured."[178]

The best evidence of the dangers faced by plummeting airmen were the severe injuries sustained by returning POWs. Thirty-eight percent of navy repatriates required "five days or more hospitalization" as a result of injuries suffered during shootdown.[179] Upon ejection from his aircraft, John McCain fractured his left arm, broke his right arm in three places, broke his right knee, and lost consciousness. Landing in a lake in downtown Hanoi, he nearly drowned before inflating his life vest, only to be dragged from the lake and bayoneted in the ankle and groin by an angry mob, which also broke his right shoulder in the process.[180] Stockdale broke his left leg and left shoulder upon ejection and was shot at repeatedly by villagers once he hit the ground.[181] Thompson was shot in the face and so severely burned in his shootdown that he could not stand for two weeks, and he suffered from chronic dysentery and malaria throughout captivity.[182]

All three were initially listed as MIA, and their return suggests why each MIA case, no matter how grim, offered hope of survival. However, in each case, evidence of their survival surfaced in enemy propaganda within six months of their disappearance, moving them to the POW list. Men listed as POWs or MIAs who never appeared in enemy propaganda and were never reported in prisoner mail or the testimony of returned prisoners surely succumbed to similar or worse traumas. Even in cases with some indication that a man survived shootdown, "we were left with the anguished judgment, conclusion, that, despite those earlier indications, some of which were years earlier, something had happened" in the intervening years, as Sieverts told Senate investigators.[183] Such cases were most common in Laos, where downed pilots who were not recovered by search and rescue teams faced grim prospects due to that country's harsh climate, sparse population, extreme poverty, and brutal civil war.[184]

Yet once a given individual was listed as POW or MIA it was politically impossible to downgrade him to KIA/BNR, even when years of intelligence gathering failed to establish his captivity. Status upgrades from MIA to POW happened regularly, but never the other way. "There were very few status changes made prior to '73," Shields recalled. "They would be made if you recovered remains on the battlefield," but that only happened "in a couple of instances."[185] Any reclassification based solely on wartime intelligence, enemy reporting, or the passage of time was refused. When Shields recommended a finding of death for twenty men the DRV reported to have died in captivity in December 1970, Laird refused for fear "that some of the families would not stand for it."[186] Over time this had the effect of whittling the MIA roster down to a list of the dead, though officials were unwilling to admit it.

To MIA families and concerned citizens, the fact that "few of those previously carried as 'missing' were on the lists" of homecoming prisoners came as a devastating blow.[187] After the last POWs were repatriated, MIA sister Gail Innes wrote to Nixon, "I still can't realize that we only got so few back. I feel that they are holding back more." Suspicion that "the North Vietnamese are holding out" was widespread among activists, who begged Nixon to "please do something. We are to [sic] great of a country to let that rotten little country run all over us."[188] With administration officials busy promoting Operation Homecoming as proof that they had won peace with honor, League families grew "alarmed that the other side might erroneously conclude that the lists will go unchallenged by the American people. We cannot let this happen," they told Scowcroft. "Our organization does not intend to keep silent indefinitely."[189]

As that remark suggests, the League was coming to distrust not just the Vietnamese communists, but the Nixon administration that seemed content with communist cooperation. As MIA brother Dermot Foley told New York congressmen who held ad hoc hearings on the issue in May, "It is a disgrace to tolerate the abandonment of these Americans to discretionary disposal by a guilty enemy who has only hate and contempt for us. To do so by failure to act effectively on the available evidence is equally wrong." VIVA's New York chairman added, "I have been very bitter, and contrary to some of the people here, I feel there were two parties involved in this war and they are both wrong, damn wrong."[190] Developments at the League's 1973 meeting in July showed how disenchanted its members had become with Nixon's handling of the issue. The first act of its new executive director, MIA father Scott Albright, was to write the White House to insist "that all United States Government officials (military and civilian) immediately cease using such phrases as 'all POWs returned;' 'we have no evidence of any POWs still alive in Southeast Asia;' and 'our involvement in Southeast Asia is over;' and speak instead in terms of the discrepancies in the accounting of our POW/MIAs." "The families are expressing a growing sense of frustration at the inability of our Government to get a satisfactory and full accounting of these missing men," he concluded, and "their patience is wearing extremely thin."[191]

There were logical flaws in assuming the communists had returned some MIAs but not others. The PRG's belated release of Robert White on 1 April 1973, the day after Operation Homecoming formally ended, was particularly revealing in this regard. An MIA held in solitary confinement in the Mekong Delta since 1969, White was a perfect candidate to hold hostage had the communists wished to do so.[192] Instead they turned him over to U.S. authorities, making him the last American to be repatriated in Operation Homecoming. As one DRV official professed upon handing over the list of Americans captured in Laos, "we have not come this far . . . to hold on to a handful of Americans, after all what would that prove?"[193]

But MIA activists saw things differently—if the Vietnamese held one American back, even for a day, they could hold more—and they refused to "take the word of the enemy about these men." "These are the same men who violated the Geneva Conventions in regard to p.o.w.'s and m.i.a.'s," one relative explained, so "why must we trust them now?"—especially when the president had told them not to trust the Vietnamese for his entire first term.[194]

The short answer was that they had no choice, since the communists controlled the areas where MIAs were lost. Another reason to believe the Vietnamese was that returnees largely verified enemy claims. POWs who spent years compiling "a memorialized chronology of contacts and acquaintances that could some day, God willing, when papers and pencils were available, allow you to present to the world a history, in the worst case, of who was last known to be where" reported many missing men dead, but provided no tales of captive Americans who did not return. POW "memory banks" who memorized "every American prisoner who had ever been sighted, whispered to, tapped to by any other American" were an exceedingly trustworthy source of information regarding captives in Indochina.[195] As a longtime supporter of the POW/MIA cause, Congressman Clement Zablocki, reported during May 1973 hearings into the matter, "In testimony received from returnees, and we have had officers as well as an enlisted man, they expressed the view that there are no missing in action or prisoners of war in Southeast Asia at this time that they believe are alive." Even in cases where they could not confirm death, "the fact that reports from our returned prisoners of war indicate that many others apparently did not enter the captivity environment" pointed toward death, since no

American could survive indefinitely outside the prison system.[196] Given the returnees' "firm opinion that none of the other missing men entered the captivity system," Acting Secretary of Defense William Clements advised the president in July, "a determination of death should now be made in these cases."[197]

In a letter to Clements, the Corpus Christi National League of Families chapter objected: "MIA families have been told that our men would be considered missing in action until there is evidence that they are dead. And we have been assured time and time again that a search for our men would be conducted." Since "the return of the known POWs," it continued, "the message we are getting is that the sooner you can sweep this under the rug, the better you will like it. And we will not tolerate that, you can be sure." "The fact is, *you have no proof our men are dead*," the letter insisted. "Why are you so willing to believe the enemy on this subject when they do not tell the truth on any other subject?" "With every negative statement that comes out of the Department of Defense," it warned, "we are all the more convinced that if anyone must pursue this dilemma and see that these men are not forgotten, it is us—as usual."[198]

THE LONG-AWAITED PRISONER return proved not that the war was finished, only that it had switched to a new theater in which Americans would fight with each other over what had gone wrong in Vietnam and whom to hold accountable. The emergence of the POW/MIA issue in the late 1960s heralded the beginning of that contest, but once Americans ceased direct military involvement in Southeast Asia, those mobilized for the fight focused their energies and their outrage inward. Even in the joyous first months of Operation Homecoming, Americans fought over the prisoners' meaning and purpose, while those in the MIA lobby broke ranks with the Nixon administration over its sanguine assessment of the war. The promise of redemption and restoration offered by returnees proved unattainable as they inserted themselves into the raging political debates about the war. Their affiliation with a disgraced president suggested to cynics and supporters alike that even these heroic figures could not avoid being corrupted by the Vietnam War.

Meanwhile, the families, friends, and allies of those still missing had legitimate questions about what happened to the MIAs. They were led to believe that the primary, perhaps the only remaining war aim of the United States in Vietnam was to win the release of POWs. To impart a sense of urgency to this mission, the Nixon administration updated and embellished age-old tales of Oriental treachery to imply Vietnamese duplicity, while slandering antiwar activists whose sympathy for the enemy allegedly endangered captive Americans. Those who invested time, energy, and emotion in the cause clung to these war-inducing ideas long after they no longer served the interests of a president who had decided to exit Vietnam on the best terms he could get.

3

As It Has in the Past

A Short History of Oblivion

Unable to bring the missing back to life or recover their remains, the Department of Defense looked to precedent to resolve the MIA issue. "The decision to change status should not be unalterably tied to the inspection of combat sites, the recovery of remains, or the personal desires of family members," Acting Secretary of Defense William Clements advised in his July 1973 proposal to proceed with presumptive findings of death. "In a significant number of cases, only faint hope was ever held for the individual's survival," he concluded. "In the interest of consistency and fairness, the well defined system for status determination should function as prescribed by law as it has in the past."[1]

As Clements told Nixon, recovery of the war dead is not a timeless American tradition. Nor is American history a linear narrative of growing devotion to the dead. Public commitment to the recovery of the war dead emerged fitfully in the mid-nineteenth century as the Mexican War and the Civil War resulted in American soldiers dying far from home. Though persistent, this commitment has waxed and waned in the years since, often honored more in the breach than in the observance. Created in response to the mass deaths of the Civil War, graves registration units were unable to recover or identify at least 170,000 Union dead, and ignored 260,000 Confederate dead entirely until the turn of the century.[2] World War I left another 2,800 to 3,300 Americans missing and unidentified.[3] Some 78,000 Americans were never found after World War II and another 8,500 were recovered but never identified, while over 8,000 Americans were left missing or unidentified in the Korean War.[4] In this history of oblivion, the

2,505 Americans missing after the Vietnam War were neither numerous nor new.

Against the bloody canvas of twentieth-century warfare, they were less remarkable still. More than half of the nine million men killed in the First World War were never found.[5] Two to three million Russians disappeared in World War II, as did six million Jews in the Holocaust.[6] One and a half million Germans were missing in 1945; nearly half a million were never found.[7] So many Japanese were unaccounted for after the war that the radio program "Missing Persons," which helped families search for missing loved ones, aired until 1962.[8] The numbers missing in Vietnam were similarly vast, though Americans represented less than 1 percent of the war's unrecovered casualties—the number of Vietnamese missing is estimated at 300,000, but so many lives were obliterated that the exact number is unknown.[9]

Faced with such loss, postwar societies relied on symbolism, ritual, and law to resolve the fate of the missing. Beginning with the burial of an Unknown Warrior at Westminster Abbey and interment of the *soldat inconnu* beneath the Arc de Triomphe on 11 November 1920, the burial of an unidentified set of remains became the customary means to honor those never found. The United States followed suit with the interment of an Unknown Soldier at Arlington National Cemetery on 11 November 1921, adding remains from World War II and the Korean War to the Tomb of the Unknowns in 1958. Making a virtue of necessity, these ceremonies comforted survivors while imposing limits on the search for the missing. For millions there would be no accounting, only the presumption of death.

Throughout history the passage of time without proof of life has been grounds for the presumption of death. There are cases where this presumption proved premature, but the common law principle that "after the lapse of seven years, without intelligence concerning the person, the presumption of life ceases" proved a practicable basis for resolving missing persons cases.[10] Early in World War II, this principle was codified in the United States Code through the Missing Persons Act, which established "a lapse of time without information" as sufficient grounds for a determination of death.[11] Over the next two decades, that law authorized presumptive findings of death in the absence of remains for nearly 100,000 missing American servicemen. Those findings generated scattered complaints but nothing like the organized opposition to status changes after the Vietnam War.

The problem of the missing dead was not unique to the Vietnam War, nor was Clements's proposed solution. What was unique was the reaction of MIA families who filed suit two days after Clements's proposal in an effort to prevent presumptions of death. Represented by Dermot Foley, an MIA brother and future legal counsel to the National League of Families, these families sought an injunction against future status changes and damages for those already underway on the grounds that they violated the constitutional right of due process.[12] Their suit made clear that the activists who dominated the League's membership were determined to resist official efforts to define the missing as dead.

For all its novelty, League opposition to the presumption of death developed in response to earlier memorial traditions. Likewise, the actions and intentions of federal authorities built on their understanding of memorialization of the war dead as an official state prerogative. Too often scholars treat American memory of the Vietnam War in isolation, overlooking transnational and transhistorical influences in favor of an overdetermined "Vietnam" capable of explaining all things. Everything is attributed to the trauma of Vietnam.[13] Yet the war was not the most bloody or divisive conflict in American history, nor did it compare to earlier cataclysms of the twentieth century, at least not for Americans. And given that U.S. intervention in Vietnam grew out of the Second World War and marked the culmination of nearly a century of American combat in Asia dating to the Philippine-American War, the study of the war's memory could benefit from the same broadened frame of reference that has reinvigorated its diplomatic history. Only with the perspective gained through comparisons of post-Vietnam memory to other memorial contexts, and through archival research into evolving practices of remembrance, can historians grasp the peculiarities of post-Vietnam memory, much less explain them.

Like all who comment on or commemorate the past in public, MIA activists and state authorities used "images and gestures derived from their broader social experience," including precedent, to advance their construction of MIA absence. At stake for each were questions of who would speak for the missing and what they would say. What meaning would they draw from their sacrifice? What memory would they make from their loss? The competing memories they put forward were "socially framed," shaped in part by immediate concerns arising from the war and in part by traditions of mourning the missing.[14] This chapter charts the development of those traditions in order to highlight what was at stake in the post-Vietnam struggle over MIAs. Since the Civil War, national elites had constructed narratives of heroic sacrifice for the state through memorializing missing warriors. And with the telling exception of the Reconstruction-era South, federal officials largely succeeded in using the missing to legitimate their authority—until Vietnam.

It goes without saying that death is the most universal human experience and that burial of the dead is a basic human institution. "Humanity in its distinctive features is through and through necrocratic," Robert Pogue Harrison has theorized, "a way of being mortal and relating to the dead. To be human means above all to bury."[15] Funerary rites are intrinsic to community formation. Shared customs and common burial grounds bind people into groups, while differences in such rituals and those they honor distinguish one group from another.

Mourning is essential to state creation and continuity. As spelled out in *Antigone* in 441 B.C., burial bounds the state by defining whom it will remember. By burying Antigone's brother Eteokles "with full and just and lawful honors due the dead" while insisting that their brother Polyneices remain unburied, Kreon, king of Thebes, policed the boundaries of his state. "Eteokles, who fought in defense of the nation and fell in action, will be given holy burial," he decreed. But Polyneices, "who descended with fire to destroy his fatherland and family gods, to drink our blood and drive us off slaves, will have no ritual, no mourners, will be left unburied so men may see him ripped for food by dogs and vultures." "I shall honor the friends of the state while they live, and when they die," Kreon decreed, "and I shall not befriend the enemy of this land. For the state is safety."

In penning Kreon's defense, Sophocles showed how foundational funerary rites were to social order. Yet he also presented burial as a fundamental human right and suggested that Kreon's denial of this right, even to a traitor, wreaked havoc on society. "Death is a god who wants his laws obeyed," Antigone proclaims after burying Polyneices in defiance. Kreon learns death's authority when he orders Antigone buried alive, prompting his wife and son to take their own lives in return. "Your devotion *is* a kind of reverence," the chorus chants as Antigone goes to her grave. Having embarked on his course to save the state, Kreon is warned by the prophet Teiresias that "the state is sick. You and your principles are to blame."[16]

The point here is not that all people in all places and times have sought to recover or identify the dead in the same way or for the same reasons, but to show that political communities rely on commemoration of the dead to produce "feelings of profound sociability and belonging through the primitive construction of the social out of the flesh and blood of group members."[17] Affiliative groups like the Christian church similarly organized around the body and blood of Christ and other martyrs whose sacrifice for their faith established boundaries between Christians and their persecutors.[18] "Since bodies are common to all of us," as Carolyn Marvin and David Ingle put it, "they are useful for representing socially important things," including the reciprocal obligations that bind people into communities.[19]

Even more than their ancient predecessors, modern nations depend on symbols and ideals to give them substance. The nation, as Benedict Anderson famously observed, "is an imagined political community." "The members of even the smallest nation will never know most of their fellow-members, meet them, or even hear of them, yet in the minds of each lives the image of their communion." And while nations are composed of diverse and competing persons, groups, and interests, they are "always conceived as a deep, horizontal comradeship" for which millions have killed and died.[20] Dead soldiers are particularly important to such idealization, as their deaths ostensibly occurred in defense of the community and therefore can reinforce or fracture notions of national fraternity. If properly honored, the war dead can sanctify the nation, binding citizens to the state by making the soldier the ideal against which all citizens are measured.[21] But if the nation is seen as unworthy of their sacrifice, then the war dead may widen rifts created by their loss. Having caused or failed to prevent the death of its soldiers, the nation-state must simultaneously accept and evade responsibility for—in a sense, take credit for—their loss, something it has done through memorialization.[22]

As Anderson and others have shown, the way states memorialized the war dead changed significantly as mass literacy, print capitalism, and participatory politics gave rise to popular nationalism. As hereditary monarchs gave way to democratic politics and conscript armies, memorialization became increasingly inclusive, culminating in the "democracy of death" of World War I, when the United States, Britain, France, and other combatant nations went to great lengths to find, identify, and bury every fallen soldier.[23]

Such memorial exhaustiveness is in stark contrast to the experience of early Americans. "Except for officers or militia men killed close to their homes, the burial of the war dead during the Revolution had been a haphazard affair," according to G. Kurt Piehler.[24] With little sense of national identity, the Continental army had no reason (or resources) to recover its dead. In the tradition of the dynastic armies from which it sprang, George Washington's army honored men of rank, as did its British adversary. "The most important factor determining funeral rites was the rank of the deceased," not national identity. "Burial rituals reinforced the divisions of rank" more than communal ties. While Continental army general Enoch Poor was buried in a mahogany coffin with "a regiment of light infantry, several fieldpieces, and six generals" as an honor guard, dead privates received less care. A British officer recorded that his men crammed in "fifteen, sixteen, and twenty" Americans per hole after the British victory at Freeman's Farm. Similarly, a Boston shoemaker recalled "British corpses 'chucked' into an open pit in the town commons."[25]

While such neglect might be attributed to the exigencies of war, even in peacetime Americans were slow to honor their dead, as demonstrated in their neglect of 11,000 Americans who perished aboard British prison ships off the coast of Brooklyn. Buried in shallow graves or left to rot in the open air, their bodies languished for decades, with "skulls and feets, arms and legs, sticking out of the crumbling bank in the wildest disorder." Lone voices made sporadic calls to reinter the bones, but property owners refused and petitions to Congress were rejected.

Not until 1808 did the New York state legislature grant the Tammany Society $1,000 to bury the prison ship dead. The act was less a sign of blooming nationalism than a measure of the intense partisanship of the early republic. With President Thomas Jefferson's Embargo Act threatening the political fortunes of Jeffersonians in the seaport of New York, the Tammany ceremony stoked anti-British, anti-Tory, anti-Federalist fires among workingmen by recalling the common soldiers and sailors whose revolutionary sacrifices had been forgotten as Federalists promoted the memory of Washington over radical patriots. In a slap at the cult of Washington, the *Public Advertiser* claimed that the reinterment had not been "for a single admiral, or general, which might pamper an aristocratic pride . . . but to the grateful remembrance of eleven thousand five hundred brave defenders of their country." The Federalists would have none of it, deriding the ceremony as "political necromancy" conducted by "hypocrites to answer some political purpose." Others undercut the reinterment's significance by suggesting that the remains included Hessian and horse bones. Charges of political expediency seemed borne out when the wooden vault built for the remains soon fell into disrepair. Before long the bones were again "exposed in a neglected and dilapidated tomb." Finally, in 1873 the remains were relocated to a stone crypt at nearby Fort Greene Park. A congressional appropriation of $100,000 and $125,000 in local funds financed construction of a 150-foot granite column there in 1908, one hundred years after their initial reburial.[26]

Much had changed in the years between the open-air disposal of the prison ship dead and the dedication of the Prison Ship Martyrs' Monument, as president-elect William Howard Taft explained in his dedicatory address. "Efforts from time to time have been made to put into permanent form an expression of the gratitude of this Government and its people to those who thus offered up their lives rather than be unfaithful to their country's cause," Taft told 20,000 onlookers gathered in a freezing rain, "but not until now by Governmental aid has a suitable testimonial been reared in memory of these heroes and martyrs." With the rise of the nation-state—Government with a capital G—nationalism came to dominate memory of the Revolution. In place of the economic and partisan memory of the prisoner ship dead that Tammany had asserted a century before, Taft made them martyrs to the nation alone. "No list of those who died survives to enable us to identify its victims," he avowed. "We know this: the men who were there confined were Americans" whose example would inspire "future unselfish and unheralded sacrifice to maintain our institutions of liberty and civilization."[27]

Taft's memory would have made little sense to those he memorialized; his vision of a national memorial culture in which the sacrifices of anonymous dead men inspired sacrifices from anonymous men of the future would have been equally foreign. Until the mid-nineteenth century memorial activity remained primarily local and religious rather than national and civic. Religious traditions that presented death as divinely ordained, combined with the rapidity of decomposition before embalming came into wide use in the Civil War, led to an emphasis on the fate of the soul over disposition of the body. "Why care for these bodies?" Henry David Thoreau asked as he watched shipwrecked emigrants wash ashore in an 1849 essay, musing that "it is hard to part with one's body, but, no doubt, it is easy enough to do without it once it is gone."[28]

Early instances of wartime and postwar body recovery were initiated and financed by the families of the dead rather than by the nation-state, and they were undertaken to return the dead to his local community rather than to his national homeland. During the Revolution and the War of 1812, officers and those who died close to home stood the best chance of recovery because their relatives were best positioned to do the work themselves. Only with the Seminole Wars of the Jacksonian era did military officials become directly involved in recovering the dead. Even then they agreed only to forward lead-lined coffins provided by families to a quartermaster who exhumed the desired remains and returned them to the family at their expense, a luxury only the wealthiest could afford.[29]

In the Mexican War, federal authorities assumed additional responsibilities, including the establishment of a cemetery for the American dead in Mexico City. But even this act served to reinforce the institutional and ideological limits of the American nation-state. At least one state, Kentucky, repatriated its dead to a cemetery built in their honor two years before Congress created the Mexico City cemetery in 1850. By the time Congress acted, only 750 of the 13,000 men who died in the campaign could be found, and none were identified. "Removed from the vicinity of the Mexico City garbage dump," their bones were placed at the foot of an unimposing obelisk that fails to name the war in which they died or the cause for which they fought, more a monument to forgetfulness than to memory.[30]

FROM THESE HONORED DEAD WE
TAKE INCREASED DEVOTION

Indifference to the war dead finally subsided under the weight of the corpses left by the Civil War. As it snuffed out the lives of 620,000 military personnel—nearly 2 percent of the American population—"the war created a veritable 'republic of suffering'" in which wartime "sacrifice and the state became inextricably intertwined."[31] "The most immediate and pressing problem posed by this scale of both military and civilian deaths was a logistical one," according to Drew Gilpin Faust—"what to do with the bodies." The problem of so many dead bodies so close to civilian populations brought home the war's physical and political dangers, as the sheer numbers killed "destabilized the definitions of human identity and dignity that burial customs symbolized." By threatening identity, the war threatened the foundations of familial, local, regional, religious, racial, and national communities, prompting unprecedented efforts to reassert those communities through recovery of the dead.[32]

The Civil War confirmed what the Mexican War hinted: military commanders were ill prepared to cope with the carnage of industrial warfare. The war's battles often left thousands, sometimes tens of thousands dead and missing. When the losing army finally quit the fight, the corpse-choked field fell to the victors, who buried the dead, especially the enemy dead, with little regard for their identification. A member of one Gettysburg burial party recorded his crew's haphazard routine: "We collected the dead men into rows, as usual laying one against another, heads all one way, Union and Confederate in separate rows . . . while the majority of men buried them in trenches. . . . These burial trenches were dug here, there and everywhere over the field and contained three or four or fifty as the number of dead near required. Few of these men had anything about them by which they could be identified, and were buried as 'unknown.'" Half of all Union dead and two-thirds of the Confederate dead at Gettysburg were

Bodies of the Confederate dead gathered for burial at Antietam, September 1862.
(Civil War Photographs, Prints and Photographs Division, Library of Congress)

buried as unknowns. When attempted, identifications were unreliable, based on material effects and guesswork. Of the 1,100 marked Confederate graves at Gettysburg, roughly half are considered misidentified. Numerous soldiers identified as dead at Gettysburg later turned up alive.[33]

Such problems were not unique to Gettysburg. One reporter found "long trenches, where many hundred rebel soldiers lie uncoffined and unknown" at Antietam. "On one headboard is written '147 buried here.'"[34] Part of the challenge of identifying the dead was the failure on both sides to issue identification discs or "dog tags" that identified the dead. Such tags were not standard equipment until the Spanish-American War, though the fact that some soldiers bought their own suggests an awareness of their utility. Others pinned names to their uniforms before going into battle, though such markings could be destroyed in battle or overlooked by burial crews. In fact, burial details and other survivors often robbed the dead of the very things likely to carry traces of their identity—watches, knives, and other valuables that possessed inscriptions or were known to be owned by a given individual.[35] By the war's last year, careless burial practices literally haunted the war's combatants. As General Grant made his final assault on Richmond in 1864, his army stumbled over the bones of its predecessors as it fought for the same ground in the Wilderness and Spotsylvania Court

House battles that it had fought over at Chancellorsville one year prior. It was as if the war had turned the entire eastern seaboard into "a vast bone yard."[36]

In the absence of effective government caretaking, the families of the fallen set out in search of their loved ones. After the Union victory at Fort Donelson, General George Cullum reported the arrival of "hordes of brothers, fathers, mothers, sisters, cousins, &c" who came looking for missing men.[37] These pilgrims encountered sights that only compounded their grief. One visitor to Gettysburg discovered "festering corpses at every step; some still unburied; some, hastily and rudely buried with so little of the earth upon them that the appearance presented was almost as repulsive as where no attempt had been made." Another counted "over forty dead bodies within a circle of fifty feet" near Little Round Top, "swollen and turned black with mortification, and millions of maggots could be seen rioting upon their flesh." "Arms and legs and sometimes heads protrude," local attorney David Wills wrote to Governor Andrew Curtin of Pennsylvania, "and my attention has been directed to several places where hogs were actually rooting out the bodies and devouring them."[38]

To contend with such horrors, relatives of the dead and missing called on local citizens and entrepreneurs like Aaron Good of Sharpsburg, Maryland, near Antietam who, for a fee, helped them "identify and recover the bodies of their friends who fell in the battle" using his "list of the dead that were buried on the battle field." Relatives could write to Good to arrange the shipment of their loved one's remains at the cost of "at least sixty dollars," the price quoted to one father from Georgia.[39] Embalmers, virtually unheard of before the war, stood ready to preserve the dead for the journey home for twenty-five to fifty dollars.[40] But most families could not afford such services, and even if they could, locating a missing man often proved impossible for profiteers and families alike. "Some have to go away cheerless and unsatisfied, the last resting-place of their friends not being identified, from the vast amount that were hurried into their mother-earth," the Gettysburg *Sentinel* observed in reference to distraught relatives who made their way to Gettysburg. "This is painful to a father, a mother, a wife, a sister; but such is the inevitable consequence of a fearful and tremendous battle."[41]

Not all shared the *Sentinel*'s complacency. David Wills took the time to report corpse-eating hogs to Governor Curtin not from indifference but to win support for his plan to rebury the war dead at public expense. With Curtin's blessing, Wills contacted other governors to secure funding for a military cemetery at Gettysburg and put out bids for reburial work—

the winning bid was $1.59 per body. Construction began in October 1863, and President Lincoln delivered his Gettysburg Address at the cemetery's dedication a month later.[42] Standing in the "Soldiers' National Cemetery" with the recovery and reburial of the dead going on around him, Lincoln recalled the nation's founders, who brought forth "a new nation, conceived in Liberty, and dedicated to the proposition that all men are created equal." Resolving "that from these honored dead we take increased devotion to the cause for which they gave the last full measure of devotion," Lincoln pledged that "this nation, under God, shall have a new birth of freedom—and that government of the people, by the people, for the people, shall not perish from the earth." It is not too much to say that these words "remade America," as Garry Wills put it, or that they marked the origins of modern American nationalism by allowing citizens to transcend death through the survival of the nation-state. Mixing Christian imagery of resurrection with the democratic ideals of Athenian funeral orations, Lincoln made the war dead sacred symbols of the new social order that the war promised and the national state would secure.[43]

Lincoln delivered these words from what one early visitor described as "one vast hideous charnel house" where "in some cases nothing but a few mutilated fragments and pieces of flesh were left of what had been so late a human being following his flag to death."[44] The transubstantiation of these fragmented remains into the nation's lifeblood required more than words; it required the physical reordering of the battlefield. In place of rooting hogs, rioting maggots, and protruding heads, David Wills and architect William Saunders reordered the Union dead by state in curving ranks of what Saunders called "simple grandeur" without "any intermixture or meretricious display of ornament." Grouping the dead by state, or even separating the Union from the Confederate dead, was nearly as difficult as identifying them by name. When the reburial effort ended in March 1864, 3,354 reinterments had been completed, with 1,664 unknown by name and 979 unknown by name and state. "A great percentage were erroneously identified," with misspellings of names the most common error and the burial of at least three Confederates among Union soldiers the most serious.[45]

Despite these limits, reburial allowed Lincoln to enlist the dead in the leading ranks of the imagined community by imposing nationalist discipline on the disordered dead. The importance attached to states at Gettysburg showed that the nation had not supplanted locality and region as the source of communal allegiance and political identity, even for the Union dead, but the fact that all who died for the nation were buried in an identical manner regardless of rank and at public expense, while none who opposed the nation were so honored, at least at that time, significantly advanced the national significance of the war dead. In place of the hierarchical burial of earlier wars, Gettysburg's uniform rows suggested a democratic citizenship, albeit one based "not on the individual's claim to rights" but on individual subordination to the state.[46] All who served the nation were equal in death, if not in life, according to this nationalist aesthetic. "Death does its work, obliterates a hundred, a thousand — President, general, captain, private — but the nation is immortal," Walt Whitman wrote.[47]

Of course, as Drew Faust has argued, "the very efforts Americans expended to transform death suggest the threatening power of their underlying fear that these war deaths, that even the war itself might be meaningless."[48] Soldiers and civilians staved off their fear of erasure through memorialization that linked the fragile human body to the imperiled but more permanent nation-state.[49] At the same time, federal authorities faced down the war's threats to the nation by reassuring citizens that they would do everything possible for the fallen.[50]

The establishment of a system of national cemeteries in July 1862 and the creation of a Graves Registration Service in July 1864 gave institutional expression to these commitments.[51] The 1864 Annual Report for the Quartermaster maintained that these measures had "entirely dissipated the prevailing opinion of those living remote from Washington, that soldiers were irreverently or carelessly buried."[52] While such an assessment went too far in light of ongoing identification problems — only 1,500 of the 5,350 Union dead at the battles of Wilderness and Spotsylvania Court House in May 1864 were identified — national cemeteries and graves registration at least rescued loyal soldiers from indifference.

When recovery of the Union dead ended in 1871, seventy-four national cemeteries had been established holding 303,536 remains. Another 13,575 Union dead were buried in private plots and post cemeteries. Of the 360,000 Union soldiers estimated to have died in the war, 315,555 had been recovered and 172,109 positively identified.[53] This was a stunning memorial achievement, unprecedented in human history to that time. The graves registration effort was remarkable not only for its scale but for the fact that it sought to recover, identify, and reinter every fallen Union soldier, regardless of rank. While the dead were not always treated equally (officers were allowed larger headstones than were enlisted men at Arlington National Cemetery, for instance), each Union soldier was accorded the honor of an individual grave and marker at public expense. Such uniform treatment of the war dead represented an American precursor to the "democracy of death" and "cult of the fallen soldier" that Thomas Laqueur and George Mosse have noted in European memorialization after World War I.[54]

Despite the achievements of Civil War graves registration, equally remarkable was the horrific toll of unrecovered and unidentified dead. The remains of 26,125 Union soldiers were still missing when recovery operations ceased. Added to the 143,466 recovered but unidentified remains, some 169,571 Union dead—almost half of the federal dead—were lost, with no grave for loved ones to visit. The Civil War Tomb of the Unknowns at Arlington contains not one set of remains, like its twentieth-century successor, but the commingled remains of 2,111 men from the single battle of Bull Run.[55] Such a record of oblivion is unimaginable today.

The war's memorial innovations cushioned the blow by translating pain into political agency, elevating self-sacrifice to the highest form of citizenship and anonymity as the purest form of national identity. To borrow Franny Nudelman's analysis, nationalists sought "not to know the dead but to unknow them." "The scene at Gettysburg—simple headstones arranged in orderly ranks, the president paying homage to a generic heroism—suggests the contours of a nationalist aesthetic that favors abstraction over detail and vies with commemorative traditions that dwell on the material properties of the corpse." Walt Whitman's "The Million Dead, Too, Summ'd Up," for instance, evoked "soldiers Cemeteries of the Nation" in which "we see, and ages yet may see, on monuments and gravestones, singly or in masses, to thousands or tens of thousands, the significant word UNKNOWN." For those who embraced the democracy of death that emerged from the Civil War, the body's decomposition inside new national cemeteries erased all social markers save nationality, essentializing national identity and immortalizing the nation.[56]

THE SOUTH IS NOW UNITED BY A BAND OF GRAVES

These new aesthetics of mourning were not meant for everyone. They did not include all Americans, nor did they comfort them all. National cemeteries did little to assuage the grief and rage of Southerners who lost a smaller number but higher percentage of men than their northern adversaries. Two hundred and sixty thousand Confederates died in the war, and there are no known numbers for how many of them were found or identified, since the federal government made no effort to account for them until decades later. Most Civil War battles took place in the Confederacy or border states, making it easier for Southerners to recover their dead, but whatever advantage the South gained from its proximity to

An unburied Confederate lies next to the marked grave of a Union soldier at
Antietam, September 1862. (Civil War Photographs, Prints and Photographs
Division, Library of Congress)

battle was offset by losing the war to Union forces who took little interest
in recovering Confederate remains and actively opposed their inclusion in
national cemeteries. "Including Confederate soldiers was beyond the pale"
when the national cemetery system was created, according to historian
John Neff; "hence *national cemetery* is best thought of as a synonym for
Union cemetery."

As New Jersey governor Marcus Ward put it, "National cemeteries are
consecrated to the loyalty of the nation, and those who died for their country should not, in my opinion, share a common grave with those who would
have destroyed it."[57] Because national cemeteries were designed to preserve such distinctions, they were a source of division as much as unity.
That Quartermaster General Montgomery Meigs and Secretary of War
Edwin Stanton chose General Robert E. Lee's abandoned Arlington estate
as the burial ground for Union soldiers who died in the vicinity of Washington, circling it with so many graves that it became uninhabitable, strongly
suggests that "the initial motivations governing creation of the national
cemeteries were born of the hostility of war." That Arlington and other
national cemeteries honored ex-slaves who fought for the Union while
banishing Confederates or marking their graves with the word REBEL
shows that these spaces imagined the nation along ideological rather than

racial lines.[58] That vision was eventually replaced by a reunionist vision that elided divisions between white Americans at the expense of black citizenship, but even then the war dead remained contested. As Frederick Douglass insisted at an 1894 Memorial Day speech, typical of many such speeches he delivered late in life, "Death has no power to change moral qualities. What was bad before the war, and during the war, has not been made good since the war."[59]

Douglass, it would seem, lost the argument. Speaking before the Georgia legislature in December 1898, President William McKinley announced that the time had come "when in the spirit of fraternity we should share with you in the care of the graves of Confederate soldiers." Amid the burst of nationalistic feeling that accompanied the Spanish-American War, the announcement won praise from North and South, and Congress quickly authorized funds to gather Confederate remains for burial at Arlington. Additional appropriations soon followed to build a towering memorial there and to find and rebury the estimated 30,000 southern whites who died in northern hospitals and prisons.[60] This newfound concern for the Confederate dead was just one element of a broader sectional reconciliation that emerged near the turn of the century, which numerous scholars have noted.[61]

But the very richness of the scholarship on Civil War memory indicates that Douglass's sense that "there are no bygones in the world, and the past is not dead and cannot die," was as true for southern whites as it was for African Americans.[62] This was particularly true when it came to the war dead—"reconciliation would always run counter to the undeniable fact that many young men lay in graves because of the actions of the enemy, and no reunion, encampment, or political oration could deny that essential reality."[63] McKinley's move to care for the Confederate dead pleased most white Southerners, but did little to diminish the grudge they bore against the federal government for its earlier neglect. The white women who assumed responsibility for the Confederate dead decades earlier had no intention of relinquishing control over their martyrs to the Lost Cause. As officials readied Confederate remains for burial at Arlington, the Ladies of the Hollywood Memorial Association, the Daughters of the Confederacy, and the Confederated Southern Memorial Association forced them to delay until families who wished to do so had the chance to repatriate their dead to southern soil. During this delay, Katie Behan of the Confederated Southern Memorial Association sought to lay claim to all who were slated for burial.[64] "We want our dead and . . . we are going to have our dead," Janet Randolph of the Daughters of the Confederacy declared, though eventually over 400 Southerners were interred around the Confederate Memorial at Arlington.[65]

These women and their organizations opposed yoking the Confederate dead to national unity, preferring a memory that made southern loss the source of southern separateness. That memory was forged in the immediate aftermath of the war when the government's disregard for the southern dead was seized on as a sign of federal vindictiveness and illegitimacy. "The nation contemns our dead," wrote one Richmond editor. "They are left in deserted places to rot into oblivion."[66] If exclusion from national cemeteries marked Confederates as less than full citizens, it nourished a unifying hostility toward the nation and a sense of southern identity. "So often have I been in the national cemetery at Chattanooga and wished that our Confederate dead could have their graves so well kept by the government," one Georgia woman wrote, "and in my heart felt rebellious that it was not so." "I almost wish I was dead, & in the grave with them, when I think of our state of degradation," another young woman noted in her journal after attending the 1866 Decoration Day ceremonies in Charlottesville.[67] For her and millions like her, the fate of the dead was a way to conceptualize and articulate the experience of defeat.

For white Southerners as much as their enemies, the loss of the war dead was intensified by the absence of physical remains. "Oh my child, I feel at times as though I could submit to this great affliction," one South Carolinian wrote her daughter in 1862. "I sometimes think [Jim] is not dead, it might have been a mistake."[68] But unlike families of the Union dead, they could not rely on federal authorities to recover their missing. Within a year of the South's defeat, Ladies Memorial Associations sprang up to reclaim the remains of the fallen and tend to their graves.[69] They recovered thousands of bodies from Washington and Gettysburg, drumming up support for their efforts through incendiary claims that Confederate bones rested alongside the bodies of black "contrabands" or were being ground up for fertilizer by avaricious Northerners.[70]

Since federal graves registration units ignored the Confederate dead until the turn of the century, southern body recovery could be seen as a substitute for federal efforts rather than a form of competition. But if the Ladies Memorial Associations started as a stand-in for federal authority, they eventually came to rival it. Though they claimed to represent "neither party, nor section, nor division," the Ladies Memorial Associations forged an oppositional southern nationalism using the same memorial practices as federal authorities, making the Confederate dead into a unifying force. "The South is now united by a band of graves," proclaimed the Rev. J. E.

Edwards at the Oakwood Memorial Association's inaugural Decoration Day in May 1866.[71]

If anything, their work was more successful in fostering community than that of federal officials. Because white women led the effort to save the Confederate dead, their efforts could be presented as sentimental rather than political, which made the community they constructed more authentic in the eyes of its members and more difficult to oppose. When the *Chicago Tribune* criticized the ladies of Richmond for decorating the graves of the dead, the *Richmond Whig* shot back: "Political significance is not attached to these funeral ceremonies. . . . It is not the habit of Southern ladies to form political conspiracies."[72] Definitions of white womanhood as private, and Victorian mourning rituals that emphasized sincerity, allowed the Ladies Memorial Associations to hide their politics in plain view even as those cultural norms enhanced their legitimacy.

The history of southern body recovery suggests the ways in which the materiality and particularity of the dead can resist abstraction when memory activists make them a source of grievance against the nation-state. It also suggests the agenda of MIA activists a century later. The white women who memorialized the Confederate dead shared much in common with those who pursued an accounting of Americans missing in Vietnam. In the Reconstruction-era South and again after the Vietnam War, defeated Americans demonstrated an urge to recover the war dead from the land of the enemy and an unwillingness to rely on national authorities to carry out that mission.[73] In both instances, those who emphasized their sacrifice at the hands of the state rather than on its behalf made the missing into artifacts of loss, insisting on their recovery as a way of publicizing their sacrifice. And in both, women led the ranks of mourners who vied with public agencies for control over the dead. Whenever possible, these activists took physical possession of the dead in order to deprive the nation of their symbolic power and to wield that power against the state.

In her study of resurrection belief in the early Christian church, Caroline Walker Bynum argued that "the horror that resurrection overcomes is finally not so much torture or execution as the dishonor of being treated as a common criminal after death."[74] As in the early church, with its devotion to the bones of martyrs, the recovery of war remains may serve as a secular form of resurrection that overcomes the dishonor of wartime defeat. The defeated community resurrects itself around the graves of its honored dead. In contrast to victorious wars, where recovery and memorialization were left to the nation-state, often with lackluster results, in the post–Civil War South and after the Vietnam War private groups took the lead, returning remains to their families and local communities in order to lay claim to these powerful emblems of grief.

PERCHED ON A MOUNTAIN OF CORPSES

The Civil War's memorial innovations were refined amid the carnage of World War I.[75] Shortly after the outbreak of hostilities in August 1914, combatants organized elaborate graves registration services to find, identify, and, when possible, bury the dead. But despite the use of identification discs — first issued to American troops in the Spanish-American War — and unprecedented efforts at body recovery after the war, over half of those killed in the Great War "were lost as corpses in the wilderness of the battlefield, an astounding number considering that 9,000,000 soldiers died in the war."[76] In its aftermath, a postwar world "perched on a mountain of corpses" struggled to contain the catastrophe through commemoration.[77]

The trench warfare that defined the western front posed severe challenges to casualty resolution. Once the war settled into stalemate in September 1914, its major battles consisted of sporadic mass offensives featuring artillery barrages and machine-gun fire that killed with lunatic efficiency. Of the 100,000 British troops that attacked German lines at the river Somme on 1 July 1916, 20,000 were killed, many in the first minutes of attack. When the offensive ended four months later, 419,655 British, 194,451 French, and 600,000 German soldiers were dead or wounded. Similarly, the German assault on French fortifications at Verdun consumed 200,000 soldiers from each side during its most intense phase, and 600,000 by war's end. "The earth around us was literally stuffed with corpses," wrote one French soldier stationed there.[78]

With battle lines moving slowly or not at all, those who fell between the trenches, even if only wounded, often could not be retrieved.[79] Upon occasion the effort was made despite the risk. General John J. Pershing, who commanded the American Expeditionary Force, described the work of an American graves registration unit that "began their work under heavy shell of fire and gas, and, although troops were in dugouts, these men . . . gathered many bodies which had been first in the hand of the Germans, and were later retaken by American counterattacks." Despite the unit's bravery, he concluded that "identification was especially difficult, all papers and tags having been removed, and most of the bodies being in a terrible condition."[80]

Due to its risks, body recovery was often delayed until identification proved impossible. Though American soldiers wore dog tags, artillery shells often rendered them useless by tearing bodies "along no anatomical lines but rather divided as capriciously as the fragmentation in the burst of a high explosive shell," as Ernest Hemingway put it.[81] Even "bodies that seemed quite whole," one soldier bemoaned, "became like huge masses of white, slimy chalk when we handled them . . . and I have had to pull bodies to pieces in order that they should not be buried unknown. And yet, what a large number did pass through my hands unknown, not a clue of any kind to reveal the name by which the awful remains were known."[82]

Those who handled the dead often found the task more terrible than enemy fire, though they often endured both. "Many men who have stood it all, cannot stand this clearing of the battlefield," reported another chaplain. British burial parties were issued a double rum ration, ostensibly to kill the germs they inhaled but also, no doubt, to dull their senses.[83] The segregated U.S. Army ordered African Americans to carry out work of graves registration. "They prove to be efficient in the disagreeable task," the quartermaster reported.[84]

Millions of bodies were never recovered, or were buried so hastily or in such numbers that they reemerged to haunt those who tunneled, ate, slept, and fought among them. "There must be hundreds of German dead buried here," reported a British commander at Passchendaele, "and now their own shells are reploughing the area and turning them up."[85] Where it proved impossible to dig or reinforce trenches without unearthing the dead, bodies were used "to build the support walls for the fortified ditches; yellowing skulls, arms, legs could be seen packed tight into the dank, black soil." "We stood and sat on bodies as if they were stones or logs of wood," a German recalled, "as long as one didn't have to sit in the mud."[86]

After the war, body recovery could proceed in relative safety, though unexploded shells still posed risks.[87] Postwar battlefield cleanup was the most extensive ever conducted. Britain's Imperial War Graves Commission, France's Public Commemoration Division of the Ministry of the Interior, and the Graves Registration Service of the U.S. Army oversaw the exhumation and concentration of remains, but the "vastness of the work" invited the participation of civil society as well. Throughout the 1920s the Red Cross, Boy Scouts, and local civic groups labored in the corpse-infested fields of Belgium and France.[88] But grieving families were prohibited from taking part. Britain outlawed private exhumation of the war dead, while France and the United States repatriated the dead only at the request of next of kin, insisting on state control of the process.[89] Only in the defeated nations of Germany and Austria did private groups emerge to recover and commemorate the dead, in part due to restricted official access to German and Austrian graves under the Treaty of Versailles, but also due to the same distrust of public officials that led defeated Americans to seek out missing remains in the post–Civil War South and after Vietnam.[90]

In terms of numbers, post–World War I body recovery was catastrophically unsuccessful. Of the million British war dead, 517,000 were never found or, if found, never identified.[91] The French fared as bad if not worse, identifying only 700,000 of the 1.3 to 1.7 million French dead.[92] The record of Germany, Russia, Austria, and Turkey must have been worse still, as these states were ruined by war and had limited access to the areas where their men fell. Only the United States succeeded in finding most of its dead. Graves registration teams recovered and identified all but about 3,000 of the 80,000 Americans who died in Europe, leaving roughly 4 percent missing when recovery efforts ended in 1922.[93] American success rested on their late entry and limited involvement in the war. The main American offensives came in the war's final months, by which time the fighting was more mobile and more conducive to casualty resolution. Experience gained in the Civil War and Spanish-American War also contributed to American success.

That success facilitated the repatriation of remains to the United States, continuing a practice that began with the Spanish-American War. Though some prominent Americans, including Theodore Roosevelt and William Howard Taft, advocated burying the war dead where they fell, most Americans rejected this idea. "You took my son from me and sent him to war," one mother wrote Secretary of State Robert Lansing, "and now you *must* as a duty of yours bring my son back to me." Formed in 1919, the Bring Home the Soldier Dead League called for "an American tomb in America for every American hero who died on foreign soil." Capitalizing on the nativism of the war's backwash, opponents maintained that France would hold the American dead hostage, forcing further interventions in European affairs to safeguard their graves. Ultimately, authorities allowed next of kin to choose the disposition of remains, with roughly 70 percent opting for repatriation. The rest were buried in the disciplined rows of national cemeteries built throughout Belgium, Britain, and France under the direction of the American Battle Monuments Commission, established in 1923 to ensure that overseas cemeteries tastefully represented the democracy of death.[94]

The American policy of elective repatriation resembled a similar compromise reached in France after fierce debate, though the greater number of unidentified dead, the reduced distance to the front, and the French government's willingness to pay for yearly visits there for immediate family members meant that a larger number and proportion of the French dead were interred in the four massive military cemeteries built at the front.[95] British authorities permitted no such accommodations, prohibiting the return of all British dead and mandating that their remains be concentrated in overseas cemeteries. A marked departure from British military tradition, this policy reflected the dynamics of industrialized warfare, with its reliance on mass armies and mobilized civilians. Allowing only the rich and powerful to repatriate their dead in accordance with British custom would have run counter to the ideal of national unity essential to voluntary enlistment in Britain's "New Armies." But universal repatriation would have confronted civilians with the war's unimaginable toll. Either way, the fate of the war dead would have worked against official interests. The solution arrived at in a series of decisions in early 1915 was to outlaw the return of the war dead while creating the Graves Registration Commission to gather their remains for burial in austere, rigidly uniform military cemeteries.[96]

National cemeteries attained their full form and function in interwar Europe. By the time it completed its post–World War I work in 1938, the British Imperial War Graves Commission had built 1,850 military cemeteries with 557,520 soldiers interred in marked graves and 180,861 buried in individual graves marked "unknown." The French preferred to mass their dead. Some 130,000 unidentified remains are gathered at Douaumont Ossuary at Verdun, with 15,000 French soldiers buried in marked graves at the adjacent Douaumont cemetery. In those cases where no body could be found or identified, the names of the missing were memorialized at the national cemetery nearest where they fell. Sir Edwin Lutyens's Monument to the Missing of the Somme at Thiepval is inscribed with the names of 73,367 British dead. Menin Gate at Ypres contains another 58,600. The walls of the French ossuaries are similarly covered with the names of the missing, and every village in France erected a monument listing the names of those it sent off to war who never returned. American national cemeteries in Europe and those in the United States not only followed these forms, they were in some sense the model. "When you see the admirable cemetery for 25,000 Americans at Romagne, you will want us to have comparable ones wherever our sons distinguished themselves," future French president Paul Doumer told the National War Graves Commission.[97]

"During the war and after," Thomas Laqueur observed of this effort, "the state poured enormous human, financial, administrative, artistic, and diplomatic resources into preserving and remembering the names of individual common soldiers."[98] Yet if the dominant feature of World War I

A large crowd gathered at Arlington National Cemetery to observe the burial of the Unknown Soldier from World War I on 11 November 1921. (National Photo Company Collection, Prints and Photographs Division, Library of Congress)

commemoration was its exhaustiveness, its defining act was the burial of a single Unknown Soldier who had given "even his name" to the nation. Britain and France inaugurated this practice on the second anniversary of the war's end with the burial of an Unknown Warrior at Westminster Abbey and a *soldat inconnu* beneath the Arc de Triomphe. On the same day one year later, the United States buried an Unknown American at the Tomb of the Unknown Soldier in Arlington National Cemetery.

Stripped of all markers of individuality save nationality and gender, the Unknown Soldier could be claimed by any group and associated with any form of military service, while always emphasizing sacrifice to the state as the highest form of citizenship and identity. Lacking a name, the Unknown was able to stand in for all who were lost on the western front, indeed to stand in for the nation itself. But because the Unknown Soldier was in all probability a dead foot soldier, his elevation above men of the highest rank seemed proof, as the *London Times* put it, "that we are all equal, all members of one body, or rather one soul . . . that we may, indeed, all become members of one body politic and of one immortal soul."[99] This transubstantiation of the human body to the body politic, the transformation of death to eternal life, was the ultimate act of faith, or imagination, based on a body not seen, "known but to God."

The Tomb's symbolism was even stronger in the United States, since it concealed not only class distinctions between officers and enlisted men but also the ethnic, racial, regional, and religious diversity that made the American nation uniquely difficult to imagine. In a process meant to ensure anonymity and ordinariness, the Unknown Soldier was selected from four identical caskets by a decorated combat veteran. Once chosen, the Unknown was awarded the Congressional Medal of Honor, the Distinguished Service Cross, and other awards for valor while lying in state at the Capitol rotunda. President Warren Harding delivered the eulogy at a funeral attended by members of Congress and the Supreme Court, former president Woodrow Wilson, and other dignitaries who, by so honoring an ordinary soldier, showed their subordination to the people and made restitution for their sacrifices.[100]

The elaborateness of these rites showed that government leaders could not take national unity for granted, but they also revealed their faith in the Unknown Soldier as a symbol capable of masking or containing divisions within American society. If multicultural notes were struck at the Unknown's funeral—a rabbi intoned the Twenty-third Psalm and Chief Plenty Coups of the Crow nation placed his war bonnet on the crypt— his Tomb submerged alternative communities within the nation, just as the Unknown Soldier sacrificed his personal identity for his national one. Skeptics like John Dos Passos questioned the Tomb's inclusiveness—"make sure he ain't a dinge, boys / make sure he ain't a guinea or a kike."[101] But for those who sought a nation free from such distinctions, including many who felt their sting, the Tomb offered an idealized community open to all who served it in war. In years to come millions of Americans would stake their claim to full citizenship on the grounds of military sacrifice.

WHEN YOU LIVE NEAR THE GRAVEYARD,
YOU CAN'T WEEP FOR EVERYONE

Unlike World War I, when most American casualties came in a handful of ground engagements covering a few hundred miles in northeastern France, World War II scattered dead Americans over the four corners of the earth where 78,794 were permanently lost and another 8,532 were recovered but never identified, over one-fifth of the 405,000 Americans killed in the war.[102] Pearl Harbor offered a portent of things to come—only

229 of the 1,177 sailors trapped inside the battleship *Arizona* when it sank were recovered before the effort to retrieve them was called off.[103] In the four years that followed, the loss of other warships, bombers, and island outposts resulted in the disappearance of many men under circumstances that precluded their retrieval. Larger forces deployed further afield with more firepower aimed at them and at their disposal made it easier than ever before for Americans to vanish without a trace.

Staggeringly imprecise casualty reports from the Office of War Information suggest the difficulty the armed forces faced in apprehending the fate of their men. The first comprehensive list of American casualties, released in July 1942, showed 4,801 dead and 36,124 missing.[104] By February 1943 the number missing had climbed to 44,181, still more than four times the number of known dead.[105] The number of Americans listed as killed in the conflict did not surpass the number carried as missing until February 1944, and only then because the services reclassified many men originally listed as missing to the status of killed in action or prisoner of war.[106]

The number of missing prompted legal and institutional changes during the war itself, not just at its end. At the outset, it was standard practice for the War Department and Department of the Navy to stop a serviceman's pay and allowances when he was reported missing, but his next of kin could not collect death benefits until he was declared dead. If a man spent significant time in missing status, these procedures imposed serious hardship on his family. This punitive tradition was retired in early 1942 when Congress passed the Missing Persons Act, which authorized service secretaries to pay a missing man's family for one year after he became missing or until he was declared dead, whichever came first. On Christmas Eve 1942, recognizing "failures of an enemy to comply with international agreements in reporting deaths and captures," Congress amended the act to allow payment beyond twelve months if a missing man's status could not be discerned. In mid-1944 Congress revisited the act once more in light of "unanticipated situations and circumstances . . . pertaining to the fiscal entitlements of absent and deceased personnel and their dependents." Only this time, instead of extending payment, Congress authorized service secretaries to issue findings of death on the basis of "a lapse of time without information" that might lead to "a reasonable presumption that any person in a missing or other status is no longer alive." Lawmakers signaled their contentment with the amended legislation by extending it in one-year increments until 1957, at which time they made it a permanent part of the United States Code.[107]

Aside from the expanded financial and legal obligations of the Missing Persons Act, efforts to account for the missing during and after World War II did not depart significantly from precedent set in World War I and the Civil War. However, advances in weaponry and mobility that produced so many missing servicemen posed new challenges to their recovery and identification. The prominence of naval and aerial war proved particularly troublesome, as scuttled sailors and downed airmen often disappeared under circumstances that guaranteed they would never be found. Two-thirds of American bomber crews in 1943 failed to complete their requisite twenty-five missions before crashing or being shot down, often over enemy territory, remote mountains, or vast seas. One airman recalled a bombing run where "a crewman went out of the front hatch of a plane and hit the tail assembly of his own plane. No chute. His body turned over and over like a bean bag tossed into the air."[108] If recoverable, victims of such incidents were usually so charred, mangled, fragmented, or decomposed that identification proved impossible. To identify such remains the army set up specialized Central Identification Units composed of forensic anthropologists who correlated bone measurements, dental records, and fingerprints to the known characteristics of the missing. With their help, nearly 97 percent of recovered casualties were identified after World War II.[109] In light of post-Vietnam identification problems, it is certain that some of these identifications were in error, though it is impossible to know how many given that few families challenged the military's expertise and countervailing forensic technology did not exist.[110]

As in the First World War, individual identification allowed Congress to pass legislation providing for final disposition of the dead based on the wishes of primary next of kin. Roughly 60 percent chose repatriation, the remainder opting for burial in one of fourteen national cemeteries established outside the continental United States.[111] Tellingly, 75 percent who lost a loved one in the Pacific chose repatriation, and only three national cemeteries were built there, all in territories controlled by Americans—the Manila American Cemetery in the Philippines, the National Memorial Cemetery of the Pacific in Hawaii, and the comparably tiny Fort Richardson National Cemetery in Alaska—suggesting longstanding unease with interring American warriors in a region associated with racial others.[112] The families of many of those memorialized at these sites had no choice in the matter—36,285 names are inscribed on the Tablets of the Missing in Manila, and the Courts of the Missing in Hawaii display another 18,094.

These names remind us that in tens of thousands of cases there were no remains to bury. To cite one notorious example, nearly 900 Americans were lost at sea when the heavy cruiser *Indianapolis* was torpedoed in 1945,

A bugler blows taps at Margraten Military Cemetery in the waning days of World War II. Many of the remains in this photo were later repatriated to the United States. Today over 8,300 Americans are buried at Margraten, and 1,722 names are inscribed on the tablets of the missing there. (Courtesy National Archives)

many consumed by sharks during the five days they spent awaiting rescue. Nearly half of all Americans left missing were lost at sea.[113] Pilots and airmen were similarly hard to find. A UC-78 aircraft that disappeared after departing Douglas Army Airfield in Arizona in 1943 was not discovered until 1974 when hikers stumbled upon its wreckage and the remains of its crew.[114] If airmen could be lost in southern Arizona, it was far simpler to disappear overseas. A single raid over Ploesti, Romania, on 1 August 1943 resulted in 532 lost airmen, including over 200 buried at the scene, half of whom were so "carbonized" that they were never identified.[115]

Given such losses, official accounting efforts were both massive and inadequate. At its peak, graves registration occupied 13,000 personnel at a cost of nearly $164 million.[116] Yet given the numbers of missing, body recovery operations were surprisingly abbreviated, ending in the European theater by September 1949 and in Asia and the Pacific by the year's end. Graves registration searched New Guinea for just a few months before Juanita Allred, whose husband disappeared over the island in 1944, was notified that "the War Department must now terminate your husband's absence by presumptive finding of death," since "no information has been received which would support a presumption of his continued survival."

His body was not found until 1981, and only then through the chance discovery by two villagers on a hunting trip.[117]

Juanita Allred coped with the loss of her husband like many grieving Americans must have, writing to army authorities seeking information on unidentified patients from the South Pacific and to officers leading the search and recovery effort about the likelihood of finding her husband's plane. One officer searching for Americans lost in South America wrote her "that the chances of locating a crash in the jungle are virtually nonexistent." After devoting most of 1946 to her search for answers, she bought an illuminated chancel cross for her church with a small brass plate inscribed, "To the Glory of God and In Memory of Robert E. Allred—World War II," before remarrying in February 1948.[118]

Not all relatives were so easily dissuaded. Ida Mae Reitz Stichnoth, the mother of a man who was shot down during the Ploesti raid, refused to believe her son was dead despite accounts from other fliers that his plane burst into flames before crashing. She persisted in her belief that her son was imprisoned in a Soviet Gulag until the end of her life despite the fact that four members of his ten-man crew were identified and returned for burial, and the Adjutant General conducted a study showing that "the total number of dead buried by the Roumanians closely approximates the number of men lost in Roumania who cannot be accounted for otherwise." Her activism attracted coverage in *Stars and Stripes* and various California newspapers, winning her pride of place as the nation's "first POW activist" in the eyes of those who followed in her footsteps after Vietnam.[119]

Claims of secret captivity resonated with few Americans. Stichnoth's charges attracted attention only because they concerned the Soviet Union, the source of growing anxiety in the war's aftermath. Because U.S. forces physically occupied enemy territory and had access to liberated and allied lands, U.S. officials and most Americans assumed that men not found in captivity were surely dead. When 91,252 Americans turned up in German prison camps in 1945, nearly 14,000 of whom had been in missing status, the War Department announced "substantially all" Americans in Europe were accounted for.[120] Those whose bodies were not found were presumed dead based on the passage of time without proof of life, as in the Allred case, or using mathematical formulas like the one offered to Stichnoth.

But more than logic, it was the curious nearness of death mixed with the public's lack of direct exposure to it that may have made body recovery more perfunctory than it had been in the past or would be in the future.[121] Despite the privatism that infused official and popular notions of what Americans were fighting for, the war's massive scope and scale, the way it involved and targeted entire populations, and the aggressive nationalism it reflected and fueled all encouraged Americans to conceptualize sacrifice "in aggregate more than individual terms," particularly the mass death American bombers rained on German and Japanese civilians, but also to American deaths.[122] "When you live near the graveyard, you can't weep for everyone," according to a Russian proverb, and the war cost so many lives that Americans became inured to its tragedy. Of the 27 million Russian dead, two to three million were never found, 540,000 Japanese were missing more than a year after the war, the Germans abandoned hundreds of thousands of dead men as they retreated across the eastern front, and the yet-to-be-named Holocaust obliterated six million Jewish lives, leaving only traces — shoes, shorn hair, stolen art, and ashes — behind.[123]

Millions of Americans grieved for friends and loved ones lost to war, but public memory in the postwar period displayed neither the sepulchral mania that characterized official memory after the Great War nor the dislocation, paradox, and irony that marked popular memory of the earlier war. Its most noteworthy sculpture, Felix DeWeldon's monumental replica of Joseph Rosenthal's Iwo Jima flag-raising photo, was triumphant rather than mournful, busy rather than austere, and in no way suggested that three of the six men it depicted died at Iwo Jima. More intent on preparing for the next war than recalling the last, the nation's leaders invoked the war dead as cautionary symbols of worse fates to come should Americans fail to remain vigilant.[124] Ordinary Americans were more intent on reaping the rewards of wartime service through living memorials such as highways, airports, stadiums, and parks than in supplementing the memorial landscape inherited from earlier wars.[125] With the Cold War's dawning, there was little time to reflect on wartime loss before more menacing conflicts loomed. Graves registration teams ended their recovery effort just in time to begin work in Korea, which produced a fresh crop of dead Americans. In terms of memorialization, the wars seemed to bleed together, with Unknown Soldiers from both conflicts buried in the same ceremony on the same day in 1958.

THE GRAVES OF YOUNG AMERICANS
SURROUND THE GLOBE

Nothing better demonstrated how rapidly search and recovery operations ended after World War II than how unprepared the graves registration service was when the Korean War broke out in June 1950. Citing a still secret military history of graves registration in Korea, RAND researcher Paul Cole reports that at the start of the war "the entire graves registration effort consisted of one group, the 108th QM GRS Platoon," comprising thirty men led by a laundry officer. Incapable of matching the pace of combat, this inexperienced and understaffed crew scattered American graves wherever troops fell. As UN forces retreated down the Korean peninsula in the summer of 1950, those graves were abandoned. When General Douglas MacArthur staged an amphibious invasion at Inchon in September, more graves followed his push into North Korea. Concerned that graves would be lost in the chaos, the quartermaster ordered that American remains be consolidated in the city of Kaesong along the 38th parallel, but fuel and manpower shortages, along with uncertainty about where scattered American graves were located, slowed compliance.[126] When Chinese forces entered the war in November, precipitating another UN retreat, they captured 5,000 to 6,000 American prisoners and at least 1,500 American graves as they advanced southward. Thousands more Americans went missing in the retreat, trapped or dead behind enemy lines.

The war settled into a stalemate near the 38th parallel by June 1951, but MacArthur's assault on North Korea and subsequent retreat "complicated the immediate problem in Graves Registration and greatly intensified the one of final recovery for the UN dead."[127] Having lost territory littered with remains, UN forces were incapable of retrieving them without retaking North Korea. Realizing the folly of battlefield burials, graves registration instituted a policy of "concurrent return" in December 1950, shipping dead Americans directly to Kokura, Japan, for identification by a central identification unit before returning them to the United States for burial. Concurrent return not only meant that new casualties were never interred in Korean soil, it led to the excavation of American remains under UN control. Beginning in January, remains from the war's early months were exhumed for processing at Kokura and transshipment home. The first "floating hearse" reached Oakland in March, bearing the remains of fifty-seven Americans. An army spokesman hailed its arrival as "the first time the United States has returned battlefield casualties from a war theatre while hostilities were continuing." Americans had always been reluctant to bury their war dead in Asia, and after 1950 they would never willingly do so again.[128]

But thousands of Americans were already lost. Thousands more joined them as some 2,700 Americans died in prison camps before the war ended, along with unknown numbers who died before, during, and immediately after capture.[129] Anxiety over the fate of these men mounted as the seesaw struggle stabilized at the 38th parallel. In December 1951 anxiety became outrage when the communists provided a list of American POWs as part of ongoing peace negotiations. "The list contains the names of only 3,198 of the 11,042 Americans reported missing," the *New York Times* complained, raising "an insistent question: Where are the others?" "Only two possibilities remain: the Communists are withholding the names of prisoners whom they are attempting to keep for their own purposes, as the Russians are still keeping hundreds of thousands of Europeans and Japanese," or "a large number of those missing and unaccounted for have been massacred or have died in Communist prison camps."[130] President Harry Truman joined the chorus: "This country has no way of verifying whether the list is accurate or inaccurate, true or false, complete or incomplete. For the sake of the families whose sons are missing in action, everyone should treat the list with skepticism."

The problem of independent verification was real but hardly unique to the Korean War. As one source recalled, "The bodies of one-third of the men listed as missing during the Italian campaign [in World War II] were never recovered nor their graves established despite careful checking."[131] Soldiers vanished in war; Korea would be no different. But in Korea the missing were turned into a justification for war in ways that had happened only late and haltingly during World War II.[132] Complaining of "wide discrepancies" in the Chinese list of American POWs, the UN Command announced on 23 December 1951 that it would not return communist prisoners who declined repatriation.[133] From that point on, the Korean War was fought over POWs and MIAs.

As was later the case in Vietnam, the shift toward fighting over the prisoners and missing both reflected and responded to mounting frustration with a war that promised little hope of victory. While officials were genuinely concerned over Americans missing from Chinese captivity rolls, UN commander General Matthew Ridgway had already accused the communists of murdering as many as 6,000 Americans in November 1951, and the secretary of the army repeated these charges before a Senate subcommittee in January 1952, suggesting that authorities suspected unlisted MIAs were already dead. Officials familiar with the bloody and confused fighting that resulted in the loss of these men found the Chinese list a pessimistic but plausible picture of MIA mortality, and its names and serial numbers matched up with missing personnel.[134] But by the time the list arrived, Truman had decided to make the fate of POWs the decisive issue in an otherwise limited war by insisting that the return of communist POWs in UN custody would be voluntary. Having been advised that as many as 45,000 enemy prisoners professed no desire to return home, Truman hoped to turn their defections into a Cold War propaganda coup.[135]

Given that the UN command unveiled this controversial proposal at the height of public outrage over the fate of American MIAs, it is possible that the Truman administration encouraged perceptions of concealed prisoners to help sell its plan to withhold enemy captives to a war-weary public. Since Americans cared more for their own men than for Asian captives, both sides of the prisoner equation were needed to convince them to sacrifice for the principle of non-repatriation. Two days before UN officials broached their decision not to return enemy prisoners who declined repatriation, reporter Hanson Baldwin railed that "the release of the names of the prisoners of war allegedly held by the enemy in Korea reveal[s] . . . an enemy set apart from the nations of the West by lack of civilized restraint." He apprised readers that "some of those in our stockades have turned against communism and a return of these men to the enemy would be equivalent to a death sentence." He closed by weaving the two POW populations into a tapestry that revealed how the current "struggle of two worlds is not merely power politics, not only national rivalries, but a conflict of man against savagery, of man against power and evil, of man for his soul."[136] Cotton Mather could not have divined greater moral imperatives from captivity, though this was surely the first time in history that men were asked to kill and die to liberate prisoners already in the custody of their own command.

The superficial accounting effort that followed the Korean War further calls into question the sincerity of official claims that Americans were secretly imprisoned. Once the ceasefire was reached in July 1953, military officials declared missing Americans dead with lightning speed. One month after 3,746 American POWs returned to U.S. custody in the two prisoner exchanges that concluded the war, the Pentagon announced, "It is now the considered opinion of the Department of Defense that most of these [missing] men must eventually be presumed dead."[137] There was little eventuality involved. At the time of the press release, service secretaries had already reclassified 687 MIA cases based on reports of death from returning POWs. By year's end they had issued another 3,386 findings of death. "The Missing Persons Act was about to expire," the Adjutant General's Office explained in a 1954 study of these status changes, "and decision was made to get as many determinations made as possible." After Congress extended the legislation, another 2,465 determinations of death were issued immediately. Within six months of the prisoner exchange, only 226 men remained in missing status, awaiting "dispatch as the year required by the Missing Persons Act expires."[138]

Presumptions of death should not be confused with the recovery and identification of remains. In most of these cases, no body was ever found to confirm death. Nearly 8,200 Americans were left missing or unidentified after the Korean War. They represented over 22 percent of the 36,576 American deaths in Korea, even higher than the percentage of war dead left missing after World War II.[139] Though the ceasefire agreement authorized graves registration teams to recover the fallen from enemy territory, body recovery provisions were violated due to distrust on all sides. In February 1954, the U.S. Commander in the Far East decided against "'search and recovery' operations (i.e., looking for unrecorded graves) since authorization . . . would require granting reciprocal privileges for communist teams to roam throughout South Korea."[140] Soon each side began recovering enemy remains in order to deny the other entry into its own zone of control, an arrangement formally agreed to by both sides in August. Between the first of September and end of October, UN forces returned 14,000 remains to communist forces and the communists returned 4,219 bodies in an exchange dubbed "Operation Glory." Of these, 2,944 were thought to be Americans, though hundreds could not be identified. By January 1956 the Kokura identification facility was closed and the Korean accounting effort was at an end.[141]

Operation Glory hardly answered all questions regarding missing Americans. As late as August 1953 UN Commander General Mark Clark alleged that the enemy "might be holding 2,000 to 3,000 more prisoners" than they would repatriate.[142] Immediately following the final release of American POWs in September, the UN command requested an accounting for 3,404 personnel, including 944 Americans thought to be in enemy custody.[143] POW debriefings and graves registration halved this list of "discrepancy cases" by 1955, but the lack of information on these men so rankled Congressman Clement Zablocki that he introduced a House Resolution in May 1957 calling on President Dwight Eisenhower to "make the return of the four hundred and fifty American prisoners of war still imprisoned by Communist forces the foremost objective of the foreign policy of the United States."[144] "In a land where the individual welfare of all citizens is paramount," the mother of one missing soldier wrote the president that year, "why has there been . . . no public fervor over the missing in action in the Korean War?" Another wrote: "My son is always in my mind and heart," but "it seems to me that he has been forgotten by his country."[145]

FROM THIS SEAT TO ONE IN THE UN?

John Fischetti's 1953 cartoon depicting a Chinese soldier with a bloody knife atop the grave of "Missing American PWs" suggests that the suspicions surrounding the fate of the missing after the Vietnam War were present in muted form after the Korean War. (Courtesy Karen Fischetti Trust)

For some, the fate of these men symbolized the weakness and lack of will inherent in the policy of containment. Columnist David Lawrence first broke the "humiliating story" of "the forgotten 944 Americans" who were "spirited away to hiding places behind the Iron Curtain" as an example of what happens when troops "were not permitted to use maximum power to win the victory." Chafing at the limits of containment, he painted a picture of "fearful," "buck-passing" officials who "soft-peddled" communist tyranny "because our Allies did not approve." "Once upon a time," he wrote, warming to his tale, the United States "would take drastic measures to secure respect for its troops."[146] *U.S. News & World Report* sharpened these charges a few days later. "The United States did not win the war in Korea. As a result, it cannot demand and expect to receive any reliable accounting for those still missing."[147] Rage over the inability to charge behind the Iron Curtain and retrieve missing Americans still boiled in the House chamber years later as Zablocki's resolution was debated. Massachusetts congressman Thomas J. Lane mourned the passing of "a time when we were unafraid," when "in clear and explicit terms we would set a date by which these men must be released—or else."[148] The inability to reclaim the missing, or insist upon their return, proved that an imagined age of American omnipotence had passed into oblivion, somewhere behind the DMZ, along with the unrecovered, unavenged American dead—the final and most painful proof of American defeat.

Yet despite expressions of anger over the fate of MIAs, no organized interest group emerged on their behalf as after Vietnam. Small groups engaged in isolated acts of protest, but fifteen mothers sending their son's medals to the White House with the message that "our sons want your loyalty, not your medals" hardly fazed the national security state.[149] Unlike those lost in Vietnam, most MIAs in Korea were unmarried foot soldiers from poor families who were unorganized and unaccustomed to speaking in public. "I have fought many a silent battle over the subject," an MIA father told Zablocki's committee, but "I realize that just one individual is essentially helpless to do anything." The federal government was too powerful and dissent too dangerous for MIA parents to reproach it. "I lie awake at night composing strong letters to the State Department," one mother told a *Baltimore Afro-American* reporter. "Then I never send them because I am afraid the State Department will call me a communist." "All of the parents who have contacted me," the reporter testified, "seem for some reason or other to tremble when they come to Washington and try to deal with officials."[150]

In the waning days of the Vietnam War, the disappearance of so many MIAs in Korea was cited as a disgrace not to be repeated, but in the intervening years the main lesson drawn from the experience was that Americans needed to commit more fully to the anticommunist crusade. A strict new Code of Conduct was the chief reform to emerge from the crucible of North Korean prison camps—the same code that American prisoners in Hanoi would cling to with such determination a decade later. "I am an American fighting man," the new Code began. "I serve in the forces which guard my country and our way of life. I am prepared to give my life in their defense." Equating the Code of Conduct to the Ten Commandments and the Constitution, its authors exhorted American servicemen to "remember that the United States of America will neither forget, nor forsake him, and that it will win the ultimate victory."[151] In this formulation, the pain and anger of the Korean War were harnessed to a renewed commitment to the nation-state as the only force on earth capable of transcending death. Like a modern priest rousing his flock with the bones of saints and the example of Christ, John F. Kennedy noted that "the graves of young Americans who answered the call to service surround the globe," invoking them as proof of his rousing inaugural pledge that he would "pay any price, bear any burden, meet any hardship, support any friend, oppose any foe to assure the survival and the success of liberty."[152]

ACTING DEFENSE SECRETARY CLEMENTS turned to this historical paradigm when he told the White House in 1973 that it was time for the

Pentagon to resolve the MIA issue "as it has in the past." Past resolution had come not only through field operations to recover dead bodies but through concomitant, even antecedent presumptions of death. Though the JCRC was still pursuing MIA remains on the ground, by mid-1973 senior Pentagon officials and their counterparts at the State Department and White House were ready for symbolic resolution. Reflecting on the mood in the Pentagon at the time, Frank Sieverts told Senate Select Committee investigators that "military people of higher rank who had been through earlier wars might well have believed in '73 that the time had come to follow the practices of the past and simply declare people dead on the ground, that that was the kindest, fairest way to do this."[153]

This conviction rested on several considerations, ranging from the danger and difficulty of casualty resolution to the disquiet many officials felt over the fact that the families of the missing continued to receive pay and benefits denied to the families of those killed in action. But also at work, though seldom expressed, were deep-rooted traditions—presumptions of death transformed missing warriors into mute but sacred objects that could be claimed as defenders of the nation rather than brandished as its victims. Seeking to discredit those who challenged state authority over the dead, Clements dismissed MIA activism as "rumor-mongering by charlatans," insisting "there is not a shred of evidence, not one hard piece of evidence, that would give us hope that there are survivors among the MIAs."[154]

In an angry letter to former secretary of defense Melvin Laird that quoted Clements's remarks and similar comments from other officials, League leader Gladys Brooks recalled Nixon's promises "that he was not going to forget the MIAs—we are beginning to think he meant they were going to erect a monument or something." In the past a monument might have sufficed, but no more. "The memorial act implies termination," as David Lowenthal observed. "We seldom erect monuments to ongoing events, or to people still alive."[155] For MIA relatives, the very idea of memorializing the missing represented betrayal. "We're going, 'Wait a minute, it wasn't six months ago you were saying, "We know they're lying. We know they haven't admitted all the POWs. Don't give up hope. Keep fighting,"'" future League executive director Ann Mills Griffiths later recalled. "Then all of a sudden because we have a peace agreement . . . we're supposed to just stop."[156]

Their angry letters, protests, resolutions, and advertisements made clear that MIA activists did not trust officials to honor their wartime commitments, much less the Code of Conduct's lofty promises. They suspected that military officials would follow precedent. "They are planning to tidy up this whole mess by changing all MIAs to KIA—whether grounds exist or not," one MIA wife wrote to VIVA, "thereby leading the public to believe that everyone has been accounted for." But unlike MIA families in the past, this woman and others like her had no intention of accepting such a result.

"Just about everyone thinks that the war is over," she closed. "It will never be over for me." [157]

Fullest Possible Accounting

The Persistence of the Past

As communist forces made their final assault on the Government of South Vietnam, President Gerald Ford sought to stave off its imminent collapse by requesting $722 million in emergency military aid. Lawmakers refused, with Congressman Les Aspin warning that more arms would only lead to further "fighting, casualties, and maybe, worst of all, American POWs."[1] To ward off that worst-case scenario, Congress authorized $300 million to evacuate Americans from the region. The specter of captive Americans had gone from the main reason to stay and fight to the best justification to cut and run. All that remained was a mad dash for the exits.

As Americans in Saigon scrambled to the top of the U.S. embassy to await airlift, Ford urged those back home to avert their eyes. "America can regain the sense of pride that existed before Vietnam," he counseled in a 23 April 1975 commencement address, "but it cannot be achieved by re-fighting a war that is finished as far as America is concerned."[2] Days later, as the last marines were whisked from the embassy roof, Ford implored Americans "to close ranks, to avoid recrimination about the past, to look ahead to the many goals we share, and to work together on the great tasks that remain to be accomplished."[3]

Ford's presidency was awash with such talk. "My fellow Americans, our long national nightmare is over," the new president pronounced upon taking the oath of office in August 1974. "Let brotherly love purge our hearts of suspicion and of hate."[4] Determined "to hasten the healing process," Ford stunned those accustomed to the blood sport of Nixonian politics by traveling to the Veterans of Foreign Wars convention ten days later to announce his support for the "earned re-entry" of draft evaders and military deserters.[5] A few weeks later he shocked Americans once more by granting his predecessor "a full, free, and absolute pardon." "I cannot prolong the bad dreams that continue to reopen a chapter that is closed," he declared. "Only I, as President, have the constitutional power to firmly shut and seal this book."[6]

But the power of an unelected, accidental president proved insufficient "to bind up the nation's wounds" and to force "the reconciliation of all our people and the restoration of the essential unity of Americans," as Ford's plummeting approval rating soon proved.[7] Nothing exposed the limits of Ford's healing hand more than his failure to resolve the festering MIA issue. MIA activists were among those most incensed by Ford's no-fault approach to the past. When Ford announced he would show leniency toward draft evaders, the League's executive director fired off a letter to the White House calling it "inconceivable that our Commander-in-Chief would show greater concern in a speech to Veterans for those who *chose to leave the United States* . . . than he does for over 1,300 U.S. Servicemen who are still unaccounted for in Southeast Asia." Unlike "dodgers and deserters," the letter continued, "our men have earned their re-entry whether they be alive and walking or in a casket."[8] "Amnesty, conditional or otherwise, should not have been considered until (1) the return of all POW's from Southeast Asia, (2) the fullest possible accounting of all Missing-in-Action, and, (3) the fullest possible repatriation of the remains of all servicemen who died, serving our country," complained a League press release condemning the decision.[9]

Such arguments were vintage Nixon, who, as president, repudiated calls to forgive and forget with the acrid pronouncement, "Let us not dishonor those who served their country by granting amnesty to those who deserted America."[10] Their persistence showed that some citizens preferred Nixon's scorekeeping to Ford's see-no-evil approach. Though always more ambivalent about the war than Nixon represented, most Americans, and certainly most League activists, shared his sense that the war was the paramount issue of the day, along with his conviction that its outcome hinged less on enemy action than the decisions and behaviors of Americans. Despite their differences over the war, virtually all Americans agreed that something had gone terribly wrong in Vietnam and many anticipated, even relished, debate over who and what to blame. "It is all very well for you to counsel the nation to turn our backs on defeat and address the future," a retired army general wrote Ford, "provided that first the factual record be set straight."[11]

Despite their reputed amnesia toward the war and its veterans in the mid-1970s, millions of Americans shared this compulsion to set the record straight, to establish the war's meaning, to praise its heroes and punish its villains—in short, to construct its memory—putting them at odds with official amnesia. "There is much to be said for this Ford approach," wrote the Catholic journal *Commonweal*, "but there is also a real danger that it means only sweeping our past sins under the rug."[12] Though he disagreed with his liberal co-religionists about the war's lessons, conservative William F. Buckley agreed that Ford should "stop talking about the causes of South Vietnamese defeat in all those nice formulations whose common denominator is that it wasn't our fault."[13] The one thing commentators agreed on was that "the misbegotten American crusade in Vietnam isn't over," as Rod MacLeish wrote for the *Washington Post*. "We will be memory cursed by how it all went wrong," with "each side seeking to prove the other's evil by the evidence of the cause's ruin."[14]

The war that dominated American politics for over a decade was not about to go away, not without some score-settling. And though debate about the war ranged well beyond the MIA issue, expressions of concern for missing Americans offered a familiar and potent means to sway public opinion. In the face of Ford's amnesty announcement, 65,000 Christmas cards addressed to MIAs flooded the White House in December 1974.[15] Fearing "that the United States government has deemed it expedient to forget the fates of these men and their families," the Maryland Senate passed a resolution in March 1975 calling on President Ford "to create a Special Commission to develop and execute a plan for an acceptable accounting for the missing in action."[16] Governor Daniel Evans of Washington told Ford that "this loose thread from an era you recently said was at an end, must be cut from this country's past by achieving a full accounting of those missing soldiers as soon as possible. Only with this action can we in good faith turn away from this aspect of our country's past."[17] By recalling those lost in Vietnam, these voices insisted that the war's costs be remembered; by seeking an accounting, they demanded that someone be held accountable. A May 1975 letter to Congress requested an "accounting of every American life lost in Viet Nam. By that I mean to say, who, under what circumstances, and *why*."[18]

Satisfying such a demand was impossible. That was precisely the point. So long as the infinitely elastic standard of a "full accounting" went unmet, any effort to declare the war over could be called premature. By insinuating that missing Americans still suffered in Southeast Asia, MIA activists maintained the war as an ongoing problem requiring redress. MIA activism was one way Americans articulated the war's continued presence, a means to address the pain and anger it still caused, and a weapon with which to attack those deemed responsible. In their search for the missing, activists pursued their enemies at home and abroad, constructing public memory of the war as a cautionary tale of patriotic white American men betrayed by a faithless state and its feckless leaders. The nightmare of American servicemen held captive by implacable dark-skinned evildoers not only delayed normalization of relations with the Socialist Republic of Vietnam, it helped reignite the Cold War and sparked an aggrieved nationalism that has yet to abate, becoming an early iteration of the narratives "of impotence and castration, captivity and restraint" that dominated American politics in the 1970s.[19] The failure of centrists from either party to remedy this perceived injustice accelerated the revolt against midcentury liberalism that began with Barry Goldwater's 1964 nomination, continued with Richard Nixon's victories in 1968 and 1972, and culminated in Ronald Reagan's election in 1980, which marked the start of nearly three decades of Republican ascendancy. MIA activists did not cause these things to happen single-handedly, but by perpetuating bitter memories of betrayal in Vietnam they sustained a sense of danger and distrust that lent itself to such causes.

WE ARE ENTERING A DIFFICULT PERIOD

On 31 May 1974, New York attorney and MIA brother Dermot Foley wrote the General Counsel for the Defense Department concerning "the current friction between MIA families and the Administration" that led him to file suit challenging the right of military service secretaries to issue presumptive findings of death. Over five single-spaced pages, Foley made his case that "those who used and merchandised us and then lied to us now are seeking to abandon us" by "declaring dead the servicemen who would be subjects of such accounting." "We are not, as a group, oriented antagonistically toward the military or the war effort or the President," Foley professed, only compelled "to press for substantive accomplishments by our Government in MIA accounting. . . . If we fail, we will help hide the identity of those who bear the historic guilt for surrendering the MIA's to discretionary disposition by the other side and for the aggregation of military, diplomatic, and administrative mismanagement that helped bring it about."[20]

Foley copied his memo to Jack Marsh, a key adviser to then Vice President Ford, and it may have been on Marsh's mind as he prepped Ford for an August meeting with League leaders. "We are entering a difficult period in terms of the MIA issue," Marsh warned. "The issue is both complex and emotionally charged, involving the motivations of agencies, groups, and individuals which are not always clear." Noting that "divisions and fissures are appearing among key groups," Marsh sensed that "any solution in terms of this issue will leave some elements dissatisfied," calling it "a time of caution for you in regards to the MIA problem."[21]

As Marsh predicted, the National League of Families experienced significant upheaval during these years as the return of American POWs and the Pentagon's determination to pursue presumptive findings of death for the remaining MIAs forced relatives to decide whether their activism should continue. Differences of opinion over whether to remain politically active were compounded by differences over how to proceed, bringing the League to a crossroads that left it a smaller, more reactionary organization than it had been just a few years earlier.

Even before the war ended, the League was contracting and becoming more militant as moderate members, including high-profile POW wives like Louise Mulligan, left the group to speak out against the war. With the prisoners' release in 1973, most remaining POW wives left the League, seeing little reason to agitate on behalf of men now safely home. MIA families were more likely to persist, though those who were never very active or who never had much hope of repatriation also drifted away after 1973, particularly wives who decided to move on with their lives.

Their exodus reduced the League's size and reoriented its politics, as the ambivalence of the many gave way to the fervor of the few. Instead of the "smartly dressed young women" who had once dominated League meetings, a reporter found "mostly parents, or brothers and sisters" at the 1973 meeting, with turnout down to "about 500 family members, most of whom are related to MIAs." An April 1974 report estimated the group's membership at just over 2,000 members, with only 16 percent related to POWs, and with parents and siblings outnumbering wives four to one.[22] The League's leaders reflected these changes, with MIA father Scott Albright becoming the first MIA parent, and first man, ever appointed to the League's top post in 1973.[23]

Postwar attrition was not surprising given that most League members, at least initially, saw their mobilization as a temporary departure from their prevailing political quietism. But the departure of so many so quickly was accelerated by and inflected with politics. Foley's lawsuit, in particular, pushed many members to leave the League. By seeking to invalidate the Missing Persons Act, Foley's litigation exacerbated tensions already roiling the League. On one side were families like the five who joined Foley's suit, who saw status changes as another sign that the missing were being written off by the federal government. On the other were those ready to accept the death of their loved ones, who saw Foley's suit as a delusional attack on governmental leaders and institutions they held dear. Their fight involved emotional, financial, and personal differences often expressed in bitter terms. But it was also about whether a group once aligned with the nation-state and deeply invested in its Cold War vision should break with the state as a result of its mistakes in Vietnam. In that sense it was also political.

As soon as Foley's *McDonald v. McLucas* complaint was filed in July 1973, the U.S. District Court for the Southern District of New York issued an injunction that prohibited "any official report of death or any finding of death with respect to any MIA" without a written request from his primary next of kin.[24] After hearing oral arguments in October, a three-judge panel ruled in February 1974 that the Missing Persons Act was unconstitutional insofar as it denied those with "a property interest at stake in the continuation of the entitlements granted to them" the procedural protections required under the due process clause. But the judgment rested on narrow procedural grounds rather than broad constitutional principles, spelling out an easily met remedy that allowed reviews to proceed. "Notice must be given of a status review and the affected parties afforded a reasonable opportunity to attend the review," the court ordered, where next of kin would have "access to the information upon which the reviewing board will act" and would be "permitted to present any information which they consider relevant to the proceeding." "Once this is done," the judges ruled, "the requirements of due process have been satisfied."[25]

This solution fell short of the constitutional prohibition Foley sought. He immediately appealed the ruling, but the Supreme Court declined the case in November, leaving the District Court ruling in effect. At that point the military services were free to resume status reviews so long as they met the new procedural requirements. But the services, fearful of political fallout, left the ban on unsolicited reviews in place until August 1977. At first they stalled while waiting for a rumored presidential or congressional review of the issue. When such an investigation was slow to materialize, military officials requested White House permission to resume involuntary reviews in July 1975, only to be turned down by National Security Adviser Brent Scowcroft, who worried that "the impact, so far as the President is concerned, would be wholly negative." Noting legislation before Congress to create a Select Committee on MIAs, Scowcroft anticipated that "we will be in a stronger political position to resolve these cases after the Congress has reviewed the whole issue."[26] Once the House Select Committee was created, it asked the military services to delay involuntary reviews until it completed its investigation. Matters were further postponed due to the 1976 election and the transition from the Ford to the Carter administration.

Though Foley failed to invalidate the Missing Persons Act, his suit hindered its operation for more than four years. During those years, whether a man remained in missing status or was presumed dead depended on the desires of his primary next of kin. As of August 1976, 590 of the original 1,300 MIAs had been presumed dead, 437 at the request of the primary next of kin.[27] With the disposition of each case left to the discretion of family members, presumptive findings of death divided the League as no other issue could.

Though Foley filed suit on behalf of "all next-of-kin," the court rejected the petitioners' standing as a class, viewing the status review question as two-sided. Its *McDonald v. McLucas* ruling noted an "emotional breach" between those "like the plaintiffs who understandably still hope for the return of their loved ones" and "those who have accepted the apparent fate of death . . . and who desperately want the services to make immediate determinations of death so that emotionally and actually they might begin their lives anew." "The court believes that it can — and indeed must — accommodate the interests of both groups of families," which is one reason it refused to prohibit voluntary reviews.[28] Its assessment conformed to observations from inside the League. In her July 1973 League newsletter, National Coordinator Helene Knapp asked "each of you to be cognizant of the fact that there are two sides to this very important and delicate issue."[29]

Most observers understood this divide as a disagreement between MIA wives and their in-laws. "A father or mother or sister or brother can wait forever for a finding," Knapp told a reporter, "but wives and children cannot."[30] Another woman elaborated, "wives (unlike sisters, parents, or brothers) have much to lose 'if status changes are disallowed,'" since a finding of death was the only way these women could remarry or control jointly owned assets.[31] Less constrained by their status, MIA parents and siblings were more apt to view presumptions of death in wholly negative terms. And since wives were the primary next of kin in two-thirds of MIA cases, they usually decided whether to initiate a reclassification, which upset parents and siblings who felt their position and interests usurped.[32]

Though most families denied it, financial considerations further separated wives from parents. As the court recognized in *McDonald v. McLucas*, the benefits of MIA status gave the dependents of missing men a "property interest" in prolonging that status. So long as a man was classified as MIA, his dependents received his base pay, combat pay, housing allowance, family separation allowance, and unused leave pay, all tax-free. And because MIAs were promoted alongside their non-missing peers, each year spent in missing status brought his beneficiaries higher pay and the promise of larger benefits when he was presumed dead. An air force captain declared missing in 1966, for instance, would have been promoted to lieutenant colonel by 1974. Assuming he was married with three children, by 1975 his dependents would have received $98,000 more in pay and allowances than they would have received had he been declared dead when he was shot down.[33] That year the remaining 700 MIA families received $9 million more in pay and allowances than they would have received if all MIAs had been presumed dead, giving them powerful incentives to maintain MIA status.[34]

Though both benefited financially from MIA status, wives and parents had different interests at stake when it came to status reviews. Parents of unmarried MIAs seldom qualified as legal dependents of their missing sons, meaning that few of them received immediate monetary benefits as a result of their son's loss. Nor could they look forward to Social Security survivor benefits if their son was declared dead, as MIA wives and children did. Still, parents of unmarried MIAs usually stood to inherit their son's uncollected pay when he was presumed dead, which had been collecting 10 percent annual interest in the Uniformed Services Savings Deposit Program (USSDP). By 1976 the remaining MIA USSDP accounts were worth over $40 million, with 100 accounts in excess of $100,000. Though parents inherited these funds only after a status review, giving them an incentive to seek a finding of death, once their son was reclassified his pay stopped and his parents lost access to the unusually secure and lucrative savings program.[35] By delaying their son's status review, parents collected more in accumulated savings while preserving hope of his eventual return.

In contrast, MIA wives drew most of their husband's salary in direct pay, reducing their USSDP deposits. However, wives stood to collect their own windfall from a status change since Social Security regulations allowed legal dependents to collect survivor benefits back to the date an MIA became missing. Since most MIAs were lost before 1968, most wives stood to collect years of retroactive Social Security benefits with a presumption of death. Like parents, the longer these women delayed a status review, the larger their payout became, but unlike parents, whose benefits ceased after a status review, wives and minor-age children earned survivor benefits on an ongoing basis after receiving their retroactive Social Security benefits. In other words, after receiving all the wages they would have earned if their husbands were alive — tax free — MIA wives were awarded the Social Security benefits they would have received had their husbands been dead all along, only at a higher rate based on the higher rank attained in missing status — again tax free — before collecting survivor benefits on an ongoing basis. Had the wife of the hypothetical MIA captain shot down in July 1966 requested a status review for her lieutenant colonel husband in July 1975, she and her three children would have received a lump sum Social Security payment of $82,555 and monthly survivor benefits of $985 after that, substantially less than the $2,300 per month they received before the status review, but not the full stop imposed on primary next-of-kin parents. All told, with a presumptive finding of death in mid-1975, this hypothetical but typical MIA family would have received $165,000 more in total compensation than if the downed captain had been declared dead when he was shot down.[36]

These were large sums of money when median family income was under $14,000 per year, large enough to prompt hard feelings and disagreement.[37] Given that most MIAs were married and that their parents and siblings had little incentive to pursue a presumption of death while wives stood to benefit a great deal, competing interests created the potential for bitter rifts within families and, by extension, in the League. MIA wife Maerose Evans, an outspoken foe of Foley's lawsuit, complained of "some family members or organizations (that have made money because of this problem) getting headlines or prolonging this agony because it has become a way of life for them."[38] MIA mother Iris Powers confessed that "we are in a comfortable position financially. Some may not be willing to change that. I know that sounds terrible, but one must be realistic."[39] Most family members avoided discussing money due to the discomfort involved, but parents and siblings clearly had less financial or emotional interest in status reviews than did wives. Considering that any given case involved multiple biological relations, but only two-thirds of all cases involved a wife, opponents came to dominate the League. Outnumbered, wives found their authority challenged as never before, prompting women already ambivalent about continued activism to leave. "The National League of Families is run largely by the *parents* of MIAs," former Nevada coordinator Eva Brown told Congress in 1976; "it is *their* self-interest that is served by continual opposition to status changes."[40]

If money factored obliquely into the split between wives and parents, it factored directly into mounting tensions between MIA activists and federal officials. On the eve of the League's 1974 annual meeting, UPI reported "suspicion among many members of Congress and Pentagon officials that some of the families active in the movement to slow or halt official death declarations are interested mainly in their own pocketbooks," noting anger among senior military officers that MIA relatives enjoyed "fringe benefits and elite status that the families of guys who were just flat-out killed over there never enjoyed."[41] "There are a lot of people making money off this," insisted one unnamed official, and "these groups have a vested interest in keeping this going."[42] These charges were repeated, again without attribution, in a 60 *Minutes* report aired that same summer.[43]

Not surprisingly, activists were incensed by the whispering campaign. MIA sister Ann Mills Griffiths called it "an insult to the families of these men to attempt to belittle their efforts with this type of slanderous, inflammatory mud-slinging" and professed the willingness of MIA families to "give all the money deposited in the accounts receiving 10% interest, and in many cases match it dollar for dollar, just to receive definite information as to the fate of their loved one."[44] MIA wives Kay Bosiljevac and Anne Hart pretended to do precisely that, signing over their husbands' paychecks as "ransom" to the secretary of defense "on the condition that the United States make some attempt to account for the men rather than declaring them all dead." The stunt convinced few League critics—when confronted by an air force casualty officer at the League's 1974 meeting, Bosiljevac confessed that "all she signed was a piece of paper which went nowhere"—and suspicion that MIA activists were in it for the money poisoned their relations with government officials.[45]

Yet for all this talk of money, it is worth remembering that primary next of kin, whether parents or wives, stood to benefit whether they requested a status review or not; only the mix of immediate and long-term rewards changed. It must also be emphasized that Congress and the Nixon administration authorized the lavish benefits for POW and MIA families and were responsible for the inequities created. "We do not know who is suddenly profiteering," VIVA leader Gloria Coppin complained in a letter to Melvin Laird. "DOD had made no such claims for the past three years," she reminded him.[46] That officials did so only at war's end was taken as further proof of their duplicity.

Money played its part, but the status review controversy was also about memory. For families on both sides and for those in the middle, no amount of money could compensate for their loss. What was at stake was how that

Far from a closed book

Douglas Borgstedt's 1976 cartoon published in the *Alameda Times Star*, hometown newspaper of Alameda Naval Air Station, shows how missing Americans stood in the way of calls for closure. (Courtesy of *Alameda Times Star*)

loss should be remembered. Many who requested a presumptive finding of death saw it as a way to honor their loved one's service. "We place our complete trust in you and in the Secretary of the Army to review Jerry's case," the parents of one MIA wrote to the Adjutant General. "We take comfort in this—because we know it is the way he would have wanted it. . . . He was a gallant soldier dedicated to his country and devoted to his job."[47] "My husband knew what he was doing and he went willingly," Maerose Evans wrote to Defense Secretary James Schlesinger. "It is more than time to have status changed. No other group in military history has received such privileges and concern."[48] For these families, status reviews brought comfort by situating death in Vietnam within a noble military tradition. "The agony I have experienced over eight years as an MIA wife must now be ended with the same dignity as that with which my husband proudly served his country," beseeched Bernice Smith.[49] Anything less would, in the eyes of Maerose Evans, "degrade my husband and all who serve their country."[50] Embracing the military and its preferred abstractions of wartime death, they portrayed their sacrifice as honorable and freely given.

But their opponents insisted that presumptions of death were another betrayal of those who served in Vietnam. "A [presumptive finding of death] by the U.S. simply writes him off—forgotten—a closing of the book with no recognition, no honor and *no dignity*," one MIA wife complained in a letter to Congress. "An official and accurate accounting," she insisted, "is the only possible way his family can ever really say a final goodbye and that the U.S. can say 'we remember that you gave.'"[51] Anything short of this standard was a dereliction of duty that exacerbated rather than ennobled her loss. Questioning this notion, *60 Minutes* asked Kay Bosiljevac "how could it possibly be in the interest of the United States government to declare these men dead if, in fact, there is a possibility that they are alive?" "Many of the families, myself included, feel that the U.S. government will be relieving themselves [*sic*] of responsibility for these men," she answered. "In other words, their books are closed." To Bosiljevac, closure was premature, regardless of the wishes of primary next of kin. "It's wrong," she insisted, "to declare a man dead to accommodate his wife." "It was the man who served his country, not his wife."[52] In a harsh rebuttal to Maerose Evans along these lines, MIA father Earl Hopper accused her of "working against the majority of families of these missing men" and "working against the men themselves. To change the status of these men without first as complete of an accounting as possible," he alleged, "is to deprive them of the individual liberties and rights they are assured of by the Constitution."[53]

Tension over these matters came to a head at the League's fifth annual meeting held in Omaha in June 1974. Repeatedly jeered and interrupted at the opening session of the four-day event, Executive Director Scott Albright announced, "I can't chair this meeting. Does somebody else want to do it?" and abruptly left the podium. Arizona coordinator Earl Hopper stepped in to take charge.[54] The transition brought a changing of the guard that left the League diminished in size but radicalized in spirit. With Albright went the last of the League moderates. In their place came memory activists who, in Albright's view, "dedicated themselves to nothing short of a full accounting, no matter *what* that takes."[55] After Omaha, their fight for an accounting became a fight against forgetting, with the U.S. government and large subsets of the American people defined as the enemy.

Albright was an early casualty. By January 1974, he hardly recognized the group he was elected to lead six months prior, telling the Senate Foreign Relations Committee, "One year ago today, our organization had more than 3,000 members. Today we have only a little more than half of that number," consisting mainly of "hardcore infighters."[56] One week earlier, Albright narrowly escaped becoming their victim when he uncovered a plot by dissident board members to elect a new board without his knowledge using VIVA's pirated mailing list of MIA families. In a letter alerting the membership, Albright called the attempted coup "one of the most blatant, presumptuous acts I have ever encountered." He defiantly vowed to reject "suggestions which appear to be non-productive," but the "please help!" that concluded his missive made clear his influence was waning.[57]

According to a perceptive but overly sanguine analysis prepared for the Senate Foreign Relations Committee, by the time Albright appeared before the committee in January he hoped to bring the League to an end: "Many of the League's national leaders have come to recognize that there is little more to be done. Some of them would prefer to see the League quietly fold rather than continue an increasingly futile campaign which they fear will degenerate into strident militancy. They are opposed by a minority element in the League which accuses the leaders (such as today's lead witness, Scott Albright) of having given up and sold out to the Administration."[58] But the more quiescent League moderates became, the more determined activist members were to keep up the fight. As Ann Mills Griffiths recalled, "Some of the families who were in the original leadership of the League at the end of the war wanted to shut down the issue with honor," but "some of us said, 'no way, we're not shutting down with honor' and kept it going."[59] While outsiders may have been correct that militants represented a minority of all POW and MIA families, they made up the majority of the League's active members and were determined to take charge.

At the Omaha convention, activist relatives finally claimed the League's top leadership posts. E. C. "Bus" Mills, described as "a representative of the militants" by the Senate Foreign Relations analyst, replaced Albright as executive director; Kay Bosiljevac of 60 Minutes fame became national coordinator; George Brooks, who led the January uprising against Albright, returned to the League board as its vice chairman; Earl Hopper took over coordination of the League's appeal of the McDonald v. McLucas ruling; and Foley became League counsel.[60] In a sign of its transformation, the composition of the board went from five parents and ten wives to eight parents, two siblings, and five wives on the incoming board, and the new board had more men in leadership positions than ever before.[61] Accusing their predecessors of "refusing to rock the boat," the new board members promised to be more "active" in taking on the government.[62] As a step in that direction, they secured a mandate to seek legislation prohibiting presumptive findings of death, which passed by a vote of "around 300 to stop status changes and only 8 against stopping them" after moderate members departed the meeting in disgust.[63]

The Omaha convention began a new chapter in League history, defined by constant suspicion of and frequent hostility toward federal authority. The anti-government turn appalled many members, who responded with a flood of mail complaining that their organization had been hijacked by radicals. "I have just returned from the Annual meeting," Maerose Evans wrote Secretary Schlesinger, and "am most distressed by many of the statements and happenings there."[64] "The League is not speaking for its entire membership but only its vocal minority," insisted self-proclaimed representatives of the old guard, Nancy and Gordon Perisho.[65] "Less than 250 of the missing men were represented at the meeting," Bernice Smith told the White House.[66] "The National League of Families does not speak for me," another MIA wife told her congressman.[67]

Leading studies of the MIA issue second such charges, claiming that militants tipped the scales in their favor by bringing VIVA activists with no relation to missing Americans "into the League staff and hierarchy" in return for monetary contributions. Evidence for this claim is spotty.[68] League newsletters make no mention of a financial contribution; in fact, the August newsletter worried that the Omaha meeting generated only $4,000.[69] More important, Albright's farewell address heralded the fact that "the families voted once again, this time overwhelmingly, to restrict voting membership to family members." His parting shot at "*outsiders* who seem to feel that they are actually more concerned than the family members" confirms that VIVA was present at Omaha, but stops short of suggesting a takeover or infiltration.[70] A fierce VIVA critic, Albright would have condemned any incorporation of its concerned citizens into the League's voting membership.

VIVA did not take over the League so much as finance the efforts of activist relatives who were jockeying for control. There were longstanding ties between VIVA and the League, with state and local League chapters selling VIVA bracelets on consignment in return for a share of the profits.[71] The support and involvement of MIA families in VIVA's operation gave legitimacy to what otherwise would have seemed a crass attempt to profit from their loss, while VIVA's bracelets and advertising enhanced public awareness of the League's cause. With both groups worried about declining interest in the MIA issue, VIVA supported anything that kept MIAs on the public agenda, making it an ally of League militants like Ann Mills Griffiths, who joined VIVA's board. In time VIVA ceased to have any function other than funding the activist element of the League and enriching its own leadership. "When I left [in 1974] we had more than five million dollars in the bank," Gloria Coppin told Christian Appy. "I still don't know what happened to the money."[72]

Among other things, it helped propel Griffiths, already a League board member, to the League's executive director post in 1978, a role she still holds. When VIVA closed its doors in 1976, it transferred its assets to Support Our POW/MIAs, a Southern California group under Griffiths's control. The amount involved was never disclosed, but it may have been significant, given that an August 1975 audit showed VIVA with $191,000.[73] And before Griffiths took the helm, bracelet inventor Carol Bates served as executive director for two years, which might be seen as a sign of a VIVA takeover given that she was not related to an MIA. But in some ways Bates's appointment reflected VIVA's weakness rather than its strength, both because it was motivated by VIVA's collapse, and because it was arranged by League power brokers for their own self-serving reasons. Neither Mills nor Hopper, the League's executive directors in 1974 and 1975, wished to remain in the post due to its Washington residence requirement. Thus to control the group from afar, they named Bates as their successor. With no independent standing in the League, she served at their pleasure and could not challenge their authority as Albright had and as Griffiths would later do.[74]

Whether levied by League moderates or by historians, the charge that VIVA "bought out the League" implied that "'professional' crusader[s]" had radicalized the group for political or profit motives when most families preferred to bring it to an end. Critics buttress this idea by pointing out that the post-Omaha League permitted any "lawful relative of the American who is now or has been a prisoner or missing in Southeast Asia and his or her spouse" to qualify as family members, and even allowed non-relatives to become honorary members by "adopting" an MIA for $5 per month.[75] Though unable to vote in League elections, such people were often vigorous participants in League affairs, and their prominence made the group illegitimate in the eyes of some. "I bitterly resent having 'concerned citizens' hysterically telling me that they care more about my son than I do!" Iris Powers protested in 1975. "Good God, I wonder what motivates these people who have made our problem their crusade?"[76]

Her question is key to understanding the persistence of the MIA issue. Essentially she asked how and why a small group of MIA families and non-family activists from VIVA and elsewhere were able to dictate public memory of the war when she considered herself better suited and more entitled to the task. "The League represents only a small portion of families," Powers insisted, with many members remaining on the rolls "just to get the League newsletter."[77] Powers was hardly alone in voicing such complaints, which various commentators have embraced. But as Jay Winter and Emmanuel Sivan point out, "collective memory is not what historians say about the past," nor is it simply "what everybody thinks about war." It is, rather, those representations that predominate in the public sphere. It is the act of remembering in public that produces public memory, and political and profit motives often fuel such acts of remembrance. When it comes to public remembrance, "some act; others — most others — do not," Winter and Sivan write, and the motives of memory activists are seldom simple.[78]

The "some act, most others do not" formula certainly held true for the League after 1973. League voters favored an activist approach by wide margins, with Mills, Brooks, and Bosiljevac tallying twice as many votes in the 1975 election as moderates like Emma Hagerman. But while League leaders boasted that "of the 944 members who voted, 739 agreed with present policy of the League," these numbers were a fraction of all POW and MIA families.[79] Considering that multiple members of activist families voted for the same slate of candidates, the 833 votes cast for Mills, the League's top vote getter in 1975, hardly represented family opinion in its totality. To the contrary, such a small number of votes showed that two-thirds of the League's wartime membership no longer voted.

But if the League's membership had dissipated, it remained the only legitimate entity for treating the MIA issue, as the Pentagon's begrudging airlift to its annual meeting and perfunctory briefings to its members made clear. If its prominence faded in the mid- to late 1970s, so did late war suspicions that it was an administration mouthpiece, and compared to government agencies and officials or to groups like the American Legion, the VFW, or Vietnam Veterans against the War, the League retained unparalleled political legitimacy and moral authority, rarely challenged or condemned by anyone of consequence save in unattributed whispers. The League had never been representative so much as self-referential; in that sense its declining membership mattered little so long as it retained its standing as the official POW/MIA family organization, a status that government officials and media outlets reinforced every time they engaged the League in public discourse about the war. Since most of those who left the League retreated into private life, they posed no real threat to its status. Their departure did little more than purify the position of those who remained, allowing a small subset of disgruntled radicals to masquerade as something more significant.

Critics who portray the story of the post-Vietnam League as one of outsiders usurping the rightful place of mothers and wives reinforce the idea that nuclear families, particularly those that conform to a nonpolitical, private ideal, represent the rightful community of mourners, and that the participation of those motivated by political or public concerns is always less pure, even improper. But the idea that the family trumps the community was the very bludgeon that League activists used to assert their memorial authority. The grave has always been "a point of tension between the family and the community," but the privileging of the family over the community in this context dates to the Victorian era, when intense public displays of grief over the death of a loved one became an outward sign of the bourgeoisie's rich interior life in contrast to a sterile public world.[80] This separate-spheres framework was always ill suited to death in war, which necessarily occurs in a social context, and which has prompted public mourning rituals that make Victorian funerary rites pale by comparison. To take the nuclear family as the sole and rightful arbiters of wartime memory reduces historical analysis to an argument over whether the League was or was not representative of MIA families, when an interrogation of how all memory activists used the family's privileged position to shape public memory is more fruitful.

In the state-dominated memorial culture of modern nations, historian Daniel Sherman argues, "the term 'family' designated not only the group that held a name in common, but also the beneficiaries of state-funded exhumations and the interest groups calling for them."[81] This model, where the state constructs the family by enlisting it in commemoration of the war dead, and where the family gains legitimacy through its involvement therein, helps explain how the League remained central to public memory despite its contested representativeness. Having granted the National League of Families legitimacy during the war, neither the state nor the press could easily take that legitimacy away, even when the group came to include people with no legal relationship to missing Americans.

An adoptive League member whom one study cites as an example of professional crusaders posing as genuine family members illustrates the elusiveness of such categories. After joining the League as an "adoptive sister" of her MIA boyfriend, Cheryl Eller became state coordinator for the League's Connecticut chapter in 1974. Not content to remain "related only by God's wish that we reach out to one another in love and mutual support as brothers and sisters are wont to do in time of great crisis," she legally changed her name to Cheryl Eller Boyd in September 1974, taking the surname of her late boyfriend in order "to carry on the fight for POW-MIAs in his name." Accusing the government of trying "to sweep the POW-MIA issue under the rug," Eller Boyd insisted that "the families, sweethearts, and friends of these missing men wouldn't let them get away with it."[82] By taking her lover's name, she showed that the family was defined by law, custom, practice, and affiliation as much as biology. However tenuous her claims to MIA status, Eller Boyd and others like her became the face of MIA families by mourning the missing in public. They became what Jay Winter has called "fictive kin." As their detractors departed public life, these "agents of remembrance" recalled the loss of American men in Vietnam as an unforgivable betrayal.[83]

WE WILL STRIKE BACK IN EVERY WAY POSSIBLE

President Ford's announcement that he would grant clemency to draft evaders brought him into immediate conflict with the League. "I can't see how you can possibly think about giving the cowards amnesty [sic]," MIA mother Eleanor Cordova raged in a letter to the White House. "What do you tell the families of the men that are lying in our cemeteries? That they would be alive if they ran away." "Take care of our servicemen first," she demanded.[84] Telling Ford that "we are not satisfied that you and others will always *remember the missing*," the new League board did all it could to remind him, calling a press conference where chairwoman Maureen Dunn pronounced that "justice is now missing in action in the United States of America." "The families of the men have waited too long already," Mills concluded; "We will now strike back in every way possible to achieve our goal."[85]

As protests poured in, Ford told his staff that "the amnesty/MIA issue should be separated." "There is not a great deal we can do to influence the North Vietnamese," so why delay amnesty until after an accounting that might never come?[86] Yet for League activists, the unlikelihood of accounting for the missing was all the more reason to reject amnesty. As they saw it, their loved ones had sacrificed for the state; to allow those who refused to make the same sacrifices to go unpunished would be "a travesty of justice."[87] Since the suffering of MIA families continued, so should the suffering of their opposition. "The draft dodgers and deserters have suffered little compared to the men still prisoner or missing," Ann Mills Griffiths editorialized.[88]

While he denied any connection between clemency and MIAs, Ford saw both (and most other difficult issues he faced) as divisive residues of a war he was anxious to leave behind, which led him to link them despite his better judgment. His clemency announcement tied the two issues together from the start. Referring to the period of "armed hostilities in Southeast Asia" as a time of "great losses," he noted that "thousands died in combat, thousands more were wounded, others are still listed as missing in action," and "the status of thousands" more who avoided military service "remains unresolved." Ford hoped to move past all these sacrifices at once — "I do not want to delay another day in resolving the dilemmas of the past," he declared. "Reconciliation calls for an act of mercy to bind the Nation's wounds and to heal the scars of divisiveness."[89]

Ford's rhetoric conforms to literary critic Keith Beattie's claim that Americans have used a "wound metaphor" to represent the Vietnam War, whereby the conflict "is foregrounded as a rupturing presence within American culture while *at the same time* it is used to evoke the need for unity." Representations of the war as a debilitating breach of a presumably natural national unity, Beattie argues, compose an "ideology of unity" that privileges social and political cohesion over division and debate, ideological consensus over criticism and complaint. According to Beattie, the wound metaphor makes the war "the scar that binds," so that "the divisions exposed by the war are negated, difference is elided, unity prevails."[90]

But Ford's experience with amnesty shows it was easier to "evoke the need for unity" than to establish unity among Americans accustomed to conflict. While it offers a brilliant deconstruction of official rhetoric, Beattie's argument fails to note how MIA activists and their supporters used the "wound metaphor" not to unify Americans but to assert a fundamental difference between those who "suffered and bled" and those who "deserted and fled."[91] Whereas Ford wanted to elide the difference between the two, League activists and their allies accentuated the distinction. This was clear not only in the League's rhetorical demands but in formal acts such as the resolution put before the Senate Armed Services Committee by freshman senator Jesse Helms:

> Whereas two and one-half million United States servicemen served honorably during the conflict in Southeast Asia, and
> Whereas 58,000 servicemen lost their lives while performing their duty in service to their country in that conflict, and
> Whereas nearly 1,300 American servicemen remain unaccounted for in Southeast Asia.
> Now, therefore be it resolved that:
> It is the sense of the Senate that no amnesty, conditional or otherwise, be considered for any United States citizen who knowingly evaded the draft in order not to serve in the conflict in Southeast Asia, or who knowingly deserted from the armed services while serving our country, until such time as there is
> (a) The fullest possible accounting of all Americans still missing in action or otherwise unaccounted for in Southeast Asia; and
> (b) A return of all Prisoners of War; and
> (c) The fullest possible accounting for and repatriation of the remains of those American servicemen who died in conflict in Southeast Asia.[92]

"Death is the definitive boundary," social theorists Carolyn Marvin and David Ingle have written; "detached from death, differences are negotiable," but "death . . . distinguishes who submits from who does not" in ways that are impossible to ignore.[93] And while submission to the state had been commemorated after earlier wars as a way to establish the essential unity of all Americans, the inequities of the Vietnam-era draft, combined with the political discord the war inspired, made an assertion of unity more difficult after Vietnam. "The tremendous number of unfortunate families who lost someone in Southeast Asia must feel outraged upon thinking that their men could have 'deserted and fled rather than served and bled,'" League polemicists spat, none more than MIA families. Not even the families of the war dead suffered so much, since "at least there is no uncertainty for them."[94] By promoting the possibility that MIAs might still be alive — might still be suffering in service to their country—the League created a boundary even more definitive than death because it could be extended indefinitely.

Wielding their grief as a scourge, League members lashed out at the permissiveness and license that they blamed for the clemency board and for defeat in Vietnam. "The great virtues of duty to country, honor or respect for our flag, patriotism, died to a great degree when greater concern was shown for those who burned our flag, paraded and rallied around the Viet Cong flag shouting 'Hell, no, we won't go,' than for the 1,300 U.S. servicemen still unaccounted for in Southeast Asia," Mills thundered at the League's anti-clemency news conference in September. "We don't know how these virtues can be resurrected," he concluded, but he suggested the first step should be "the return of all POWs," "the fullest possible accounting of the Missing," and "the return of the remains of those whose bodies can be recovered."[95] Only the return of missing warriors could restore honor and integrity to the fallen nation.

Reclaiming, reconfiguring, and repositioning bodies is among the best-established ways of "reordering worlds of meaning," as Mills's use of resurrection language suggests. In her analysis of the reburial of nationalists in postsocialist Eastern Europe, anthropologist Katherine Verdery explains that, "because at the time of their deaths these men had achieved visibility around certain values, which then receded or were suppressed, handling them recalls those values to the ones lately prevailing."[96] Though activists denied that MIAs were dead, their calls for a full accounting served the same purpose. Just as "parading the dead bodies of famous men [used] their specific biographies to reevaluate the national past," the evocation of white, patriotic, middle-class airmen betrayed by faithless citizens and corrupt public officials cast clemency as a continuation of the war rather than a remedy to it. Their "empty chairs and fatherless homes are evidence that the United States of America has tragically and shamefully abandoned the very men who serve her while the resistors and deserters are welcomed home," an MIA father wrote to Senator Bob Packwood. "This is not the America I grew up in."[97]

Such letters evinced little hope of reversing the nation's decline, at least in the near term. Instead, they amplified the nation's fall in order to establish blame. A 1975 mailing from Steve Kiba that sought to enlist Americans as adoptive members of the League was surpassingly dark. "It is difficult if not impossible to imagine just how horrible the life of an MIA is," Kiba declared as he depicted a captive American forced to eat "worms, small white stones, large and yellowish toenails with dirt and crud caked on them,

[and] slivers of wood" as "obnoxious guards hack and spit phlegm" at him. "Forced to wallow in his own excrement" until "infested with parasites and covered with fungi infections," he "cries out anguishly [sic] for help, but no one hears his pitiful plea." Worse than his physical condition is his knowledge of "the shameful truth that he HAS BEEN ABANDONED and FORSAKEN by his government—the very government which sent him abroad to fight for freedom." "Most American people are too busy and wrapped up in their own private little worlds and can not trouble themselves to give the deplorable plight of the MIA a second thought," Kiba concluded, imploring readers to "wake up and once again start behaving as true Christian-Americans."[98]

Kiba's waking nightmare, sprawled over three single-spaced, legal-sized pages, represented what Bruce Franklin called a "reimaging of the history of the Vietnam War," which depicted "American white working class men as crucified prisoners of the Vietnamese." This "myth of imprisonment" made "Vietnam the source of the imprisonment, powerlessness, and alienation felt by many Americans in an epoch when alien economic, technological, and bureaucratic forces dominate[d] much of their lives."[99]

Yet while Franklin focused on the ways in which the MIA issue reversed the war's victimology—accusing the Vietnamese who suffered at American hands of atrocities against Americans—what is striking about MIA activism after 1973 is its inattention to the Vietnamese relative to its hostility toward domestic foes. Widely held and well-documented racial enmity toward the Vietnamese hardly disappeared, but it increasingly found expression in disputes having less to do with real Vietnamese than with their alleged American sympathizers, allies, and dupes. Unable to shed their contempt for the Vietnamese or their unshakable faith in American power, activists tended to blame their countrymen for MIA suffering. They were no longer prisoners of war, in the eyes of one wife, but "prisoners of peace," sacrificed by corrupt Americans who placed their own comfort ahead of the common good.[100]

Consider the scalding agitprop entitled "Missing the Missing in Action" published by the National Review in early 1975. Written by Stephen Rudloff, who spent the last eight months of the war in a Hanoi prison, the article forgoes customary depictions of Vietnamese cruelty in favor of a New Journalism pastiche of national dishonor, mixing news clippings on amnesty, the Code of Conduct, even the burial of Smokey the Bear to paint a hallucinogenic portrait of MIAs as Christ-like martyrs. "These are the forgotten Americans," Rudloff seethed, "the men who sacrificed so much, and yet who ask for so little in return. 'My God, my God, why hast Thou *forsaken me?'"* In a frenzy of righteous indignation, he closed, "the MIA has been 'properly disposed of' by Congress and the people. His memory makes a fitting bier for the coffin of American integrity. Let his epitaph read BETRAYED."[101]

Comparing the MIAs to Christ on the cross, Rudloff tapped into the richest narrative of betrayal and redemption available. Like Christ, MIAs were betrayed by their own people and forsaken by the omnipotent power they served, sacrificed for a sinful, undeserving community. Their descent from the heights of American power to earthbound ignominy was the human equivalent of Christ's descent from heaven. Christ was stabbed in the side; the MIAs were stabbed in the back. Yet, like Christ, they might still be redeemed if the people would repent their sins. There was still time to roll the stone away from the tomb and resurrect American integrity. Analyzing similar iconography in representations of missing Germans after the Second World War, Frank Biess notes both the "profoundly antimodernist, culturally pessimistic message" of such images alongside the possibility of salvation offered through the survival of men who adhered to "allegedly timeless and essential German values."[102] By making MIAs into national martyrs, MIA activists condemned the present while holding out hope for national deliverance.

Though the League had shrunk in size and influence from its early 1970s heyday, it remained capable of rallying large numbers of Americans to its side. During the war, the League directed its letter drives and lobbying efforts at the communist officials and international agencies it blamed for American captivity. But with the shooting war at an end, those energies turned inward as it took aim at Capitol Hill, Foggy Bottom, even the White House and Pentagon as the source of the nation's ills. As she forwarded 65,000 Christmas cards addressed to MIAs to the White House in 1974, the League's Pennsylvania coordinator Elaine Worrell told Ford that "we are frustrated and sometimes even bitter," that "we must not only fight the North Vietnamese to get them to live up to the terms of the Paris Peace Agreement, but our own State Department."[103]

As the 65,000 cards attest, Worrell was not alone in her frustration. Philip Jenkins, Bruce Schulman, Natasha Zaretsky, and other historians of the 1970s have shown Americans to have been widely dissatisfied with the state of national affairs during the decade, with those on the left angry that so little had changed while those on the right were angry that so much had, and virtually everyone worried about runaway inflation, high unemployment, crime, and corruption. They voiced their displeasure in myriad ways over myriad issues, but most embraced a discourse of "dangerous, conspiratorial outsiders" bent on their destruction, an idea the MIA issue reinforced as well as any, with the added advantage of linking present problems to an unpopular war.[104] Many Americans emerged from the war angry over what historian Peter Clecak has called "the structure of advantage" exposed by its inequities. And though millions enjoyed the personal freedoms and expressive cultural styles that flowered after the mid-1960s, most were unhappy with the quality of political leadership over the same period. While the liberal reformers who controlled Congress expressed their displeasure by exposing CIA and FBI abuses of power and reining in the executive branch, conservative activists were, for a time, unable to find an official channel for their grievances. Ill at ease with a compunctious Ford administration filled with Nixon holdovers and largely locked out of a Congress more antiwar than any since the 1930s, they experienced the frustration of those who had been encouraged to voice their opinions even though no one was listening. The highly expressive culture of MIA activism offered them an unassailable means of dissent "from the culture of modernism, dissent from the social ethics of liberalism, and dissent from the politics of the welfare state."[105]

ABSOLUTELY NO HOPE OF SOLUTION

Thrown on the defensive by League hostility, the Ford administration searched for some way for "the President to do something soon with the MIA wives to show his concern and to blunt some of the amnesty business."[106] The September release of CIA pilot Emmet Kay, captured in Laos in May 1973, offered Ford an opportunity to drown out the League's anti-clemency press conference scheduled for the same day, and he seized it without hesitation.[107] Citing Kay's release as "a major positive step" toward "peace and reconciliation," Ford admonished North Vietnam for allowing no similar "progress on accounting for the missing and no further arrangements for the return of the remains of the dead" following its repatriation of twenty-three American remains in March. Taking a page from Nixon's playbook, he proclaimed "there should be no political or military controversy about this humanitarian problem."[108]

If Ford hoped to separate the MIA issue from amnesty, his high-profile reaction to Kay's release two days after creating the clemency board had the opposite effect. League activists who urged him to make "a strong statement condemning the DRV" could rightly conclude that he had done so as a result of the pressure they brought to bear.[109] Rather than appease his critics, Ford's words only convinced League hardliners of the wisdom of their

National League of Families chairman E. C. Mills places a POW/MIA lapel pin on
President Gerald Ford in the White House Cabinet Room on 22 July 1975.
(Courtesy Gerald R. Ford Library)

confrontational approach. On Veterans Day, 350 MIA activists marched in
front of the White House, where they threw 1,300 red carnations onto the
lawn in remembrance of the missing.[110]

Among their goals was the creation of a "Presidential MIA/POW Task
Force, modeled along the lines of the Presidential Amnesty Commission"
that, according to Ford's military aide General Richard Lawson, would
"review, clarify, and coordinate current MIA/POW activities."[111] "Lawson
strongly favors the idea," the State Department's POW/MIA expert Frank
Sieverts told Secretary of State Henry Kissinger when the proposal surfaced in October, "seeing it as a means, however imperfect, of resolving
this sensitive question." Sieverts's Pentagon equivalent Roger Shields "also
spoke for it," sharing Lawson's eagerness to hand off the vexing MIA issue
to someone with the authority to bring it to rest.[112]

Support for a presidential commission among officials who dealt with
the MIA issue on a daily basis reflected their growing recognition that the
MIA problem was not going to resolve itself. Sieverts had been working on

the POW/MIA issue for nearly a decade, and found it more vexing in 1974 than when he first became involved in 1965. As the Nixon holdover and League confidant Lawson explained to Ford, the League had "not dissolved as they have in the aftermath of previous conflicts" and it was clear that they would "not 'go away' without an overt action on the part of the government." The Supreme Court's decision not to review the ruling on status reviews promised further controversy.[113] Kissinger, Scowcroft, and other senior officials were skeptical that a presidential commission could accomplish much, but the League's Christmas card campaign and grumblings from Capitol Hill convinced them that "if the President does not establish such a special MIA board, the Congress will."[114]

The second anniversary of the Paris agreement offered an ideal date to announce such a step and imparted urgency to White House deliberations. By offering "proof that the country did care," Lawson maintained, the commission would leave MIA families with no other option than to accept its "final resolution to their problem." With nowhere else to go, MIA activists would "disband, and return to their private lives."[115] Everyone in the administration shared Lawson's goal of easing MIA activists from the public sphere. But some were unconvinced that a commission would do the trick. "Simply because we do not know what else to do," Scowcroft cautioned, was no reason to create a body that might "embarrass the President without in any way contributing to the solution of the problem." There was nothing "further which can usefully be done" to recover MIAs, he argued, and a blue ribbon panel would "put the families through another cycle of hope and despair without affecting their determination to continue their struggle." Scowcroft preferred to leave "what appears to be a 'no win' situation" to Congress, as did domestic counsel Ken Cole, who warned Ford that "such a Board runs the substantial risk of thrusting you personally into an area of past controversy which you bore no responsibility for creating and for which there is absolutely no hope of solution."[116]

The anniversary of the Paris agreement came and went without word on the proposal. Internally, the decision was made to "postpone the creation of any such Board pending possible Congressional action," but the League was not told this, prompting it to step up its pressure.[117] Meanwhile, congressional hawks continued to crow on the subject, with the chairman of the Senate Armed Services Committee, John Stennis, calling on Ford to create a commission.[118] He noted that the idea had the support of veterans groups and many on Capitol Hill, something the White House hardly needed to be told after receiving "six thousand letters and petitions requesting support for the establishment of the Presidential Task Force" from "all of the major service organizations." Calling the issue a "matter of transcendent importance," the vfw cabled Ford that "failure to keep faith here would mean we have already become a country different from our proud beginnings."[119]

The White House heard these voices of protest, but by March even Lawson admitted that "as long as the families persist in their dictum that the primary and initial objective of a Presidential commission must be a complete accounting of the missing," it "would appear doomed from the start." On the other hand, "a rejection of the proposal made by the families might lead to a violent reaction on their part with its attendant sensational publicity." Rather than confront the League as he had the vfw with his clemency proposal, Ford decided another postponement was the best policy in hopes that Congress would assume "responsibility for developing a solution to the problem."[120]

Ford reaffirmed his do-nothing approach on 10 March, the same day that communists captured the city of Ban Me Thuot in Vietnam's Central Highlands, beginning the rout of South Vietnamese forces that toppled the Saigon regime on 30 April.[121] His requests for additional aid to South Vietnam refused, Ford ordered the evacuation of all Americans from Saigon, declaring, "This action closes a chapter in the American experience."[122]

But Saigon's collapse presented more reasons to revisit the Vietnam experience than to foreclose it. In particular, it offered new opportunities to address the MIA issue, which might finally be pursued with fewer dangers and less rancor. All interested parties moved to capitalize on the changed environment. Each viewed its actions as a means to resolution, though their competing visions of what resolution required had the effect of keeping the MIA issue unresolved.

Eager to collect the reconstruction aid promised in the Paris agreement, the communists reopened the accounting issue before their victory was even complete. Signaling their intent to move forward on the issue as an inducement to diplomatic exchange, communist officials wrote to Senator Edward Kennedy in April, promising to repatriate three sets of American remains sometime in August. Having signaled their willingness to cooperate, they then demanded concessions. Throughout the coming months, party organs like *Nhan Dan* and Radio Hanoi asserted that the search for American MIAs could only proceed if economic assistance was forthcoming. In a letter to two dozen congressmen, Prime Minister Pham Van Dong called on the United States to fulfill "its obligation to contribute to the healing of the wounds of war" and "create the conditions for the establishment of normal relations," laying out his position that would remain essentially unchanged for the next two years.[123]

By raising the MIA issue early, often, and independently of American initiatives, and by linking it to unmet provisions of the Paris agreement, Vietnamese officials showed they were just as determined to address the war's unfinished business as the activists in the League. Above all, they were intent on extracting the billions in reconstruction aid that Nixon had promised them. Communist officials were naive to insist on fulfillment of Nixon's secret agreement, given that not a single elected U.S. official other than Nixon knew its full details until early 1976.[124] New Hampshire senator Norris Cotton's position that "no matter what have been the terms of these agreements, Congress wasn't party to them" and was under no obligation to carry them out was unlikely to change.[125] With Kissinger bitter over his defeat and reluctant to have his concessions made public, the Ford administration was even less likely to concede to Vietnam's demands.

As it had with the subject of an MIA commission, the White House ignored Vietnamese overtures while it privately sought a way to reject them. The administration knew that "if at some point we do not follow up on the information provided to Senator Kennedy, we will be accused by MIA families, members of Congress and others of being disinterested," but feared "being hit with DRV demands in exchange for cooperation."[126] Assistant Secretary of State Philip Habib devised a one-way street out of this dilemma by crafting a policy which held that "the other side has effectively repudiated the [Paris] Agreement by its actions and, as a result, the United States no longer has any obligations under it." "As a theoretical legal matter, North Vietnam is still obligated to give us an accounting for our missing in action," but Habib saw "no practical way of enforcing that claim."[127]

Habib's construction was self-serving. As he knew, the ceasefire never went into effect—communist forces that captured South Vietnamese territory the night before it began were counterattacked in the morning. "Ceasefire or no," one observer noted, "operations are continuing much as before."[128] Despite hopes that the communist victory would bring the MIA issue to a close, the same could be said of MIA diplomacy after the fall of Saigon—operations continued much as before. As Edwin Martini puts it, Kissinger and Ford continued the war "by other means," imposing crippling economic sanctions on Vietnam.[129]

Because this postwar conflict involved economic coercion rather than armed combat, and because Americans enjoyed even more lopsided advantages in international finance than they did in military strength, Martini rightly paints the United States as the aggressor in that struggle. As he shows, U.S. policy was motivated by no strategic goal or national interest, but by a desire for vengeance, with the MIA issue serving as a pretext for punitive acts.[130] Yet as Christopher Jespersen has established, the Vietnamese played an active if often counterproductive part in this struggle.[131] Communist officials pursued MIA diplomacy as aggressively as ever. Ambassador Vo Van Sung reminded congressmen at a Paris meeting in December that the DRV had already repatriated the remains of twenty-three Americans and offered to return three more. At the same time he insisted that "while we who suffered most from the war were generous," the United States refused to "meet its commitments as laid down by Article 21." "We cannot be asked to do everything," Sung lectured, "while the other side does nothing and actually does negative acts." "We have won the war," Deputy Foreign Minister Phan Hien reminded an American delegation to Hanoi later that month as he handed over the three remains promised to Kennedy in April; "how can we carry out 8(b) and not 21?"[132]

As in the American case, Vietnamese policy reflected not just objective self-interest but the politics of memory. American restitution toward "healing the wounds of war" represented implicit confirmation that the Vietnamese people had "suffered the most from the war," a claim central to official memory in Vietnam, and crucial to the communist party's image.[133] Before they could gain an accounting for MIAs, Americans who used the MIA issue to assert their own exclusive victimization in the Vietnam War were forced to confront the competing claims of their former enemy. Since the Ford administration refused to do so, it fell to Congress to undertake that thankless task.

TO LEAVE NO ROOM FOR FURTHER COMPLAINT

On 11 September 1975, Congress authorized the ten-member House Select Committee on Missing Persons in Southeast Asia under the chairmanship of G. V. "Sonny" Montgomery, a conservative Mississippi Democrat, World War II and Korean War veteran, and Vietnam War hawk.[134] Charged with bringing "final resolution to all aspects of the missing in action" issue, over the next fifteen months the bipartisan committee took testimony from over fifty witnesses, reviewed more than 200 MIA case files, flew to Paris, Geneva, Hanoi, and Vientiane to confer with Vietnamese and Laotian officials, met twice with Secretary Kissinger, twice with President Ford, and once with President Jimmy Carter. It secured the release of sixty-eight Americans stranded in Vietnam at war's end, and facilitated the return of five sets of American remains.[135] Most important, it fostered dialogue between American and Vietnamese officials, without which there could be no progress on MIAs.

Despite its achievements, when the committee issued its *Final Report* in December 1976, the National League of Families accused it of an "early disposition to prejudge and pave-over the MIA issue, rather than really investigate it." Seeking to discredit the committee it helped bring into being, the League dismissed its findings "that no Americans are still being held as prisoners in Indochina" and that "a total accounting for all 2,546 Americans who did not return from Southeast Asia is not now, and never will be, possible" as "wildly speculative."[136] Its dismissal of the committee's work as a "whitewash" brought the League as close as it had yet come to charges of official conspiracy.[137] Scowcroft's prediction that a government investigation would fail to appease the families seemed prophetic.[138] Still, it is worth considering how the realization of the League's year-long campaign for an official investigation became its latest evidence of official betrayal, particularly in light of the fact that the House Select Committee was the most serious and sustained state effort to address the problem of the missing war dead in American history to that time.

Like body recovery efforts discussed in chapter 3, the House Select Committee was both more and less than a search for information about the missing. In the committee's words, it was, above all, a bipartisan effort to write "the last chapter on the long war in Indochina."[139] Its determination growing as its work progressed, the committee sought to create an official memory of the war untroubled by MIAs and all they represented. In place of well-worn claims that the Vietnamese knew more than they let on, the committee concluded that "a total accounting by the Indochinese Governments is not possible and should not be expected."[140] Refuting charges of official cover-up, it claimed that authorities "generally devoted generous attention to the needs and desires of POW/MIA next of kin," noting icily that "in every war America has ever fought, some fighting men and civilians disappeared." Instead of the usual assurances of redoubled efforts, it observed that the "massive efforts" already undertaken on behalf of the missing were "unparalleled in the history of our nation." The "problem" in Vietnam, it insisted, was not this unalterable fact of war but the impertinent "citizens and civic and veterans organizations" who "sought more responsibility and accountability than had ever been provided after previous wars."[141]

The 266-page *Final Report* was an extended treatise on how the discordant MIA issue could be incorporated into narratives of heroic self-sacrifice to the state. Its overriding message was that the missing were dead and that the dead were heroes, not victims. Their disappearance was a regrettable but "natural phenomenon," not a result of misguided foreign policy. Rather than mourn their loss, the committee celebrated their sacrifice. "Theirs was not the task to determine the political conditions under which the struggle in Southeast Asia would be waged; rather, it was their often thankless task to give of their youth in sweat and blood." Certain that the missing had "paid the ultimate price in the service of their country," committee members moved to make their deaths official, advising the military to "immediately begin individual case reviews in the manner prescribed by public law."[142] The final recommendation of their *Final Report* was "that a memorial be erected on the grounds of Arlington National Cemetery" bearing the inscription "IN GRATEFUL REMEMBERANCE [*sic*] OF THOSE WHO GAVE THEIR LIVES IN SERVICE OF THEIR COUNTRY AND WHO SLEEP IN UNKNOWN GRAVES."[143]

"Convinced that progress on the MIA issue [was] key to shifting U.S. public opinion and . . . healing the wounds of war," committee members sought Vietnamese assistance in putting the war behind them through the repatriation of remains.[144] "It would help us immeasurably if we could identify two to three hundred of the pilots," liberal Republican congressman and committee member Paul McCloskey told Phan Hien, as "that would focus public opinion to support healing the wounds of war." In return the committee made vague allusions to economic concessions, knowing that American businesses wanted access to Vietnamese markets.[145] To the committee, "reciprocal gestures" whereby Vietnamese officials traded American remains for informal economic assistance was the path to "healing" in both the domestic and international contexts.[146] Resolution would come through reconciliation, and reconciliation through implicit agreement that neither Vietnam nor the MIA lobby would insist on a frank admission of the failures and injustices of U.S. policy in Vietnam.

This vision of "building a bridge of friendship plank by plank" challenged the League's recriminatory agenda.[147] Initially pleased by the committee's creation, seeing it as a substitute for the dream deferred of a presidential commission, MIA activists were incensed when it substituted reconciliation for reckoning. When Montgomery called his December talks with Vo Van Sung "very beneficial for both parties," Executive Director Earl Hopper cautioned that "a continued sell out" was in the works. "The POW-MIA problem will be placed on the back burner and replaced with efforts directed to granting reconstruction aid, diplomatic recognition, and other concessions to the North and South Vietnamese governments," he warned.[148] When the committee visited Hanoi later that month, MIA activists were furious—its retrieval of three American remains only compounded their fury by putting the bodies of missing warriors to the purpose of peace with their former enemies.

"There was something infinitely demeaning about those four congressmen who brought the bodies of three American servicemen home from Hanoi as though they were bringing home some great diplomatic triumph," Hearst columnist Guy Wright wrote. Contending that only "barbarians . . . hold corpses for ransom," Wright condemned Vietnamese officials as "liars and peddlers of corpses" who "will sell them bones, anybody's bones, for as long as they are suckers enough to keep buying."[149] Standing history on its head, Wright failed to mention that the bodies in question fell into Vietnamese hands while Americans waged war on the Vietnamese people, that the reconstruction aid at issue was already promised by the Nixon administration, and that Vietnam received nothing but broken promises and popular hostility in return for its cooperation. Like German narratives of MIA suffering in Soviet gulags after World War II, Wright sought to turn military defeat into a moral victory "by asserting a persistent cultural superiority of the defeated over the victors."[150] Still, Wright recognized his nation's impotence—indeed, it was the source of his outrage. Despite his deceptions, Wright grasped the war's essential truth: that the Vietnamese had thwarted and continued to thwart his urge to subjugate them. In this struggle of wills, MIAs loomed large. "They are using the bodies of our honored servicemen as pawns," author Louis Fanning warned Montgomery, "in the same manner they used our captured military personnel" during the war. "These men have a keen sense of our weak points and always manage to maneuver us into positions which are to their advantage."[151]

That Montgomery, famed for snatching an antiwar banner away from peace demonstrators gathered on the House steps in 1971, fell victim to the wiles of "the Anti-Christ Vietnamese" convinced those like Fanning and Wright that their worst fears of internal corruption had come to pass.[152] "You have made us all very ashamed," Gladys Brooks scolded; "our worse crime has been believing and trusting our government."[153] "Aren't there any good people left in our Government????" asked another woman who accused Montgomery of "*Whitewashing* we *Red Blooded* Americans." Seeming to share the values of appeasement and self-abasement that MIA activists blamed for American defeat in Vietnam, the Montgomery Committee became "the last straw" in their disillusionment with the nation-state.[154] "Since there has been no accounting for the 1,300 abandoned American servicemen, it is logical to assume that there is a cover up," the Americanism chairman of the Nassau County American Legion told Montgomery.

"When a congressional committee doesn't do the job it was created to do, it is logical to assume that the committee is part of the cover up."[155]

As League criticism mounted, Montgomery began to "doubt that anything would satisfy them." Realizing that "interest groups are already attempting to discredit our final report," he decided "to come down hard on them," believing that it was "unfair to the American people to permit this problem to continue."[156] Convinced that "no one has the guts to tell those people there's no *rational* basis to believe that any of these men is [*sic*] still alive," some on the committee decided to make their *Final Report* "blunt, harsh and, while very distressing to some family members, realistic."[157]

It certainly was blunt. To dampen inflated expectations of MIA survival the committee offered reams of evidence that "death could readily occur at any point" once an American went missing. The report was also harsh, conveying the committee's "firm conviction" that belief in continued captivity could only be explained by the fact that the "public has been misled too long and too often by charlatans, opportunists, intelligence fabricators, and publicity mongers, who preyed on the hopes and sorrows of patriotic citizens."[158] In a frank assessment that scandalized the League at its 1976 meeting, the committee's staff director accused "MIA celebrities" of keeping the League going and proclaimed that "the time has come for an ending."[159] Such talk was indeed distressing to some families.[160] But tough talk aimed solely at MIA activists was hardly realistic. It created a false dichotomy between MIA opportunists and MIA families and it minimized official responsibility for encouraging opportunistic families to believe that their loved ones might still be alive. Claims that unidentified fringe elements of the MIA community perpetuated the MIA problem outraged League members not because they were brutally honest, but because they obscured official culpability.

For critics of the League, its rejection of the committee's findings confirmed that MIA activists were "so distraught and frustrated and angry that they no longer look for an accounting, but are waiting for a resurrection," as MIA wife Emma Hagerman told the committee during its last set of hearings.[161] Expatriate League members agreed, including MIA wife Phyllis Corbitt, who wrote the *Washington Post* that "the National League of Families, in keeping the MIA issue alive, is simply refusing to accept reality."[162] So, too, did members of the committee and its staff, particularly its core of seven military veterans, who developed a strong distaste for the League's singular mix of sentimentality and stridency. Korean War veterans McCloskey and staff director J. Angus MacDonald hardly hid their contempt for the League, and Montgomery, James Lloyd, and Richard Ottinger—

all veterans—soon tired of its demands. Though World War II veteran Benjamin Gilman was the most vocal supporter of the League (perhaps because his Westchester county constituents included George and Gladys Brooks, among the League's leading families), his fellow veterans had little patience for its attacks on the defense establishment.[163] That many of the League's leading lights were women who deigned to challenge the "imperial brotherhood" that led the nation to war only intensified their disdain.[164]

The conflict between the League and committee was not just psychological or personal; above all it was political. Suggestions that League complaints were irrational rested on the view that concern with MIA accounting was itself an unhealthy response to wartime loss. Why should this be so? No scholar would make such a claim about the Mothers of the Plaza de Mayo, whose efforts to recover disappeared Argentines and to fix responsibility for their loss in some sense resembled the efforts of the League.[165] It is the League's reactionary politics and compromised victim status that critics object to. As Jay Winter notes, the remembrance of war shifted over the twentieth century from an emphasis on soldiers and sailors to an emphasis on civilian victims, particularly those "moral witnesses" destroyed or disfigured by war. We like to think of these victims as innocents who speak truth to power on behalf of humanity—the Holocaust survivor is the ultimate moral witness—and cultural historians and critical theorists lionize them in the same way labor historians once praised the heroic working class.[166]

Measured against this idealized image, MIA activists are frauds whose claims to victim status are unearned and immoral. Given that many MIA activists supported the American war in Vietnam to the bitter end—an unprovoked war that cost some three million Vietnamese lives—and rarely renounced the war's aims even as they attacked its execution, skepticism toward their victim politics is warranted.

Still, whatever else may be said of them, MIA activists lost something dear to them in Vietnam, and by recalling that loss in the face of official efforts to sanitize their experience they engaged in a political act that warrants close attention. If they were not true moral witnesses, the signifying practices they used to construct and communicate their experience were comparable to those employed by moral witnesses more worthy of the term. Like contemporaries who insisted on remembering historic wrongs, they were driven by fear that those in power wished to forget their loss in order to escape its indictment of their leadership.[167]

That fear was well founded, based on memorial precedent and official rhetoric from the Ford administration and the Montgomery Committee. Memorialization has long been a means to glorify war. In light of that history, to see the League's conflict with the committee as anything but political is to ignore state power. Politicians on the committee intervened in MIA accounting for political reasons. While emotional, financial, and personal concerns shaped the League's response to committee findings, those same factors also shaped the findings. All were part of the debate about how to remember the Vietnam War. In that context, League claims were no more delusional than committee claims that the missing willingly "gave their lives in the service of their country," rather than having had them sacrificed by U.S. government officials on behalf of a corrupt and unpopular South Vietnamese regime.[168] For MIA father Robin Gatwood, such platitudes made "a mockery" of his loss, a position many scholars would endorse had it come from a more palatable source.[169]

Competing understandings of the MIA issue were ideological. Each side argued its case to mobilize support for its preferred narrative of the war. Christine Barrows, the wife of a returned POW, understood this. "I have wondered why the families and the Select Committee have been so often at loggerheads," Barrows wrote Montgomery midway through the committee's tenure. "What is the essential difference that makes each party see things so differently?" Knowing the anguish of a POW family member, but with the detachment of one who had left that status behind, she observed that the essential difference was one of "perspective." Whereas "MIA families are concerned about the men first and foremost," Barrows posited, the committee was intent on "wrapping up the whole MIA affair in such a way as to leave no room for further complaint." She sensed that from the committee's perspective, the most noteworthy element of the MIA situation was "how much the government has done already for the families," but she warned that MIA families "will not accept a Congressional investigation that does no justice to the men themselves."[170]

It was unclear how the committee could offer justice to those who had died in an unnecessary and now lost cause. But Barrows knew that resolving the MIA affair so as to leave no room for complaint was the opposite of justice. To adapt David Blight's formula from the post–Civil War context, it placed healing before justice.[171] For MIA activists, resolution on these terms meant forgetting. It meant moving forward rather than looking back, accepting the changes the war wrought, the forgoing of hope. Worst of all, resolution without accounting held no one responsible for the loss of

American lives in Vietnam. It was based on the idea that official efforts on behalf of the missing Americans were unprecedented rather than insufficient. It was an assertion that the MIA problem was one of too much memory rather than too little.[172]

THIS EVEN SPLIT REPRESENTS THE TRUE VIEWS OF THE COMMITTEE

By its own standards, the Montgomery Committee failed to resolve the MIA issue. Created with the intention of forging an anodyne collective memory, it failed to convince the American people of its version of the past, including many of its own members. Its failure showed most clearly in its inability to reach internal agreement on what to include in the "last chapter" it set out to write. Three dissenting members appended "additional and separate" views to the *Final Report*; two others sought to join them but their formal requests were made too late, hours after the report was sent to the Clerk of the House for printing, with Montgomery telling MacDonald "it was not his task nor mine to solicit Additional Views from Members."[173] Taken together, this meant that fully half of the ten-member committee expressed reservations about its findings. The day after the committee briefed President Carter, dissenter John "Joe" Moakley of Massachusetts informed the new president about the last-minute discord, advising him that "this even split must be seen as representing the true views of the Committee."[174]

The significance of the committee's differences should not be overstated. League claims that "HALF OF THE COMMITTEE DISAGREE EN-TIRELY WITH MAJOR CONCLUSIONS AND RECOMMENDATIONS OF THE REPORT" exaggerated the split.[175] Moakley stipulated that "my differences with the report are largely matters of tone," and the near-dissenters James Lloyd and Richard Ottinger spoke favorably of the committee's work when they met Carter. "We have already bitten the bullet, now you can go forward to solve the problem," Lloyd told the president. Whatever his problems with the report, his warning that "you should not go back and reopen the box" hardly conformed to League demands.[176] The *Final Report* was just one element of the record the committee assembled through hearings, diplomacy, and speeches, and its success or failure depended less on internal convictions expressed in a little-read government report than on the impression it made on the American people, particularly MIA activists and their supporters. That said, it was in the public sphere where the committee failed to make its case that the Vietnam War could best be remembered through a heroic Arlington memorial. Its internal differences were less the cause of that failure than its symptom.

Reports by committee consultant Alfonso Sellet from VFW conventions in Washington in March 1976 and in New York in August 1976 show the committee's failure to persuade those who cared most deeply about the MIA issue. In his March report to the committee, Sellet noted that "the majority" of VFW members in Washington "believe no living Americans are being held in Laos, North Vietnam, Cambodia, or anywhere else" and that "the League of Families has gone a little too far." The older veterans who dominated the group recalled "that one or two years after WWII and Korea the MIAs were classified as KIAs," suggesting that official solicitousness toward Vietnam MIAs showed "a lack of dignity in front of the world." Conflicting emotions pulsed through the group. While members wanted to "bring them all back 'once and for all,'" they dismissed government accounting efforts as "a waste of time and money," complained of being "blackmailed" for bones, and worried that the League "could go on for another 10 years." They felt "used" by all parties, including the committee, distrusting "'politics' which they feel is a major factor in this issue."[177]

By August Sellet found "a marked change" among the 40,000 members in New York. Suddenly "the MIA issue was a paramount item," and Sellet "learned that *many, many* more VFW members now share the opinion that there are, indeed, *many* survivors still in prison in Southeast Asia." "RESENTMENT and HOSTILITY is growing," especially "resentment that our fighting men have been used," "left to 'rot'" on foreign soil. "We are the losers . . . our men are still not accounted for!" he paraphrased. "The feeling still prevails with the veterans and public that our government is not actively working on the MIA issue."[178]

In six months, the veterans who made up the VFW had gone from feeling ambivalent about the MIA issue to being adamant that it symbolized their betrayal. What changed? In all likelihood its members were reacting to the growing hostilities between the League and the committee over the summer of 1976. Even more important, during that spring and summer VFW members were electrified by Ronald Reagan's bid for the GOP nomination, which featured "strident attacks on the Ford-Nixon policy of détente."[179] Never one for nuance, Reagan mixed the MIA issue together with the proposed giveback of the Panama Canal and warming relations with China and the Soviet Union as clear evidence of "the retreat of American power" under "Kissinger and Ford," charging Ford with seeking to establish "friendly relations" with North Vietnam. As if that prospect were not sufficiently infuriating, he alleged that American MIAs were being used as the pretense for appeasement. "To make this more palatable," he continued, "we are told this might help us to learn the fate of the men still listed as missing in action."[180]

By fitting the MIA issue into a pattern of national weakness, Reagan applied the narrative of betrayal developed by the post-Omaha League to a much larger set of concerns. POWs and MIAs had long been a preoccupation of Reagan's—he put Sybil Stockdale in touch with Nixon in 1968, presided over VIVA's unveiling of the POW/MIA bracelet in 1970, and hosted a lavish state dinner for returned POWs in 1973—and he used MIAs in 1976 as a popular and potent way to illustrate the destructive effects he attributed to defeat in Vietnam. His critique reverberated among Americans who "deeply resented and passionately resisted the nation's seeming loss of international dominance after the Vietnam War."[181] Though it lacked the League's commitment to the MIA issue, the VFW proved receptive to rhetoric that equated support for MIAs with support for the armed forces. Blending anticommunism with concerns over moral corruption, threats to the patriarchal family, and all manner of liberal license, the MIA issue proved the perfect vehicle for Reagan to revive, remodel, and expand Nixon's "silent majority."[182]

Desperate to fend off Reagan's challenge, Ford abandoned his know-nothing approach to the MIA issue and joined him in condemning the Vietnamese as "international pirates" at Lenoir-Rhyne College in North Carolina three days before losing that state's March primary to Reagan.[183] Kissinger groused that foreign policy should not be shaped by "the remains of Americans who died in action," but he echoed the hard line a few days later when he declared a "full accounting" was "the absolute minimum precondition without which we cannot consider the normalization of relations."[184] Their words made Ford's four-month old "Pacific doctrine of peace" inoperative, and scuttled the Montgomery Committee's painstaking MIA diplomacy.[185]

The *Nation* looked on these developments with alarm, denouncing the MIA issue as "a shibboleth of the most idly destructive kind."[186] But in blaming Reagan and Ford for its revival, the *Nation* misconstrued the MIA resurgence, which was driven as much by congressional Democrats and Vietnamese diplomats as it was by conservatives.[187] The predominantly liberal House Select Committee, as much as the Republican primaries, refocused attention on the MIA issue. Though a congressional committee on MIAs would never have been considered without League pressure, authorization resulted from near unanimous consent in the House that there was something to be gained by taking up the issue. McCloskey, for one, was confident the committee's efforts would help Ford vanquish Reagan. "I want Mr. Ford renominated, since he is more liberal than Mr. Reagan," he told Phan Hien. "To help this we need to defuse the MIA issue," he added, calling Reagan's challenge "a one-in-four year opportunity" for progress in U.S.-Vietnam relations.[188] In this he proved mistaken. But his confidence that the committee would advance his interests was widely shared.

Widespread frustration with Nixon's, Kissinger's, and Ford's foreign policy helps explain this bipartisan interest in reopening the MIA issue. Both sides of the political aisle were united in their hostility toward realpolitik, which they closely associated with Kissinger.[189] Liberals saw Kissinger's secret diplomacy and not-so-secret support for authoritarian governments as unprincipled and undemocratic. Conservatives saw his accommodation to the limits of national power as unprincipled and un-American. Regardless of their party affiliation, legislators resented Kissinger's contempt for Congress, while ordinary Americans associated him with the twinned traumas of Watergate and Vietnam. Anxious to reopen debate on these matters heading into the 1976 elections, Congress was ready to pounce on any sign of obstruction or dissembling as it sought to break free from Ford's moratorium on divisive subjects. When Kissinger answered Vietnamese offers to exchange American remains for economic aid in the most tepid possible way—granting only $800,000 in private humanitarian aid in July 1975—then vetoed Vietnam's applications for United Nations membership in August, only two days after the DRV reaffirmed its readiness to repatriate American remains, Congress authorized the Montgomery Committee.[190]

All actors, including Kissinger, knew it would benefit them if they could show progress on accounting for MIAs, but their divergent goals were bound to create conflict. The right was anxious to confront the communists, rattling the saber for a base reeling over defeat in Vietnam, while those on the left wanted to eliminate obstacles to normalization, some because they hoped to make amends with Vietnam, others because such an opening put Ford in a difficult political bind with conservatives in his party.[191] Even business interests, normally drawn to Ford's bland Republicanism, scorned Ford's embargo on Vietnam, since it locked them out of the Vietnamese economy.[192] These forces combined to bring the committee into existence, but they in no way agreed on its desired outcome. Instead, the MIA issue became a way for competing interests and groups to rally public opinion to their side, as it had during the war.[193]

The League shared the desire to reopen debate about the war. MIA activists distrusted Kissinger and his professed sympathy, with some calling his donation of $50,000 in Nobel prize money to the children of POWs and

MIAs "blood money" meant to assuage his war guilt.[194] Their suspicions were confirmed in early 1976 when the committee revealed for the first time the explicit nature of the $4.75 billion he and Nixon had promised North Vietnam.[195] That disclosure offered further ammunition to Kissinger haters in the League, and the organization formally demanded his resignation as the GOP headed into its still too-close-to-call nominating convention.[196]

The League's call for Kissinger's resignation was a clear attempt to throw the nomination to Reagan. Reagan suggested such a step in a telegram to the League's 1976 annual meeting in July. Telling League members that "if you had had the kind of action you have been seeking you would not have to be gathering for a 7th annual meeting," he pledged "the first week that I am president, a new secretary of state will begin immediately taking every reasonable and proper step to return any live Americans still being held in Southeast Asia."[197] A pitch-perfect rendition of League rhetoric, Reagan's cable showed the depth of disillusionment with Kissinger's foreign policy among conservatives, of a piece with the push to incorporate a "Morality in Foreign Policy" plank into the Republican Party platform "in which secret agreements, hidden from our people, will have no part."[198]

Reagan fell short of the nomination, but the "Morality in Foreign Policy" plank survived. As Ford beat back Reagan's challenge in the days before the convention, he made his third consecutive appearance at the League's annual meeting, where the limits of his no-fault vision were on full display. "We are employing every effective means to account for your loved ones," he assured the League. But instead of the heroes and villains that Reagan conjured, Ford offered the same cold comfort coming out of the Montgomery Committee. "We must be honest," he told the League. "It is a tragic fact—and it makes me, as well as you and millions like you, very, very sad—that every missing man or information concerning that individual may never be available, regardless of any superhuman effort by the most and the best in our Government."[199] Oregon coordinator Barbara Parker was nonplussed. Confronting Ford after his speech, she told him she "didn't think he was doing everything he could."[200] His bland assurances were no more welcome than Montgomery's address the day before. "We must face the cruel, but hard, facts that our MIAs lost their lives in the service of their nation," he reiterated, prompting one bystander to shout back, "You are not God!"[201]

Those ready to face facts had left the League years earlier; those who remained wanted miracles. Needless to say, they were disappointed. So, too, were Ford, Montgomery, McCloskey, and others who thought they could substitute a conciliatory official memory for the memory of betrayal recalled by the League. Instead of closure, the House Select Committee helped reignite passions over the Vietnam War in the politically charged atmosphere of a presidential election. The debate that followed not only split the committee, but split the Republican Party as well, moving its activist base to the right. While Democrats benefited from that split in 1976, with Jimmy Carter winning the votes of many League members, the committee's push for resolution nourished populist distrust of government that led to long-term conservative gains.

OFFICIAL RHETORIC OF CLOSURE during the Ford years confirmed League activists in their belief that the U.S. government wanted to forget them and their men. In fact, there had never been a group of American war dead so obsessively remembered. National leaders wanted not so much to forget the missing as to forget the war they fought in and the discredited reasons for which they died. The memory activists in the post-Omaha League were unwilling to allow that. "We want a simple answer to a simple question," wrote one. "Why are these Americans being abandoned? Who is responsible for leaving them behind?"[202]

Framing the question in this way implied an answer. As MIA activists saw it, American servicemen were not lost by accident or through the skill and determination of their Vietnamese adversaries; they were abandoned by disloyal Americans and dishonest politicians. Worse still, their betrayal continued, as those who sent them to war now turned their loss to the purpose of friendship with their enemies. "We cannot demand loyalty on the battlefield and in the prisoner of war camps if there is no loyalty in Washington!!" wrote one wife.[203] "What in the hell do you think our Sons are—'cannon fodder?'" asked another writer.[204] "Don't come looking for more of my sons to fight your shitty wars."[205]

Bitterness over the Vietnam War was universal by the mid-1970s, which may explain why politicians continued to revisit the MIA issue despite the League's declining membership. With help from its critics as much as its supporters, the League's influence spread even as its numbers dwindled. Its narrative of patriotic white male abandonment reinforced related notions of government conspiracy, family disintegration, and national decline that were omnipresent in 1970s political culture. In the years since, such issues have been encoded as conservative, but they drew their initial force from widespread dissatisfaction with the status quo that transcended partisan boundaries. In 1976 a pacifist who "spent a term in prison for refusing to register for the draft" wrote Montgomery that it was "unconscionable that a country which asked—demanded—such sacrifices of its young men can now be so unconcerned about their fate."[206]

This was rhetoric Jimmy Carter deployed as easily and profitably as Ronald Reagan. Antiwar sentiment began on the left, as did public concern for POWs. But whereas Reagan and the conservative movement promised to act aggressively against internal and external enemies to reclaim missing Americans and restore national honor, Carter planned to rebuild popular faith in the government, pledging, "I'll never lie to you." Both agendas proved unworkable, but Carter had the misfortune of failing first, and his failure was more predictable insofar as his strategy had already been tried and failed, first by Ford, then by the House Select Committee.

5

The Wilderness Years

Life after Death

When President Jimmy Carter ordered the Pentagon to resume involuntary status reviews in August 1977, the ranks of Americans missing in Southeast Asia entered what all parties considered an inevitable decline. "There is little chance that any of the 712 currently listed as prisoners or missing will remain in that status," the National League of Families warned its members. "No family member should remain under the illusion that due to the facts in their man's case, he will not be re-classified to killed in action."[1] Active elements of the League still fought reclassification through tactics ranging from litigation to refusing to "accept phone calls from the casualty office," but the slide in MIA numbers was inexorable.[2] By the time Carter left office, all but seventeen MIAs had been presumed dead.[3] As the number neared zero, Douglas Clarke concluded the first serious study of the MIA issue with the thought that "the MIA's cannot long survive as a dramatic issue capable of having domestic or international impact without men still in missing status."[4]

Yet as the MIA issue neared its seemingly unavoidable end, it achieved new life. Public interest in MIAs surged at the decade's close, in ways connected to but obscured by the Iran hostage crisis, which itself echoed earlier anxieties over the fate of Vietnam POWs and other foreign policy setbacks in the Carter years. By the time the League's long-time patron Ronald Reagan was inaugurated as president in 1981, the MIA issue was securely reestablished in political debate and rapidly making its way back into popular culture. In the most extraordinary marker of this reversal, the prospect of continued captivity was no longer limited to the handful of "discrepancy cases" once thought to be prisoners who failed to return from

Vietnam, or even to the 1,392 men in MIA status at war's end. Beginning in 1980, Americans were told that as many as 2,500 servicemen could be in captivity. This previously unheard number included 1,113 casualties classified as "killed in action/body not recovered" (KIA/BNR), a status reserved for cases in which "available information indicates beyond any reasonable doubt that a missing person could not have survived" but remains were never found.[5] As presumptive findings of death eliminated distinctions between the missing and the dead, the POW/MIA population paradoxically grew rather than declined.

As in the Nixon years, misleading rhetoric and manipulated intelligence encouraged optimistic expectations of survival among this indeterminate population. Months before his secretary of the navy issued the final presumptive finding of death for a missing American from the Vietnam War,[6] President Reagan told the White House press corps, "There are some more than 2,000, close to 2,500, around there, names of individuals missing in action." When asked if he thought any of those men were still held in captivity Reagan answered, "I don't think we can afford to believe there aren't."[7]

The contradiction between Reagan's rhetoric and the realities of the situation, as reflected in the findings of death issued by the military services, is further evidence of the degree to which the era he presided over was consumed by fantasy. "To look back over the public record of the late 1970s and 1980s," Frances FitzGerald wrote of the Reagan years, "is to enter a world of phantoms and mirages."[8] Philip Jenkins has called the mid-1970s to mid-1980s "a decade of nightmares."[9] Nowhere were the phantoms more haunting or the nightmares more florid than in the claim that Americans still languished in Vietnamese captivity. Because of Reagan's ties to the MIA lobby, his even deeper ties to the movie industry, his admitted tendency to confuse war movies with reality, and his aggressive revisionism of the Vietnam War as a "noble cause," Reagan is usually seen as the essential source of renewed interest in the MIA issue, and his presidency as the obvious focus of critical analysis.[10] The "noble cause" idea represented "denial so extreme that fantasy would become the norm in perceiving the reality of something called 'Vietnam,'" H. Bruce Franklin argued, with the "POW/MIA myth" being "the most pervasive." "Who could resurrect those missing American fighting men?" Franklin asked. "This was a job for true heroes, led by one of VIVA's original sponsors, Ronald Reagan."[11]

Reagan was undeniably key to the revival of the issue.[12] Had he continued the efforts of Ford, Carter, and the House Select Committee to silence the League, it is possible that it would have disappeared. Instead, he embraced the League, granting it greater prominence and power during his presidency than it enjoyed at any time since the war's end. Yet Reagan's preoccupation with MIAs cannot fully explain the public's rediscovery of missing Americans during the Carter years. Overstating his role risks misunderstanding the League's adversarial relationship to state power and its challenge to official memory.

More than anything Reagan said or did, the reemergence of POW/MIA politics depended on the persistence of the League. Had the group ceased to exist under Carter, it would have been difficult for Reagan to revive. Instead, League leaders pioneered a new style of activism in the late 1970s that emphasized the possibility that missing Americans were still alive, soliciting "live-sighting reports" from refugees to compel a governmental response. If government agencies refused to follow up on these reports, the League claimed a cover-up. If officials pursued them only to prove them false, it claimed a conspiracy. By cultivating an independent source of information, MIA activists forced official involvement in what was increasingly a no-win situation for government authorities.

Reagan did not cause renewed interest in missing Americans so much as he capitalized on it. The MIA issue fused public and private loss, and this fusion was crucial to conservative ascendancy in the late 1970s. By linking the alleged victimization of patriotic white men in Vietnam to concerns about national decline, MIA activists created a sense of continuity between wartime ignominy and the "crisis of confidence" in the Carter years that disaffected Americans found familiar and compelling. The anguish of MIA families dramatized the costs of national weakness in ways that complemented arguments advanced by conservatives and neoconservatives. Their alleged abandonment illustrated claims that national weakness and a bloated bureaucracy threatened middle- and working-class whites. Their bruised patriotism and catch-all contempt for the recent past resonated within and beyond the conservative movement, accelerating the rightward turn in American politics and giving MIA activists new relevance and new life by decade's end.

NOW IS A CONVENIENT MOMENT TO TERMINATE THAT HOPE

While Reagan and Ford fought for the GOP nomination in 1976, Jimmy Carter campaigned hard on the MIA issue for much the same reason as congressional Democrats—it offered a platform to call attention to the foreign policy failures of Nixon, Kissinger, and Ford, and suggested a change of direction was in order. Conservative Republicans were not the only Americans bothered by the sense of drift and dejection under Nixon and Ford. Many Democrats were disturbed by what they saw as the nation's loss of leadership and moral vision, with liberals promoting an enlightened internationalism chastened by the experience of Vietnam, while the party's conservative elements sought a return to the crusading nationalism of the early Cold War. Many in the latter camp soon bolted the party over what they perceived as weakness and vacillation on Carter's part, aligning with the conservative movement as "neoconservatives."[13] But in 1976 these strands largely held together in their shared rejection of the past and their hope for salvation, sentiments Carter appealed to by emphasizing his outsider status and his disdain for Ford's do-nothing approach to MIAs. On the same day that Ford appeared before the League's 1976 convention, the Democratic nominee cabled the League that "internal Republican party politics" had "deprived our MIA families of their best chance to know the fate of their sons, fathers, and husbands." "Our MIA will be fully accounted for," he told them, "only through an open, gradual negotiation of outstanding issues," which only Carter was prepared to deliver.[14]

Negotiations had less appeal for the League than Reagan's more belligerent (but vague) approach. In February the board had reaffirmed League policy "that our government must not make any concessions" to the communist governments of Southeast Asia "without built-in safeguards that will insure an honorable accounting."[15] Yet Ford's sanctions policy had produced only stalemate, and with Reagan out of the race after August, many League members preferred Carter's promised diplomacy to Ford's inaction. Carter impressed the group when he went after Ford on the subject during their foreign policy debate in October, blasting the lack of "aggressive action on the part of the President . . . to get that information which has kept the MIA families in despair and doubt" as one of Ford's "most embarrassing failures." His proposal to appoint a presidential task force if elected president, and a position statement promising not to "normalize relations with the Vietnamese government until I am convinced that they have made a complete accounting of those who are missing," reassured League hardliners.[16]

The League had never endorsed a candidate in its history and was not about to start with Jimmy Carter. In the end, though, many League members voted for him, and, like many Carter voters, they did so less because of what he said or did than because of who he was—an outsider so bland that wildly disparate groups identified with him. In the League's case, a critical element of Carter's biography gave League members hope that he would understand their situation: Carter shared the agony of having been an MIA relative. In the opening days of World War II, Carter's uncle Tom Gordy was captured by the Japanese while stationed on Guam. After hearing no news of Tom for two years, the Carter family was notified that he was dead, prompting his wife, Dorothy, to remarry. When the war ended, Carter's uncle turned up emaciated but alive among a group of Americans working on a Japanese railroad. Tom and Dorothy never reconciled and the incident left a vivid impression on the teenage Carter, who cited it in his campaign memoir as one of the reasons he attended the U.S. Naval Academy.

More harrowing still, Carter nearly became an MIA himself on a dark and stormy night in 1948 when a wave ripped him from the deck of his surfaced submarine. Losing his grip on the handrail, Carter found himself "swimming literally within the huge wave, completely separated from the submarine" until the wave deposited him "thirty feet aft of where I had been standing." "Had the currents been even slightly broadside," he wrote, "I never would have landed on the ship as the wave receded, and would undoubtedly have been lost at sea."[17] Aware of his brushes with their experience, "a lot of families voted for President Carter" because "they figured he would automatically be sympathetic" to their plight.[18]

In his first month in office the League praised Carter's "initiatives to pursue diplomatic discussions between the U.S. and Vietnam in an attempt to gain an accounting."[19] But as those initiatives bore fruit, MIA activists condemned the steps they had once praised as a "maneuver by the Administration to dispose of this 'unpleasant problem.'" Though Carter achieved unprecedented results in accounting for the missing during his first two years in office, Executive Director Carol Bates soon charged that he had "systematically broken each and every promise he made to the families in regard to Vietnam and the POW/MIA accounting."[20]

It was a familiar pattern of raised hopes and dashed expectations. Its familiarity suggests that the League's habitual sense of betrayal revealed more about its own impossible expectations than something peculiar to the Carter administration. Clearly the League was less interested in resolution than it claimed. But while accurate, such an analysis assumes continuity only on the part of the League, overlooking the shared goals of state actors who interacted with the League and their constant, overriding concern with resolving the MIA issue despite party differences. As Robert McMahon has shown, post-Vietnam presidents were surprisingly consistent in their historical revisionism, with otherwise disparate men presenting "a highly selective, unabashedly patriotic memory" of U.S. involvement in Vietnam, "one that would not disrupt, challenge, or subvert the glorious master narrative of U.S. history" with troublesome thoughts of government betrayal propagated by MIA activists.[21] Personally and politically invested in transcending the poisonous legacy of his predecessors, Carter was less interested in avoiding the residue of the Vietnam War, as Ford had been, than he was in confronting it.[22] But the goal for both men was transcendence, something that would never satisfy those dedicated to historical accountability.

"It's now a time for healing," Carter proclaimed upon accepting his party's nomination.[23] Hoping to succeed where Ford had failed, he delivered on his campaign promise of a presidential pardon for draft evaders on his first day in office, drawing complaints from veterans' groups and returned POWs, but no formal complaint from the League, which held fire in hopes of shaping Carter's plans to appoint a presidential envoy to Hanoi.[24] Like the pardon, the envoy idea originated during the campaign, with Carter's future secretary of state Cyrus Vance suggesting the step as a way to make good on Carter's promised healing, and Carter announcing it in his October foreign policy debate with Ford.[25] The House Select Committee urged him on when it briefed the new president on its *Final Report* in January. When Carter met with League leaders on 11 February to discuss the plan, he assured them of the "special responsibility" he felt to handle the issue "carefully, compassionately and fully" as part of his personal commitment to "healing our war wounds."[26]

Carter's plan underestimated the severity of the wounds in question and miscalculated their amenability to the cures he envisioned. That is not to say that he or his staff were blind to the challenges they faced. The NSC's East Asia hand Michel Oksenberg informed National Security Adviser Zbigniew Brzezinski that the commission Carter proposed would need to be carefully chosen since "a major portion of the Mission is to defuse the political issue and remove—as much as possible—the emotional rancor" surrounding MIAs. Great care went into selecting a group that could bargain effectively with the Vietnamese while still gaining respect from the League.[27] On 25 February, the State Department announced that United Auto Workers president Leonard Woodcock would head up the commission, and that House Select Committee chairman Sonny Montgomery, former senator Mike Mansfield, Children's Defense Fund director Marian Wright Edelman, and Ambassador Charles Yost would accompany him to Hanoi where they would "obtain the best possible accounting for MIAs and the return of the remains of our dead."[28]

Before it left, the Woodcock Commission came in for criticism from the League, which protested Montgomery's inclusion on the grounds that he

Normalization talks in 1977–78 resulted in the repatriation of forty-eight American remains from Vietnam and Laos, including eleven depicted here, which returned to Travis Air Force Base on 29 March 1977 following the Woodcock Commission's mission to Hanoi. (Courtesy Sergeant Mike Dial, Department of Defense, #NN33300514 2005-06-03)

had already made up his mind, clamoring for a League member to be appointed in his place. Though the League request was endorsed by forty-five members of Congress, Brzezinski dismissed it out of hand, writing Bates that "it would be difficult — perhaps impossible — to assemble a delegation dealing with the tragic legacy of the Vietnam War on which every member won universal acclaim."[29] He was right, but his assessment augured poorly for Woodcock's ability to accomplish his mission.

Brzezinski might have recognized this, but he was focused on other things, ordering his staff to "keep ZB out of MIA thing as much as possible." Following his boss's lead, Oksenberg asked, "Who is to bear this burden?" upon receiving Brzezinski's note, admitting, "I prefer not to."[30] With minimal NSC oversight, the Woodcock Commission was run out of the State Department, where Secretary Vance and Assistant Secretary for East Asia and the Pacific Richard Holbrooke shared Carter's commitment to healing the wounds of war, with healing defined as consigning the MIA issue to the past.[31] As the Woodcock Commission departed for Asia, Vance assured Carter that it would "do everything possible to assist the Administration in putting the problem behind us."[32]

When Woodcock returned with twelve sets of remains, Carter proclaimed "every hope we had for the mission has been realized." Though one of the remains was not American, Carter called it "an honest mistake" and announced that high-level talks would resume "without delay, to resolve other issues that might be an obstacle to peace."[33] Asked if he was over-estimating the importance of a few remains, Carter replied that the Vietnamese had "acted in good faith" and assessed that "I think this is about all they can do." "I don't have any way to prove that they have accounted for all of those about whom they have information," he confessed, revealing his pledge to "personally" see to it that Vietnam "had done everything humanely possible to provide a complete accounting of our men who are listed as missing" as an empty promise.[34] Indeed, one of Woodcock's goals was "to make clear that we do not expect the impossible and are well aware of the fact that no information will ever be found on many of the men."[35]

Carter had little hope for a full accounting, only one sufficient to remove the MIA issue as a roadblock to domestic reconciliation and diplomatic normalization. As Holbrooke told a reporter, Carter was "interested in normalizing relations with Vietnam as a symbol."[36] Carter "seemed to look at the opening to Vietnam less as part of a new comprehensive Asian strategy for the United States than as symbolically writing *finis* to an unhappy chapter," concluded Frederick Brown from the State Department's Indochina desk. Carter's motives were "historical-moral," according to Brzezinski. "The President wanted to heal the wounds of the Vietnamese war in general, both inside America and in terms of America's external policies."[37] Progress in one area would bring progress in others. The Montgomery Committee had attempted such an approach, which it "likened to a bridge that one builds, board after board," but found its efforts thwarted by Ford's refusal to compromise.[38] Now with Woodcock's and Montgomery's help, Carter picked up where the House Select Committee left off, asserting "that no accounting will ever be possible for most of the Americans lost in Indochina" but that "the best hope for obtaining the proper accounting for MIAs lies in the context of such improved relations."[39]

But as Deputy Foreign Minister Phan Hien warned, "it was impossible to completely sever the future from the past."[40] Vietnamese officials continued to insist on the "undeniable responsibility" the United States bore for Vietnam's devastation, while Carter and the Congress continued to refuse direct economic assistance.[41] As Holbrooke left for Paris in May to discuss normalization, he was told to offer only "mutual recognition without preconditions," meaning he was not to discuss reconstruction aid. Following orders, Holbrooke told Hien, "Let's leave aside the issues that divide us" and "go outside and jointly declare to the press that we have decided to normalize relations." Hien refused, insisting that the U.S. honor its commitments to "healing the wounds of war," an idea as powerful for aggrieved Vietnamese as it was for MIA activists.

In making this demand, Vietnamese leaders may have mistaken "antiwar sentiment in the U.S. for pro-Vietnamese sentiment," as historian Steven Hurst put it. Perhaps they misread polls showing that two-thirds of Americans supported humanitarian aid for Vietnam but only one in five supported monetary aid.[42] More likely they were engaged in the same politics of memory that engaged the League, insisting that the United States ameliorate Vietnamese suffering in return for their help in resolving the fate of missing Americans. Hien raised the adverse effects of the American war in Vietnam as a way of asserting that Vietnam's claims under Article 21 were every bit as morally freighted as American claims under Article 8(b).[43] When Hien made such a linkage at their meeting in Hanoi, Woodcock warned him that "you are saying in a sense that you will sell us the remains of our MIAs. . . . No American President or Congress could approve such a deal."[44] Woodcock assumed Vietnam was powerless to press its case. Congress made the same assumption when it passed legislation prohibiting the administration from "negotiating reparations, aid, or any other form of payment" to Vietnam after Hien reiterated his demands in public. In June it passed an amendment to the foreign aid bill renouncing Nixon's secret pledge of $4.75 billion to Vietnam. Yet Americans could not rewrite treaties by fiat. When Holbrooke informed Hien of this legislation in June, Hien replied, "What would you do if I said the Vietnamese National Assembly had passed a law prohibiting searches for the MIAs?"[45]

"When one considers the Vietnamese statements as well as Congressional votes against aid to Vietnam, we see the inability of two bitter enemies to place the past behind them," Oksenberg assessed in a memo to Brzezinski as the talks broke down. Given that Carter "had raised public expectations," Oksenberg worried that "this will place the President in a difficult political position."[46] Like the three previous administrations, the Carter White House was getting a crash course in the perils of POW/MIA diplomacy. Responding as its predecessors had, the administration tried to compensate for its inability to dominate Vietnam by manipulating the MIA lobby. Since Vietnam had few bargaining chips other than American remains, Carter's foreign policy team tried to diminish the importance of those remains by reducing the profile of the MIA issue. Predicting that Vietnam would "dole out these remains slowly whenever they wanted to be applauded," Oksenberg counseled that "sometimes it pays to feign lack of interest."[47]

The problem with his approach was that the administration could not feign disinterest in MIAs without angering the always-vigilant League. Only by making MIAs less valuable in the United States could they be made less valuable to the Vietnamese. Joseph Lelyveld noted this conundrum in the *New York Times Magazine.* Quoting an MIA father who called his son "too valuable" for the Vietnamese to kill, Lelyveld observed that there was "something odd in the notion" that "enemies attached a higher value to American lives than we attached to theirs."[48] Something odd and untrue, as it was the constant assertion of MIAs' importance at home that gave them diplomatic exchange value, and Carter could not change one half of this equation without confronting the other.

The only, hence the obvious, step open to Carter as he sought to de-emphasize the MIA issue was to revisit the four-year-old moratorium on involuntary status reviews. In his February meeting with the League, Carter had promised to uphold the ban, but the Woodcock Commission had seconded the House Select Committee's suggestion that status reviews be resumed upon its return, giving the president political cover to reverse himself. In April Carter asked Secretary of Defense Harold Brown to consider such a step, which Brzezinski believed would "diffuse the MIA issue as an anti-Vietnam rallying point in the U.S."[49] When normalization talks bogged down later that summer, deliberations on status reviews assumed the added dimension of reducing Vietnamese expectations that they would receive aid in return for remains.

In late May, Brown came back with a recommendation to reinstitute mandatory reviews. There was "no reason to believe that continuing to carry servicemen as missing in action puts pressure on Hanoi to provide information on our missing men," he concluded. "In fact, the opposite probably is true" since the heightened expectations that flowed from the moratorium "puts pressure on us to make concessions to Hanoi. Given the overwhelming probability that none of the MIAs will ever be found alive," he recommended that mandatory status reviews proceed, which Brzezinski forwarded to Carter with his own concurrence and that of the State Department. The moratorium, Brzezinski observed, "perpetuates the hope that some MIAs may be held prisoner. Now is a convenient moment to terminate that hope." "I agree," Carter wrote.[50]

The decision was made in June, but it was not announced until August to avoid having it coincide with the League's July convention. The League suspected the worst when, for the first time in its history, it was denied free military transport to its annual meeting. Nixon began the military airlift to League events in 1970 under the pretense of bringing POW and MIA families to Washington for official briefings when its true purpose was to facilitate their attendance at Bob Dole's Appeal for International Justice. It was one of many things he did to keep the League in the public eye. Now with anti-League sentiment growing in Washington, the practice was discontinued with the hope that the League would go away.[51] The 18 August 1977 announcement that status reviews would resume was made with the same hope.

THE WILDERNESS YEARS

Initially, the resumption of mandatory status reviews seemed to have precisely the effect the White House intended, removing MIAs as a roadblock to normalization by reducing the ranks of the missing and marginalizing their relatives. Six months after it returned eleven American remains to Woodcock and Montgomery, Vietnam repatriated another twenty-two American remains in return for admission to the United Nations. Whereas Ford once cited Vietnam's failure to account for MIAs in vetoing its UN application, Carter justified its admission on the basis of its rapid repatriation of remains.[52] Talks aimed at normalization resumed in December, resulting in an agreement to send Vietnamese officials to the U.S. Army's Central Identification Laboratory in Hawaii (CILHI) to learn forensic identification techniques. When the Vietnamese team arrived at the lab in July 1978, delegation chief Vu Hoang professed his government's willingness to drop reconstruction aid as a precondition to normalization.[53] In August the Vietnamese repatriated eleven more remains to Montgomery, who traveled to Hanoi to receive them and to meet Prime Minister Pham Van Dong. After collecting four more sets of remains in Laos on the same trip, Montgomery returned to Washington to recommend "full diplomatic and trade ties with Vietnam."[54] In eighteen months, Carter's strategy of engagement had accounted for forty-eight American MIAs, surpassing the total accounted for in the four years prior, and moving the United States to the brink of normalization with Vietnam.[55]

Over those same eighteen months, presumptive findings of death reduced the number of Americans listed as missing by forty percent, further weakening the League, whose membership had fallen to roughly 500 relatives and fewer than 700 total members.[56] Deprived of its military airlift for the second straight year, the League held its 1978 convention in San Diego, within driving distance for its predominantly Sunbelt membership, but thousands of miles away from Washington. A Pentagon official who attended called it "an extremely sad, emotional, and, I must add, bizarre event."[57] In less populous states, the group neared extinction. "Our chapter is not active lately," the Indiana state coordinator wrote Congressman Dan Quayle; "the years of discouragement has [sic] taken its toll."[58] For Ann Mills Griffiths, who became executive director in 1978, these were "the wilderness years."[59]

Midway through his first term, Carter appeared well on his way toward resolution of the MIA problem. Having pushed the League to the margins, he promoted his own chastened vision of the Vietnam War as the nation's official memory through pursuit of normal diplomatic relations with Vietnam. Officials could point to the rapid return of remains that accompanied normalization talks as proof that the nation's post-Vietnam president was putting the war in the past as he reduced its painful human legacy.

But just when it appeared that the MIA issue was coming to a close, it resurfaced like the demonic villain from one of the era's classic horror films. The rapid pace of remains repatriation represented not just progress but desperation. Menaced by China to the north and the Chinese-backed Khmer Rouge that controlled Cambodia to the west, Vietnam pursued normalization less for economic assistance than for the security it offered from Chinese attack. The likelihood of such an attack increased over the course of 1978 as Vietnam's border dispute with the Khmer Rouge and its crackdown on its ethnic Chinese population prompted waves of refugees to flee. Anxious to secure U.S. support before war broke out, Deputy Foreign Minister Nguyen Co Thach proposed normalization without precondition on 27 September.

By the time Vietnamese officials reconciled themselves to forgoing monetary aid, Carter had cooled toward normalization. Heeding Brzezinski, Carter delayed until after normalizing with China. By choosing China over Vietnam, Carter hoped to intensify the Sino-Soviet split as he slid toward a policy of Soviet containment in the second half of his presidency. In this great power game, Vietnam once more became a pawn in a reinvigorated Cold War. Not only would normalizing with China antagonize the Soviets, but by tipping the regional balance of power in China's favor, the move compelled its historic Vietnamese rival to seek Soviet protection and predisposed the Soviets to grant it lest they lose influence throughout Indochina. With tensions rising and hopes of normalization with the U.S. fading, Vietnam signed a friendship treaty with the Soviets shortly before it invaded Cambodia on 25 December 1978. Determined "to put a restraint on the wild ambitions of the Vietnamese," Deng Xiaoping, during his visit to the White House in January 1979, informed Carter of his plans to teach Vietnam "an appropriate limited lesson," a promise he made good when China invaded Vietnam's northern provinces the following month.[60]

In the domestic context, Carter's decision to forgo normalization sacrificed symbolic resolution of the Vietnam War to resurgent anticommunism. As Carter alternately promoted and acquiesced in the Cold War's renaissance, sullen grievances over its most recent and bloody conflict resurfaced. With renewed fighting in Indochina and the mass exodus of refugees that accompanied it, Americans unreconciled to the war's outcome found fresh evidence that Vietnamese communists were expansionistic, illegitimate, even evil. Carter seemed to endorse their assessment by cutting off contact with Vietnam once it invaded Cambodia, accusing it and other Soviet-backed regimes of human rights abuses. But while he encouraged Cold Warriors in their hatred of communists, his unwillingness to take military action against them only inflamed popular animosity toward Vietnam by recalling the limits of American power. Fond of lectures, Carter scolded Vietnam without punishing it, fueling resentments of himself along with the Vietnamese.

Whatever Carter's failings, popular attitudes toward "Vietnam"—the war and the place—were shaped less by his foreign policy than by its critics. After forgoing normalization, Carter turned his attention elsewhere, focusing on the Middle East for the remainder of his presidency. Yet even as Vietnam receded in U.S. foreign policy, it retained its primacy in political culture. Picking up where Reagan left off in 1976, Republicans and neoconservatives worked to discredit domestic reform and the constraints of post-Vietnam foreign policy by tying both to the war in Vietnam. Citing an all-encompassing "culture of appeasement" as "the dangerous legacy of Vietnam," neoconservative Norman Podhoretz warned "that, far from having put Vietnam behind us, we are still living with it in a thousand different ways."[61]

This message united the disparate strands of the conservative movement. Composed of countless single-issue groups with diverse, sometimes even competing interests, the conservative movement was unified above all by its pervasive sense of disorder and decline that it traced back to defeat in Vietnam. While conservatives in these years saw themselves menaced by all manner of enemies and threats, they tended to view those threats in similar ways. Implacably evil and bent on the destruction of all they held dear, their foes were unleashed and emboldened by the failure of national will exposed in Vietnam. Defeat in Vietnam was the ultimate symbol and source of national enervation; it was "the new 'Munich,'" in the words of historian Andrew Bacevich, the accommodation with evil that must never be repeated yet seemed to threaten with each new crisis. Knitting the wartime past to the embattled present through a web of think tanks, direct mailings, tent revivals, and in-house journals, conservative ideologues generated a sense of "imminent apocalypse" that could be harnessed to their pet causes.[62]

Though their ranks were shrinking at a time of expansion on the right, MIA activists and their most singular single issue remained central to the conservative movement as its leaders revisited and revised the history of the Vietnam War. Reagan, for one, was not about to let the MIA issue drop, authoring the introduction to a collection of POW biographies in 1977. Intended as a celebratory volume, *We Came Home* possessed a curiously strident tone. Dusting off themes from Nixon's "silent majority" speech, Reagan vowed that "whenever again men are asked to fight and die for this Nation, the voice of the traitor will not be allowed."[63] His combative words revealed affinities between the politics of loss and the populist backlash that fueled conservative gains in the Ford and Carter years.

Natasha Zaretsky provides a partial explanation for the continued importance of the MIA issue to conservative discourse, arguing that narratives of MIA abandonment presented defeat in familial, hence familiar, terms. By publicizing families left fatherless by the war, MIA discourse presented the family "as a wounded and violable space of national injury."[64] Linking this thread of MIA family endangerment to other constructions of families in peril from later in the decade, Zaretsky argues that such concerns only intensified after the war, but her brief treatment of the MIA issue after 1973 only suggests what must be emphasized: it was the assertion of continued, ongoing abandonment that made MIAs so important in the late 1970s. Their spectral presence was central to conservative and neoconservative claims that the Vietnam War was an ongoing but recuperable loss. Their fallen state, like the grim state of the nation, testified to the past and present dangers of liberal governance while suggesting the redemptive possibilities of a return to older values.

Andrew Bacevich's summary of the six core beliefs of neoconservative thought shows how ideally suited MIAs were to advancing such claims in the Carter years. Bacevich identifies the key claims of leading neoconservative thinkers as follows: First, "evil is real." Second, "only the possession of—and willingness to employ—armed might" can defeat evil. Third, "alternatives to or substitutes for American global leadership simply did not exist." Fourth, radical assaults on tradition "undermined efforts to fulfill America's calling abroad." Fifth, "the United States after Vietnam confronted a dire crisis; absent decisive action to resolve that crisis, unspeakable consequences awaited." Sixth, "the antidote to crisis is leadership."[65] Claims of patriotic white men abandoned to the predations of their racial and ideological enemies by the corrupt government they served (and still relied on for salvation) illustrated each of these ideas in ways that were familiar and true for those who participated in MIA activism. By making the war a morality tale, MIAs transformed U.S. defeat in Vietnam from a failure of force to a failure of will—a failure that continued but could still be reversed.

As assumptions and institutions that had seen the nation through the Great Depression and Second World War came unraveled at the end of the Vietnam War, millions of Americans beyond the League entered what felt like the wilderness years. The League's narrative of dual victimization at the hands of Vietnamese communists and treacherous American elites offered these lost souls a means to understand and address their condition. Updating arguments from the war, MIA activists presented the war as an ongoing conflict between Americans, rather than a contest already won by the Vietnamese. After Reagan's introduction looking forward to the next war, Ann Mills Griffiths concluded *We Came Home* with a reminder that the last war was not yet finished. "POW/MIA families and concerned Americans continue to press our own government and those in Southeast Asia for a resolution," she wrote. "Hopefully the United States will not desert her own."[66]

THESE ARE EXCITING TIMES

Over the coming years, Reagan and Griffiths led the League's resurgence, with Griffiths playing the more vital role. Griffiths took over as executive director of the League in August 1978, backed by her father, who occupied the post during the tumultuous year of 1974–75.[67] Her appointment marked the end of whatever claims the League once had to being representative of all MIA families. Her ties to her father and her predecessor and friend Carol Bates, whom she met through VIVA, indicated that a coterie of militants firmly controlled the group, an impression confirmed by the fact that, three decades later, Griffiths still runs the League. But if the League no longer represented most MIA families, under Griffiths it again attracted the attention and support of influential interest groups and government insiders.

As Stockdale had a decade earlier, Griffiths cultivated relationships with powerful men receptive to her cause. Yet where Stockdale started on the inside of the defense establishment and worked her way out into the public sphere, Griffiths came from the outside and worked her way in. Her reverse trajectory reflected her hardscrabble roots and a very different relationship to the nation and its military. Other than their adopted home state of California, Griffiths and Stockdale had little in common. Even their California ties suggest their differences. Born and raised in New Haven, Connecticut, Stockdale summered at her family's cottage on the shore and attended a private day school, matriculating to Mount Holyoke, then Stanford, before settling in picturesque Coronado.[68] In comparison, Griffiths's girlhood journey from tiny Stigler, Oklahoma, to gritty Bakersfield, where her father was principal at Bakersfield High, seemed torn from *The Grapes of Wrath*. Leaving Bakersfield for Orange County, Griffiths, who never finished college, spent a number of years working for a manufacturer of acrylic aircraft glazes in Garden Grove, home of Robert Schuller's Crystal Cathedral, before joining Support Our POW/MIAs in nearby Los Alamitos. Socioeconomic differences were compounded by generational ones. Having come of age during World War II, Stockdale was middle-aged when she organized the League, whereas Griffiths entered adulthood during the Vietnam War and was still young when she became active in POW/MIA organizing. And though she shared Stockdale's low opinion of antiwar activists and other reform-minded contemporaries, Griffiths emulated their frank and confrontational cultural style. In contrast to Stockdale's studied femininity, Griffiths dressed simply, spoke bluntly, and smoked heavily, giving her a voice that could strip bark from a tree. While Stockdale practiced maternalist politics, Griffiths seldom discussed her missing brother in sentimental terms and never alluded to her family life, knowing that as a divorced mother of three she did not fit the mold of the waiting POW wife that Stockdale popularized a decade earlier.[69]

For all her pearls and grace, however, Stockdale was forceful and direct when necessary. And despite her just-one-of-the-boys brusqueness, Griffiths soon proved a sophisticated political operative and bureaucratic infighter. In terms of her lower-middle-class background and limited cultural capital, Griffiths was little different from many relatives who remained active in the League after the group's old guard departed in Omaha. The League was a decidedly less respectable organization after the war. What set Griffiths apart from the men who led the League in the mid-1970s, including her father, was that she shared Stockdale's conviction that she stood a better chance of shaping policy from inside the government than she could from the outside. But in order to do this she first had to infiltrate a national security bureaucracy that had grown hostile toward the League.

She began by seeking intelligence of MIA survival that could be used to pressure and persuade uncooperative officials. Soon after Griffiths became executive director, the League intensified its effort to solicit information on American MIAs from the hundreds of thousands of refugees then fleeing Vietnam. The plan was pioneered by Dermot Foley, after a motion he filed on behalf of missing Americans was dismissed due to lack of evidence that the plaintiffs were still alive. Foley appealed, launching a series of motions in which he introduced "reports of actual sightings . . . from two totally separate refugee groups."[70] For Foley, these "live-sighting reports" not only proved that presumptive findings of death were premature, they "exposed the inertia of the political and bureaucratic vermin who had refused to really exert themselves."[71]

The U.S. Court of Appeals for the Second Circuit rejected his claims, holding that "the government is acting generously and compassionately in sparing no pains to ascertain as conclusively as possible what has actually happened to those missing in action."[72] But live-sighting reports proved more persuasive in the court of public opinion. At the League's 1978 meeting, Ngo Phi Hung held the assembled members and media rapt with tales of having seen forty-nine American captives between 1975 and 1977. "When Hung finished his story, there was elation," according to one account.[73] A month later, Hung was invited before the House Subcommittee on East Asia and Pacific Affairs to reiterate his claims.[74] Later that year, U.S. relations with Vietnam soured, bringing the flow of American remains to a standstill. These developments, which promised further uncertainty for MIA families, brought jubilation to League hardliners. "These are exciting times," gushed one board member. "All we need is a picture, a finger print or some handwriting to prove there are live Americans in Southeast Asia."[75]

The return of marine POW Robert Garwood from North Vietnam in March 1979 after a thirteen-year absence seemed to provide that proof. To those like Donna Long, who became his advocate, lover, and financier, Garwood's "mere existence as a POW still in Vietnam . . . was the answer to a dream."[76] To Foley, who served as his lawyer for a time, Garwood offered a fresh opportunity to expose official mendacity. "He'll use this case to do everything he can to get back at the government," Foley's friend and League chairman Earl Hopper told reporters.[77]

But for Hopper, Griffiths, and other League leaders, Garwood was a disappointment. Unlike the long-suffering heroes they imagined, Garwood was a suspected deserter, known collaborator, and probable defector who was widely reviled by other POWs, Vietnam vets, and active-duty marines. Though crucial details concerning his capture and captivity will never be known given the absence of eyewitnesses, Americans in prison with him prior to his 1969 departure from their camp reported that Garwood spoke Vietnamese, carried a gun, received extra food, and "greeted his captors with hugs and smiles." They accused him of striking a fellow prisoner—a capital offense—and of indoctrinating, interrogating, and informing on his fellow inmates. He was convicted on these charges upon his return to the United States, suffering a reduction in rank, loss of pay, and dishonorable discharge as punishment.[78]

Garwood's greatest crime in the eyes of most Americans, certainly those in the League, was the likelihood that he had refused repatriation at war's end, a charge he denied. For those who viewed the Vietnam War in strict moral and racial dichotomies, this possibility undermined all the League's claims about the war—he did not resist, he collaborated; he did not keep faith with his fellow prisoners or his homeland, he embraced the enemy; he was not held back or kept in secret captivity, he stayed behind willingly and lived openly, contacting a western journalist when he wished to leave. At no point was Garwood a secret prisoner. Though Vietnam's government denied his survival, homecoming POWs reported his departure for the North during their debriefings, and U.S. government agencies suspected his existence, along with that of another deserter who later died in Cambodia. The House Select Committee *Final Report* noted that "at least one deserter [McKinley Nolan] and one defector [Robert Garwood], the latter currently listed as a POW, were alive, in Indochina in the early 1970s and may still be alive."[79] Instead of exposing official duplicity, Garwood's return only confirmed such official claims. Activists who sought to use Garwood "to bring them to their knees" eventually gave up. Adopting a policy of neutrality toward Garwood's return and court-martial, the League turned its attention to live-sighting reports.[80]

Unlike Garwood, the refugees who poured out of Vietnam told League leaders what they wanted to hear—that Americans were suffering in secret captivity—and the group devoted its resources to cultivating and communicating that message to the proper authorities and the American people. In Griffiths's first year as executive director the League exceeded its $57,000 budget by $20,000, an overrun she attributed to the "placement of ads in Vietnamese and Laotian publications" seeking information from "refugee centers throughout Southeast Asia and Europe." To keep the reports coming, the League board approved a budget of over $88,000 for 1979–1980, more than three times its available reserves. "Efforts to obtain irrefutable proof of live prisoners is time-consuming and expensive," Griffiths acknowledged in a donor appeal, "however, productive results are increasing."

How the League financed these efforts is unclear. Its dwindling membership probably could not cover the costs on its own. One possible source was VIVA funds in the account of Support Our POW/MIAs. Griffiths used the account of the defunct organization, periodically refreshed by conservative donors, as a slush fund in the 1980s, and she may have tapped the same source for earlier operations.[81] Wherever it found the funds, the League got what it paid for. Word that Americans wanted MIA information prompted over 400 live-sighting reports in 1979, swamping the three-man JCRC unit in Bangkok.[82]

The influx of live sightings was so overwhelming that the House Subcommittee on East Asia and Pacific Affairs spun off the House Task Force on American Prisoners and Missing in Southeast Asia under the direction of Tennyson Guyer, who dissented from the Montgomery Committee's *Final Report*. With Guyer and fellow Republican and Select Committee dissident Benjamin Gilman as its leaders, the Task Force instantly became the institutional base for MIA activism on Capitol Hill.[83] Joined by archconservative Robert Dornan—the inspiration behind VIVA's POW/MIA bracelets who was elected to Congress in 1976 out of western Los Angeles—Guyer and Gilman held hearings to publicize refugee reports, sparking stories in conservative journals that soon spread to more mainstream publications.[84]

Congressional activism pressured executive agencies to pay attention to the MIA issue and compelled the White House to modulate its hostility toward the League, as Foley hoped when he proposed the refugee strategy. With refugee reports on the rise, Oksenberg advised Brzezinski that it was "politically wise for the President to indicate his own continued concern with the MIAs." "This is a 'right wing' issue, and I think it gains the President some politically to indicate his continued interest."[85] "The idea is to say the President is determined to pursue any lead concerning live MIAs," he counseled, without offering "an opinion as to whether these leads are realistic."[86]

As Oksenberg later told the Senate Select Committee on POW/MIA Affairs, there was ample reason to consider live-sighting reports unrealistic. "The imprecision of the recollection, the lack of consistency in the reporting," and the probability that "refugees may have concluded that if they reported live sightings, they would receive some kind of beneficial treatment" left government experts convinced that the League was "putting words in some of these people's mouths."[87] Frank Sieverts, who became deputy assistant secretary for refugees in 1979 after fifteen years as the State Department's authority on POW/MIA matters, concluded that refugees were motivated by "the hope that this would give them a special status in the refugee flow."[88] Those suspicions were shared by the field agents who investigated the vague and implausible reports of Americans wandering the countryside. Despite those doubts, official investigations fostered refugee hopes by making clear that Americans valued news of MIAs.

The debriefing of Ngo Phi Hung, the League's first high-profile refugee, revealed the complex interplay of individuals and interests that fueled the live-sighting reports. Like many who fled Vietnam at the time, Hung was an ethnic Chinese who left Saigon amid growing tensions with China. Like many Chinese in the South, Hung was a businessman who profited during the war and was later targeted as a class enemy by the communist regime.[89] Upon arrival at the Song Khla refugee camp in Thailand, Hung came across a notice in *Trang Den* magazine, billing itself as the "Voice of non-communist Vietnamese," that called on "anyone who has any information regarding American persons who are missing in Vietnam" to contact Le Thi Anh in Cheverly, Maryland. Anh, herself a refugee who fled Vietnam in 1975 to take up the anticommunist cause, assured *Trang Den*'s readers that "this work will be of unlimited benefit to our just cause."

Hung replied immediately, claiming "knowledge of a number of prisoners" and boasting of three years in the National Restoration Resistance Forces. In a second letter, he vowed to "do anything that will benefit the United States government" and "to satisfy all of the families who still have members missing in Vietnam, as soon as I step foot in the United States," unaware of the tension between the two parties, even as he indicated that his primary interest in either case was his own resettlement. Hung urged Anh to "request the United States government to allow me to go earlier than planned." Two months later he arrived in San Diego, just in time for his appearance at the League convention and subsequent testimony before Congress.[90]

League activists openly exploited the personal and political interests that inspired refugee reports. Contrary to her depiction in the conservative press as a selfless anticommunist, Anh was on the League payroll as a translator and consultant, and the group financed her work with the refugee community until 1984 when U.S. intelligence warned the League that she was not anticommunist at all, but actually a double agent generating false reports of captive Americans in order to pressure the United States to normalize relations. Whether this claim was true or whether it was a ploy by the Reagan administration to curtail live-sighting reports that were no longer welcome is not clear, though it suggests the tangle of interests that motivated the various players in the MIA saga.[91]

Rather than distrusting self-interested refugees, League members considered them ideal witnesses to Vietnamese treachery. In this they mirrored a tendency among conservatives who turned Carter's concern with human rights to their own ends in the late 1970s by celebrating communist dissidents like Aleksandr Solzhenitsyn who condemned communist repression.[92] An old practice made new, the testimony of ex-communists had long been central to domestic countersubversion.[93] Richard Hofstadter observed the tendency within the "paranoid style" of politics to attach great significance to "the renegade from the enemy cause . . . who has been in the secret world of the enemy, and brings forth with him or her the final verification of suspicions which might otherwise have been doubted by a skeptical world."[94] A 1981 *National Review* article on live sightings proved his acuity when it explained "why would the Vietnamese continue to hold Americans" with the assertion that "we are dealing with . . . an Eastern mind that has been contaminated by Communism." "There doesn't have to be a logical Western reason."[95] Mixing old assumptions of American innocence and Oriental barbarism with claims of liberal naivete, MIA activists freed themselves from offering reasons for the behavior they attributed to their enemies.

In late 1979, the League's refugee strategy paid its biggest dividends yet, when an ethnic Chinese refugee from Hanoi named Tran Vien Loc appeared in Hong Kong claiming first-hand knowledge of the whereabouts of more than 400 American remains.[96] Loc identified himself as a mortician who had personally "processed" two to three hundred American remains for storage at a former prison camp in downtown Hanoi from 1969 to 1977, and had observed an estimated 400 boxes of remains at the same facility. After he failed his initial polygraph, U.S. officials arranged for his transport to Washington, where he passed a second polygraph.[97]

Though controversy later arose over Loc's veracity, the DIA emerged from his two-week debriefing convinced that "the mortician," as the anonymous intelligence source would come to be known, was who he purported to be—an official assigned to inter and disinter American remains in preparation for their return to the United States. DIA director General Eugene Tighe advised the Joint Chiefs of Staff that Loc possessed "a great deal of accurate information," and Tighe's staff briefed the Subcommittee on East Asia and Pacific Affairs to that effect, at which point Loc's story became known to Griffiths, who attended classified DIA briefings to the subcommittee.[98]

While the White House suspected that Loc's testimony was part of "an epidemic of false reports, motivated by the refugees' passionate hatred of the Vietnamese communist regime," administration officials felt "obliged to follow up on and check all these reports."[99] Carter authorized New York congressman Lester Wolff to lead a congressional delegation to Hanoi, where Wolff confronted Vietnamese officials with charges of warehoused remains and demanded to visit the building where they were allegedly stored. Upon his return, Wolff called a press conference to report that the Vietnamese "declined to permit on site inspection," as though this act alone proved their guilt.[100] Six months later, as MIA activists gathered in Washington for their 1980 meeting, Wolff called Loc to testify before the Subcommittee on East Asia and Pacific Affairs in an identity-concealing helmet, prompting the first mainstream press coverage of his claims.[101]

Warehoused remains rang true to those who followed the MIA issue because Vietnamese officials had clearly traded remains for diplomatic gain in the past. Since their war with France, Vietnamese leaders had used remains as bargaining chips, returning bones when it suited them, usually for payment or diplomatic advantage.[102] This pattern was equally apparent in postwar negotiations with the United States, as Vietnam dramatically modulated the number of remains it returned depending on its prospects for normalization.[103] This practice infuriated MIA activists, who accused the Vietnamese of inhumanity and accused Carter of "playing along with the Communist's act."[104] Such charges were unfair and one-sided. The Vietnamese "doled out bones," as Neil Sheehan explained, only "to keep a dialogue going with the United States because Washington was not interested in discussing any other subject."[105] They asked only for what they were promised, and were willing to settle for less — by the end they sought only trade and humanitarian assistance, and even then Americans were unwilling to make peace. As for barbarism, at least six Vietnamese skulls were seized by U.S. customs agents during the war, taken from returning GIs. Covered in graffiti, converted to candle holders and ashtrays, the skulls still sit in a drawer at Walter Reed Army Medical Center.[106]

Still, the fact that Vietnam repatriated remains at advantageous moments did not prove Loc's veracity. While Vietnam may have possessed surplus remains when he left Hanoi, how many it held, whether they were American, and whether they were stored in a "warehouse" is unclear. When Loc fled the country, Vietnam had repatriated over seventy American remains, meaning he could have processed large numbers without leaving behind a vast storehouse.[107] By his admission, Loc processed only about half the remains he reported seeing, estimating the remainder from boxes stacked in an adjacent room. Since he "was never allowed in that room," according to DIA, and "all his observations were made through a doorway," he could not know if American remains were inside boxes in a room he never entered.[108] Vietnam's refusal to allow Wolff to visit the reputed warehouse at 17 Ly Nam De Street was taken as proof of guilt, but reporters who searched the premises a few months later found "nothing to indicate the compound had ever been used as a 'warehouse' for men missing in action."[109]

If Vietnam held American remains in 1979, it was doubtful that they numbered anywhere near 400, and impossible to verify in any event, which became clear as analysts failed to confirm Loc's testimony. "Given the roughness of the mortician's various estimates," an Intelligence Community Assessment assessed in 1996, "we cannot conclude with a high degree of certainty that Hanoi held 400 sets of remains in 1977."[110] An intelligence estimate two years later cast doubt on Loc's story, attributing it to "the unsupported testimony of a single unreliable source."[111] Earlier DIA studies expressed more confidence in Loc's claims, but the two-decade effort to establish Loc's veracity suggests that initial reports of his "irrefutable" testimony were overblown.[112]

Even at the time, California congressman George Danielson, a member of Wolff's Subcommittee on East Asia and Pacific Affairs, cautioned against putting too much stock in "a story told by a single refugee," who "may have had a variety of motives in presenting his account."[113] When his colleagues ignored his concerns, Danielson submitted additional and separate views to the committee's report on its trip to Vietnam, noting that the subcommittee's endorsement of Loc's story rested almost entirely on the fact that he had passed one of two polygraphs in which he described the building at 17 Ly Nam De. "Any normal adult person who has lived in a given city for more than 40 years can describe at least one fairly large building which is at some designated location in that city," Danielson chided. Doing so proved nothing about what was inside the building. Disputing claims that Loc had no reason to lie, Danielson noted that a former high-ranking refugee "may have a resentment or animosity against the Hanoi establishment and may wish to retaliate by causing problems for them." If Loc was impervious to resentment, surely he was susceptible to enticement. "By telling his story he has achieved an instant and highly desired betterment of his own status," which left Danielson convinced that Loc had ample cause to exaggerate.[114]

While others shared Danielson's doubts, he was the only government official to challenge Loc's story at the time. The political consensus created by Loc's claims was on display at Wolff's January 1980 press conference, where Wolff, Griffiths, the Task Force on POW/MIAs, and DIA representatives were all on hand to endorse Loc's story.[115] Even White House skeptics played along, issuing a statement reaffirming the "personal importance" the president attached to "pursuing information about any live MIAs that may still be in Indochina."[116] Fourteen years after Sybil Stockdale invited POW wives to her house for lunch and seven years after the return of American POWs, the idea that Americans required rescue from Vietnam still resonated.

AMERICA HELD HOSTAGE

Many factors contributed to the renewal of the MIA issue, none more powerfully than the Iran hostage crisis. That ordeal began on 4 November 1979 — the same week that Loc arrived in Washington — when Iranian militants seized the U.S. embassy in Tehran and the sixty-six Americans stationed there. For the next 444 days the press, the president, and all his rivals and critics encouraged Americans to view their ordeal as a national crisis. Watching the footage his reporters sent back from Tehran, ABC News president Roone Arledge remarked, "Look what's happening to the psyche of the American people. We really are being held hostage." As the head of the only network news division with cameras in Tehran, Arledge created the nightly news program *America Held Hostage* that provoked and sustained the crisis atmosphere. Clambering to get on top of the story, Carter's staff presented him as directly managing events. According to Assistant Secretary of State Hodding Carter, "The decision was made for there to be a very visibly concerned president."[117] Yellow ribbons tied to flagpoles, fence posts, and old oak trees offered striking evidence of the hostages' hold on the imagination.[118] In a *New York Times Magazine* piece, Steven Roberts declared 1980 "The Year of the Hostage," when it felt as though "the whole nation had been blindfolded and hogtied, hauled through the streets of a strange city with people taunting them in a foreign tongue."[119]

Haynes Johnson dismissed the hostage crisis as "self-induced" hysteria "that affected national behavior and attitudes in a manner unworthy of a mature world power."[120] While fair, Johnson's critique prompts the question of why Americans were so moved by the event. Americans perceived the hostage taking as a crisis, David Farber has answered, "because they believed that the U.S., at the end of the 1970s, was already a nation in crisis." For most, "the hostages were a simple way of thinking about the state of their nation and the men who were supposed to lead it."[121] They were also a way to envision the threat that post-Vietnam lassitude posed to middle-class families, as Melani McAlister and Natasha Zaretsky have shown.[122]

Memories of American losses in Vietnam gave the Iran hostage crisis its strange urgency. To Roberts and many of those he interviewed for his "Year of the Hostage" article, the current crisis began not in Iran but in Vietnam. "When I went into the service, the United States had respect," retired air force officer Frank Kennedy recalled, and "then along came Vietnam."[123] Reagan reinforced this reading of events by diagnosing "the deepening crisis in Iran" as "a symptom of a larger crisis."[124] "How did we come to the point that a rag-tag revolutionary mob can invade an embassy of ours, seize our people, and now be holding them into the third month, and we seem unable to do anything about it?"[125] For Reagan and the growing numbers who backed his candidacy, it went without saying that the larger crisis originated in Vietnam, the place where Americans first became captive to dark revolutionaries. The failure of the April rescue mission Carter sent to free the captives, and the resulting images of American corpses and crashed helicopters littering the sands, sealed the connection. "We tried, we failed, and we have paid a price: the bodies of eight young Americans still lie in the Iranian desert," ABC anchor Frank Reynolds intoned after the debacle, using all-too-familiar words and images.[126]

Aside from differences in landscape and vegetation, depictions of the hostage crisis were strikingly similar to Vietnam POW imagery. The blindfolded American hostages that became the iconographic images of the event bore a striking resemblance to a famous photograph of the bandaged and barefoot James Lindbergh Hughes being marched through the streets of Hanoi, and they were almost identical to the famous photo that purported to show Ron Dodge in communist hands that appeared on the 10 November 1972 cover of *Life* magazine and which MIA activists widely reproduced as proof of postwar captivity.[127] Each presented a lone white American man in a white shirt with white bandages around his head surrounded by threatening dark-skinned captors who unleashed their fury on the helpless figure. Interviews with hostage families recalled similar domestic dramas with POW and MIA families, as did briefings between administration officials and hostage families. Iranians inadvertently reinforced these connections by granting early release to women and black men, echoing the release of minority POWs in Vietnam. Many of those released early sympathized with their captors, angering the same superpatriots enraged by similar episodes during the Vietnam War, while their release purified the hostage population to the same white male core that had endured captivity in Vietnam.[128]

Images from the Iran hostage crisis recalled iconic images of American captivity in Vietnam, as these photos illustrate. The top image shows Lieutenant Colonel James Lindbergh Hughes being led through the streets of Hanoi in May 1967. The bottom image shows a blindfolded American hostage in Tehran in November 1979. (Top photo © Bettman/Corbis; bottom photo © Kaveh Kazemi/Corbis)

It was as if history were repeating itself. POW families briefed hostage families on how to endure captivity.[129] Congressman Bob Dornan adapted the POW/MIA bracelets he had inspired during the Vietnam War to the new crisis, sending "every major figure in government . . . an Iranian hostage bracelet with the name of Air Force Lieutenant Colonel David Roeder inscribed on it along with the message, 'Never Again.'"[130] The implicit reference to defeat in Vietnam and MIA abandonment was unmistakable. By choosing a military officer to represent the largely civilian hostage population, Dornan deepened the association. Reagan sealed the connection when he insisted on calling the hostages "prisoners of war" at his first cabinet meeting. And upon their return to the United States he replayed Operation Homecoming, hosting a lavish reception in their honor.[131]

League families were acutely aware of these ties, alternately envious of the attention hostages received and hopeful that their captivity would spark renewed interest in Americans missing in Southeast Asia. Griffiths complained bitterly when the administration flew hostage families to Washington for official briefings after it ended the League's airlift in 1977, while New York coordinator Gladys Brooks credited the Iran hostages for "a great surge of interest in our POW/MIA issue."[132] Those outside the League were likely less conscious of the connections between captivity in Vietnam and the hostage crisis, even when they blamed American defeat in Vietnam for American humiliation in Tehran. Still, captivity had been key to popular perceptions of defeat in Vietnam. Now it returned as a way to understand the war's continuing grip, while recent POW activism offered Americans accustomed means of confronting its threat. Reprising wartime roles, politicians publicized their efforts on the hostages' behalf while reporters headed into the hinterland to interview hostage families. Ordinary citizens showed their support through yellow ribbons and hostage bracelets.

What at first glance seems hysterical about the response to the hostage taking can be understood as a continued conversation about the consequences of defeat in Vietnam. When the crisis began, Americans had imagined their countrymen in captivity for more than a decade. As Melani McAlister has argued, reactions to the crisis could be reduced to a "deep commitment to this simple proposition: It is time to get our people out of there." That commitment first arose in Vietnam and was first articulated in the context of POW activism. The hostage families were not "a new kind of figure in American public life," as McAlister would have it. The National League of Families preceded them, and its success in sentimentalizing U.S. foreign policy through association with the middle-class family paved the way for the Iran hostage families to do the same.[133] Unlike the hostage families, though, the League was built to last. Its missing loved ones could never be found, its fullest possible accounting agenda could never be satisfied, and its persistence was about to pay off.

THE MUCH IMPROVED SPIRIT OF COOPERATION

With the eyes of the nation fixed on Tehran, Loc's claims of warehoused remains played out as a minor story deep inside leading newspapers and largely absent from network news.[134] His reports were handled at much the same level inside the government. After 1978, Carter seldom devoted attention to MIAs, even after the influx of refugee reports convinced his staff that he should feign interest. He had more pressing concerns and was content to leave the MIA issue to mid-level officials, limiting his involvement to the establishment of National POW/MIA Recognition Day in 1979.[135]

With Carter's national security staff focused on Iran and Afghanistan and his domestic advisers preoccupied with his reelection bid, those who once kept the League in check no longer did so. At the same time, there were some within the government who sympathized with the League, as there always had been. Their numbers and influence grew as refugee reports converged with events in the Middle East to convince many in the administration that U.S. foreign policy was dangerously adrift.[136]

The first sign that things were changing came on 16 November 1979 — two weeks after the U.S. embassy was seized—when DIA director Eugene Tighe granted Ann Mills Griffiths "limited access to classified information." Tighe's decision to allow Griffiths to attend classified briefings on Loc's claims of warehoused remains necessitated the arrangement.[137] Since Loc's testimony was the first refugee report endorsed by the DIA, Tighe may have hoped to lessen the heat his agency was under from the League for dismissing earlier live sightings.[138] He shared the League's discontent with the Carter administration, and by giving Griffiths "a broader base upon which to represent the League in her dealings with those in the Government," he sought to "contribute to the much improved spirit of cooperation which all of us desire."[139]

Seizing on the crisis atmosphere that gripped Washington, Griffiths used Loc's testimony and Wolff's visit to Hanoi to organize and claim a seat on the Inter-Agency Group on POW/MIA Affairs, also known as the PW/MIA Interagency Group or IAG, which held its first meeting in March 1980.[140] Within weeks of receiving her security clearance, Griffiths met with Deputy Assistant Secretary of State for East Asian and Pacific Affairs

John Negroponte, Deputy Assistant Secretary of Defense for International Security Affairs Nick Platt, and NSC East Asia expert Roger Sullivan to suggest that "a 'task force' should be established to meet on a regular basis, realistically determine the status of efforts and formulate policy to meet the requirements for obtaining an honorable conclusion."[141] In addition to State, Defense, and the NSC, Griffiths recommended representatives from DIA, the Joint Chiefs of Staff, the Subcommittee on East Asian and Pacific Affairs, the House POW/MIA Task Force, and the League. With her newly minted security clearance, she nominated herself as the League liaison.

Her handpicked roster stacked the IAG membership in her favor, with the League's long-time friend General Richard Lawson, who acted as the Joint Chiefs' representative to the IAG, joining Tighe and the IAG members from the House as League allies.[142] More importantly, Griffiths found an affinity with State Department representative John Negroponte, a career diplomat who saw Vietnam's invasion of Cambodia in 1978, the Sandinista uprising that seized power in Nicaragua in 1979, and the Soviet invasion of Afghanistan later that year as evidence that communism was on the march, and who interpreted Carter's inaction on hostages and MIAs as a sign of his impotence.[143] Unlike other early IAG members, Negroponte survived the 1980 election, serving as Reagan's ambassador to Honduras, ambassador to Mexico under George H. W. Bush, ambassador to the Philippines under Bill Clinton, and ambassador to the United Nations, ambassador to Iraq, director of national intelligence, and deputy secretary of state under George W. Bush.[144] Negroponte and Griffiths "grew up together" in the IAG, and his support was key to its survival in the Reagan and Bush administrations.[145]

From the beginning, career civil servants and congressional representatives outnumbered and outgunned Carter administration appointees on the IAG, shifting policy in directions favored by the League. As its early organization gave way (at Griffiths's insistence) to a more select, secretive group from the NSC, Defense, State, the Joint Chiefs, and the League in the 1980s, the IAG became "the focal point of U.S. policy formulation on the POW/MIA issue."[146] As its authority grew, Griffiths's influence grew with it. Immune from the electoral constraints other members faced, and untrammeled by their obligation to the public interest, Griffiths became the group's sole permanent member and plenipotentiary. Using her access to senior officials and classified information to manipulate and intimidate League members and government employees, she soon turned her IAG seat into an unassailable stronghold. When the Senate Select Committee learned the extent to which she had ensconced herself in the government's lead POW/MIA policymaking body, it denounced "the close connection between private interests and U.S. government actions that the League's membership on the IAG effectuates," opining that "the League's central role — often as the driver of Government policies — raises serious questions about whether it has unduly influenced U.S. policy." Answering those questions proved difficult given "the IAG's failure to keep regular minutes of its meetings" after 1983, but sufficient evidence of Griffiths's influence survived to inspire the Senate Select Committee to call on the Clinton administration to review "the role of the IAG and issues of membership on it."[147]

When the IAG formed in the spring of 1980, few of its founders could have dreamed it would exist thirteen years later, much less exert such influence. Not only did such interagency groups, a common policymaking and coordinating mechanism within modern presidencies, seldom survive the administration in which they were formed, the PW/MIA IAG seemed destined to encounter the same constraints that doomed earlier accounting efforts.[148] Predictable grassroots skepticism was already evident at the League's 1980 convention, where some members saw Griffiths's seat on the IAG as a form of "government seduction."[149] Before the convention, Dermot Foley and Earl Hopper resigned their positions in protest after learning that Griffiths had signed a secrecy agreement to gain her security clearance, which they considered a threat to League autonomy.

The scolding tone of their public resignations suggests that they were upset, at least in part, by the fact that a young woman they regarded as their subordinate suddenly held sway with the same powerful men who had shown them such contempt. This stung Hopper in particular, a retired Army colonel who insisted that Griffiths could not possibly possess a security clearance, the exclusive preserve of "persons within the military or government."[150] But their suspicion of government motives was also rooted in the League's history. "What I see happening now reminds me all too well of the stroking that led a few poor souls to oppose litigation [against status reviews] in 1973," Foley admonished in his letter of resignation. If "we are prepared to capitulate to a collection of smiling functionaries," he predicted, "we will deserve what you know and I know we are going to get, once our objections have been silenced or controlled."[151]

By the mid-1980s such suspicions of the IAG and its influence over Griffiths prompted many MIA activists to leave the League in favor of more radical splinter cells. But in the IAG's infancy, few League members followed Foley and Hopper in condemning the IAG. Though the League had been at odds with the federal government since 1973, most members saw the IAG as an improvement over their recent obscurity. To the extent that they were aware of what went on inside the IAG, which was reported sparingly in the League newsletter, all signs suggested that it was advancing League goals. Shortly after its formation, DIA assigned additional personnel to investigate MIA issues, the Subcommittee on East Asian and Pacific Affairs called Loc to testify during the League's convention, and the State Department elevated MIA accounting to "a more frequent and explicit point of emphasis in appropriate official policy statements."[152] Skeptics dismissed these steps as empty gestures. But in ordering executive agencies to "discontinue USG use of the statement that 'we have no credible evidence to indicate that any U.S. servicemen are alive in captivity and being held against their will in Southeast Asia'" in favor of a *public information campaign* focused on the possibility of MIA survival, the IAG paved the way for the League's resurgence.[153]

If League history taught anything, it was that POW/MIA rhetoric put as much pressure on American leaders as it did on those in Vietnam. The IAG public information campaign raised the profile of the MIA issue, and the pressure to resolve it, by changing the way missing personnel were counted so as to increase dramatically the number of "unaccounted for" Americans. Until 1980 the MIA population exclusively comprised servicemen who were missing without clear evidence of death. The exact number of these men varied depending on the date and source, but there was general consensus among all interested parties, the League included, that just over 1,300 Americans met this criterion. The League routinely used that number in advertisements and newsletters, as did politicians and the press.[154] However, the 1,300 figure did not represent the full universe of Americans lost in Southeast Asia. In addition to 1,300 MIAs, U.S. officials also pursued an accounting for 1,100 persons classified as Killed in Action/Body Not Recovered who had never been counted among the missing, since they were known dead.[155] These distinctions were erased on 27 June 1980 when Tighe appeared before the Subcommittee on East Asian and Pacific Affairs to endorse Loc's warehouse testimony and abruptly announced that there were "approximately 2,500 Americans unaccounted for in Southeast Asia" and that any "distinction between the terms" POW, MIA, and KIA/BNR would now be "treated only administratively by DIA." Addressing the committee later that year, Tighe reasoned that because "the status of most of these 2,500 Americans has since been changed by the military services to that of presumed dead . . . there is no distinction between these terms as far as DIA is concerned."[156]

Tighe was right to question the continued relevance of wartime categories that divided missing Americans into presumed living and presumed dead. By 1980 status review boards had concluded that all but a handful of

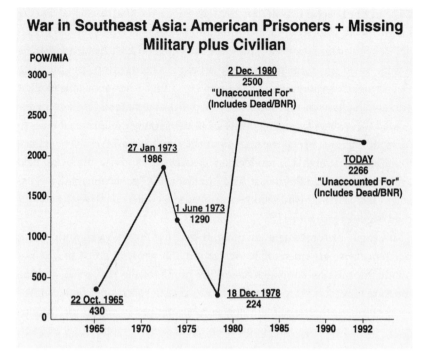

War in Southeast Asia: American Prisoners + Missing Military plus Civilian

This chart from the Senate Select Committee on POW/MIA Affairs illustrates the POW/MIA population boom in 1980 through the addition of KIA/BNR to the number of "unaccounted for" Americans. (Reprinted from Senate Select Committee on POW/MIA Affairs, *Hearing on Americans Missing or Prisoner in Southeast Asia, The Department of Defense Accounting Process*, 1375)

MIAs must be presumed dead. But in the context in which they were made, Tighe's words carried precisely the opposite meaning, suggesting the fate of 2,500 Americans was in doubt when there were at best a few dozen cases with even a remote possibility of survival. As the Senate Select Committee noted in 1992, Tighe's lumping "created the anomalous situation of having more Americans considered unaccounted for today than we had immediately after the war."[157] MIA inflation could be seen in copies of *Newsweek* that arrived in mailboxes the day before the 1980 election. Whereas the magazine had written of "1,363 Americans on the MIA rolls" heading into the 1976 election, it sympathized with "families of some of the 2,500 servicemen missing in action" on the eve of the 1980 balloting.[158] Around the same time, the *National Review* wondered if "the 2,546 Americans originally listed as Missing in Action" were "lost or merely forgotten," while retired general John Singlaub, later implicated in the Iran-Contra scandal, asked readers of the *American Legion*, "Were 2,800 POW/MIAs forsaken to 'normalize' relations with Vietnam?" Singlaub's formulation was particularly absurd, adding 389 MIAs from Korea to the 2,490 he counted for the Vietnam War.[159]

Such figures could not have been more misleading. Under military regulations, in order for a man to be classified KIA/BNR "the facts must be such that death is the only plausible alternative under the circumstances." Given the incentives for commanders to place unrecovered casualties in MIA status, had there not been overwhelming evidence of death, men in KIA/BNR status would have been listed as missing. Whatever confusion existed between these categories resulted from overly optimistic assessments that placed dead men in MIA status, not the other way around. Combat conditions and historical precedent dictated that the majority of MIAs were KIA/BNR, not vice versa, as the House Select Committee concluded and the status review process confirmed.[160] That only one KIA/BNR turned up alive during Operation Homecoming was the exception that proved the rule: these men were dead.[161] DIA's decision to count them as missing implied otherwise, with the obvious intention of exaggerating the MIA population.

The time and place Tighe chose to announce his decision underlined his intent. Tighe appeared before Congress on the same day that Loc made his second appearance on Capitol Hill, and the testimony of both men was scheduled for the first day of the League's convention. The two events were carefully coordinated by the IAG to allow League members to hear Tighe's and Loc's testimony. Tighe knew League members would be in attendance when he announced that distinctions among unrecovered Americans no longer applied; had he expected anything but their enthusiastic approval, he would have chosen another forum, or none at all, leaving the status quo in place. His announcement was another sign of the improved spirit of cooperation he desired, motivated by League worries that MIA ranks were nearing zero as the missing were presumed dead. Griffiths later took credit for the POW/MIA amalgamation in an IAG memo.[162]

The League had its own part to play in orchestrating this affair, which further highlights its political implications. Two weeks after the first IAG meeting and two months before Reagan secured the GOP nomination, Griffiths wrote to Reagan campaign consultant (later his national security adviser) Richard Allen to suggest the League's June meeting as a perfect "forum for the Governor to provide the media with yet another failure of the Carter Administration."[163] In a second letter she condemned Carter's "impotence to obtain the long-promised accounting" and repeated her hope that Reagan could "visit with our members."[164] With her invitation to turn the League convention into a campaign stop, the Wolff Subcommittee's invitation to Loc to testify, and Tighe's decree that the POW/MIA population had doubled overnight, IAG members promoted the Reagan campaign from inside the Carter administration.

RATHER THAN ADDRESS the League, Reagan went before the Veterans of Foreign Wars in August to declare that "it is time we recognized that [in Vietnam] ours, in truth, was a noble cause." Wrapping his revisionism in the mantle of the war dead, he insisted, "We dishonor the memory of 50,000 young Americans who died in that cause when we give way to feelings of guilt." Had he stopped there, Reagan might have offended those still angry over the war's failures, including the government's failure to account for missing Americans. But he brought the VFW to its feet with a vague but passionate indictment of those who opposed the war: "Let us tell those who fought in that war that we will never again ask your men to fight and possibly die in a war our government is afraid to win."[165] A contradictory speech that celebrated the war's purpose but condemned its execution, Reagan's remarks reflected the ambivalence of the war's memory in the late 1970s and resolved its tensions through anti-government rhetoric.[166]

Reagan, who inserted the "noble cause" line into his speech against the advice of his staff, had been saying such things for years. His combative "Reaganisms" had long stirred his party's right wing, but they also earned him a reputation as an extremist, one he retained even after his 1976 primary run.[167] Throughout the 1980 campaign reporters derided his "glib formulations" as "wonderfully suited for the early 1950s," but "wholly out of touch with the context and content of current events."[168] With his "noble cause" speech, commentators assumed he had "again created unnecessary problems for himself" in "the defiant way he courted controversy over one of the most painful episodes in American history." "He may yet auto-destruct," Howell Raines predicted.[169] Sharing that hope, Carter spent the campaign calling Reagan "dangerous" and "disturbing."[170] For those in the Carter camp, it was obvious that calling the Vietnam War noble disqualified Reagan as a national leader.[171]

To their chagrin, Reagan's message proved surprisingly popular. Voters gave him a landslide victory in an election dominated by foreign policy and defense.[172] More surprising still, conservatives gained control of the Senate for the first time since 1954 as Frank Church, George McGovern, Birch

Bayh, and other liberal critics of the war were replaced by its defenders like former POW Jeremiah Denton.[173] Beyond obvious reasons for the swing to the right, most notably a dismal economy that bred anti-incumbent sentiment, there were deeper reasons that took time to unravel, including deindustrialization that sapped organized labor of its strength, growing rifts between African Americans and white ethnics who were essential to Democratic success, demographic shifts to the conservative South and Southwest, and increased political participation among evangelicals.[174] With powerful forces reshaping the political landscape, few analysts considered Reagan's "noble cause" speech that significant, except insofar as they credited him with overcoming such comments.

Later, as Reagan embellished his noble cause rhetoric, commentators began to suspect that his historical revisionism was key to his success.[175] Yet Reagan did not alter public memory of the war so much as he capitalized on its prevailing sense of loss. His views on the war had changed little since the 1960s, when he argued that the war could be won through sufficient force, including nuclear weapons if necessary.[176] To him, those who advocated anything less were to blame for the war's failures. As those failures mounted, he was the first politician to embrace POW/MIA families as a means of focusing on the war's American victims, beating even Nixon to the punch. And when South Vietnam collapsed, he insisted that the war was lost only because unnamed elements of the government were "afraid to win."[177] But he was hardly alone in recasting the conflict in these terms, joined by a phalanx of returned POWs, retired officers, emergent neoconservatives, even Nixon and Kissinger, all of whom held that the war was winnable but that its warriors were stabbed in the back by the press, pacifists, bureaucrats, or some other murky combination of liberal elites. No group was more committed to the idea that the war and its soldiers were forfeited than the League, and none was better suited to remind Americans of the war's unfinished business. After battling government officials for the better part of a decade, League members had come to see their struggle, above all, as a war between Americans. Frustrated by Carter's neglect, they found other outsiders who helped them generate new evidence of disloyalty and defeatism inside the American government.

Those unreconciled to the Vietnam War's outcome seized on that evidence, no matter how dubious, to "raise questions about the U.S. commitment to obtaining an adequate MIA accounting," questions that implied more pressing questions about the national commitment to winning the war in the first place. "Our State Department has in effect abandoned the

MIAs and their families," Paul Gigot concluded for the *National Review* on the eve of the hostage crisis.[178] As grim as such thinking was, it gave ammunition to those still determined to wage war on the Washington battlefront. "Until we have a positive statement and preferably the return of their bodies, we shall not consider that the war is over," the *American Legion* vowed on the eve of the 1980 election.[179]

214

— ◦ —

Highest National Priority

Resurrection and Retribution

President Ronald Reagan could have marked the tenth anniversary of U.S. withdrawal from Vietnam in any number of ways. That he chose to address the National League of Families was a clear sign of the group's return to power. League members flown to Washington for the event must have felt the world restored to its rightful order as air force transports lifted them to heights not seen since the Nixon years. As in those heady early days, the League sampled public service announcements urging Americans to "ask for an accounting," beheld a "head table richly stocked with congressmen, generals and service secretaries," and basked in presidential rhetoric of overdue discovery after undeserved neglect.

Standing before the League's black and white flag—the words "You Are Not Forgotten" emblazoned beneath the silhouette of an American POW—Reagan deplored the disinterest of the recent past, which left MIA activists "on the outside, driven in some cases to demonstrate for attention in front of the White House gates." "You, the families, of our missing men were trying to be heard, and yet you were sometimes unfairly and cruelly branded as emotionally distraught groups that ignored reality and simply hoped against hope." "Today, your long vigil is over." In his administration, "the return of all POWs, the fullest possible accounting for the still missing, and the repatriation of the remains of those who died serving our nation" would be "the highest national priority." "I've been waiting fifteen years to hear something like that," one MIA mother told a reporter. "He's given us hope."[1]

Reagan gave the League more than hope. A League ally since the 1960s, he worked wonders for the group, which enjoyed more money, media

President Ronald Reagan addresses the National League of Families to mark the tenth anniversary of the Paris Agreement, 28 January 1983. (Courtesy Ronald Reagan Library)

coverage, and political influence during his presidency than at any time in its history. "If the President is personally interested in something, then the Government is interested in it," a White House aide told a reporter, "and Mr. and Mrs. Reagan are personally very interested in MIAs."[2]

By all accounts, Reagan was consumed by thoughts of captive Americans. National Security Adviser Richard Allen recalled "many, many conversations" where Reagan "indicated to me that he believed that there were

. . . Americans being held against their will in Southeast Asia."[3] Allen's successor, Robert "Bud" McFarlane, reported, "Reagan's obsession with freeing the hostages overrode anything else."[4] Chief of Staff Donald Regan traced Reagan's fixation to Reagan's star turn in the 1954 film *Prisoner of War*. "He puts himself into the part," Regan reasoned; "all of a sudden he's envisioning himself as a captive alone in a dank, damp prison, and where's the president of the United States? . . . Ronald Reagan eats his heart out over this."[5] In a 1984 address to former POWs, Reagan cited his performance in *Prisoner of War* as "the only experience that I had that was at all in keeping with what you have gone through."[6] If "one side of Reagan's temperament was a passive disengagement from" most issues, biographer Lou Cannon noted in explaining Reagan's "awesome stubbornness" on the hostage issue, "the other side was an intense, almost passionate commitment to causes he visualized in personal terms." The actor-turned-president visualized the plight of POWs and MIAs in the most personal way possible.[7]

Like most issues Reagan took to heart, captive and missing Americans put a human face on a political problem. For him, they symbolized the national decline caused by the Vietnam War. Reagan embraced them for complex, even contradictory reasons, mixing a compulsion to transform public memory of the Vietnam War from national tragedy to triumphal "noble cause" with a darker impulse to attack those he blamed for American defeat. To Reagan, these men and their families had done "nothing to deserve [their] terrible emotional ordeal," which made them potent symbols of national victimization in a war where Americans were aggressors.[8] Honorable and blameless, they could be rescued from the nightmare of Vietnam, giving the war an air of nobility. At the same time, their continued absence preserved the war as a cautionary tale of liberalism run amok, of bureaucrats who could not be trusted, of the dangers of military weakness and un-American dissent.

While Reagan's memorial politics were complicated, his tactics were not, re-creating Nixon's Go Public offensive but infusing it with his trademark charm. According to the *Final Interagency Report of the Reagan Administration on the POW/MIA Issue in Southeast Asia*, he launched "an aggressive public awareness campaign" midway through his first term that "raised domestic consciousness of this issue to the highest level since the end of the war."[9] Reagan's January 1983 appearance before the League, his interment of an Unknown Soldier from the Vietnam War in 1984, along with his participation in the dedication of the Vietnam Veterans Memorial in 1982 and his formal acceptance of "The Wall" in 1984, highlighted his commitment to the missing and harnessed their plight to his revisionism.[10] Footage from these events was packaged into stirring commercials with titles such as "America is Back" and "Morning Again in America" that became the centerpiece of Reagan's reelection bid. Such ads were not subtle about what America was coming back from or where it had been the night before — viewers knew that they were returning from Vietnam, with Reagan leading the way home.

The return of missing Americans was integral to Reagan's claims to have saved the nation from the crippling memory of Vietnam. When recovering MIAs proved too slow and insufficient, Reagan asked their families to serve as surrogates, making them recipients of the national redemption he had wrought. The League's success assured larger constituencies — soldiers and veterans, southern whites, evangelicals — that their days of being forgotten and disrespected were over. Even Reagan's critics cited his success in bringing "the country back together" as reason enough to reelect him.[11] For Americans in the 1980s, nothing sounded what Abraham Lincoln called "the mystic chords of memory, stretching from every battlefield, and patriot grave, to every living heart and hearthstone" so soothingly as the restoration of MIA families to a place of honor.[12]

But for many in the League, something more than symbolism was needed to repair the breach between citizens and the state. League firebrands like Earl Hopper called on Reagan to fulfill "his pledge of resolving this problem on a 'high national priority' basis with the only result satisfactory to us being *the return of our live prisoners*." "We do not wish to listen to repetitive rhetoric," he spat, "after listening to the same story for so many years." "We want our men home, and home this year."[13] For those like Hopper, only a full accounting — an infinitely elastic standard — could set things right. While Reagan professed sympathy with them, his "Morning in America" crowing was oblivious to their anguish. "Ronald Reagan, Sympathetic or Just Acting?" asked one newsletter popular among MIA malcontents.[14]

If Reagan won reelection by acting out a melodrama of national reconciliation, by his second term it was increasingly clear that the show lacked substance. Americans longed to recover from the Vietnam War, but they disagreed about what recovery would look like or how it would happen. The urge to celebrate Vietnam veterans could not conceal its source: the widespread sense that their sacrifice was a waste. For Americans who cared deeply about the war, resolution could come only through fixing responsibility for its failures. This was particularly true for MIA activists who reacted to reconciliationist rhetoric with as much suspicion as satisfaction.

By the time Reagan took office, MIAs had come to represent, more than anything else, the betrayal of those who served in Vietnam, by the state, the press, the public, the establishment, or some combination of the above. As a presidential contender running against Washington and those unworthy enough to depend on it, Reagan felt little compunction about embracing such symbolism. But the return of the MIA issue during his presidency hardly showed that Americans accepted his claims that the Vietnam War was a noble cause. Just the opposite — it suggested a growing consensus that the war was a tragedy, that the men who fought it were victims, and that the fullest possible accounting for what went wrong was essential, even the highest national priority. As they imagined MIAs in continued captivity, Americans expressed their sense that abandonment, betrayal, and deceit were the defining features of U.S. involvement in Vietnam. By encouraging expectations of accountability for the missing that he could not satisfy, Reagan reinforced those attitudes, leaving many Americans convinced that the war's legacy of official misconduct stretched into the present and that state efforts to evade responsibility for the war were ongoing.

LAZARUS COME FORTH

Asked by the Senate Select Committee on POW/MIA Affairs how Reagan changed MIA accounting efforts, Ann Mills Griffiths credited him with bringing "massive," "total," "180 [degree] change right down the line." "We knew he would be serious," she continued, using the royal "we" she habitually adopted after years of speaking on the League's behalf, "because he had been serious throughout when he was governor, between that time and when he was a candidate for President."[15]

In Reagan's first year she expressed a more circumspect view. At a June meeting of the Inter-Agency Group on POW/MIA Affairs, she voiced "impatience with accounting progress" and complained bitterly that the military airlift of MIA families to the League's convention had not been reinstated under Reagan even though such transportation was provided to Iran hostage families. Explaining her urgency, she warned that she was having "problems with some board members" who had been "told that progress has been made, but they don't see concrete results." "Cooperation had improved," she admitted, but "the families' suspicions had not been allayed."[16]

It was a portent of things to come and a reminder of things past. The League had a long history of dashed expectations; its history with Reagan would be no different. The fundamental hurdles to a full accounting — wartime oblivion and Vietnamese intransigence — had not gone away. If anything, Reagan's election made accounting less likely by empowering policymakers more interested in confronting the Vietnamese than in co-operating with them. Hanoi was condemned rather than rewarded for re-patriating three sets of remains in 1981 when it was discovered that one of the three belonged to Ron Dodge, a celebrated "discrepancy case" that MIA activists assumed was still alive. After years of demanding answers about Dodge, activists greeted evidence of his death with grotesque allegations that the Vietnamese had murdered him in order to cash in his remains for diplomatic favors.[17]

Little cooperation was possible in such a climate, and little progress was made. The administration put a positive spin on its efforts in the 1982 POW-MIA *Fact Book*, but admitted only "a degree of progress has been made," since "Indochinese governments have been unwilling to provide informa-tion to U.S. officials."[18] Presidential pledges to "work unceasingly until a full accounting is made" were welcome, but evidence of Reagan's com-mitment was scarce.[19] The Defense Intelligence Agency's (DIA) POW/MIA shop had just twelve analysts in 1983, down from fourteen when Reagan took office.[20] The staff at the army's Central Identification Lab (CILHI) fell from twenty-six to fifteen in Reagan's first term, with a single scien-tist whose highest educational attainment consisted of a bachelor's degree from the University of Tokyo.[21] With a 25 percent reduction in Joint Casu-alty Resolution Center (JCRC) billets since 1976 and just twenty-two sets of remains returned in Reagan's first term—fewer than half the number repatriated under Carter—there was little work for the lab anyway.[22] While Reagan declared MIAs the "highest national priority," one staffer recalled the mission "wasn't just low priority, [it] was no priority" when he joined the JCRC in 1981, so short on cash that he had to drive his own 1969 Toyota Corona to interview refugees.[23]

Those who wished could take comfort in the fact that the new deputy assistant secretary of defense, Richard Armitage, traveled to Hanoi in 1982 and again in 1984 as assistant secretary of defense. But MIA activists pre-ferred deeds to words and tough talk to diplomacy, which may explain why, at the 1983 meeting of the Association of Southeast Asian Nations, Secre-tary of State George Shultz blasted Vietnam for warehousing remains.[24] Such belligerence pleased activists, but it stood in the way of account-ing progress, as Foreign Minister Nguyen Co Thach made clear when he warned that "there will be no more cooperation if they continue to use the issue as a political weapon against us."[25]

Rather than deliver results, Reagan offered spectacle. In addition to his many speeches paying lip service to the MIA cause, Reagan authorized a series of ostensibly covert operations that failed to find missing Americans but captivated MIA activists. The first sent U.S.-backed indigenous mercenaries into Laos in April 1981 to find and photograph Americans after satellite imagery showed shadows in a Laotian prison that "looked too long for Asians but just right for Caucasians." The operation, commanded by the DIA representative to the IAG, failed to find Americans, but it did find the front page of the *Washington Post*, suggesting that the camera-wielding Laotians were deployed to generate publicity rather than real intelligence. Unnamed Pentagon sources confessed that "the story [w]as helpful to the Reagan administration's effort to convince prisoner of war families that it is determined to pursue every avenue to rescue any Americans," while Secretary of Defense Caspar Weinberger promised "appropriate action if any of these reports prove to be true."[26]

Appropriate or not, further action followed in November 1982, when retired Green Beret and Vietnam veteran James "Bo" Gritz led four Americans and fifteen Laotian "resistance fighters" on a rescue mission into Laos he dubbed "Operation Lazarus." Within twenty-four hours Gritz was ambushed by a local militia, which captured one of his American POW hunters and killed two of his Laotian mercenaries. Beating a retreat to Thailand, Gritz ran into the Pathet Lao, which chased him to the border. Intended to bring American soldiers back from the dead, Lazarus left two Laotians dead and one American behind. The American was soon released for "$17,500 and forty boxes of medicine," raising obvious questions as to why Laotian officials would not similarly ransom American POWs if they held them, as Gritz alleged.[27]

As this comedy of errors came to light, Gritz and his men were ridiculed as beer can commandos unable to leave the war behind. Even before Lazarus, Gritz compromised his warrior credentials by conducting training exercises at a Florida cheerleading camp. An overwrought "Intelligence Summary and Situation Report" issued on the eve of his foray further undermined his credibility. Proclaiming it "time the POWs came home," Gritz boasted, "If I and my people don't do it, I don't know anyone in Washington who will. . . . Teddy Roosevelt and John Wayne are dead. Hopefully, like the name of this operation, their spirit and resolve live today in the heart of our president, resurrected as those declared dead by our system soon will be." Having placed himself in the pantheon of self-invented warriors, Gritz became a laughingstock when his men told *Soldier of Fortune* that he shed his clothes and equipment as he fled the Pathet Lao, ultimately crossing the Mekong River in his underwear.[28]

Yet Gritz was not the only one to see himself as a hero. Clint Eastwood and William Shatner helped finance his misadventure by paying Gritz

$40,000 for rights to his story. These exemplars of Hollywood masculinity saw Gritz as a "square-jawed, ramrod-straight professional soldier from central casting" who could compete with *Rambo* at the movies.[29] "A modern-day Sergeant York," Shatner raved to Johnny Carson, Gritz was an attractive figure to millions of Americans. "I'm gonna have an orgasm!" ex–Green Beret Terry Smith gushed as he envisioned "shoot[ing] the first commie" as a member of Gritz's team.[30] ROTC instructor Fred Leenhouts admitted that "when I got called for the mission I got goosebumps."[31] For those disgruntled with the recent past, Gritz recalled an earlier ideal of white male dominance. A real-life version of the Hollywood "hard bodies" of the era, Gritz waged war on behalf of those who felt debilitated by feminism, the civil rights movement, and American defeat in Vietnam.[32] Men who derided his failure to live up to the warrior ideal did so not because they disdained that ideal but because Gritz threatened to call it into question by falling short of its purest expression.

At the White House, Gritz was considered "a lone ranger, a swashbuckler, a derring-do type," much like Reagan's on-screen role as Brass Bancroft in the 1940 film *Murder in the Air*, but with real medals and bigger biceps. Reagan shared Gritz's desire to "get something done" for those defeated by Vietnam. "He didn't take five seconds" to authorize the 1981 Laos raid, Richard Allen recalled in his deposition to the Senate Select Committee on POW/MIA Affairs.[33] Its failure did little to diminish Reagan's "belief in the presence of POW's," and in July army intelligence made Gritz "a principal in confirming/denying and definitively locating live PWs," giving him $25,000 in cash and equipment.[34] The army later claimed that it severed ties with Gritz in December, but when Clint Eastwood visited Reagan's Rancho del Cielo to seek final presidential approval for Gritz's raid, Deputy National Security Adviser Bud McFarlane directed John Poindexter "that we not provide a 'green' nor 'red' light to the operation . . . but state only that we must have valid information." "*DIA has told Bo Gritz*," he continued, "*that if it proves valid, we will take action.*"[35]

For a true believer, this was more than enough encouragement. Like Reagan and his staff, Gritz had no use for bright lines of responsibility, congressional oversight, or international law. Rather than discourage him, Reagan's desire to keep him at arm's length fed Gritz's heroic pretensions. "Because none of us are in uniform," he told his men, "it lets the U.S. government off the hook. If we get caught they can say, 'we couldn't control those crazy bastards.' But if we bring back just one live American POW, he becomes the ante for the biggest poker game this nation will ever play."[36]

Here was the authentic voice of the Reagan administration, explaining its preferred mode of foreign policy—privatized and paramilitary, with a heavy dose of the theatrical.[37] Where state institutions had failed, the lone white warrior would succeed. Success was elusive—Gritz failed to rescue POWs—but his mission was less to rescue American POWs than to convince the public that they existed and that Reagan would save them. Gritz saw little difference between publicizing POWs and liberating them. By acting like John Wayne, he would inspire Reagan to act like Teddy Roosevelt; by resurrecting the warrior ethos, he would resurrect missing warriors; by empowering himself he would empower those who followed him.

"Covert operations actually function as spectacle," political scientist Michael Rogin argued in an incisive postmortem of the Iran-Contra affair. His counterintuitive analysis helps explain why Reagan relied on blustering narcissists like Bo Gritz and Oliver North to carry out clandestine foreign policy. "Even where the particular operation is supposed to remain secret, the government wants it known it has the power, secretly, to intervene."[38] In the Lazarus case, Allen predicted leaks but reasoned that Gritz "gave you plausible deniability," so "there was no need to be limp-wristed about this sort of thing."[39] Indeed, Gritz proved better at talking than fighting—in addition to selling his story to Shatner and Eastwood, Gritz gave an interview to *Penthouse* magazine *before* leaving for Laos, inspired a special edition of *Soldier of Fortune*, and appeared on the *Today* show, *20/20*, and *Nightline* upon his return.[40] He even testified before Congress, where he accused skeptical Democrats of covering up MIA abandonment.[41] Hardly "limp-wristed," Gritz became a hero of male bathroom literature, and everyone assumed that Reagan approved, though he never had to say so.

The genius of Reagan's privatized foreign policy was that "paramilitary romanticism and emotional instability . . . *discredit* the operatives if they ever go public," even as these qualities assure that the operative will do precisely that, allowing the president to profit from the publicity without taking responsibility for the failure.[42] This is not to say that Reagan wanted Gritz to fail. "Fantasies about our enemies," Rogin reminds us, "operate not in the first place in popular culture but at the most secret levels of decision making." Reagan surely hoped Gritz would succeed. But knowing the risks, his staff disavowed his involvement in "the spectacle they produce[d] for one another" while assuring MIA insiders that "the operations that are going on are of a covert nature."[43]

"When many Americans felt deeply wounded by failure in Vietnam, profoundly afraid of risks that might repeat it, yet still determined that their nation police the world's bullies," covert missions provided an illusion of power.[44] High-stakes, low-cost paramilitary operations were espe-

All seventy-two pages of the Spring 1983 issue of *Soldier of Fortune* were devoted to the POW/MIA issue, nearly half to Bo Gritz's clandestine border crossings. (Courtesy *Soldier of Fortune* magazine)

cially pleasing to the movement conservatives who controlled the federal government but still associated it with the liberalism of an earlier age. To conservatives, national revival could only originate from outside the liberal state. Its agents could not save the white men abandoned in Vietnam. Only those free from its corrupting influence could restore order. By funneling public power and money into privatized paramilitary operations, conservative leaders mediated between their disdain for the state and their desire to wield its weapons.

The public-private partnerships that resulted gave great sway to unelected activists, none more than Ann Mills Griffiths, who took part in a little-known operation under Reagan to funnel funds to anticommunist "Lao resistance elements" in return for MIA remains and information. The plan, hatched by the IAG in 1982, exposed by reporters in 1987, and documented by the Senate Select Committee in 1992, involved the deposit of private donations into the bank account of Support Our POW/MIAs (SOP), the California-based group Griffiths controlled before taking over the League, then transferring those funds to Southeast Asia.[45] Between 1982 and 1985 this scheme diverted between $150,000 and $500,000 to operatives in the region, much of it to a shadowy figure named Mushtaq Ahmed Diwan with no clear ties to the MIA issue.[46] At the same time, Republican congressmen and MIA activists John LeBoutillier of New York and Billy Hendon of North Carolina distributed $200,000 in medical supplies inside Laos.[47] Having been first elected on Reagan's coattails, LeBoutillier and Hendon also solicited conservative donors on SOP's behalf. Burt Hurlburt, Nelson Bunker Hunt, and Ellen St. John Garwood, famous for their contributions to Nicaraguan Contras, gave thousands of dollars to the scheme, which was coordinated by NSC Director of Political Affairs Richard Childress.[48] Griffiths, who worked closely with Childress on the IAG, then directed her contacts at SOP to transfer the funds.[49]

Griffiths and Childress acknowledged their involvement in this scheme to the Senate Select Committee, but called LeBoutillier the driving force behind the operation and pleaded ignorance of his activities. LeBoutillier, Hurlburt, and the leaders of SOP painted a different picture, telling committee investigators that Griffiths and Childress ran the operation.[50] Much of the archival record that could settle this question remains classified or, in the case of the IAG, nonexistent, but available evidence strongly suggests White House coordination. Reagan knew about and supported LeBoutillier's activities in Laos, approving $200,000 in "medicinals" purchased at public expense, and an additional $8,000 in travel expenses. "We should make it plain we are impressed with what they have accomplished," Reagan told his chief of staff James Baker in a handwritten note pertaining to LeBoutillier and Hendon, adding that "a live one [POW] would be sensational."[51] Days later the DIA representative to the IAG, Admiral Allan Paulson, noted in his PW/MIA Daily Report that the two men "had the ear of the president."[52] As late as January 1983 Childress wrote to National Security Adviser William Clark recommending that the NSC "continue monitoring and helping, as possible, the LeBoutillier initiative."[53] Both Childress and his White House superiors, up to and including the president, approved of LeBoutillier's attempts to trade goods and cash for captives. Combined with the fact that Griffiths and Childress went out of their way to facilitate the money transfers, and later used the SOP account to finance Griffiths's travel to Vietnam as part of the 1984 Armitage delegation, it is hard to believe that they were LeBoutillier's pawns. To the contrary, all evidence suggests this "was something that had more than the casual blessing of the White House," as one donor to Griffiths's SOP account put it.[54]

The IAG enterprise bore a striking resemblance to the subsequent Iran-Contra scandal. Like Oliver North's "neat idea" of trading arms for hostages and giving the proceeds to contra rebels, it used funds intended to win the release of American captives to finance anticommunist "freedom fighters," only in this case the captives and guerillas were in the same country, and unlike the Beirut hostages, the captives in Laos were imagined rather than real. The 6,000–8,000 man Laotian resistance was smaller and less organized than the contras—more like the "Iranian moderates" North claimed to be working with than an effective fighting force.[55] But the basic plan, players, and preoccupations were the same, with the same Texas tycoons donating large sums of money at the behest of eerily similar NSC officials. Both Vietnam veterans, Childress and North came to the White House in January 1982 as active-duty mid-career officers on loan from the Pentagon. Assigned to "hold charts" for Allen as he briefed senators on the sale of military aircraft, each turned his assignment into something more permanent by freelancing on behalf of captive Americans after Allen was forced out of the NSC soon after their arrival.[56] Moving to the political-military affairs directorate upon its creation in 1983, both men served there until the office was abolished in late 1986 once the scope of its illegal activities became clear, at which point Childress became Director of Asian Affairs and North was shown the door.[57]

There is no evidence that Childress inspired North's activities, but their remarkable physical, institutional, and ideological proximity makes it impossible to believe that they were ignorant of one another's schemes. Still, it must be emphasized that these men represented a movement, not a criminal conspiracy. They moved in the same circles and shared similar concerns not from some sinister plot but because they were part of an administration and a movement enthralled by captivity in Vietnam. Each called on operatives from the MIA lobby to carry out his plans—Childress used Griffiths and LeBoutillier while North tapped John Singlaub and Richard Secord to run his "Enterprise" and Ross Perot to finance his operations—because they knew and trusted them.[58] Such people were not hard to find in the conservative movement. Their prominence in the Reagan administration reflected their importance to the movement he led.

Commentators have long recognized the hold that hostages had on Reagan. Others have held that Iran-Contra was an institutional or ideological response to defeat in Vietnam. "Absent Vietnam there would have been no Iran-Contra," journalist Robert Timberg wrote in a succinct statement of what he helped make conventional wisdom.[59] Yet no one has noted that captivity was the connection between Vietnam and Iran-Contra for Reagan and those around him. Reagan made no distinction between hostages and prisoners of war—"last night I got out of the habit of calling them hostages," he remarked in the fourth sentence of his inaugural cabinet meeting; "I called them prisoners of war."[60] His history with the League taught him that there was a seamless progression leading from the abandonment of MIAs in Southeast Asia to the seizure of American hostages in the Middle East. And if Reagan's customary "inscrutability allowed his bureaucratic servants to project upon him their fondest hopes," his obvious emotional connection to American captives—Griffiths recalled "tears in the president's eyes when I've talked to him about it"—encouraged his staff to be particularly aggressive in pursuing them.[61]

NOT TO RESOLVE THE ISSUE BUT TO KEEP IT GOING

"A cottage industry specializing in the creation and dissemination of false POW/MIA information and 'POW/MIA hunting' has emerged," the Senate Select Committee noted in its *Final Report*. "Certain individuals provide, for a fee, illegal cross-border transportation . . . armed escort, mission coordination and related services. It appears these same individuals and others provide the 'intelligence' that prompts the mission in the first instance—a textbook perfect industry because it creates the demand and fills it too."[62] This indictment pinpointed the power and pitfalls of Reagan's POW/MIA policy. As in Iran-Contra, where Americans were taken hostage to preserve a triangle trade that served not just their captors but lined the pockets of Americans and their Contra allies, perverse incentives produced the illusion of American captivity in Southeast Asia. Political, diplomatic, and financial rewards, along with ideological imperatives, produced a flood of bone fragments, fingerprints, dog tags, and photos, mostly fake, along with rescue missions, congressional hearings, and media events that served the MIA lobby and its administration allies but soon escaped official control.[63] The goal for all sides, one DIA analyst told Select Committee investigators, became "not to resolve the POW, remains, bones or dog tag problems soon, but to keep it going."[64]

Because no proof of life was required, producing and peddling information pertaining to POWs was far easier than hostage taking. With IAG money to be had and bounties like the $2.4 million reward put up by the American Defense Institute for the return of a live POW, profiteers produced ample evidence of captive Americans.[65] Thousands of "live sightings" and "dog tag reports" gave the impression that Vietnam and Laos were crawling with Americans. Based on military identification discs, such reports grew in number to over 1,000 per year by decade's end. Their sheer volume convinced many Americans that their countrymen remained in bondage.[66] More careful observers knew that nearly all these reports were obvious fakes. Only 3 percent referred to American MIAs—the rest named Americans who had already returned from the war.[67]

So many reports flooded in that by mid-decade DIA analysts were convinced that they represented "a Vietnamese directed misinformation campaign."[68] Like the contemporaneous warning that Le Thi Anh was a communist double agent, this analysis may have been meant to slow refugee reports that were swamping government agencies, or to prevent them from dictating U.S. foreign policy toward Vietnam and Laos. It also may have reflected the attribution of occult powers to Asian foes, mixed with the rise of "Straussian" intelligence after the Vietnam War, whereby assumptions about the nature of repressive regimes was given greater weight than verifiable data about them.[69] Retired DIA director Eugene Tighe sensed "a centuries old display of Oriental superiority"—"a ritual of victory" reflecting "the ingenuity of Asiatic labyrinthine thought."[70] But when the DIA questioned refugee reports of POW survival, MIA activists alleged an official "mindset to debunk" evidence pointing to captive Americans, creating further tension between activists and government agencies.[71]

Despite the limits and prejudices of DIA's analysis, there were reasons to suspect that communist officials facilitated the rash of live sightings and dog-tag reports. Party officials, particularly at the local level, were susceptible to the same incentives that enticed American officials to trade in such information. Though most of the millions put up to rescue MIAs ended up in the hands of unscrupulous Americans, the percentage that made it into Vietnam and Laos represented a fortune in a region where per capita income was $250 per year.[72] Party leaders did not have to deal directly with Americans to profit—like their American counterparts, they were more likely to work through middlemen who knew the value of MIA information in refugee camps and on the black market. And the fact that the same names associated with the same locales appeared again and again in refugee reporting indicated that such information may have come from a single source rather than being generated spontaneously by thousands of individuals.[73]

There were also historical reasons for DIA's suspicions. Since the Paris Peace Talks, Vietnamese officials had linked accounting to economic aid, and they continued this linkage in the 1980s. In the midst of negotiations over the first JCRC field excavation inside Vietnam since the war's end, the party newspaper *Nhan Dan* called it "preposterous that while Mr. Reagan is imposing on Vietnam the responsibility of seeking American MIAs . . . he is washing his hands of all responsibility of the United States for having caused suffering and death to millions of Vietnamese, and its duty to help heal the wounds of war in Vietnam."[74] Mutually understood code for reconstruction aid, "healing the wounds of war" remained the price for Vietnamese cooperation. While Americans refused to pay state-to-state reparations, when Nguyen Co Thach told Childress "a contribution was needed for the purpose of continuing the [accounting] efforts" in 1984, Childress told him that the U.S. government would "underwrite the costs of such surveys and excavations."[75] The JCRC paid $120,665 in labor costs and rental fees to conduct a three-week search of a crash site near Hanoi the following year. No remains were found, but a framework was established that allowed "joint field operations" in return for steep fees. Though far short of the billions Nixon promised, the fees were substantial—$9.5 million annually throughout the 1990s—adding up to a considerable sum over time.[76]

Vietnamese policymakers never hesitated to demand money in return for an accounting. "If we can help the Americans on MIAs," Foreign Minister Thach told reporters in 1987, "then the Americans can help us heal our wounds of war."[77] This does not prove that they planned or coordinated the dissemination of MIA reports to American authorities and activists, but clearly the trade intensified concern for MIAs inside the United States and placed pressure on Reagan to act on their behalf, which raised the value of Vietnam's MIA bargaining chips. At the very least, Vietnamese officials were unlikely to rein it in.

Those who see the MIA issue solely as an American creation have viewed MIAs as a pretext to punish Vietnam—a ruse to deny it reconstruction aid, an excuse to lock it out of the global economy, a myth to reverse the war's outcome and responsibility for waging it.[78] Hesitant to blame the victim and reluctant to parrot dubious theories from the MIA lobby, scholars have ignored or minimized Vietnam's part in MIA diplomacy and focused on

U.S. officials. But the Vietnamese were never mere victims of the war—they were also its victors. They won by finding ways to endure U.S. aggression and to ultimately turn it to their advantage.

As crazed as Tighe's "ritual of victory" theory may seem, it properly identifies the war's winners and losers and it accurately perceives that the Vietnamese pursued their own agenda in the postwar period, often in opposition to historical revisionists on the American side. Vietnam's insistent linkage of its "wounds of war" to MIA accounting was a persistent reminder of its own official memory of the war, where righteous sacrifice in pursuit of ultimate victory loomed large. To Americans it may seem that Vietnam won little worth having and paid an enormous price in the process. From its admission to the UN in 1977 to the end of the U.S. trade embargo in 1994, Vietnam profited little from MIAs save for a few million dollars in crash-site concessions and humanitarian assistance. Yet even this paltry aid was more than what vengeful Americans wanted to give. And by refusing to relinquish their official memory of the war, party leaders preserved something that may have been more valuable to them—their legitimacy as national leaders.

But no one benefited more from the resurgence of the MIA issue than the League, though even here the story was complicated. At first glance, League membership skyrocketed in the 1980s. "The upswing is amazing," former executive director Carol Bates told reporters at the League's 1981 meeting.[79] If League leaders are to be believed, the group's growth under Reagan was astonishing. In a 1988 interview Griffiths claimed 3,600 League members, up from just 500 ten years prior.[80] Like the surge in the POW/MIA population after 1980, though, League growth in the Reagan years was largely an illusion.

It is hard to penetrate to the reality of League numbers, since the group became secretive about its membership after Griffiths took the helm, but it clearly had far fewer members than it claimed. According to her critics inside the POW/MIA movement, Griffiths used her exclusive control over League member data to exaggerate the League's membership and misrepresent its views. One board member informed Congress that "hundreds of family members are counted as members because they filed an original application years ago. In fact, many do not participate in the League actively because they disagree with the current positions of the League."[81] The NSC estimated that "700 family members" attended Reagan's 1988 address to the group, which is probably an accurate measure of its active membership since those who declined free travel to a presidential event were unlikely to take part in less exalted League activities.[82] This number would indicate that some 200 relatives joined the League in the 1980s, growth that came primarily from MIA children too young to join in the 1970s and the admission of KIA/BNR families ineligible for membership until the League relaxed its bylaws in 1983.[83] Few if any of the "Old Guard" who left the League in the 1970s returned, meaning the group remained smaller than it was during the war.[84]

If the League's membership grew more modestly than reported, its finances grew more rapidly than most observers knew. When Reagan took office the League was nearly bankrupt, with $27,000 in the bank and expenditures exceeding income by $2,540 per month.[85] By 1982 its revenues approached $600,000, and by 1983 they exceeded $900,000.[86] Over these same three years, Griffiths's salary doubled from the $22,677 to $45,000. When Reagan left office her salary had reached $61,000, while the League's payroll had grown to $145,871. With revenues of $3.5 million between 1988 and 1990, Griffiths could afford to add staff.[87] She could also pay for the publicity campaigns and direct-mail fundraisers that kept the money coming, and which gave the appearance of a far larger organization.

In fact, the League represented only a portion of a vast POW/MIA fundraising operation that the Senate Select Committee calculated had raised over $30 million between 1985 and 1992.[88] Some POW/MIA organizations were little more than a single activist backed by professional fundraisers who used the unprincipled front man to "prospect" among donors.[89] Operation Rescue, Inc., a POW rescue outfit out of Thailand consisting of a lone retired army officer named Jack Bailey, raised $2.2 million between 1985 and 1990, spending $2 million of that sum on further fundraising. Rather than finding missing Americans, Operation Rescue's true purpose was to create "dissatisfaction with the status quo" that would drum up financial contributions.[90] Its fundraiser, Bruce Eberle of Bruce W. Eberle & Associates, Inc., called the shots, not Bailey. When Bailey tried to "discontinue all prospecting mail," Eberle "ran up a tremendous amount of bills for prospecting and postal loans . . . against our wishes."[91] A direct mail pioneer who raised millions for Reagan in 1976 and 1980 before taking on as clients Congressman Jack Kemp, Senator Orrin Hatch, and the College Republican National Committee, Eberle used Operation Rescue to build donor lists and pad his bottom line while keeping frustrated grassroots conservatives mobilized.[92]

Privately, Griffiths worried that such profiteering could compromise League legitimacy, siphon off contributions from her flagship organization, and confuse concerned citizens, but there was little she could say or do publicly without calling the MIA lobby she led into disrepute.[93] Besides, the fervor that fringe groups drummed up enhanced her stature as the movement's leader, just as the League's reputation as a "non-partisan" family organization lent legitimacy to those who used the MIA issue to profit from MIA donors.

Clearly, the League benefited from the public concern that more aggressive groups generated. But as in the Nixon years, it also profited from official assistance that belied its anti-government rhetoric. Reagan's staff went out of its way to help Griffiths and her organization as "a friend of this administration."[94] After meeting with League leaders in 1982, McFarlane asked Childress, "What kinds of follow-up action would be most effective in meeting the grievances that were expressed?" "Board members stated that Defense contractor contributions had trailed off," he added, before offering "to see if Liddy Dole's office can't put the squeeze on the contractors."[95] Soon even the president was calling on all Americans "to give these families your help and your support."[96]

Despite little movement on MIA accounting in Reagan's first term, such assistance brought satisfaction to MIA activists. Secretary of Defense Weinberger's appearance at the League's 1982 meeting was the first by a senior official since Gerald Ford's visit in 1976. Weinberger also arranged for commercial air carriers to offer free flights to League families traveling to the event. When Reagan reinstated the military airlift for his January 1983 address to the League, he confirmed that the group was back where it belonged.[97] Legislation passed later that year perpetuated the airlift until 1996, when the Clinton administration reverted to commercial travel vouchers.[98] With presidential appearances before the League in 1983, 1984, and 1988 along with speeches by Vice President George Bush in 1985, by National Security Adviser Bud McFarlane in 1984 and 1985, by the chairman of the Joint Chiefs of Staff in 1986, and by Secretary of State George Shultz and National Security Adviser Colin Powell in 1987, the League meeting was a hot ticket once more. And speeches by President Bush and Secretary of Defense Dick Cheney in 1989 suggested a seamless transition after Reagan stepped down.

Appearances mattered. Just as League members applauded Reagan's covert operations—despite their failure to find MIAs—as a sign of presidential willingness to act on their behalf, they welcomed face time with senior officials as a sign of respect for their sacrifice, which they defined as the loss of their rightful place in the social order as much as the loss of a loved one. By restoring them to prominence, Reagan rectified their marginalization. With more members, more money, and more access, the League could put pressure on government agencies and attract media coverage.

For Griffiths, money and power were ends in themselves, and not for megalomaniacal reasons alone, as her critics would have it, but as the just rewards for MIA sacrifice. These rewards restored the social contract that was broken when Nixon, Ford, Carter, and the House Select Committee minimized the suffering of MIA families. A sentimental nationalist himself, Reagan understood the League's desire for recognition. When he assured its members that "their government . . . would be *semper fi*—'always faithful,'" or when he made their black and white banner the first flag other than the American flag ever flown over the White House, he embraced MIA families and their symbols of sacrifice in a way that moved them emotionally and elevated them politically.[99] League newsletters celebrated "the tremendous boost" such acts gave the group—attracting TV coverage, generating a spike in donations, and putting the group "in a better position, with a more positive prognosis for resolving the issue, than at any time since the League originated."[100] Whether presidential rhetoric moved the League any closer to "resolving" the MIA issue was debatable. Board chairman Earl Hopper responded to Griffiths's sanguine assessment with a sour rejoinder: "Effort should be devoted to securing results" rather "than to flattering and misleading the families."[101] But official flattery paid dividends for the League.

None was more remarkable or ultimately more divisive than the League's incorporation into the Reagan and Bush administrations through the person of Ann Mills Griffiths. As "a vital member of the POW/MIA Interagency Group," Griffiths "participated as a delegation member in all policy-level negotiations on the POW/MIA issue since 1982," according to the Reagan administration's *Final Interagency Report*.[102] Between 1982 and 1992 she "participated in at least 20 of the 25 official and semi-official meetings" with the Vietnamese, and met privately with them at least four times.[103]

Without IAG minutes, not regularly kept after 1982, it is impossible to reconstruct a complete picture of Griffiths's influence, but it was clearly extraordinary given that she had no more than a high school diploma, held no public office, and possessed no foreign policy experience before joining the IAG.[104] Soon after William Clark became the new national security adviser in 1982, Childress briefed him on Griffiths, detailing her "frustrations that need to be understood" before Clark met this "de-facto member of the government," an inversion of the expected hierarchy.[105] Frank Carlucci was similarly advised to meet Griffiths when he took the top job at NSC in 1986, with Childress noting that she had met "the President on several occasions and *all* of your predecessors."[106] A 1984 memo from Bud McFarlane to the Secretaries of State and Defense and the Joint Chiefs of Staff relayed a list of League demands, including the blacklisting of the powerful House Veteran's Affairs Committee chairman Sonny Montgomery for his leadership of the House Select Committee, along with the directive that "we would appreciate a report on actions to address their other expressed concerns" in three weeks time.[107] Democratic congressman Stephen Solarz, who worked with Griffiths frequently as head of the subcommittee on Asian and Pacific Affairs, understated the case when he told the *New York Times* that "Griffiths has carved out a very interesting role for herself."[108] Griffiths, he assessed, "kept this issue alive in the hearts of the American people and the consciousness of Congress."[109]

The IAG was the source of her influence. There was never any thought of ending the IAG after Reagan's election, only plans for its expansion. At its first meeting in the new administration, Richard Allen dropped by to express "the President's interest in the PW/MIA issue" and to offer "his help when the group thought it appropriate."[110] Learning that Deputy Assistant Secretary of Defense for East Asia Richard Armitage was "very interested in SEA [Southeast Asia] and POW/MIA," its members invited him to join them, and by the end of the year he had replaced Negroponte as the IAG's ranking member.[111] With Childress's arrival in January 1982, the group's nucleus was complete. Griffiths, Childress, and Armitage remained in place and grew in power through Reagan's two terms, with Armitage named assistant secretary of defense for international security affairs in 1984 and Childress ascending to director of Asian affairs in 1987. Griffiths rose alongside them, accompanying Armitage, Childress, and Paul Wolfowitz, the assistant secretary of state for East Asian affairs, to Hanoi in 1986 for the most senior bilateral talks since the war's end—her fifth trip there in four years—and briefing the president and his top advisers for forty-five minutes upon her return.[112] At the League convention later that year, Solarz remarked that "in a very real sense she has become a part of the governmental team here in Washington."[113] The State Department's director of Vietnam, Laos, and Cambodia affairs at the time called her "the fourth branch of government."[114] Even the Vietnamese knew her importance, citing her as "the leader of 20 million Republicans" in one intelligence report.[115]

From her IAG redoubt, Griffiths elevated the MIA issue to "the highest national priority." Though always more rhetorical than real, this designation resulted in significant policy changes. The official line on the likelihood of live prisoners went from "we have no indications at this time that there are any Americans alive in Indochina" to the "assumption that at least some Americans are still held captive."[116] Impossible to disprove, this formulation became the basis for a government-run "public awareness"

Ann Mills Griffiths briefs President Ronald Reagan and his national security advisers upon her return from an official visit to Vietnam in January 1986. The officials depicted in the top photo include, from left, Deputy Assistant to the President for National Security Affairs Don Fortier, White House Chief of Staff Donald Regan, National Security Adviser John Poindexter, Assistant Secretary of State for East Asian Affairs Paul Wolfowitz, President Reagan, Ann Mills Griffiths, NSC Director of Political-Military Affairs Richard Childress, Vice President George Bush, and Secretary of State George Shultz. (Courtesy Ronald Reagan Library)

campaign that "served to sensitize the American people to the need for support of revitalized official efforts." It also moved MIA accounting to the top of the U.S. agenda in Indochina, elevating it as a "humanitarian" problem that must be solved before the "political issues" put forward by the SRV could be addressed.[117] Because the Vietnamese insisted that their own humanitarian issues be resolved in return for accounting, the two sides were at an impasse through most of Reagan's presidency, with progress coming only late in his second term.[118] Even with the 1987 appointment of the retired chairman of the Joint Chiefs, General John W. Vessey Jr., as the special presidential emissary to Hanoi on the POW/MIA issue, normalization of relations was six years away, thanks in part to Griffiths, whom Secretary of State Lawrence Eagleburger later called a "significant factor" in slowing normalization. A survey of twenty policymakers from the Reagan, Bush, and Clinton administrations found that officials ranked the League the most important force in shaping policy toward Vietnam, with twice the muscle of business lobbyists and three times that of pro-normalization groups.[119]

Why Griffiths supported a stalemate on the MIA issue is unclear. The League criticized Gerald Ford and Henry Kissinger for refusing to negotiate for MIAs in the mid-1970s, and Griffiths "suggested moving the accounting discussions to a higher government to government level" as late as June 1981, to "find out what *quid* the SRV wants."[120] Once such discussions began in 1982, she routinely reported her involvement to the League, suggesting its members welcomed diplomacy. But as she became immersed in the give-and-take of diplomacy, she grew more concerned with thwarting Vietnamese advantage than with rapid accounting, prompting some League members to question her priorities. In one of his increasingly strident attacks on Griffiths, Hopper charged that "White House puppeteers were confident they could fatten her ego with a unique, exciting, and glamorously visible place in world diplomacy, a world she would fight to keep herself in at all costs."[121] According to this view, Griffiths so identified with the Reagan administration that she could no longer distinguish between its interests, her self-interest, and League interests.

"Tremendous progress" had occurred under Reagan, Griffiths reassured restive members, "but it is often very difficult to see." Efforts to recover POWs, she scolded, "must *not* be visible if they are to be successful." In place of results, she cited "high level government statements" as proof of the "high priority assigned by President Reagan."[122] But skeptics sensed a winking disingenuousness in Reagan's references to "sacrifices they made, and may still be making," given his lack of urgency to recover missing men.[123]

When the administration announced in 1985 that Vietnam had accepted "the US-proposed two-year plan to expedite resolution of the issue," former League chairwoman Anne Hart asked, "Does that mean really resolving it or just clearing the books?"[124] "I'm just distrustful of the government's position," Gregory McDonald told reporters when his brother's remains were returned in 1985. "I don't know what [its] motivation is."[125]

Whether Reagan still sought accountability or was ready to accept a 1970s-style resolution was the question that haunted MIA activists headed into his second term. Alert to their concerns, Reagan included the lines "we write no last chapters; we close no books" when he addressed the MIA issue in the 1984 campaign and beyond. In this sense he evoked the war as a disruptive presence in American life while simultaneously using it to assert the need for national unity. But to turn the MIA issue, which Reagan called the war's "sorest wound," into Keith Beattie's "scar that binds" required not just proof of injury, but signs of healing.[126] And as Reagan enlisted the League as the beneficiaries of his healing powers, a growing number rejected him and his intermediary, Ann Mills Griffiths.

THIS WASN'T ANYTHING THAT WAS NOBLE

The MIA movement's suspicions intensified during Reagan's 1984 reelection campaign, which was designed to "paint Reagan as the personification of all that is right with, or heroized by, America."[127] Watching as the White House "kept apple pie and the flag going the whole time" alienated those still haunted by the ghosts of Vietnam, especially when the remains of missing servicemen were placed at the center of the celebration.[128] The first sign of rebellion surfaced in April after Caspar Weinberger announced plans to bury an Unknown Soldier from the Vietnam War at the Tomb of the Unknowns in Arlington National Cemetery on Memorial Day 1984. The news was greeted with alarm by MIA activists, who worried that the ceremony marked an end to the war they were still waging.

The League had opposed plans to bury a Vietnam Unknown since the idea was first broached in the 1970s, and Griffiths had beat back an attempt to inter an Unknown early in Reagan's first term by threatening "to inform the families" that "sufficient information is already available to narrow the identification process to a small number of individuals" on both sets of remains being considered for interment.[129] With her security clearance, Griffiths knew "the state of identification on each set of remains, the fact that records have been shredded and the propensity of the Army to push for early action," Childress warned his superiors.[130] Should she publicize all she knew, "rather than 'heal the wounds' of Vietnam, they would be reopened."[131]

At Childress's insistence, the Pentagon delayed interment and resumed its investigation of the available remains. But the urge to bury a Vietnam Unknown persisted. For those who shared the vision of noble war, only the Tomb of the Unknowns could restore "the dignity of the soldier and the dignity of the nation by linking the two at the root."[132] As League activists worked to scuttle the idea, the vfw rank and file demanded the burial of a Vietnam Unknown at that group's 1982 convention, and forty-four members of Congress co-sponsored House Concurrent Resolution 413, urging such a step, later that year.[133]

Weinberger's decision to proceed with interment in April 1984 ostensibly followed "an exhaustive effort to identify the few unidentified remains" in U.S. custody.[134] "We used every trick, but we can't match him to any known missing soldier," Pentagon spokesman Robert Shields avowed.[135] Subsequent revelations proved that such claims were exaggerated. Based on the time and place of their recovery, the remains designated for the Tomb had to belong to air force lieutenant Michael Blassie or army captain Rodney Strobridge, with all the material effects found with the bones—including a flight suit, parachute, life raft, ejection seat, and Michael Blassie's ID and dog tags—pointing to Blassie. The remains were designated "Believed to be Blassie" from the time of their recovery in 1972 until that designation was lifted in 1980 on the basis of two unreliable identification procedures that pointed to Strobridge.[136] In declaring the remains "unknown" on the basis of conflicting forensic and material evidence, authorities sought "not to know the dead but to unknow them," to revisit Franny Nudelman's characterization of the nationalist aesthetic.[137] As one unnamed lab official later professed, declaring the remains Unknown "was politically expedient. At best it was premature. . . . Perhaps it was appropriate to the Vietnam War. So much else about it was political."[138]

In that sense, the controversy that followed Weinberger's announcement that "we are now able to honor our Vietnam veterans by placing one of their fallen comrades-in-arms alongside the national heroes of previous wars at the Tomb of the Unknowns" was also appropriate.[139] Once the administration decided to proceed, Griffiths warned her restive board that the League could not afford to "alienate the highest levels of the U.S. government and the political side of the White House" through continued opposition to interment.[140] Ignoring her counsel, the League board declared interment "morally wrong" and urged Reagan "to postpone this ceremony until any Americans still held captive are returned."[141] And it threatened legal action to force officials to provide it with information on the remains selected for the Tomb, a step Griffiths blasted as "a political embarrassment during an election year."[142] With burial just a month away, the board hardly had time to mount a serious legal challenge. But behind the scenes disapprobation inspired an abortive attempt to replace Griffiths at that summer's convention.[143] And lingering hard feelings moved MIA activist Ted Sampley, one of Griffiths's harshest critics, to pursue information on the remains in the Tomb until he established in the July 1994 edition of his *U.S. Veteran Dispatch* that they indeed belonged to Michael Blassie, charges which led to the exhumation and identification of the Vietnam Unknown as Blassie in 1998.[144]

More immediately, League opposition manifested itself in the conflicted eulogy Reagan delivered at the interment ceremony. Calling the Vietnam War a noble cause three times in his ten-minutes address, he expressed hope that by honoring a Vietnam Unknown, Americans "could transcend the tragedies of the past" and "trust each other again." Yet as he spoke of transcendence, he acknowledged that some "fear this ceremony writes a final chapter, leaving those they love forgotten." Reagan spoke of MIAs at such length—one-third of his address was devoted to their loss—that the nation he sought to reinvigorate seemed subordinate to "a small but brave group of Americans—the families of those still missing in action."[145] That such concessions were necessary demonstrated the difficulty even a master illusionist like Reagan faced in conjuring the nation as a "deep, horizontal comradeship" after the bloody triage of Vietnam.[146]

Seeking to repair relations with the League, Reagan invited MIA families to the White House for POW/MIA Recognition Day in July.[147] One of many stirring scenes that made up his Rose Garden campaign, Reagan's pledge that "we will not rest until that formation is complete," as the Navy's Blue Angels aerobatic team roared through a missing-man formation over the South Lawn, played well on the nightly news.[148] And by extending such an invitation to the families on the eve of the League convention, Reagan's White House handlers helped Griffiths gather enough loyal voters in Washington to replace "adversarial members of the League Board" with those Childress called "believers," in hotly contested elections at the League's 1984 meeting. After sitting on the dais with Reagan and receiving his personal endorsement, Griffiths remained executive director, which helped earn Childress McFarlane's hearty praise. "It's been a stormy year Dick," McFarlane wrote in his own hand, "but you've made real gains which will last. Very, very well done."[149]

Among those gains were two notable achievements announced at the

Surrounded by American flags and U.S. servicemen, President Ronald Reagan presides at the funeral for an Unknown Soldier from the Vietnam War at the Arlington National Cemetery Memorial Amphitheater, Memorial Day, 1984. (Courtesy Ronald Reagan Library)

Recognition Day ceremony: the repatriation of "the remains of several more U.S. servicemen" from Vietnam, and an agreement reached the night before to excavate the crash site of an AC-130 gunship shot down near Pakse, Laos, in 1972.[150] After the stasis of the past six years, these steps marked an important acceleration in accounting efforts. The first operation of its kind since the war's end, the Pakse excavation would soon yield 50,000 bone fragments, which CILHI quickly identified as the thirteen men aboard the AC-130 when it was shot down.[151] Hailed as a "big, big breakthrough" by the League's front office, the Pakse agreement became the basis for an ongoing program of joint field activities, beginning with the first U.S.-led excavation inside postwar Vietnam in November 1985.[152] In each case, the Reagan administration paid for communist cooperation, with famine-stricken Laos receiving 5,000 tons of rice, $5,000 in medicine, and $101,848 in fees, and the Vietnamese government earning $120,665.[153] With Reagan reelected to a second term and their own economy in freefall, the Vietnamese could no longer afford to hold out for more.[154] "1985 will be a year of progress on the MIA issue," Vietnam's UN ambassador told Griffiths in January. In March 1985, Vietnam accepted the IAG's two-year plan, returning thirty-eight American remains over the course of the year, and allowing the crash site's excavation in November.[155] A corner had been turned. "We know of hundreds more such sites," League spokesperson Mary Currall told reporters, "and hope there will be many more excavations."[156]

Others were less hopeful. When Anne Hart was notified that her husband's remains were found at Pakse, "the news made her 'edgy . . . because it's not that neat and tidy.'" A League firebrand purged from the board after the Unknown Soldier fight, Hart refused to accept the identification, demanding a second opinion, which the army refused. Taking her case to court, she won a court order allowing Dr. Michael Charney, the director of the Center for Human Identification at Colorado State University, to examine the remains. Charney was "horrified" by what he found: seven bone fragments, none greater than six inches in length. "The fragments were so minute, there was no way they could be identified," Charney reported, calling the identification "incompetence of the worst sort." While some Pakse families considered Hart's actions "intolerable and outrageous," others who might have accepted remains now had doubts. James Fuller's family opened his flag-draped coffin to find a "total amount of remains [that] could have fit in the palm of one hand" atop a neatly pressed uniform.[157] Families who had buried remains from earlier repatriations also grew suspicious. "Was this what I buried?" Kathryn Fanning asked, "a handful of bones?" Exhuming the remains she buried eleven months before, she asked Charney and forensic anthropologist Dr. Clyde C. Snow to review the remains. Both ruled out a positive identification from the bone fragments CILHI had given her.[158] A third forensic expert, Dr. George Gill of the University of Wyoming, reviewed the Fuller and Fanning remains, along with those of Captain Milton Vescelius. He concluded the identifications reflected "carelessness, incompetence, fabrication of data, or some combination of these things."[159]

Outraged, Hart, Fanning, and Fuller called a press conference in September where they displayed Fuller's remains before the assembled news media. Footage from the event was later featured on ABC's newsmagazine 20/20 in a segment appropriately titled "MIAs: The Story That Will Not Die." Meanwhile, Fuller's nephew continued to exhibit what may or may not have been his uncle's remains as an example of government deceit. "They can't threaten me," he told a reporter, "because I've got the bones. . . . I said they'll be returned only when Mr. Fuller is declared missing again and they actively look for him."[160]

Public reaction to this bizarre controversy focused on the quality of science at CILHI rather than its more macabre elements, though a ghoulish quality lurked beneath the surface of most media coverage. Three leading forensic experts were dispatched to the lab in December to review its procedures. They reported to Congress that while "the routine cases reviewed over the past three years have been strong identifications," the lab's facilities and staff were "between inadequate and barely adequate." They concluded that "hopelessly commingled remains," such as those found at Pakse, were "unidentifiable" and "should be accepted and presented as such." The fault, all agreed, was not in concluding that the crewmembers onboard the AC-130 that crashed at Pakse were dead, but in bending the evidence to prove it. "Most of these men have died," Charney told the Investigations Subcommittee of the House Armed Services Committee in September 1986, but "what has to be done is not to give them fragments of bone and say this is yours and this is yours and this is yours."[161]

Instead of imposing new standards for the identification of commingled remains, lab authorities responded to this criticism by quadrupling their staff and purchasing $200,000 worth of equipment, including sinks with hot water and air conditioning. "To give us the credibility that is felt we need," as he grudgingly explained in 1987 testimony before Congress, the lab's commander, Lieutenant Colonel Johnnie Webb, replaced head scientist Tadao Furue, whose lowly bachelor's degree had become an embarrassment, with Dr. Ellis Kerley from the University of Maryland.[162] Kerley, whom Webb would fire in 1991 while he was serving as president of the American Academy of Forensic Sciences, soon realized he had been brought on board for cosmetic reasons. As Kerley told Senate Select Committee investigators that year, Webb's attitude was "sort of like getting educated by owning books, rather than reading them." Webb, who had run the lab since 1976, "refused to admit that there was ever anything amiss in the operation of CILHI."[163] So did Griffiths. As if to illustrate Kerley's point about buying books but not reading them, she informed her members that Furue "will continue as the Senior Anthropologist" but had "finally been given the opportunity" to "begin studies part-time at the University of Hawaii to gain additional academic credentials" and to publish his "self-developed techniques of anthropological comparison" for scientists unfamiliar with his methods.[164] Furue's sudden death in 1988 ended this arrangement, but both Webb and Griffiths continue to lead their respective organizations today.

Regardless of their refusal to acknowledge wrongdoing, something was amiss at the lab. Furue's science was clearly part of the problem. Identifications were botched, leaving already distrustful MIA families angry and suspicious. However, scientific deficiencies alone cannot explain the passion of MIA activists in opposing the lab's findings. If the qualifications of the lab's chief scientist or the conditions in which he worked really were the cause for complaint, why had no activists expressed concern before Pakse? Furue had been the lab's lone scientist since 1977 and had identified dead soldiers for the U.S. military since 1951. In a misguided attempt to defend him after 20/20 questioned his credentials, Richard Armitage protested that Furue had personally identified "over 26,000 combat remains" in his thirty-five years with the army.[165] Of course, this did nothing to prove the validity of those identifications; it only prompted the question of why there were no challenges to Furue's work before 1985, especially given that leading anthropologists were aware of his limited academic training well before then.[166]

In fact, arcane questions of forensic science offered a singularly poor explanation for the medieval character of the CILHI controversy, in which tiny shards of bone were made the source of moral authority for those who would speak publicly about the Vietnam War. Junk science was merely the means by which MIA activists challenged military officials for control over the war dead. Fuller's nephew did not travel the country exhibiting bones that he denied were his uncle's in order to expose scientific fraud. He undertook this pilgrimage to contest the government's claim that it had honorably discharged its duty to account for his uncle. On this mission of memory, the bones were more meaningful to him broken and manipulated than they would have been whole and unimpeachable. A complete skeleton with a bullet hole in the skull would have allowed the military to claim that it had accounted for Fuller and brought his family closure. A handful of bone shards—"they believe this is not even part of a human anatomy," correspondent Tom Jarriel remarked ominously as 20/20 broadcast images of fragmented bone—proved that it had not. "He is owed more than that by this country," his nephew insisted. "It's that simple."[167]

In the weeks between the Pakse identifications and the press conference when Fuller's bones were displayed, Vice President Bush hailed the Pakse excavation as "a major step towards a sustained pattern of progress." By returning American remains, he told the League at its 1985 convention, the Reagan administration was "helping bring America home." Hidden inside flag-draped coffins borne by honor guards to the hallowed grounds of national cemeteries, repatriated remains proved that "America has always honored the splendid men who have fought to protect liberty," in Vietnam no less than in earlier wars.[168] But exposed as pulverized and manipulated, the same bones offered visible signs that American soldiers were still being exploited "by the same despicable politicians and bureaucrats in Washington who sent them there in the first place to deliberately lose a war, and, perhaps, to die in the process."[169] Like holy relics, they offered proof of martyrdom and the promise of resurrection.

Grasping the symbolic power attached to MIA remains helps explain why their recovery became so controversial in the 1980s and 1990s. Even before 50,000 bone shards returned from Pakse, activists distrusted the administration's growing reliance on body recovery as the main means to account for MIAs, and the concomitant neglect of the covert operations Reagan had once emphasized. "Is the act of picking up a shovel to be considered a mark of success after 12 years?" MIA rabble-rouser Michael Van Atta asked. "How long will it take before the U.S. Government shifts its emphasis to rescuing the live POWs?"[170]

Such sentiments had a long history in the League — "We want the living men released, not just the remains of those who didn't survive," one MIA family told the House Select Committee in 1976 — but they became more pronounced in the 1980s as Reagan and his advisers speculated on the existence of live POWs and activists grew proficient at generating evidence of their survival.[171] So long as remains repatriation was limited, skepticism toward it was reserved for extraordinary cases like Ron Dodge. But the increased tempo of crash-site excavations after Pakse, and the flood of remains those excavations brought, alarmed those awaiting the return of live POWs. "There is the appearance that more emphasis is being placed on recovering remains than release of live men," the board chairman of the National Forget-Me-Not Association wrote to Secretary of Defense Weinberger; "I am sure you will agree which is more important."[172]

That appearance intensified in 1986, which opened with a second excavation in Laos that resulted in the recovery of nine more American remains and saw the return of thirteen remains from Vietnam. Reagan's appointment of General John Vessey as his emissary to Hanoi on the POW/MIA Issue in 1987 resulted in the handover of seventy more American remains in the last eighteen months of Reagan's presidency. By decade's end Vietnam had repatriated fifty more American remains.[173] At last, Griffiths and her partners in the Reagan and Bush administrations could point to real progress in accounting for missing Americans. At the end of 1986, Griffiths claimed that the recent upswing in remains repatriation supplied "answers" to "the families of 85 American heroes."[174] Most of those families were relieved to have a grave where they could mourn, even if it contained only a few fragments. Ten of thirteen families accepted the Pakse remains, even after Hart called them into question, no doubt because they brought an end to the nightmare of uncertainty.

But every MIA identified meant one less live POW, and committed activ-

In this cartoon from the October/November 1986 edition of *Bamboo Connection*, a newsletter popular among MIA activists, bones are repatriated while live POWs are left behind. (Courtesy Ted Sampley)

ists saw the return and identification of remains not as an accounting so much as a death sentence. "You cannot separate the POW issue, the live POW issue from the Central Identification Lab," Hart told Congress. "Once a man is accounted for there, he is finished." If her husband was identified, "they would never again be looking for Tom Hart."[175] For some, resolution in this form was impossible to accept. "I don't want my brother's bones," said one man who traveled to Thailand to advertise a $2.4 million dollar reward for a live American POW. "I want the flesh and blood—the living man. And if I can't get him, I want another P.O.W."[176] "My son and others are not waiting at the crash site to be rescued," said another leading activist. "My God, we've got to work on the living."[177]

Such claims were so irrational as to be easily dismissed. "That woman wouldn't believe her husband died if it happened right in front of her," one army official said of Hart.[178] There was virtually no chance, for instance, that the men shot down at Pakse had survived. Their aircraft was seen to explode in a "fireball" before it plummeted to the earth and it continued to erupt for several hours afterward as its ordnance burned off. Two crew members who parachuted to safety before the explosion were rescued by an American search and rescue team later that night, but the team could not make radio contact with any other crew members nor locate any survivors in the area using heat-sensing equipment. The next day a Royal Laotian Army unit inspected the site and found a dismembered arm and bloody bandages but no survivors.[179] The prospect of surviving this catastrophe while going undetected by American and Laotian rescue teams on the scene was negligible. The prospect that any survivor would still be alive in captivity fifteen years later in some of the harshest social and environmental conditions on earth was even less likely. Dismissive administration officials started calling those who refused to face such realities "crazies" and "Rambos," in reference to the eponymous POW rescue film released in May 1985, while critics on the left held that belief in POW survival reflected "a profound psychological sickness."[180]

But the Pakse dispute, and the critique of body recovery it touched off, only appeared to be about whether the remains in question adequately proved that an MIA was, in fact, dead. As MIA activists pointed out time and again, what they really objected to was the attempt to use body recovery to "close the books" or "write off" the missing by making it seem that they were properly accounted for. As Anne Hart asked, "Is the identification of remains actually to account for individuals who are missing or is it to wipe the slate clean?"[181] In a letter inviting Dr. Kerley to examine her husband's remains, Kathryn Fanning admitted that "my husband *may* be dead," but she refused to allow "my own government to withhold information or make a spurious identification in order to settle another case."[182] "I'm convinced that the remains are his, but in my mind that doesn't end it," Bobbe Lindland raged. "I'm still mad. I'm still furious. . . . The hope is gone. The bitterness and hatred are not."[183]

The common theme in much of this criticism was that body recovery was "only a lie and a trick to get your support," that the "trickle of remains" was a "hoax" that offered an illusion of progress as it condemned "the POWs to slow death" and "*us* to endless pain and suffering."[184] If the administration was serious about accounting for the missing, the argument ran, it would "go to the prisons instead of the crash sites." But to do so would expose it to scrutiny by exposing the U.S. government's abandonment of American soldiers in Vietnam.[185] "They're still there to this day," actor Charlton Heston explained in a mid-1980s telephone pitch for an MIA rescue outfit, "locked in bamboo cages . . . used as slaves, forced to drag plows in rice paddies." But their presence was "too hot" for Washington to handle, too "embarrassing and destructive to international relations."[186] "If there should develop a clamor for a public investigation of this problem," the MIA hunters in another group called Homecoming II Project explained in November 1986, "U.S. government officials and bureaucrats will be exposed for their illegal conduct and for lying to the American people."[187]

It was in this notion, that the government could not withstand the outcry if its treachery were revealed, that the MIA activist worldview was most fanciful. Official lies, misdeeds, cover-ups, and abuses of power during the Vietnam War were already well established and had brought down the presidencies of Lyndon Johnson and Richard Nixon, yet the national security apparatus kept growing in size, power, and secrecy. The MIA issue remained a perennial presence in post-Vietnam politics because Americans distrusted virtually everything their government leaders said or did with regard to the war in Vietnam, and various national leaders, Reagan most prominent among them, had, until taking office, found it in their interest to cultivate that distrust.

Yet it was also in this idea—that MIAs could inflict retribution on the state and its leaders—that the aims of MIA activists were made manifest. In his 1985 *Manifesto on the Indochina POW-MIA Issue*, MIA brother Jeff Donahue declared, *"There is no greater moral imperative than accounting for the men who served their country,"* yet *"there is no one in the government who is accountable on the issue." "The efforts of the government were turned solely toward its perpetuation and the protection of those involved,"* not toward finding the missing. "The absence of *accountability* on the POW-MIA issue has changed the nature of our adversary," he concluded. "He is no longer without; he is within."[188] When asked by 20/20 if he would ever reach a point where he gave up, Donahue replied that he foresaw a day when he would find his brother and he could tell "the State Department and you guys in the Defense Department, I'm coming back, and I'm going to inflict upon you the suffering you've given me and my mother and my brother all these years, and we're going to settle up."[189] In the absence of live POWs, misidentified remains could serve the same purpose, exposing the dark deceits of the war. "I want them to know every friggin' thing the government did that was wrong," Vietnam vet and POW/MIA webmaster Sarge Hulbein said in 1992. "Even if nobody walks out of that jungle, I can't let them forget what happened. . . . This wasn't anything that was noble."[190]

This remembrance formed in opposition to Reagan's "noble cause" rhetoric, intensifying alongside Reagan's attempts to escape the limits the Vietnam War imposed on U.S. foreign policy. "The real issue which separates 'them from us,'" Homecoming II wrote in reference to administration officials, "is our differing views of the importance of the faith of the American people in our elected leaders. They believe that faith is essential, we believe it is dangerous." Dangerous because such faith led to war in Vietnam, resulting in the loss of 58,000 American lives. By exposing "the truth of the POW issue, the record of 13 years of lies and deception," MIA activists hoped to "shake the blind faith and confidence of the American people in their officials, which is so essential to our elitist leaders. It is only that blind faith which allows them to govern in the way they choose even though the people would (stupidly, they believe) oppose them if the truth were known."[191]

"HISTORIANS HAVE LONG RECOGNIZED that belief in resurrection tends to emerge in response to persecution," historian Caroline Walker Bynum has written. "The persecuted want to claim that those who die for their faith will be rewarded in another life."[192] Reagan resurrected the League and rewarded its faithful service to the nation and his own political fortunes, but he could not resurrect the men the League hoped to find. Neither could the League, though with Reagan's help it managed to conjure their spectral presence. As their relationship frayed in the face of immovable reality, it became increasingly clear that their common project did not share a common purpose. Whereas the League wished to resurrect the missing to establish the injustice and inequity of the Vietnam War, Reagan wished to use the group to ennoble a war that its members, and many of his supporters, despised. That dynamic drove the politics of loss in the 1980s.

After a slow start, the Reagan administration increased its accounting efforts, especially its ongoing effort to recover and identify American remains. Redoubled recovery efforts were matched, even outpaced, by renewed rhetoric on the issue and restored political access for MIA families. Yet these steps failed to resolve the MIA problem. Instead, they aggravated suspicions that Americans were still in captivity and radicalized MIA activists to an unprecedented degree. The more progress Reagan demonstrated, the more dissatisfied activists became; the more he offered resolution, the more it was scorned. "I hope that Reagan understands," John LeBoutillier wrote in a 1985 op-ed piece, "that 'the issue that won't go away' won't go away until all the POWs come home."[193]

Both Reagan and the League were committed to revising public memory of the Vietnam War. But as each moved to do so they came into conflict over what that memory should be and how the MIA issue should be used to construct it. If Reagan used the issue as "the scar that binds," to return to Beattie's term—and clearly he tried, citing it as the war's "sorest wound"—the memory activists in the MIA movement used it to bind in the other sense of the word—to constrain, hinder, restrain, or restrict any attempt to declare their wounds healed or to make them relinquish their grievances against those they blamed for their suffering.[194] The poem "I Am Alive" answered Reagan's pledge to MIA families that "you'll never be alone again" with the toxic rejoinder that "I am still here, still captive, still waiting / I am not yet just remains / not fragments . . . not dental records," "my pain is mine alone."[195]

Not to Close the Door, but to Open It

The Ambiguity of Recovery

As his presidency came to an end, President Bill Clinton visited Vietnam in November 2000. The first sitting president to journey there since Richard Nixon, Clinton and his family began the second day of their three-day stay by traveling to an MIA excavation site north of Hanoi where an American F-105 Thunderchief piloted by Captain Lawrence Evert crashed in 1967. There he told the twelve-member American search team and the 150 Vietnamese villagers combing through the dark, heavy mud in search of bone and metal that "our nation has made a commitment that we will not rest until we have achieved the fullest possible account for our lost veterans." But whereas this commitment once seemed an insurmountable obstacle to bilateral relations, Clinton used it to cement the bonds between the searchers. "This common endeavor we make as friends is unprecedented in all of human history," he told them. "Once we met here as adversaries. Today we work as partners."

His message was meant for the families of missing Americans—represented by Dan and David Evert, who joined him in the field where their father disappeared—as much as the people of Vietnam. By the end of his eight years in office, Clinton knew he could not please them all, but he had learned that by aggressively pursuing the recovery of MIA remains he could garner enough support to neutralize critics. In contrast to League officials who condemned Clinton's trip, David Evert affirmed that "we are absolutely grateful the president came here" and assured the Vietnamese that "we love them and don't hold any animosity at all." When asked what he would say to those who felt different, Veteran Affairs Secretary Hershel

President Bill Clinton observes Vietnamese locals as they search for the remains of Captain Lawrence Everet, missing in action since his plane crashed near Tien Chau, Vietnam, in 1967. Everet's sons Daniel and David Evert look over the president's shoulder. (Courtesy William J. Clinton Presidential Library)

Gober answered, "Some will never be satisfied but I suggest they be like these Vietnamese and put the past behind them."[1]

These words, and the setting in which they were delivered, demonstrate the remarkable changes in U.S.-Vietnam relations during the 1990s, and the importance of MIA recovery to that transformation. Beginning in the late 1980s and accelerating in the 1990s, the search for MIAs that had once caused such acrimony between the two states became a source of reconciliation, helping to usher in normal diplomatic relations in July 1995 and over $1 billion in annual trade by decade's end.[2] The most obvious explanation for this rapid turnaround was the end of the Cold War, which forced Vietnamese leaders to implement economic reforms, reshuffled the regional and international security environment, and allowed a new generation to come to power on both sides.[3] Yet what is striking about Clinton's trip to the Evert crash site is how little it reflected such changes, clinging to a decades-old preoccupation with missing Americans, even as it put their loss and recovery to new ends.

It may seem perverse to argue that the recovery of missing Americans played a vital part in the normalization of relations. Traditionally, scholars have viewed the POW/MIA issue as an impediment to reconciliation, an interpretation that is accurate when applied to the 1970s and 1980s.[4] Robert Schulzinger suggests a more mutable role for MIAs in the 1990s, showing how important the MIA issue was to bilateral relations in the Bush and Clinton years, but his focus on foreign policy leaves ample room to fill in the complicated domestic backstory that allowed for such sweeping policy reversals.[5] This chapter seeks to provide that story, within the limits imposed by a still incomplete archival record.

However much the Cold War's end created the conditions for change, political and cultural shifts inside the United States were needed to normalize relations. Among the most important and least noted was the evolution of MIA activism in the Reagan and Bush years. As MIA activists shifted responsibility for their suffering from Vietnamese communists in the late 1960s to liberal bureaucrats in the late 1970s to the Reagan and Bush administrations in the late 1980s, they deprived themselves of erstwhile supporters and created a political controversy that cried out for a bipartisan response. Paradoxically, the MIA lobby's growing influence contained within it the seeds of its own destruction, giving officials from both parties reasons to put to rest its more outlandish claims, even as it enhanced the value of Vietnam's MIA bargaining chips. Suspicion on all sides dictated slow progress, but the way forward was clear. By the end of the Reagan years American and Vietnamese officials were working ever more closely to increase the flow of remains, with Vietnam earning valuable enticements and rewards in return. These developments infuriated those who awaited the rescue of live POWs, but they had only themselves to blame. By placing such emphasis on the missing, MIA activists helped re-create the dynamic of the war's last years, when getting Americans home became more important than continuing to fight in their name.

Rather than happening all at once at Cold War's end, normalization occurred in fits and starts, beginning with the two-year plan to resolve the MIA issue in 1985. The timetable proved wildly optimistic, but by prompting the first significant remains repatriation since 1978 and the first U.S.-led remains recovery operation in Vietnam since 1973, the plan laid the basis for future cooperation and prompted MIA radicals to break with Reagan.[6] These patterns hardened over the next decade as annual crash-site excavations and the regular return of remains led first to a "Roadmap to U.S.-SRV Normalization" in early 1991, the end of the trade embargo in 1994, normalization of relations in 1995, and a bilateral trade agreement in 2001, all accompanied by cries of outrage from the MIA lobby.[7]

There were many important steps along the way, none more so than the formation of the Senate Select Committee on POW/MIA Affairs in August 1991. The committee included most of the Senate's Vietnam veterans and was led by John Kerry and John McCain, whose status as Vietnam combat veterans allowed them to contest claims of MIA abandonment. McCain's POW status gave him a moral authority that vaulted him ahead of the committee's MIA lobby mouthpieces. Knowing that "sympathy, monuments, medals, benefits or flags" had failed to "reestablish trust between our government and our people," Kerry and McCain pursued exposure, not closure. Through 200 hours of public hearings, over 200 sworn depositions, the declassification of millions of records, and a 1,200-page report on their findings, they brought transparency to the MIA issue and scrutiny to its proponents.[8] "This report is not intended to close the door on this issue," they wrote in the committee's unanimous final report in January 1993; "it is meant to open it."[9]

That open door was welcomed by the Clinton administration, which delayed its decision to lift the trade embargo imposed on Vietnam nineteen years earlier until Kerry and McCain had engineered passage of a Senate resolution calling for its repeal. Adopting a similarly cautious approach, Clinton positioned Kerry and McCain beside him as he normalized diplomatic relations, embracing each the moment he finished speaking.[10] MIA families like the Everts—those who eschewed memory politics but still sought answers about the fate of their loved ones—also welcomed the open door as it resulted in the recovery of roughly 500 identifiable American remains between 1991 and 2006, a 100 percent increase over the previous fifteen years.[11]

These developments were less welcomed by MIA activists, who viewed the bipartisan push for bilateral relations as their final betrayal. Given the progress toward the accounting they claimed to seek, they could not easily oppose these endeavors, but they slowed them, postponing normalization that was widely anticipated at the end of the first Bush administration, and they exacted a political price for cooperation, abandoning Bush for the third-party candidacy of Ross Perot in 1992, hounding Clinton relentlessly through his eight years in office, and going after Kerry and McCain in their presidential runs. If their opposition failed to prevent change, it shaped that change, just as it continued to shape public memory.

LOOSE CANNON

Ross Perot was among those energized by the building MIA mania of the mid-eighties. Still much admired among MIA activists for his part in the Go Public campaign, Perot continued his one-man war against those who would imprison Americans into the postwar era, hosting a ticker-tape parade for returned POWs in 1973, arranging a dramatic rescue when top executives from his Electronic Data Systems were imprisoned in Tehran in 1979, and giving funds and frisson to Bo Gritz and other would-be POW rescuers in the 1980s. "Every nutcase, everybody claiming to have information, all found their way to him," Griffiths complained.[12] MIA hunters fed Perot's fondness for conspiracy with tales of POW abandonment and official drug running, tales that became more credible as the remains identification controversy and the Iran-Contra scandal unfolded in 1986 and after. Their murmurs convinced him that he alone could keep the forces of darkness at bay.

Like those around him, Perot was disturbed when Reagan seemed to turn his back on POW hunters in favor of remains excavations. "I don't care about bones," he told Griffiths. "I only care about live prisoners." "Dead men tell no tales," he complained, which in his view was why authorities were keen to recover them. When "you look at the standards we require to show you that there is one live American still in Vietnam or Laos and compare that to what we send home in caskets," he told Congress, "it's apparent we've got ourselves a double standard." "I don't know how you define coverup," he continued, but the government's rush to "close the books with the tiniest shred of information" met his definition.[13]

Such charges were common among radical MIA activists, but unlike some in the Rambo set, Perot was not easily ignored. His great wealth and public profile made it difficult for the White House or the League to dismiss him for fear of jeopardizing his $2.5 million pledge to the Reagan library, among other dangers. "We didn't want this man mad," recalled Reagan's deputy chief of staff, James Cannon. Instead of confronting him, DIA Director General Leonard Perroots asked Perot to join another dangerous critic of Reagan's MIA effort, retired DIA Director Eugene Tighe, in reviewing "the current case files and handling of those files, looking for any indications of impropriety or 'cover up,'" an invitation Perot declined, citing a busy schedule.[14] When Tighe came back with a report in May 1986, released to the public in September, pointing to "a large volume of evidence" that Americans were still alive in Southeast Asia, he added to the drumbeat of criticism coming from the increasingly restive MIA community.[15] Calling Reagan's highest national priority rhetoric "so much boilerplate," and citing "an amazing lack of any government activity," Tighe concluded that "worse than a 'cover-up,' the mindless effort of those involved to make the issue go away is a great tragedy."[16] Knowing that "the public will compare [Tighe's report] with this Administration's statements and say 'cover-up,'" Richard Childress penned a nine-page rebuttal that IAG members could use to refute the report.[17] But the damage was done. By October, House Concurrent Resolution 129, which called for the creation of a Perot Commission on Americans Missing in Southeast Asia, had 275 cosponsors.[18]

Desperate to prevent passage of such legislation, Childress e-mailed National Security Adviser John Poindexter about plans to bottle up "the monster" in the House Subcommittee on Asian and Pacific Affairs, a strategy complicated by the fact that three of the committee's ten members had cosponsored the measure. He suggested calls to Perot and to committee chairman Stephen Solarz from the NSC, the League, and Vice President George Bush voicing opposition to the move and proposing an amendment that made any commission "contingent on Presidential approval." Solarz lent assistance by asking colleagues who favored the bill to skip hearings on the matter and by lining up proxies for others.[19] But Perot's allies on the committee nearly foiled this plan by arranging for him to appear in the audience to provide "spontaneous" testimony before the committee, testimony where he likened the effort to find proof of American captives to "putting 18 inches of additional concrete on a road already paved." What was needed, he told the committee, was not more evidence but some horse-trading to win their release — "I have a horse. You want to buy it; you say, 'Ross, do you want to sell your horse or not?' That is where we start." But Perot's amateurish ideas left the committee cold, and a commanding performance by Griffiths, who opposed the plan for fear that it would pick up where the House Select Committee and Woodcock Commission left off, killed the deal. The bill was tabled when Solarz cast his vote and three proxy votes against it, equaling the four votes cast for the measure, though he was the only member to actually vote against it. To MIA radicals this preordained outcome was further proof of a government conspiracy, but Solarz was unfazed, telling his colleagues, "I can't see . . . how any member would have a problem justifying a vote against a resolution that is opposed by the National League of Families."[20]

Griffiths's opposition did nothing to diminish the resolve of those like Vietnam veteran Gino Casanova, then waging a hunger strike while locked inside a bamboo cage at the Vietnam Veterans Memorial in order to force Reagan to appoint a Perot Commission, one of many such stunts carried out over the winter of 1986–87.[21] Perot was equally unpersuaded, taking Bush's phone call on the eve of the Solarz hearing as an invitation to "dig into this issue — go all the way to the bottom of it," as he told reporters.[22] Given that the purpose of Bush's call was to ward off a Perot Commission, it is unclear where Perot got this idea, but the White House was reluctant to rein him in. Perot took this as implicit approval for his activities, right up to the point where he departed for Hanoi in March 1987. Perot's trip was in response to an invitation from Foreign Minister Nguyen Co Thach, who had just joined the Politburo at the Sixth Party Congress.[23] Whether Perot went with Reagan's blessing, however, remains unclear to everyone except Perot. "I didn't tell anyone in Washington," Perot later explained in typical cloak-and-dagger style. "See, they wanted me to go. I was working on a task force for him, a one-man task force for the president."[24]

While Reagan's staff was apoplectic over Perot's trip, no one at the NSC should have been surprised by it.[25] Perot had long been a leading player in Reagan's privatized foreign policy, fronting $300,000 to ransom Beirut hostages in 1985 and promising $2 million rewards for their release on at least four separate occasions since 1982.[26] The NSC briefed the president on Perot's plans on the eve of his departure for Hanoi, and both Perot's and Reagan's diaries refer to a presidential directive authorizing the trip, though if such a document exists it remains classified.[27] For many conservatives, such freelance diplomacy was part of the romance of the Reagan years. "There were young men who were always just in from the bush or back from the border," Peggy Noonan recalls of the Reagan White House. "They hated communism because communism was the state sitting on the individual, so they went to where the individuals were fighting back and joined in however they could."[28] Perot was in some sense the progenitor for such crusaders, with off-the-record exploits dating back to the Nixon years.

The problem with such "paramilitarism as state policy" was that it empowered people who were impossible to control.[29] When Perot returned from Vietnam demanding to see the president, then went public with news of his trip, praising Hanoi's attitude as "very open" and "constructive," even Reagan concluded he had become "a loose cannon on the POW matter."[30] Within twenty-four hours of Perot's leak, the White House announced the appointment of General John Vessey as special presidential emissary to

Hanoi on the POW/MIA issue.[31] Since few NSC papers from Reagan's second term have yet been opened for research, the origins of the Vessey mission remain murky.[32] Administration spokesmen, League officials, even Perot himself claimed that such a mission was contemplated before Perot's trip to Hanoi, most likely by Colin Powell and Frank Carlucci, who had been brought in to clean up Reagan's dysfunctional NSC after the tenures of Poindexter and McFarlane. But Childress, the League, and perhaps the full IAG opposed such a mission. The timing of the announcement suggests that Perot forced the issue in Vessey's favor, with Reagan calling Perot to the Oval Office a few days later to tell him that Vessey would "be our sole negotiator with Hanoi" and to persuade him "to step back & not indicate we should try normalizing relations—trade, etc. until we get the truth on our POW's."[33] Having written talking points for Reagan to read, Powell and Carlucci were on hand to make sure the message was delivered and received. They needn't have worried—Reagan read one of his index cards twice.[34]

AMERICA CANNOT MOVE FORWARD BY LEAVING HER MISSING SONS BEHIND

Vessey's appointment was a major breakthrough in U.S.-Vietnam relations, building on the progress that began with the 1985 two-year plan. With the Democrats retaking the Senate in November 1986 and the selection of economic reformers Nguyen Van Linh as party general secretary and Vo Van Kiet as vice premier in December, both sides appeared ready for change. And Thach's promotion to the Politburo suggested an opening to the United States was high on Vietnam's agenda, considering he had been the SRV's chief intermediary with the IAG since 1983.[35] His invitation to Perot was a step in that direction—Perot returned from Hanoi to report that the other side sought "a presidential negotiator."[36]

If a presidential mediator was his goal, then Thach succeeded. Reappointed by Presidents Bush and Clinton, Vessey remained in his post until 1993, meeting with Vietnamese officials more than a dozen times and acting as a tough but fair negotiator. A former infantryman who fought in North Africa and Italy as a noncommissioned officer in World War II before winning a battlefield commission, Vessey knew the realities of war.[37] Like many military men, he had limited patience for those who harbored unrealistic expectations of MIA survival, telling JCRC personnel in Bangkok that "when you have a war, you have casualties; it's time to move on."[38] He pursued discrepancy cases aggressively, but unlike most U.S. officials, his conception of the fullest possible accounting had limits, which gave the Vietnamese goals to work toward and MIA activists cause for alarm. But Vessey's uniform, combat record, and advanced age largely shielded him from their attacks.

In Vessey, Thach finally found a way around the IAG, but Griffiths and Childress still had cards to play, traveling as an advance team to Hanoi soon after his appointment "to establish a realistic agenda and determine whether a valid basis exists for a Vessey mission." Finding Thach unimpressed, Griffiths warned that the Vietnamese were "hoping the domestic pressure in the United States will aid their purposes rather than our own, as happened during the war. . . . Our loss has been tragic and still continues," she concluded; "however, selling out the basic purpose for which so many Americans lost their lives, were imprisoned and may still be captive, would be tantamount to treason."[39]

This remarkable statement put Vessey on notice for what he would face if he crossed the League. But it did not dissuade Vietnam's leaders, who, having embarked on market reforms, were committed to ending the U.S.-imposed trade embargo. Between Griffiths's departure and Vessey's arrival, Thach insisted that if the United States expected help on MIAs, "then the Americans can help us on our wounds."[40] While this sparked the usual rebukes at the League's annual meeting a few days later, when Vessey arrived in Hanoi for three days of talks in August, he carried a letter from Reagan expressing hope that "the United States and Vietnam can work together to finally put the war behind us by resolving issues which are clearly humanitarian in nature."[41]

The letter marked a change in tone, if not yet in policy, and it demonstrated the threat Vessey posed to Griffiths, since talk of resolution remained anathema to the League. Either Reagan's letter was drafted without her knowledge or her input was ignored. And while Griffiths and Childress accompanied Vessey on his mission, they appeared to have little influence on him. When Thach reiterated the need "to address both sides of the problem," Vessey replied that he was prepared to send medical experts and supplies to help Vietnam's 1.4 million war-disabled citizens in return for Thach's help in resolving the seventy most compelling discrepancy cases.[42] Agreement was quickly reached and over the next year Vietnam returned seventy-seven sets of remains while American NGOs shipped over $100,000 in medical supplies to Vietnam.[43]

This was the most rapid progress toward the professed goals of either side since war's end, but it satisfied no one. Given their conviction that Vietnam warehoused remains, few activists applauded the surge in repatriations.[44]

Instead, they blasted the U.S. government for showing Vietnam that "the USG is not that concerned with Live POWs and they will be glad to settle for remains."[45] Vietnam was likewise dissatisfied with the size and shape of American aid. Thach told reporters that he could "accept nongovernmental organization aid, but there must be at least some from the Government." Complaining that the humanitarian teams sent to Vietnam were "not of a high enough level," he insisted that "the establishment of relations should not wait but should be as soon as possible."[46] As he returned twenty-seven remains to Senator Larry Pressler, a South Dakota Republican and Vietnam veteran, Thach suggested that Washington "consider offering food to areas of Vietnam where rural people are asked to help search for the remains of Americans."[47]

Thach's strategy of pursuing closer relations through remains repatriation seemed to bear fruit when Tom Ridge and John McCain, both Vietnam veterans, introduced resolutions in the House and Senate in March 1988 calling for the creation of "interest sections" in Washington and Hanoi in order to facilitate accounting. Vietnam quickly endorsed the plan, and Thach proposed the resumption of joint field activities in a June meeting with Vessey in New York.[48] In between, Vietnam's Foreign Ministry announced plans to withdraw 50,000 troops from Cambodia by December, showing flexibility on the other major hurdle to normalization with the United States (and with China) and signaling its determination to end Vietnam's international isolation.[49]

Despite progress, the interest section idea fell victim to League opposition. Reagan's stance toward Vietnam vacillated over his last two years in office as his staff tried to show progress on the MIA issue without further alienating MIA activists.[50] Mixed signals were the order of the day, with Vessey pursuing cooperation while the IAG remained oppositional. Reagan's reluctance to resolve disputes among subordinates, along with political instincts that made it impossible for him to confront the League, meant that Griffiths remained a force to be reckoned with, and her position was clear.[51] "*Interest sections demonstrate clear movement toward normalization of relations*," she thundered in her April newsletter. "The League has long been firmly opposed to linking resolution of the POW/MIA issue to normalization of relations," out of a professed fear that linkage would hold MIA accounting hostage to "political" differences between the two countries.[52] With Griffiths opposing Ridge and McCain, their resolution was scuttled at congressional hearings scheduled to bookend the League convention in July. As State Department officials advocated Vietnam's continued isolation on Capitol Hill, Reagan told League members meeting a few blocks away: "There have always been those rushing to say that it was time to forget." "To them I say: America cannot move forward by leaving her missing sons behind."[53]

Disappointed, Vietnam rescinded its offer of joint field activities, complaining that the United States had "failed to respond appropriately to our goodwill."[54] Then, perhaps thinking better of taking Griffiths's bait, Thach told Vessey in late August that excavations could proceed. Americans arrived in Hanoi in late September to conduct the most extensive casualty resolution operations to date. Over three months, U.S. military teams investigated twenty-six crash sites and interviewed countless eyewitnesses to determine the fate of missing Americans. Recovering two remains through excavations and collecting fifty-nine from Vietnamese officials, they doubled the progress of the last year in just eighty days. All told, one hundred and thirty remains returned from Vietnam in 1988, with three more recovered from Laos. Nearly half were identified as Americans, including fourteen of Vessey's seventy most compelling cases, and searchers visited sites associated with another eighteen such cases. As many MIAS were accounted for during the last eighteen months of Reagan's presidency as had been in the previous eight years.[55]

To JCRC chief Paul Mather, this achievement showed Hanoi had made "a conscious decision . . . to remove the issue of Americans unaccounted for in Southeast Asia as a divisive obstacle to better relations."[56] The enhanced cooperation was likely meant as a message to the incoming Bush administration that Vietnam was eager to resolve outstanding issues that stood in the way of normalization, conforming to a pattern of enhanced POW/MIA activity on the eve of transfers of power dating back to 1968.[57] Joint field activities were also a source of income for cadres who arranged and participated in the investigations, with costs ranging from $25 per day for every laborer assigned to the effort to $1,200 landing fees to $1,500 organizing fees for each province that took part in a search. While incidental to Americans, these charges added up to many thousands of dollars per "iteration," as each field investigation was called, sizable sums to cash-strapped party officials.[58] Finally, MIA progress was a way to engage in "people's diplomacy," providing evidence of Vietnam's good nature to pro-normalization opinion makers in the United States while undermining anti-normalization groups like the League.[59] Though dissatisfied with the unofficial and subterranean aid provided in return for his efforts, Thach must have been pleased when the Washington Post featured a lengthy article on Christmas Day that called for greater aid to Vietnam. Written by Vietnam veteran and prosthetics expert Frederick Downs Jr., who had made four trips to Vietnam as part of Vessey's 1987 commitment to help the war-disabled, the article asserted that "resources currently available fall far short of the overwhelming needs" and that "the families of our men still missing in action as well as the disabled child in Hanoi can benefit from the private generosity for which our country is so well known."[60]

SUNDERED BY MEMORY

When President George H. W. Bush declared in his inaugural address in January 1989 that "the final lesson of Vietnam is this: no great nation can long be sundered by a memory" and subsequently reappointed Vessey to his post, normalization seemed just around the corner, prompting the Politburo to hasten the withdrawal of Vietnamese forces from Cambodia to the following September.[61] Field activities continued at an all-time high, with crash-site visits and interviews throughout the year, resulting in the identification of thirty-three Americans that year.[62] Regarding all this, Democratic congressman Chet Atkins urged "normalization—not to diminish the importance of outstanding divisive issues between us, but to improve the chances of resolving them."[63] But reluctant to make sudden moves, Bush refused to accept the legitimacy of Vietnam's pullout from Cambodia, or other evidence of the Cold War's end. Declaring Vietnam's withdrawal "not enough," the State Department imposed new demands, including a comprehensive Cambodian peace agreement and further progress on MIAs. "The issue of missing American servicemen must first be resolved" before normalization, declared Secretary of State James Baker.[64]

In an uncertain international environment, MIAs were a means for Bush to keep relations with Vietnam moving without moving too fast. Among the stalling tactics that constituted the Bush "pause" of 1989 and 1990, MIA accounting became a means to justify his slow steps toward normalization.[65] Bush sought a similar balance in the domestic sphere, as he tried to show progress on MIAs without causing an open split with those already angry over what one activist called "the ridiculous dig-up-a-crash-site game."[66]

A continuation of Reagan's approach, this strategy of progress amid stasis was now even less satisfactory. After years of being told that their occupation of Cambodia and recalcitrance on MIAs prevented normalization, the Vietnamese believed they had met American conditions but "that the Americans had moved the goal posts."[67] Meanwhile, "for those Americans who believe the evidence that many living POWs are still alive and held captive, the return of remains does not signal progress, but only delay," as an attorney for Homecoming II argued.[68] In a nation still sundered by memory, Bush's balancing act proved impossible.

Demonstrating continuity with Reagan's "highest national priority" stance was important to Bush. "Leadership of P.O.W.-M.I.A. organization is concerned about whether the new administration will continue our work in seeking information & remains," Reagan noted in his diary after his last meeting with Griffiths.[69] Bush sought to ease those fears by voicing concern for "Americans who are held against their will in foreign lands" in his inaugural address and by echoing Reagan in his keynote at the League's 1989 convention.[70] Similarly, he sent Griffiths and Vessey to New York to consult with Vietnamese officials in October before they traveled to Hanoi later that month. Anticipating normalization, Thach agreed to expand joint efforts to account for a growing list of "compelling" cases while Vessey agreed to send $250,000 in medical equipment to Vietnam through NGOs.[71]

Such steps did little to persuade Bush's doubters, or the growing mob of Griffiths haters. Bush's comments at a November press conference, where he praised Vietnam's "stepped-up spirit of cooperation" and endorsed its claims "that there are no government holding facilities for remains," shocked the MIA community, as it challenged one of its key articles of faith—the remains warehouse, without which Vietnam's remains repatriation would have to be taken seriously and rewarded.[72] Indeed, Bush's performance suggested such a shift was underway. Sensing danger, Griffiths observed in her newsletter that Bush's claim was "countered by facts known to the League and the U.S. Government."[73]

Her retort no doubt pained Griffiths, who treasured her proximity to presidential power, but it was necessary to save face with her constituents. As the "live POW" factions that sprang up in the mid-eighties multiplied and gained strength at decade's end, they posed a growing threat to her leadership. While her position at the League was secure thanks to her iron grip over its mailing list and annual meetings, where she used "sergeants-at-arms" to maintain order, the proliferation of splinter cells featuring former League leaders made it difficult for Griffiths to portray herself as the authoritative voice of MIA families. Her standing hinged on her ability to communicate a united front between government officials and MIA families, both in the press and in her dealings with Hanoi. If she could not deliver that impression, they would have little use for her. At the same time, the perception that Griffiths was too close to official Washington was poison to those convinced of a government conspiracy to cover up the existence of live POWs. Caught between conflicting demands, her position became untenable.

The attacks on Griffiths were vicious and relentless, with one self-styled "Rambo faction publication" branding her "the mistress of deceit" and "a 2,000 pound Government whore." "All Griffiths talks about is bones," it alleged, accusing her of endorsing "the continuing slaughter of our missing men by pointing to the growing pile of bones and calling it 'significant progress.'"[74] Earl Hopper regularly sent her long letters accusing her of "blind obedience to your government masters."[75] Another man sent her a picture of his ".44 magnum capable of clean neck shots on deer (or traitors) at 1000 yards" in a rambling death threat.[76] As in the past, men seemed most inclined to indulge in such aspersions, drawing on virgin/whore dichotomies and gendered tropes of warrior abandonment to embellish their stabbed-in-the-back narratives. Making her representative of the feminists and neutered bureaucrats they blamed for American defeat, their misogynistic fantasies appealed to a sizable subculture of American men, including a significant part of the MIA lobby.[77] As the League gathered for its 1990 convention, past and future board member Jeff Donahue advised his fellow members that "our Executive Director is being wined and dined at the White House to make sure the truth is not told and to make sure the live POWs do not come home," crafting a modern David and Bathsheba morality tale.[78]

Griffiths gave as good as she got, devoting considerable staff resources and ample space in her newsletters to rebutting her critics. But without Childress and Armitage to back her up—Perot torpedoed Armitage's appointment as secretary of the army as an act of vengeance for his alleged involvement in the POW cover-up—and with the League's Ford administration nemesis Brent Scowcroft back in charge at NSC, Griffiths was unable to change the policy that ultimately threatened her authority.[79] Despite Bush's interest in MIA continuity, he and the foreign policy realists he brought with him rarely expressed the deep-seated grievances over the Vietnam War that had once emanated from the Reagan White House. The difference was hard to articulate but palpable, reflecting the defining fissures of the modern Republican Party—between movement conservatives and the party establishment, the neocons and the realists, the "fundamentalists and their ferocity and their I VISITED HERITAGE VILLAGE T-shirts" and the "nice men in their blue suits from Brooks," as Peggy Noonan put it.[80] Shared outrage over the conduct, outcome, and legacy of the Vietnam War brought these two strands together in the late seventies; Reagan's great gift was his ability to make both feel at home in his party and his administration. Bush possessed no such gift. Having never trusted or been trusted by conservatives close to Reagan, he took the blame for Reagan's failures, on MIAs and everything else, while receiving little credit for his victories. "Reagan true believers always knew that [Bush] was not one of them, and never would be," David Halberstam explained. "They did not have to give him a test to know that if they did, he would in some way fail it."[81]

The collapse of communist governments across Eastern Europe in 1989 and the Soviet Union's subsequent demise presented Bush with a series of tests that seemed designed to split him from the militant right. Making an anachronism of the anticommunism that had lent form and substance to conservative politics for more than forty years, the Cold War's end reopened the foreign policy debates that rocked the Republican Party in 1976 and gave the losing side another chance to demonstrate the value of pragmatism in world affairs. After a period of hesitation, Bush, Scowcroft, Baker, and Baker's deputy and eventual successor Lawrence Eagleburger, establishment Republicans with little regard for the "morality in foreign policy" wing of the party, moved to realize opportunities presented by the Soviet decline. As they did, they came into conflict with those who "wanted to fight the war a little bit longer," including those in the MIA movement.[82]

The reorientation of U.S. policy was especially pressing in Indochina, where Vietnam's withdrawal from Cambodia left the Hanoi-installed government in Phnom Penh largely defenseless against the American-backed "noncommunist resistance," ironically allied with the Chinese-backed Khmer Rouge. A grotesque legacy of the Reagan administration's knee-jerk anti-Vietnamese sentiment, this policy of indirect support to the genocidal Khmer Rouge had produced civil war throughout the eighties.[83] Now, minus Vietnam's counterbalance, it risked bringing the Khmer Rouge back to power, prompting a refugee crisis.[84] Its attention focused elsewhere, the Bush administration hoped the United Nations could broker a peace agreement, but its support for the resistance gave the Khmer Rouge little reason to compromise. Only when Congress moved to cut off funds to Cambodia did Baker act, announcing on 18 July 1990 the end of U.S. support for the rebel coalition and his intent to begin talks with Hanoi aimed at resolving the conflict.[85]

The media-savvy Baker received most of the credit for the move, but some media-savvy Vietnam veterans in the Senate laid the groundwork for the change, beginning with Nebraska's Bob Kerrey, whose nine-day fact-finding mission to Cambodia in April attracted new attention to its problems. A rising star in the Democratic Party, Kerrey used the trip to introduce voters to his impressive biography — he won the Congressional Medal of Honor and lost his right foot in Vietnam before returning to Nebraska and becoming a self-made millionaire — as he prepared for a presidential bid.[86] Lest the telegenic Kerrey win all the acclaim, fellow freshman Democrat and Vietnam vet Chuck Robb of Virginia revealed in June that he had visited Phnom Penh in February to confer with resistance leader Prince Norodom Sihanouk and Prime Minister Hun Sen, whose government the State Department had previously refused to recognize, as well as unnamed Vietnamese officials. Calling on Bush "to take a lead on this issue," Robb advocated "a truly independent and neutral Cambodia," a goal that became more attainable later that same day when Sihanouk and Hun Sen formed a Supreme National Council that the Khmer Rouge refused to join.[87] To give Baker a final push, Robb went before the League on 13 July to announce an agreement with the Hun Sen government to allow the JCRC to retrieve remains believed to belong to missing Americans, a step Griffiths warily endorsed.[88] Robb proposed the step to Hun Sen and Vietnam's Deputy Foreign Minister Nguyen Manh Cam during his visit to Cambodia, and "the Vietnamese were receptive to expanding cooperation in this area of the relationship."[89]

What part this offer played in the decision five days later to terminate U.S. support for the Cambodian resistance is unclear. Sihanouk's decision to make peace, the Soviet's desire to remove Cambodia as a stumbling block to better relations with China and the United States, and congressional pressure to resolve a growing crisis all converged to force a change. However, the timing of the moves, with Baker's reversal sandwiched between the offer to repatriate remains and the JCRC's arrival in Phnom Penh twelve days later, suggests that the remains repatriation was an important symbol of progress meant to appease those who might otherwise oppose a policy shift. Considering that the Cambodian government had never before made such an offer, and that it did so for the first time when Vietnam was using MIA cooperation to cultivate closer ties to the United States, the Robb agreement was yet the latest sign of body recovery's diplomatic utility.

With the Cambodian impasse resolved, U.S.-Vietnam relations became more fluid. In late September Baker met Thach in New York for the highest-level discussions between the two nations since 1973. Baker thanked Thach for the constructive role Vietnam played in Cambodia and urged him to redouble his MIA efforts to position the two sides for normalization once a Cambodian settlement was reached. To allow for further talks, Baker invited Thach to meet Vessey and Griffiths in Washington in October, waiving the travel ban that restricted Vietnamese officials to within twenty-five miles of the UN.[90] In Washington they hammered out an agreement granting U.S. officials limited access to archival materials on MIAs that would help them identify promising excavation sites in return for the promise that the United States would consider opening an MIA office in Hanoi should the workload warrant it.

Both sides saw such an office as the first step toward normalization and, it seemed, both sides were on the verge of such a step. "If Vietnam is forthcoming on P.O.W.-M.I.A. affairs, then this will facilitate the rapid movement toward normalization," an unnamed senior official told the *New York Times* after the Thach-Vessey session.[91] With signs of recession increasingly apparent, the trade embargo was an anachronism the United States could no longer afford.[92] Even old friends of the MIA lobby like John LeBoutillier, writing for the *Wall Street Journal*, backed trade and investment as "the best way to encourage the Vietnamese government to continue its economic reforms" and "settle the POW issue."[93]

But not all were ready to bury the hatchet. Days before Thach's October visit to Washington, archconservative Jesse Helms took to the Senate floor to denounce what he called "the mock burial of MIAs." Claiming that the Pentagon was burying empty coffins as men it professed to have accounted for, the senator from North Carolina suggested that body recovery was a "charade" meant to deceive Americans into accepting relations with "a government that may well be concealing the fate of many other American MIAs."[94] Three weeks later Helms released an "Interim Report on the Southeast Asian POW/MIA Issue" that alleged "several hundred living American POWs remained in captivity in Southeast Asia."[95] Issued under the imprimatur of the Foreign Relations Committee's Republican members, but without their knowledge, the eighteen-page report was little more than a compendium of the MIA lobby's favorite innuendos. But with Helms fighting for his political life in a close reelection campaign, it attracted credulous press coverage and put the Vietnamese and the Bush administration on notice that the Foreign Relations Committee's ranking Republican was not about to surrender the Vietnam War, a message that resonated with voters in his military-friendly state.[96] Running a campaign that emphasized the victimization of white men at the hands of liberal elites and their minority allies, Helms won reelection with 53 percent of the vote.[97]

Helms's desperate, no-holds-barred reelection bid was undoubtedly the main reason for his MIA activism. But the Iraqi invasion of Kuwait in August 1990, and the aggressive Bush response, may have provided another reason for Helms's rediscovery of the MIA issue. Today the Persian Gulf War is remembered as something akin to a summer blockbuster—escapist fun soon forgotten—but at the time the build-up of U.S. forces in the region touched off serious anxiety, and not just on the antiwar left. MIA activists like Red McDaniel saw history repeating itself. "My advice to the boys in the Middle East is: Don't get captured," McDaniel told reporters upon reading the interim report.[98] For the report's principal author, a Republican staffer named Tracy Usry, the parallels were unmistakable. In a January 1991 letter to his staff director, Usry requested additional resources to finish his final report, which he called "very important, now more than ever. As the ground war increases, more Allied and US prisoners will be lost. The US is still doing the same thing," he warned in reference to POW abandonment, and "we need to act."[99] Memories of Vietnam stopped few conservatives from supporting the war—Charles Grassley, among the Senate's most reliable MIA voices, was one of only two Republicans to vote against the use of force—but they lurked beneath the surface on the eve of war, as Helms must have sensed when he released Usry's interim report.

In the war's lightning-fast execution, the ghosts of Vietnam were supposedly laid to rest. "The specter of Vietnam has been buried forever in the desert sands," Bush exulted once the 100-hour war came to an end.[100] "There will be no repeat of Vietnam," Dana Priest declared in her reporting on the rapid return of prisoners from Iraq; "no cottage industry of POW groups. No political fodder for those who would attempt to say the war was a mistake."[101] Even Usry admitted that "the war was so brief and so powerful that all prisoners were returned without question" in his final report in May.[102] Looking to capitalize on the triumphal mood, Bob Kerrey and John McCain traveled to Indochina to advocate a diplomatic presence in Phnom Penh and an MIA office in Hanoi.[103] Following this push from two of the Senate's most prominent Vietnam veterans, Bush dispatched Assistant Secretary of State Richard Solomon to New York to present a "roadmap" to normalization to Ambassador Trinh Xuan Long. Outlining a four-phase process whereby the United States would reward Vietnam for a Cambodian peace agreement and MIA repatriation, the roadmap committed both sides to eventual normalization.[104] Upon its delivery, Vessey left for Hanoi to arrange for an MIA office to open there in June in return for a $1.3 million grant from the Agency for International Development.[105] The JCRC staff was doubled to handle the increased workload.[106]

But the triumphalism of early 1991 proved fleeting, and the gains it allowed in U.S.-Vietnam relations were challenged from the start. On 23 May 1991 Helms issued the final draft of Usry's "Examination of U.S. Policy

Toward POW/MIAs," again without consulting his fellow Foreign Relations Committee members but with enthusiastic support from Grassley and Republican Bob Smith of New Hampshire, elected to the Senate in November after six years in the House. Released the day before Charles Krauthammer's "In Praise of Parades" appeared in the *Washington Post*, the Helms-Usry report proved that claims of vanquishing the ghosts of Vietnam were premature. While Krauthammer celebrated "the endless stream of homecoming parades" as an "expiation for our shabby treatment of Vietnam vets," the Helms-Usry report alleged that tens of thousands of American soldiers had been knowingly abandoned to the communists in conflicts dating back to the First World War. To make matters worse, Helms wrote, as these men were discarded to communist captivity, "our government pursued policies intended to make diplomatic recognition and financial support of the revolutionary regimes possible," just as it was now doing in Vietnam.[107]

A remarkable document that harkened back to the hucksterism of the McCarthyite right, the report proved such an embarrassment to the Foreign Relations Committee that it eventually compelled Helms to fire Usry and eight other members of the committee's minority staff.[108] Unlike the poorly sourced interim report, its flaw was not a lack of facts or footnotes, but the extravagant claims it built from innocuous details, claims that called into question the entire project of U.S. engagement with the world in the twentieth century.[109] Distrusting its outlandishness and lacking an easily recognizable political context for it, reporters ignored the release, but the 100,000 copies printed at taxpayer expense circulated widely among MIA believers.[110] And while the press ignored the report, its epilogue—a reprint of the letter Colonel Millard Peck stapled to his office door when he resigned as head of DIA's POW/MIA office in February—prompted congressional hearings that threatened to derail MIA diplomacy.

In an extraordinary report, Peck's letter may have been the most extraordinary element. Alternately sentimental and incisive, it pulled back the cloak of government secrecy to confirm the worst fears of MIA radicals. After asserting his commitment to the MIA cause, which he viewed as a "holy crusade," Peck alleged "that the entire issue is being manipulated by unscrupulous people in the Government or associated with the Government." "That national leaders continue to address the prisoner of war and missing in action issue as the 'highest national priority,' is a travesty," he continued. "Any soldier left in Vietnam was, in fact, abandoned years ago, and the farce that is being played is no more than political legerdemain done with 'smoke and mirrors,' to stall the issue until it dies." While "the puppet masters play a confusing, murky role," Peck confided, one thing was clear: Ann Mills Griffiths was "more than meets the eye. As the principal actor in the grand show, she is in the perfect position to clamor for 'progress,' while really intentionally impeding the effort."[111]

Aside from its intemperance, Peck's letter mirrored much of the scholarship on the issue. Not once did Peck mention the Vietnamese in his five-page screed; aside from Griffiths, who called his claims "ludicrous," he hardly mentioned anyone at all, taking aim instead at disembodied state power that worked its will through "smoke and mirrors," the poor man's "ideology of unity."[112] If taken seriously, Peck's letter suggests that the politics of the MIA issue was more complicated than scholars have yet grasped: it shows an agent of the state charged with carrying out its accounting agenda turning the very terms of that agenda against the state with the support of conservative nationalists like Jesse Helms. "I'm not criticizing Vietnam as much as I am our own Government," Helms insisted.[113]

Among Helms's professed goals in releasing his report was the creation of a Select Committee on POW/MIA Affairs. Senator Bob Smith introduced legislation to establish such a body in March, citing Helms's interim report as one reason. Returning the favor, Helms called for passage of Smith's resolution in the cover letter to his May report.[114] Smith, an MIA firebrand in the House who now looked to bring his signature issue to the upper chamber, insisted such a step was needed lest the failures of Vietnam be forgotten amid the euphoria of the Gulf War. "We did it right this time," he allowed. "However, we did not do it right in Vietnam. We did not do it right in North Korea. And this senator, through this committee, is going to get the truth."[115] Along with Chuck Grassley, the other main proponent of the bill, Smith and Helms used Usry's report and Peck's resignation to promote their agenda, with Smith notifying his colleagues of Peck's charges and calling for an investigation "to get to the bottom of it."[116]

When that failed to spur action, Smith and his supporters went public with photographic proof, albeit manufactured, of the existence of American POWs. On 17 July Red McDaniel of the American Defense Institute released a blurry black-and-white photograph of three paunchy men holding a sign reading "LD-25-5-1990 NNTK! K.B.C.19." MIA families, taking the sign as some sort of date reference, immediately claimed the men as their missing loved ones, prompting USA Today to publish the photo on its front page. Newsweek followed suit with its next cover. Days later Smith went on the Today show with another set of photos claimed by another MIA family. Then Jack Bailey, whose fundraising prowess was discussed in chapter 6, released a third photo purported to depict yet another POW.

All these photos were shown to be fake within a matter of months, with McDaniel's photo originating in a 1923 issue of *Soviet Life* magazine from the Phnom Penh Soviet Cultural Center, while the Smith and Bailey photos were proven to depict, respectively, a Laotian tribesman and a German bird trader in Bangkok.[117] But evidence of their contrivance came too late to stop the momentum they gave Smith's legislation. When the McDaniel photo surfaced, John Kerry of Massachusetts and Hank Brown of Colorado, both Vietnam veterans, announced plans to hold hearings before the Senate Foreign Relations Committee. As more photos came to light, the urge to respond, particularly among the Senate's veterans, grew irresistible. With the Soviet Union on the verge of collapse, the Gulf War at an end, and MIA militants on the march, Kerry decided that "you need something here that bridges the gap, that is approaching this with bona fides that are real, that ought to reestablish credibility between citizen and government."[118] Casting his weight behind the Smith bill, Kerry volunteered to lead the last battle of the Vietnam War.

THE BEGINNING OF THE END

A few days before the Senate Select Committee on POW/MIA Affairs was authorized on 2 August 1991, McDaniel, pleased with his handiwork, raved to a reporter, "We're on a roll. This used to be a lonely battle, but it isn't anymore. We're beginning to see the beginning of the end."[119] He was more right than he knew. The end was beginning to come into view, but it turned out differently than McDaniel envisioned. Rather than proving the POWs' existence, the Senate Select Committee made significant strides toward putting the issue to rest.

Borne of the most militant elements of the MIA movement, the committee's membership was stacked with MIA advocates like Smith, Grassley, and Helms. And while Democrats controlled Congress, half of the committee's seats went to Republicans. John McCain, Hank Brown, and Nancy Kassebaum rounded out the GOP caucus. McCain and Kassebaum were on record as favoring relations with Vietnam, but Brown had supported MIA legislation in the past. Further stacking the deck, Smith named a number of MIA activists to the committee staff, including former congressman Billy Hendon. On the other side were many of the Democratic Party's future heavyweights, including John Kerry, Tom Daschle, Harry Reid, and Bob Kerrey, but except for Kerrey, perceived by some as the frontrunner for the 1992 presidential nomination, none of these men were as prominent as they would become and none had much history on the MIA matter.[120]

Sensing disaster, a Kerry staffer worried "about this stampede to form a Select Committee on POWs/MIAs. The Committee has all the potential to become another Un-American Activities Committee, open-ended, full of loose cannons, resolving nothing." It would be composed of "Senatorial and staff dregs," he predicted, and "your image as a serious Senator would be eroded as the Smiths and Helms on this Committee and their staffs dragged you deeper and deeper in the search for phantom missing Americans."[121] It was sage advice, similar to that which Scowcroft gave President Ford in 1975 and largely borne out by Sonny Montgomery's experience on the House Select Committee. Every time government officials set out to silence the MIA lobby, through cooptation or confrontation, they added to its legitimacy and determination. There were always those like Smith and Helms whose interests would be served by playing on the raw nerve of American defeat. But while Smith was sure to be the committee's most zealous member, he would not wield the most influence. On such emotionally fraught terrain, influence was a function of biography as much as zeal, and on this score League members always trumped everyone else. But this time they faced more formidable foes.

Of the committee's twelve members, eight had served in the Vietnam-era armed forces, six in the Vietnam theater, and five in combat roles. The combat veterans—John Kerry, John McCain, Bob Kerrey, Chuck Robb, and Hank Brown—were hardly of one mind on the war or each other.[122] Their party differences—McCain and Brown were Republicans, Kerry, Kerrey, and Robb were Democrats—were exacerbated by personal animus. Bitter over Kerry's antiwar activism in the early 1970s, McCain had traveled to Massachusetts in 1984 as a freshman congressman to campaign against Kerry in a vain attempt to prevent his election to the Senate. While McCain's impertinence angered John Kerry, his sanctimony enraged Bob Kerrey, who regarded McCain with contempt that dated back to Operation Homecoming. "I thought to myself, 'these guys are getting parades? What did they do?'" Kerrey told a reporter. "'They got shot down and sat in jail for six years. Who gives a shit?'"[123] That all but Brown harbored presidential aspirations heightened their mutual distrust. But with their political fortunes inextricably tied to the war, each had a vested interest in resolving the volatile MIA issue.

Given this shared need, the panel's vets found themselves working together, along with Kassebaum, Daschle, and Reid, to limit the influence of the committee's MIA activists. None were more vigilant than Kerry and McCain, who attended countless hours of hearings and shuttled back and forth to Hanoi repeatedly in 1991 and 1992. It seems obvious that these two would emerge as committee leaders given that Kerry was its chair and McCain was a former POW. Yet their commitment to the committee's work also revealed the multiple registers on which the wounded patriotism of the MIA issue resonated. Kerry and McCain were as engaged by the politics of loss as Smith and Helms, but their engagement was rooted in different experiences and served different ends.

"I felt betrayed," Kerry answered when asked why he was leading the committee. "There is an obligation owed to everybody who served in Vietnam, everybody who was affected by Vietnam, and every American. And it pisses me off that they lie. It pisses me off that we are sitting here, thirty years later, struggling to get information."[124] It was an answer that might have come from a hardened MIA activist, whose trajectory from patriotic volunteer to activist critic was not so different from Kerry's evolution as a young man who returned from war to become a leading voice in Vietnam Veterans against the War.[125] Yet because that evolution, shared by millions in his generation, had come to be seen as the source of POW/MIA victimization rather than something akin to it, Kerry's record left him vulnerable to charges of hypocrisy that dogged him throughout his career.[126] Through his work on the committee, Kerry sought common ground with the war's critics on the right, restoring coherence to his life story. Or as he put it, in decidedly drier tones, "This gives me a chance to show I can work with a very broad range of ideological types and hopefully come up with some sound results."[127]

McCain's motives were different. He was looking for redemption, first from the savings and loan scandal that left him branded as one of "the Keating Five."[128] More than that, he sought national redemption. McCain never voiced the same bitterness over the war that Kerry did, but his outrage at the antics of MIA activists was apparent from his opening statement on the committee's first day, when he exposed the photos Smith peddled on the *Today* show as frauds and blasted their release.[129] He often sparred with activists who appeared before the committee, and during one committee meeting he became so angry at Chuck Grassley that Kerrey feared the two would come to blows, with McCain snarling, "You know what your problem is, Senator? You don't listen"—before calling Grassley "a fucking jerk."[130] McCain attributed his anger to concern for the emotional well-being of MIA families, whom he believed were being manipulated, but given that many of the groups he criticized were led or supported by MIA relatives, that rationale made little sense. Indeed, McCain has engaged in heated confrontations with activist families that have charged him with claims of MIA abandonment.[131] What really upset him was the fact that others sought to use the POW experience—his experience—to sully the memory of the war he fought in and to tarnish the reputation of men and institutions he admired, including his father, who served as commander-in-chief of U.S. forces in the Pacific at the height of the Vietnam War. McCain was as angry at the war's outcome as were those in the MIA movement, but he focused his anger at the movement itself, blaming the war's critics for its ill effects rather than the underlying policy. "The issue has painfully lingered in the hearts of us all," he conceded, "but this should not be a question that divides us. It should be the one question in our national affairs that firmly unites every single American."[132] Through the committee, he sought to forge a public memory of his war that he deemed worthy of those he served with in Vietnam and in Washington.

The MIA militants who pushed for the creation of a Senate committee paid little thought to its members, so long as it included Smith, Helms, and Grassley. Believing that any thorough investigation into the matter would reveal the truth of POW captivity, they naively assumed it was just a matter of time before their heroes delivered results. "Within the next sixty to ninety days we will have at least one or more living POW or MIA," Helms pledged on the committee's first day.[133] With a longer history in the movement, Griffiths was less sanguine. "Some who will be debating the POW/MIA issue have other agendas," she advised.[134]

Griffiths had been fighting against a special committee since the Perot Commission, and always for the same reason: she knew that such an entity would seek to resolve the issue that gave her influence. "The POW/MIA issue can't afford another 'conclusion,'" she warned in a League position paper on the subject.[135] That the committee was formed despite her opposition was a testament to her decline. In contrast to 1986, when she helped sink the Perot Commission, her objections to the Select Committee only stoked the determination of Smith, Grassley, and Helms, who took umbrage at her attempts to deny them access to files she perused. They cited this inversion of Washington's customary power dynamics to goad associates into investigating the source and legitimacy of her influence, and on this score they found otherwise skeptical colleagues more receptive. The veterans on the committee showed the same exasperation toward Griffiths that her critics in the MIA movement evinced.[136] But unlike her intemperate opponents in the MIA movement, the Senate committee brought impressive bona fides and a media megaphone to its showdown with Griffiths. Nor could Griffiths count on support from the Bush administration, which after Desert Storm was determined to put Vietnam behind it and could count on Vessey and a bevy of Gulf War general officers to guard its right flank.

Riding high on record approval ratings, "George Bush is no longer afraid of attacks from the ultra-conservatives on what he does in Southeast Asia," a State Department source told *U.S. News & World Report* in August.[137]

Griffiths knew all this, which is why she was alarmed. With the signing of a Cambodian peace accord in October and the collapse of the Soviet Union in November, the MIA issue was all that stood in the way of lifting the trade embargo against Vietnam, a step that Bush was under growing pressure to take given the worsening U.S. economy. In October, Vietnam's new prime minister, Vo Van Kiet, pledged his "unconditional coopera-tion" in resolving the MIA issue, prompting Baker to lift the travel ban on Vietnamese diplomats in the United States and end travel restrictions on Americans who wished to visit Vietnam as stipulated in phase I of the roadmap.[138] Vessey endorsed these measures in his November testimony before the select committee, where he cast doubt on the existence of a remains warehouse and told the senators that the likelihood of discovering live Americans was "considerably lower than I thought it was when I took on this job."[139]

Vessey's testimony threatened League efforts to portray Vietnam's co-operation as inadequate. While Vietnam allowed greater access to war records and crash sites than ever, few of the remains it repatriated in 1991 had yet been identified, leaving room for Griffiths and others to allege it was still dragging its feet. "The *activity level* has been high, and the Viet-namese have received immense credit despite the lack of accountability," the League newsletter complained in November. "It is past time for Viet-nam . . . to rapidly provide information and remains in their possession."[140] Since Vietnam was providing both, this was code for repatriating ware-housed remains, something the League still insisted it had failed to do de-spite the return of hundreds of remains since the late 1980s.

Vessey was no longer willing to accept this line, in part because it im-pugned the real progress he had made. In a January 1992 memo to Scow-croft, Baker, and Secretary of Defense Dick Cheney, he criticized a DIA report on warehoused remains. Calling the DIA estimate that 255 American remains were in storage "way too high," Vessey asked, "Why would Viet-nam, which by its own admission desperately needs to resolve the differ-ences with the U.S., continue to hold remains?" Its leaders "could surely have given up a few sets of bones to resolve the discrepancy cases and ac-crue immense value for their country in getting the trade embargo lifted and moving toward normalization. I have searched my mind over and over again for an explanation. There may be one, but I can't find it." "Setting the standards to which we will hold the Vietnamese is at the heart of our movement down the 'roadmap,'" he ended. "Maybe the Vietnamese have a large stock of remains, but if they don't, and we continue to insist that they do, we will never get the answers to our questions."[141]

In words Griffiths likely had a hand in crafting, the IAG responded by accusing Vessey of perpetuating an "illusion that activity equates with progress," charging that "General Vessey does not agree with the established USG policy."[142] Given his stature, this was a greater problem for Griffiths than for Vessey. When Griffiths questioned Vietnam's cooperation at her final appearance before the committee in December 1992, Kerry's response showed Vessey had won the debate. "Excuse me, Ms. Griffiths," Kerry cut in, "the guys in the field, on the team doing the work do not think they are holding remains." When she persisted, Kerry snapped, "I know exactly who made the estimate. I also know that other people do not agree with it." "You folks ought to be jumping up and down and saying we feel good," he chided, but "you do not want to see the progress."[143]

The committee, on the other hand, recognized Vietnam's efforts, which it witnessed firsthand in its visits to Vietnam. In April, Kerry, Smith, Robb, Brown, and Grassley spoke with Vietnam's foreign, defense, and interior ministers and general secretary. They reiterated commitments Vessey and Assistant Secretary of State Richard Solomon reached with their Vietnamese counterparts before splitting into teams for short-notice inspections of Vietnamese prisoners.[144] Before they departed, the State Department announced it would permit telecommunication links with Vietnam. And upon their return it lifted the ban on commercial sales of food and medicine to meet basic human needs and ended all restrictions on NGOs in Vietnam, meeting most of the steps stipulated in phase II of the roadmap.[145]

This was noteworthy progress, but with presidential elections looming, the committee sought more. Staff director Frances Zwenig traveled to Hanoi in July to insist on further action, reminding officials that time was of the essence. Shortly thereafter a DIA researcher in Hanoi was given access to previously unseen wartime records pertaining to American POWs. These discoveries led to an October meeting between Secretary of State Eagleburger and Secretary of Defense Cheney and Foreign Minister Nguyen Manh Cam and a trip to Hanoi by Vessey and McCain later that month. When Vessey and McCain arrived in Hanoi they were presented with an agreement granting access to archival records relating to POWs and MIAs, a concession Bush heralded as a "real breakthrough" in a Rose Garden ceremony the next week. "Finally," he declared, "we can begin writing the last chapter of the Vietnam War."[146]

Hanoi Army Museum director Colonel Nguyen Trong Dai presents Senator John McCain's flight helmet to Senator John Kerry during Kerry's visit to Hanoi on 18 November 1992 as chairman of the Senate Select Committee on POW/MIA Affairs. (Hoang Dinh Nam/ AFP/Getty Images)

With this achievement under their belt, Kerry, Daschle, and Brown traveled to Hanoi in November and Kerry and Smith returned in December as Kerry maneuvered the committee into issuing a unanimous final report. Under pressure to recognize Vietnam's concessions, Bush allowed U.S. firms to open offices in Vietnam and sign preliminary contracts there, and blessed Japan's decision to loan $375 million to Vietnam, completing phase II of the roadmap.[147] But despite hints that he would go further, Bush proved unwilling to normalize relations.

SHUT UP AND SIT DOWN

Had he been reelected, Bush might have normalized U.S.-Vietnam relations early in his second term. But the munificence he espoused in 1991 disappeared amid a bruising campaign in which Bush revived the Vietnam War he claimed to have buried in the Arabian sands, only to see its MIA golem cost him the presidency in the form of Ross Perot. Perot's appeal was based on more than his history with the POW/MIA issue, of course, and his candidacy, which won nineteen million votes—nearly one out of every five ballots cast—drew support away from both major party candidates. And while Perot supporters were usually Republican men—older, wealthier, and whiter than the general public—since many would not have voted, or would have picked Bill Clinton without Perot on the ballot, it is hard to prove that he hurt Bush.[148] Exit polls suggest that he cost Bush only the single state of Ohio, not enough to make up Bush's 200-vote electoral college deficit.[149]

But what use are exit polls and voter surveys in explaining a candidate who chose Patsy Cline's "Crazy" as his theme song? In a campaign where

Perot claimed to have been targeted for assassination by a Black Panther hit squad backed by the Vietnamese government, then went on *60 Minutes* to accuse the Bush campaign of seeking to ruin his daughter's reputation by sending provocateurs to her wedding to distribute doctored photos of her engaging in lesbian sex acts, polls seem to lose their explanatory power.[150] Perot's success was about his sensibility and tone, not policy, which he gleefully professed "I don't know a thing about."[151] Perot was a protest candidate and a vote for him was a vote against Bush, but also against the government. More than party or ideological identification, and far more than policy positions, what Perot supporters shared was contempt for government. "Nearly all—95 percent—believed that they could trust the federal government only some of the time or almost never," compared to three in ten average voters. They viewed Bush, Congress, even business and the military in far more negative terms than most voters, and held Bush in far lower regard than Clinton despite being twice as likely to call themselves conservative and identify as Republicans.[152]

What was it about Perot that moved these people to support him? He was an outsider, he was unorthodox, he was nonpartisan, he promised change. But more than this, Perot shared their distrust of government, even fueled it. While pundits saw Perot's conspiratorial proclivities as a weakness, for Perot diehards it was the source of his appeal. Perot's paranoid claims and bizarre behavior—dropping out of the race in July to protect his daughter from Bush's alleged plans to ruin her wedding only to rejoin it in October to expose his devilry—were less distractions from his candidacy than dramatizations of its central theme: that the government preyed upon its own people. If that message cost him an electoral majority, it guaranteed him the support of millions, including many in the MIA lobby. One political scientist found that Perot voters "became exceptionally more cynical . . . as a result of the Perot candidacy."[153]

Seen in this light, Perot's POW/MIA advocacy was key to his campaign. Everything he did had a POW subtext, starting with his decision to run. Perot had harbored ill will toward Bush since their encounters concerning the aborted Perot Commission, blaming Bush for Reagan's rebuff and suspecting Bush of shutting down his investigation to protect corrupt officials.[154] To say that this sparked Perot's presidential ambitions would go too far, but the idea of a presidential run was already in the air at a gala in his honor in April 1987, the very moment Perot was engaged in personal diplomacy with Vietnam over missing Americans. As men in combat fatigues accompanied Perot onto a stage set up like a dungeon with "an angry-looking banner behind him written in Arabic," a woman's voice rose from the crowd—"Run Ross! Run for president!"—while a hotel clerk clad in POW garb and greasepaint stood chained to an hors d'oeuvre table nearby. "If I were real, he'd set me free," the clerk told journalist David Remnick.[155]

That idea, that Perot could rescue Americans from their post-Vietnam imprisonment, was at the heart of his campaign five years later. Soon after he announced he would run, Perot named former POW Jim Stockdale as his running mate. When he published his campaign book he entitled it *United We Stand: How We Can Take Back Our Country*, borrowing the title from his 1969 POW publicity effort. When his volunteers formed a national campaign, they named it "United We Stand America," settling for a variation on the theme after discovering that a gay and lesbian organization now held rights to the original name. And when it came time to select the first president of the new group, former POW Orson Swindle was asked to lead, making him Perot's campaign manager.[156] Even the half-hour infomercials that became his main campaign tool featured Perot's POW activism and made explicit claims of the government's prisoner abandonment.[157]

Perot's fixation on captivity, conspiracy, and the politics of loss played a key part in his fateful decision to drop out of the race, a step that redefined the election when it was a virtual dead heat, and which came about through Perot's association with one of the MIA movement's most notorious charlatans, Scott Barnes. Barnes, who claimed involvement in Operation Lazarus and an earlier POW rescue mission into Cambodia, attracted Perot's attention in the mid-eighties with fantastical conspiracy theories, later published in his book BOHICA: *A True Account of One Man's Battle to Expose the Most Heinous Cover-up of the Vietnam Saga!* An acronym for "Bend Over, Here It Comes Again," BOHICA included Barnes's Ramboesque account of finding two "caucasians" in a Laotian prison only to be ordered to "liquidate the merchandise."[158] Even in the florid paramilitary community Barnes was considered a con man—his *Soldier of Fortune* profile was titled "Scott Barnes: My Favorite Flake"—but that did not keep him from convincing Perot of a Republican plot against him, allegedly meant to prevent Perot from telling the Senate Select Committee the truth about POW abandonment. Fearing Republican dirty tricks, Perot cancelled his appearance before the committee in June. Then, after further word from Barnes that Bush operatives had compromising photos of his daughter, he abruptly withdrew from the race.[159]

Only when Perot went public with Barnes's story after reentering the race in October did Americans learn the details behind his spasmodic campaigning. Even then, the details were too strange for most people to take seriously. When *Newsweek* asked, on the heels of the 1992 balloting, "Does Perot rely too much on stories that are not backed up by hard evidence?" half of all voters said yes, compared to one-third who answered no. In stark contrast, 71 percent of Perot voters answered no.[160] Some even saw Perot's revelations as confirmation of what they suspected all along. MIA daughter Robin Sampley, who spent weeks gathering signatures to get Perot on the North Carolina ballot only to see him drop out, guessed that "they must have threatened his family. The reasons he gave didn't seem to make sense. It doesn't seem like him to back down." Asked who "they" were, she answered, "I just don't know."[161] But her ties to the MIA movement gave her plenty of ideas, and when Perot went on *60 Minutes* to tell Barnes's tale it only proved what she already surmised. Perot performed the conspiracy his supporters wanted to believe.

The crippling effect this performance had on Bush's electoral prospects became apparent at the League's 1992 convention. Making his first appearance at the event since 1989, Bush must have known the League rank and file preferred Perot. But with Perot's withdrawal the week before, he likely anticipated at least a polite reception at an event where he could win back the disaffected right by reminding conservatives of his military service in World War II, his military victory in Iraq, and his opponent's evasion of the Vietnam-era draft. Though he had once boasted of ending the Vietnam Syndrome, Bush's attacks on Clinton's draft record showed that the cure was at best partial—Vietnam remained the defining battleground in late-twentieth-century politics. And for a quarter of a century when presidents wanted to do battle over the Vietnam War and its meaning, they went before the League. His was the ninth presidential address to the League. It was also the last.

The room Bush looked out upon as he stepped to the microphone was ready to explode, and his triumphal remarks supplied the spark. Extending a hearty thanks to Griffiths and a salute to Dick Childress, he began: "We live in a marvelous time." It was as if his words were designed to provoke League dissidents, who viewed recent developments as anything but marvelous and saw Griffiths and Childress as part of the problem. Five minutes into his speech, several dozen audience members began chanting, "No more lies! Tell the truth!" At that point "the place just turned into bedlam," according to dissident board member Jeff Donahue, who joined the protest from his place on the dais. "Mr. President, this is just symptomatic of twenty-three years of deceit and lies and neglect," Donahue shouted at Bush. "The government has been lying about the whole thing all along. The families are fed up with being lied to." "Are you calling me a liar?" Bush shot

President George Bush confronts a restive National League of Families at its annual meeting in July 1992. (Courtesy George Bush Presidential Library)

back. "If you want these people to vote for you," Donahue replied, "bring our loved ones back home." As the audience chanted, "We won't budge! Tell the truth!" Griffiths tried to restore order. "Maybe if the media will stop taking pictures of the minority, they'll go away," she lectured in her typical Oz-like manner. When Bush resumed his speech only to be interrupted almost immediately, both embattled leaders lost their cool. "Sit down!" Griffiths thundered at her rebellious membership; then Bush, his jaw tightening and finger wagging, exploded at them: "Would you please shut up and sit down!"

The commandment quieted the crowd long enough for him to finish, but the damage was done. The confrontation led the nightly news and ran on the front page of the morning papers as further evidence of Bush's troubles with his conservative base. Sensing the danger he was in, Bush tried to appease his assailants for the remainder of his speech, referring to the death of his three-year-old daughter in 1953 and the loss of seven of the fifteen men in his squadron in World War II as evidence of his sympathy for their loss. But nothing he said could erase his eagerness to forget Vietnam sixteen months earlier. Even his famously garbled syntax served up a fresh reminder: "Others say, 'Look, the war is over. Let's move on.' And that is something we can and will never say."[162]

Visiting POW House, "a combined crash pad and propaganda factory for the POW/MIA movement" in Annandale, Virginia, shortly after the Bush speech, a reporter found stacks of T-shirts bearing a caricature of an irate Bush over the words, "SHUT UP AND SIT DOWN: George Bush's Policy on POW/MIAs," alongside "Perot pamphlets, posters, and shirts."[163] The National Vietnam Veterans Coalition declared it the "quote of the summer," vowing "we will not shut up and sit down!"[164] Even the *New York Times* editorialized that given Bush's involvement "with government decision-making in this area for most of the nineteen years since U.S. troops left Vietnam . . . the Vietnam syndrome cannot be declared properly buried until the executive branch itself sets the record straight on those missing in action."[165]

But the visceral rage at the League meeting, and the efforts to sustain it into November, worked against the MIA movement as much as the Bush administration. The League's outsized influence had always depended on two things: public sympathy and the support of public officials. Over the course of 1992, the League and its spin-offs squandered both. As much as they hated the government, MIA activists depended on it. Without the support of at least some element of the U.S. government, they could not influence U.S. policy and public opinion. The League had enjoyed the support of agencies and officials over the years because it served their interests. As it grew more extreme, it broke faith not just with Bush but with his party and with the political mainstream, which could no longer comprehend its Byzantine conspiracy theories and bitter infighting. Its erratic behavior presented fresh evidence of the irrationality of U.S. policy toward Vietnam. "Relations between our two countries have been taken hostage in the hands of some strong MIA lobbies," Vietnam's ambassador to the UN complained, and a growing number of Americans were inclined to agree.[166] It was not just Bush's reception before the League that led many politicians and opinion makers to break ranks with the group; it was also the work of the Senate Select Committee, which exposed the MIA movement as more corrupt, divided, and exiguous than previously thought.

Believing that "nothing has done more to fuel suspicion" than "unnecessary secrecy," the committee defined its mission as "demystifying the process" by "getting the books opened" and "building a public record."[167] But as the committee began declassifying millions of government documents and deposing scores of public officials, it only energized MIA believers who, much as Usry had done, took bits and pieces of the record the committee was creating and used it to insinuate a government conspiracy. Making matters worse, Smith's staff leaked anything that cast doubt on official efforts, including committee work product and classified records. When the committee cracked down on such behavior, dismissing Smith's top aides from its staff, it drew the ire of militants. McCain came under particularly harsh attack, in part because he was the most outspoken critic of MIA fraud, but more than that because his POW status gave him such credibility. Ted Sampley, whose *U.S. Veteran Dispatch* was required reading for the MIA hardcore, accused McCain of having been brainwashed while held captive in Hanoi, while the same man who had mailed death threats to Griffiths began a campaign to defeat him in his 1992 Senate reelection bid.[168] "IF YOU'RE SERIOUS ABOUT WANTING TO BRING HOME LIVE POWS," he wrote to Arizona veterans, "HELP GET OUT THE VOTE AGAINST JOHN MCCAIN, LIAR, TRAITOR, COMMUNIST SYMPATHIZER AND BETRAYER OF EVERYONE WHO EVER SERVED IN THE U.S. ARMED FORCES."[169] When the committee came to McCain's defense, Sampley turned his fire on Kerry, accusing him of seeking to inflate the "MIA body count" in order to "dismiss the issue" and pave the way for normalization.[170]

As its efforts emboldened its critics, the committee began an aggressive investigation of the MIA lobby, over Smith's strenuous objections. "While there have been several congressional attempts to provide an accounting of governmental efforts regarding the POW/MIAs, there has never been any attempt at an accounting of private sector efforts," committee investigator Hilton Foster wrote in a memo addressing Smith's concerns. "We owe people the same level of scrutiny, investigation, and accounting that we have applied to governmental efforts."[171] Together with a series of ABC News reports that revealed the 1991 POW photos as elaborate frauds, the committee exposed a contemporary MIA lobby composed of charlatans, cynics, and ideologues that bore little resemblance to the teary POW wives and MIA mothers of the early 1970s. And while the most egregious travesties unearthed concerned the fundraising practices of the little-known splinter cells that proliferated in the late eighties, the League did not escape unscathed. Griffiths's role funneling money for the IAG played prominently in the committee's final report and was at the heart of its recommendation to disband that body. More important, the League suffered from guilt by association, since the committee made clear that there were no bright lines between it and more mercenary organizations, with most committed activists belonging to multiple groups. The MIA lobby was surprisingly small, it turned out, and this revelation was the most damaging of all, with many politicians concluding that its bark was worse than its bite.[172]

McCain's unbridled rebuke at the committee's final hearings in December exhibited none of the deference usually shown to MIA promoters. "The people who have done these things are not zealots in a good cause. In my opinion, they are criminals and some of the most craven, most cynical, and most despicable human beings to ever run a scam." Expressing indifference to their motives, he concluded, "I would hope when the facts are known in detail that the American people will forever hold these activists in the contempt they deserve and view their credibility with the suspicion they have earned."[173] It was a remarkable statement that showed how the committee's work, along with the third-party challenge of Perot's candidacy, changed the political calculus of the POW/MIA issue. The League was not defeated nor its influence at an end—few officials could get away with speaking the way McCain had—but its reputation had been dealt a blow from which it never fully recovered.

NOTHING LIKE IT IN ALL THE HISTORY OF WARFARE

Two weeks before Bill Clinton was elected president, Thomas Vallely, a Vietnam veteran at the Harvard Institute for International Development, warned Vietnam's Foreign Ministry that the conventional wisdom that a "Democratic administration will close the book on America's war with Vietnam" was naive. "Clinton will have two basic problems with vastly improving relations with Vietnam," Vallely predicted: his party's traditional concern for human rights, and the League. "The political controversy that surrounds his own avoidance of military service will make it difficult for him to offer any new policy initiatives. He, too, will be afraid of Ann Mills Griffiths."[174]

Vallely's prognosis proved insightful in the short term. If one lesson to be drawn from Clinton's victory was that most Americans accepted his efforts to avoid serving in Vietnam, he seemed more impressed by the stridency of those who did not. After suffering further slings and arrows in his bid to allow gays and lesbians to serve openly in the armed forces, Clinton showed little stomach for further fights with the guardians of patriotic correctness over relations with Vietnam. He did not, however, halt the deliberate progress of recent years, instead letting it play out to its predictable end. While normalization took longer than it might have had Bush been reelected, not coming until July 1995, it occurred through familiar means—body recovery and the forceful intervention of prominent Vietnam veterans.

General Vessey was among the most important of those veterans. Clinton asked him to stay on as his presidential envoy, extending Vessey's tenure into its sixth year, and in April 1993 Vessey made his first trip to Hanoi under the new administration. On the eve of his departure, a research associate at Harvard's Center for International Affairs, and a longstanding critic of the Vietnamese government and the American antiwar movement, unearthed a "secret document" in the Soviet archives that purported to show 1,205 Americans in North Vietnamese custody as of September 1972. Like the fake photos of 1991, this Russian translation of an alleged briefing to Vietnam's Politburo was hailed as confirmation of the enemy's duplicity by MIA commentators and media talking heads, though its vastly inflated POW figure was contradicted by reams of U.S. intelligence.[175] It seemed that the production of such "evidence" might forever thwart closer relations. But Vessey repudiated the document, returning from Vietnam with records to disprove the report and bluntly insisting, "we haven't found any of the facts to be accurate."[176] Vietnam was "bending over backward" to account for missing Americans, he told reporters after briefing the president on the controversy.[177]

Kerry and McCain spoke volumes about their opinion of the report when they journeyed to Hanoi a month later with Democratic congressman and former POW Pete Peterson, visiting Hoa Lo prison. Like Vessey, they returned to tell Clinton he should reward Vietnam's efforts on MIAs, which had resulted in the recovery of fifty-eight remains in 1992 and the return of twenty-one more in the months since Clinton took office.[178] A few days later, Kerry accompanied Clinton to Boston for a commencement address, where he continued to press his case.[179] And on 1 July, Kerry, McCain, and Peterson joined nineteen members of Congress who had served in Vietnam in signing a letter that urged Clinton to relax sanctions against Vietnam. Given the "significant progress on many of our unresolved POW/MIA cases," they wrote, "if Vietnam is not given a signal by our government that it recognizes the significant contributions it is making, it may well discontinue its efforts."[180] "I've been a hard-liner," Republican senator Larry Pressler told Winston Lord, the nominee for assistant secretary of state for East Asian and Pacific affairs in his confirmation hearings. "I'm a Vietnam veteran and served two tours." But the time had come to "recognize Vietnam."[181]

On 2 July Clinton announced he would no longer block international financial institutions from lending money to Vietnam, clearing the way for nearly $1 billion in loans from the World Bank, the International Monetary Fund, and the Asian Development Bank. At the same time he announced plans to send Lord and other U.S. officials to Hanoi to discuss additional steps toward "the fullest possible accounting."[182] Griffiths declared the move "the most disastrous decision in all these years," but with the IAG disbanded there was little she could do but complain. While the League held its annual meeting later that month, Lord was in Hanoi arranging to station U.S. diplomats there to help MIA families visiting Vietnam to search for missing loved ones. Lord denied that it was a step toward diplomatic relations, but their consular presence allowed day-to-day contact between the two governments.[183] At the same time Lord gave Vietnam microfilm containing millions of pages of captured communist documents from the war, the first time the United States had ever made an effort to help account for missing Vietnamese.[184]

Clinton was not the first to use the MIA issue as an impetus for closer relations rather than an impediment, but he and his congressional allies perfected the strategy, and Vietnam's vigorous cooperation made it credible. At the heart of this strategy was an emphasis on field activities—archival research, short-notice site inspections, and, above all, crash-site excavations. These operations had grown exponentially since the MIA office known as The Ranch opened in Hanoi in 1991, with several hundred Americans engaged in the effort in Vietnam, Laos, and Cambodia, or in support roles in Hawaii and Washington. In 1993, seventeen Americans were stationed in Hanoi with two three-man teams in Saigon and Danang and seven ten-man teams roving the countryside. Their efforts were supplemented by hundreds more Vietnamese officials and a large network of locals supplying labor and supplies. To oversee this enterprise—operationally known as Joint Task Force–Full Accounting (JTF-FA), which replaced the JCRC in 1992—a deputy assistant secretary of defense for POW/MIA affairs post was created in 1991, and in 1993 the Defense Prisoner of War/Missing in Action Office (DPMO) was established at the Pentagon.[185]

This expanded accounting effort cost over $100 million per year, which divided by the number of remains recovered in 1992 translated to $1.7 million per remains. Because some remains were so fragmentary they could not be identified, the cost per identification was even higher, a fact that struck some observers as unseemly, even immoral, in light of the hundreds of thousands of missing Vietnamese and the millions more disabled by the war. As Neil Sheehan wrote in the New Yorker, in 1992 the accounting effort cost more than thirty times the value of U.S. humanitarian aid paid to Vietnam, though he also noted that many of those funds ultimately ended up in the hands of Vietnamese officials.[186] For one letter writer to the New York Times, the "grisly bureaucratic enterprise" was no better than "the adventurous racketeers" it replaced, with both exhibiting callous indifference to Vietnamese suffering.[187]

Administration officials presented the effort in a more positive light, as a sign not only of their commitment to MIA accounting but of Vietnam's cooperation. When Lord visited Vietnam in July, he took representatives from Vietnam Veterans of America, the American Legion, the VFW, and other veteran's groups (though not the League) to impress on them the enormity of the search and sway them toward the administration's view that the best way to find MIAs was through closer cooperation. Lord failed to win over the Legion, but the VFW joined the Vietnam Veterans of America in endorsing closer ties.[188] Lord returned to Hanoi in December to take part in a repatriation ceremony that otherwise would have attracted limited attention. Upon his return the debate over the embargo resumed, with those who favored its end noting the return of sixty-seven remains in 1993.[189] In January the JTF-FA began its twenty-seventh and largest field activity to date, sending seven dozen specialists to thirteen sites with Admiral Charles Larson, the commander of U.S. forces in the Pacific, and a Senate delegation that included Kerry in tow.[190]

When Kerry returned, he and McCain introduced a resolution calling for an end to the embargo. Speaking for the measure, Kerry cited "the most significant remains retrieval and identification effort in the history of warfare" as proof that both governments were doing all they could to account for the missing. He detailed his visits to excavation sites and showed pictures of Americans and Vietnamese working together to find remains. When McCain joined him on the Senate floor, he came with endorsements from Admiral Larson, General Vessey, and various field commanders working to resolve cases inside Vietnam. "JTF personnel are responsible for locating more information, for resolving more of the mystery surrounding this question than all the professional malcontents, conspiracy mongers, con artists, and dime store Rambos who attend this issue have ever or will ever contribute," McCain snapped.[191]

Their resolution passed by a vote of sixty-two to thirty-eight, which gave Clinton political cover to make a decision that was sure to anger some on the right.[192] Many supporters approved the measure in pursuit of economic opportunities. Thanks to economic liberalization and the growing porousness of the embargo, Vietnam's economy made a striking turnaround in the early nineties, with annual growth of 5 to 8 percent. As foreign investors grabbed the low-hanging fruit, American firms worried that nothing would be left by the time they gained access to the Vietnamese market.[193] These concerns were well represented in the debate over the embargo, with numerous speakers protesting that the embargo cost Americans more than the Vietnamese.

Yet important as the economic rationale was, it was overshadowed by the MIA issue, both in the Senate debate and in presidential pronouncements. When asked if he was under pressure from the business lobby to lift the embargo, Clinton acknowledged that he was. "But that cannot be the sole criteria," he continued. "Our first concern has to be for the POWs and the MIAs."[194] The same priorities were displayed in the Senate. When trade was mentioned, its influence on MIA accounting was paramount, not its effect on the pocketbook. Debate became far more heated than an ordinary trade dispute as senators spoke in personal terms of their long involvement with the issue. "I am just worn out by these people," Larry Pressler said of MIA activists who questioned his patriotism. "It is time for those of us who are Vietnam veterans to stand up and say that enough is enough from this very small group." Republican senators Frank Murkowski and Alan Simpson joined him, remembering their disgust at the antics of MIA activists who came before the Veterans Affairs Committee in 1986. Simpson pointed out that his first cousin was among the tens of thousands still missing from World War II. Democrat John Glenn noted how many of his fellow World War II and Korean War comrades remained missing, and added to this total 300,000 Vietnamese. "Do we have adequate records on all those people?" he asked, noting the absurdity of expecting the enemy to provide a full account of the American dead. Republican John Chafee recalled burying a friend who fought alongside him at the Battle of Guadalcanal only to be unable to find his body after the battle; he remained missing until discovered by a farmer plowing his fields in 1989. So many war stories were told and military experts cited in the debate that Smith objected: "I do not think having a medal or having a great, illustrious military career which is fantastic is the criteria we ought to use to judge whether or not the Vietnamese are making the full accounting."[195]

But in Washington medals and military careers mattered, particularly to a White House under attack from the military establishment. With Kerry, Robb, Kerrey, and Pete Peterson at his side, Clinton announced on 3 February 1994 that he was ending the trade embargo. He took the step, he told reporters, "because I am absolutely convinced it offers the best way to resolve the fate of those who remain missing," citing the return of remains and reduction in discrepancy cases as proof that his approach was working.[196]

Though invited, Griffiths boycotted the ceremony, saying Clinton had "broken his promise."[197] "President Clinton has sold the morality of the American people for just a few pieces of silver," MIA sister Dolores Alfond seethed.[198] Both women rejected the idea that the hundreds of remains returned in recent years represented progress, noting that only three of the sixty-seven remains repatriated in 1993 had been identified. "They have thrown a few flight suits at us," Alfond spat. "They haven't given us noth-

President Bill Clinton and Senator John Kerry shake hands after President Clinton announces normalization of relations with the Socialist Republic of Vietnam on 11 July 1995. Also present, from left, are Vice President Al Gore, Secretary of State Warren Christopher, Defense Secretary William Perry, Senator John McCain, and National Security Adviser Anthony Lake. (Courtesy William J. Clinton Presidential Library)

ing."[199] But media outlets challenged this claim, noting that it often took years to identify the fragmentary remains from Vietnam.[200] The League's own data later showed that more MIAs were recovered and identified in Clinton's first term—258 in all—than in any four-year period before or since.[201]

Aside from the furor from predictable quarters, there was little public outcry over Clinton's move. If anything, there were more entreaties to complete the process by normalizing diplomatic relations than outcries against the embargo's end. Polls showed that Americans backed such a step by wide margins, with 61 percent favoring recognition and 27 percent opposed.[202] As Clinton inched toward that end over the next year and a half, he retraced his earlier steps. In late February the administration dispatched an even larger JTF-FA contingent than the one it sent to Vietnam in early January, with over 100 searchers.[203] Over the coming year, sixty-one additional remains were returned. In May the two sides agreed to establish liaison offices in Hanoi and Washington to "facilitate progress on all issues of concern, particularly POW/MIA accounting."[204] And on Memorial Day 1995, Clinton unveiled a POW/MIA postage stamp on the South Lawn and spoke of his continued commitment "to leave no stone unturned" in the search for the missing. "More than 200 sets of remains have been returned since I became President," he reminded critics; "there is nothing like it in all the history of warfare."[205]

When Kerry and McCain dropped by the Oval Office that week, any close observer could have guessed what was coming. On 11 July, Clinton announced the normalization of diplomatic relations with Vietnam, citing rapid accounting progress. Again he thanked Kerry, McCain, Robb, Kerrey, and Peterson for helping "America to move forward on Vietnam." Then, reaching his peroration, he concluded, "This moment offers us the opportunity to bind up our own wounds. They have resisted time for too long."[206]

NORMALIZATION OF RELATIONS did not bring an end to the MIA issue or the politics of loss. Secretary of State Warren Christopher's visit to Hanoi in August began with a ceremony at the Hanoi airport in which four caskets containing Americans were returned to U.S. custody. Only after this display of dedication to MIAs did Christopher and Foreign Minister Nguyen Manh Cam sign the documents that established diplomatic relations between their two governments.[207] In the years to come, such scenes of fidelity became obligatory for visiting American dignitaries. When former president George Bush traveled to Hanoi in 1995 he visited an ongoing excavation, as did Secretary of Defense William Cohen when he visited in 2000 and President Clinton during his visit later that year.[208] Secretary of State Colin Powell brought the practice into the second Bush administration when he returned to Vietnam in 2001 to mark the ratification of a bilateral trade agreement, lighting incense at The Ranch in honor of seven Americans and nine Vietnamese who died in a helicopter crash en route to an excavation site in April.[209]

Added to those killed in JCRC recovery operations in 1973, these deaths brought the total number killed in the U.S. accounting effort to eight Americans and eleven Vietnamese. While their mission resulted in the recovery of hundreds of American remains, their lives were a high price to pay for an effort scorned by those it was meant to appease. "We are being asked to once again believe in a tooth fairy," Donna Long wrote in 1994, "by our political parent, Uncle Sam, and his concubines, Vietnam and Laos. This new tooth fairy . . . sells the teeth of unreturned American prisoners of war and missing in action for billions of dollars in trade. . . . But the criteria for belief in tooth fairies is the same — in order to believe, you must remain sound asleep."[210]

Minus Long's overwrought tone, many Americans would agree that there was something untoward about the MIA accounting effort and the purposes to which it was put in the 1990s.[211] Sending Americans to their deaths in search of bits of bone was a macabre endeavor. Tied to a policy that sought to open Vietnamese markets to international trade and investment, it became a mercenary one. But cast in different terms—terms of healing and closure—Americans regarded the body recovery effort with more sympathy. And while such a characterization can be fraught with nationalistic overtones, it can also become the basis for humanistic aspirations to re-create the brotherhood of man after the horrors of war.[212] Skeptics might argue that Clinton's talk of partnership at a multi-million-dollar excavation site as he turned a blind eye to the suffering of Vietnamese wartime survivors ignored the power imbalance between the United States and Vietnam, and the differences between ordinary Americans and their government. At the same time, such sentiment was key to easing the hostility that defined U.S.-Vietnam relations for so long, and was actively cultivated by Vietnamese leaders.

While the bipartisan comity of the Senate Select Committee proved that Americans with opposing views on the war could find common ground in their shared appreciation for wartime sacrifice, the committee's effectiveness depended on the same narratives of self-victimization that the MIA lobby had long propagated. The same stricken national conscience that allowed MIA activists to go unchallenged for so many years permitted Vietnam veterans in the Senate to rebut them. Feelings of guilt and shame left those Americans who never served in Vietnam on the sidelines, unable to argue over the war for fear of further victimizing those it had already harmed. Long before he took office, Clinton learned that he could not address the war without being called a draft dodger, which is why he surrounded himself with veterans whenever he spoke about the war. That Vietnam veterans and POWs helped him turn the accounting effort toward resolution rather than retribution only confirmed for those in the MIA movement that the nation's leaders could not be trusted and that all were, in some sense, responsible for defeat in Vietnam.

Conclusion

This Thing Has Consumed American Politics for Years

"This is a fascinating untold story, an incredible story," John Kerry remarked midway through his tenure as Senate Select Committee chairman. "The more you raise it, the more complicated it becomes." "There is not a place I have gone in the last years in this country where someone has not come up to me and said, 'Why are you not doing anything on this?'" Kerry professed. Given its hold on the public imagination, it was "hardly appropriate for us to just turn our backs and say, this is not relevant," he counseled. "This thing has consumed American politics for twenty years."[1]

In the years after Kerry's remarks, most observers concluded that the Senate Select Committee and the passage of time had finally brought the controversy surrounding missing Americans to rest. By the mid-nineties the National League of Families and its splinter groups were in eclipse, with dwindling memberships that no longer commanded the attention of presidents and top policymakers. Bill Clinton's 1996 reelection over the disabled war veteran and League patron Bob Dole in the face of opposition from the League and other watchdogs of patriotic orthodoxy seemed to prove that the politics of loss no longer moved voters. Days before Clinton's victory, James Carroll wrote glowingly of how John Kerry and John Mc-Cain, "two heroes who came home on different sides of the war made their peace — and the nation's," in a long *New Yorker* article titled "A Friendship That Ended the War."[2]

In the area of U.S.-Vietnam relations, there was ample evidence to support this sanguine view. Despite tensions surrounding Vietnam's human rights record and U.S. foot-dragging in addressing the devastating health and environmental effects caused by its use of dioxins during the war, diplomatic and trade relations between the two nations advanced under both Clinton and George W. Bush.[3] Bush followed Clinton's 2000 visit to Vietnam with a Hanoi trip of his own in November 2006, where he spent just fifteen minutes at The Ranch.[4] After this perfunctory show of support for the MIA accounting effort, Bush welcomed Vietnam's President Nguyen Minh Triet to the Oval Office in June 2007. Reporting on the historic visit of Vietnam's highest-ranking official highlighted human rights and trade—which reached $9.4 billion that year—with scarce mention of the MIA cause.[5]

But the war was not yet over on the home front, as the two men Carroll credited with ending it learned firsthand in their respective 2000, 2004, and 2008 presidential bids. In each case Kerry and McCain suffered vicious attacks from MIA militants administering payback for their work on the Senate Select Committee. The first to test the presidential waters in 2000, McCain was the first to feel the slings and arrows of MIA activists. After an unlikely double-digit victory over Bush in the New Hampshire primary, McCain was derailed through a furious smear campaign that vaulted Bush to an eleven-point win in South Carolina. As the campaign entered South Carolina, ugly rumors began to circulate—that McCain frequented prostitutes and suffered from sexually transmitted diseases, that his wife was addicted to drugs, that his adopted Bangladeshi daughter was his half-black love child—that addressed the fears and prejudices of conservative evangelicals who turned out for Bush by wide margins.

Though these charges, distributed via flyers, e-mail, and push polls from little-known or fictitious organizations, eventually achieved notoriety, most attracted little immediate media coverage. That was the point—to raise issues that mattered to the party base that were too disreputable or from sources too unreliable for the Bush camp to air in the open, and to do so without leaving footprints that could be traced back to the campaign. "I paint my face and travel at night," Bush operative Ralph Reed boasted. "You don't know it's over until you're in a body bag."[6] But there was one notable exception to this rule, one issue that Bush supporters openly promoted to raise doubts about McCain: that his years in captivity left him prone to violent fits of temper, perhaps even rendered him mentally unstable.

This idea had been floating around since the Senate Select Committee's tenure when Ted Sampley accused McCain of having succumbed to communist brainwashing while in captivity in his *U.S. Veteran Dispatch* article, "John McCain: The Manchurian Candidate." Calling McCain a "counterfeit hero," Sampley used his popular broadsheet, distributed to subscribers and available at the Vietnam Veterans Memorial and through his web site, to turn McCain's war record from a strength to a weakness, an agenda that McCain's rivals embraced as his campaign gained momentum.[7] Starting in late 1999 and intensifying through the South Carolina primary, Bush surrogates, including prominent Senate Republicans, began telling reporters, as one put it, that McCain returned from Vietnam "with a loose screw," often citing his heated exchanges with MIA activists as proof of his volatility.[8]

The "Manchurian Candidate" charge garnered more media attention than other elements in the anti-McCain smear campaign, and grew louder and more explicit as that campaign wore on, leading to a fiery moment in a mid-February debate. "You should be ashamed," McCain scolded Bush for campaigning with MIA activist J. Thomas Burch, who told crowds at Bush rallies that McCain "came home [and] forgot us."[9] But Bush was unapologetic. Days before the South Carolina vote, the conservative patriarch Paul Weyrich reported that the "Khmer Rouge has claimed that 'McCain is a Vietnamese agent'" in an e-mail distributed through his Free Congress Foundation, adding that MIA families considered McCain "a traitor." Proof of McCain's disloyalty was elusive, Weyrich admitted—Sampley's web site was his only source—but "there must be some basis for the emotions expressed by otherwise rational people."[10]

This claim, with its slippage from emotion to reason, prompts the question of why McCain's mental health achieved a notoriety that other elements of the Bush whispering campaign never did. In part it had to do with its grain of truth: McCain was famous for his temper. And it picked up on the most widely known fact about McCain. He and his supporters had long promoted his POW status. Therefore statements about that experience carried greater weight than unproven aspersions about McCain's private life, and were more easily adjudicated by reporters. But other rumors about McCain bore some semblance to reality. McCain's wife, Cindy, really was addicted to painkillers in the early 1990s, McCain was a notorious playboy before and after his years in Vietnam, and his adopted South Asian daughter had far darker skin than the ghostly white McCains. By the same token, the "Manchurian Candidate" idea went well beyond anything known or knowable about McCain. That it was spoken more freely and taken more seriously than other calumnies against him reflected institutional and cultural developments rooted in the history of the POW/MIA issue more than any basis in reality.

McCain's temper may have become a campaign issue no matter what, but it would not have mutated into rumors of a disloyal automaton without the efforts of MIA activists and the legitimacy they had achieved through decades of POW/MIA advocacy. Though Sampley, the chief peddler of the

"Manchurian Candidate" rumor, was not related to an MIA, and lacked the esteem enjoyed by Ann Mills Griffiths (who despised Sampley, and sat out his anti-McCain crusade), he commanded a sizable audience in MIA circles. As his allegations were picked up and repeated by other activists, they acquired an appearance of grassroots authenticity that other "astro-turf" whispering efforts lacked. In an environment where no Bush strategist wished to be seen orchestrating the assault on McCain, the zeal of the MIA movement was key. "The value of having this whole network of people who all come out of the same influence," South Carolina Republican political consultant Rod Shealy told *Vanity Fair*, was that "you don't have to tell them" what to do or how to do it. "You don't have to say, 'you know, wouldn't it be a great thing if this happened?'"[11] Those like Sampley were self-starting and self-sustaining. All Bush had to do was welcome and repeat their smears rather than repudiate them.

While Bush gave license to attacks on McCain's POW record, they resonated with voters for deeper reasons. Decades of POW/MIA activism had taught Americans to regard Vietnam veterans generally, and POWs in particular, as more victims than heroes. Though most who participated in POW/MIA politics did so to honor and support those who served in Vietnam, their expressions of support were more often mournful than celebratory, more aggrieved than triumphal. That plaintive public memory had often clashed with positive constructions of the war, whether from presidents or from former POWs themselves. While McCain owed much of his political success to the fact that he did not appear embittered by his captivity, the heroic image he promoted was less familiar to Americans than the image of the broken and betrayed veteran encouraged by Sampley. McCain's fellow veteran and campaign co-chair Senator Chuck Hagel recognized the dilemma, telling columnist Maureen Dowd, "It's an orchestrated effort, very subtle, very clever. . . . They say, 'you can't blame John for acting half-nuts sometimes. He's a hero. Anyone who went through that experience would be half-nuts.'" He called such talk "despicable rumor-mongering about a guy who has given so damn much to his country by a lot of guys who have never given anything and never worn uniforms."[12] But even in his assessment, Hagel reinforced the image of the veteran as victim. When McCain refused to play that role, and expressed impatience with those who did, he attracted the ire of the MIA activists who popularized it, causing confusion among Americans accustomed to thinking of the war as a tragedy rather than a triumph of the human spirit.

More than McCain, however, John Kerry bore the brunt of MIA lobby rage, and it was Kerry's 2004 presidential campaign that showed the persistence of the politics of loss. Vietnam was arguably the defining issue of the 2004 election. Kerry won his party's nomination on the strength of his Vietnam War record, he made his military service the centerpiece of his campaign, and his opponents attacked that service throughout his run for the White House. From Kerry's Vietnam-studded nominating convention in July to the Swift Boat Veterans For Truth attacks on him that consumed the late summer and fall, through the *60 Minutes* scandal surrounding Bush's Texas Air National Guard duty in September and on to Sinclair Broadcast Group's proposal to air the anti-Kerry film *Stolen Honor: Wounds That Never Heal* in October, Vietnam displaced Iraq, Afghanistan, Osama bin Laden, Al Qaeda, Abu Ghraib, and other pressing foreign policy issues at the center of media coverage and political debate. And though it might seem that the war's prominence would benefit Kerry—a decorated veteran who volunteered for two tours of duty campaigning against two men who deliberately avoided military service in Vietnam— doubts about Kerry's conduct during and after the war dealt a fatal blow to his presidential prospects. One post-election survey showed that three-quarters of all voters were familiar with attacks on Kerry's Vietnam record, and when asked which campaign advertisements made the biggest impression, those of Kerry's Swift Vet critics were cited as often as all other "527" advocacy ads combined.[13]

Some bemoaned Vietnam's prominence as a distraction, but none should have been surprised by it. For four decades the war in Vietnam had dominated discussion of U.S. foreign policy and shaped public attitudes toward the nation and its leaders, and Kerry was a key contributor to that conversation from the start. Long before his service on the Senate Select Committee, Kerry burst onto the national scene in April 1971 when he famously asked the Senate Foreign Relations Committee, "How do you ask a man to be the last man to die in Vietnam? How do you ask a man to be the last man to die for a mistake?" His testimony lent a veteran's voice to the chorus of complaint emanating from POW wives, whose revolt took place that same spring. Kerry was in Washington to take part in a weeklong demonstration in which a thousand members of Vietnam Veterans against the War (VVAW) encamped on the National Mall, and the resulting confluence of protest unnerved the Nixon White House. "They're really killing us because they run the veterans' demonstration every night," H. R. Haldeman wrote in his diary, "and we have no way to fight back."[14]

Nixon hit-man Chuck Colson soon devised a response, tearing into Kerry's record to tell his boss that "this fellow Kerry . . . turns out to be really quite a phony." "He is sort of phony, isn't he?" Nixon replied, in what may have been the first recorded instance of the claim that Kerry "flip-flopped."[15] In an attempt to promote warriors who more closely conformed to the silent majority ideal, Nixon implemented Colson's plan for a $150 million Ad Council campaign focused on POWs and their families and invited prowar veteran John O'Neill to the White House to demonstrate the proper role for veterans: "The President does our talking for us," said O'Neill.[16] Kerry "was a thorn in our flesh," Colson later recalled. "He forced us to create a counterfoil. We found a vet named John O'Neill and formed a group called Vietnam Veterans for a Just Peace. We had O'Neill meet the President, and we did everything we could to boost his group."[17]

These same parties—O'Neill, POWs, and hard-bitten activists like Sampley, bankrolled by oil tycoons and real estate developers—led the charge against Kerry three decades later. Through a $25 million barrage of TV ads, direct mail, digital media, a best-selling book, and a short film, the O'Neill-led Swift Boat Veterans for Truth accused Kerry of lying about his war record and slandering those who served in Vietnam.[18] Their attacks on Kerry's military service, his war wounds, and his medals and commendations fired up the Republican base, but were dismissed by all but the most conservative media outlets as slurs "no informed person can seriously believe."[19] Their more damaging charges came in the form of Swift Vet attacks on Kerry's antiwar record, recalled through endless loops of his 1971 Senate testimony. Using clips where Kerry condemned the war's atrocities, his critics cast him not as an opponent of U.S. policy but as an enemy of American soldiers. One Swift Vet ad spliced footage of him reporting atrocities with veterans proclaiming that his words "betrayed us."[20] Sampley, who founded the less-well-financed Vietnam Veterans against Kerry, gave verisimilitude to these charges by distributing photoshopped images of Kerry and Jane Fonda sharing a speaker's platform at an antiwar rally. The Fonda photo was soon exposed as a fake, but not before Kerry's alleged ties to "Hanoi Jane" were cited by critics as proof of his disloyalty to men in the field.[21]

Calling the Swift Vets a "front" for the Bush campaign, Kerry dismissed their attacks as "so petty that it's almost pathetic."[22] John McCain also condemned their ads, though not in the strenuous terms Kerry would have liked.[23] And while the media was criticized for paying them undue attention, most mainstream commentators treated Swift Vet attacks on Kerry's war record with skepticism (reporters showed fewer qualms when it came to repeating attacks on his antiwar activity). Still, the smear campaign refused to dissipate, in part because O'Neill had $25 million to burn, in part because he enjoyed the support of the Bush White House, but equally important because the Swift Vets tapped into emotions and ideas that resonated powerfully with American voters.[24] As O'Neill explained in telling terms, "We learned from some former POWs that when they were captive in Vietnam, they developed a 'tap code' to communicate with each other without the guards knowing." To reach voters without attracting the opprobrium of media watchdogs, "we realized we needed our own tap code to talk to the public."[25]

Who better to teach the Swift Vets to tap the politics of loss than former POWs? In late September O'Neill announced that he was joining forces with seventeen Vietnam POWs as the "Swift Vets and POWs for Truth." The rechristened group immediately launched a multimillion dollar ad campaign and released its new forty-minute film *Stolen Honor: Wounds That Never Heal*, in which former POWs and their wives blamed Kerry for extending their captivity and worsening their suffering.[26] The key component in O'Neill's coded message, the former prisoners and their wives offered seemingly incontrovertible proof of Kerry's treason from a source few dared question. "John Kerry gave aid and comfort to the enemy," they reported, encouraging "the North Vietnamese to keep us in captivity longer, which meant more torture, more lost years and, sadly, more death."[27] According to this view, Kerry's words were deadly weapons aimed at the hearts of American prisoners. "Who was the last POW to die languishing in a North Vietnamese prison, forced to listen to the recorded voice of John Kerry disgracing his service by dishonest testimony?" O'Neill asked, joining POW Paul Galanti in blaming Kerry for adding "thousands of additional names" to the Vietnam Veterans Memorial.[28]

These charges were baseless. Communists broadcast antiwar statements inside Hanoi's prisons, but the torture of American prisoners ended in 1969.[29] And though some prisoners and their families resented it, the historical record makes clear that peace activists secured the release of dozens of American POWs and facilitated improvements in their living conditions. Many captives granted early release joined Kerry and the VVAW in condemning the war, as did a sizable minority of the POW population inside Hanoi, and their example was more upsetting, though no more fatal, to American prisoners than anything that Kerry said.[30]

Differences among POWs remind us that countless soldiers and veterans, like most Americans, opposed the war by the time Kerry condemned it in 1971.[31] Yet in the Swift Vets' telling, Kerry, "the one who got credit for serving with distinction in combat, then, through the eyes of the veterans in this film, went home to discredit the men left behind," was responsible for widespread doubts about the war, "literally creating the images of those who served in combat as deranged drug-addicted psychopaths," as *Stolen*

Honor's director Carlton Sherwood put it. Kerry's "betrayal," Sherwood attested, produced "an inner hurt no surgeon's scalpel could remove," and the marine combat veteran "want[ed] him to answer for his lies."[32] Sherwood's subjects evinced a similar determination to make Kerry pay for their "stolen honor," with POW James Warner going so far as to blame Kerry for his mother's appearance at the Winter Soldier investigation and her subsequent antiwar testimony before Congress in April 1971.[33]

Their angry words exploited public memory of the war more than they altered it. Because most Americans considered the war not just mistaken but "unjust"—an assessment that remained consistent in opinion polling throughout the postwar period and into 2004—they took Swift Vet and POW outrage seriously, and because most people regretted the war, few were inclined to question their claims.[34] In the midst of the Swift Vet fracas, even the neoconservative *Weekly Standard* admitted, "Virtually all Americans agree that Vietnam was a tragedy."[35] Plenty of people regretted Swift Vet attacks as harmful in their own right, but few begrudged them their anger. After all, the notion that American servicemen were damaged by the war and mistreated upon their return was even more common than the conviction that the war was wrong. In the eyes of many Americans, the harm it did to American soldiers was *why* it was wrong.

Kerry helped promulgate this view throughout his career, whether in his 1971 Senate testimony, which was more concerned with the psychic damage Americans suffered as they carried out atrocities than with the costs inflicted on their Vietnamese victims, or through his work on the Senate Select Committee, which hammered home the idea that American soldiers were betrayed. And in 2004 he frequently recalled the lies and deceptions of the Vietnam War to remind Americans of the costs of unnecessary wars, and to reassure Americans that he would avoid repeating the mistakes of the past. In each case his claims moved millions of Americans to support him. His ability to use his combat record to harness the grief and anger Americans felt over the Vietnam War and turn it to his own ends was why Nixon recognized him as a threat in 1971 and helps to explain his rise to the top of the Democratic Party thirty-three years later.

But in the end Kerry fell victim to his own success. "They used the energy that we had created about Vietnam to turn it against us," one adviser explained. That energy came not from the 2004 campaign alone but from Kerry's entire life's work. His skill at navigating the politics of loss and using its passions to promote peace rather than conflict enraged his enemies, who were particularly incensed by the ways Kerry seemed to profit from their pain. It was this sense—that Kerry professed to speak for

Americans who suffered in Vietnam while promoting rather than punishing the antiwar movement and the Vietnamese people whom many blamed for their ordeal—that led critics to accuse him of hypocrisy, of wanting it both ways, of flip-flopping. "It's not just what he said in '71, it's what he did in the '90s," Bob Kerrey told reporters when asked about the Swift Vets. "If John Kerry had been one of the leaders in saying 'Hell no, we're not going to recognize Vietnam,' this would not be happening." But because he blurred the boundaries between villain and victim, "they full-bore hate him."[36]

To these Americans, only exposing Kerry as a fraud could settle the score. As one Florida billboard put it, "Defeating John Kerry Would Give Vietnam Veterans The Homecoming They Never Had."[37] How many Americans felt this way, or, more important, how many were persuaded to cast a vote against Kerry they might otherwise have cast for him, is impossible to say.[38] But Swift Vet advertising took a toll. Kerry's favorability ratings plummeted from 53 percent to 44 percent in the first month the Swift Vet ads went on the air, and by November they had neutralized what had been Kerry's greatest strength.[39] The Swift Vets "never fully convinced voters that Mr. Kerry 'betrayed' his country," Republican pollster Frank Luntz wrote in an election postmortem, "but they did raise nagging and unresolved doubts about Mr. Kerry's character and judgment at the very moment that voters had begun to make up their minds," doubts that proved costly in a razor-close election.[40]

If nothing else, the Swift Vets showed that the Vietnam War was not over for many Americans, that its memory aroused passions like little else. Those passions remained dark and divisive, with little ability to inspire confidence or forge an electoral majority, as John McCain learned when he again failed to turn his prisoner of war status into a winning presidential platform in 2008. His failure came through no lack of effort. In a campaign widely criticized as erratic, the one constant was the McCain camp's emphasis of his POW experience. Convinced that the election was "not about issues" but about character, McCain and his advisers cited his captivity ordeal as the crucible that forged his "country first" code.[41] When his campaign nearly went bankrupt in 2007, McCain invited former Hanoi prison mates to join his "No Surrender" tour, reviving his political fortunes by reminding Republicans that he alone among the GOP contenders had "sacrificed for his country."[42] After clinching his party's nomination with this show of steel, McCain launched his "Service to America" tour in which he traveled to posts from his martial past while releasing the companion ad "Service to America: 624787." As his first TV commercial of the general election, the spot featured grainy black-and-white footage of McCain shortly after his capture, his arm in a cast, his eyes fever bright, providing his military rank and serial number to an unseen interrogator while the narrator asked, "What must a president believe about us? About America? That she is worth protecting? That liberty is priceless? Our people, honorable?" And "what must we believe about that president? What does he think? Where has he been? Has he walked the walk?" Intercut with POW scenes was footage of McCain at a campaign stop where he rallied the crowd with moral imperatives he had derived from his Vietnam days: "Keep that faith. Keep your courage. Stick together. Stay strong. Do not yield. Stand up! We're Americans, and we'll never surrender!"[43] McCain revisited these themes in his acceptance speech at the Republican nominating convention, where he spoke of captivity as his life's defining moment before he closed, "Stand up to defend our country from its enemies!" to thunderous applause. "Stand up and fight! Nothing is inevitable here! We're Americans, and we never give up! We never quit! We never hide from history. We make history!"[44]

No doubt such rhetoric, and the life story behind it, stirred many Americans, including some who were otherwise unimpressed by McCain. Yet it failed to inspire a majority of voters to support him over Barack Obama, a man who never served in Vietnam or in military uniform at all, for that matter. Contrary to the expectations of his staff, McCain's war record was not the election's decisive issue. Nor was it the unalloyed asset they envisioned. For a growing number of voters the problem was one of relevance. In 2008 nearly half of all voters were born after McCain's 1967 capture, meaning that most had no living memory of the Vietnam War. They were closer in that sense to Obama, who was still a child when the war ended and was largely untroubled by, even impatient with, its ancient grievances. Two-thirds of all voters under the age of thirty picked Obama and 54 percent of thirty-somethings did likewise, whereas McCain dominated among older voters, particularly older whites who had long identified with the Vietnam POWs.[45] "My argument with John McCain is not his biography, it's his policies," Obama remarked whenever McCain brought up his war record. Obama's generational rebuff—"John McCain's politics are of the past, and we are the party of the future"—played well in the midst of an economic crisis that made McCain's record seem ill suited to the defining issues of the day.[46]

The other problem McCain faced was that the lessons he had drawn from his own life's story were often at odds with the significance that story possessed for those most receptive to it. McCain's amanuensis Mark Salter liked to sound the story's grace notes of self-sacrifice for the greater good. But this heroic narrative of Americans standing together to fight the nation's foes coexisted uneasily alongside memories of Vietnam-era doubt and discord that the POW/MIA issue provoked. And it was only when his running mate, Alaska governor Sarah Palin, waded into the debate to sound these deeper notes that the conservative base embraced McCain. After warming up her large, mostly white crowds with stories of Obama's association with "domestic terrorist" William Ayers, Palin would deliver one of her biggest applause lines. "Since he won't say it on his own behalf, I'm gonna say it for my running mate here: There is only one man in this race who has ever really fought for you, and that man is John McCain." When McCain followed these remarks with the reminder, "I've been fighting for this country since I was seventeen and I have the scars to prove it," the crowd erupted, as much in indignation as in adulation. In Obama's unearned rise over the resolute but wounded veteran, McCain supporters saw the latest evidence of warrior abandonment.[47]

This was the message that roused the conservative faithful, though it was not a case that McCain, the "happy warrior," was especially keen to make, as Palin's "since he won't say it on his own behalf" preamble acknowledged. Still, with the White House slipping from his grasp, McCain did not hesitate to use his POW status to revive the culture wars. And in so doing he may have done himself more harm than good. His decision to use his war record to question his opponent's patriotism and moral fiber cost him the support of moderates, most notably former secretary of state and fellow Vietnam veteran Colin Powell, who otherwise might have embraced his brand of moderate Republicanism.[48] And it invited harsh new scrutiny of McCain's military service that he otherwise might have avoided. In mid-October *Rolling Stone* published a scathing fourteen-page article entitled "Make-Believe Maverick" that ridiculed McCain as a self-serving playboy and the navy's "bottom gun," and which featured a number of former POWs who challenged McCain's wartime heroics. "John allows the media to make him out to be the hero POW, which he knows is absolutely not true," scoffed returnee Phil Butler. "If it really were country first, John McCain would probably be walking around without one or two arms or legs—or he'd be dead," snarled the renowned POW hardliner John Dramesi, who refused to cooperate with his captors even after a thwarted escape attempt subjected him to relentless torture. Others, like Larry Wilkerson, a Vietnam veteran and Colin Powell's former chief of staff, cited McCain's POW years as a mark against him. "I'm not sure that much time in a prisoner of war status doesn't do something to you," he cautioned, "that might make you a little more volatile, a little less apt to listen to reason, a little more inclined to be volcanic in your temperament."[49]

Once only whispered, such doubts emerged with new force amid wars in Afghanistan and Iraq and with looming threats in Iran, Pakistan, and Russia. Was "getting shot down" really the best "qualification to become president?" retired general Wesley Clark, himself a Vietnam vet, asked CBS's Bob Schieffer on *Face the Nation*.[50] Not according to Rand Beers, an adviser to the Obama campaign. "Because he was in isolation essentially for many of those years and did not experience the turmoil here or the challenges that were involved for those of us who served in Vietnam," Beers told ABC News, "to some extent his national security experience in that regard is sadly limited, and I think it is reflected in some of the ways that he thinks about how U.S. forces might be committed to conflicts around the world."[51] "John McCain is not somebody I would like to see with his finger near the red button," Phil Butler warned in a widely viewed YouTube video.[52] Such attacks came from the right as well as the left, with Ted Sampley's web site VietnamVeteransAgainstJohnMcCain.com serving as a digital clearinghouse for all manner of smears on McCain's character and psychological stability, deliberately tailored to the concerns of veterans and their families.[53] Whatever its origin, such talk reminded voters that the American experience in Vietnam was hardly a success. McCain's claims that "We're Americans, and we never give up! We never quit!" were contradicted by the nation's own history in Vietnam, a history he seemed determined to rewrite on the streets of Baghdad.[54]

In the end, it is doubtful that critical exposés on John McCain's past prompted many Americans to revise their opinion of his wartime service. Yet Americans could admire McCain without voting for him. Indeed, many of his fans breathed a sigh of relief when he relinquished his partisan scourge and resumed his role as a self-sacrificing war hero in his election night concession speech. Whether his concession to the nation's first post-Vietnam president brings an end to the POW/MIA issue in American politics is difficult to say. If nothing else, McCain may be the last Vietnam veteran to seek the nation's highest office, given that his loss marks the third straight defeat for a Vietnam veteran presidential nominee.[55]

Whatever the future holds, the specter of warrior abandonment continues to shape the national conversation about war and the warrior's relationship to the national state. Though MIA activism has tapered off in recent years, the "leave-no-man-behind" ethos it engendered has taken deep root in American culture. Since the Senate Select Committee ended its work, the accounting effort has been institutionalized through the creation of the Defense Prisoner of War/Missing Personnel Office (DPMO) at the Pentagon in 1993, and the Joint POW/MIA Accounting Command (JPAC) in

Hawaii in 2003.[56] These commands have expanded the accounting effort to Korea, Europe, and the Pacific in pursuit of lost casualties dating back to the Second World War while pioneering policies and procedures that have helped to minimize the number of missing casualties in recent conflicts.[57]

These institutions are as much markers as they are agents of change, visible signs of a less obvious preoccupation with the protection, rescue, and recovery of American servicemen and women that has come to influence how and why Americans wage war. As chapter 3 argued, the leave-no-man-behind ethic is not the timeless tradition many Americans assume. It emerged as a moral imperative within the warrior class of the all-volunteer force in response to perceptions of warrior abandonment after Vietnam. Formalized in the Ranger Creed of 1974—"I will never leave a fallen comrade to fall into the hands of the enemy"—this pledge of fidelity to the fallen formed a kind of unofficial foreign policy in the decades that followed.[58] Since that time a striking number of U.S. military operations have been rescue missions—the rescue of the crew of the *Mayaguez* in 1975, the attempted rescue of hostages from Iran in 1980, the invasion of Grenada to save medical students in 1983—or have been punctuated by spectacular recovery efforts—the deadly Battle of Mogadishu to retrieve downed helicopter crews in Somalia in 1993, the celebrated snatch-and-grab of air force pilot Scott O'Grady in Bosnia in 1995, the fierce fight to retrieve a dead Navy Seal during Operation Anaconda in Afghanistan in 2002, and the pseudo-rescue of Jessica Lynch during the invasion of Iraq in 2003. While these operations often involved great courage, in each case, individual salvation took priority over strategic objectives, suggesting that a kind of "casualty aversion" had taken hold within the upper reaches of the U.S. government that effectively limited the use of military force as a policy instrument.[59] The box office success and critical acclaim that greeted *Saving Private Ryan*, *Black Hawk Down*, and a host of lesser warrior rescue films from the post-Vietnam era implied that the public largely endorsed these priorities.

After the September 11, 2001, terrorist attacks, commentators from across the political spectrum predicted a lessened concern with casualties amid a renewed sense of national purpose. The Bush administration's immediate response to those attacks, with its emphasis on military retaliation and "bring 'em on" swagger, seemed to bear out those predictions, as did early opinion polls which indicated that Americans would, on average, accept 29,853 war dead to prevent Iraq from obtaining weapons of mass destruction and that most were prepared to stay in Iraq "as long as necessary to complete the process, even if it takes as long as five years," a seeming eternity in 2003.[60] Given the apparent bloodlust, pollster John Zogby assessed, "we may finally be exiting the post-Vietnam era in terms of public opinion."[61]

A few years later, such predictions of historic transformation appeared premature. As the wars in Iraq and Afghanistan dragged on, the Bush administration felt compelled to conceal their costs in human lives. Images of the war dead, their coffins, and in some cases their funerals were deemed too disturbing for broadcast or publication.[62] Yet even as he hid the war dead from the American people, Bush cited them as the reason he would not leave Iraq, arguing that any withdrawal short of "victory" would mean that Americans who died there had died in vain.[63] This was essentially the same argument John McCain made in the September 2008 presidential debate on U.S. foreign policy when he brandished the bracelet he wore bearing the name of Matthew Stanley, an American soldier killed in Baghdad in 2006. "Senator McCain," he recalled Stanley's mother telling him as she gave him the bracelet, "promise me that you'll do everything in your power to make sure that my son's death was not in vain." Spurning Bush's reluctance to compare the Iraq War to Vietnam, he spoke of "a war that I was in, where we had an Army, that it wasn't through any fault of their own, but they were defeated. And I know how hard it is for an Army and a military to recover from that. And it did and we will win this one, and we won't come home in defeat and dishonor."[64] Once himself the warrior whose name was on the bracelet and whose sacrifice was cited as a cause for war, McCain had become the bracelet wearer, using another man's loss to vindicate his own. To withdraw, he argued, would be to abandon his warrior brethren once more.

Faced with such Nixonian logic, administration critics rediscovered the power of captive and missing Americans to illustrate the costs of endless war. Only in this case, the hostages in question were not POWs—rare in this war given American air supremacy and the military's emphasis on force protection, and usually killed by their captors in any case—but military personnel and their families hijacked by the "forever war."[65] Stop-loss policies that prevented soldiers from leaving the military when their service contracts expired and multiple deployments that sent troops into combat again and again with only brief return trips home came in for intense criticism as proof of the heavy and unequal burdens the Iraq War placed on those in the volunteer force.[66] So, too, the life-long wounds so many troops suffered and the shoddy care they received at Walter Reed Army Medical Center and other stateside military hospitals were highlighted as hidden costs of war that would haunt Americans for years to come.[67] Critics of the war forced the Pentagon to overturn its ban on photographs of flag-draped coffins to better document the war's human cost.[68] And while media figures and political elites often conveyed these messages to the public, they usually did so in conjunction with grassroots groups like Military Families Speak Out, Iraq Veterans against the War, Gold Star Families for Peace, and grieving family members like Cindy Sheehan, which gave antiwar rhetoric its power and appeal.[69] When McCain brought up his bracelet, Obama had a ready response. "I've got a bracelet too," he replied, "from the mother of Sergeant Ryan David Jopeck, and she asked me, 'Can you please make sure that another mother is not going through what I'm going through?'"[70]

The bracelet debate would have been familiar to voters in 1972, though its final outcome, in the form of Obama's election, might have surprised them. That the terms of debate were so similar indicates that the ways Americans waged and regarded war were still very much shaped by the memory of Vietnam. That the debate's result was different than it had been in the early 1970s, when the war hawk who promised peace with honor defeated his antiwar opponent, suggests that the decades spent mourning those lost in Vietnam had left Americans leery of open-ended military commitments like those in Iraq and Afghanistan, and suspicious of promises to win an honorable peace. New wars amplified old doubts about the competence and integrity of the nation's leaders, and raised new questions about whether its people were worthy of the sacrifices they demanded of soldiers. It remains to be seen if those doubts will dissipate or intensify in the coming years. But as this book shows, wars do not end when the shooting stops. They cast long shadows. And in that regard the unending war over Vietnam will color, however subtly, what is to come.

ABBREVIATIONS

The following abbreviations appear in the notes.

GRFL	Gerald R. Ford Library, National Archives, Ann Arbor, Mich.
LOC VNDC	The U.S. Department of Defense Vietnam-Era POW/ MIA Documentation Collection in Microform, Microform Reading Room, Library of Congress, Washington, D.C. (Microfilm (o) 92/300 MicRR)
NPMS	Nixon Presidential Materials, National Archives, College Park, Md.
PPP	*Public Papers of the Presidents of the United States* (Washington, D.C.: U.S. Government Printing Office, 1957–2007)
RG46 SSC	Record Group 46, Records of the United States Senate, Records of the Senate Select Committee on POW/MIA Affairs, 102d Congress, 1991–1993, National Archives, Washington, D.C.
RG233 HSC	Record Group 233, Records of the United States House of Representatives, Records of the Select Committee on Missing Persons in Southeast Asia, 94th Congress, 1975–1976, National Archives, Washington, D.C.
RG330	Record Group 330, Records of the Office of the Secretary of Defense, National Archives, College Park, Md.
RG338 POW/MIA	Record Group 338, Records of U.S. Army Commands, 1941–, Records of the U.S. Army Office of POW/MIA Affairs, National Archives, College Park, Md.
RG407	Record Group 407, Records of the Adjutant General's Office, National Archives, College Park, Md.

RRL   Ronald Reagan Library, National Archives, Simi Valley, Calif.

VIVA KSU   VIVA Collection, Kent State University Archives, Kent, Ohio

VNA TTU   The Vietnam Archive, Texas Tech University, Lubbock, Tex.

VVMF LOC   Vietnam Veterans Memorial Fund Collection, Manuscript
Division, Library of Congress, Washington, D.C.

WHCF   White House Central Files

WHSF   White House Staff Files

INTRODUCTION

1   Senate Select Committee on POW/MIA Affairs, *Hearings on the Paris Peace Accords: Hearings before the Select Committee on POW/MIA Affairs*, 102d Cong., 2d sess., 22 September 1992, 259.

2   Senate Select Committee, *Hearings on the Paris Peace Accords*, 258, 361.

3   Franklin, *M.I.A. or Mythmaking in America*, xv.

4   Bush, *PPP, 1992–93*, Book I, 1168–71; Maureen Dowd, "Kin of Missing G.I.'s Heckle President," *New York Times*, 25 July 1992, A1.

5   There were at least fifty-eight congressional hearings on Vietnam POWs and MIAs between 1969 and the hearings at which Kissinger testified in 1992.

6   As I establish throughout the book, casualty figures are always inexact. The figures here are approximations based on a range of available evidence. Most sources report 2,505–2,583 Americans who failed to return from Vietnam and 78,000 Americans missing from World War II. Under post-Vietnam formulations, the 8,500 Americans whose remains were recovered but not identified after World War II would also be considered unaccounted for. For Civil War figures, see Steere, "Genesis of American Graves Registration," 161. For subsequent conflicts see House Select Committee on Missing Persons in Southeast Asia, *Americans Missing in Southeast Asia: Final Report Together with Additional and Separate Views of the Select Committee on Missing Persons in Southeast Asia*, 94th Cong., 2d sess., 13 December 1976, 73–77, 145.

7   Steere, "Genesis of American Graves Registration," 150; Anders, "With All Due Honors," 21; Piehler, *Remembering War the American Way*, 41–42; the Department of Defense lists 3,350 MIAs for World War I at http://www.dtic.mil/dpmo/ powday/2000_powmia_day_guidance.htm (accessed 21 July 2008).

8   Neil Sheehan, "Prisoners of the Past," *New Yorker*, 24 May 1993, 46; Brenda Smiley, "Excavating MIAs," *Archaeology* (March-April 1996), 20.

9   Seth Mydans, "U.S. Combs Indochina for Clues to the Missing," *New York Times*, 20 July 2002, A6.

10   Rachel Louise Snyder, "MIA," *American Heritage* (February-March 2005), 30. While the U.S. military has conducted searches for casualties from the Korean War and World War II since the 1990s, it remains focused on Vietnam. The Joint POW/MIA Accounting Command web site lists sixteen locations where it will conduct search and recovery operations in 2008–9. Of those sites, seven are in Indochina, and all three of its overseas detachments are located in Southeast Asia. See http://www.jpac.pacom.mil/ (accessed 9 April 2009).

11 Ken Ringle, "Vietnam: Why the Wait?," *Washington Post*, 12 July 1995, D13.

12 "Garwood's Conviction Is Upheld by Camp Lejeune Commandant," *New York Times*, 9 June 1981, B10. Other American captives such as the Ban Me Thout twelve, a group of American missionaries released in 1975, returned from Vietnam after the war ended, though none of these parolees were prisoners of war.

13 As of 1 March 2009 904 Americans had been accounted for. Updates of the latest statistics available at http://www.pow-miafamilies.org/stats.html, which features official DOD data (accessed 9 April 2009).

14 Statement of John A. C. Fellows, 2 December 1992, Minnesota Won't Forget, Box 13, Investigator's Case Files, Hilton Foster, RG46 SSC.

15 Zaretsky, *No Direction Home*, chap. 1, also notes the importance of gender and family to the League's appeal.

16 "Until the last man comes home" is a common rallying cry within the POW/MIA movement, seen on pins, patches, and bumper stickers, and featured as the tagline for the 1984 POW rescue fantasy film *Missing in Action*. O'Daniel, *Missing in Action*, 238, writes: "The thing to remember is that the war is not over until all our men, alive and dead alike, are home again."

17 Sheehan, "Prisoners of the Past," *New Yorker*, 24 May 1993, 46.

18 Appy, *Patriots*, 488.

19 Jenkins, *Decade of Nightmares*, chap. 2, addresses this phenomenon on the left.

20 McMahon, "Contested Memory: The Vietnam War and American Society," 184, makes much the same observation. The literature treating aspects of the Vietnam War's legacy or memory includes Beattie, *Scar That Binds*; Doyle, "Unresolved Mysteries," 1–18; Franklin, *Vietnam & Other American Fantasies*; Franklin, *M.I.A. or Mythmaking in America*; Gibson, *Warrior Dreams*; Gruner, *Prisoners of Culture*; Hass, *Carried to the Wall*; Hawley, *Remains of War*; Howes, *Voices of the Vietnam POWs*; Isaacs, *Vietnam Shadows*; Jeffords, *Remasculinization of America*; Jeffords, *Hard Bodies*; Kinney, *Friendly Fire*; Lembcke, *Spitting Image*; Martini, *Invisible Enemies*; Michalowski and Dubisch, *Run for the Wall*; Morris and Ehrenhaus, *Cultural Legacies of Vietnam*; Neu, *After Vietnam*; Rowe and Berg, *Vietnam War and American Culture*; Schulzinger, *Time for Peace*; Searle, *Search and Clear*; Sturken, *Tangled Memories*; Turner, *Echoes of Combat*; Zaretsky, *No Direction Home*.

21 Jenkins, *Decade of Nightmares*, 6–8, makes much the same point. Some excellent books suggest the Vietnam War's political consequences, including Bacevich, *New American Militarism*; Mann, *Rise of the Vulcans*; Timberg, *Nightingale's Song*, but most works that touch on 1970s politics do so through presidential biographies or adopt a broader social or cultural framework that transcends Vietnam, like that found in Schulman, *Seventies*; McAlister, *Epic Encounters*; Zaretsky, *No Direction Home*.

22 Jenkins, *Decade of Nightmares*, 15–16, and Zaretsky, *No Direction Home*, 2–3, argue that only by combining political and cultural concerns can historians make sense of the 1970s and 1980s. Schulzinger, *Time for Peace*, presents the war's diplomatic, social, cultural, and political legacies in four separate parts with little sense of how these strands interrelate.

23 Confino, "Collective Memory and Cultural History," 1386–1403, makes many of these criticisms of the history of memory more generally.

309

— • —

24 Quotes taken from Rogin, "Healing the Vietnam Wound," 708; Lembcke, *Spitting Image*, 184.

25 Winter and Sivan, "Setting the Framework," 6–10.

26 Winter, *Remembering War*, 3–5, 135–53.

27 For an introduction to this literature, see Bradley and Young, *Making Sense of the Vietnam Wars*; Logevall, "Bringing in the 'Other Side,'" 77–93.

28 Examples include Brennan, *Turning Right in the Sixties*; Farber and Roche, *Conservative Sixties*; Lassiter, *Silent Majority*; McGirr, *Suburban Warriors*; Schoenwald, *Time for Choosing*.

CHAPTER 1.

1 Smith, *P.O.W.*, 302n16; Seymour Topping, "Asian Communists Sure Public Opinion in U.S. Will Force War's End," *New York Times*, 28 November 1965, 1, 87.

2 Smith, *P.O.W.*, 281, 304n19; "Two Freed G.I.'s Say U.S. Should Quit Vietnam," *New York Times*, 1 December 1965, 1; Rochester and Kiley, *Honor Bound*, 249–50.

3 Howes, *Voices of the Vietnam POWs*, 205–10, is the lone exception.

4 Schell, *Time of Illusion*, 231. This analysis first appeared in Jonathan Schell, "Reflections—The Nixon Years, pt. IV," *New Yorker*, 23 June 1975, 76.

5 Quotes taken in order from Franklin, *M.I.A.*, 40, 48; Neil Sheehan, "Prisoners of the Past," *New Yorker*, 24 May 1993, 45; Isaacs, *Vietnam Shadows*, 117; Kimball, *Nixon's Vietnam War*, 167; Schulzinger, *Time for War*, 293; Martini, *Invisible Enemies*, 43; Zaretsky, *No Direction Home*, 236. For the most recent articulation of this idea see Perlstein, *Nixonland*, 618. Perlstein presents a more nuanced assessment closer to that offered here on page 703.

6 The number of American captives granted early release is open to debate. My research suggests that the DRV and NLF freed fifty-seven Americans between 1954 and the general prisoner release in 1973. I arrived at this figure by subtracting prisoners released by Cambodia and Laos from the list of "U.S. Personnel Captured in Southeast Asia, 1961–1973 (and Selected Foreign Nationals)" in Rochester and Kiley, *Honor Bound*, 600–620, and using contemporary reporting to confirm the details of early releases, adding the five Americans released in 1954.

7 Davis, *Long Road Home*, 210.

8 Laird quoted in Davis, *Long Road Home*, 202. For an example of the significance attributed to this event see Franklin, *M.I.A.*, 49.

9 "Laird Appeals to Enemy to Release U.S. Captives," *New York Times*, 20 May 1969, 1, 3.

10 Davis, *Long Road Home*, 204.

11 "Free POWs, Laird Tells Cong," *Chicago Tribune*, 20 May 1969, 15.

12 Bradley, *Imagining Vietnam and America*, 122–23; Duiker, *Sacred War*, 43–44.

13 Rochester and Kiley, *Honor Bound*, 25–27.

14 Zinoman, *Colonial Bastille*, 1–4, 227, 287, 299–300; Brigham, *Guerrilla Diplomacy*, 7, 16, 79; Young, *Vietnam Wars*, 5–6. Nguyen Co Thach, who helped lead efforts to normalize relations with the United States in the early 1990s as Viet-

nam's foreign minister, also served time in Hanoi's Hoa Lo prison in the 1930s. See McCain, *Worth the Fighting For*, 223–35.

15 Figures based on Rochester and Kiley, *Honor Bound*, 600–620.

16 Seymour Topping, "Red Is Executed in Saigon Square," *New York Times*, 22 June 1965, 1; "Execution of G.I. Termed Murder," *New York Times*, 26 June 1965, 1.

17 Rochester and Kiley, *Honor Bound*, 68–72, 235, 245.

18 Davis, *Long Road Home*, 60–61. The murder of communists continued as evidenced most famously by General Nguyen Ngoc Loan's execution of a manacled prisoner during the Tet Offensive.

19 Brigham, *Guerrilla Diplomacy*, chap. 3.

20 Rochester and Kiley, *Honor Bound*, 67, 231–32.

21 Ibid., 188–92.

22 Davis, *Long Road Home*, 68–74; Rochester and Kiley, *Honor Bound*, chap. 10.

23 "Hanoi's Kind of Escalation," *Time*, 22 July 1966, 12.

24 "An Instructive Episode," *Nation*, 8 August 1966, 108; James Burnham, "Hanoi's Special Weapons System," *National Review*, 9 August 1966, 765.

25 Davis, *Long Road Home*, 79.

26 Memo from Frank Sieverts to Frank Borman, August 1970, Folder 9, Box 6, Records Received: State Department, Selected Records of Frank A. Sieverts, RG46 SSC.

27 "Rusk Warns Hanoi Not to Try Captives," *New York Times*, 15 July 1966, 1, 3.

28 "18 Senate 'Doves' Urge Hanoi Spare Captured Pilots," *New York Times*, 16 July 1966, 1, 3.

29 "Thant Bids Hanoi Spare U.S. Fliers," *New York Times*, 17 July 1966, 1, 8; "An Instructive Episode," *Nation*, 108.

30 Lyndon B. Johnson, *PPP, 1966*, Book II, 744–51.

31 "Trial and Error?," *Newsweek*, 1 August 1966, 36.

32 "An Instructive Episode," *Nation*, 8 August 1966, 108; Davis, *Long Road Home*, 83–84.

33 Deposition of Frank Sieverts, 1 May 1992, Transcripts of Depositions, RG46 SSC, 30–31.

34 Ann Martin, "Families of Vietnam War POW's and MIA's: The Ordeal Continues," *USA Today*, May 1984, 32–37, reprinted in Long, *Vietnam Ten Years After*, 81.

35 "An Instructive Episode," *Nation*, 8 August 1966, 108, italics in original; see also "The Endangered Prisoners," *New York Times*, 17 July 1966, 10E.

36 Rochester and Kiley, *Honor Bound*, 260.

37 Brigham, *Guerrilla Diplomacy*, 72; Davis, *Long Road Home*, 101–7; Rochester and Kiley, *Honor Bound*, 449.

38 Engelhardt, *End of Victory Culture*, 240; Thompson, *To Hanoi and Back*, 186.

39 "U.S. Prisoners in North Vietnam," *Life*, 20 October 1967, 21–32.

40 Translated text of "Practical Military Matters," column titled "Capturing Parachuting Pilots," in *Quan Doi Nhan Dan*, 5 December 1970, Folder 1, Box 2, Records Received: State Department, Selected Records of Frank A. Sieverts, RG46 SSC.

41 Freida Lee Mock and Terry Sanders, *Return with Honor*, American Film Foun-

dation, 1998; Stockdale, *In Love and War*, 179–82. See also McCain, "Code of Conduct and the Vietnam Prisoners of War," 4, 26.

42   Howes, *Voices of the Vietnam POWs*, 205–31.

43   Rochester and Kiley, *Honor Bound*, 173–75, 239.

44   Ibid., 600–620; Hershberger, *Traveling to Vietnam*, 139–42, xxi.

45   "Three U.S. Pilots Arrive in Laos From Hanoi," *New York Times*, 3 August 1968, 1, 7.

46   Joe Hill Collective, "POWs—The Big Lie" [1971], Unmarked folder, Box 25, VIVA KSU.

47   Berman, *No Peace, No Honor*, 101.

48   Appy, *Patriots*, 322.

49   Stockdale, *In Love and War*, chap. 6.

50   Hunter and Phelan, "Army, Navy and Marine Corps Prisoners of War and Missing in Action," 15.

51   Stockdale, *In Love and War*, 145–46; House Subcommittee on National Security Policy and Scientific Developments, *American Prisoners of War in Southeast Asia, 1970: Hearings before the Subcommittee on National Security Policy and Scientific Developments of the Committee on Foreign Affairs*, 91st Cong., 2d sess., 29 April, 1 May, 6 May 1970, 60–61; Clarke, *Missing Man*, 31.

52   Brown, "Bye, Bye Miss American Pie," 113.

53   Howes, *Voices of the Vietnam POWs*, 242–47.

54   Judy Klemesrud, "Navy Wives Who Find Comfort in Sharing a Common Anguish," *New York Times*, 25 August 1970, 36M.

55   Moreau, *Waiting Wives*, xiii–xxii, 30.

56   Louise Mulligan formed a similar group in Virginia Beach in mid-1966, which merged with Stockdale's group when the League was incorporated in 1970. Keenan, *Every Effort*, 44.

57   A survey of 215 POW/MIA families conducted by the Center for Prisoner of War Studies found that 80 percent had children. See McCubbin, Hunter, and Dahl, "Residuals of War," 99.

58   Stockdale, *In Love and War*, chap. 2.

59   Loudon Wainright, "When Johnny Comes Marching Home Again—Or Doesn't," *Life*, 10 November 1972, 37.

60   McCubbin, Hunter, and Dahl, "Residuals of War," 98–107; McCubbin, Hunter, and Metres, "Adaptation of the Family to the PW/MIA Experience," 21–47.

61   Karen Thorsen, "A Campaign to Get a Husband Home," *Life*, 29 September 1972, 42.

62   Lassiter, *Silent Majority*; McGirr, *Suburban Warriors*. See also Nickerson, "Moral Mothers and Goldwater Girls."

63   Nickerson, "Moral Mothers and Goldwater Girls," 52.

64   McCubbin, Hunter, and Dahl, "Residuals of War," 98–107; McCubbin, Hunter, and Metres, "Adaptation of the Family to the PW/MIA Experience," 23–47.

65   Moreau, *Waiting Wives*, xv; Keenan, *Every Effort*, 88–89.

66   Gruner, *Prisoners of Culture*, 89.

67   Beverly Beyette, "Navy Wife Keeps Vigil for Captive Pilot," *San Diego Union*, 27 October 1968, 1, 8.

68 Stockdale, *In Love and War*, 52, 203, 222.

69 Lunch and Sperlich, "American Public Opinion and the War in Vietnam," 25.

70 Stockdale, *In Love and War*, 131–48, 194–98, 220.

71 Ibid., 220–22.

72 Ibid., 295–301. The *San Diego Union* "adhered to staunch Republican lines," according to McGirr, *Suburban Warriors*, 37. On the Code of Conduct, see Davis, *Long Road Home*, 13–19.

73 Beyette, "Navy Wife Keeps Vigil for Captive Pilot," 1, 8.

74 Stockdale, *In Love and War*, 299–303.

75 McGirr, *Suburban Warriors*, chap. 1 and 214–16. Despite his California roots, Nixon's victory there was by no means assured absent these developments, as his defeat in California's 1962 gubernatorial race made clear.

76 Stockdale, *In Love and War*, 304, 314; memo from Gwen King to Bromley Smith, 22 January 1969, Ex ND 18-3/CO 165 Beginning—12/31/69 [1 of 2], Box 1, WHCF, NPMS. Though Stockdale claims 2,000 telegrams on inauguration day, the handwritten tally on King's memo reports only 904 in Nixon's first three days in office. I have used Stockdale's figure on the assumption that telegrams continued to arrive in the coming days.

77 Ann Mills Griffiths, interview with the author, tape recording, Washington, D.C., 8 November 2000.

78 Franklin, *M.I.A.*, 50–53, 190, and 240n48.

79 Joseph Lelyveld, "Dear President Nixon—the P.O.W. Families," *New York Times Magazine*, 3 October 1971, 56.

80 Haldeman, *Ends of Power*, 81.

81 Kimball, *Nixon's Vietnam War*, 151–69, esp. 160–61. See also Sherry, *In the Shadow of War*, 313–14.

82 Berman, *No Peace, No Honor*, 44.

83 Memo from Alexander Butterfield to Richard Nixon, 15 December 1969, Ex ND 18-3/CO 165 Beginning—12/31/69 [2 of 2], Box 1, WHCF, NPMS; Davis, *Long Road Home*, 242, 394; Stockdale, *In Love and War*, 306–12.

84 Press Briefing, 24 June 1969, Folder 2, Box 21, Records Received: State Department, Selected Records of Frank A. Sieverts, RG46 SSC.

85 Lelyveld, "Dear President Nixon—the P.O.W. Families," 56.

86 Memo from Frank Sieverts to William Rogers, 26 June 1969, Folder 3, Box 22, Records Received: State Department, Selected Records of Frank A. Sieverts, RG46 SSC.

87 Stockdale, *In Love and War*, 314–15; "Wives Organizing to Find 1,332 G.I.'s Missing in War," *New York Times*, 31 July 1969, 31.

88 Deposition of Frank Sieverts, 1 May 1992, Transcripts of Depositions, RG46 SSC, 39–40.

89 Porter, *Peace Denied*, 82.

90 Davis, *Long Road Home*, 393.

91 Rochester and Kiley, *Honor Bound*, 373, 477. For an example of the growing profile of the POW problem before Nixon took office see Joseph B. Treaster, "Vietnam: The Knotty Problem of the Prisoners," *New York Times*, 5 January 1969, E2.

92   Davis, *Long Road Home*, 231–33.

93   Kimball, *Nixon's Vietnam War*, 151.

94   For analysis of the NLF plan and administration reaction see Brigham, *Guerrilla Diplomacy*, 86–87; Mann, *Grand Delusion*, 632–35.

95   Kimball, *Nixon's Vietnam War*, 160–61. Italics in the original.

96   Ambrose, *Nixon*, 305, 326, 659.

97   "Text of President Nixon's Address to the Nation on U.S. Policy in the War in Vietnam," *New York Times*, 4 November 1969, 16.

98   James Reston, "Nixon Makes His Stand," *New York Times*, 4 November 1969, 1, 17.

99   Carroll, *It Seemed Like Nothing Happened*, 6.

100 Memo from William Safire to H. R. Haldeman, 22 October 1969, Memoranda received October–December 1969, Box 8, Alexander P. Butterfield Correspondence File, WHSF, NPMS.

101 Memo from Lyn Nofziger to Alex Butterfield, 9 October 1969, Memoranda received October–December 1969, Box 8, Alexander P. Butterfield Correspondence File, WHSF, NPMS.

102 Franklin, *M.I.A.*, 49; Turner, *Echoes of Combat*, 101.

103 Memo from H. R. Haldeman to Henry Kissinger, Herb Klein, Ron Ziegler, 23 September 1969, Ex ND 18-3/CO 165 Beginning 12/31/69 [2 of 2], Box 1, WHCF, NPMS.

104 Memo from H. R. Haldeman to Dwight Chapin, 23 September 1969, Ex ND 18-3/CO 165 Beginning 12/31/69 [2 of 2], Box 1, WHCF, NPMS; memo from Melvin Laird to Richard Nixon, 25 September 1969, Ex ND 18-3/CO 165 Beginning 12/31/69 [2 of 2], Box 1, WHCF, NPMS.

105 Memo from Alexander Haig to Dwight Chapin, 9 October 1969, Ex ND 18-3/CO 165 Beginning 12/31/69 [2 of 2], Box 1, WHCF, NPMS; memo from Alexander Haig to Dwight Chapin, 18 October 1969, Ex ND 18-3/CO 165 Beginning 12/31/69 [2 of 2], Box 1, WHCF, NPMS. Though Haig authored these memos, he specified that he was communicating Kissinger's views.

106 Memo from Harry S. Dent to H. R. Haldeman, 20 October 1969, Ex ND 18-3/CO 165 Beginning 12/31/69 [2 of 2], Box 1, WHCF, NPMS.

107 Memo from Dwight Chapin to Alexander Haig, 17 October 1969, Ex ND 18-3/CO 165 Beginning 12/31/69 [2 of 2], Box 1, WHCF, NPMS.

108 Memo from Henry Kissinger to Dwight Chapin, 10 November 1969, Ex ND 18-3/CO 165 Beginning 12/31/69 [2 of 2], Box 1, WHCF, NPMS.

109 Davis, *Long Road Home*, 206–9, 395–96; Louis R. Stockstill, "What You Can Do for American Prisoners in Vietnam," *Reader's Digest*, November 1969, 61–66; Robert Frishman, "I Was a Prisoner in Hanoi," *Reader's Digest*, December 1969, 111–15. For reporting on Frishman's claims see Seymour Hersh, "POW Life 'An Ordeal of Horror,'" *Dayton Journal Herald*, 13 February 1971, 1; Seymour Hersh, "POW's Tale Doubted," *Dayton Journal Herald*, 15 February 1971, 1; and Jon M. Van Dyke, "Were They Tortured?," *Nation*, 6 October 1969, 334.

110 Memo from Frank Sieverts to William Rogers, 13 October 1969, Folder 7, Box 15, Records Received: State Department, Selected Records of Frank A. Sieverts, RG46 SSC; Stockdale, *In Love and War*, 323–25.

111 Different versions of Perot's ads appeared in different papers on different days, including 6, 7, 9, 10, and 16 November. See "The Majority Speaks," *Chicago Tribune*, 10 November 1969, 7. For coverage of Perot's effort see Jon Nordheimer, "Billionaire Texan Fights Social Ills," *New York Times*, 28 November 1969, 41; James Naughton, "How the President Feels the Nation's Pulse," *New York Times*, 12 December 1969, 33. For Perot's ties to Nixon see Posner, *Citizen Perot*, chap. 5; and Davis, *Long Road Home*, 222.

112 Stockdale, *In Love and War*, 318; Davis, *Long Road Home*, 220.

113 House Subcommittee on National Security Policy and Scientific Developments, *American Prisoners of War in Vietnam*, 45.

114 Stockdale, *In Love and War*, 318; Haldeman, *Ends of Power*, 8; Ambrose, *Nixon*, 325–26; Kimball, *Nixon's Vietnam War*, 161; Reeves, *President Nixon*, 37, 155.

115 Memo from Alexander Butterfield to Richard Nixon, 15 December 1969, Ex ND 18-3/CO 165 Beginning 12/31/69 [2 of 2], Box 1, WHCF, NPMS.

116 Memo from Alexander Butterfield to James Hughes, 4 December 1969, Ex ND 18-3/CO 165 Beginning 12/31/69 [1 of 2], Box 1, WHCF, NPMS; Briefing from Stephen Bull to Richard Nixon, 12 December 1969, Ex ND 18-3/CO 165 Beginning 12/31/69 [2 of 2], Box 1, WHCF, NPMS.

117 Engelhardt, *End of Victory Culture*, 13.

118 By February the White House had received 118,000 letters and Perot had received "over 1 million letters" on POWs, according to a memo from Alexander Butterfield to Anne Higgins, 6 February 1970, Ex ND 18-3/CO 165 1/1/70–8/31/70, Box 2, WHCF, NPMS.

119 "Nixon Declares 'Silent Majority' Backs His Speech," *New York Times*, 5 November 1969, 1; Naughton, "How the President Feels the Nation's Pulse," *New York Times*, 12 December 1969, 33, 47; "Drive to Help U.S. Prisoners," *U.S. News & World Report*, 22 December 1969, 11.

120 Holland, "Washington Snowstorm" cartoon, *Chicago Tribune*, 9 November 1969, 1.

121 "Tell Drive to Compile Huge Wire to Nixon," *Chicago Tribune*, 5 November 1969, 12.

122 Reeves, *President Nixon*, 145, 155; Kimball, *Nixon's Vietnam War*, 175, 2.

123 Rochester and Kiley, *Honor Bound*, 477.

124 "Freed POW Lauds Treatment by Cong," *Chicago Tribune*, 10 November 1969, 1.

125 Davis, *Long Road Home*, 212.

126 House Subcommittee on National Security Policy and Scientific Developments, *American Prisoners of War in Vietnam, 1970*, 1–3.

127 Davis, *Long Road Home*, 244.

128 Ibid., 212.

129 "Peace Group Lists 59 as Held by Hanoi," *New York Times*, 27 November 1969, 12.

130 Memorandum for the Record, author redacted, 2 December 1969, OSS-92-4260, Box 68, Declassified Files, RG46 SSC; Senate Select Committee, *Report of the Select Committee on POW/MIA Affairs*, 103d Cong., 1st sess., 13 January 1993, S. Rep. 103-1, 142.

131 Memo from Richard Capen to Daniel Henkin, 2 January 1970, Folder 203, Box 1,

— ∙ —

Records Received: Department of Defense, Office of Secretary of Defense, Policy Files, RG46 SSC.

132 Henry Giniger, "U.S. Gives Enemy List of Missing," *New York Times*, 31 December 1969, 1.

133 "Hanoi Aides in Paris Bid U.S. Wives to Protest War," *New York Times*, 16 October 1969, 40; Stockdale, *In Love and War*, 322.

134 Senate Select Committee, *Report of the Select Committee on POW/MIA Affairs*, 141–42; Davis, *Long Road Home*, 374–76; Deposition of Roger Shields, 24 March 1992, Transcripts of Depositions, RG46 SSC, 249.

135 Memo from Neal Kravitz to Frances Zwenig, 4 October 1992, Cora Weiss, Box 6, Investigator's Case Files, Neal E. Kravitz, RG46 SSC.

136 Letter from COLIAFAM to classified family member, 7 April 1970, Folder 2, Box 4, Records Received: State Department, Selected Records of Frank A. Sieverts, RG46 SSC.

137 Press release and letter to John N. Mitchell, 25 March 1970, Folder 6, Box 4, Records Received: State Department, Selected Records of Frank A. Sieverts, RG46 SSC.

138 Letter from General Counsel to Chairman of the House Judiciary Committee, undated [spring 1970], Change to HR 14626, Box 13, Records re: Americans Taken Prisoners of War or Reported Missing in Action in Southeast Asia, 1961–1992, RG338 POW/MIA.

139 House Subcommittee on National Security Policy and Scientific Developments, *American Prisoners of War in Southeast Asia, 1970*, 17–18, 4.

140 A. D. Horne, "Agnew Says U.S. Won't Forget Hanoi's Mistreatment of POWs," *Washington Post*, 2 May 1970, A6; Marie Smith, "Support for Families of Hanoi's Captives," *Washington Post*, 2 May 1970, C1; "Appeal for International Justice," *Commanders Digest*, 23 May 1970, 1–3.

141 Horne, "Agnew Says U.S. Won't Forget Hanoi's Mistreatment of POWs," A6.

142 House Subcommittee on National Security Policy and Scientific Developments, *American Prisoners of War in Southeast Asia, 1970*, 16.

143 "Appeal for International Justice," 1 May 1970, program, Iris R. Powers Collection, Unfoldered, Box 3, Hoover Institution Archives, Palo Alto, Calif.; Reeves, *President Nixon*, 198–99, 210–11.

144 House Subcommittee on National Security Policy and Scientific Developments, *American Prisoners of War in Southeast Asia, 1970*, 96–98; Deposition of Roger Shields, 24 March 1992, Transcripts of Depositions, RG46 SSC, 249.

145 Ambrose, *Nixon*, 348–49.

146 Keenan, *Every Effort*, 204.

147 Stockdale, *In Love and War*, 375–76; National League of Families, "Background Information," 1 August 2000 (unpublished flier available through League, in author's possession); Davis, *Long Road Home*, 408.

148 Clarke, *Missing Man*, 34–35; Davis, *Long Road Home*, 410–13.

149 League newsletter, 11 January 1971, Folder 207, Box 2, Records Received: Department of Defense, Office of Secretary of Defense, Policy Files, RG46 SSC; Stewart letter, December 1970, National League of Families, Box 4, VIVA KSU. Lelyveld, "Dear President Nixon—the P.O.W. Families," 59.

150   Seymour Hersh, "Pentagon Directs Efforts by Wives," *Dayton Journal Herald*, 16 February 1971, 14.

151   Memo from Jeb Magruder to Dwight Chapin, 8 December 1970, ND 18-3 Prisoners [1969–70], Box 1, WHCF, NPMS; Jimmy Stewart mass mailing, National League of Families, Box 4, VIVA KSU.

152   Another Mother for Peace pamphlet, February 1971, Folder 207D, Box 3, Records Received: Department of Defense, Office of Secretary of Defense, Policy Files, RG46 SSC.

153   Howes, *Voices of the Vietnam POWs*, 13; Appy, *Working-Class War*, chap. 1; Shafer, "The Vietnam-Era Draft," in Shafer, *The Legacy*, 67–72.

154   Of the 5,353 American airmen shot down in Southeast Asia, 51 percent were recovered through search and rescue operations, 10 percent were captured, and the rest were dead or missing. See House Select Committee, *Final Report*, 45, 205.

155   Howes, *Voices of the Vietnam POWs*, 4–5; Briefing for Maxwell Taylor, 7 September 1971, Folder: Briefing for Gen. Taylor, Box 9, Records re: Americans Taken Prisoners of War or Reported Missing in Action in Southeast Asia, 1961–1992, RG338 POW/MIA.

156   Three hundred and fifteen of the 324 air force prisoners (97 percent), all 138 navy prisoners (100 percent), 15 of 26 marine prisoners (57 percent), and 29 of 77 army prisoners (37 percent) were officers, for a total of 497 out of 565 POWs, or 87.96 percent. See Howes, *Voices of the Vietnam POWs*, 4. The percentage of officers in the MIA population was lower because it had a heavier concentration of army infantry. See "Percentage of Officers, Warrant Officers, and Enlisted Men of the Captured and Missing Personnel in Southeast Asia," 22 September 1972, Status of PW/MIA (DAAG Summaries), Box 4, Records Received: Records of the Department of the Army Relating to POW/MIA Affairs, 1965–1980, RG46 SSC; Hunter and Phelan, "Army, Navy, and Marine Corps Prisoner of War and Missing in Action," 17; Clarke, *Missing Man*, 10, table 2, for MIA figures.

157   Hunter and Phelan, "Army, Navy, and Marine Corps Prisoner of War and Missing in Action," 12, 17.

158   Shafer, "The Vietnam-Era Draft," 69; Appy, *Working-Class War*, 19; Howes, *Voices of the Vietnam POWs*, 4. Statistics on the POW population seldom reported race, but roughly 95 percent were white according to Howren and Baldwin Kiland, *Open Doors*, 155.

159   Rochester and Kiley, *Honor Bound*, 173–75, 239.

160   Ibid., 175.

161   See Hunter, "Army, Navy, and Marine Corps Prisoner of War and Missing in Action," 15, and Appy, *Working-Class War*, 26, table 2.

162   Howren and Kiland, *Open Doors*, 156.

163   Rochester and Kiley, *Honor Bound*, 268.

164   Hunter and Phelan, "Army, Navy, and Marine Corps Prisoner of War and Missing in Action," 13.

165   "Percentage of Married and Single Men of Captured and Missing Personnel," 22 September 1972, Status of PW/MIA (DAAG Summaries), Box 4, Records Received: Records of the Department of the Army Relating to POW/MIA Affairs,

1965–1980, RG46 SSC; Hunter and Phelan, "Army, Navy, and Marine Corps Prisoner of War and Missing in Action," 15–17; Davis, *Long Road Home*, 311.

166 House Select Committee, *Final Report*, 165, for 1966 pay scale, and Klemesrud, "Navy Wives Who Find Comfort in Sharing a Common Anguish," 36M, for 1970 pay scale. 1970 median family income in 1970 dollars from the U.S. Census Bureau, Table F-7, "Type of Family, All Races by Median and Mean Income: 1947 to 2006," http://www.census.gov/hhes/www/income/histine/f07ar.html (accessed 9 April 2009).

167 Davis, *Long Road Home*, chap. 20, quote on 448.

168 Howes, *Voices of the Vietnam POWs*, 88.

169 Rochester and Kiley, *Honor Bound*, Appendix 3, 600–620.

170 Howren and Kiland, *Open Doors*, 160, 155, 101.

171 Deposition of Frank Sieverts, 1 May 1992, Transcripts of Depositions, RG46 SSC, 36.

172 Schell, *Military Half*, is the exception that proves this rule. For more on attempts to publicize the air war see Franklin, *Vietnam & Other American Fantasies*, chap. 4.

173 Since World War II, American soldiers have been increasingly cast as victims of U.S. government policy, and that tendency intensified in Vietnam, though POWs were the most visible and sympathetic symbols of that victimization for reasons that this chapter explains. See Huebner, *Warrior Image*, 11–12, 210, 269.

174 Gruner, *Prisoners of Culture*, 30–31.

175 Young, *Vietnam Wars*, 255–58; Lembcke, *Spitting Image*, chaps. 3–4.

176 Appy, *Working-Class War*, 38–43; Farber, "Silent Majority and Talk about Revolution," 296–305.

177 Keenan, *Every Effort*, 92.

178 Klemesrud, "Navy Wives Who Find Comfort in Sharing a Common Anguish," 36M; Priscilla Buckley, "They Also Serve," *National Review*, 28 July 1970, 786.

179 "Living with Uncertainty; The Families Who Wait Back Home," *Time*, 7 December 1970, 18–19; Margery Byers, "At Home with the Prisoners' Families," *Life*, 20 October 1967, 34B; Ryan, "Pentagon Princesses and Wayward Sisters," 140, 144.

180 Grace Paley, "The Man in the Sky Is a Killer," *New York Times*, 23 March 1972, 43.

181 "Living with Uncertainty; The Families Who Wait Back Home," *Time*, 7 December 1970, 18–19.

182 Stockdale, *In Love and War*, 322–24; Brown, "Bye, Bye Miss American Pie," 326.

183 Barbara Mullen, an eventual leader of the antiwar group Families for Immediate Release, was told to "sit down! Your husband is a murderer!" at her first COLIAFAM meeting. While this did not dissuade her from joining the movement, it would have dissuaded most League members. Keenan, *Every Effort*, 118.

184 Lembcke, *Spitting Image*; Young, "Ho, Ho, Ho Chi Minh, Ho Chi Minh Is Gonna Win," 219–30; Carroll, *It Seemed Like Nothing Happened*, chaps. 4 and 6; Franklin, *Vietnam & Other American Fantasies*, 47–70.

185 Letter from Paula Woods to John Holdridge, 15 November 1969, Ex ND 18-3/CO 165, 1/1/70–8/31/70, Box 2, WHCF, NPMS.

186   Letter from J. W. Williams to Richard Nixon, 14 February 1973, Ex ND 18-3/CO 165-1 [2/21/73–2/28/73], Box 6, WHCF, NPMS.

187   Appy, *Patriots*, 268.

188   "Living with Uncertainty; The Families Who Wait Back Home," *Time*, 7 December 1970, 18–19.

189   Stockdale, *In Love and War*, 53.

190   Lelyveld, "Dear President Nixon—The P.O.W. Families," 59. Kathleen Robinson was identified only as "Mrs. Robinson Risner" in Lelyveld's article.

191   Taylor Branch, "Prisoners of War, Prisoners of Peace," *Washington Monthly*, August 1972, 43.

192   Stockdale, *In Love and War*, 366.

193   Letter from Sybil Stockdale to James Hughes, 3 January 1970, Ex ND 18-3/CO 165, 1/1/70–8/31/70, Box 2, WHCF, NPMS.

194   Memo from Frank Sieverts to Elliot Richardson, 4 June 1970, Folder 3, Box 8, Records Received: State Department, Selected Records of Frank A. Sieverts, RG46 SSC.

195   Press Conference of Frank Borman, 2 September 1970, Folder 9, Box 6, Records Received: State Department, Selected Records of Frank A. Sieverts, RG46 SSC. Borman was chosen only after Governor Thomas Dewey and Ambassador Robert Murphy declined.

196   Intelligence Brief, 17 September 1970, North Vietnam—Negotiations 1968–73 (4), Box 10, National Security Adviser NSC Vietnam Information Group: Intelligence and other reports, 1967–1975, GRFL; Berman, *No Peace, No Honor*, 77; Kimball, *Nixon's Vietnam War*, 232–33.

197   Brigham, *Guerrilla Diplomacy*, 98. Brigham is analyzing a similar 1971 proposal here, but his analysis works equally well for Binh's 1970 plan.

198   Kimball, *Nixon's Vietnam War*, 227.

199   Mann, *Grand Delusion*, 672. Italics in the original.

200   Letter from Mrs. T. E. Collins III to Richard Nixon, 16 September 1970, Folder 204B, Box 2, Records Received: Department of Defense, Office of Secretary of Defense, Policy Files, RG46 SSC. Emphasis in the original.

201   Davis, *Long Road Home*, 266.

202   Thompson, *To Hanoi and Back*, 193–98; Kimball, *Nixon's Vietnam War*, 2373–78. Air strikes supporting the Son Tay raiders flowed into a distinct, second set of strikes dubbed "Operation Freedom Bait" that didn't begin until 4:00 AM, after the Son Tay raiders had returned, and continued until halted by a typhoon six hours later.

203   Stockdale, *In Love and War*, 381.

204   Barbara Ondrasik, "The Prison Raid Raised Hopes . . . ," *New York Times*, 8 December 1970, A47.

205   "Fulbright Questions Reasons for Raid on Reported P.O.W. Camp," *New York Times*, 9 December 1970, 13; John Finney, "Discord Building over Sontay Raid," *New York Times*, 13 December 1970, 5; "The Politics of Rescue," *National Review*, 15 December 1970, 334.

206   "More Armed Adventurism," *St. Louis Post-Dispatch*, 24 November 1970, 2B; "Victory through Air Power," *New York Times*, 24 November 1970, 40.

207   "The Wives Tell What It's Like," *Life*, 4 December 1970, 40; Thompson, *To Hanoi and Back*, 198.

208   Cora Weiss, ". . . But It Avoided the Real Facts," *New York Times*, 8 December 1970, A47.

209   Ambrose, *Nixon*, 429.

210   Nixon, *PPP, 1971,* 389; "U.S. Discloses Figures on P.O.W.'s and Missing," *New York Times*, 6 March 1971, 3; Murrey Marder, "The POWs in Political Crossfire," *Washington Post*, 21 May 1971, A22; Seymour Hersh, "POW Propaganda War Was Numbers Game," *Dayton Journal Herald*, 17 February 1971, 6. See also Franklin, *M.I.A.*, 64–74.

211   Nixon, *PPP, 1971*, 541; "Nixon Bars Halt in Raids Till Foe Frees All P.O.W.'s," *New York Times*, 17 April 1971, 1.

212   Anthony Lewis, "Hanoi Aide Says P.O.W. Agreement Can Be Separate," *New York Times*, 7 July 1971, A1, A14; Chalmers Roberts, "N. Viets Demand Aid End," *Washington Post*, 9 June 1971, A1, A10.

213   Kimball, *Nixon's Vietnam War*, 273.

214   Marder, "U.S. Accuses Hanoi of POW Deception," *Washington Post*, 10 June 1971, A1, A11.

215   Mann, *Grand Delusion*, 682; Herring, *America's Longest War*, 300.

216   Richard Halloran, "Tactics Disputed in Fight to Win Release of P.O.W.'s," *New York Times*, 7 June 1971, 3; Lelyveld, "Dear President Nixon," 14.

217   Memo from Alexander Haig and Dick Smyser to Henry Kissinger, 24 January 1971, Vietnam January–June 1971 Vol. II [1 of 2], Box 121, NSC Vietnam Subject Files, NPMS.

218   Memcon, Henry Kissinger, Alexander Haig, and 17 representatives of the National League of Families, 25 January 1971, Vietnam January–June 1971 Vol. II [1 of 2], Box 121, NSC Vietnam Subject Files, NPMS.

219   Letter from Mrs. Tom Beyer to Richard Nixon, 30 March 1971, Folder 1, Box 21, Records Received: State Department, Selected Records of Frank A. Sieverts, RG46 SSC. Emphasis in the original.

220   Keenan, *Every Effort*, 141; letter from Barbara Mullen to Melvin Laird, 31 October 1971, and responding letter from Laird to Mullen, undated, Folder 207D, Box 3, Records Received: Department of Defense, Office of Secretary of Defense, Policy Files, RG46 SSC.

221   "Please Mr. President," *Washington Post*, 27 May 1971, A4.

222   Keenan, *Every Effort*, 95.

223   "Some 'POW' Relatives Say They Are Misled by American Officials," *Wall Street Journal*, 30 September 1971, 1, 27.

224   Lelyveld, "Dear President Nixon," 54.

225   "Hope for the POWs," *Virginian Pilot*, 6 May 1971, A12.

226   Don McLeod, "Kin of Missing and Captive GIs Urge War's End," *Washington Post*, 29 May 1971, A12.

227   "Proportional Repatriation," *Nation*, 15 March 1971, 324.

228   Memo from H. R. Haldeman to Richard Nixon, 14 April 1971, Rusty Lindley Background Docs, Box 17, Investigator's Case Files, Hilton Foster, RG46 SSC.

229 Memo from James Hughes to Richard Nixon, 15 April 1971, Ex ND 18-3, Prisoners 1/1/71–[1972], Box 1 (2), WHCF, NPMS.

230 Memo from H. R. Haldeman to James Hughes, 26 April 1971, Rusty Lindley Background Docs, Box 17, Investigator's Case Files, Hilton Foster, RG46 SSC.

231 Memo from Melvin Laird to Richard Nixon, 17 May 1971, Vietnam January–June 1971 Vol. II [1 of 2], Box 121, NSC Vietnam Subject Files, NPMS.

232 Memo from H. R. Haldeman to Richard Nixon, 14 April 1971, Rusty Lindley Background Docs, Box 17, Investigator's Case Files, Hilton Foster, RG46 SSC.

233 Memo from James Hughes to Richard Nixon, 15 April 1971, Ex ND 18-3, Prisoners 1/1/71–[1972], Box 1 (2), WHCF, NPMS.

234 Memo from James Hughes to H. R. Haldeman, 27 April 1971, Rusty Lindley Background Docs, Box 17, Investigator's Case Files, Hilton Foster, RG46 SSC.

235 Memo from James Hughes to H. R. Haldeman, 29 April 1971, Rusty Lindley Background Docs, Box 17, Investigator's Case Files, Hilton Foster, RG46 SSC; memo from James Hughes to Richard Nixon, 10 June 1971, Prisoner of War, Box 104, Charles Colson Subject Files, WHSF, NPMS; memo from James Hughes to Charles Colson, 15 May 1971, Prisoner of War, Box 104, Charles Colson Subject Files, WHSF, NPMS; Advertising Council Contact Report, 22 July 1971, Folder 2, Box 28, Records Received: State Department, Selected Records of Frank A. Sieverts, RG46 SSC; Nixon, *PPP, 1971*, 1009–10; Stockdale, *In Love and War*, 390.

236 "POWs Group Got GOP Help in Fund-Raising," *Washington Post*, 22 January 1972, A4.

237 Davis, *Long Road Home*, 421.

238 Don Hill, "Many POW Families Changing Attitudes," *Virginian Pilot*, 24 July 1971, 29; Lelyveld, "Dear President Nixon," 60. As discussed below, League membership rolls have always been shrouded in secrecy, allowing League leaders to suppress internal dissent and avoid external scrutiny.

239 Branch, "Prisoners of War, Prisoners of Peace," *Washington Monthly*, August 1972, 43; Lelyveld, "Dear President Nixon," 14. These internal divisions are explored in more detail in subsequent chapters.

240 Davis, *Long Road Home*, 421. Whatever overlap existed between these dissident groups was likely offset by the fact that dissident families were less likely to attend official briefings than pro-administration figures and hence less likely to be counted by Shields.

241 Stockdale, *In Love and War*, 389–90; League Board of Directors Election Statements, 1971–72, undated with hand notation "Nov. 6–7," Folder 1, Box 21, Records Received: State Department, Selected Records of Frank A. Sieverts, RG46 SSC.

242 Lelyveld, "Dear President Nixon," 14; Davis, *Long Road Home*, 425.

243 "Proportional Repatriation," *Nation*, 15 March 1971, 324.

244 Letter from Wendall Wyatt to Henry Kissinger, 25 March 1971, Ex ND 18-3/CO 165-1, [1/1/71–3/31/71], Box 5, WHCF, NPMS.

245 Letter from Charles Bennett to Richard Nixon, 9 June 1971, Ex ND 18-3/CO 165, [1/1/71–12/31/72], Box 2, WHCF, NPMS.

246 Schulzinger, *Time for War*, 293.

247 Marilyn Berger, "Clifford Is Hopeful on POW Release," *Washington Post*, 9 June 1971, A1, A10; Chalmers Roberts, "N. Viets Demand Aid End," *Washington Post*, 9 June 1971, A1, A10. These articles ran side by side.

248 Terrence Smith, "Rogers Bars the Abandonment of U.S. Goals to Free Captives," *New York Times*, 16 June 1971, A17.

249 Berman, *No Peace, No Honor*, chap. 4.

250 Porter, *Peace Denied*, 101.

251 Berman, *No Peace, No Honor*, 95, 97.

252 James Doyle, "Non-Candidate Hits Nerve," *Washington Star*, 3 October 1971, A1.

253 "The Truth about Vietnam Now," *New York Times*, 13 September 1972, A35; Thorsen, "A Campaign to Get a Husband Home," *Life*, 29 September 1972, 35.

254 Memo from Alexander Haig to Spiro Agnew, 13 September 1972, Vietnam (POW) Vol. V July–December 1972, Box 2, National Security Council Files POW/MIA, NPMS.

255 Porter, *Peace Denied*, 153–54, 161–62; Brigham, *Guerilla Diplomacy*, 106–12; Rochester and Kiley, *Honor Bound*, 569. Brigham suggests the communists reopened the POW issue when talks broke down not only to threaten the United States but because the NLF was unhappy over the DRV's agreement in October to repatriate American POWs without the release of political prisoners in South Vietnam. "There is no reason why we should free American prisoners while our compatriots remain in jail," Madame Binh declared on 8 December, simultaneously threatening the Americans and protesting the DRV's earlier concessions.

256 Joseph Lelyveld, "P.O.W. Arithmetic," *New York Times*, 3 October 1971, 60.

257 Tom Gillem, "Problems Hit POW-MIA Organization," *Tennessean*, 11 March 1973, 1; Tom Gillem "'Almost as If I've Adopted Him' — One of 4 Million Bracelet Reasons," *Tennessean*, 13 March 1973, 13; memo from Robert E. Treese to VIVA Office Directors, 11 October 1973, October–December 1973 Inter-Office Memo, Box 2, VIVA KSU; Franklin, *M.I.A.*, 57, for POW/MIA bracelet wearers.

258 Articles of Incorporation, filed 10 April 1967, Articles of Incorporation, Amendments and Registration as a Charitable Organization, Box 1, VIVA KSU.

259 Russell Kirk, "Students for Victory," *National Review*, 31 May 1966, 535; Koenigsamen, "Mobilization of a Conscience Constituency: VIVA and the POW/MIA Movement," 78; Tom Gillem, "VIVA Changes Name, Image," *Tennessean*, 12 March 1973, 4.

260 Letter from Stephen Frank to Doug Anderson, 20 September 1970, Fund Soliciting Correspondence, Box 2, VIVA KSU.

261 Isserman and Kazin, *America Divided*, 213; Koenigsamen, "Mobilization of a Conscience Constituency," 5.

262 Appy, *Patriots*, 489.

263 Gillem, "VIVA Changes Name, Image," 4; Koenigsamen, "Mobilization of a Conscience Constituency," 35.

264 Salute to Armed Forces Ball program, 7 June 1968, Fund Soliciting Correspondence, Box 2, VIVA KSU; Appy, *Patriots*, 490. Yorty, though a Democrat, was

a populist leader of white backlash—see McGirr, *Suburban Warriors*, 199–201. Curtis was Nixon's staunchest defender throughout the Watergate affair—see "Senator Carl T. Curtis, 94, Staunch Nixon Ally," *New York Times*, 26 January 2000, C29.

265   Coppin, Frank, Bates, and a full-time executive director made up VIVA's leadership, according to Koenigsamen, "Mobilization of a Conscience Constituency," 32.

266   Gillem, "VIVA Changes Name, Image," 4.

267   Prospectus, 1970, Folder: Prospectus (3), Box 1, VIVA KSU.

268   Letter from Stephen Frank to Signal Oil Company, 12 August 1970, Folder: Prospectus (3), Box 1, VIVA KSU; Koenigsamen, "Mobilization of a Conscience Constituency," 44–45; Appy, *Patriots*, 490.

269   Gillem, "Problems Hit POW-MIA Organization," 1, 16; Koenigsamen, "Mobilization of a Conscience Constituency," 45, 87. In 1972 VIVA executive compensation totaled $147,520 and it distributed 18,728,000 brochures, 13,808,000 bumper stickers, 11,892,000 form letters, 5,898,000 mini-stickers, and 4,828,000 buttons.

270   Appy, *Patriots*, 490.

271   Letter from Robert Treese to *Newsweek*, 27 July 1972, January–July 1972 Inter-Office Memos, Box 2, VIVA KSU.

272   Bernadine Morris, "Bracelet That Stands for a Cause," *New York Times*, 17 June 1972, A16.

273   Pat Samson, "I Lost My Brother . . . ," *Record*, 21 January 1971, 8.

274   Gillem, "'Almost as If I've Adopted Him,'" 13.

275   List of black POWs, Folder A, Box 6, VIVA KSU.

276   Letter from Cliff Lee to VIVA, 26 March 1973, January–April 1973 Inter-Office Memos, Box 2, VIVA KSU; letter from Darlene Tamanini to VIVA, 9 August 1972, Correspondence: 1972 Bracelets, Box 2, VIVA KSU.

277   Harris poll data from "Hope for the POWs," *Virginian Pilot*, 6 May 1971, A12.

278   Gillem, "'Almost as If I've Adopted Him,'" 13.

279   Letter from George Smith to VIVA, 22 June 1972, APO/FPO, Box 4, VIVA KSU.

280   Gillem, "'Almost as If I've Adopted Him,'" 13.

281   Franklin, *M.I.A.*, 54. Evidence of how simulated imagery has permeated memory of the war can be seen on the cover of *Honor Bound*, DOD's official history of the Prisoner of War experience in Vietnam, which features a photo of an emaciated wax-figure POW commissioned by Ross Perot for the U.S. Capitol Crypt Room. For reporting on this diorama see "Grim Reminder of POW's," *Commanders Digest*, 13 June 1970, 1–3.

282   Don McLeod, "Kin of Missing and Captive GIs Urge War's End," *Washington Post*, 29 May 1971, A12.

283   Branch, "Prisoners of War, Prisoners of Peace," *Washington Monthly*, August 1972, 54.

284   For an example, see Logevall, *Choosing War*.

285   For more on captivity narratives, see Slotkin, *Regeneration through Violence*; Engelhardt, *End of Victory Culture*, chaps. 2–3; Gruner, *Prisoners of Culture*, chap. 2.

286 Memo from Alexander Haig to H. R. Haldeman, 5 May 1971, Vietnam Vol. II January–June 1971 [2 of 2], Box 121, NSC Vietnam Subject Files, NPMS.

CHAPTER 2.

1   Richard Nixon, *PPP, 1973*, 234.

2   Lance Morrow, "A Celebration of Men Redeemed," *Time*, 19 February 1973, 13.

3   "Home at Last!," *Newsweek*, 26 February 1973, 16. Figures of 45,943 KIAs and 1,334 MIAs are both low—1,392 Americans were missing in action at the end of Operation Homecoming.

4   Tom Wicker, "Red Carpets and Other Hypocrisies," *New York Times*, 15 February 1973, 43.

5   Until the late 1970s MIA status was reserved for those who disappeared with no conclusive evidence of death, as distinguished from KIA/BNR status assigned to cases with evidence of death but no recovered remains. The House Select Committee reported that 1,392 Americans were missing without proof of death at the end of Operation Homecoming and that 1,113 were KIA/BNR. Fifteen years later the Senate Select Committee reported 1,325 Americans in missing status at the conclusion of Operation Homecoming. House Select Committee, *Final Report*, 22; Senate Select Committee, *Report of the Select Committee on POW/MIA Affairs*, 145.

6   "POW Reaction Hailed by Nixon," *Washington Post*, 17 February 1973, 2.

7   Letter from Mrs. George L. Brooks to Melvin Laird, 5 July 1973, Gen ND 18-3/CO 165-1 5/1/73–[8/9/74], Box 11, WHCF, NPMS.

8   Major C. Wells, "Relatives of MIAs Ask Congress' Aid in Seeking Return," *Washington Post*, 16 November 1973, A14.

9   Letter from Charles J. Neal to General Daniel "Chappie" James, 14 February 1973, Folder 204, Box 1, Records Received: Policy Files of the Office of the Secretary, Department of Defense, RG46 SSC.

10 "Home at Last!," *Newsweek*, 26 February 1973, 16; "Brass Bands in a Low Key," *Newsweek*, 26 February 1973, 24.

11 Wayne King, "Returning P.O.W.'s Are Flooded with Offers of Gifts and Other Benefits," *New York Times*, 15 February 1973, 18; "Brass Bands in a Low Key," *Newsweek*, 26 February 1973, 24; Davis, *Long Road Home*, 432–34, 440; Howes, *Voices of the Vietnam POWs*, 158–62.

12 Richard Nixon, Proclamation #4188, 13 February 1973, Ex ND 18-3/CO 165-1 [2/1/73–2/14/73], Box 6, WHCF, NPMS.

13 "Brass Bands in a Low Key," *Newsweek*, 26 February 1973, 24; Bill Kovach, "Scituate, Proud of Its Historic Symbolism, Is Split by Flag Dispute," *New York Times*, 17 January 1973, 16.

14 Michael A. White III, "Letters," *Newsweek*, 12 March 1973, 4.

15 Sam Bunge, "Letters," *Time*, 12 March 1973, 5.

16 Steven V. Roberts, "20 Former P.O.W.'s Land in California," *New York Times*, 15 February 1973, 16.

17 Morrow, "A Celebration of Men Redeemed," *Time*, 19 February 1973, 16.

18 Memcon, Richard Nixon, Andrew Goodpaster, Brent Scowcroft, 15 February 1973, Folder Feb. 15, 1973 — Nixon, General Andrew Goodpaster, Box 1, National Security Adviser Memoranda of Conversations, 1973–1977, GRFL.

19 Memcon, Richard Nixon, Elliot Richardson, Joint Chiefs, Brent Scowcroft, 15 February 1973, Folder Feb. 15, 1973 — Nixon, Defense Secretary Elliot Richardson, Box 1, National Security Adviser Memoranda of Conversations, 1973–1977, GRFL.

20 Memcon, Richard Nixon, H. R. Haldeman, Brent Scowcroft, 15 February 1973, Folder Feb. 15, 1973 — Nixon, H. R. Haldeman, Box 1, National Security Adviser Memoranda of Conversations, 1973–1977, GRFL.

21 Memcon, Richard Nixon, Roger Shields, Brent Scowcroft, 11 April 1973, Folder April 11, 1973 — Nixon, POW/MIA Coordinator Roger Shields, Box 1, National Security Adviser Memoranda of Conversations, 1973–1977, GRFL.

22 Davis, *Long Road Home*, 43–48, chaps. 8–9.

23 Ibid., 287–97.

24 Memo from Daniel Henkin to Service Secretaries, 3 August 1972, Ex ND 18-3/CO 165-1 [1/1/73–1/31/73], Box 6, WHCF, NPMS. See also Robert C. Maynard, "Return of the Prisoners: Script by the Military," *Washington Post*, 21 February 1973, A18; Davis, *Long Road Home*, 330–40.

25 "Home at Last!," *Newsweek*, 26 February 1973, 19.

26 James Sterba, "First Prisoner Release Completed," *New York Times*, 13 February 1973, A1.

27 "A Nixonian Mood of Ebullience," *Time*, 26 February 1973, 14.

28 Memo from Joseph Ulatoski to Brent Scowcroft, 15 March 1973, ExND 18-3/CO 165-1 [3/9/73–3/16/73], Box 7, WHCF, NPMS; memo from Bruce Kehrli to Pat Buchanan, 20 March 1973, Vietnam (POW) Vol. VI January 1973 [1 of 2], Box 2 (3), White House NSC Files: POW/MIA, NPMS.

29 Editorial from 24 February 1973, quoted in Howes, *Voices of the Vietnam POWs*, 8.

30 James P. Sterba, "Clark Base Gets Thanks of P.O.W.'s," *New York Times*, 15 February 1973, A16.

31 Maynard, "Return of the Prisoners: Script by the Military," *Washington Post*, 21 February 1973, A18.

32 Kimball, *Nixon's Vietnam War*, 368–69.

33 See "Home at Last!," *Newsweek*, 26 February 1973, 20, for an example of how South Vietnam POWs were tightly controlled.

34 Memo from Jerry Friedheim to Elliot Richardson, 22 February 1973, Vietnam (POW) Vol. VI January 1973 [2 of 2], Box 2 (4), White House NSC Files: POW/MIA, NPMS.

35 Howes, *Voices of the Vietnam POWs*, 8–9, chap. 3.

36 Leroy Aarons, "40 More POWs Back, Thanking God," *Washington Post*, 16 February 1973, A22.

37 Cable from Brent Scowcroft to Henry Kissinger, 13 February 1973, HAK Bangkok — Vientiane — Hanoi — Hong Kong — Peking — Tokyo Trip — To HAK — 66-140 — 7–20 Feb. 1973, Box 5 (32), White House NSC Files: POW/MIA, NPMS.

38 Conversation 893-13 between Nixon and Roger Shields, 11 April 1973, 12:04–12:29 PM, White House Tapes Release: Prisoners of War (POW), 28 August 1997, NPMS.

39 Memcon, Richard Nixon, Roger Shields, Brent Scowcroft, 11 April 1973, Folder April 11, 1973 — Nixon, Roger Shields, National Security Adviser Memoranda of Conversations, 1973–77, GRFL.

40 Memo from Bruce Kehrli to Pat Buchanan, 20 March 1973, Vietnam (POW) Vol. VI January 1973 [1 of 2], Box 2 (3), White House NSC Files: POW/MIA, NPMS.

41 Steven Roberts, "The P.O.W.'s: Focus of Division," New York Times, 3 March 1973, A16.

42 Betty Medsger and Donald Baker, "Tragedy of POW Years Put Aside," Washington Post, 17 February 1973, A1.

43 Stefan Kanfer, "The Returned: A New Rip Van Winkle," Time, 19 February 1973, 31.

44 David Brinkley, NBC Nightly News, 13 February 1973, Network evening newscasts relating to DoD activities during the Vietnam War, 1965–76, RG330. To acclimate returning POWs, the Pentagon compiled "a 219-page synopsis of news events dating back to 1965" summarizing "the emergence of black militancy, radical antiwar movements, the assassinations of the late 60s, and so forth." See Leroy F. Aarons, "Quiet Reception Awaits Returning POWs at California Base," Washington Post, 13 February 1973, A11.

45 Gruner, Prisoners of Culture, 23.

46 Ryan Ross, "Letters," Time, 12 March 1973, 5; Mrs. Walter H. Goodhue, "Letters," Newsweek, 12 March 1973, 4.

47 Leroy F. Aarons, "Ex-POW: Re-Entering a New World," Washington Post, 18 February 1973, A1, A20.

48 Roberts, Civilization without Sexes, 5; Beattie, Scar That Binds; Jeffords, Remasculinization of America; Lembcke, Spitting Image. See also Mosse, Fallen Soldiers, 166.

49 Peter Arnett, "Bunnies Await the POWs," Omaha World-Herald, 29 January 1973, quoted in Davis, Long Road Home, 496–97.

50 Don Oberdorfer, "143 POWs: An Emotional Return to Freedom," Washington Post, 13 February 1973, A8. Since Playboy had been around since 1953, the message readers were meant to take away from such prurient reporting was that POWs were shocked by depictions of female genitalia.

51 "Home at Last!," Newsweek, 26 February 1973, 19–20; Eugene L. Meyer, "POW Family Tells of Camp Incidents," Washington Post, 18 February 1973, A15, for story about POWs receiving Playboy.

52 Daily news summary cable from White House situation room to Henry Kissinger, 17 February 1973, Folder: HAK Bangkok — Vientiane — Hanoi — Hong Kong — Peking — Tokyo Trip — To HAK — 66–140 — 7–20 Feb. 1973, Box 5 (34), White House NSC Files: POW/MIA, NPMS.

53 Philpot, Glory Denied, 244.

54 "An Emotional, Exuberant Welcome Home," Time, 26 February 1973, 13.

55 Carroll, It Seemed Like Nothing Happened, 97; Philpot, Glory Denied, 244.

56 Maynard, "Return of the Prisoners: Script by the Military," *Washington Post*, 21 February 1973, A18.

57 Memo from Dwight Chapin to H. R. Haldeman, 18 January 1973, Ex ND 18-3/CO 165-1 [1/1/73–1/31/73], Box 6, WHCF, NPMS.

58 Four-photo sequence in "An Emotional, Exuberant Welcome Home," *Time*, 26 February 1973, 12–13; "P.O.W.S: A Needed Tonic for America," *Time*, 19 March 1973, 19.

59 "Home at Last!," *Newsweek*, 26 February 1973, cover.

60 "Total Amnesty Has No Precedent," *San Diego Union*, 20 February 1973, 9.

61 "Letters," *Newsweek*, 12 March 1973, 4; "An Emotional, Exuberant Welcome Home," *Time*, 26 February 1973, 14; Howren and Kiland, *Open Doors*, 31. *Newsweek*'s cover story for the issue containing these letters was titled "The Broken Family" and reported on rising divorce rates.

62 "The Prisoners Return," *Time*, 19 February 1973, cover, 14; Loudon Wainwright, "When Johnny Comes Marching Home Again—or Doesn't," *Life*, 10 November 1972, 36–37.

63 Timberg, *Nightingale's Song*, 173–74, 240; Paul Farhi, "The Separate Peace of John and Carol," *Washington Post*, 6 October 2008, C1. Even before McCain met Hensley in 1979, he engaged in what he called "dalliances" with other women.

64 Hunter, "Prisoners of War: Readjustment and Rehabilitation," 753; Philpot, *Glory Denied*, 264–65.

65 McCubbin, Hunter, and Metres, "Adaptation of the Family to the PW/MIA Experience," 27.

66 Aarons, "Ex-POW: Re-Entering a New World," *Washington Post*, 18 February 1973, A1. During Operation Homecoming the Pentagon announced that 39 of the 420 married returnees "have either gotten or are getting divorces," according to Howes, *Voices of the Vietnam POWs*, 11.

67 Rochester and Kiley, *Honor Bound*, 587.

68 Philpot, *Glory Denied*, 263; Hunter, "Prisoners of War: Readjustment and Rehabilitation," 753.

69 See "A Needed Tonic for America," *Time*, 19 March 1973, 19; Metres, McCubbin, and Hunter, "Families of Returned Prisoners of War."

70 Howren and Kiland, *Open Doors*, 79.

71 Hunter, "Prisoners of War: Readjustment and Rehabilitation," 753; Howren and Kiland, *Open Doors*, 163–64; Farhi, "The Separate Peace of John and Carol," *Washington Post*, 6 October 2008, C1. The divorce rate for non-POWs who were married and served in Vietnam was 11 percent.

72 Philpot, *Glory Denied*, 277.

73 Howes, *Voices of the Vietnam POWs*, 145, 12. Abel Kavanaugh also killed himself shortly after homecoming, possibly because he was facing litigation from other POWs for collaboration. See Metres, McCubbin, Hunter, "Families of Returned Prisoners of War," 153.

74 Philpot, *Glory Denied*, chaps. 33–44; Jim and Alyce exchange on 263; Alyce quoted on 305.

75 Wainwright, "When Johnny Comes Marching Home Again—or Doesn't," 36.

76 Gruner, *Prisoners of Culture*, 89–90.

77 Philpot, *Glory Denied*, 291.

78 Metres, McCubbin, Hunter, "Families of Returned Prisoners of War," 151.

79 McDaniel quoted in Gruner, *Prisoners of Culture*, 94; Meyer in Philpot, *Glory Denied*, 291.

80 Engelhardt, *End of Victory Culture*, 274.

81 "P.O.W.S: And Now a Darker Story," *Time*, 5 March 1973, 14; "The Permanent War Prisoners," *Newsweek*, 5 March 1973, 23.

82 "Home Again," *New York Times*, 13 February 1973, 36.

83 Steven Roberts, "Former P.O.W.'s Charge Torture by North Vietnam," *New York Times*, 30 March 1973, A1.

84 Steven Roberts, "The P.O.W.'s: Focus of Division," *New York Times*, 3 March 1973, A16.

85 Seymour Hersh, "Pilot Recalls 'Bad Attitude' Made Him Suffer in Hanoi," *New York Times*, 1 April 1973, A1.

86 Robert Jay Lifton, "Heroes and Victims," *New York Times*, 28 March 1973, A47.

87 Steven Roberts, "The Horrors of Captivity," *New York Times*, 1 April 1973, 234.

88 Engelhardt, *End of Victory Culture*, 3–5, presents an excellent sketch of "the American war story" in which "the band of brothers, the small patrol, or, classically, the lone white frontiersman gained the right to destroy through a sacramental rite of initiation in the wilderness. In this trial by nature, it was the Indians who, by the ambush, the atrocity, and the capture of the white woman (or even of the frontiersman himself)—by, in fact, their very numbers—became the aggressors and so sealed their own fate."

89 Steven Roberts, "P.O.W.'s Felt Their Mission Was to Resist," *New York Times*, 30 April 1970, 63.

90 Steven Roberts, "Captain Says Resistance by P.O.W.'s Forced Captors to Be Brutal," *New York Times*, 31 March 1973, 4.

91 Ibid.; Howes, *Voices of the Vietnam POWs*, 30–32. Howes offers a thorough and sophisticated analysis of torture and resistance to it.

92 Stockdale, *In Love and War*, 11–25, 112–16, 158, 162, 168, 182–84, 435–36. Stockdale was in the air over the USS *Maddox* and USS *Turner Joy* on the night of the alleged attack and knew that there had been no attack. The fear that his captors would exploit his knowledge of "the fraud of the United States government's trumped-up charges in the Tonkin Gulf" haunted him throughout his imprisonment.

93 Schell, *Time of Illusion*, chap. 6, esp. 341, 363–67.

94 Stockdale, *In Love and War*, 445–46. Not only was Stockdale the first warrior in U.S. history to earn the nation's highest commendation for a suicide attempt, but he and fellow POW George "Bud" Day, awarded the Medal of Honor on the same day, were the first men to earn the award for acts undertaken as prisoners of war. Traditionally, falling into enemy hands had been stigmatized. To date, seven Vietnam POWs have been awarded the Medal of Honor, nearly 3 percent of the war's total recipients, with five earning the award specifically for valor during captivity.

95 Steven Roberts, "Ex-P.O.W.'s Say Ordeal Was Not in Vain," *New York Times*, A12.

96 "P.O.W. Hails Nixon, Scores War Foes," *New York Times*, 27 February 1973, A9.

97 Seymour Hersh, "Pilot Recalls 'Bad Attitude' Made Him Suffer in Hanoi," *New York Times*, 1 April 1973, A1, A62.

98 Steven Roberts, "Two Pilots, Two Wars," *New York Times Magazine*, 10 June 1973, 60.

99 Letter from Jeremiah Denton to Richard Nixon, 27 February 1973, ND 18-3/CO 165-1 [2/21/73–2/2873], Box 6, WHCF, NPMS.

100 "Notes on People," *New York Times*, 19 August 1977, 14; Wendell Rawls, "Two Conservatives Fight Close Battle for Senate in Alabama," *New York Times*, 1 November 1980, 10. For more on Denton's political career see http://www.denton foundation.org/ (accessed 21 July 2008).

101 Letter from Harry Dent to Anne Armstrong, 3 May 1973, Vietnam (POW) Vol. VI January 1973 [1 of 2], Box 2 (3), White House NSC Files: POW/MIA, NPMS; Douglas Kneeland, "G.O.P.'s War Hero Candidate Offers McGovern a Stiff Race," *New York Times*, 22 July 1974, 31, 46.

102 "All Prisoners of War Lose Congress Races," *New York Times*, 7 November 1974, 40; "Democrat Wins Dakota Recount," *New York Times*, 20 December 1978, A16.

103 Kneeland, "G.O.P.'s War Hero Candidate Offers McGovern a Stiff Race," 46.

104 Mosse, *Fallen Soldiers*, 50.

105 Matt Bai, "The McCain Doctrines," *New York Times Magazine*, 18 May 2008, 40; David Kirkpatrick, "In '74 Thesis, The Seeds of McCain's War Views," *New York Times*, 15 June 2008, A1.

106 Mark Danner, "Obama and Sweet Potato Pie," *New York Review of Books*, 20 November 2008, 12–20, argues that McCain's wartime trauma was both a powerful draw and ultimate impediment to his presidential prospects in 2008.

107 Slotkin, *Regeneration through Violence*, 129. Denton's declension model of 1960s history can be usefully compared to Puritan Jeremiads, which warned of a fall from a divine state and threatened doom unless the community was refounded on its original Godly principles.

108 Gruner, *Prisoners of Culture*, chap. 2, and Howes, *Voices of the Vietnam POWs*, chap. 6, both offer comparisons between Puritan and POW captivity narratives.

109 Slotkin, *Regeneration through Violence*, 94.

110 Quoted in Cora Weiss, "Adventures in the P.O.W. Trade," *Ramparts*, June 1973, 15.

111 Roberts, "The P.O.W.'s: Focus of Division," *New York Times*, 3 March 1973, 16.

112 Ngo Vinh Long, "Their Glory Is All Moonshine," *Ramparts*, May 1973, 11, 13.

113 Cable from Charles Evers to Richard Nixon, 15 February 1973, ND 18-3/CO 165-1 [2/21/73–2/2873], Box 6, WHCF, NPMS. Harlem congressman Charles Rangel noted the same: House Subcommittee on National Security Policy and Scientific Developments, *American Prisoners of War and Missing in Action in Southeast Asia, 1973*, 93d Cong., 1st sess., 23, 30, and 31 May 1973, 50.

114 Letter from Mrs. William Steward to Daniel James, 5 March 1973, Folder 204 A, Box 1, Records Received: Department of Defense, Office of Secretary of Defense, Policy Files, RG46 SSC.

115 Reeves, *President Nixon*, 575–609; James Naughton, "Gallup Poll Hints Scandal, Dims G.O.P.'s '74 Outlook," *New York Times*, 10 May 1974, 36.

116 John Herbers, "Ex-P.O.W.'s Cheer," *New York Times*, 25 May 1971, 1, 16.

117 "Nixon Throws a Party," *Time*, 4 June 1973, 32; "Veterans Give Nixon Plaque," *New York Times*, 25 May 1973, 71.

118 Herbers, "Ex-P.O.W.'s Cheer," *New York Times*, 25 May 1971, 1.

119 "Nixon at Low Point in Gallup Poll," *New York Times*, 26 July 1974, 15.

120 Advertisement, *Washington Post*, 12 February 1973, A7. Over the next six weeks, this ad ran in ninety-one newspapers in thirty states only to be replaced by another like it that appeared in ninety-five papers in thirty-four states, according to Koenigsamen, "Mobilization of a Conscience Constituency," 85. The photograph in the ad, which originally appeared in the March 1967 *Paris Match*, was identified as Dodge by his family and still circulates in POW/MIA circles as proof of Dodge's survival despite the fact that returned POW Ron Bliss claimed that the photo depicted his capture in 1966, not Dodge's. Footage of Bliss discussing the photo's signature features — a full head bandage and torn white T-shirt — as elements of his own captivity can be seen in the documentary film *Return with Honor*.

121 Memo from Sven Kraemer to Brent Scowcroft, 16 February 1973, ExND 18-3/CO 165-1 [2/15/73–2/20/73], Box 6, WHCF, NPMS.

122 Brent Scowcroft briefing for Richard Nixon, 10 April 1973, Vietnam (POW) Vol. VI January 1973, Box 7, NSC Files, POW/MIA, NPMS; Conversation 893-13 between Richard Nixon and Roger Shields, 11 April 1973, 12:04–12:29 PM, White House Tapes Release: Prisoners of War (POW), 28 August 1997, NPMS.

123 Hawley, *Remains of War*, 24, 157, 159.

124 For full text of the Paris Peace Accords, see Gettleman et al., *Vietnam and America*, 472–87.

125 Mather, *M.I.A.*, 10–11, 31–32; Edward P. Brynn and Arthur P. Geesey, Project CHECO Report, "Joint Personnel Recovery in Southeast Asia," 1 September 1976, Project CHECO Office of History, HQ PACAF, 14, 17, available through Maxwell Air Force Base.

126 Thomas Lippman, "Viet Body Search Frustrating Task," *Washington Post*, 1 July 1973, A1, A19.

127 Brynn and Geesey, "Joint Personnel Recovery in Southeast Asia," Project CHECO Office of History, 3.

128 Brynn and Geesey claim 276 losses over water, whereas Mather claims "over 400." Brynn and Geesey, "Joint Personnel Recovery in Southeast Asia," Project CHECO Office of History, 3; Mather, *M.I.A.*, 15–16.

129 Herring, *America's Longest War*, 257–62.

130 Senate Select Committee, *Report of the Select Committee on POW/MIA Affairs*, 110–11; "P.O.W. Complaints Bring Red Threat," *New York Times*, 5 April 1973, 15.

131 Mather, *M.I.A.*, 21.

132 Ibid., 14; Lippman, "Viet Body Search Frustrating Task," *Washington Post*, 1 July 1973, A19.

133 A. W. Saunders, "Letters," *Newsweek*, 7 May 1973, 7.

134   House Subcommittee on National Security Policy and Scientific Developments, *Missing in Action in Southeast Asia, 1973: Hearing before the Subcommittee on National Security Policy and Scientific Developments of the Committee on Foreign Affairs*, 93rd Cong., 1st sess., 5 December 1973, 46.

135   Mather, *M.I.A.*, 14, 19–20.

136   House Subcommittee on National Security Policy, *Missing in Action in Southeast Asia, 1973*, December Hearings, 29.

137   Mather, *M.I.A.*, 21–23; PRG delegates made these charges openly in Four-Party meetings; see Stern, *Imprisoned or Missing in Vietnam*, 17.

138   Letter from Steven Davis to George McGovern, 23 January 1974, Folder 7, Box 10, Records Received: State Department, Selected Records of Frank A. Sieverts, RG46 SSC; memo from Vice Adm. V. P. de Poix to CJCS, 20 February 1974, Folder 4, Box 2, Records Received: Department of Defense, Joint Chiefs of Staff, RG46 SSC. See also Lippman, "Viet Body Search Frustrating Task," A1; and Clarke, *Missing Man*, 60, for U.S. suspicions of DRV misuse of MIA accounting.

139   Mather, *M.I.A.*, 25–26.

140   Stern, *Imprisoned or Missing in Vietnam*, 17.

141   Mather, *M.I.A.*, 35–40, 49.

142   Senate Select Committee, *Report of the Select Committee on POW/MIA Affairs*, 116–17; 89–90.

143   Berman, *No Peace, No Honor*, 211, 231, 206.

144   Senate Select Committee, *Report of the Select Committee on POW/MIA Affairs*, 121; Reeves, *President Nixon*, 592. Berman, *No Peace, No Honor*, 255–59, modulated the Watergate thesis, correctly citing POWs as a more important restraint from February through April.

145   Reston quoted in Berman, *No Peace, No Honor*, 258; Senate Select Committee, *Report of the Select Committee on POW/MIA Affairs*, 88.

146   Senate Select Committee, *Report of the Select Committee on POW/MIA Affairs*, 120. Aspin quoted in Schulzinger, *Time for War*, 320. Aspin made this argument in opposition to Gerald Ford's request for $300 million in emergency funds for South Vietnam in January 1975, but the logic of his argument applies equally well to earlier proposals to enforce the ceasefire.

147   Isaacs, *Without Honor*, 135–36.

148   Berman, *No Peace, No Honor*, 240; Asselin, *Bitter Peace*, 178. I agree with Asselin's claim that Washington did not control the war on the ground or at the bargaining table. We disagree only in our assessment of Negroponte's point—I take his quote to be an admission of American impotence rather than an assertion of American power.

149   *Rambo: First Blood Part II*, directed by George P. Cosmatos, TriStar Pictures, 1985.

150   Asselin, *Bitter Peace*, 162–63.

151   Senate Select Committee, *Report of the Select Committee on POW/MIA Affairs*, 83–84; Asselin, *Bitter Peace*, 163, 180.

152   Senate Select Committee, *Report of the Select Committee on POW/MIA Affairs*, 78, 82, 145.

153 Stern, *Imprisoned or Missing in Vietnam*, 13; Clarke, *Missing Man*, 65–67; Isaacs, *Without Honor*, 131–37; Herring, *America's Longest War*, 327.

154 Isaacs, *Without Honor*, 132.

155 Everett R. Holles, "Unit for P.O.W.'s Has New Project," *New York Times*, 26 February 1973, 5.

156 Nixon claimed "1,600 Americans in North Vietnam jails" and the Congress passed Concurrent Resolution 582, which claimed "over 1,500 American servicemen are imprisoned by Communist forces." See Nixon, *PPP, 1971*, 389; and Franklin, *M.I.A.*, 70.

157 Taylor Branch, "Prisoners of War, Prisoners of Peace," *Washington Monthly*, August 1972, 44.

158 Keenan, *Every Effort*, 82.

159 Memo from Warren Nutter to Melvin Laird, 22 December 1970, OSS-92-4260, Box 68, Declassified Files, RG46 SSC; and memo from Warren Nutter to Melvin Laird, 23 December 1970, page 14, Folder U-353, Box 8, Records received: Department of Defense/Central Documentation Office, RG46 SSC.

160 This is Nutter's summary of the position of Deputy Assistant Secretary of Defense for Public Affairs Richard Capen. I was unable to find Capen's memo on the Kennedy/Fulbright lists in the files of the Senate Select Committee. Memo from Nutter to Laird, 23 December 1970, page 14, Folder U-353, Box 8, Records received: Department of Defense/Central Documentation Office, RG46 SSC.

161 Davis, *Long Road Home*, 228; Transcript of morning briefing, 23 December 1970, Folder 203B, Box 1, Records Received: Department of Defense, Office of Secretary of Defense, Policy Files, RG46SSC.

162 Quotes taken from Deposition of Roger Shields, 24 March 1992, Transcripts of Depositions, RG46 SSC, 359–60 and 251.

163 Senate Select Committee, *Report of the Select Committee on POW/MIA Affairs*, 144–46. The ratio of POWs to MIAs in the DOD and DIA lists were in inverse proportion to each other, as a higher number of POWs resulted in a lower number of MIAs and vice versa.

164 Engelhardt, *End of Victory Culture*, 212.

165 Appy, *Patriots*, 442.

166 Deposition of Frank Sieverts, 1 May 1992, Transcripts of Depositions, RG46 SSC, 163, 169, 171.

167 Senate Select Committee, *Report of the Select Committee on POW/MIA Affairs*, 82.

168 Franklin, *M.I.A.*, 124.

169 Because of the many analyses conducted over three decades that sought to delineate the number of discrepancy cases, the figures I cite here should be considered approximations. Of course, it is this very ambiguity that allows activists to discount any study, no matter how extensive, that minimizes or contradicts their claims of POW survival.

170 Senate Select Committee, *Report of the Select Committee on POW/MIA Affairs*, 148. In congressional testimony in May 1973, Shields indicated "some 82 status changes have been made since the return of our men . . . based upon the testi-

mony of our men and the information that they had." See House Subcommittee on National Security Policy, *American Prisoners of War and Missing in Action in Southeast Asia, 1973*, May Hearings, 75.

171 Senate Select Committee, *Report of the Select Committee on POW/MIA Affairs*, 146, and Shields's testimony before the House Select Committee quoted in Franklin, *M.I.A.*, 92. Of the sixty-three Americans reported to have died in captivity, thirty-four were listed as POWs in DIA's higher estimates.

172 Senate Select Committee, *Report of the Select Committee on POW/MIA Affairs*, 146. At the signing of the peace accords, DIA carried fourteen servicemen as POWs that DOD did not. By the end of Operation Homecoming DIA had reconciled its list of military POWs with the military services with a single exception.

173 On KIAs who returned, see memo from Roger Shields to J. Angus MacDonald, 5 December 1975, Briefing by MIA Staff, Box 1, Select Committee Files, RG233 HSC.

174 See Shields's testimony in Franklin, *M.I.A.*, 92.

175 Ibid. Franklin's figures are based on 593 estimated POWs, which is two higher than the 27 January estimate on which I have based my calculations.

176 Deposition of Roger Shields, 24 March 1992, Transcripts of Depositions, RG46 SSC, 359–60.

177 Clarke, *Missing Man*, chap. 3, 15.

178 House Select Committee, *Final Report*, 63.

179 Ibid., 46–51.

180 McCain, *Faith of My Fathers*, 189–93. McCain believes his captors intended to let him die until they realized his father was Commander in Chief of Pacific Forces.

181 Stockdale, *In Love and War*, 101–7, 171.

182 Philpot, *Glory Denied*, 94–101.

183 Deposition of Frank Sieverts, 1 May 1992, Transcripts of Depositions, RG46 SSC, 170. Shields makes the same point, that "we knew that at one time there were some Americans live there and we hadn't heard from them for years," in Deposition of Roger Shields, 24 March 1992, Transcripts of Depositions, RG46 SSC, 157–58.

184 Rochester and Kiley, *Honor Bound*, chap. 15; Franklin *M.I.A.*, 108–13. It is worth noting that aviators shot down over Laos actually had a higher rate of survival than those lost over North Vietnam due to the fact that 61 percent were rescued *before* falling into communist hands. See Defense Intelligence Agency Background Paper on Laos and the "Black Hole" Theory, undated [1976], Unmarked folder 1, Box 3, Working Files of Frances Zwenig, RG46 SSC.

185 Deposition of Roger Shields, 24 March 1992, Transcripts of Depositions, RG46 SSC, 174.

186 Senate Select Committee, *Report of the Select Committee on POW/MIA Affairs*, 140.

187 League Newsletter, February 1973, Folder 207: Organizational Support, Reel 89, LOC VNDC.

188 Letter from Gail Innes to Richard Nixon, 17 April 1973, GenND 18-3/CO 165-1

[5/1/73–8/9/74], Box 11, WHCF, NPMS; Steven V. Roberts, "U.S. Has Cautious Hope of Finding More P.O.W.'s," *New York Times*, 26 February 1973, 4.

189 Letter from Helene Knapp to Brent Scowcroft, 20 February 1973, Vietnam (POW) Vol. VI January 1973 [2 of 2], Box 2 (4), White House NSC Files: POW/MIA, NPMS.

190 House Subcommittee on National Security Policy, *American Prisoners of War and Missing in Action in Southeast Asia, 1973*, May Hearings, 113, 126.

191 Letter from Scott Albright to Richard Nixon, 14 August 1973, ExND 18-3/CO 165-1 [6/1/73–12/31/73], Box 8, WHCF, NPMS.

192 Rochester and Kiley, *Honor Bound*, 462, 587. The same argument can be made about the lone KIA released by the DRV in Operation Homecoming.

193 Senate Select Committee, *Report of the Select Committee on POW/MIA Affairs*, 84.

194 Letter from Charles J. Neal to Daniel "Chappie" James, 14 February 1973, Folder 204, Box 1, Records Received: Department of Defense, Office of Secretary of Defense, Policy Files, RG46 SSC.

195 Testimony of James Stockdale, Senate Select Committee, *Report of the Select Committee on POW/MIA Affairs*, 910.

196 House Subcommittee on National Security Policy, *American Prisoners of War and Missing in Action in Southeast Asia, 1973*, May Hearings, 55, 77.

197 Memo from William Clements to Richard Nixon, 17 July 1973, Vietnam (POW) Vol. VI January 1973, Box 7, White House NSC Files: POW/MIA, NPMS.

198 Letter from name redacted [Sandy Olsen] to William Clements, 11 June 1973, Folder S-529, Box 2, Records received: Department of Defense/Central Documentation Office, RG46 SSC. Emphasis in the original.

CHAPTER 3.

1 Memo from William Clements to Richard Nixon, 17 July 1973, Vietnam (POW) Vol. VI January 1973, Box 7, White House National Security Files: POW/MIA, NPMS. Roger Shields drafted Clements's memo, and both he and the Assistant Secretary of Defense for International Security Affairs endorsed reclassification. See memo from Roger Shields to Robert Hill, 25 June 1973, Clements, Box 1, Investigator's Case Files, Neal E. Kravitz, RG46 SSC; memo from Robert Hill to William Clements, 6 July 1973, Clements, Box 1, Investigator's Case Files, Neal E. Kravitz, RG46SSC.

2 Only rough estimates of the unrecovered and unidentified Union dead are possible. There were 143,446 recovered but unidentified Union dead after the war and anywhere from 26,125 to 46,000 unrecovered dead, depending upon various estimates of the total death toll. See Steere, "Genesis of American Graves Registration," 161; Faust, *This Republic of Suffering*, 236. For Confederate casualties see Neff, *Honoring the Civil War Dead*, 7; Blair, *Cities of the Dead*, 179, 193.

3 Combat and disease claimed between 112,000 and 115,000 American lives during World War I, but only 79,000 to 81,000 of these died in Europe and were subject to wartime graves registration recovery efforts. For numbers left missing see Frie et. al., "Fallen Comrades," 32–34. The Defense Prisoner of War/Missing

Personnel Office lists 3,350 MIAs for World War I at http://www.dtic.mil/dpmo/
powday/2000_powmia_day_guidance.htm (accessed 21 July 2008).

4   House Select Committee, *Final Report*, 73; Cole, *POW/MIA Issues*, vol. 1, 15. Most
    sources report 78,000 Americans missing from World War II. Under prevailing
    post-Vietnam formulations, however, the 8,500 Americans whose remains were
    recovered but not identified would also be considered unaccounted for, since
    their remains were buried as "unknown." See Remarks of Karl D. Jackson to the
    American Legion POW/MIA Forum, 29 February 1988, Karl D. Jackson Testi-
    mony, Box 20, Foreign Relations Committee Minority Staff Files—Tracy Usry,
    RG46 SSC.

5   Keegan, *First World War*, 5–6; Webster, *Aftermath*, 62.

6   Tumarkian, *Living and the Dead*, 12–14.

7   Biess, *Homecomings*, 19, 45.

8   Dower, *Embracing Defeat*, 50–60.

9   Malarney, "The Fatherland Remembers Your Sacrifice," 71, 76n42.

10 S. Greenleaf, *Treatise on the Law of Evidence*, sec. 41, at 138–40 (16th ed. 1899),
    quoted in Clarke, *Missing Man*, 22. At the end of the Vietnam War, this principle
    was enacted as state law in forty-one states, while four states presumed death
    after five years and five used a longer or variable timeframe. See "Selected State
    Laws Concerning Prisoners of War and Missing in Action," undated, Folder 7,
    Box 3, Records Received: State Department, Selected Records of Frank A. Siev-
    erts, RG46 SSC.

11 Stahl, "New Law on Department of Defense Personnel Missing as a Result of
    Hostile Action," 97–101; Clarke, *Missing Man*, 19–21.

12 House Select Committee, *Final Report*, 179.

13 Hass, *Carried to the Wall*, is an exception to this rule.

14 Winter, *Remembering War*, 22.

15 Harrison, *Dominion of the Dead*, ix–xi.

16 Sophocles, *Antigone*, trans. Braun, 29, 226–46, 634–35, 1020–23, 1170–71.

17 Marvin and Ingle, *Blood Sacrifice and the Nation*, 7.

18 Brown, *Cult of the Saints*, 31.

19 Marvin and Ingle, *Blood Sacrifice and the Nation*, 42.

20 Anderson, *Imagined Communities*, 6–7.

21 See Mosse, *Fallen Soldiers*; Verdery, *Politics of Dead Bodies*.

22 The nationalist's contradictory need to acknowledge and disavow responsibility
    for wartime loss results in what Keith Beattie has called "the wound metaphor"
    in post-Vietnam discourse, whereby "'Vietnam' is foregrounded as a rupturing
    presence within American culture while *at the same time* it is used to evoke the
    need for unity." This dialectic is present in all war memorials, but it was more
    pronounced after the Vietnam War for reasons that this chapter seeks to explain.
    Beattie, *Scar That Binds*, 1.

23 Laqueur, "Memory and Naming in the Great War," 151. Mosse, *Fallen Soldiers*,
    105, describes this same phenomenon as the "cult of the war dead."

24 Piehler, *Remembering War the American Way*, 26.

25 Cox, *Proper Sense of Honor*, 163–64, 174, 182; Cray, "Commemorating the Prison
    Ship Dead," 571–72.

26 Cray, "Commemorating the Prison Ship Dead," 565–90; Cox, *Proper Sense of Honor*, 250–51; "Taft and Hughes at Martyrs' Shaft," *New York Times*, 15 November 1908, 1.

27 "Taft and Hughes at Martyrs' Shaft," *New York Times*, 15 November 1908, 3.

28 Laderman, *Sacred Remains*, pt. I, esp. 56, 65.

29 Sledge, *Soldier Dead*, 32.

30 Steere, "Genesis of American Graves Registration," 150; Anders, "With All Due Honors," 21; Piehler, *Remembering War the American Way*, 41–42.

31 Faust, *This Republic of Suffering*, xi, xiii; Neff, *Honoring the Civil War Dead*, 7, 20.

32 Faust, "Riddle of Death," 10, 13.

33 Coco, *Strange and Blighted Land*, 88–89, 93, 107, 122. Steere maintains that 82 percent of the Union dead at Gettysburg were identified. The true figure appears lower. Of the 5,100 federal troops killed there, roughly 1,500 were shipped home for private burial upon positive identification and another 869 buried at Gettysburg National Cemetery were identified. The remaining 2,700 — over half — were buried as "unknown" or lost. See Coco, *Strange and Blighted Land*, 388n66, 122.

34 Miles, "A Visit to Antietam," *Portland Daily Press*, 11 May 1863, 1.

35 Coco, *Strange and Blighted Land*, 88, 104; Laderman, *Sacred Remains*, 105.

36 Steere, "Genesis of American Graves Registration," 154; Coco, *Strange and Blighted Land*, 317.

37 Faust, "Riddle of Death," 13.

38 Coco, *Strange and Blighted Land*, 40–41, 31–32, 83, 105; Wills, *Lincoln at Gettysburg*, 21.

39 Letter from James R. Carlton to Aaron Good, 19 July 1867, Claim of Aaron Good, Antietam Battlefield letters from Family Members, Committee on War Claims (House), National Archives, Washington, D.C.

40 Laderman, *Sacred Remains*, 109–16.

41 Coco, *Strange and Blighted Land*, 105.

42 Wills, *Lincoln at Gettysburg*, prologue.

43 Ibid., esp. chaps. 1–2.

44 Coco, *Strange and Blighted Land*, 40.

45 Wills, *Lincoln at Gettysburg*, 23; Coco, *Strange and Blighted Land*, 107, 112, 122.

46 Nudelman, *John Brown's Body*, 37.

47 Faust, "A Riddle of Death," 24.

48 Ibid., 25.

49 Ibid., 17.

50 Laderman, *Sacred Remains*, 104.

51 Ibid., 118–22; Piehler, *Remembering War the American Way*, 49–52; Steere, "Genesis of American Graves Registration," 151–56.

52 Steere, "Genesis of American Graves Registration," 153.

53 Faust, *This Republic of Suffering*, 236; Steere, "Genesis of American Graves Registration," 160–61. Faust reports that 54 percent of the Union dead were identified. Steere's numbers suggest a slightly lower 48 percent.

54 Laqueur, "Memory and Naming in the Great War," 161. Mosse, *Fallen Soldiers*, 46.

55 Steere, "Genesis of American Graves Registration," 161; Bigler, *In Honored Glory*, 30.

56 My analysis here leans heavily on Nudelman, *John Brown's Body*, 6, 39, 76–79; and Redfield, "Imagi-Nation," 66–69.

57 Neff, *Honoring the Civil War Dead*, 132, 121. Italics in the original.

58 Bigler, *In Honored Glory*; Neff, *Honoring the Civil War Dead*, 132–33. See also Blair, *Cities of the Dead*, 174, 177. Neff's Appendix A reveals that fifty-eight of seventy-two national cemeteries created after the Civil War were located in Confederate states or border states, and these cemeteries contained 91 percent of the Union dead, making them, in a sense, federal outposts in enemy territory.

59 Blight, "'For Something Beyond the Battlefield,'" 1175, 1178.

60 Blair, *Cities of the Dead*, 182, 188, 193, 201, 205.

61 Blight, *Race and Reunion*; Neff, *Honoring the Civil War Dead*.

62 Blight, "'For Something Beyond the Battlefield,'" 1175.

63 Neff, *Honoring the Civil War Dead*, 6.

64 Krowl, "In the Spirit of Fraternity," 151–86.

65 Blair, *Cities of the Dead*, 189; Bigler, *In Honored Glory*, 405.

66 Blair, *Cities of the Dead*, 53.

67 Ibid., 59.

68 Faust, "A Riddle of Death," 20.

69 Blair, *Cities of the Dead*, chap. 4, esp. 80–81.

70 Coco, *Strange and Blighted Land*, 93, 127, 136–37; Blair, *Cities of the Dead*, 80, 96.

71 Blair, *Cities of the Dead*, 59.

72 Ibid., 88.

73 Germany and Austria also saw private memorial associations emerge to care for the war dead after World War I, in contrast to the victorious Allies where official entities carried out the recovery and memorialization of the dead. See Mosse, *Fallen Soldiers*, 82.

74 Bynum, *Resurrection of the Body in Western Christianity*, 48.

75 To look at "photographs of early American military cemeteries, means anticipating the military cemeteries of the First World War," as George Mosse put it. Mosse, *Fallen Soldiers*, 46.

76 Keegan, *First World War*, 5–6. On dog tags see Anders, "With All Due Honors," 22; Laqueur, "Memory and Naming in the Great War," 158.

77 Keegan, *First World War*, 423; Winter, *Sites of Mourning*, 46, 17.

78 Hanson, *Unknown Soldiers*, 144–45; Keegan, *First World War*, 285, 299; Mosse, *Fallen Soldiers*, 68, 93.

79 Hanson, *Unknown Soldiers*, 87, 54.

80 Anders, "With All Due Honors," 23.

81 Hemingway, "A Natural History of the Dead," quoted in Douglas, *Terrible Honesty*, 204.

82 Hanson, *Unknown Soldiers*, 123.

83 Ibid., 121–23.

84 Sledge, *Soldier Dead*, 224.

85 Keegan, *First World War*, 361.

86   Hanson, *Unknown Soldiers*, 87.

87   In work that continues to this day, France's Département du Déminage has collected and destroyed 18 million artillery shells and 10 million grenades littering French soil since World War I. See Webster, *Aftermath*, chap. 1.

88   Ibid., 69; Sherman, *Construction of Memory in Interwar France*, 48.

89   Winter, *Sites of Memory, Sites of Mourning*, 25; Sherman, *Construction of Memory in Interwar France*, 75–83; Piehler, *Remembering War the American Way*, 95–96.

90   Mosse, *Fallen Soldiers*, 82; Hanson, *Unknown Soldier*, 419. The American edition of Hanson's book does not include discussion of German commemoration.

91   Laqueur, "Memory and Naming in the Great War," 155–56.

92   Winter, *Sites of Memory, Sites of Mourning*, 26. Keegan estimates 1.7 million French dead while Daniel Sherman claims 1,327,000 in his "Art Commerce, and the Production of Memory in France after World War I," in Gillis, *Commemorations*, 187.

93   As with all combatants, U.S. casualty data is imprecise. I have based my figures only on European deaths that were subject to wartime graves registration efforts. For data, see Steere, "Genesis of American Graves Registration," 161; Frie, "Fallen Comrades," 32–34. The Defense Prisoner of War/Missing Personnel Office lists 3,350 MIAs for World War I at http://www.dtic.mil/dpmo/powday/2000_powmia_day_guidance.htm (accessed 21 July 2008).

94   Piehler, *Remembering War the American Way*, 95–101. Interestingly, the United States exhumed and moved Americans who died in Russia, Germany, or the former Austria-Hungarian empire to Western Europe or the United States.

95   Sherman, *Construction of Memory in Interwar France*, 75–83.

96   Hanson, *Unknown Soldiers*, 228–29; Laqueur, "Memory and Naming in the Great War," 152–56.

97   Laqueur, "Memory and Naming in the Great War," 154–55; Sherman, *Construction of Memory in Interwar France*, chap. 2. The number of remains in the Douamont ossuary has been estimated at anywhere from 32,000 to 130,000. See Sherman, *Construction of Memory in Interwar France*, 82, 353n80.

98   Laqueur, "Memory and Naming in the Great War," 155.

99   *London Times* quoted in Laqueur, "Memory and Naming in the Great War," 158.

100   Burns, "Known But to God," 38–41.

101   Dos Passos quoted in Piehler, *Remembering War the American Way*, 121.

102   House Select Committee, *Americans Missing in Southeast Asia*, 73–74.

103   Linenthal, *Sacred Ground*, 175; Priit J. Vesilind, "Oil and Honor at Pearl Harbor," *National Geographic*, June 2001, 98.

104   "War Casualties of U.S. at 44,143," *New York Times*, 22 July 1942, 7.

105   "Casualties Reach a Total of 65,380," *New York Times*, 21 February 1943, 7.

106   "War Casualties Now 146,186; 33,153 Dead," *New York Times*, 1 February 1944, 11.

107   House Select Committee, *Americans Missing in Southeast Asia*, 173–76; Stahl, "New Law on Department of Defense Personnel Missing as a Result of Hostile Action," 97–101.

108   Kennedy, *Freedom from Fear*, 606–8.

109 U.S. Army Central Identification Laboratory, *Not to Be Forgotten*, 5; Sledge, *Soldier Dead*, 100–101, 111–12.

110 Sledge, *Soldier Dead*, 121–24. The inexactitude of identifications based on long-bone measurements was a frequent point of controversy in the 1980s and 1990s.

111 Shomon, *Crosses in the Wind*, 131, 146–47; Piehler, *Remembering War the American Way*, 132.

112 Sledge, *Soldier Dead*, 151; Piehler, *Remembering War the American Way*, 130–32.

113 Nenninger, "United States Prisoners of War and the Red Army," 771.

114 Summary of Events, U.S. Army Memorial Affairs Agency, undated, Folder 283, Reel 52, LOC VNDC.

115 Nenninger, "United States Prisoners of War and the Red Army," 779.

116 House Select Committee, *Americans Missing in Southeast Asia: Hearings before the House Select Committee on Missing Persons in Southeast Asia*, 94th Cong., 2d sess., Part 5, 17, 25 June, 21 July, and 21 September 1976, 6; House Select Committee, *Final Report*, 73; Sledge, *Soldier Dead*, 151.

117 Sledge, *Soldier Dead*, 73–77; Susan Sheehan, "A Missing Plane," pts. 1 and 3, *New Yorker*, 12 May 1986, 48; 26 May 1986, 75–76.

118 Sheehan, "A Missing Plane," pt. 3, *New Yorker*, 26 May 1986, 76–77.

119 Nenninger, "United States Prisoners of War and the Red Army," 770, 779–81. Nenninger delivers a damning rebuttal to Stichnoth's claims and the activists who have promoted them.

120 Senate Select Committee, *Report of the Select Committee on POW/MIA Affairs*, 417; "10,000 Ex-Captives Coming by Week-End; Army Sees All in Europe Accounted For," *New York Times*, 1 June 1945, 6.

121 Sherry, *In the Shadow of War*; Roeder, *Censored War*.

122 On privatism, see Westbrook, "Fighting for the American Family," 195–221. On the tendency to imagine death in national rather than individual terms at mid-century, see Sherry, "Death, Mourning, and Memorial Culture," 156–59; Fenrich, "Mass Death in Miniature," 122–33.

123 Tumarkian, *Living and the Dead*, 8, 12–14; Dower, *Embracing Defeat*, 50–58; Webster, *Aftermath*, chap. 2. For American reactions to the dead of the Holocaust and atomic bombs see Fenrich, "Mass Death in Miniature," 125–26.

124 Sherry, "Death, Mourning, and Memorial Culture," 156–59.

125 Piehler, *Remembering War the American Way*, 133–38.

126 Cole, *POW/MIA Issues: The Korean War*, vol. 1, 50–55; Coleman, "Recovering the Korean War Dead, 1950–1958," 187–93; Anders, "With All Due Honors," 24.

127 *Graves Registration Service in the Korean Conflict: An Unofficial History*, quoted in Cole, *POW/MIA Issues*, 55.

128 Cole, *POW/MIA Issues*, 55–56, 62; "Ship Brings Home 57 U.S. War Dead," *New York Times*, 23 March 1951, 3.

129 "2,730 of 7,190 Americans Died in Captivity during Korean War," *New York Times*, 18 August 1955, 1. Estimates on the number of Americans killed after capture but before reaching enemy prisons, what are called post-capture killed, range from 365 to 6,000. See Cole, *POW/MIA Issues*, 23–36.

130 "The Missing Prisoners," *New York Times*, 12 December 1951, 30.

131 Austin Stevens, "Truman Advocates Skepticism on List of Reds' Captives," *New York Times*, 20 December 1951, 1, 9.

132 The Office of War Information publicized Japanese atrocities committed against American prisoners in 1944–45 as a way of sustaining American enthusiasm for the war and as justification for bombing Japanese civilians. Avenging American prisoners per se, however, never became the justification for war against Japan; rather, the abuse of American prisoners was added to a long list of grievances Americans harbored toward the Japanese. See Dower, *War without Mercy*.

133 Lindesay Parrott, "Allies, Foe Charge Lists of Prisoners Lack Many Names," *New York Times*, 22 December 1951, 1; Lindesay Parrott, "Foe Urged to Visit Pusan to Witness Captive Screening," *New York Times*, 23 December 1951, 1.

134 Stevens, "Truman Advocates Skepticism on List of Reds' Captives," *New York Times*, 20 December 1951, 1.

135 For full treatment of the origins of the non-forcible repatriation plan and the coercive conditions under which enemy prisoners made their "voluntary" choice never to return home, see Foot, *Substitute for Victory*. Foot claims that Truman had decided on the plan as early as October 1951.

136 Hanson W. Baldwin, "Captives are Red Pawns," *New York Times*, 21 December 1951, 4.

137 Determination Section, Chronology of Events, 13 May 1954, File 204–58 Korea or Korea War, 1527, 374, Box 103, Adjutant General's Office Legislative and Policy Precedent Files, 1943–75, RG407; "Most of War Missing to be Presumed Dead," *New York Times*, 9 October 1953.

138 Determination Section, Chronology of Events, 13 May 1954, File 204–58 Korea or Korea War, 1527, 374, Box 103, Adjutant General's Office Legislative and Policy Precedent Files, 1943–75, RG407.

139 Cole, *POW/MIA Issues*, 20–23. Coleman, "Recovering the Korean War Dead, 1950–1958," 217–18, suggests a considerably lower figure of 7,000 missing and unidentified Americans, but the 8,200 figure is more commonly cited in official sources, and the American Battle Monuments Commission lists the names of 8,196 missing Americans from the Korean War at the National Memorial Cemetery of the Pacific in Hawaii. As Cole points out, "Korean War casualty data have always been dynamic."

140 Cable from CINCFE to Dept. of the Army, 11 February 1954, RG349-1a, Box 7, Defense Prisoner of War/Missing in Action Office, Copies of records relating to Korean War POW/MIAs, 1951–1958, RG330.

141 Coleman, "Recovering the Korean War Dead, 1950–1958," 213, 217; U.S. Department of Army Central Identification Laboratory, *Not to Be Forgotten*, 5.

142 "Back From Red Death Camps, POW's Rediscover Freedom," *Newsweek*, 17 August 1953, 29.

143 "Blackmail Scheme," *Time*, 21 September 1953.

144 House Subcommittee on the Far East and the Pacific, *Return of American Prisoners of War Who Have Not Been Accounted For by the Communists: Hearings on H. Con. Res. 140*, 85th Cong., 1st sess., 27 May 1957, 1. Zablocki later played a

leading role in POW/MIA politics during the Vietnam War, as discussed in chapter 1.

145 Coleman, "Recovering the Korean War Dead, 1950–1958," 218.

146 David Lawrence, "Case of 944 Missing G.I.s Called Buck-Passing Fiasco," *Washington Star*, 16 December 1953.

147 "Where Are 944 Missing GI's?," *U.S. News & World Report*, 18 December 1953, 27.

148 House Subcommittee on the Far East and the Pacific of the Committee on Foreign Affairs, *Return of American Prisoners of War Who Have Not Been Accounted For by the Communists*, 17, 19.

149 Senate Select Committee, *Report of the Select Committee on POW/MIA Affairs*, 548.

150 House Subcommittee on the Far East and the Pacific of the Committee on Foreign Affairs, *Return of American Prisoners of War Who Have Not Been Accounted For by the Communists*, 45, 53.

151 Secretary of Defense's Advisory Committee on Prisoners of War, *POW: The Fight Continues after the Battle* (Washington, D.C.: U.S. Defense Advisory Committee on Prisoners of War, 1955), 17–23; Anthony Leviero, "New Code Orders P.O.W.'s to Resist in 'Brainwashing,'" *New York Times*, 18 August 1955, 1, 8.

152 Kennedy quoted in Neu, "The Vietnam War and the Transformation of America," in Neu, *After Vietnam*, 10.

153 Deposition of Frank Sieverts, 1 May 1992, 368, Transcripts of Depositions, RG46 SSC.

154 DOD Press Division Query, 5 June 1973, Folder: Misc., Box 17, VIVA KSU. Clements's remarks, quoted in the *Dallas Time Herald*, soon spread throughout the POW/MIA community. See letter from Mrs. George L. Brooks to Melvin Laird, 5 July 1973, Gen ND 18-3/CO 165-1 5/1/73–[8/9/74], Box 11, WHCF, NPMS.

155 Letter from Mrs. George L. Brooks to Melvin Laird, 5 July 1973, Gen ND 18-3/CO 165-1 5/1/73–[8/9/74], Box 11, WHCF, NPMS; David Lowenthal, *The Past Is a Foreign Country* (New York: Cambridge University Press, 1985), 323, quoted in Crossland, "Buried Lives," 154.

156 Ann Mills Griffiths, interview by author, tape recording, Washington, D.C., 8 November 2000.

157 Letter from Mrs. Charles E. Darr to Carol Bates, 15 May 1973, Families against PFD, Box 27, VIVA KSU.

CHAPTER 4.

1 Herring, *America's Longest War*, 334; Schulzinger, *Time for War*, 320. Aspin later served as Bill Clinton's first secretary of defense from January 1993 until February 1994.

2 Ford, *PPP, 1975*, Book I, 569; McMahon, "Contested Memory," 164.

3 Ford, *PPP, 1975*, Book I, 605.

4 Ford, *PPP, 1974*, 2.

5 Ford, *Time to Heal*, 141; Ford, *PPP, 1974*, 25, 136–37.

6 Ford, *PPP, 1974*, 102–4.

7 Ibid., 136–37; Carroll, *It Seemed Like Nothing Happened*, 162.

8 Letter from E. C. Mills to Gerald Ford, 20 August 1974, ND8-1, Box 8, WHCF, GRFL.

9 Press release, 5 September 1974, Missing in Action — National League of Families (1), Box 16, Theodore C. Marrs Files, 1974–1976, GRFL.

10 Nixon, *PPP, 1973*, 235.

11 Letter from F. J. Chesarek to Gerald Ford, 30 April 1975, Folder: 20–21 May 1975, Box 14, NSC East Asian and Pacific Affairs Staff: Files (1969) 1973–76, GRFL.

12 "After Vietnam," *Commonweal*, 23 May 1975, 131.

13 William F. Buckley, "On the Collapse of South Vietnam," *National Review*, 25 April 1975, 470.

14 Rod MacLeish, "Vietnam: It's Not the End," *Washington Post*, 1 May 1975, A22.

15 Memo from Richard Lawson to Gerald Ford, 20 January 1975, MIA/Amnesty/NLF (1), Box 10, Presidential Subject File, GRFL.

16 Senate Resolution No. 72, 5 March 1975, Missing in Action Public Mail (3), Box 17, Theodore C. Marrs Files, 1974–1976, GRFL.

17 Letter from Daniel Evans to Gerald Ford, 18 June 1975, ND8-1 casualties 6/16/75–7/7/75, Box 9, WHCF, GRFL.

18 Letter from George H. Copelin to Joseph Fisher, 12 May 1975, Folder 283, Reel 52, LOC VNDC. Emphasis in the original.

19 Jenkins, *Decade of Nightmares*, 20.

20 Memo from Dermot Foley to Martin Hoffman, 30 May 1974, Folder 3, Reel 19, LOC VNDC.

21 Memo from John "Jack" Marsh to Gerald Ford, 30 July 1974, MIA-POW 6 July–8 August 1974, Box 61, Ford Vice Presidential Papers, GRFL.

22 "League Representation," attached to 29 April 1974 Newsletter, Folder 6, Box 38, Records Received: State Department, Selected Records of Frank A. Sieverts, RG46 SSC.

23 Donald P. Baker, "MIA Status Debated in Convention," *Washington Post*, 29 July 1973, B1. Traditionally, the board chairman had been the most powerful position in the League, followed by the national coordinator. This structure changed with the creation of the paid position of executive director in 1973. Albright was the first MIA father to occupy any of these top posts, and the first to be paid for his labors.

24 House Select Committee, *Final Report*, 179.

25 *McDonald v. McLucas*, 371 F. Supp. 831, 836 (S.D. N.Y. 1974) (three-judge court), aff'd mem., 419 U.S. 297 (1974).

26 Memo from Martin Hoffman to Theodore Marrs, 9 July 1975, ND8-1 Casualties 7/8/75–7/16/75, Box 9, White House Central File, GRFL; memo from Brent Scowcroft to Philip Buchen, 18 July 1975, MIA/Amnesty/National League of Families (2), Box 10, Presidential Subject File, GRFL.

27 As of 31 July 1974, the military had reclassified 376 MIAs, 223 at family request and 153 on the basis of POW debriefings or recovered remains. An 18 August 1976 list provided to the House Select Committee showed 437 status reviews had

been requested by next of kin as of that date. Assuming this figure includes the 223 family-initiated reviews noted in the July 1974 report, and adding these 437 voluntary reviews to 153 involuntary reviews, I calculate 590 status changes as of August 1976. See Status Changes, 31 July 1974, Folder 26, Reel 21, LOC VNDC; and Memorandum from Roger Shields to J. Angus MacDonald, 18 August 1976, Folder 278, Reel 49, LOC VNDC.

28 *McDonald v. McLucas.*

29 League Newsletter, 9 July 1973, Richardson 704, Reel 14, LOC VNDC.

30 Baker, "MIA Status Debated in Convention," *Washington Post*, 29 July 1973, B4.

31 Letter from Charlotte Lannom to Ann Mills Griffiths, 4 June 1973, Families against PFD, Box 27, VIVA KSU.

32 Department of Defense, "Percentage of Married and Single Men of Captured and Missing Personnel in Southeast Asia, by Service," 22 September 1972, Status of PW/MIA (DAAG Summaries of/Rosters of PW/MIA), Box 4, Records of the Department of the Army Relating to POW/MIA Affairs, RG46 SSC.

33 House Select Committee, *Final Report*, 163–68. Between July 1974 and July 1975 this hypothetical MIA would have earned $27,000 in pay and allowances.

34 "MIAs: Lives in Limbo," *Newsweek*, 9 August 1976, 26.

35 House Select Committee, *Final Report*, 191–92; Davis, *Long Road Home*, 433, 438–40.

36 House Select Committee, *Final Report*, 165–67; Davis, *Long Road Home*, 435.

37 For 1975 median family income see http://www.census.gov/hhes/www/income/histinc/f12ar.html (accessed 21 July 2008).

38 Letter from Maerose Evans to James Schlesinger, 6 July 1974, Unfoldered, Box 3, Maerose J. Evans Collection, Hoover Institution Archives, Palo Alto, Calif. Evans repeated these charges in testimony before the House Select Committee in 1976.

39 "MIAs: Lives in Limbo," *Newsweek*, 9 August 1976, 26.

40 House Select Committee, *Final Report*, 186. Italics in original.

41 "Some Kin Fight for MIA Status for the Money, Pentagon Says," *Orange County Register*, 20 May 1974, A3.

42 "MIA Relatives Attack DOD 'Money' Story," *The Voice*, June 1974, Pay and Allowances, Box 11, RG233 HSC.

43 *60 Minutes* transcript, 28 July 1974, MIA-POW 6 July–8 August 1974, Box 61, Ford Vice Presidential Papers, GRFL.

44 Letter from Ann Mills Griffiths to James Schlesinger, 21 May 1974, Folder 5, Box 38, Records Received: State Department, Selected Records of Frank A. Sieverts, RG46 SSC.

45 "MIA Relatives Attack DOD 'Money' Story," *The Voice*, June 1974, 1; A. W. Gratch, "Casualty Documentation Record," 3 July 1974, Pay and Allowances, Box 11, RG233 HSC.

46 Letter from Gloria Coppin to Melvin Laird, 14 September 1973, Folder 6, Box 29, Records Received: State Department, Selected Records of Frank A. Sieverts, RG46 SSC.

47 Letter from Dale and Dorothy Shriver to Verne L. Bowers, 26 April 1974, Folder 36, Reel 22, LOC VNDC.

48 Letter from Maerose Evans to James Schlesinger, 6 July 1974, Unfoldered, Box 3, Maerose J. Evans Collection, Hoover Institution Archives, Palo Alto, Calif.

49 Letter from Bernice Smith to Richard L. Lawson, 22 July 1974, MIAs/POWs July–September 1974, Box 1, Milt Mitler Files, 1973–77, GRFL.

50 Letter from Maerose Evans to James Schlesinger, 6 July 1974, Unfoldered, Box 3, Maerose J. Evans Collection, Hoover Institution Archives, Palo Alto, Calif.

51 Letter from Donna Silver to G. V. Montgomery, 31 November 1975, Status Changes/General, Box 13, RG233 HSC. Emphasis in the original.

52 60 Minutes transcript, 28 July 1974, MIA-POW 6 July–8 August 1974, Box 61, Ford Vice Presidential Papers, GRFL.

53 Letter from Earl Hopper to Maerose Evans, 6 August 1974, Folder 26, Reel 21, LOC VNDC.

54 Frank Santiago, "POW, MIA League Argue over Direction," Omaha World Herald, 29 June 1974, 17.

55 Scott Albright, Newsletter, 19 July 1974, Folder 5, Box 38, Records Received: State Department, Selected Records of Frank A. Sieverts, RG46 SSC. Emphasis in the original.

56 Senate Committee on Foreign Relations, U.S. POW's and MIA's in Southeast Asia: Hearing before the Committee on Foreign Relations, 93d Cong., 2d sess., 28 January 1974, 4–5.

57 Letter from Scott Albright to League, 21 January 1974, Folder 6, Box 38, Records Received: State Department, Selected Records of Frank A. Sieverts, RG46 SSC. VIVA compiled its mailing list through its bracelet business, which required it to contact POW/MIA families to obtain permission to use their loved one's name. Throughout its history, the League has exercised strict control over its mailing list in order to prevent such challenges to its leaders, and the VIVA list came as a shock to Albright.

58 Memo from Dick Moose to U.S. Senate Foreign Relations Committee, 28 January 1974, U.S. Senate—Data, Box 3, RG233 HSC. In a common occurrence, this briefing marked "for committee use only" made it into League hands, where it was taken as "positive proof of the abandonment of POWs/MIAs."

59 Ann Mills Griffiths, interview by author, tape recording, Washington, D.C., 8 November 2000.

60 Scott Albright, Newsletter, 19 July 1974, Folder 5, Box 38, Records Received: State Department, Selected Records of Frank A. Sieverts, RG46 SSC. For characterization of Mills see memo from Dick Moose to U.S. Senate Foreign Relations Committee, 28 January 1974, U.S. Senate—Data, Box 3, RG233 HSC.

61 Four of the seven League officials who met with Ford on 2 August 1974 were men. See memo from Ric Sardo to Jack Marsh, 1 August 1974, MIA-POW 6 July–8 August 1974, Box 61, Ford Vice Presidential Papers, GRFL; memo from Richard Lawson to Brent Scowcroft, 5 August 1974, MIAs/POWs July–September 1974, Box 1, Milt Mitler Files, GRFL; Scott Albright, Newsletter, 19 July 1974, Folder 5, Box 38, Records Received: State Department, Selected Records of Frank A. Sieverts, RG46 SSC.

62 "Omaha Held Clues for One MIA Family," Omaha World Herald, 30 June 1974, 4B.

63　Letter from Earl Hopper to Maerose Evans, 6 August 1974, Folder 26, Reel 21, LOC VNDC. Albright reported that over 500 people attended the Omaha convention. Hopper's vote tally suggests that not all who attended voted on League resolutions, and it is likely that many moderates followed Albright's example and left the convention.

64　Letter from Maerose Evans to James Schlesinger, 6 July 1974, Unfoldered, Box 3, Maerose J. Evans Collection, Hoover Institution Archives, Palo Alto, Calif.

65　Letter from Dr. and Mrs. Gordon Perisho to James Schlesinger, 20 July 1974, MIA-POW 6 July–8 August 1974, Box 61, Vice Presidential Papers, GRFL.

66　Letter from F. Berenice Smith to Richard Lawson, 22 July 1974, MIAs/POWs, July–September 1974, Box 1, Milt Mitler Files, 1973–77, GRFL.

67　Letter from Mary Jane Jensen to Jim Lloyd, 5 October 1975, Status Changes/General, Box 13, RG233 HSC.

68　Clarke, *Missing Man*, 40; Franklin, *M.I.A.*, 84–85, 224n12. Franklin and Clarke cite interviews with David Burgess as their source. According to Franklin, Burgess conducted hundreds of interviews with MIA families in 1974 but "never completed the study and has no idea what happened to his notes and rough draft."

69　E. C. Mills, Newsletter, 14 August 1974, Folder 6, Box 38, Records Received: State Department, Selected Records of Frank A. Sieverts, RG46 SSC.

70　Scott Albright, Newsletter, 19 July 1974, Folder 5, Box 38, Records Received: State Department, Selected Records of Frank A. Sieverts, RG46 SSC.

71　Letter from Robert Treese to all VIVA offices, 11 October 1973, October–December 1973 Inter-Office Memo, Box 2, VIVA KSU.

72　Appy, *Patriots*, 491.

73　According to its August 1975 audit, VIVA had $191,602 in assets as of 31 August 1975. In her June 1976 newsletter Griffiths denied rumors "regarding large sums of money being involved," but did not specify how much she inherited. See Griffiths, "The Missing Man" (newsletter), June–July 1976, Misc. Interest Groups, Box 4, RG233 HSC.

74　Ann Mills Griffiths, interview by the author, tape recording, Washington, D.C., 8 November 2000; Carol Bates Brown, interview by the author at 32d Annual Meeting of the National League of Families, notes, 21 June 2001. Bates maintains that Griffiths wanted to take over the position in 1976 but that neither Mills, Griffiths's father, nor Hopper wanted her in the post and so they hired Bates instead.

75　Clarke, *Missing Man*, 40; Franklin, *M.I.A.*, 84–85.

76　Iris Powers testimony before the House Select Committee, 12 November 1975, Binder III, Box H296, Paul N. McCloskey Papers, Hoover Institution Archives, Palo Alto, Calif.

77　Notes on conversation with Iris Powers and Nancy Perisho, 1 October 1975, Chairman Gillespie V. Montgomery, Box 3, RG233 HSC.

78　Winter and Sivan, *War and Remembrance in the Twentieth Century*, 8–10.

79　Vote summary, undated [summer 1975], National League of Families, Box 5, RG233 HSC. Some voters chose not to indicate whether they supported or opposed League policy, perhaps because the policy was not clear.

80 Brown, *Cult of the Saints*, 24; Halttunen, *Confidence Men and Painted Women*, 130–34.

81 Sherman, *Construction of Memory in Interwar France*, 99.

82 Letter from Cheryl Eller Boyd to House Select Committee with cover memo from Jennei [no last name] to J. Angus MacDonald, undated, Potential Witnesses, Box 1, RG233 HSC. Eller Boyd is used as an example of a "professional crusader" in Clarke, *Missing Man*, 40.

83 Winter, *Remembering War*, 136–37.

84 Letter from Eleanor Cordova to Gerald Ford, undated, MIAs/POWs June 1976, Box 1, Milt Mitler Files, 1973–77, GRFL.

85 Letter from E. C. Mills to Gerald Ford, 20 August 1974, ND8-1, Box 8, WHCF, GRFL; "Accounting before Amnesty, Says NLF," *The Voice*, October 1974, 7, Folder 5, Box 38, Records Received: State Department, Selected Records of Frank A. Sieverts, RG46 SSC. Emphasis in the original.

86 Letter from William Timmons to Brent Scowcroft, 2 September 1974, MIA/Amnesty/National League of Families (1), Box 10, Presidential Subject File, GRFL; Memorandum for the Record, 3 September 1974, MIA/Amnesty/National League of Families (1), Box 10, GRFL.

87 Press release, 17 September 1974, Missing in Action—General (3), Box 16, Theodore C. Marrs Files, 1974–76, GRFL.

88 Ann Mills Griffiths, "Accounting Must Be before Amnesty, Says MIA Sister," *The Voice*, October 1974, 2, 8, Folder 5, Box 38, Records Received: State Department, Selected Records of Frank A. Sieverts, RG46 SSC.

89 Ford, *PPP, 1974*, 136–38.

90 Beattie, *Scar That Binds*, 1–9.

91 League press release, 17 September 1974, Missing in Action—General (3), Box 16, Theodore C. Marrs Files, 1974–76, GRFL. In his rush to chronicle the Reagan era, which he identifies as "the height of the ideological assertion of unity," Beattie largely overlooks the presidencies of Gerald Ford and Jimmy Carter.

92 "Helms Says MIAs Must Be Priority over Amnesty," *The Voice*, October 1974, 7, Folder 5, Box 38, Records Received: State Department, Selected Records of Frank A. Sieverts, RG46 SSC. For DUTY quote see Griffiths, "Accounting Must Be before Amnesty, Says MIA Sister," *The Voice*, October 1974, 8, Folder 5, Box 38, Records Received: State Department, Selected Records of Frank A. Sieverts, RG46 SSC.

93 Marvin and Ingle, *Blood Sacrifice and the Nation*, 73.

94 Griffiths, "Accounting Must Be before Amnesty, Says MIA Sister," *The Voice*, October 1974, 2, 8, Folder 5, Box 38, Records Received: State Department, Selected Records of Frank A. Sieverts, RG46 SSC.

95 Press release, 17 September 1974, Missing in Action—General (3), Box 16, Theodore C. Marrs Files, 1974–76, GRFL; "Accounting before Amnesty, Says NLF," *The Voice*, October 1974, 1, Folder 5, Box 38, Records Received: State Department, Selected Records of Frank A. Sieverts, RG46 SSC.

96 Verdery, *Political Lives of Dead Bodies*, 19–20.

97 Letter from Robert Brett to Bob Packwood, 16 December 1974, ND8-1, Box 8, WHCF, GRFL.

98 Steve Kiba, "The MIA—Portrait of Frustration," 26 December 1975, Folder K, Box 17, RG233 HSC. Capitalization in the original.

99 Franklin, *M.I.A.*, 133; Franklin, *Vietnam & Other American Fantasies*, 189.

100 Louise Sweeney, "Missing GIs—Viet 'Sightings' Add to Anxiety," *Christian Science Monitor*, 3 February 1975, 6.

101 Stephen A. Rudloff, "Missing the Missing in Action," *National Review*, 14 February 1975, 163. Emphasis in the original.

102 Biess, *Homecomings*, 101–2.

103 Letter from Elaine Worrell to Gerald Ford, 12 December 1974, ND8-1 Casualties, 12/1/74–1/31/75, Box 10, WHCF, GRFL. For total cards see memo from Lawson to Gerald Ford, 20 January 1975, MIA/Amnesty/NLF (1), Box 10, Presidential Subject File, GRFL.

104 Jenkins, *Decade of Nightmares*, 11.

105 Clecak, *America's Quest for the Ideal Self*, 140–41. See also Farber, "Silent Majority and Talk about Revolution," 291–316.

106 Memo from Tom Korologos to Brent Scowcroft, 2 September 1974, MIA/Amnesty/National League of Families (1), Box 10, Presidential Subject File, GRFL.

107 Ford's military assistant recommended "a statement [on Kay] at this time would help blunt" League protests. Memo from Richard Lawson to Gerald Ford, 17 September 1974, ND8-1, Box 8, WHCF, GRFL.

108 Ford, *PPP, 1974*, 163. See chapter 2 for discussion of March 1974 repatriation of remains.

109 Letter from E. C. Mills to Gerald Ford, 20 August 1974, ND8-1, Box 8, WHCF, GRFL.

110 "Area Again Celebrates Veterans Day," *Washington Post*, 12 November 1974, C1, C4.

111 Memo from Richard Lawson to Gerald Ford, 18 October 1974, MIAs/POWs, October–December 1974, Box 1, Milt Mitler Files, 1973–77, GRFL.

112 Memo from Frank Sieverts to Henry Kissinger, 8 November 1974, Folder 2, Box 38, Records Received: State Department, Selected Records of Frank A. Sieverts, RG46 SSC.

113 See discussion above on page 9. See also memo from Richard Lawson to Gerald Ford, 20 January 1975, MIA/Amnesty/ National League of Families (1), Box 10, Presidential Subject File, GRFL.

114 Memo from Sven Kraemer and William Stearman to Brent Scowcroft, 9 January 1975, MIA/Amnesty/National League of Families (1), Box 10, Presidential Subject File, GRFL.

115 Memo from Richard Lawson to Gerald Ford, 20 January 1975, MIA/Amnesty/ National League of Families (1), Box 10, Presidential Subject File, GRFL.

116 Memo from Brent Scowcroft to Dick Lawson, 21 January 1975, Missing in Action—Pres. Board or Commission, Box 17, Theodore C. Marrs Files, 1974–1976, GRFL; memo from Ken Cole to Gerald Ford, 22 January 1975, MIA/Amnesty/National League of Families (2), Box 10, Presidential Subject File, GRFL.

117 Memo from Ken Cole to Gerald Ford, 22 January 1975, MIA/Amnesty/National League of Families (2), Box 10, Presidential Subject File, GRFL. On the six-week postponement see letter from E. C. Mills to Gerald Ford, 31 March 1975, Missing

in Action—National League of Families (3), Box 17, Theodore C. Marrs Files, 1974–1976, GRFL.

118 News release from John Stennis and letter from John Stennis to Gerald Ford, 27 February 1975, Box 9, ND8-1, Casualties 3/1/75–3/31/75, Box 9, WHCF, GRFL.

119 Cable from John Stang to Gerald Ford, 14 February 1975, 20–21 May 1975, Box 14, NSC East Asian and Pacific Staff Files (1969) 1973–76, GRFL.

120 Memo from Richard Lawson to Gerald Ford, 11 March 1975, Convenience File— Far East POW/MIA (2), Box A3, National Security Council Staff Convenience Files—Operations Staff for East Asian and Pacific Affairs, Henry Kissinger and Brent Scowcroft Files, (1972) 1974–1977, GRFL.

121 Herring, *America's Longest War*, 332–33.

122 Ford, *PPP, 1975*, 605.

123 Stern, *Imprisoned or Missing in Vietnam*, 18–19; Hurst, *Carter Administration and Vietnam*, 18–20; Menétrey-Monchau, *American-Vietnamese Relations*, 27–31.

124 Nixon's pledge was publicly revealed by Leslie Gelb, "Hanoi Says Nixon Pledged 3 Billion as Postwar Aid," *New York Times*, 2 February 1976, 1.

125 Isaacs, *Without Honor*, 136. See also Schulzinger, *Time for Peace*, 6.

126 Memo from William Stearman to Henry Kissinger, 27 June 1975, MIA/Amnesty/ National League of Families (2), Box 10, Presidential Subject File, GRFL.

127 Memo from Philip Habib and Monroe Leigh to Henry Kissinger, 14 June 1975, Vietnam (25), Box 20, National Security Adviser Presidential Country Files for East Asia and the Pacific, 1974–1977, GRFL.

128 Isaacs, *Without Honor*, 71, 78–79.

129 Martini, *Invisible Enemies*, 12, 80.

130 Ibid., 18–24; Franklin, *M.I.A.*, 123–26.

131 Jespersen, "Bitter End and the Lost Chance in Vietnam," 265.

132 Ibid., 265, 278; Memorandum for the Record, 6 December 1975, Folder 3, Box 30, Records Received: State Department, Selected Records of Frank A. Sieverts, RG46 SSC.

133 Tai, *Country of Memory*, esp. Tai, "Introduction: Situating Memory," and Malarney, "'The Fatherland Remembers Your Sacrifice.'" The "suffered the most" quote comes from Ambassador Vo Van Sung, Memorandum for the Record, 6 December 1975, Folder 3, Box 30, Records Received: State Department, Selected Records of Frank A. Sieverts, RG46 SSC.

134 Montgomery later became famous for modernizing the "Montgomery GI Bill" in his capacity as chairman of the House Veteran's Affairs Committee.

135 "House Creates a Committee to Probe Missing in Action," *Washington Post*, 12 September 1975, A2; press Release, undated, Committee Objectives, Box 1, RG233 HSC; House Select Committee, *Final Report*, chaps. 1–2.

136 For committee findings see *Final Report*, vii and chap. 10, esp. 241. For League reaction, see Analysis of the Final Report of the House Select Committee on Missing Persons in Southeast Asia, 18 February 1977, NLF OTF, Box 13, Foreign Relations Committee Minority Staff Files—Tracy Usry, RG46 SSC.

137 Letter from Gladys Brooks to G. V. Montgomery, 19 May 1976, Select Committee Members Memoranda to and from, Box 2, RG233 HSC.

138 Memo from Brent Scowcroft to Dick Lawson, 21 January 1975, Missing in Action—Pres. Board or Commission, Box 17, Theodore C. Marrs Files, 1974–1976, GRFL.

139 Quote taken from a letter conveying the committee's *Final Report* to president-elect Jimmy Carter, 15 December 1976, Carter-Mondale Campaign, Box 7, RG233 HSC.

140 House Select Committee, *Final Report*, vii.

141 Ibid., 1–2, 240.

142 Ibid., vii.

143 Ibid., 248.

144 Memorandum for the Record re: House Select Committee meeting with Pham Van Dong, 22 December 1975, Dinner Meeting with Pham Van Dong, Prime Minister (DRV) 12/22/75, Box 29, RG233 HSC.

145 Memorandum for the Record, 21 December 1975, Dinner Meeting with Phan Hien, Deputy Foreign Minister—Hanoi 12/21/1975, Box 29, RG233 HSC; Memorandum for the Record, 22 December 1975, Dinner Meeting with Pham Van Dong, Prime Minister (DRV) 12/22/75, Box 29, RG233 HSC; letter from Edwin W. Beeby to G. V. Montgomery, 21 January 1976, Misc. Interest Groups, Box 4, RG233 HSC.

146 Memcon, 26 January 1976, Folder: January 26, 1976—Ford, House Select Committee on MIAs, Box 17, National Security Adviser Memoranda of Conversations, GRFL.

147 Memo from Paul N. McCloskey to Max Friedersdorf, Frank Sieverts, and Brent Scowcroft, 3 February 1976, CO 165-1 Vietnam (North), Box 59, WHCF, GRFL.

148 "Hanoi Sets Return of 3 Bodies," *Baltimore Sun*, 7 December 1975, 1; Hopper press release, 7 December 1975, Folder 3, Box 30, Records Received: State Department, Selected Records of Frank A. Sieverts, RG46 SSC.

149 Guy Wright, "Hanoi's Peddlers of Corpses," *San Francisco Examiner*, 8 January 1976, 31.

150 Biess, *Homecomings*, 105.

151 Letter from Louis Fanning to G. V. Montgomery, 2 January 1976, Folder F, Box 17, RG233 HSC. Fanning would go on to write *Betrayal in Vietnam* (New Rochelle: Arlington House, 1976), which accused liberals of betraying American servicemen in Vietnam.

152 Letter from Royal Cresap to G. V. Montgomery, 11 December 1975, Folder C, Box 17, RG233 HSC; William L. Claiborne and Bart Barnes, "1,200 Protestors Arrested at Capitol," *Washington Post*, 6 May 1971, A1.

153 Letter from Gladys Brooks to G. V. Montgomery, 19 May 1976, House Select Committee Members Memoranda to and from, Box 2, RG233 HSC.

154 Letter from Alice McDuffie to G. V. Montgomery, 20 February 1976, Folder Mc, Box 17, RG233 HSC. Emphasis in the original.

155 Letter from Bob Schroder to G. V. Montgomery, 16 March 1976, Folder S, Box 18, RG233 HSC.

156 Letter from G. V. Montgomery to Richard Ottinger, 21 January 1976, Richard L. Ottinger (D-NY), Box 3, Select Committee Files, RG233 HSC; memo from G. V.

Montgomery to Select Committee, 1 June 1976, House Select Committee Members Memoranda to and from, Box 2, RG233 HSC; Memorandum for the Record, 13 April 1976, Box 29, Executive Session Mtg. 13 April 1976, Box 29, RG233 HSC.

157 Committee member Paul McCloskey, quoted in "MIA's: Lives in Limbo," *Newsweek*, 9 August 1976, 26; Clarke, *Missing Man*, 98.

158 House Select Committee, *Final Report*, 51, 44, chap. 4.

159 Kathy Sawyer, "MIA Families Fight a Lonely Battle," *Washington Post*, 18 July 1976, A1, A12.

160 Letter from Earl Hopper to G. V. Montgomery, 28 July 1976, Interest Groups, Box 5, RG233 HSC; see also "Analysis of the Final Report of the House Select Committee on Missing Persons in Southeast Asia," 18 February 1977, NLF OTF, Box 13, Foreign Relations Committee Minority Staff Files—Tracy Usry, RG46 SSC.

161 Emma Hagerman testimony, *Americans Missing in Southeast Asia: Hearings before the House Select Committee*, 94th Cong., 2d sess., 17, 25 June, 21 July, 21 September 1976, pt. 5: 20–21. Franklin, *M.I.A.*, 9, 168, and Clarke, *Missing Man*, 168, quote Hagerman approvingly.

162 Phyllis Corbitt, "Rethinking our Position on MIAs," *Washington Post*, 25 October 1976, A14.

163 Seven of the committee's ten members were veterans and its two chief staffers, J. Angus MacDonald and Henry "Hank" Kenny, served in Vietnam. Early in his career MacDonald had processed American POWs at the end of the Korean War as part of the U.S. effort to account for missing personnel and his expectations of MIA accounting were clearly colored by his experience in Korea, which he discussed in his 1961 master's thesis at the University of Maryland, "The Problems of U.S. Marine Corps Prisoners of War in Korea." He retired from active duty as a colonel in 1973. See Staff biographies, Box 3, RG233 HSC.

164 Dean, *Imperial Brotherhood*.

165 Crossland, "Buried Lives," 146–59.

166 Winter, *Remembering War*, 238–71, esp. 240–42.

167 Ibid., 244–46, 270.

168 House Select Committee, *Final Report*, 248.

169 Letter from Robin Gatwood to G. V. Montgomery, 20 December 1976, Comments on Committee Files, Box 2, RG233 HSC.

170 Letter from Christine Barrows to G. V. Montgomery, 1 June 1976, Misc. Interest Groups, Box 4, RG233 HSC.

171 Blight, *Race and Reunion*, 3.

172 House Select Committee, *Final Report*, 209.

173 Memorandum for the record, J. Angus MacDonald, 9 December 1976 and 13 December 1976, memo for the Record, Box 28, RG233 HSC.

174 Letter from John Moakley to Jimmy Carter, 1 February 1977, Folder 5, Box 31, Records Received: State Department, Selected Records of Frank A. Sieverts, RG46 SSC; Memoranda for the record, 9 December 1976 and 13 December 1976, memo for the Record, Box 28, RG233 HSC.

175 "Analysis of the Final Report of the House Select Committee on Missing Persons in Southeast Asia," 18 February 1977, NLF OTF, Box 13, Foreign Relations Committee Minority Staff Files—Tracy Usry, RG46 SSC. Emphasis in the original.

176 Memorandum for the Record, 31 January 1977, Document 1720, Fiche 145, The Declassified Document Reference System, Issued 1994.

177 Letter and memo from Alfonso Sellet to House Select Committee, 17 March 1976, Al Sellet, Consultant, Box 9, RG233 HSC.

178 Letter and memo from Alfonso Sellet to House Select Committee, 28 August 1976, Al Sellet, Consultant, Box 9, RG233 HSC. It is unclear why the VFW had two conventions within five months; however, the August convention was the group's national convention and appears to have been the larger of the two.

179 Wills, *Reagan's America*, 390.

180 Ford, *Time to Heal*, 373; Carroll, *It Seemed Like Nothing Happened*, 199; "The MIA Families," *Washington Post*, 28 July 1976, A20.

181 Schulman, *Seventies*, chap. 8, esp. 199.

182 McGirr, *Suburban Warriors*, 225–26, offers insight into the changing structure and evolving concerns of the conservative movement in the 1970s.

183 Jespersen, "Bitter End and the Lost Chance in Vietnam," 284–85.

184 Hurst, *Carter Administration and Vietnam*, 21–23.

185 Ford, *PPP, 1975*, 1950–55. Ford announced the Pacific Doctrine on December 7, the "date which will live in infamy," showing that even in the best diplomatic relationships, the past was never truly forgotten.

186 "MIA: The Heartless Ploy," *Nation*, 25 September 1976, 260.

187 In October the *Nation* published an article alleging "the importance of the MIA issue was first contrived as a propaganda weapon early in the tenure of Richard Nixon," consolidating the emerging origins narrative I sought to complicate in chapter 1. It could be argued that this claim arose out of willful amnesia on the left, which erased its own role in publicizing the POW/MIA issue by assigning responsibility to Nixon. Robert K. Musil, "Manipulating the MIAs," *Nation*, 9 October 1976, 331–34.

188 Memorandum for the Record, 21 December 1975, Dinner Meeting with Phan Hien, Deputy Foreign Minister—Hanoi 12/21/1975, Box 29, RG233 HSC.

189 Ford, *Time to Heal*, 354–57, 373–74.

190 For sequence of events see cable from Henry Kissinger to American Embassy Paris, 29 August 1975, Vietnam (12), Box 11, National Security Adviser Presidential Country Files for East Asia and the Pacific, 1974–1977, GRFL; see also Hurst, *Carter Administration*, 20.

191 Dovish GOP congressman Paul McCloskey complained to president Carter that "Kissinger had a feeling of petulance on Vietnam." See Memorandum for the Record, 31 January 1977, Document 1720, Fiche 145, The Declassified Document Reference System, Issued 1994.

192 Letter from Edwin W. Beeby to G. V. Montgomery, 21 January 1976, Misc. Interest Groups, Box 4, RG233 HSC.

193 In May 1976 the State Department's East Asia specialist assessed "church groups and anti–Vietnam war Congressman have decided that the accounting for POW/

MIA's is the best vehicle for promoting their interest in normalization of relations and assistance to Vietnam." See memo from Arthur Hummel to [no first name] Wilson, 10 May 1976, Folder 6, Box 36, Records Received: State Department, Selected Records of Frank A. Sieverts, RG46 SSC.

194 Letter from Mary Jane Lewis to G. V. Montgomery, 19 January 1976, Chairman Gillespie V. Montgomery, Box 3, RG233 HSC.

195 Committee consultant Gareth Porter leaked the story through Senator McGovern's office and was consequently fired. See Gelb, "Hanoi Says Nixon Pledged 3 Billion as Postwar Aid," *New York Times*, 2 February 1976, 1. For Kissinger's attempts to obstruct committee efforts to learn of the agreement, see memo from John J. Taylor to Henry Kissinger, 31 October 1975, MIA/Amnesty/National League of Families (2), Box 10, National Security Adviser, Presidential Subject File, 1974–1977, GRFL.

196 Letter from Earl Hopper to Gerald Ford, 27 July 1976, National League of Families, Box 2298, WHCF, GRFL.

197 Telegram from Ronald Reagan to the League convention, 24 July 1976, MIA/POW—National League of Families Convention (2), Box 21, John Marsh Files, 1974–1977, GRFL.

198 Mann, *Rise of the Vulcans*, 72–73; Jenkins, *Decade of Nightmares*, 60.

199 Ford, *PPP, 1976*, 2085.

200 "Ford Vows to Aid Search for G.I.'s," *New York Times*, 26 July 1976, A6.

201 Remarks of G. V. Montgomery before the National League of Families, 23 July 1976, Dear Colleagues and Press Releases, Box 1, RG233 HSC. For "you are not God" quote see Kathy Sawyer, "No Hope, MIA Families Told," *Washington Post*, 24 July 1976, A1, A6.

202 Letter from Angela Ucci to G. V. Montgomery, 25 May 1976, Folder U, Box 18, RG233 HSC.

203 Ibid. Exclamation points in original.

204 Letter from L. W. Griffin to G. V. Montgomery, 10 December 1975, Folder F, Box 17, RG233 HSC.

205 Letter from Mrs. Paul Crone to House Select Committee, 30 September 1975, Status Changes/General, Box 13, RG233 HSC.

206 Letter from Christopher Hodgkin to G. V. Montgomery, 3 March 1976, Folder H, Box 17, RG233 HSC.

CHAPTER 5.

1 Carol Bates, Newsletter, 30 August 1977, PC-1043 Army Status Review, Box 5, POW/MIA Affairs Office, Records re: Americans Taken Prisoners of War or Reported Missing in Action in Southeast Asia, 1961–1992, RG338 POW/MIA.

2 Carol Bates, Newsletter, 13 December 1977, NLF OTF, Box 13, Foreign Relations Committee Minority Staff Files—Tracy Usry, RG46 SSC.

3 Ann Mills Griffiths, Newsletter, 7 October 1980, NLF #1, Box 13, Investigator's Case Files, Hilton Foster, RG46 SSC.

4 Clarke, *Missing Man*, 109.

5   Ibid., 14–15.

6   DIA PW/MIA Weekly Report, 15 September 1983, POW/MIA Weekly Reports, September 1983–December 1985, Box 16, Records Received: Central Documentation Office, Department of Defense, RG46 SSC. Charles Shelton, shot down over Laos in 1965, remained "administratively" classified as a POW until 1994 as a purely "symbolic gesture by Air Force officials" meant "to keep the nation, and the bureaucracy, from forgetting the human toll of war." See Molly Moore, "Lest We Forget," *Washington Post*, 16 September 1988, A25.

7   Ronald Reagan, *PPP, 1983*, Book I, 470.

8   FitzGerald, *Way Out There in the Blue*, 16.

9   Jenkins, *Decade of Nightmares*.

10 Cannon, *President Reagan*, 40; McMahon, "Contested Memory," 168.

11 Franklin, *Vietnam & Other American Fantasies*, 3, 27, 29, and Franklin, *M.I.A.*, 132.

12 McMahon, "Contested Memory," 168.

13 Zaretsky, *No Direction Home*, 171–81.

14 Telegram from Jimmy Carter to the League convention, 24 July 1976, MIA/POW—National League of Families Convention (2), Box 21, John Marsh Files, 1974–1977, GRFL.

15 Memo from Earl Hopper to Ben Gilman, 4 February 1976, Folder 4, Box 35, Records Received: State Department, Selected Records of Frank A. Sieverts, RG46 SSC.

16 All Carter statements were reported in the League Newsletter, 26 October 1976, National League of Families, Box 5, Select Committee Files, RG233 HSC. For Carter's campaign pledges pertaining to MIAs see Hurst, *Carter Administration and Vietnam*, 30.

17 Carter, *Why Not the Best*, 37–38, 47–48.

18 Ann Mills Griffiths, interview by author, tape recording, Washington, D.C., 8 November 2000.

19 "Analysis of the Final Report of the House Select Committee on Missing Persons in Southeast Asia," 18 February 1977, NLF OTF, Box 13, Foreign Relations Committee Minority Staff Files—Tracy Usry, RG46 SSC.

20 Carol Bates, Newsletter, 30 August 1977, PC-1043 Army Status Review, Box 5, Records re: Americans Taken Prisoners of War or Reported Missing in Action in Southeast Asia, 1961–1992, RG338 POW/MIA.

21 McMahon, "Contested Memories," 165–71.

22 Sherry, *In the Shadow of War*, 344–45.

23 Carroll, *It Seemed Like Nothing Happened*, 197.

24 "Pardon: How Broad a Blanket," *Time*, 17 January 1977, 22; "Keeping His First Promise," *Time*, 31 January 1977, 15.

25 Chanda, *Brother Enemy*, 147; Jespersen, "Bitter End and Lost Chance in Vietnam," 288.

26 Memo from Zbigniew Brzezinski to Jimmy Carter, 10 February 1977, Document 1721, Fiche 145, The Declassified Document Reference System, Issued 1994.

27 Jespersen, "Politics and Culture of Nonrecognition," 405.

28 Ibid., 405–6; Mather, *M.I.A.*, 51.

29 Letter from Zbigniew Brzezinski to Carol Bates, 3 March 1977, Sheldon, Box 28, Foreign Relations Committee Minority Staff Files—Tracy Usry, RG46 SSC; Mather, *M.I.A.*, 52.

30 Handwritten notation on memo from Michel Oksenberg to Zbigniew Brzezinski, 31 January 1977, Sheldon, Box 28, Foreign Relations Committee Minority Staff Files—Tracy Usry, RG46 SSC; Ron Martz, "Carter Files Suggest MIA Kin Misled," *Atlanta Journal-Constitution*, 28 February 1987, 1A, 14A.

31 Brzezinski, *Power and Principle*, 228.

32 Memo from Cyrus Vance to Jimmy Carter, 11 March 1977, Document 1725, Fiche 145, The Declassified Document Reference System, Issued 1994.

33 Jimmy Carter, *PPP, 1977*, Book I, 489.

34 Mather, *M.I.A.*, 57; League Newsletter, 26 October 1976, National League of Families, Box 5, Select Committee Files, RG233 HSC.

35 Memo from Cyrus Vance to Jimmy Carter, 11 March 1977, Document 1725, Fiche 145, The Declassified Document Reference System, Issued 1994. See also Chanda, *Brother Enemy*, 147.

36 Holbrooke shared these motivations. See Chanda, *Brother Enemy*, 146, 150.

37 Hurst, *Carter Administration and Vietnam*, 28.

38 Memorandum for the Record, 6 December 1975, Folder 3, Box 30, Records Received: State Department, Selected Records of Frank A. Sieverts, RG46 SSC.

39 Senate Committee on Foreign Relations, *U.S. MIA's in Southeast Asia: Hearing before the Committee on Foreign Relations*, 95th Cong., 1st sess., 1 April 1977, 1–2.

40 Chanda, *Brother Enemy*, 148.

41 Mather, *M.I.A.*, 53–54.

42 Hurst, *Carter Administration and Vietnam*, 39–40.

43 Jespersen, "Politics and Culture of Nonrecognition," 408–9.

44 Hurst, *Carter Administration and Vietnam*, 33.

45 Chanda, *Brother Enemy*, 151–57; Menétrey-Monchau, *American-Vietnamese Relations*, chaps. 2–3.

46 Memo from Michel Oksenberg to Zbigniew Brzezinski, 25 May 1977, Oksenberg Memo, Box 6, Working Files of Staff Director Frances A. Zwenig, RG46 SSC.

47 Deposition of Michel Oksenberg, 18 June 1992, 62, Transcripts of Depositions, RG46 SSC.

48 Joseph Lelyveld, "Prisoners of Hope," *New York Times Magazine*, 20 March 1977, 110.

49 Memo from Zbigniew Brzezinski to Jimmy Carter, undated [June 1977], Document 2397, Fiche 210, The Declassified Documents Reference System, Issued 1998.

50 Memo from Harold Brown to Jimmy Carter, 26 May 1977, S-783, Box 3, Records received: Department of Defense, Central Documentation Office, RG46 SSC; memo from Zbigniew Brzezinski to Jimmy Carter, undated [June 1977], Document 2397, Fiche 210, The Declassified Documents Reference System, Issued 1998.

51 Memo from Walter Slocombe to Charles Duncan, 9 June 1977, OSS-92-3822, Box 116, Declassified Files, RG46 SSC.

52 Clarke, *Missing Man*, 106, 110n25; Mather, *M.I.A.*, 60.

53 Stern, *Imprisoned or Missing in Vietnam*, 25; Mather, *M.I.A.*, 62.

54 Repatriation discussed in Mather, *M.I.A.*, 68n26; Dong's meeting with Montgomery discussed in Hurst, *Carter Administration and Vietnam*, 96; Montgomery's advice discussed in Chanda, *Brother Enemy*, 271.

55 Forty-two Americans had been accounted for when Carter took office: sixteen through JCRC field operations and twenty-six through unilateral Vietnamese repatriations.

56 Reduction estimated on the basis of the League's claim of "712 currently listed as prisoners or missing" in August 1977 and DOD's claim that "there are 430 unresolved cases" in late June 1978. See Carol Bates, Newsletter, 30 August 1977, PC-1043 Army Status Review, Box 5, POW/MIA Affairs Office, Records re: Americans Taken Prisoners of War or Reported Missing in Action in Southeast Asia, 1961–1992, RG338 POW/MIA; memo from Deanne C. Siemer to Charles W. Duncan, 23 June 1978, OSS 92-3822, Box 116, Declassified Files, RG46 SSC. Carol Bates, Newsletter, 9 June 1978, NLF #1, Box 13, Hilton Foster Investigator Case Files, RG46 SSC.

57 Letter from Frank Wright to Walter Slocombe, 19 July 1978, OSS-92-3068, Box 71, Declassified Files, RG46 SSC.

58 Letter from Bob Ammon to Rep. Dan Quayle, 17 October 1977, Folder 7, Box 30, Records Received: State Department, Selected Records of Frank A. Sieverts, RG46 SSC.

59 Griffiths quoted in Josh Getlin, "Hearts & Bones," *Los Angeles Times Magazine*, 12 October 1986, 13.

60 The conflict between China, Vietnam, and Cambodia and the Carter administration's response to it is the subject of Nayan Chanda's indispensable *Brother Enemy*. For more on the U.S. role in the conflict see Hurst, *Carter Administration and Vietnam*; and Brzezinski, *Power and Principle*, 228, 409, 417, which includes Brzezinski's account of Deng Xiaoping's warning that China intended to invade Vietnam, and Vance's position "that our neglect of Vietnam was driving Vietnam into the hands of the Soviets."

61 Norman Podhoretz, "The Culture of Appeasement," *Harper's*, October 1977, 25.

62 "Munich" from Bacevich, *New American Militarism*, 74; "imminent apocalypse" from Jenkins, *Decade of Nightmares*, 16.

63 Ronald Reagan, "Introduction," in *We Came Home*, ed. Barbara Powers Wyatt, unpaginated.

64 Zaretsky, *No Direction Home*, 27–29.

65 Bacevich, *New American Militarism*, 73–77.

66 Ann Mills Griffiths, "Missing Man Essay," in *We Came Home*, ed. Barbara Powers Wyatt, unpaginated.

67 Carol Bates, Newsletter, 9 June 1978, NLF #1, Box 13, Investigator's Case Files, Hilton Foster, RG46 SSC.

68 Stockdale, *In Love and War*, chap. 2.

69 Ann Mills Griffiths, interview by author, tape recording, Washington, D.C., 8 November 2000; Deposition of Ann Mills Griffiths, 1 October 1992, Transcripts of Depositions, RG46 SSC, 18. Cathryn Donohoe, "A Support Group's Turmoil,"

Washington Times, 13 October 1991, A1, A6. My impressions are also based on interviews, correspondence, and telephone conversations with Griffiths, as well as observations from the 2001 League annual meeting.

70 Dermot Foley, Deposition, 17 April 1978, Folder 5, Box 31, Records Received: State Department, Selected Records of Frank A. Sieverts, RG46 SSC. Foley made these claims while prosecuting the civil action *Hopper, Jr. v. Carter*. Unlike the League's earlier *McDonald v. McLucas* litigation, the *Hopper* complaint was filed directly on behalf of MIAs themselves rather than their next of kin.

71 Dermot Foley, "Letter of resignation as League counsel," 17 June 1980, given to author by Bahar Hess, original in author's possession.

72 Stahl, "New Law on Department of Defense Personnel Missing as a Result of Hostile Action," 124–25.

73 O'Daniel, *Missing in Action*, 30.

74 Letter from Frank Wright to Walter Slocombe, 19 July 1978, OSS-92-3068, Box 71, Declassified Files, RG46 SSC; "DIA Findings on the Report of U.S. PWs in Vietnam From Refugee Ngo Phi Hung," December 1978, Unfoldered, Box 13, Investigator's Case Files, Neal E. Kravitz, RG46 SSC.

75 George Shultz, letter to family members and concerned citizens, undated, included in Ann Mills Griffiths, Newsletter, 27 November 1979, Folder: NLF, Box 2, VVMF LOC.

76 Groom and Spencer, *Conversations with the Enemy*, 325.

77 Robert Sam Anson, "The Vietnamization of Dermot Foley," *American Lawyer*, June 1979, 20.

78 Groom and Spencer, *Conversations with the Enemy*, chaps. 12–15, pp. 347, 391–93; Rochester and Kiley, *Honor Bound*, chap. 14.

79 House Select Committee, *Final Report*, 238–39, 26. In addition to Garwood, deserter McKinley Nolan was also thought to be alive in Southeast Asia. See Deposition of J. Angus MacDonald, 21 October 1992, 119–24, Transcripts of Depositions, RG46 SSC.

80 Foley was kicked off Garwood's defense team in June 1979 according to Groom and Spencer, *Conversations with the Enemy*, 353. League neutrality discussed in Anson, "The Vietnamization of Dermot Foley," *American Lawyer*, June 1979, 22.

81 See discussion in chapter 6.

82 Mather, *M.I.A.*, 75. See also George Shultz, letter to family members and concerned citizens, undated, included in Ann Mills Griffiths, Newsletter, 27 November 1979, Folder: NLF, Box 2, VVMF LOC.

83 Most congressional MIA hunters eventually served time on the Task Force, including Bob Smith of New Hampshire, Billy Hendon of North Carolina, John LeBoutillier of New York, and Gilman, Guyer, and Dornan.

84 Paul A. Gigot, "Lost or Merely Forgotten?," *National Review*, 17 August 1979, 1035–1038; John K. Singlaub, "Let's Find Our Missing Men!," *American Legion*, August 1980, 10–11, 42–45; "The Search for Missing Servicemen," *Newsweek*, 10 November 1980, 16.

85 Memo from Michel Oksenberg to David Aaron, 12 March 1979, Sheldon, Box 28, Foreign Relations Committee Minority Staff Files—Tracy Usry, RG46 SSC.

86 Senate Select Committee, *Report of the Select Committee on POW/MIA Affairs*, 154–55. See also Ron Martz, "Carter Files Suggest MIA Kin Misled," *Atlanta Journal-Constitution*, 28 February 1987, 1-A, 14-A.

87 Deposition of Michel Oksenberg, 18 June 1992, Transcripts of Depositions, RG46 SSC, 73.

88 Deposition of Frank Sieverts, 1 May 1992, Transcripts of Depositions, RG46 SSC, 375–77.

89 Given his claims to have "abandoned a wealth much larger than a half-a-billion in cash" and his professed involvement in anticommunist groups, party cadres were right to suspect Hung. Chanda, *Brother Enemy*, 234–39; "DIA Findings on the Report of US PWs in Vietnam From Refugee Ngo Phi Hung," 4–5, 77, December 1978, Unfoldered, Box 13, Investigator's Case Files, Neal E. Kravitz, RG46 SSC.

90 Translations of advertisement in "DIA Findings on the Report of US PWs in Vietnam From Refugee Ngo Phi Hung," 76, 81, 85, December 1978, Unfoldered, Box 13, Investigator's Case Files, Neal E. Kravitz, RG46 SSC.

91 Gigot, "Lost or Merely Forgotten," *National Review*, 17 August 1979, 1038. On Anh's "possible affiliation or association with the other side," see Addendum to memo from Richard Childress to Leonard H. Perroots, 18 June 1986, Unfoldered, Box 14, Records Received: Department of Defense, Central Documentation Office, RG46 SSC.

92 Sherry, *In the Shadow of War*, 347, 349, 357–58. For discussion of Aleksandr Solzhenitsyn and the influence of his work *The Gulag Archipelago, 1918–1956* in the late 1970s, see Steven Merritt Miner, "The Other Killing Machine," *New York Times Book Review*, 11 May 2003, 11.

93 Ellen Schrecker, *Many Are the Crimes*, 76–78.

94 Hofstadter, *The Paranoid Style in American Politics and Other Essays*, 34–35.

95 Thomas D. Boettcher and Joseph A. Rehyansky, "'We Can Keep You . . . Forever,'" *National Review*, 21 August 1981, 958, 960.

96 Loc is an intelligence source commonly referred to as "the mortician." His name appears in the table of contents of Edward D. Valentine, "Disposition of U.S. Skeletal Remains in the Socialist Republic of Vietnam," May 1981, OSS 92-3824, Box 116, Declassified Files, RG46 SSC, and is published in Bell, *Leave No Man Behind*, 127.

97 Loc's claims have become the subject of heated debate within the intelligence community, resulting in repeated reassessments of his story. I have based my account on the earliest DIA accounts, which are the least "corrupted" by subsequent debates that ultimately concern the implications of Loc's charges rather than their substance — memo from A. L. Kelln to David C. Jones, enclosure 3, 16 November 1979, OSS 92-4422, Box 58, Declassified Files, JCS Files-TS-703 (3 of 10), RG46 SSC; memo from Eugene F. Tighe to David C. Jones, 28 November 1979, TS-522, Box 7, Records Received: Department of Defense, Central Documentation Office RG46 SSC.

98 Memo from Eugene Tighe to David C. Jones, 28 November 1979, TS-522, Box 7, Records Received: Central Documentation Office, Department of De-

fense, RG46 SSC. Griffiths's presence discussed in memo from Peter Tarnoff to Zbigniew Brzezinski, 21 December 1979, Document 2240, Fiche 186, The Declassified Documents Reference System, 1994.

99 Memo from Peter Tarnoff to Zbigniew Brzezinski, 21 December 1979, Document 2240, Fiche 186, The Declassified Documents Reference System, 1994.

100 Statement of Lester Wolff, 30 January 1980, Unmarked folder (4), Box 8, Records Received: Department of Defense, Office of Secretary of Defense, Policy Files, RG46 SSC.

101 Michael Hirsley, "POW-MIA Kin Cling to New Hope," *Chicago Tribune*, 8 July 1980, 1; "Story of POW Bodies in Hanoi," *San Francisco Chronicle*, 28 June 1980, 6.

102 Testimony of Anita Lauve on the French POW/MIA experience after the first Indochina War, House Select Committee, *Hearings before the House Select Committee on Missing Persons in Southeast Asia*, Part 4, 94th Cong., 2d sess., 7 April 1976, 5–8, 12, 16–17.

103 After repatriating forty-four remains in the first eighteen months of Carter's presidency, for instance, Vietnam repatriated only twenty-two remains over the next seven years, then returned fifty-four sets in nine months' time. Defense Prisoner of War and Missing Personnel Office, "Vietnam's Collection and Repatriation of American Remains," June 1999, 28, figure 8; Mather, *M.I.A.*, 126–28; Stern, *Imprisoned or Missing in Vietnam*, 34; Neil Sheehan, "Prisoners of the Past," *New Yorker*, 24 May 1993, 45.

104 Carol Bates, "Newsletter," 30 August 1977, NLF OTF, Box 13, Foreign Relations Committee Minority Staff Files—Tracy Usry, RG46 SSC; see also Guy Wright, "Hanoi's Peddlers of Corpses," *San Francisco Examiner*, 8 January 1976, 31, for popular opinion on the subject.

105 Sheehan, "Prisoners of the Past," *New Yorker*, 24 May 1993, 45.

106 To her credit, Ann Mills Griffiths has called for the skulls to be returned to Vietnam. See Michelle Boorstein, "Eerie Souvenir from the Vietnam War," *Washington Post*, 3 July 2007, A11; Lori Andrews, "The Bones We Carried," *New York Times*, 22 June 2007, A21.

107 Defense Prisoner of War and Missing Personnel Office, "Vietnam's Collection and Repatriation of American Remains" (Washington, D.C.: Department of Defense, June 1999), 27–28, figure 8.

108 See Richard C. Bush, Intelligence Community Assessment, *Vietnamese Storage of Remains of Unaccounted US Personnel*, October 1996, ICA 96-05, 2.

109 "Hanoi Disproves Charge of Hiding US Bodies," *Alameda Times-Star*, 5 August 1980, 12. Instead of a morgue, journalists found "dust caked on piles of discarded film cans" left over from the war. According to DOD's official history of the POW experience in Vietnam, 17 Ly Nam De served "as a showplace for displaying captives to visiting delegations and conducting photo sessions and other propaganda activities," which may explain the film cans and coal-fired projectors that UPI discovered in 1980. See Rochester and Kiley, *Honor Bound*, chap. 18.

110 Richard C. Bush, *Vietnamese Storage of Remains of Unaccounted US Personnel*, Intelligence Community Assessment (ICA) 96-05, October 1996, 2.

111 National Intelligence Council, *Vietnamese Intentions, Capabilities, and Perfor-*

mances Concerning the POW/MIA Issue, National Intelligence Estimate (NIE) 98-03, April 1998, 18. This challenge to Loc's credibility outraged MIA activists, and was subsequently refined in a joint DOD/CIA review: "We believe that the mortician was truthful in explaining his knowledge of warehoused remains, but that his information regarding the numbers of remains was not accurate." This hair-splitting suggests that Loc did not mean to lie, but did not know what he was talking about. See Donald Mancuso and L. Britt Snider, *A Review of the 1998 National Intelligence Estimate on POW/MIA Issues and the Charges Levied by A Critical Assessment of the Estimate*, (1999-5974-IG), (00-OIR-04), 29 February 2000, 60, document given to author by Senator Bob Smith's office.

112   DIA official J. O. Tuttle quoted in Ann Mills Griffiths, Newsletter, 25 February 1980, Unmarked folder (1), Box 8, Records Received: Department of Defense, Office of Secretary of Defense, Policy Files, RG46 SSC.

113   Danielson quoted in Ann Mills Griffiths, Newsletter, 25 February 1980, Unmarked folder (1), Box 8, Records Received: Department of Defense, Office of Secretary of Defense, Policy Files, RG46 SSC; "Wolff Says Hanoi Holds Remains of Servicemen," *Washington Post*, 31 January 1980, A13.

114   "Additional and Separate Views of Representative George E. Danielson," House Special Study Mission to Asia, *Asian Security Environment, 1980: Report Submitted by a Special Study Mission to Asia*, 96th Cong., 2d sess., May 1980, H382-20, 37–38.

115   Memo from Ann Mills Griffiths to Board of Directors, Counsel, Regional & State Directors, 31 January 1980, Unmarked folder (4), Box 8, Records Received: Department of Defense, Office of Secretary of Defense, Policy Files, RG46 SSC.

116   Carter quoted in Ann Mills Griffiths, Newsletter, 25 February 1980, Unmarked folder (1), Box 8, Records Received: Department of Defense, Office of Secretary of Defense, Policy Files, RG46 SSC.

117   Farber, *Taken Hostage*, 138–40, 149; McAlister, *Epic Encounters*, 205.

118   McAlister, *Epic Encounters*, 206–8; see Gerald E. Parsons, "How the Yellow Ribbon Became a National Folk Symbol," *Folklife Center News* 13, no. 3 (1991): 9–11, available at the Library of Congress American Folklife Center web site, http://www.loc.gov/folklife/ribbons/ for discussion of the yellow ribbon as a symbol of fidelity (accessed 9 April 2009).

119   Steven V. Roberts, "The Year of the Hostage," *New York Times Magazine*, 2 November 1980, 26.

120   Johnson, *Sleepwalking through History*, 33.

121   Farber, *Taken Hostage*, 14, 141.

122   McAlister, *Epic Encounters*, 198–234; Zaretsky, *No Direction Home*, 234–38.

123   Roberts, "The Year of the Hostage," *New York Times Magazine*, 2 November 1980, 26.

124   Terence Smith, "President Critical," *New York Times*, 22 October 1980, A1; Roberts, "The Year of the Hostage," *New York Times Magazine*, 2 November 1980, 66.

125   Zaretsky, *No Direction Home*, 230.

126   The failure of "Operation Eagle's Claw" is described in McAlister, *Epic Encounters*, 212–14; and Johnson, *Sleepwalking through History*, 35–36.

127 As discussed above, it is more likely that the photograph showed returned POW Ron Bliss.

128 McAlister, *Epic Encounters*, 210; Jenkins, *Decade of Nightmares*, 152, 158.

129 "Hostages' Families Talk to Vietnam Ex-P.O.W.," *New York Times*, 5 May 1980, A10.

130 Rudy Maxa, "Vietnam POWs, Dissident Scharansky, and New Hostages," *Washington Post Magazine*, 20 April 1980, 2.

131 Ronald Reagan, *PPP, 1981*, 27, 38.

132 Letter from Ann Mills Griffiths to John Negroponte, 24 March 1980, Unmarked folder (3), Box 8, Records Received: Department of Defense, Office of Secretary of Defense, RG46 SSC; Newsletter by Gladys Brooks, March 1981, Legal: POW/ MIA 1980–7/1981 [7 of 9], Box OA90300, Robert Kimmit Files, WHSF, RRL.

133 McAlister, "A Cultural History of the War without End," 447, 451; McAlister, *Epic Encounters*, 207–10. See also Zaretsky, *No Direction Home*, 235.

134 "Wolff Says Hanoi Holds Remains of Servicemen," *Washington Post*, 31 January 1980, A13; "Story of POW Bodies in Hanoi," *San Francisco Chronicle*, 28 June 1980, 6. The *Chicago Tribune* ran a front-page story on the League that included discussion of warehoused remains by Hirsley, "POW-MIA Kin Cling to New Hope," *Chicago Tribune*, 8 July 1980, 1.

135 The National League of POW/MIA Families, "POW/MIA Recognition Day: Background," available at http://www.powmiaff.org/recognitionday.html (accessed 21 July 2008).

136 Brzezinski, *Power and Principle*, 44, 480; E. J. Dionne, "Fear of War or Weakness Resonating in Campaign," *New York Times*, 24 October 1980, A18.

137 Secrecy agreement appended to Dermot Foley, "Letter of resignation as League counsel," 17 June 1980, supplied to author by Bahar Hess, original in author's possession.

138 According to Griffiths, "Tighe gave me a lower level security clearance . . . so that I could reassure the families of the legitimacy of what they were doing." Ann Mills Griffiths, interview by author, tape recording, Washington, D.C., 8 November 2000.

139 Memo from Eugene Tighe to Charles Walker, 27 June 1980, Unmarked folder (4), Box 8, Records Received: Department of Defense, Office of Secretary of Defense, Policy Files, RG46 SSC.

140 Memorandum for the Record (Minutes of first IAG Meeting), 14 March 1980, Folder 4, Reel 19, LOC VNDC.

141 Ann Mills Griffiths, Newsletter, 25 February 1980, Unmarked folder (1), Box 8, Records Received: Department of Defense, Office of Secretary of Defense, Policy Files, RG46 SSC.

142 Ann Mills Griffiths, memo to PW/MIA Interagency Group Members, 8 October 1981, Folder 17, Reel 20, LOC VNDC. Lawson's relationship with the League dated back to his years as military assistant to President Ford, when he advocated a presidential POW/MIA task force. He was director of plans and policy for the JCS when the IAG was formed in 1980. The League board unanimously selected him as keynote speaker for the 1980 convention.

143 Negroponte National Security Archive interview at http://www.gwu.edu/

~nsarchiv/coldwar/interviews/episode-18/negroponte1.html (accessed 21 July 2008).

144 Linda Cooper and Jim Hodge, "Appointees Spark Controversy," *National Catholic Reporter*, 10 August 2001, 7; Bart Jones, "Three Tarnished Reagan Figures Have Hands in Bush Foreign Policy," *National Catholic Reporter*, 10 January 2003, 6.

145 Ann Mills Griffiths, interview by author, tape recording, Washington, D.C., 8 November 2000.

146 For early IAG membership see Ann Mills Griffiths, Newsletter, 25 March 1980, Unmarked folder (5), Box 8, Records Received: Department of Defense, Office of Secretary of Defense, Policy Files, RG46 SSC. For Griffiths's role in streamlining the IAG see Ann Mills Griffiths, memo to PW/MIA Interagency Group Members, 8 October 1981, Folder 17, Reel 20, LOC VNDC. For the IAG's policy role see Senate Select Committee, *Report of the Select Committee on POW/MIA Affairs*, 272.

147 Senate Select Committee, *Report of the Select Committee on POW/MIA Affairs*, 31, 272, 280. The IAG's secrecy under Reagan and Bush also makes it difficult for historians to penetrate the inner workings of the group after 1981.

148 Senate Select Committee, *Report of the Select Committee on POW/MIA Affairs*, 272.

149 Hirsley, "POW-MIA Kin Cling to New Hope," *Chicago Tribune*, 8 July 1980, 1.

150 Letter from Earl Hopper to Ann Mills Griffiths and Board of Directors, 26 March 1980, Folder: Hopper, Box 7, Investigator's Case Files, Hilton Foster, RG46 SSC.

151 Dermot Foley, letter of resignation as League counsel, 17 June 1980, supplied to author by Bahar Hess, original in author's possession. Foley's letter was circulated at the League's 1980 convention along with Hopper's letter of resignation and a copy of Griffiths's DIA Secrecy Agreement. See also letter of resignation from Earl Hopper to League Board of Directors, 12 April 1980, Unmarked folder (4), Box 8, Records Received: Department of Defense, Office of Secretary of Defense, Policy Files, RG46 SSC.

152 DIA personnel discussed in Memorandum for the Record (Minutes of first IAG Meeting), 14 March 1980, Folder 4, Reel 19, LOC VNDC; policy language from Joint Chiefs of Staff, "POW/MIA Policy," 1 July 1980, Folder 1, Box 4, Records Received: Department of Defense, Joint Chiefs of Staff, RG46 SSC; see also Ann Mills Griffiths, Newsletter, 7 October 1980, NLF #1, Box 13, Investigator's Case Files, Hilton Foster, RG46 SSC.

153 Joint Chiefs of Staff, "POW/MIA Policy," 1 July 1980, Folder 1, Box 4, Records Received: Department of Defense, Joint Chiefs of Staff, RG46 SSC. Emphasis in the original.

154 League advertisement, "He'd Have a Better Chance If He Were an Orphan," undated [context suggests 1975], Folder 206A, Box 2, Records Received: Department of Defense, Office of Secretary of Defense, Policy Files, RG46 SSC, cites "1300 U.S. Servicemen who are classified POW or MIA"; for testimony from government officials using the 1,300 figure see Senate Select Committee on POW/MIA Affairs, *Hearing on Americans Missing or Prisoner in Southeast Asia, The Department of Defense Accounting Process: Hearings before the Select Committee*

on *POW/MIA Affairs*, 102d Cong., 2d sess., 24–25 June 1992, S. HRG. 102-966, 13–20.

155 House Select Committee, *Final Report*, 21–22.

156 Senate Select Committee, *Hearing on Americans Missing or Prisoner in Southeast Asia, The Department of Defense Accounting Process*, 21.

157 Senate Select Committee, *Report of the Select Committee on POW/MIA Affairs*, 158.

158 "MIAs: Lives in Limbo," *Newsweek*, 9 August 1976, 26; "The Search for Missing Servicemen," *Newsweek*, 10 November 1980, 16.

159 Gigot, "Lost or Merely Forgotten," *National Review*, 17 August 1979, 1035–38; Singlaub, "Let's Find Our Missing Men!," *American Legion*, August 1980, 10–11, 42–45.

160 "The widespread practice of classifying an individual as MIA at the time of loss, based mainly on not recovering the individual, led to many questionable classifications as MIA" according to the House Select Committee, *Final Report*, 238; see also Clarke, *Missing Man*, 13–25.

161 Memo from Roger Shields to J. Angus MacDonald, 5 December 1975, Briefing by MIA Staff, Box 1, Select Committee Files, RG233 HSC.

162 Memo from Ann Mills Griffiths to the IAG, 25 March 1986, OSS-92-3070 ISA/ Roger Shield Files: POW/MIA Policy, Box 47, Declassified Files, RG46 SSC. Griffiths explained that "it was not until . . . 1979, that the League finally convinced the Defense Department that presumptions of death do not mean accountability, and the policy was changed to reflect the total number of Americans 'missing or otherwise unaccounted for in Southeast Asia.'" See also memo from Eugene Tighe to Charles Walker, 27 June 1980, Unmarked folder (4), Box 8, Records Received: Department of Defense, Office of Secretary of Defense, Policy Files, RG46 SSC.

163 Letter from Ann Mills Griffiths to Richard Allen, 26 March 1980, Unmarked folder (3), Box 8, Records Received: Department of Defense, Office of Secretary of Defense, Policy Files, RG46 SSC.

164 Ibid.

165 McMahon, "Contested Memory," 168; Lou Cannon, "Reagan: 'Peace through Strength,'" *Washington Post*, 19 August 1980, A1.

166 Cannon, *President Reagan*, 290.

167 Reagan had been delivering the same basic speech since the 1950s, using apocrypha to illustrate American decline brought on by big government. See Wills, *Reagan's America*, chap. 3; Cannon, *President Reagan*, 66–71.

168 For contemporary coverage critical of Reagan's rhetoric see Robert Kaiser, "Those Old Reaganisms May Be Brought Back to Haunt Him," *Washington Post*, 2 September 1980, A2; Philip Geyelin, "Rip Van Reagan," *Washington Post*, 23 June 1980, A15.

169 Haynes Johnson, "Reagan's Combative Rhetoric is Working against Him," *Washington Post*, 24 August 1980, A3; Peter Goldman, "The Battle of the Button," *Newsweek*, 1 September 1980, 18; Howell Raines, "Reagan Campaign Problems," *New York Times*, 27 August 1980, A17.

170 Hedrick Smith, "Examining What President Says on Reagan and War," *New York*

Times, 28 October 1980, A24; Lou Cannon and Edward Walsh, "War, Peace Dominate Debate," *Washington Post*, 29 October 1980, A1.

171 Timberg, *Nightingale's Song*, 15; Adam Clymer, "Behind Every Defense Policy There Lurks a Political Idea," 24 August 1980, *New York Times*, D4.

172 Lou Cannon and Edward Walsh, "War, Peace Dominate Debate," *Washington Post*, 29 October 1980, A1; E. J. Dionne, "Fear of War or Weakness Resonating in Campaign," *New York Times*, 24 October 1980, A18; David Broder, "Republicans Surge Ahead in New Poll," *Washington Post*, 6 July 1980, A1.

173 Martin Tolchin, "Republican Majority Is Possible in the Senate," *Washington Post*, 5 November 1980, A1; Michael Getler, "Direct Hit Scored on Defense Policy," *Washington Post*, 6 November 1980, A7.

174 Schulman, *Seventies*, chaps. 4, 8–9.

175 Cannon, *President Reagan*, 435, 582; Schaller, *Reckoning with Reagan*, 36; Gibson, *Warrior Dreams*, 269.

176 Kaiser, "Those Old Reaganisms May Be Brought Back to Haunt Him," *Washington Post*, 2 September 1980, A2.

177 Cannon, *President Reagan*, 290.

178 Gigot, "Lost or Merely Forgotten," *National Review*, 17 August 1979, 1035–36.

179 Singlaub, "Let's Find Our Missing Men!," *American Legion*, August 1980, 45.

CHAPTER 6.

1 Chip Brown, "MIA Families Gather Here to Apply Renewed Pressure," *Washington Post*, 28 January 1983, A1; Chip Brown, "Reagan Pledges Search for Men Missing in Vietnam," *Washington Post*, 29 January 1983, A4; Ronald Reagan, *PPP, 1984*, Book I, 130–32.

2 James Rosenthal, "The Myth of the Lost POWs," *New Republic*, July 1985, 19.

3 Deposition of Richard V. Allen, 23 June 1992, Transcripts of Depositions, RG46 SSC, 20, 92.

4 Cannon, *President Reagan*, 54.

5 Ibid., 541.

6 Reagan, *PPP, 1984*, vol. II, 1054. Reagan also played a downed flyer shot down behind German lines in the World War II film *Desperate Journey*. See Rogin, *Ronald Reagan, the Movie*, 13.

7 Cannon, *President Reagan*, 559.

8 Brown, "Reagan Pledges Search for Men Missing in Vietnam," *Washington Post*, 29 January 1983, A4.

9 *Final Interagency Report of the Reagan Administration on the POW/MIA Issue in Southeast Asia*, 19 January 1989, Interagency Report on POW/MIA Issue in Southeast Asia, Box 6, Foreign Relations Committee Minority Staff Files—Tracy Usry, RG46 SSC.

10 Wills, *Reagan's America*, 379; Cannon, *President Reagan*, 31–35.

11 Blumenthal, *Our Long National Daydream*, 106–12, 118–24; Cannon, *President Reagan*, 451–3; FitzGerald, *Way Out There in the Blue*, 233–35.

12 Kammen, *Mystic Chords of Memory*, 100.

13 Memo from Earl Hopper to League regional and state coordinators, 12 January

1984, Folder: Hopper, Box 7, Investigator's Case Files, Hilton Foster, RG46 SSC. Emphasis in the original.

14 Ted Sampley, "Ronald Reagan, Sympathetic or Just Acting," *Bamboo Connection*, 14 February 1988, 10.

15 Deposition of Ann Mills Griffiths, 1 October 1992, Transcripts of Depositions, RG46 SSC, 18.

16 IAG Minutes, 7 April 1981, Folder 5, Reel 19, LOC VNDC; Draft Memorandum for the Record, 2 June 1981, Folder 5, Reel 19, LOC VNDC; Memorandum for the Record, 2 June 1981, OSS-92-3358, Box 48, Declassified Files, RG46 SSC; memo from Ann Mills Griffiths to IAG members, 8 October 1981, Folder 17, Reel 20, LOC VNDC.

17 Mather, *M.I.A.*, 125–27. Thomas D. Boettcher and Joseph A. Rehyansky, "'We Can Keep You . . . Forever,'" *National Review*, August 1981, 958, 960.

18 Department of Defense, *POW-MIA Fact Book* (Washington, D.C.: Department of Defense, 1982), 2.

19 Ann Mills Griffiths, Newsletter, 21 December 1982, POW/MIA NLF—January 1983 National League of Families Meeting, Box OA92407, Richard Childress Files, RRL.

20 For DIA staff reduction compare Memorandum of Inspection, 24 March 1983, Folder 154 (DIA & CIA Reports), Box 21, Investigator's Case Files, Hilton Foster, RG46 SSC; and Memorandum for the Record (Minutes of first IAG Meeting), 14 March 1980, Folder 4, Reel 19, LOC VNDC.

21 1981 CILHI staff levels from *Final Interagency Report of the Reagan Administration on the POW/MIA Issue in Southeast Asia*, 19 January 1989, Interagency Report on POW/MIA Issue in SEA, Box 6, Foreign Relations Committee Minority Staff Files—Tracy Usry, RG46 SSC; 1985 CILHI staff levels from Robert Lee Hotz, "Putting Names to the Dead: No Easy Task," *Atlanta Journal-Constitution*, 11 August 1985, 1A, 14A; and William R. Maples, "Status Report on US Army Central Identification Laboratory (Hawaii)," Undated, Unmarked folder (1), Box 5, Investigator's Case Files, John Erickson, RG46 SSC; Susan Sheehan, "A Missing Plane," pt. 2, *New Yorker*, 19 May 1986, 47.

22 Deputy Assistant Secretary of Defense for POW/Missing Personnel Affairs, *Vietnam's Collection and Repatriation of American Remains* (Washington, D.C.: Department of Defense, 1999), 28, http://www.dtic.mil/dpmo/vietnamwar/remains_study.htm (accessed 21 July 2008); Department of Defense, *POW-MIA Fact Book*, July 1982, 20. For 1976 levels see Mather, *M.I.A.*, 49.

23 Bell, *Leave No Man Behind*, 145, 153.

24 Mather, *M.I.A.*, 127–29; National League of Families, "POW/MIA Agreements Between the US and SRV, February 1982–Present," undated [1992], NLF #9, Box 13, Investigator's Case Files, Hilton Foster, RG46 SSC.

25 "Hanoi Says U.S. Exploits Issue of Missing G.I.'s," *New York Times*, 23 February 1982, A5.

26 George C. Wilson and Art Harris, "Mercenaries Sent to Laos Seeking MIAs," *Washington Post*, 21 May 1981, A1, A10.

27 William Branigin, "Thais Probe Adventurers' Search for POWs in Laos," *Washington Post*, 22 February 1983, A1, A11.

28 Ibid.; Wilson and Harris, "Mercenaries Sent to Laos Seeking MIAs," *Washington Post*, 21 May 1981, A10; Art Harris, "Bo Gritz: The Glory and the Search," *Washington Post*, 3 March 1983, D1; Jim Graves and Jim Coyne, "Operation Lazarus: The Inside Story," *Soldier of Fortune*, Spring 1983, 8.

29 Philip Geyelin, "Bo Gritz Is Not the Issue," *Washington Post*, 31 March 1983, A23; Harris, "Bo Gritz: The Glory and the Search," *Washington Post*, 3 March 1983, D1.

30 Harris, "Bo Gritz: The Glory and the Search," *Washington Post*, 3 March 1983, D1.

31 Wilson and Harris, "Mercenaries Sent to Laos Seeking MIAs," *Washington Post*, 21 May 1981, A10.

32 Jeffords, *Hard Bodies*, 89.

33 Deposition of Richard V. Allen, 23 June 1992, Transcripts of Depositions, RG46 SSC, 41, 43–45, 60.

34 Memo for the Director of the Army Staff, 21 December 1987, Department of Army Inquiry on Lt. Col. Bo Gritz, Box 6, Records Received: Department of Defense, Office of Secretary of Defense, Policy Files, RG46 SSC.

35 Memo from Robert McFarlane to John Poindexter, 30 November 1982, POW/MIA Vol. I (3) 1/20/81–7/31/84, Box 85, Executive Secretariat, NSC: Subject Files, RRL. Emphasis in the original.

36 Harris, "Bo Gritz: The Glory and the Search," *Washington Post*, 3 March 1983, D1.

37 For a contemporary critique of Reagan's "privatized diplomacy," see "Franchising the Reagan Doctrine," *New York Times*, 8 February 1987, E22.

38 Rogin, "'Make My Day!,'" 116.

39 Deposition of Richard V. Allen, 23 June 1992, Transcripts of Depositions, RG46 SSC, 59.

40 *Penthouse* interview discussed in Branigin, "Thais Probe Adventurers' Search for POWs in Laos," *Washington Post*, 22 February 1983, A11; other appearances in Dona DuVall, "Gritz-est Show on Earth," *Soldier of Fortune*, Spring 1983, 44.

41 Geyelin, "Bo Gritz Is Not the Issue," *Washington Post*, 31 March 1983, A23.

42 Gibson, *Warrior Dreams*, 283.

43 Rogin, "'Make My Day!,'" 102; letter from Ronald Reagan to Mr. and Mrs. Fleckenstein, 19 May 1982, Folder DOD, Reel 13, LOC VNDC.

44 Sherry, *In the Shadow of War*, 396; Rogin, "'Make My Day!,'" 107, 116.

45 VIVA transferred its assets to Support Our POW/MIAs when it dissolved. Griffiths's use of this account for the IAG operation suggests that she may have used it as a slush fund even before 1981, as suggested in chapter 5.

46 Senate Select Committee, *Report of the Select Committee on POW/MIA Affairs*, 304–9; memo from Sedgwick Tourison to Hilton Foster, 10 November 1992, Folder: 154 (DIA and CIA Reports), Box 21, Investigator's Case Files, Hilton Foster, RG46 SSC; Ron Martz, "U.S. Backed MIA Effort Despite Ban," *Atlanta Journal-Constitution*, 28 June 1987, A1.

47 Memo from Robert McFarlane to James Baker, signed and notated by Ronald Reagan, 1 June 1982, POW/MIA Vol. I (3) 1/20/81–7/30/84, Box 85, Executive Secretariat, NSC: Subject Files, RRL.

48 Letter from John LeBoutillier to Ted Sampley, 10 October 1992, Veterans of the Vietnam War, Box 2, Hilton Foster Investigation Case Files, RG46 SSC.

49 Deposition of Ann Mills Griffiths, 1 October 1992, Transcripts of Depositions, RG46 SSC, 48–81, 102–17.

50 Senate Select Committee on POW/MIA Affairs, *Report of the Select Committee on POW/MIA Affairs*, 304–9.

51 Memo from Robert McFarlane to James Baker signed and notated by Ronald Reagan, 1 June 1982, POW/MIA Vol. I (3) 1/20/81–7/30/84, Box 85, Executive Secretariat, NSC: Subject Files, RRL.

52 Allan G. Paulson, PW/MIA Daily Report, 4 June 1982, June 1982 DIR Reports, Box 6, Records received: Department of Defense/Central Documentation Office, RG46 SSC.

53 Memo from Richard Childress to William Clark, 31 January 1983, POW/MIA 1/20/81–7/31/84 (2), Box 85, Executive Secretariat, NSC Records Subject Files, RRL.

54 Deposition of Ann Mills Griffiths, 1 October 1992, Transcripts of Depositions, RG46 SSC, 108–9; Martz, "U.S. Backed MIA Effort Despite Ban," A1.

55 See Senate Select Committee, *Report of the Select Committee on POW/MIA Affairs*, 303, for DIA assessment of the Lao resistance. See Johnson, *Sleepwalking through History*, 245–371, for more on the Iran-Contra affair.

56 Deposition of Richard Childress, 30 July 1992, Transcripts of Depositions, RG46 SSC, 12–22; Deposition of Richard Allen, 23 June 1992, Transcripts of Depositions, RG46 SSC, 30–33.

57 James Bamford, "Carlucci and the N.S.C.," *New York Times Magazine*, 18 January 1987, 26, 38, 76.

58 Singlaub publicized the MIA issue in his article "Let's Find Our Missing Men!" before going on to raise funds for the contras from wealthy donors, including Hurlburt, who belonged to his World Anti-Communist League. Secord was involved in air force intelligence on downed pilots in Laos in the early 1970s and headed the 1980 Iran hostage rescue attempt before becoming North's arms broker in Iran-Contra. On at least four separate occasions, Perot put up $2 million rewards for Iranian hostages, and provided at least $300,000 to North for an elaborate ransom scheme. See Bernard Weinraub, "Decision for Meese," *New York Times*, 2 December 1986, A1; Stephen Engelberg, "Detailing 'the D.E.A. Caper': Bungled Bid to Buy Hostages," *New York Times*, 31 May 1987, 1, 10.

59 Timberg, *Nightingale's Song*, 18–19.

60 Reagan, *PPP, 1981*, 27.

61 FitzGerald, *Way Out There in the Blue*, 269; Cannon, *President Reagan*, 541; Joanne Omang, "Convention on MIAs to Open Amid Dissension, High Hopes," *Washington Post*, 18 July 1985, A6.

62 Senate Select Committee, *Report of the Select Committee on POW/MIA Affairs*, 316.

63 Ibid., 316–28.

64 Memo from Alex Greenfield to Bill Codinha, 19 February 1992, Folder 48, Box 4, Investigator's Case Files, Hilton Foster, RG46 SSC.

65 Senate Select Committee, *Report of the Select Committee on POW/MIA Affairs*, 327.

66 Memo from Joseph Schlatter to Ann Mills Griffiths, 20 May 1989, Homecoming II vs. NLF, Box 13, Foreign Relations Committee Minority Staff Files—Tracy Usry, RG46 SSC; "Dog Tag Sources Reporting by Year" graph, 30 November 1992, Unlabeled folder, Box 12, Working Files of Staff Director Frances A. Zwenig, RG46 SSC.

67 Senate Select Committee, *Report of the Select Committee on POW/MIA Affairs*, 324–25.

68 Bell, *Leave No Man Behind*, 202.

69 Dower, *War without Mercy*; Mann, *Rise of the Vulcans*, 26–28, 73–75.

70 Eugene Tighe, "The Tighe Task Force Examination of DIA Intelligence Holdings Surrounding Unaccounted for United States Military Personnel in Southeast Asia," 27 May 1986, Tighe Task Force Review of DIA's PW/MIA Analysis Center, Box 1, Records received: Department of Defense/Central Documentation Office, RG46 SSC.

71 Senate Select Committee, *Report of the Select Committee on POW/MIA Affairs*, 10, 178.

72 Keith B. Richburg, "In South Vietnam, It's Business as Usual," *Washington Post*, 15 July 1987, A1.

73 Senate Select Committee, *Report of the Select Committee on POW/MIA Affairs*, 325; memo from Alex Greenfield to Bill Codinha, 19 February 1992, Folder 48, Box 4, Investigator's Case Files, Hilton Foster, RG46 SSC.

74 Quang Cat Loi, "Reagan's Resentment and Grudge," *Quan Doi Nhan Dan*, 12 June 1985, White House/NSC Documents, Box 9, Investigator's Case Files, Neal E. Kravitz, RG46 SSC.

75 Memorandum for the Record, 17 October 1984, POW/MIA Policy 1976–1985 [2 of 3], Box OA92407, Richard Childress Files, RRL.

76 Schulzinger, *Time for Peace*, 222–23, 272–73, 417, 426; National Intelligence Council, *National Intelligence Estimate: Vietnamese Intentions, Capabilities, and Performance Concerning the POW/MIA Issue* (Langley, Va.: Central Intelligence Agency, 1998), 9 available at: http://www.foia.cia.gov/pow_mia.asp (accessed 21 July 2008). The framework of rental fees and labor costs described here pertains to the present day.

77 Neil A. Lewis, "Hanoi Said to Agree to Meet on Missing," *New York Times*, 19 July 1987, A3.

78 Franklin, *M.I.A.*, 122–23; Martini, *Invisible Enemies*, 18–24.

79 "For Kin of MIAs, the War Goes On," *New York Daily News*, 24 July 1981.

80 Steven Erlanger, "Missing in Action: From a Lost War, a Haunting Echo That Won't Be Stilled," *New York Times*, 31 August 1988, A6; Bates, Newsletter, 9 June 1978, NLF #1, Box 13, Hilton Foster Investigator Case Files, RG46 SSC.

81 Patricia O'Grady Aloot to House Subcommittee on Asian and Pacific Affairs, undated [1986], Folder 53a, Box 5, Investigator's Case Files, Hilton Foster, RG46 SSC. When I asked Griffiths, "Can you tell me how many members the League has?" she answered, "I don't know exactly," claiming that the computer with the

membership roll was in need of repair, "but it's gone up and down." Griffiths, interview with the author, tape recording, Washington, D.C., 8 November 2000.

82 Memo from Paul Schott Stevens to Frederick J. Ryan, 18 March 1988, Folder 281, Reel 51, LOC VNDC.

83 Change in League by-laws discussed in National League of Families, "Report Concerning Misinformation on the Issue of American Prisoners of War and Missing in Action in Southeast Asia," undated, NLF #1, Box 13, Investigator's Case Files, Hilton Foster, RG46 SSC.

84 At the 2001 League convention I attended, numerous references were made to the League's declining membership.

85 Ann Mills Griffiths, Newsletter, 7 October 1980, NLF #1, Box 13, Investigator's Case Files, Hilton Foster, RG46 SSC.

86 See 1982–83 Annual Report, POW/MIA National League of Families 1982–83, Box OA92407, Richard Childress Files, RRL; 1983 revenues from Ann Mills Griffiths, Newsletter, 14 August 1984, TS-671, Box 3, Records Received: Central Documentation Office, Department of Defense, RG46 SSC.

87 Salaries and staff size from "List of names and salaries of each employee who received $20,000 or more," 30 September 1992, Folder: NLF, Box 13, Investigator's Case Files, Hilton Foster, RG46 SSC; 1988 revenue from 1988 IRS filing, Folder: DIWAN, Box 2, Investigator's Case Files, Hilton Foster, RG46 SSC.

88 Memo from Hilton Foster to Senate Select Committee Staff, 9 September 1992, Plan of Investigation of Fraud and Private Efforts, Box 1, Investigator's Case Files, Hilton Foster, RG46 SSC. Committee staff documented $30 million in donations but believed "that a significantly larger amount of money may have been raised."

89 Memo from Mary Nell Crowe to Bill Pittenger, 11 March 1985, Unmarked folder (6), Box 3, Working Files of Hilton Foster and Alex Greenfield, RG46, SSC.

90 Senate Select Committee, *Report of the Select Committee on POW/MIA Affairs*, 329–35; Deposition of Bruce Eberle, 20 October 1992, Transcripts of Depositions, RG46 SSC, 90–94.

91 990 Part I Note to the File pertaining to 1988 tax filing, undated, Unfoldered bundle 5, Box 39, Investigator's Case Files, Hilton Foster, RG46 SSC; letter from Krista Eppley to Ben Brannock, 2 February 1988, Unfoldered bundle 5, Box 39, Investigator's Case Files, Hilton Foster, RG46 SSC; letter from Linda Canada to Jack Bailey, 18 April 1985, Unfoldered bundle 5, Box 39, Investigator's Case Files, Hilton Foster, RG46 SSC.

92 Harold E. Mills, "Reagan Fund-raiser Back Home," *St. Joseph, Mo. Gazette*, undated newspaper article, Unfoldered bundle 5, Box 39, Investigator's Case Files, Hilton Foster, RG46 SSC; News Release, undated, Unfoldered bundle 5, Box 39, Investigator's Case Files, Hilton Foster, RG46 SSC. For more on Eberle see http://www.bruceeberle.com/ (accessed 21 July 2008).

93 Letter from Ann Mills Griffiths to Mike Milne, 14 October 1986, Veterans of the Vietnam War, Box 2, Investigator's Case Files, Hilton Foster, RG46 SSC.

94 Memo from Richard Childress to William Clark, 30 March 1982, POW/MIA National League of Families 1982–83, Box OA92407, Richard Childress Files, RRL.

95 Memo from Robert McFarlane to Richard Childress, 8 July 1982, Childress misc. Chrono. 1981–1985 [8], Box OA92396, Richard Childress Files, RRL. Elizabeth Dole was then White House liaison with special interest groups.

96 Reagan, *PPP, 1984*, 749.

97 Letter from Roderick Danielson to Caspar Weinberger, 20 July 1982, Folder 15663, Reel 13, LOC VNDC; Ann Mills Griffiths, League Newsletter, 21 December 1982, POW/MIA NLF—January 1983 National League of Families Meeting, Box OA92407, Richard Childress Files, RRL.

98 Memo from Richard Armitage to Director of Air Force Transportation, 20 April 1983, Folder 281, Reel 51, LOC VNDC.

99 "Semper Fi" from Reagan, *PPP, 1984*, 1064; flag discussed in Franklin, *M.I.A.*, 3. "Semper Fi" is a popular abbreviation of *semper fidelis*, the Marine Corps motto.

100 Ann Mills Griffiths, Newsletter, undated [December 1983 or early 1984], NLF, Box 2, VVMF LOC; Ann Mills Griffiths, Newsletter, 14 August 1984, TS-671, Box 3, Records Received: Central Documentation Office, Department of Defense, RG46 SSC.

101 Memo from Earl Hopper to Regional and State Coordinators, 12 January 1984, Folder: Hopper, Box 7, Investigator's Case Files, Hilton Foster, RG46 SSC.

102 *Final Interagency Report of the Reagan Administration on the POW/MIA Issue in Southeast Asia*, 19 January 1989, Interagency Report on POW/MIA issue in Southeast Asia, Box 6, Foreign Relations Committee Minority Staff Files—Tracy Usry, RG46 SSC.

103 Senate Select Committee, *Report of the Select Committee on POW/MIA Affairs*, 273; Ann Mills Griffiths, "POW/MIA Agreements Between the US and SRV," undated [1992], NLF #9, Box 13, Investigator's Case Files, Hilton Foster, RG46 SSC.

104 Since the only real "paper trail was left by the agency taking action—not the group recommending that it do so," it was impossible to distinguish Griffiths's influence from those who pushed her agenda through the bureaucracy. See Senate Select Committee, *Report of the Select Committee on POW/MIA Affairs*, 273–74, 280–82.

105 Memo from Richard Childress to William Clark, 30 March 1982, POW/MIA National League of Families 1982–83, Box OA92407, Richard Childress Files, RRL.

106 Memo from James Kelly to Frank Carlucci [drafted by Richard Childress], 21 April 1987, POW/MIA National League of Families January–December 1987, Box OA92407, Richard Childress Files, RRL. Carlucci acceded to Childress's request that he meet with Griffiths before becoming secretary of defense later that year.

107 Memo from Robert McFarlane to George Shultz, Caspar Weinberger, John Vessey, 24 December 1984, OSS-92-4417 NSC Documents-S-804, Box 72, Declassified Files, RG46 SSC.

108 Steven Erlanger, "Missing in Action: From a Lost War, a Haunting Echo That Won't Be Stilled," *New York Times*, 31 August 1988, A6.

109 House Subcommittee on Asian and Pacific Affairs, *The Vessey Mission to Hanoi: Hearing before the Subcommittee on Asian and Pacific Affairs*, 100th Cong., 1st sess., 30 January 1987, 26.

110 Minutes IAG meeting, 3 March 1981, Folder 4, Reel 19, LOC VNDC.

111 Ibid., 7 April 1981.

112 Senate Committee on Veterans' Affairs, *Live Sighting Reports of Americans Listed as Missing in Action in Southeast Asia: Hearings before the Committee on Veterans' Affairs*, vol. I, 99th Cong., 2d sess., 28 January 1986, 13; League Newsletter, 22 January 1986, POW/MIA National League of Families January–July 1986, Box OA92407, Richard Childress Files, RRL.

113 Ron Martz, "Relatives Divided on Getting POWs Home," *Atlanta Journal-Constitution*, 20 July 1986, A6.

114 Reed, "U.S.-Vietnam Relations: The Domestic Context of Normalization," 125.

115 Memo from Robert McFarlane to Ronald Reagan, 18 July 1984, POW/MIA Vol. I 1/20/81–7/31/84, Box 85, Executive Secretariat, NSC: Subject Files, RRL.

116 Department of Defense, *POW-MIA Fact Book*, July 1982, 14.

117 Background paper on Principal U.S./SRV POW/MIA Developments, 1978–1983, OSS-92-4111 (OSD & ASD for IntelSecDef), Box 71, Declassified Files, RG46 SSC.

118 Wayne Biddle, "The Ragtag and Regimental Legacies of Vietnam," *New York Times*, 30 May 1984, A20; Lucy Howard, "The VFW: An Olive Branch to Hanoi," *Newsweek*, 1 April 1985, 19; John H. Cushman, "U.S. Offers Vietnam a Negotiator," *New York Times*, 25 April 1987.

119 Reed, "U.S.-Vietnam Relations," 143, 316.

120 Memorandum for the Record re: PW/MIA IAG Meeting, 2 June 1981, OSS-92-3358, Box 48, Declassified Files, RG46 SSC.

121 Letter from Earl Hopper to Ann Mills Griffiths, 11 January 1986, Folder: Hopper, Box 7, Investigator's Case Files, Hilton Foster, RG46 SSC.

122 Memo from Ann Mills Griffiths to National Veterans Organizations, 14 November 1983, S-756, Box 3, Records Received: Central Documentation Office, Department of Defense, RG46 SSC. Emphasis in the original.

123 Ann Mills Griffiths, Newsletter, undated [December 1983 or early 1984], Folder: NLF, Box 2, VVMF LOC.

124 POW/MIA Agreements Between the US and SRV, February 1982–Present, undated [1992], Folder: NLF #9, Box 13, Investigator's Case Files, Hilton Foster, RG46 SSC; Hart quoted in Omang, "Convention on MIAs to Open Amid Dissension, High Hopes," *Washington Post*, 18 July 1985, A6.

125 "Recognition for Those Still Missing," *New York Times*, 20 July 1985, A7.

126 Reagan, *PPP, 1984*, 749.

127 Quotes from campaign plan prepared by Richard Darman, quoted in FitzGerald, *Way Out There in the Blue*, 233.

128 "Apple pie" from Reagan's campaign manager Michael Deaver, quoted in Schaller, *Reckoning with Reagan*, 36.

129 Letter from Ann Mills Griffiths to John Marsh, 11 August 1982, POW/MIA-Tomb of the Unknown [3 of 4], Box OA92409 Childress Files, RRL.

130 Memo from Richard Childress to William Clark, 9 August 1982, POW/MIA-Tomb of the Unknown [4 of 4], Box OA92409, Richard Childress Files, RRL.

131 Memo from Richard Childress to William Clark, 26 August 1982, Folder 17963, Reel 13, LOC VNDC.

132 Quote from Tod Lindberg, "Of Arms, Men & Monuments," *Commentary*, October 1984, 56. See also "Stop That Monument," *National Review*, 18 September 1981, 1064.

133 "Choose Vietnam Unknown for Burial on Memorial Day, VFW Demands," *VFW Magazine*, February 1983, 20–22.

134 Memo from Caspar Weinberger to the Joint Chiefs of Staff and the Secretaries of the Armed Services, 13 April 1984, Folder 8, Box 3, Records Received: Department of Defense, Joint Chiefs of Staff, RG46 SSC.

135 Carlyle Murphy, "Most War Victims Identified, 'Unknown' Was Hard to Find," *Washington Post*, 28 May 1984, A1.

136 "Background Paper on the Activities of the Department of Defense Senior Working Group on the Vietnam Unknown in the Tomb of the Unknown Soldiers," 24 April 1998, 2–3, http://www.defenselink.mil/news/fact_sheets/vubackgr.htm (21 July 2008).

137 Nudelman, *John Brown's Body*, 76–79.

138 Sheehan, "A Missing Plane," pt. 2, *New Yorker*, 19 May 1986, 81.

139 Press release, 13 April 1984, Folder 8, Box 3, Records Received: Department of Defense, Joint Chiefs of Staff, RG46 SSC.

140 Memo from Ann Mills Griffiths to League board, 25 April 1984, Folder S-756, Box 3, DOD/OSD Policy Files, RG46 SSC.

141 Memo from Ann Mills Griffiths to League members and concerned friends, 18 April 1984, Folder S-756, Box 3, Records Received: Central Documentation Office, Department of Defense, RG46 SSC.

142 Memo from Ann Mills Griffiths to League board, 25 April 1984, Folder S-756, Box 3, DOD/OSD Policy Files, RG46 SSC.

143 Earl Hopper, memo for Record, 9 April 1984, NLF OTF, Box 13, Foreign Relations Committee Minority Staff Files—Tracy Usry, RG46 SSC; memo from Richard Childress to Robert McFarlane, 24 July 1984, POW/MIA National League of Families January–December 1984, Box OA92407, Childress Files, RRL; League Newsletter, 14 August 1984, Folder TS-671, Box 3, Records Received: Central Documentation Office, Department of Defense, RG46 SSC.

144 Ted Sampley, "The Vietnam Unknown Soldier can be Identified," *U.S. Veteran Dispatch*, July 1994, http://www.usvetdsp.com/unknown.htm (21 July 2008). See also "Darts and Laurels," *Columbia Journalism Review*, March–April 1998, 16.

145 Reagan, *PPP, 1984*, Book 1, 748–50.

146 Anderson, *Imagined Communities*, 7.

147 Memo from Robert McFarlane to Ronald Reagan, 18 July 1984, POW/MIA Vol. I 1/20/81–7/31/84, Box 85, Executive Secretariat, NSC: Subject Files, RRL.

148 Reagan, *PPP, 1984*, Book II, 1065.

149 For Griffiths's reporting on the 1984 League election see Ann Mills Griffiths, Newsletter, 14 August 1984, Folder: TS-671 p. 18, Box 3, DOD/CDO, RG46 SSC; for Childress's reporting and McFarlane's congratulatory response see memo from Richard Childress to Robert McFarlane, 24 July 1984, POW/MIA National League of Families, January–December 1984, Box OA92407, Childress Files, RRL.

150 Reagan, *PPP, 1984*, Book II, 1064.

151 Josh Getlin, "Hearts & Bones," *Los Angeles Times Magazine*, 12 October 1986.

152 James R. Dickenson, "MIAs' Families Are Pleased, Hope for More Excavations," *Washington Post*, 15 February 1985, A28; Bell, *Leave No Man Behind*, 222–23, 272–73, 417, 426.

153 Concessions detailed in "Chronology of US/Laos Relations," August 1981–August 1984, OSS-92-4111 (OSD & ASD for IntelSecDef), Box 71, Declassified Files, RG46 SSC; and Author redacted, PW/MIA Weekly Report, 19 March 1985, POW/MIA Weekly Reports, September 1983–December 1985, Box 16, Records Received: Central Documentation Office, Department of Defense, RG46 SSC.

154 Terry Anderson, "The Light at the End of the Tunnel," 451–55.

155 National League of Families, "POW/MIA Agreements Between the US and SRV, February 1982–Present," undated [1992], NLF #9, Box 13, Investigator's Case Files, Hilton Foster, RG46 SSC.

156 Dickenson, "MIAs' Families Are Pleased, Hope for More Excavations," *Washington Post*, 15 February 1985, A28.

157 Getlin, "Hearts & Bones," *Los Angeles Times Magazine*, 12 October 1986, 15, 24–26.

158 Kathryn Fanning, "Remembering Hugh, MIA" and "Burying the Past, Burying the Truth," in *Vietnam: The Heartland Remembers*, 20, 172–77; Ann DeFrange, "MIA Wife 'Back to Square One' in Quest for Spouse," *Sunday Oklahoman*, 22 September 1985, 21.

159 George Gill testimony in House Investigations Subcommittee of the Committee on Armed Services, *Activities of the Central Identification Laboratory*, 99th Cong., 2d sess., 10 September 1986, 45.

160 Getlin, "Hearts & Bones," *Los Angeles Times Magazine*, 12 October 1986, 26; Fanning, "Burying the Past, Burying the Truth," 175; ABC News, 20/20, "MIAs: The Story That Will Not Die," 29 May 1986, show #622.

161 Ellis Kerley, Lowell Levine, and William Maples, "CILHI Identification Inspection Report," 9–12 December 1985, Unmarked folder (1), Box 5, Investigator's Case Files, John Erickson, RG46 SSC; Charney quoted in House Investigations Subcommittee, *Activities of the Central Identification Laboratory*, 61.

162 House Investigations Subcommittee of the Committee on Armed Services, *U.S. Army Central Identification Laboratory, Hawaii (CILHI)*, 100th Cong., 1st sess., 15 September 1987, 7–8, 17.

163 Letter from Ellis Kerley to John Kerry, 20 August 1991, Identification of MIA Remains—CIL Hawaii, Box 5, Investigator's Case Files, John Erickson, RG46 SSC; Memorandum of Conversation, Tom Lang and Ellis Kerley, 23 October 1991, Identification of MIA Remains—CIL Hawaii, Box 5, Investigator's Case Files,

John Erickson, RG46 SSC. Webb has ignored my repeated attempts to interview him.

164 Ann Mills Griffiths, Newsletter, 28 October 1986, POW/MIA National League of Families August–December 1986, Box OA92407, Childress Files, RRL.

165 Office of the Assistant Secretary of Defense for International Security Affairs, "Critique of ABC 20/20 May 29, 1986 Program," undated, first manila envelope (unlabeled), Box 1, Working Files of Hilton Foster and Alex Greenfield, RG46 SSC. "At the rate Furue claims to identify human remains (over 25,000??), he could do 400 in a good afternoon," Dr. Norman Sauer of Michigan State University sneered in a letter to his former student, Dr. Samuel Dunlop, entered into the record in House Investigations Subcommittee of the Committee on Armed Services, *Activities of the Central Identification Laboratory*, 102.

166 Kerley had known Furue since the two identified remains together during the Korean War, and Furue was best man at Kerley's wedding.

167 ABC News, 20/20, "MIAs: The Story That Will Not Die," 29 May 1986.

168 Remarks by George Bush to the National League of Families, 19 July 1985, White House/NSC Docs, Box 9, Investigator's Case Files, Neal E. Kravitz, RG46 SSC.

169 Pelton, *Dead or Alive*, iii.

170 Van Atta quoted in National League of Families, "Report Concerning Misinformation on the Issue of American Prisoners of War and Missing in Action in Southeast Asia," undated, NLF #1, Box 13, Investigator's Case Files, Hilton Foster, RG46 SSC.

171 Letter from Marla Shirts to Angus MacDonald, 19 February 1976, Washington State League Chapter, Box 6, Interest Groups, RG233 HSC.

172 Letter from Robert Cressman to Caspar Weinberger, 28 August 1985, Folder 281, Reel 51, LOC VNDC.

173 Figures from DPMO, *Vietnam's Collection and Repatriation of American Remains*, 28; Department of Defense, *POW-MIA Fact Book*, 14; *Final Interagency Report of the Reagan Administration on the POW/MIA Issue in Southeast Asia*, 19 January 1989, Interagency Report on POW/MIA issue in Southeast Asia, Box 6, Foreign Relations Committee Minority Staff Files—Tracy Usry, RG46 SSC.

174 Ann Mills Griffiths, Newsletter, 23 December 1986, Folder 52, Box 4, Investigator's Case Files, Hilton Foster, RG46 SSC.

175 House Investigations Subcommittee of the Committee on Armed Services, *Activities of the Central Identification Laboratory*, 98; ABC News, 20/20, "MIAs: The Story That Will Not Die."

176 Steven Erlanger, "In Indochina, New Appeals for Missing," *New York Times*, 6 October 1988, A9.

177 Paul Bedard, "U.S. Hunts for Dead, Ignores Living, POW Activists Charge," *Washington Times*, 3 April 1989, A6.

178 Getlin, "Hearts & Bones," *Los Angeles Times Magazine*, 12 October 1986, 11.

179 Details of the Pakse crash based on "Summary of Incident," 0088-86-CID208, undated, S-628, Box 9, Records Received: Central Documentation Office, Department of Defense, RG46 SSC; Getlin, "Hearts & Bones," *Los Angeles Times Magazine*, 12 October 1986, 15.

180 "MIA Protests Hurt Search, Official Says," *Fort Wayne Journal Gazette*, 12 February 1987, Folder 280, Reel 50, LOC VNDC; Franklin, *M.I.A.*, 168. Franklin calls the issue "a national psychopathology" in a jacket blurb for Elliot Gruner's *Prisoners of Culture*.

181 Hotz, "Putting Names to the Dead: No Easy Task for Army," *Atlanta Journal-Constitution*, 11 August 1985, 14A.

182 Letter from Kathryn Fanning to Ellis Kerley, 14 March 1986, S-628, Box 9, Records Received: Central Documentation Office, Department of Defense, RG46 SSC.

183 Mike Sager, "MIA Widowhood: Mix of Grief and Anger," *Washington Post*, 8 July 1983, B1.

184 Letter from Jeff Donahue to League members, July 1990, Folder 141, Box 35, Investigator's Case Files, Hilton Foster, RG46 SSC. Underlining in the original.

185 Barbara Blake, "Hendon: U.S. Hunts Bones While POWs Starve," *Asheville Citizen Times*, 16 October 1988, Sampley—U.S. Veteran, Box 17, Investigator's Case Files, Hilton Foster, RG46 SSC.

186 Bill Paul, "Actor Heston's Fiery Telephone Pitch Enlists Support to Save Vietnam POWs," *Wall Street Journal*, 27 December 1984, 19.

187 Homecoming II Newsletter, 20 November 1986, Folder 1, Box 25, Douglas Pike Collection: Unit 3, POW/MIA Issues, VNA TTU.

188 Jeff Donahue, *A Manifesto on the Indochina POW-MIA Issue*, Folder 280, reel 50, LOC VNDC. Emphasis in the original.

189 ABC News, *20/20*, "MIAs: The Story That Will Not Die."

190 Turner, *Echoes of Combat*, 116.

191 Homecoming II Newsletter, 20 November 1986, Folder 1, Box 25, Douglas Pike Collection: Unit 3, POW/MIA Issues, VNA TTU.

192 Bynum, *Resurrection of the Body in Western Christianity*, 47.

193 John LeBoutillier, "How Can Reagan Face the Indochina P.O.W.'s," *New York Times*, 16 November 1985, 27.

194 Reagan, *PPP, 1984*, 749.

195 Author unknown, "I Am Alive," Folder: Sheldon, Box 28, Foreign Relations Committee Minority Staff Files—Tracy Usry, RG46 SSC.

CHAPTER 7.

1 James Warren, "President Thanks Vietnam," *Chicago Tribune*, 19 November 2000, 3; Rajiv Chandrasekaran, "Clinton Faces War's Open Wounds," *Washington Post*, 19 November 2000, A1.

2 Mark E. Manyin, "The Vietnam-U.S. Normalization Process," CRS Issue Brief for Congress prepared by the Library of Congress Congressional Research Service, Order Code IB98033, 28 November 2001, CRS-6.

3 For an analysis that focuses on these factors see McMahon, *Limits of Empire*, 206–17.

4 Terry Anderson, "The Light at the End of the Tunnel," 443–62; Franklin, *M.I.A.*; Franklin, *Vietnam & Other American Fantasies*, chap. 9; Hawley, *Remains of War*,

chap. 6; Jespersen, "Bitter End and the Lost Chance in Vietnam," 265–93; Jespersen, "Politics and Culture of Nonrecognition," 397–412; Martini, *Invisible Enemies*, 18–24, 43–46, 163–99; and McMahon, *Limits of Empire*, 190–91.

5   Schulzinger, *Time for Peace*, 30–69.

6   Senate Select Committee, *Report of the Senate Select Committee on POW/MIA Affairs*, 376.

7   Roadmap to U.S.-SRV Normalization, 9 April 1991, OSS-91-2128, Box 61, Declassified Files, RG46 SSC.

8   Senate Select Committee, *Report of the Senate Select Committee on POW/MIA Affairs*, 2–6, 30–31, 44–59, 383–90.

9   Ibid., 4.

10 James Carroll, "A Friendship That Ended the War," *New Yorker*, 21 and 28 October 1996, 156; Douglas Jehl, "Clinton Drops 19-Year Ban on U.S. Trade with Vietnam; Cites Hanoi's Help on M.I.A.'s," *New York Times*, 4 February 1994, A1; Alison Mitchell, "Opening to Vietnam," *New York Times*, 12 July 1995, A1.

11 Figures based on the National League of Families, "Status of the POW/MIA Issue: July 4, 2008," available at: http://www.pow-miafamilies.org/stats.html (accessed 21 July 2008) and Senate Select Committee, *Report of the Senate Select Committee on POW/MIA Affairs*, 370–79.

12 Posner, *Citizen Perot*, 89–90, 100–122, 191–98; Sidney Blumenthal, "The Mission," *New Republic*, 6 July 1992, 16; Sidney Blumenthal, "On Wings of Bull," *New Republic*, 13 July 1992, 12.

13 Posner, *Citizen Perot*, 193; House Subcommittee on Asian and Pacific Affairs, *Tighe Report on American POW's and MIA's*, 99th Cong., 2d sess., 15 October 1986, 45.

14 Letter from Leonard Perroots to Eugene Tighe, 16 January 1986, Folder: Tighe TF Rev. of DIA's PW/MIA Analysis Center, Box 1, Records received: Department of Defense/Central Documentation Office, RG46 SSC; Posner, *Citizen Perot*, 198–99, 210–11; House Subcommittee on Asian and Pacific Affairs, *Tighe Report on American POW's and MIA's*, 40.

15 Eugene Tighe, "Tighe Task Force Examination of DIA Intelligence Holdings Surrounding Unaccounted for United States Military Personnel in Southeast Asia," 27 May 1986, Folder: Tighe Task Force Review. of DIA's PW/MIA Analysis Center, Box 1, Records received: Department of Defense/Central Documentation Office, RG46 SSC; Richard L. Berke, "P.O.W.'s Alive in Vietnam, Report Concludes," *New York Times*, 30 September 1986, A7.

16 Letter from Eugene Tighe to Leonard Perroots, 13 May 1986, Folder: Tighe TF Rev. of DIA's PW/MIA Analysis Center, Box 1, Records received: Department of Defense/Central Documentation Office, RG46 SSC.

17 Memo from Richard Childress to Leonard Perroots, 18 June 1986, Unfoldered, Box 14, Records received: Department of Defense/Central Documentation Office, RG46 SSC.

18 House Subcommittee on Asian and Pacific Affairs, *Tighe Report on American POW's and MIA's*, 52. The bill was originally introduced on 24 April 1985 by Billy Hendon, who played an important part in the questionable IAG activities

discussed in chapter six. Hendon was elected to the 97th and 99th Congress, serving from 1981–82 and again from 1985–86, failing to win reelection after either term. But even when he was out of office he remained an active presence in MIA politics, working on POW/MIA matters in the Pentagon from 1983–84 and serving on the Senate Select Committee staff until he was fired for leaking classified documents.

19 Tom Blanton, *White House E-Mail: The Top Secret Computer Messages the Reagan/ Bush White House Tried to Destroy* (New York: New Press, 1995), 159–64.

20 House Subcommittee on Asian and Pacific Affairs, *Tighe Report on American POW's and MIA's*, 44–46, 49–52, 67, 73–85; Homecoming II Newsletter, 20 November 1986, Folder 1, Box 25, Douglas Pike Collection: Unit 3, POW/MIA Issues, VNA TTU.

21 Homecoming II Newsletter, 30 September 1986, Folder 1, Box 25, Douglas Pike Collection: Unit 3, POW/MIA Issues, VNA TTU; Ron Martz, "Children of MIAs Fight Guerrilla War over the Fate of Their Fathers," *Atlanta Journal-Constitution*, 27 March 1987, 1-A, 8-A.

22 League Newsletter, 23 December 1986, Folder 1, Box 25, Douglas Pike Collection: Unit 3, POW/MIA Issues, VNA TTU; Posner, *Citizen Perot*, 199–201.

23 David Remnick, "Perot Negotiated Secretly with Hanoi on POW-MIA Issue," *Washington Post*, 24 April 1987, A5.

24 Posner, *Citizen Perot*, 210–15.

25 Ibid., 213.

26 Ibid., 219; Weinraub, "Decision for Meese," *New York Times*, 2 December 1986, A1; Engelberg, "Detailing 'the D.E.A. Caper': Bungled Bid to Buy Hostages," *New York Times*, 31 May 1987, 1, 10.

27 Reagan, *Reagan Diaries*, 484–85. Reagan's diaries indicate that Perot wanted "a letter from me saying I approve his going" to Hanoi, but do not say whether he granted such a letter, leaving it ambiguous whether Perot received presidential clearance for his trip. It is clear that Reagan discussed Perot's trip with his staff immediately before and after his mission.

28 Noonan, *What I Saw at the Revolution*, 103–4.

29 Gibson, *Warrior Dreams*, chap. 12.

30 Remnick, "Perot Negotiated Secretly with Hanoi on POW-MIA Issue," *Washington Post*, 24 April 1987, A5; Reagan, *Reagan Diaries*, 493.

31 John Cushman, "U.S. Offers Vietnam a Negotiator," *New York Times*, 25 April 1987, 5.

32 In July 2001 I submitted my initial Freedom of Information Act request for POW/MIA records held at the Reagan Library, at which point it was added to related FOIA requests dating back to 1995. To date 1,335 pages have been opened for research, consisting mainly of public relations materials. Few policy papers have been opened, particularly from Reagan's second term, in part due to impediments from Executive Order 13233, issued in November 2001, placed in the path of those seeking access to Reagan administration records.

33 Reagan, *Reagan Diaries*, 493.

34 Posner, *Citizen Perot*, 213–14. For Perot's more colorful account of these events,

see Monika Jensen-Stevenson and William Stevenson, *Kiss the Boys Goodbye*, chap. 23.

35 Schulzinger, *Time for Peace*, 32; Terry Anderson, "The Light at the End of the Tunnel," 452–55.

36 Cushman, "U.S. Offers Vietnam a Negotiator," *New York Times*, 25 April 1987, 5.

37 Richard Halloran, "Reagan Choice for Nation's Top Military Post," *New York Times*, 5 March 1982, B9.

38 Bell, *Leave No Man Behind*, 233.

39 League Newsletter, 29 June 1987, POW/MIA National League of Families January–December 1987, Box OA92407, Childress Files, RRL.

40 Keith Richburg, "Hanoi Keeps War Memory Alive to Fuel Prospects for U.S. Aid," *Washington Post*, 16 July 1987, A18.

41 David Ottaway, "Shultz Warns: No Trade for MIAs; Humanitarian Issues to be Focus in Hanoi," *Washington Post*, 19 July 1987, A19; letter from Ronald Reagan to Vo Chi Cong, 27 July 1987, POW/MIA 1986–88 [1 of 2], Box OA92407, Childress Files, RRL.

42 Cable from John Vessey to Frank Carlucci, 3 August 1987, OSS-92-4422, Box 61, Declassified Files, RG46 SSC; House Subcommittee on Asian and Pacific Affairs, *The Vessey Mission to Hanoi*, 30 September 1987, 100th Cong., 1st sess., 5–8; Schulzinger, *Time for Peace*, 33–35.

43 Mather, *M.I.A.*, 157–60; Senate Select Committee, *Report of the Senate Select Committee on POW/MIA Affairs*, 377–78.

44 Letter from Kelly Ann Boland to Howell Heflin, 1 August 1987, Folder 280, reel 50, LOC VNDC.

45 National Forget-Me-Not Association for POW-MIA's Inc. Newsletter, March 1988, Folder 6, Box 25, Douglas Pike Collection: Unit 3, POW/MIA Issues, VNA TTU.

46 Barbara Crossette, "Hanoi Rejects U.S. Plan on Private Aid," *New York Times*, 20 January 1988, A3.

47 Barbara Crossette, "Vietnam, Going Hungry, Seeks U.S. Aid," *New York Times*, 7 April 1988, A3.

48 League Newsletter, 26 April 1988, Folder 5, Box 25, Douglas Pike Collection: Unit 3, POW/MIA Issues, VNA TTU; Neil Lewis, "An Ex-P.O.W. Leads Drive for Hanoi Ties," *New York Times*, 1 June 1988, A20; letter from Nguyen Binh Thanh to John Vessey, 8 April 1988, POW/MIA U.S.-Vietnamese Negotiations [5 of 6], Box OA92409, Childress Files, RRL; letter from Nguyen Co Thach to John Vessey, 9 July 1988, POW/MIA U.S. Vietnamese Negotiations [6 of 6], Box OA92409, Childress Files, RRL.

49 David Ottaway, "Vietnam Reveals Plan to Withdraw 50,000 Troops From Cambodia," *Washington Post*, 26 May 1988, A14. The Cambodian troop reduction was a multilateral move, as it was meant to improve both Vietnam's and the Soviet Union's relations with China, while an accompanying nine-mile pullback from the Thai border was meant to improve Vietnam's relations with Thailand and other ASEAN nations. Vietnam could no longer afford to deploy 125,000 troops in Cambodia and 50,000 in Laos, and was hoping to increase the prospects of

— · —

aid from and trade with the Soviets, the Chinese, and the United States through troop reductions.

50 I disagree with Schulzinger's depiction of an administration that had, with the League's blessing, settled on a policy of reconciliation rather than confrontation by 1987. See Schulzinger, *Time for Peace*, 35–41.

51 Lou Cannon discusses Reagan's passive leadership style at length in Cannon, *President Reagan*, 141–71, 313–15.

52 League Newsletter, April 1988, Folder 5, Box 25, Douglas Pike Collection: Unit 3, POW/MIA Issues, VNA TTU. Emphasis in the original.

53 Ronald Reagan, *PPP, 1988–89*, Book II, 997–98.

54 "The US Side Must Bear Full Responsibility . . . ," press release, 12 August 1988, POW/MIA U.S.-Vietnamese Negotiations [5 of 6], Box OA92409, Childress Files, RRL; Ronald J. Cima, "Vietnam in 1988: The Brink of Renewal," *Asian Survey* 29, no. 1 (January 1989): 71.

55 Mather, *M.I.A.*, 127, 163–71; Senate Select Committee, *Report of the Senate Select Committee on POW/MIA Affairs*, 374–78. Seventy-two identifiable remains were recovered between 1979–1986 whereas at least seventy-one identifiable remains were returned between September 1987 and January 1989.

56 Mather, *M.I.A.*, 163–71.

57 Bell, *Leave No Man Behind*, 267.

58 Ibid., 271–73; memo from Johnnie Webb to John Vessey, 28 July 1987, Vessey Trip, Box 3, Records of the Department of the Army Relating to POW/MIA Affairs, RG46 SSC.

59 Anderson, "The Light at the End of the Tunnel," 454–55.

60 Frederick Downs Jr., "Making a Real Peace with Vietnam," *Washington Post*, 25 December 1988, B1.

61 Schulzinger, *Time for Peace*, 43; Ronald J. Cima, "Vietnam in 1989: Initiating the Post-Cambodia Period," *Asian Survey* 30, no. 1 (January 1990): 88–95.

62 Memo from Ann Mills Griffiths to League State Coordinators, 5 June 1989, Folder 7, Box 25, Douglas Pike Collection: Unit 3, POW/MIA Issues, VNA TTU; Senate Select Committee, *Report of the Senate Select Committee on POW/MIA Affairs*, 378.

63 Chet Atkins, "Normalize Relations with Vietnam," *Washington Post*, 27 September 1989, A32.

64 Charles Wallace, "U.S. Keeps Economic, Political Heat on Hanoi 15 Years after War's End," *Los Angeles Times*, 29 April 1990, 12; Atkins, "Normalize Relations with Vietnam," A32.

65 FitzGerald, *Way Out There in the Blue*, 472–73.

66 Pelton, *Dead or Alive*, 58.

67 Wallace, "U.S. Keeps Economic, Political Heat on Hanoi 15 Years After War's End," *Los Angeles Times*, 29 April 1990, 12.

68 Deposition of Ann Mills Griffiths, 6 July 1990, Homecoming II vs. NLF, Box 13, Foreign Relations Committee Minority Staff Files—Tracy Usry, RG46 SSC.

69 Reagan, *Reagan Diaries*, 634.

70 George Bush, *PPP, 1989*, 3, 1032.

71 Bill McAllister, "U.S. Plans to Send Surplus Medical Equipment to Vietnam," *Washington Post*, 9 November 1989, A62. Vessey discusses the growth of the discrepancy list from 70 to 119 cases in Senate Select Committee, *POW/MIA Policy and Process: Hearings before the Select Committee on POW/MIA Affairs*, 7 November 1991, 102d Cong., 1st sess., part I, 65.

72 Bush, *PPP, 1989*, 1470.

73 League Newsletter, 5 December 1989, Folder 7, Box 25, Douglas Pike Collection: Unit 3, POW/MIA Issues, VNA TTU.

74 Cartoon, *Bamboo Connection*, November-December 1988, 11, and James Neilson, "Ann Mills Griffiths: The Mistress of Deceit," *U.S. Veteran News and Report*, June 1991, 8, both from Sampley—U.S. Veteran, Box 17, Investigator's Case Files, Hilton Foster, RG46 SSC; "Today the League Says POWS Must Take Second Place to Other USG Foreign Policy Interests," *U.S. Veteran News and Report*, July 1990, page 5, Folder 63, Box 6, Investigator's Case Files, Hilton Foster, RG46 SSC. *Bamboo Connection* was renamed *U.S. Veteran News and Report* and later became *U.S. Veteran Dispatch*. In testimony before the Senate Select Committee, publisher Ted Sampley claimed 30,000 readers for these publication. See Senate Select Committee, *POW/MIA Policy and Process*, 537.

75 Letter from Earl Hopper to Ann Mills Griffiths, 12 December 1989, National League of Families, Box 13, Foreign Relations Committee Minority Staff Files—Tracy Usry, RG46 SSC.

76 Letter from Joe Jordan to Ann Mills Griffiths, 12 October 1992, Key Documents, Box 35, Investigator's Case Files, Hilton Foster, RG46 SSC.

77 Gibson, *Warrior Dreams*, offers a brilliant introduction to this world.

78 Letter from Jeff Donahue to League members, July 1990, Folder 141, Box 35, Investigator's Case Files, Hilton Foster, RG46 SSC.

79 Mann, *Rise of the Vulcans*, 173–75; Posner, *Citizen Perot*, 202–10. Griffiths sympathized with Armitage's fate in her June 1989 newsletter. See League Newsletter, 5 June 1989, Folder 7, Box 25, Douglas Pike Collection: Unit 3, POW/MIA Issues, VNA TTU.

80 Noonan, *What I Saw at the Revolution*, 243; Halberstam, *War in a Time of Peace*, 61.

81 Both Halberstam and Frances FitzGerald write of the hostility with which Bush, Baker, and Scowcroft ejected Reagan's staff. Halberstam, *War in a Time of Peace*, 72–73; FitzGerald, *Way Out There in the Blue*, 468–69.

82 Thomas Vallely of Harvard's Institute for International Development Indochina Program quoted in Carroll, "A Friendship That Ended the War," *New Yorker*, 21 and 28 October 1996, 152.

83 Bernard Gwertzman, "U.S. Decides to Back Resistance Groups Active in Cambodia," *New York Times*, 3 May 1981, A1. For a more thorough discussion of U.S. policy toward Cambodia and Vietnam in the 1980s, see Martini, *Invisible Enemies*, 93–115.

84 Elizabeth Becker, "Finally Facing Facts in Cambodia," *Washington Post*, 26 July 1990, A27.

85 Steven Erlanger, "Hanoi's Partial Victory," *New York Times*, 20 July 1990, A1; "U.S.

379

— • —

Switch on Cambodia Seen as Move Toward Recognition of Vietnam," *Christian Science Monitor*, 20 July 1990, 4.

86 Paul Taylor, "Vietnam War Critic on a Passage to Indochina," *Washington Post*, 13 April 1990, A8. Kerrey also participated in a massacre of thirteen unarmed women and children in the village of Thanh Phong, though that fact did not become public knowledge until 2001. See Gregory Vistica, "One Awful Night in Thanh Phong," *New York Times Magazine*, 25 April 2001, 50–57, 66–68, 133.

87 Charles Robb, "Cambodia Between Horror and Hope," *Washington Post*, 5 June 1990, A25; Steven Erlanger, "Sihanouk Widens Khmer Rouge Rift," *New York Times*, 6 June 1990, A3.

88 Kent Jenkins, "Cambodia Offers to Return Remains," *Washington Post*, 14 July 1990, A4; "Cambodia Agrees to Return Remains of 6 U.S. Missing," *Los Angeles Times*, 26 July 1990, 19.

89 Charles Robb, interview with the author, e-mail correspondence, 6 August 2007.

90 Al Kamen, "U.S., Vietnam Hold First High-Level Meeting Since 1973," *Washington Post*, 30 September 1990, A19.

91 Clifford Krauss, "Vietnam Agrees to Expand Efforts on U.S. Missing," *New York Times*, 18 October 1990, A8.

92 Jim Mann, "Are We Losing in Vietnam Again?," *Los Angeles Times*, 9 October 1990, 5.

93 John LeBoutillier, "Normalize Ties with Vietnam Now," *Wall Street Journal*, 15 September 1989, A10.

94 Jesse Helms, "The Mock Burial of MIA's," 5 October 1990, 101st Cong., 2d sess., *Cong. Rec.* 136, no. 129 S14623–25.

95 U.S. Senate Committee on Foreign Relations Republican Staff, "Interim Report on the Southeast Asian POW/MIA Issue," 29 October 1990, Folder 96, Box 27, Investigator's Case Files, Hilton Foster, RG46 SSC.

96 Many of the nation's most committed MIA activists hail from North Carolina, including Ted Sampley, who reprinted Helms's statement on MIA remains in his newspaper. See "The Mock Burial of MIAS," *U.S. Veteran News and Report*, October 1990, 4, Sampley—U.S. Veteran, Box 17, Investigator's Case Files, Hilton Foster, RG46 SSC.

97 Peter Applebome, "Divisive Victory by Helms Could Set Political Trend for Campaign Tactics," *New York Times*, 8 November 1990, B3.

98 David Evans, "Report on POWs Holds Chilling News for U.S. Soldiers in Gulf," *Chicago Tribune*, 4 November 1990, 8.

99 Memo from Tracy Usry to James P. Lucier, 31 January 1991, Folder: 1991 memos, Box 15, Foreign Relations Committee Minority Staff Files—Tracy Usry, RG46 SSC.

100 Peter Applebome, "After the War: National Mood; War Heals Wounds at Home, But Not All," *New York Times*, 4 March 1991, A1.

101 Dana Priest, "Nation Is Spared Anguish over POWs," *Washington Post*, 7 March 1991, A1.

102 U.S. Senate Committee on Foreign Relations Republican Staff, "An Examination

of U.S. Policy Toward POW/MIAs," 23 May 1991, Folder 96, Box 27, Investigator's Case Files, Hilton Foster, RG46 SSC. In later years the Gulf War acquired its own MIA celebrity in Scott Speicher. For a trenchant analysis of the Speicher case see Hawley, *Remains of War*, 244–52.

103 Dan Oberdorfer, "U.S. Details Plan for Normalizing Relations," *Washington Post*, 10 April 1991, A17.

104 Roadmap to U.S.-SRV Normalization, 9 April 1991, OSS-91-2128, Box 61, Declassified Files, RG46 SSC.

105 Schulzinger, *Time for Peace*, 47; Clifford Krauss, "U.S. to Give Vietnam $1 Million," *New York Times*, 26 April 1991, A1; Don Oberdorfer, "U.S. Awards $1.3 million to Assist Hanoi Groups," *Washington Post*, 28 September 1991, A18. AID provided $1.3 million in taxpayer-financed aid, but it was funneled through private charities.

106 Senate Select Committee, *POW/MIA Policy and Process*, 193.

107 Charles Krauthammer, "In Praise of Parades," *Washington Post*, 24 May 1991, A23; U.S. Senate Committee on Foreign Relations Republican Staff, "An Examination of U.S. Policy Toward POW/MIAs," 23 May 1991, Folder 96, Box 27, Investigator's Case Files, Hilton Foster, RG46 SSC.

108 Michael Ross, "Helms Fires GOP Staffers on Foreign Relations Panel," *Los Angeles Times*, 8 January 1992, 4.

109 "What distinguishes the paranoid style is not, then, the absence of verifiable facts," Richard Hofstadter wrote in his seminal essay on the paranoid style, "but rather the curious leap in imagination that is always made at some critical point in the recital of events. . . . The careful preparation for the big leap from the undeniable to the unbelievable." See Hofstadter's title essay in *The Paranoid Style in American Politics*, 36–38. For an equally withering objectivist critique of claims of POW abandonment in World War II, see Nenninger, "United States Prisoners of War and the Red Army," 761–81.

110 Franklin, *M.I.A.*, 179.

111 Millard Peck, "Request for Relief," 12 February 1991, Folder: DIWAN, Box 2, Investigator's Case Files, Hilton Foster, RG46 SSC. Ellipses in the original.

112 George Lardner, "Ex-Official Alleges Administration Coverup on POW/MIA Issue," *Washington Post*, 22 May 1991, A13. "Ideology of Unity" is a term Keith Beattie uses to characterize the goals of national elites who sought to repress the differences exposed by the Vietnam War. I reference the term here to refer to a constellation of such ideas in the cultural studies literature.

113 Krauss, "U.S. to Give Vietnam $1 Million," *New York Times*, 26 April 1991, A7.

114 U.S. Senate Committee on Foreign Relations Republican Staff, "An Examination of U.S. Policy Toward POW/MIAs," 23 May 1991, Folder 96, Box 27, Investigator's Case Files, Hilton Foster, RG46 SSC.

115 Bob Smith, speaking for Senate Resolution 82, 14 March 1991, 102d Cong., 1st sess., *Cong. Rec.* 137, no. 44, S3438.

116 Letter from Bob Smith to the U.S. Senate, 29 April 1991, Unmarked folder 2, Box 11, Foreign Relations Committee Minority Staff Files—Tracy Usry, RG46 SSC. Capitalization in the original.

117 Franklin, *M.I.A.*, 179–81, offers the essential debunking of these photos. See also Senate Select Committee, *Report of the Senate Select Committee on POW/MIA Affairs*, 321–24.

118 Text of Kerry/Brown press conference, 17 July 1991, Committee General, Box 5, Working Files of Staff Director Frances Zwenig, RG46 SSC.

119 Michael Isikoff, "Blurry Photograph Fuels Flames of POW-MIA Issue," *Washington Post*, 21 July 1991, A1.

120 Franklin covers this same ground and provides additional detail. He neglects to mention Kassebaum as a committee member, however, which brought the number of Republicans to seven, not the six he claims. Franklin, *M.I.A.*, 180–81.

121 Memo from Richard Kessler to John Kerry, 31 July 1991, POW/MIA Legislation, Box 5, Investigator's Case Files, Tom Lang, RG46 SSC.

122 Bob Smith served onboard a U.S. naval vessel off the coast of Vietnam and Tom Daschle and Herb Kohl served in the stateside military. I do not wish to diminish their military service by emphasizing the committee's combat veterans. I exclude them from my list of combat veterans because, in contrast to the five veterans I have named, they seldom represented themselves as Vietnam veterans and were rarely referred to as such in media coverage.

123 Carroll, "A Friendship That Ended the War," *New Yorker*, 21 and 28 October 1996, 133–34; Matt Kelley, "Six Senators Are Key to U.S.-Vietnam Ties," *Omaha World Herald*, 12 November 2000, 2A.

124 John Aloysius Farrell, "The Avenger," *Boston Globe Magazine*, 9 February 1992, 23.

125 For more on Kerry's evolution, see Brinkley, *Tour of Duty*, esp. 319–434. For studies of veteran dissent, see Moser, *New Winter Soldier*, and Nicosia, *Home to War*.

126 Appy, *Patriots*, 537, notes that "in the United States over the past quarter century only a surprisingly narrow range of Vietnam War experiences have gained widespread attention," giving us "an oddly diminished view of a vast history."

127 Farrell, "The Avenger," *Boston Globe Magazine*, 9 February 1992, 28.

128 Richard Berke, "Ethics Unit Singles Out Cranston, Chides Four Others in S & L Inquiry," *New York Times*, 28 February 1991, A1. For how deeply this scandal affected McCain see Timberg, *Nightingale's Song*, 458–61.

129 Senate Select Committee, *POW/MIA Policy and Process*, 51.

130 Jennifer Senior, "The Politics of Personality Destruction," *New York Magazine*, 11 June 2007, 32.

131 Tim Dickinson, "Make-Believe Maverick," *Rolling Stone*, 16 October 2008, 70. See also McCain, *Worth the Fighting For*, 236, 244, 248–50, 256–57.

132 Senate Select Committee, *POW/MIA Policy and Process*, 14.

133 Helms quoted in League Newsletter, 30 August 1991, Background/Comm. Delegation, Box 8, Working Files of Staff Director Frances Zwenig, RG46 SSC.

134 League Newsletter, 30 August 1991, Background/Comm. Delegation, Box 8, Working Files of Staff Director Frances Zwenig, RG46 SSC.

135 League Position Paper, "POW/MIA Special Commission," POW/MIA National League of Families, August–December 1986, Box OA92407, Richard Childress Files, RRL.

136 Senate Select Committee, *Oversight Hearings: Department of Defense, POW/MIA Family Issues, and Private Sector Issues*, 1–4 December 1992, 102d Cong., 2d sess., 212–17, 233–35, 1282–95.

137 Quote from League Newsletter, 30 August 1991, Background/Comm. Delegation, Box 8, Working Files of Staff Director Frances Zwenig, RG46 SSC.

138 Senate Select Committee, *Report of the Senate Select Committee on POW/MIA Affairs*, 381; Rone Tempest, "U.S. Opens Way for Vietnam Ties," *Los Angeles Times*, 24 October 1991, 1.

139 Senate Select Committee, *POW/MIA Policy and Process*, 68; Dara McLeod, "No Evidence of Captive Americans in Vietnam, General Vessey Reports," *Los Angeles Times*, 6 November 1991, 8.

140 League Newsletter, 20 November 1991, Folder 52, Box 4, Investigator's Case Files, Hilton Foster, RG46 SSC. Emphasis in the original.

141 Defense Intelligence Agency Special Office for Prisoner of War and Missing in Action, "Americans Missing in Indochina: An Assessment of Vietnamese Accountability," undated [10 January 1992], OSS-92-5277, Box 1, Declassified Files, RG46 SSC; memo from John Vessey to James Baker, Dick Cheney, and Brent Scowcroft, 12 January 1992, OSS-92-5336, Box 1, Declassified Files NND 982005, RG46 SSC.

142 Memo from James R. Lilley to Walter Slocombe, 21 January 1992, OSS-92-5262, Box 2, Declassified Files, RG46 SSC.

143 Senate Select Committee, *Department of Defense, POW/MIA Family Issues, and Private Sector Issues*, 223, 1282–84. See also Senate Select Committee, *Report of the Senate Select Committee on POW/MIA Affairs*, 286–89, 388–90, which suggests that if there ever was a remains warehouse it had been emptied through repatriations.

144 Senate Select Committee, *Report of the Senate Select Committee on POW/MIA Affairs*, 383–85.

145 Don Oberdorfer, "U.S. Easing Vietnam Trade Embargo," *Washington Post*, 30 April 1992, A36.

146 Senate Select Committee, *Report of the Senate Select Committee on POW/MIA Affairs*, 385–86; Schulzinger, *Time for Peace*, 50. For a detailed account of these developments, see McConnell and Schweitzer, *Inside Hanoi's Secret Archives*.

147 Senate Select Committee, *Report of the Senate Select Committee on POW/MIA Affairs*, 390; Jacob Schlesinger, "Japan to Revive Economic Ties with Vietnam," *Wall Street Journal*, 4 November 1992, A10. Japan, which had long chafed at the U.S. embargo, had its own reasons for lending money to Vietnam. Still, I surmise that the State Department gave its blessing to Japan's decision for two reasons. First, Secretary of State Eagleburger visited Tokyo a week earlier and made clear he would not oppose such a move, and second, such a step was called for under phase II of the roadmap, and the Bush administration met all the other phase II criteria.

148 McCann, Rapoport, and Stone, "Heeding the Call," 7.

149 E. J. Dionne, "Perot Seen Not Affecting Vote Outcome," *Washington Post*, 8 November 1992, A36.

150 Posner, *Citizen Perot*, 66, 307–22.

384 — • —

151 Ibid., 260.

152 McCann, Rapoport, and Stone, "Heeding the Call," 7–8.

153 Koch, "Perot Candidacy," 146.

154 Posner, *Citizen Perot*, 206, 214–15, 302.

155 David Remnick, "Our Nation Turns Its Lonely Eyes to H. Ross Perot," *Washington Post*, 12 April 1987, W25.

156 Posner, *Citizen Perot*, 253, 287–88.

157 Paul Richter, "Perot Runs Biographical 'Infomercial' Campaign," *Los Angeles Times*, 23 October 1992, 20.

158 Posner, *Citizen Perot*, 297–306; Jensen-Stevenson and Stevenson, *Kiss the Boys Goodbye*, 316–22.

159 Posner, *Citizen Perot*, 310–11; Timothy Noah, "Perot Cancels Appearance before Panel Investigating if Vietnam Holds POWs," *Wall Street Journal*, 17 June 1992, A8. Perot eventually went before the committee in August.

160 Douglas Waller and Bob Cohn, "The Strange Tales of Mr. Barnes," *Newsweek*, 9 November 1992, 24.

161 Lloyd Grove, "Still the Old Perot," *Washington Post*, 12 August 1992, C1.

162 Narrative composed from George Bush, *PPP, 1992–93*, Book I, 1168–71; Dowd, "Kin of Missing G.I.'s Heckle President," A1; Ann Devroy, "Bush Cites His Patriotism, War Record in Response to MIA Families' Heckling," *Washington Post*, 25 July 1992, A1.

163 Patrick Symmes, "Firebase Annandale," *Washington City Paper*, 4–10 September 1992, 12–13.

164 National Vietnam Veterans Coalition, *Veterans Journal*, September 1992, p. 3, Unlabeled folder [last in box], Box 14, Investigator's Case Files, Hilton Foster, RG46 SSC.

165 "What's Still Missing on M.I.A.'s," *New York Times*, 18 August 1992, A18.

166 Barbara Crossette, "Hanoi Office Sees M.I.A. Searches as Spying," *New York Times*, 9 August 1992, A17.

167 Senate Select Committee, *Report of the Senate Select Committee on POW/MIA Affairs*, 46–48, 233–44, 449–50, 456. Concurrent with the committee's creation, John McCain amended the defense appropriations bill to require the Pentagon to release all records pertaining to Vietnam POWs and MIAs, resulting in declassification of 1.5 million pages of material. In July the committee expanded that effort, asking the president to release "all documents, files, and other materials" relevant to POWs and MIAs "from all executive agencies and departments." Bush signed an executive order expediting the release of such files in July, and Clinton imposed a November 1993 deadline on that work. Finally, the committee released its own voluminous files — 285 feet of unclassified material and 93 feet awaiting declassification — when its tenure expired. Together these steps resulted in the largest declassification effort in U.S. history, creating the archival record that provides the backbone of this study. For details on the scope and content of these records see Charles Schamel, *Records Relating to American Prisoners of War and Missing in Action from the Vietnam War: Reference Information Paper 90* (Washington, D.C.: National Archives and Records Administration, 1996).

168 Letter from Ted Sampley to John McCain, 23 January 1992, Unfoldered, Box 3, Working Files of Staff Director Frances Zwenig, RG46 SSC. As discussed in note 74 above, *U.S. Veteran Dispatch* was initially named *Bamboo Connection*, then *U.S. Veteran News and Report*. To avoid confusion I refer to it by its current title in the text, while providing the contemporary title in the notes.

169 Joe Jordan, "Vote Out McCain Campaign 1992," undated, Folder: McCain, Box 6, Working Files of Staff Director Frances Zwenig, RG46 SSC. Capitalization in the original.

170 "Kerry Remains Anti-War Protestor at Heart," *U.S. Veteran News and Report*, October/November 1992, p. 8, Sampley—US Veteran, Box 17, Investigator's Case Files, Hilton Foster, RG46 SSC.

171 Memo from Hilton Foster to William Codinha (responsive to Bob Smith), 27 August 1992, Fraud, Box 5, Working Files of Staff Director Frances Zwenig, RG46 SSC.

172 Senate Select Committee, *Report of the Senate Select Committee on POW/MIA Affairs*, 301–70.

173 Senate Select Committee, *Department of Defense, POW/MIA Family Issues, and Private Sector Issues*, 261.

174 Letter from Thomas Vallely to Le Mai, 20 October 1992, Unmarked folder (9), Box 2, Working Files of Staff Director Frances Zwenig, RG46 SSC.

175 Thomas Lippmann, "POW Document Renews Bitter Arguments," *Washington Post*, 14 April 1993, A1. For the views of the researcher who discovered this document see Stephen J. Morris, "The War We Could Have Won," *New York Times*, 1 May 2005, A15; and Sheehan, "Prisoners of the Past," 47–48, which debunked the Morris document.

176 Art Pine, "U.S. Given Hanoi's Full List of POW Pilots," *Los Angeles Times*, 22 April 1993, A1. Even then Morris and his backers persisted, asserting that the vast disparities between returnee testimony and his figures could be explained by the existence of a second, secret prison system where non-returnees were held. See Stephen Morris, "Ghosts in the Archives," *Washington Post*, 12 September 1993, C3.

177 Steven Holmes, "Envoy Says P.O.W. Evidence Undermines Old Russian Report," *New York Times*, 22 April 1993, A3.

178 Sheehan, "Prisoners of the Past," 46; William Branigin, "U.S. Recovers MIA Remains in Vietnam," *Washington Post*, 9 February 1993, A12; "Vietnam Gives 16 Remains to U.S. MIA Officials," *Los Angeles Times*, 8 April 1993, 6. John Kerry, speaking for Amendment 1263 to Amendment 1262, 26 January 1994, 103rd Cong. 2d sess., *Cong. Rec.* 140, no. 2, S133.

179 Carroll, "A Friendship That Ended the War," *New Yorker*, 21 and 28 October 1996, 130, 155.

180 Goodman, "Vietnam's Post–Cold War Diplomacy and the U.S. Response," 836.

181 Elaine Sciolino, "U.S. to Send General to Vietnam, Hinting a Thaw," *New York Times*, 10 April 1993, A1.

182 Bill Clinton, *PPP, 1993*, Book I, 990–91. For investment figures see Mary Kay Magistad, "Vietnamese Hope for U.S. Trade," *Washington Post*, 6 July 1993, A12; Schulzinger, *Time for Peace*, 52, 58–59.

183 Thomas Lippman, "Clinton to Retain Embargo on Vietnam," *Washington Post*, 17 July 1993, A12; Philip Shenon, "U.S. Is to Station Officials in Hanoi," *New York Times*, 18 July 1993, A1. In a further sign of the League's fall, deputy national security adviser Sandy Berger was the most senior administration official to address the League at its annual meeting, the lowliest official to appear before the League in more than a decade.

184 William Branigin, "U.S. Team Gives Hanoi MIA Archive," *Washington Post*, 17 July 1993, A12.

185 Sheehan, "Prisoners of the Past," 46; Brenda Smiley, "Excavating MIAs," *Archaeology*, March-April 1996, 20–22; Katherine McIntire Peters, "The Endless Search," *Government Executive*, April 1996, 27–31.

186 Sheehan, "Prisoners of the Past," 46.

187 Clark Blair, "Stop Slouching Toward Vietnam War's End," *New York Times*, 9 February 1994, A20.

188 Steven Holmes, "The White House Is Moving to Ease Embargo on Hanoi," *New York Times*, 1 January 1994, A1; Senate Subcommittee on East Asian and Pacific Affairs, *U.S. Policy Toward Vietnam*, 21 July 1993, 103d Cong., 1st sess., 57–59.

189 Steven Greenhouse, "Veterans Challenging the View Hanoi Helps Fully on M.I.A.'s," *New York Times*, 31 January 1994, A2.

190 Eric Schmitt, "Admiral to Visit Hanoi as Relations Improve," *New York Times*, 6 January 1994, A10. Number of activities given in debate over Amendment 1263 to Amendment 1262, 26 January 1994, 103rd Cong. 2d sess., *Cong. Rec.* 140, no. 2, S171–72.

191 Kerry and McCain speaking in support of Amendment 1263 to Amendment 1262, 26 January 1994, 103rd Cong. 2d sess., *Cong. Rec.* 140, no. 2, S131–35.

192 James Carroll, "A Friendship That Ended the War," *New Yorker*, 21 and 28 October 1996, 156.

193 Schulzinger, *Time for Peace*, 58–59; Goodman, "Vietnam's Post–Cold War Diplomacy and the U.S. Response," 835.

194 Clinton, *PPP, 1993*, 1221.

195 Debate over Amendment 1263 to Amendment 1262, 26 January 1994, 103rd Cong. 2d sess., *Cong. Rec.* 140, no. 2, S136, S138, S148, S153, S156, S169.

196 William Clinton, *PPP, 1994*, Book I, 178–79.

197 Douglas Jehl, "Clinton Drops 19-Year Ban on U.S. Trade with Vietnam," *New York Times*, 4 February 1994, A1.

198 Tim Weiner, "Sense of Relief, and One of Betrayal, Are Evoked," *New York Times*, 4 February 1994, A8.

199 Carol Castaneda, "MIA Families Feel Betrayed by Bush," *USA Today*, 15 December 1992, 3A. Griffiths, Alfond, and most other MIA activists made similar claims throughout the 1990s.

200 Greenhouse, "Veterans Challenging the View Hanoi Helps Fully on the M.I.A.'s," *New York Times*, 31 January 1994, A2.

201 National League of Families, "Status of the POW/MIA Issue: July 4, 2008," available at: http://www.pow-miafamilies.org/stats.html (accessed 21 July 2008).

202 R. W. Apple, "Finally, Opening Door All the Way," *New York Times*, 21 July 1995, A1.

203 "Biggest MIA Search Begins," *Washington Post*, 27 February 1994, A25.

204 League Newsletter, 2 June 1994, Folder 6, Box 26, Douglas Pike Collection: Unit 3, POW/MIA Issues, VNA TTU; Norman Kempster, "U.S., Vietnam to Open Reciprocal Diplomatic Missions," *Los Angeles Times*, 28 January 1995, 8.

205 William Clinton, *PPP, 1995*, Book I, 759.

206 Carroll, "A Friendship That Ended the War," *New Yorker*, 21 and 28 October 1996, 156; Clinton, *PPP*, 1995, 1073–75.

207 Michael Dobbs, "Vietnam, U.S. Begin a New Relationship," *Washington Post*, 6 August 1995, A21.

208 Larry Light, "New World Order," *Business Week*, 10 April 1995, 6; League Newsletter, September 1995, Folder 8, Box 26, Douglas Pike Collection: Unit 3, POW/MIA Issues, VNA TTU; Robert Burns, "Cohen in Hanoi to Heal Wounds," *Chicago Tribune*, 14 March 2000, 1.

209 Jane Perlez, "Powell, in Hanoi, Pauses to Put the Past to Rest," *New York Times*, 27 July 2001, A10.

210 Donna Long, "The Tooth Fairy Is Alive and Well in Southeast Asia," *U.S. Veteran Dispatch*, May 1994, available at http://www.usvetdsp.com/story34.htm (accessed 21 July 2008).

211 Hawley, *Remains of War*, chap. 6, questions the ethics of accounting.

212 Franklin, *M.I.A.*, 168–74, presents excavations as revealing the fact that "missing Americans cannot be separated from the missing Vietnamese."

CONCLUSION

1 Quotes from Barbara Crossette, "Washington at Work: The Senator Pursues 'Untold' M.I.A. Story," *New York Times*, 8 August 1992, A13; Senate Select Committee, Senate Select Committee, *Oversight Hearings*, 221; Senate Select Committee, *Report of the Select Committee on POW/MIA Affairs*, 990.

2 James Carroll, "A Friendship That Ended the War," *New Yorker*, 21 and 28 October 1996, 130–56.

3 Anthony Faiola, "In Vietnam, Old Foes Take Aim at War's Toxic Legacy," *Washington Post*, 13 November 2006, A1; Maura Reynolds, "Bush Urges Vietnam Leader to Improve Human Rights Record," *Los Angeles Times*, 23 June 2007, A3.

4 James Gerstenzang, "Bush Hardly Looks Back, or Around, in Vietnam," *Los Angeles Times*, 19 November 2006, A14.

5 Peter Baker, "Bush Prods Vietnamese President on Human Rights and Openness," *Washington Post*, 23 June 2007, A2. Prime Minister Phan Van Khai—Vietnam's second-highest official—visited Bush in the Oval Office in June 2005. See David Sanger, "Protests Mark Visit, a First by a Leader of Vietnam," *New York Times*, 22 June 2005, A8.

6 Richard Gooding, "The Trashing of John McCain," *Vanity Fair*, November 2004, quote from 194.

7 Carroll, "A Friendship That Ended the War," *New Yorker*, 21 and 28 October 1996, 152; Ted Sampley, "John McCain: The Manchurian Candidate," *U.S. Veteran News and Report*, December 1992, http://www.usvetdsp.com/manchuan.htm (accessed 21 July 2008).

8   Elizabeth Drew, "Those Whispers about McCain," *Washington Post*, 19 November 1999, A45.

9   Ronald Brownstein, "Spirited Clashes Mark Intense GOP Debate," *Los Angeles Times*, 16 February 2000, 1; Marc Lacey, "Five Senators Rebuke Bush for Criticism of McCain," *New York Times*, 5 February 2000, A10. David Foster Wallace, "The Weasel, Twelve Monkeys and the Shrub," *Rolling Stone*, 13 April 2000, 62, makes clear that it was Bush's appearance with Burch that ultimately drove McCain to confront him.

10 Michael Powell and Tom Edsall, "Yanking His McChain," *Washington Post*, 16 February 2000, C1.

11 Gooding, "The Trashing of John McCain," *Vanity Fair*, November 2004, 202. Shealy is not specifically discussing MIA activists here. Still, his characterization accurately describes the manner in which Bush strategists worked with grassroots actors and groups in the 2000 and 2004 campaigns.

12 Maureen Dowd, "Nuts or Guts?," *New York Times*, 21 November 1999, A15.

13 John Miller, "What the Swifties Wrought," *National Review*, 29 November 2004, 18–19. See also Nick Anderson, "Small Ad Run Dwarfs Buzz of Other TV Spots," *Los Angeles Times*, 28 August 2004, A20. So-called 527 groups, named after Internal Revenue Code 527, are tax-exempt political organizations not formally affiliated with the two major parties whose activities are unregulated under the 2002 McCain-Feingold campaign finance law. The Swift Boat Veterans for Truth is arguably the most famous 527 to date.

14 Brinkley, *Tour of Duty*, 392.

15 Ibid., 378, 392.

16 Ibid., 401–2; O'Neill and Corsi, *Unfit for Command*, 15. For Colson/Nixon POW initiatives in April 1971 see discussion in chapter 1.

17 Joe Klein, "The Long War of John Kerry," *New Yorker*, 2 December 2002, 72.

18 Miller, "What the Swifties Wrought," *National Review*, 29 November 2004, 22. Readers can visit the Swift Vets web site at http://www.swiftvets.com/index.php (accessed 15 July 2008).

19 *Los Angeles Times* editorial quoted in Peter Beinart, "Apocalypse Redux," *New Republic*, 6 September 2004, 6. See also Kate Zernike and Jim Rutenberg, "Friendly Fire: The Birth of an Attack on Kerry," *New York Times*, 20 August 2004, A1.

20 Beinart, "Apocalypse Redux," 6.

21 Readers can visit Sampley's web site at http://www.vietnamveteransagainstjohnkerry.org/ (accessed 21 July 2008). For reporting on Sampley's activity and its consequences see Katie Hafner, "The Camera Never Lies, But the Software Can," *New York Times*, 11 March 2004, G1; E. J. Dionne, Jr., "Stooping Low to Smear Kerry," *Washington Post*, 27 April 2004, A21; Joe Conason, "The Vietnam Smear—From McCain to Kerry," 10 February 2004, http://dir.salon.com/story/opinion/conason/2004/02/10/kerry_smear/index.html (accessed 21 July 2008).

22 Michael Finnegan, "Kerry Accuses Bush of 'Fear and Smear,'" *Los Angeles Times*, 25 August 2004, A18.

23 Jim Rutenberg, "Anti-Kerry Ad Is Condemned by McCain," *New York Times*, 6 August 2004, A13.

24   Kate Zernike and Jim Rutenberg, "Friendly Fire: The Birth of an Attack on Kerry," *New York Times*, 20 August 2004, A1; Dan Balz and Thomas Edsall, "Lawyer Quits Bush-Cheney Organization," *Washington Post*, 26 August 2004, A1. See also John F. Harris, "Cheney Calls Kerry Unfit," *Washington Post*, 2 September 2004, A1; James Bennet, "Ex-President Bush Calls Charges of Swift Boat Group Compelling," *New York Times*, 31 August 2004, A6.

25   Miller, "What the Swifties Wrought," *National Review*, 29 November 2004, 20.

26   "Swift Boat Veterans Join Forces with POWs," press release, 29 September 2004, available at http://www.swiftvets.com/article.php?story=2004092911015589 (accessed on 21 July 2008).

27   "Swift Boat Veterans Join Forces with POWs," press release, 29 September 2004.

28   O'Neill and Corsi, *Unfit for Command*, 107–8.

29   David Kirkpatrick, "The Nixon Factor," *New York Times*, 18 June 2008, A18; Rochester and Kiley, *Honor Bound*, chaps. 22–23.

30   Rochester and Kiley, *Honor Bound*. 377. POW hardliners explained away antiwar sentiment among POWs by blaming it on "the divisive forces which had come into focus as a result of the anti-war movement in the United States," though such explanations make little sense given that most men granted early release were captured before significant stateside antiwar sentiment materialized. See David Kirkpatrick, "In '74 Thesis, the Seeds of McCain's War Views," *New York Times*, 15 June 2008, A1; McCain, "Code of Conduct and the Vietnam Prisoners of War," 13–17, 30.

31   Moser, *New Winter Soldiers*, 131; Lembcke, *Spitting Image*, 106.

32   Alessandra Stanley, "An Outpouring of Pain, Channeled Via Politics," *New York Times*, 21 October 2004, E1; Elizabeth Jensen, "Conservative TV Group to Air Anti-Kerry Film," *Los Angeles Times*, 9 October 2004, A1; Bill Toland, "Film maker Angry at Kerry Since '71," *Pittsburgh Post-Gazette*, 15 October 2004, A1; Jim Rutenberg and Kate Zernike, "Accusations and Flaws, All Serious," *New York Times*, 20 October 2004, A21.

33   Stanley, "An Outpouring of Pain, Channeled Via Politics," *New York Times*, 21 October 2004, E1. Virginia Warner anticipated that her views would be discounted by the war's defenders — "I'm sure I'm going to be labeled Communist; I'm sure I'm going to be labeled revolutionary" — and tried to head off such charges. "I am an American. I love my country . . . but this isn't the only consideration. We have to consider the people in Vietnam. What would we do, what would you and I do, if a Vietnamese plane flew over and bombed our town? How would we react to somebody that we've captured?" Her testimony was reprinted in Kerry's and the VVAW's 1971 antiwar anthology *The New Soldier*, 110.

34   Michael Tomasky, "Long Division," *American Prospect*, October 2004, 18.

35   David Gelernter, "Another Vietnam?," *Weekly Standard*, 11 October 2004, 9–10.

36   Todd Purdum, "What They're Really Fighting About," *New York Times*, 29 August 2004, WK1.

37   Billboard reported in an e-mail from Marilyn Young to author, 2 November 2004, in author's possession. This slogan and variations on this theme also appeared on conservative blogs such as freerepublic.com during 2004.

38 In the end, many of the most incendiary charges in *Stolen Honor* were never aired as the pro-Bush Sinclair Broadcast Group scrapped plans to broadcast the film on its sixty-two television stations in the face of declining stock prices, balky advertisers, and angry shareholders. Elizabeth Jensen, "Sinclair Retreats on Kerry Film," *Los Angeles Times*, 20 October 2004, A1.

39 Easton et al., "On the Trail of Kerry's Failed Dream," *Boston Globe*, 14 November 2004, 24.

40 Frank Luntz, "Why Bush Won," *Washington Times*, 5 November 2004, A21.

41 Jonathan Martin and Jim Vandehei, "McCain, Palin Push Biography, Not Issues," *Politico*, 9 September 2008, http://www.Politico.com/news/stories/0908/13275.html (accessed 9 December 2008).

42 Dan Nowicki, "Pushing Ahead, McCain Relies on POW Past," *Arizona Republic*, 22 October 2007, http://www.azcentral.com/news/specials/mccain/articles/1021mccain-pow1021-CR.html# (accessed 9 December 2008).

43 Service to America tour and ad available at http://www.johnmccain.com/service/intro.htm and http://www.johnmccain.com/tvads/ (accessed 9 December 2008).

44 See video and transcript at http://elections.nytimes.com/2008/president/conventions/videos/20080904_MCCAIN_SPEECH.html (accessed 9 December 2008).

45 See exit polls at http://www.cnn.com/ELECTION/2008/results/polls/#USP00p1 (accessed 9 December 2008).

46 http://blogs.abcnews.com/politicalradar/2008/04/obama-mccains-p.html (accessed 11 December 2008).

47 Martin and Vandehei, "McCain, Palin Push Biography, Not Issues," *Politico*, 9 September 2008; Jonathan Martin, "Might Need to Update That Palin Intro," *Politico*, 13 October 2008, http://www.Politico.com/blogs/jonathanmartin/1008/Might_need_to_update_that_Palin_intro.html (accessed 11 December 2008); Mark Danner, "Obama and Sweet Potato Pie," *New York Review of Books*, 20 November 2008, 16–20.

48 David Grann, "The Fall," *New Yorker*, 17 November 2008, 56–66.

49 Tim Dickinson, "Make-Believe Maverick," *Rolling Stone*, 16 October 2008, 56–65.

50 Josh Kraushaar, "Clark Hits McCain's Military Credentials," *Politico*, 29 June 2008, http://www.Politico.com/news/stories/0608/11425.html (accessed 11 December 2008).

51 John Berman and Mark Mooney, "Retired Gen. Wesley Clark Keeps Up Fire on McCain," *ABC News.com*, 1 July 2008, http://abcnews.go.com/GMA/Vote2008/story?id=5283442 (accessed 11 December 2008). Similar concerns were raised by a number of McCain's fellow Senate veterans in Matt Bai, "The McCain Doctrines," *New York Times Magazine*, 18 May 2008, 40–47, 62, 66, 68–70.

52 http://www.youtube.com/watch?v=_KjsEs46C70 (accessed 11 December 2008).

53 http://www.vietnamveteransagainstjohnmccain.com/ (accessed 11 December 2008). For more on Sampley's anti-McCain activities see Stephen Dinan, "McCain's Foes Buy Up Web Sites To Target Arizona Senator," *Washington Times*, 14

February 2008, A12; Elisabeth Bumiller, "McCain Parries a Reprise of '00 Smear Tactics," *New York Times*, 17 January 2008, A1.

54 Jeffrey Goldberg, "The Wars of John McCain," *Atlantic*, October 2008, 40–54.

55 It also marked the fifth straight presidential race in which a military veteran lost to a non-veteran.

56 DPMO coordinates POW/MIA policy, while JPAC carries out investigative field work and remains identification. For their official web sites see http://www.dtic .mil/dpmo/index.htm and http://www.jpac.pacom.mil/ (accessed 21 July 2008).

57 As in U.S.-Vietnam relations, the recovery of American remains has become a means for North Korea to maintain diplomatic contact with the United States while bringing in much-needed cash. See "U.S. to Get Remains of Korean War Soldiers," *Washington Post*, 10 November 2000, A5; Andrew Salmon, "Joint Mission Recovers War Dead," *International Herald Tribune*, 16 October 2004, 3.

58 See http://www.ranger.org/html/ranger_creed.html (accessed 21 July 2008).

59 On the prominence of rescue see McAlister, "A Cultural History of the War without End," 449–51. For an introduction to the vast casualty aversion literature see *Aerospace Power Journal* 14:2 (2000), which includes Record, "Force Protection Fetishism," 4–11. For a popularized synopsis of key claims and concerns within this field, see Peter Feaver and Christopher Gelpi, "A Look at Casualty Aversion," *Washington Post*, 7 November 1999, B3. One striking finding of this literature is that sensitivity to casualties is most acute among senior military officers and among military families, suggesting that fears of warrior abandonment—and a determination to avoid it—are especially intense within military culture.

60 Lawrence Kaplan, "Willpower," *New Republic*, 8 September 2003, 19.

61 Sara Fritz, "U.S. Aversion to Military Casualties Ebbs," *St. Petersburg Times*, 20 September 2001, 6A.

62 John Files, "Pentagon Agrees to Issue Photos of Coffins of Iraq War Dead," *New York Times*, 5 August 2005, A1; Mike Lupica, "Somber Reminders, G.I. Funerals a Dirty Secret," *New York Daily News*, 5 November 2006, 4.

63 Linda Kozaryn, "Bush Vows Troops Will Not Have Died in Vain," *American Forces Press Service*, 4 July 2006, http://www.defenselink.mil/news/newsarticle .aspx?id=59 (accessed 11 December 2008).

64 "Transcript of First Presidential Debate," *CNN.com*, 26 September 2008, http:// www.cnn.com/2008/POLITICS/09/26/debate.mississippi.transcript/ (accessed 11 December 2008).

65 This is war correspondent Dexter Filkins's evocative name for the war in Iraq. See Filkins, *Forever War*.

66 Julian Barnes, Press Release, "Army 'Stop-Loss' Orders up Dramatically over Last Year," *Los Angeles Times*, 9 May 2008, A16; "Webb Amendment Supports Troops through Responsible Deployment Cycles," 9 July 2007, http://webb .senate.gov/newsroom/record.cfm?id=278436 (accessed 21 July 2008); Noam Levey, "Changes to War Strategy Fail in Senate," *Los Angeles Times*, 20 September 2007, A1.

67 Dana Priest and Anne Hull, "Soldiers Face Neglect, Frustration at Army's Top Medical Facility," *Washington Post*, 18 February 2007, A1.

68 Anne Kornblut, "Ad Showing Troop Coffins Causes Clash of the Parties," *New York Times*, 14 July 2006, A16; David Carr, "Show Me the Bodies," *New York Times*, 5 June 2006, C1; Jeffrey Zaslow, "Tribute or Protest?" *Wall Street Journal*, 1 July 2006, A1.

69 Anne Kornblut, "Mother's Grief-Fueled Vigil Becomes Nexus for Antiwar Protestors," *New York Times*, 13 August 2005, A7; Petula Dvorak, "Battle Lines behind the Battle Lines," *Washington Post*, 21 September 2005, B1; Sylvia Moreno, "In Vigil on the Mall, Veteran Takes a Stand against Pentagon Policies," *Washington Post*, 29 August 2007, B2; Christopher Hitchens, "Cindy Sheehan's Sinister Piffle," *Slate.com*, 15 August 2005, http://www.slate.com/id/2124500/ (accessed 21 July 2008).

70 "Transcript of First Presidential Debate," *CNN.com*, 26 September 2008, http://www.cnn.com/2008/POLITICS/09/26/debate.mississippi.transcript/ (accessed 11 December 2008).

ARCHIVES

National Archives, Washington, D.C.
    Record Group 46. Records of the United States Senate
        Records of the Senate Select Committee on POW/MIA Affairs, 1991–93
            Records Received From Other Agencies
                Policy Files of the Office of the Secretary of Defense, 1981–88
                Declassified Documents of the Central Documentation Office,
                    Department of Defense, 1982–91
                MIA/POW Policy Documents of the Joint Chiefs of Staff, 1965–91
                Selected Records of Special Assistant Frank A. Sieverts,
                    Department of State, 1966–78
                Files of the Minority Staff of the Senate Foreign Relations
                    Committee—Tracy Usry Files, 1968–90
                Declassified Files Received from Executive Agencies
            Records of the Committee
                Working Files of Staff Director Frances A. Zwenig
                Working Files of Press Secretary Deborah DeYoung
                Working Files of Committee Investigator John Erickson
                Working Files of Committee Investigator Hilton Foster
                Working Files of Committee Investigator Alex Greenfield
                Working Files of Committee Investigator Neal Kravitz
                Working Files of Committee Investigator Tom Lang
                Working Files of Committee Investigator Sedgewick Tourison
            Transcripts of Sworn Depositions
                Richard V. Allen
                Harold Brown
                Richard T. Childress
                Bruce W. Eberle
                Ann Mills Griffiths
                Richard Holbrooke

Melvin Laird

Tran Vien Loc, aka "The Mortician"

James Angus MacDonald

Michel Oksenberg

Joseph Salta

Richard V. Secord

Charles E. Shelton Jr.

Roger E. Shields

Frank Sieverts

John E. Webb

Record Group 233. Records of the United States House of Representatives

Records of the House Select Committee on Missing Persons in
Southeast Asia, 1975–76

Select Committee Files

National Archives II, College Park, Md.

Record Group 330. Records of the Office of the Secretary of Defense

Records of the Defense Prisoner of War/Missing in Action Office

Copies of Records Relating to Korean War POW/MIAs, 1951–58

Record Group 338. Records of U.S. Army Operational, Tactical,
and Support Organizations

Records of Organizations Concerned With Prisoner of War and
Missing in Action Information

Nixon Presidential Materials, College Park, Md.

White House Central Files

Subject Categories ND 18–3, Prisoners, National Security—Defense, 1969–74

National Security Council Files

Vietnam Subject Files, 1969–74

Vietnam Country Files, 1969–74

Documents Relating to POW/MIA Matters Declassified by
Executive Order 12816, 1969–74

White House Staff Files

Alexander P. Butterfield Files, 1969–73

Charles W. Colson Files, 1969–73

Gerald Ford Library, Ann Arbor, Mich.

White House Central Files

Subject Categories ND 18–3, Prisoners, National Security—Defense, 1973–77

Subject Categories, ND 8–1, Casualties, Condolences, 1973–77

National Security Council Files

Presidential Country Files for East Asia and the Pacific, 1973–77

National Security Adviser Backchannel Messages, 1974–77

Kissinger-Scowcroft West Wing Office Files, 1968–77

East Asian and Pacific Affairs Staff Files, 1973–77

Press and Congressional Liaison Staff Files, 1975–77

Presidential Subject Files, 1973–77

Memoranda of Conversations, 1973–76
Saigon Embassy Files, 1973–75
White House Staff Files
Philip W. Buchen Files, 1974–77
John G. Carlson Files,
Richard B. Cheney Files, 1974–77
Kenneth Cole Files, 1974–75
James E. Connor Files, 1974–77
Betty Ford Files, 1973-
Gerald R. Ford Vice Presidential Papers, 1973–74
Robert T. Hartmann Files, 1974–77
Kenneth A. Lazarus Files, 1974–77
Theodore C. Marrs Files, 1974–77
John O. Marsh Files, 1974–77
Milton E. Mitler Files, 1972–77
Ron Nessen Files, 1974–77
Edward C. Schmults Files, 1974–77
Geoffrey C. Shepard Files, 1974–75
Ronald Reagan Library, Simi Valley, Calif.
National Security Council Files
National Security Council Office of the Executive Secretariat
Subject Files, POW/MIA, 1981–84
White House Staff Files
Morton C. Blackwell Files, 1981–84
Richard T. Childress Files, 1981–88
Anthony R. Dolan Files, 1981–89
Robert M. Kimmitt Files, 1981–85
Christopher M. Lehman Files, 1983–85
Edward J. Rollins Files, 1981–83
Ronald K. Sable Files, 1984–86
Library of Congress, Washington, D.C.
Records of the Vietnam Veterans Memorial Fund, 1965–94, Manuscript Division
The U.S. Department of Defense Vietnam-Era POW/MIA Documentation
Collection in Microform, Microform Reading Room

INTERVIEWS

Dolores Alfond, 2001
Carol Bates Brown, 2001
Richard T. Childress, 2000
Charles L. Cragin, 2001
Robert J. DeStatte, 2000
Ann Mills Griffiths, 2000
Vince Gonzales, 2004

Thomas D. Holland, 2001
Henry "Hank" J. Kenney, 2001
Paul D. Mather, 2000
Charles S. Robb, 2007
Frank A. Sieverts, 2001
Russ Thomasson, 2001

NEWSPAPERS AND MAGAZINES

Alameda Times-Star
American Forces Press Service
American Lawyer
American Prospect
Arizona Republic
Asheville Citizen Times
Atlanta Journal-Constitution
The Atlantic
American Legion
Baltimore Sun
Bamboo Connection
Boston Globe
Business Week
Cedar Falls Record
Chicago Tribune
Cleveland Plain-Dealer
Columbia Journalism Review
Commonweal
Dayton Journal Herald
Fort Wayne Journal Gazette
Government Executive
Harper's
Houston Chronicle
Life
Los Angeles Times
The Nation
National Catholic Reporter
National Geographic
National Review
New Republic
New York Daily News
New York Review of Books
New York Times

New Yorker
Newsweek
Omaha World-Herald
Orange County Register
Pittsburgh Post-Gazette
Ramparts
Reader's Digest
Rolling Stone
San Diego Union
San Francisco Examiner
Soldier of Fortune
St. Louis Post-Dispatch
St. Petersburg Times
Sunday Oklahoman
The Tennessean
Time
Toledo Blade
U.S. News & World Report
U.S. Veteran Dispatch
U.S. Veteran News and Report
USA Today
Vanity Fair
VFW Magazine
Virginian Pilot
The Voice
Wall Street Journal
Washington City Paper
Washington Monthly
Washington Post
Washington Star
Washington Times
Weekly Standard

GOVERNMENT PUBLICATIONS

U.S. Congress. House. Select Committee on Missing Persons in Southeast Asia. *Americans Missing in Southeast Asia: Final Report Together with Additional and Separate Views*. 94th Cong., 2d sess. Washington, D.C.: Government Printing Office, 1976.
———. Subcommittee on Asian and Pacific Affairs. *Tighe Report on American POW's and MIA's Hearing before the Subcommittee on Asian and Pacific Affairs*. 99th Cong., 2d sess., 15 October 1986. Washington, D.C.: Government Printing Office, 1986.
———. Subcommittee on Asian and Pacific Affairs. *The Vessey Mission to Hanoi:*

Hearing before the Subcommittee on Asian and Pacific Affairs. 100th Cong., 1st sess., 30 September 1987. Washington, D.C.: Government Printing Office, 1987.

————. Subcommittee on the Far East and the Pacific. *Return of American Prisoners of War Who Have Not Been Accounted For by the Communists. Hearings on H. Con. Res. 140*, 85th Cong., 1st sess., 27 May 1957. Washington, D.C.: Government Printing Office, 1957.

U.S. Congress. Senate. Committee on Foreign Relations. *U.S. MIA's in Southeast Asia: Hearing before the Committee on Foreign Relations*. 95th Cong., 1st sess., 1 April 1977. Washington, D.C.: Government Printing Office, 1977.

U.S. Congress. Senate. Committee on Foreign Relations Republican Staff. *An Examination of U.S. Policy Toward POW/MIAs by the U.S. Senate Committee on Foreign Relations Republican Staff*. Washington, D.C.: Government Printing Office, 1991.

————. Committee on Veterans' Affairs. *Live Sighting Reports of Americans Listed as Missing in Action in Southeast Asia: Hearings before the Committee on Veterans' Affairs.* Vol. I, 99th Cong., 2d sess. Washington, D.C.: Government Printing Office, 1986.

————. Select Committee on POW/MIA Affairs. *Report of the Select Committee on POW/MIA Affairs*. 103d Cong., 1st sess. Washington, D.C.: Government Printing Office, 1993.

U.S. Department of Army Central Identification Laboratory, Hawaii. *Not to Be Forgotten*. Hickam Air Force Base, Hawaii: CILHI, 1992.

————. *Remember*. Hickam Air Force Base, Hawaii: CILHI, n.d.

U.S. Department of the Army. *Identification of Deceased Personnel: Field Manual*. St. Louis: U.S. Army AG Publications Center, 1976.

U.S. Department of Defense. *POW-MIA Fact Book*. Washington, D.C.: Department of Defense, 1982.

U.S. General Accounting Office. *Report to the Chairman and Vice Chariman, Select Committee on POW/MIA Affairs, U.S. Senate: Issues Related to the Identification of Human Remains from the Vietnam Conflict*. Washington, D.C.: Government Printing Office, 1992.

PUBLISHED SOURCES

Ambrose, Stephen E. *Nixon: The Triumph of a Politician, 1962–1972*. New York: Simon & Schuster, 1989.

Anders, Steven E. "With All Due Honors: A History of the Quartermaster Graves Registration Mission." *Quartermaster Professional Bulletin* (September 1998): 30–35.

Anderson, Benedict. *Imagined Communities: Reflection on the Origin and Spread of Nationalism*. Rev. ed. New York: Verso, 1991.

Anderson, Terry. "The Light at the End of the Tunnel: The United States and the Socialist Republic of Vietnam." *Diplomatic History* 12, no. 4 (1988): 443–62.

Andrew, John A. *The Other Side of the Sixties: Young Americans for Freedom and the Rise of Conservative Politics*. New Brunswick, N.J.: Rutgers University Press, 1997.

Appy, Christian G. *Cold War Constructions: The Political Culture of United States Imperialism, 1945–1966*. Amherst: University of Massachusetts Press, 2000.

————. *Patriots: The Vietnam War Remembered From All Sides*. New York: Viking, 2003.

———. *Working-Class War: American Combat Soldiers and Vietnam.* Chapel Hill: University of North Carolina Press, 1993.

Asselin, Pierre. *A Bitter Peace: Washington, Hanoi, and the Making of the Paris Agreement.* Chapel Hill: University of North Carolina Press, 2002.

Bacevich, Andrew J. *The New American Militarism: How Americans Are Seduced By War.* New York: Oxford University Press, 2005.

Bailey, Beth, and David Farber. *America in the Seventies.* Lawrence: University Press of Kansas, 2004.

Beattie, Keith. *The Scar That Binds: American Culture and the Vietnam War.* New York: New York University Press, 1998.

Bell, Garnett. *Leave No Man Behind: Bill Bell and the Search for American POW/MIAs From the Vietnam War.* With George J. Veith. Madison, Wisc.: Goblin Fern Press, 2004.

Bender, Thomas, ed. *Rethinking American History in a Global Age.* Berkeley: University of California Press, 2002.

Berg, Rick. "Losing Vietnam: Covering the War in an Age of Technology." In *The Vietnam War and American Culture*, edited by John Carlos Rowe and Rick Berg, 115–47. New York: Columbia University Press, 1991.

Berman, Larry. *No Peace, No Honor: Nixon, Kissinger, and Betrayal in Vietnam.* New York: Free Press, 2001.

Berman, William C. *America's Right Turn: From Nixon to Clinton.* 2d ed. Baltimore: Johns Hopkins University Press, 1998.

Biess, Frank. *Homecomings: Returning POWs and the Legacies of Defeat in Postwar Germany.* Princeton, N.J.: Princeton University Press, 2006.

Bigler, Philip. *In Honored Glory: Arlington National Cemetery, The Final Post.* 3rd ed. Arlington, Va.: Vandamere Press, 1999.

Blair, William. *Cities of the Dead: Contesting the Memory of the Civil War in the South, 1865–1914.* Chapel Hill: University of North Carolina Press, 2004.

Blight, David W. "'For Something Beyond the Battlefield': Frederick Douglass and the Struggle for the Memory of the Civil War." *Journal of American History* 75, no. 4 (1989): 1156–78.

———. *Race and Reunion: The Civil War in American Memory.* Cambridge: Belknap Press of Harvard University Press, 2001.

Blumenthal, Sidney. *Our Long National Daydream: A Political Pageant of the Reagan Era.* New York: Harper & Row, 1988.

Bradley, Mark P., and Marilyn Young, eds. *Making Sense of the Vietnam Wars: Local, National, and Transnational Perspectives.* New York: Oxford University Press, 2008.

Brands, H. C. *The Strange Death of American Liberalism.* New Haven, Conn.: Yale University Press, 2001.

Brennan, Mary Charlotte. *Turning Right in the Sixties: The Conservative Capture of the GOP.* Chapel Hill: University of North Carolina Press, 1995.

Brigham, Robert K. *Guerrilla Diplomacy: The NLF's Foreign Relations and the Vietnam War.* Ithaca, N.Y.: Cornell University Press, 1999.

Brinkley, Douglas. *Tour of Duty: John Kerry and the Vietnam War.* New York: William Morrow, 2004.

Brown, Elizabeth. "Bye, Bye Miss American Pie: Wives of American Servicemen in Southeast Asia, 1961–1975." Ph.D. diss., University of Colorado, 2005.

Brown, Peter. *The Cult of the Saints: Its Rise and Function in Latin Christianity*. Chicago: University of Chicago Press, 1981.

Brzezinski, Zbigniew. *Power and Principle: Memoirs of the National Security Adviser, 1977–1981*. New York: Farrar, Straus, Giroux, 1983.

Burns, Roger A. "Known But to God." *American History* 31, no. 5 (1996): 38–41.

Butler, Judith. *Precarious Life: The Powers of Mourning and Violence*. New York: Verso, 2004.

Bush, Richard C. *Vietnamese Storage of Remains of Unaccounted US Personnel: Intelligence Community Assessment*. Washington, D.C.: National Intelligence Council, October 1996.

Bynum, Caroline Walker. *The Resurrection of the Body in Western Christianity, 200–1336*. New York: Columbia University Press, 1995.

Cannon, Lou. *President Reagan: The Role of a Lifetime*. New York: Simon & Schuster, 1991.

Carroll, Peter N. *It Seemed Like Nothing Happened: America in the 1970's*. 1982. Reprint, New Brunswick, N.J.: Rutgers University Press, 1990.

Carter, Jimmy. *Why Not The Best? Jimmy Carter: The First Fifty Years*. 1975. Reprint, Fayetteville: University of Arkansas Press, 1996.

Chanda, Nayan. *Brother Enemy: The War after the War*. New York: Harcourt Brace Jovanovich, 1986.

Cima, Ronald J. "Vietnam in 1989: Initiating the Post-Cambodia Period." *Asian Survey* 30, no. 1 (January 1990): 88–95.

Clarke, Douglas L. *The Missing Man: Politics and the MIA*. Washington, D.C.: National Defense University, 1979.

Clecak, Peter. *America's Quest for the Ideal Self: Dissent and Fulfillment in the 60s and 70s*. New York: Oxford University Press, 1983.

Clinton, Bill. *My Life*. New York: Alfred A. Knopf, 2004.

Coco, Gregory A. *A Strange and Blighted Land: Gettysburg, The Aftermath of a Battle*. Gettysburg, Pa.: Thomas Publications, 1995.

Cole, Paul M. *POW/MIA Issues*. 3 vols. Santa Monica, Calif.: Rand, 1994.

Coleman, Bradley Lynn. "Recovering the Korean War Dead, 1950–1958: Graves Registration, Forensic Anthropology, and Wartime Mobilization." *Journal of Military History* 72, no. 1 (2008): 179–222.

Confino, Alon. "Collective Memory and Cultural History: Problems of Method." *American Historical Review* 102, no. 5 (1997): 1386–1403.

Connerton, Paul. *How Societies Remember*. Cambridge: Cambridge University Press, 1989.

Cox, Caroline. *A Proper Sense of Honor: Service and Sacrifice in George Washington's Army*. Chapel Hill: University of North Carolina Press, 2004.

Cray, Robert E. Jr. "Commemorating the Prison Ship Dead: Revolutionary Memory and the Politics of Sepulture in the Early Republic, 1776–1808." *William and Mary Quarterly* 56, no. 3 (1999): 565–90.

Crossland, Zoë. "Buried Lives: Forensic Archaeology and the Disappeared in Argentina." *Archaeological Dialogues* 7, no. 2 (2000): 146–59.

Davis, Vernon E. *The Long Road Home: U.S. Prisoner of War Policy and Planning in Southeast Asia*. Washington, D.C.: Office of the Secretary of Defense, 2000.

Dean, Robert. *Imperial Brotherhood: Gender and the Making of Cold War Foreign Policy*. Amherst: University of Massachusetts Press, 2003.

Douglas, Ann. *Terrible Honesty: Mongrel Manhattan in the 1920s*. New York: Farrar, Straus, and Giroux, 1995.

Dower, John. *Embracing Defeat: Japan in the Wake of World War II*. New York: W. W. Norton, 1999.

———. *War without Mercy: Race and Power in the Pacific War*. New York: Pantheon Books, 1986.

Doyle, Robert C. "Unresolved Mysteries: The Myth of the Missing Warrior and the Government Deceit Theme in the Popular Captivity Culture of the Vietnam War." *Journal of American Culture* 15, no. 2 (1992): 1–18.

Duiker, William J. *Sacred War: Nationalism and Revolution in a Divided Vietnam*. New York: McGraw-Hill, 1995.

Engelhardt, Tom. *The End of Victory Culture: Cold War America and the Disillusioning of a Generation*. New York: Basic Books, 1995.

Enloe, Cynthia. *Bananas, Beaches, & Bases: Making Feminist Sense of International Politics*. Berkeley: University of California Press, 1989.

Fanning, Kathryn. "Remembering Hugh, MIA" and "Burying the Past, Burying the Truth?" In *Vietnam: The Heartland Remembers*, edited by Stanley W. Beesley. Norman: University of Oklahoma Press, 1987.

Farber, David. "The Silent Majority and Talk about Revolution." In *The Sixties: From Memory to History*, edited by David Farber, 291–316. Chapel Hill: University of North Carolina Press, 1994.

———. *Taken Hostage: The Iran Hostage Crisis and America's First Encounter With Radical Islam*. Princeton, N.J.: Princeton University Press, 2005.

Farber, David, and Jeff Roche, eds. *The Conservative Sixties*. New York: Peter Lang Publishing, 2003.

Farrell, James J. *Inventing the American Way of Death, 1830–1920*. Philadelphia: Temple University Press, 1980.

Faust, Drew Gilpin. *"A Riddle of Death": Mortality and Meaning in the American Civil War*. Gettysburg, Pa.: Gettysburg College, 1995.

———. *This Republic of Suffering: Death and the American Civil War*. New York: Knopf, 2008.

Fenrich, Lane. "Mass Death in Miniature." In *Living with the Bomb: American and Japanese Cultural Conflict in the Nuclear Age*, edited by Laura Hein and Mark Selden, 122–33. Armonk, N.Y.: M. E. Sharpe, 1997.

Figal, Gerald. "Bones of Contention: The Geopolitics of 'Sacred Ground' in Postwar Okinawa." *Diplomatic History* 31, no. 1 (2007): 81–109.

Filkins, Dexter. *The Forever War*. New York: Knopf, 2008.

FitzGerald, Frances. *Way Out There in the Blue: Reagan, Star Wars, and the End of the Cold War*. New York: Simon & Schuster, 2000.

Foot, Rosemary. *A Substitute for Victory: The Politics of Peacemaking at the Korean Armistice Talks*. Ithaca, N.Y.: Cornell University Press, 1990.

Ford, Gerald R. *A Time To Heal: The Autobiography of Gerald R. Ford*. New York: Harper & Row, 1979.

Franklin, H. Bruce. *M.I.A.: Mythmaking in America*. 1992. Expanded ed., New Brunswick, N.J.: Rutgers University Press, 1993.

———. *Vietnam & Other American Fantasies*. Amherst: University of Massachusetts Press, 2000.

Fraser, Steve, and Gary Gerstle, eds. *The Rise and Fall of the New Deal Order, 1930–1980*. Princeton, N.J.: Princeton University Press, 1989.

Frie, Arnd, Thomas Moody, Garth Yarnall, Jamie Kiessling, Benett Sunds, Gerard L. McCool, and Robert Uppena. "Fallen Comrades: Mortuary Affairs in the U.S. Army." *Quartermaster Professional Bulletin* (Winter 1998): 30–35.

Fussell, Paul. *The Great War and Modern Memory*. Anniversary ed. New York: Oxford University Press, 2000.

Geertz, Clifford. *The Interpretation of Cultures*. New York: Basic Books, 1973.

Gettleman, Marvin E., Jane Franklin, Marilyn B. Young, and H. Bruce Franklin, eds. *Vietnam and America: The Most Comprehensive Documented History of the Vietnam War*. New York: Grove Press, 1995.

Gibson, James W. *Warrior Dreams: Violence and Manhood in Post-Vietnam America*. New York: Hill and Wang, 1994.

Gillis, John R. *Commemorations: The Politics of National Identity*. Princeton, N.J.: Princeton University Press, 1994.

Goodman, Allan. "Vietnam's Post–Cold War Diplomacy and the U.S. Response." *Asian Survey* 33, no. 8 (1993): 832–47.

Griffiths, Ann Mills. "Missing Man Essay." In *We Came Home*, edited by Barbara Powers Wyatt. Toluca Lake, Calif.: P.O.W. Publications, 1977.

Groom, Winston, and Duncan Spencer. *Conversations With the Enemy: The Story of PFC Robert Garwood*. New York: G. P. Putnam's Sons, 1983.

Gruner, Elliott. *Prisoners of Culture: Representing the Vietnam POW*. New Brunswick, N.J.: Rutgers University Press, 1993.

Gusterson, Hugh. "Nuclear War, the Gulf War, and the Disappearing Body." *Journal of Urban and Cultural Studies* 2, no. 1 (1991): 45–55.

Hagen, Edward A. "The POW-MIA Issue: A Case of Cultural Impotence." *Connecticut Review* 15, no. 2 (1993): 63–69.

Halberstam, David. *War in a Time of Peace: Bush, Clinton, and the Generals*. New York: Scribner, 2001.

Haldeman, H.R., with Joseph DiMona. *The Ends of Power*. New York: Times Books, 1978.

Halttunen, Karen. *Confidence Men and Painted Women: A Study of Middle-Class Culture in America, 1830–1870*. New Haven, Conn.: Yale University Press, 1983.

Hanson, Neil. *Unknown Soldiers: The Story of the Missing of the First World War*. New York: Vintage Books, 2005.

Harrison, Robert Pogue. *The Dominion of the Dead*. Chicago: University of Chicago Press, 2003.

Hass, Kristin Ann. *Carried to the Wall: American Memory and the Vietnam Veterans Memorial*. Berkeley: University of California Press, 1998.

Hawley, Thomas M. *The Remains of War: Bodies, Politics, and the Search for American Soldiers Unaccounted for in Southeast Asia*. Durham, N.C.: Duke University Press, 2005.

Herring, George C. *America's Longest War: The United States and Vietnam, 1950–1975*. 4th ed. New York: McGraw-Hill, 2002.

———. "The 'Vietnam Syndrome' and American Foreign Policy." *Virginia Quarterly Review* 57, no. 4 (Autumn 1981): 594–612.

Hershberger, Mary. *Traveling to Vietnam: American Peace Activists and the War*. Syracuse: Syracuse University Press, 1998.

Hofstadter, Richard. *The Paranoid Style in American Politics and Other Essays*. 1965. Reprint, Cambridge: Harvard University Press, 1996.

Holland, Thomas D. *Problems and Observations Related to the Forensic Identification of Human Remains Repatriated to the United States by North Korea*. Santa Monica, Calif.: Rand, 1993.

Howes, Craig. *Voices of the Vietnam POWs: Witnesses to Their Fight*. New York: Oxford University Press, 1993.

Howren, Jamie, and Taylor Baldwin Kiland. *Open Doors: Vietnam POWs Thirty Years Later*. Washington, D.C.: Potomac Books, Inc., 2005.

Huebner, Andrew J. *The Warrior Image: Soldiers in American Culture from the Second World War to the Vietnam Era*. Chapel Hill: University of North Carolina Press, 2008.

Hunter, Edna J. "Prisoners of War: Readjustment and Rehabilitation." *Handbook of Military Psychology*. New York: John Wiley & Sons, 1991.

———. *Prolonged Separation: The Prisoner of War and His Family*. San Diego: Center for POW Studies, Naval Health Research Center, 1977.

Hunter, Edna J., and James D. Phelan. "Army, Navy and Marine Corps Prisoners of War and Missing in Action: A Demographic Profile." In *Family Separation and Reunion: Families of Prisoners of War and Servicemen Missing in Action*, edited by Hamilton I. McCubbin. Washington, D.C.: Government Printing Office, 1974.

Hurst, Steven. *The Carter Administration and Vietnam*. New York: St. Martin's Press, 1996.

Isaacs, Arnold R. *Vietnam Shadows: The War, Its Ghosts, and Its Legacy*. Baltimore: Johns Hopkins University Press, 1997.

———. *Without Honor: Defeat in Vietnam and Cambodia*. Baltimore: Johns Hopkins University Press, 1983.

Isserman, Maurice, and Michael Kazin. *America Divided: The Civil War of the 1960s*. New York: Oxford University Press, 2000.

Iverson, Kenneth V. *Death to Dust: What Happens to Dead Bodies?* Tucson, Ariz.: Galen Press, 1994.

Jeansonne, Glen. *Women of the Far Right: The Mothers' Movement and World War II*. Chicago: University of Chicago Press, 1996.

Jeffords, Susan. *Hard Bodies: Hollywood Masculinity in the Reagan Era*. New Brunswick, N.J.: Rutgers University Press, 1994.

———. *The Remasculinization of America: Gender and the Vietnam War*. Bloomington: Indiana University Press, 1989.

Jenkins, Philip. *Decade of Nightmares: The End of the Sixties and the Making of Eighties America*. New York: Oxford University Press, 2006.

Jensen, Jay R. *Six Years in Hell: A Returned Vietnam POW Views Captivity, Country and the Future*. Rev. ed. Orcutt, Calif.: P.O.W. (Publications of Worth), 1989.

Jensen-Stevenson, Monika, and William Stevenson. *Kiss the Boys Goodbye: How the United States Betrayed Its Own POWs in Vietnam*. New York: Dutton, 1990.

Jespersen, T. Christopher. "The Bitter End and the Lost Chance in Vietnam: Congress, the Ford Administration, and the Battle Over Vietnam, 1975–76." *Diplomatic History* 24, no. 2 (2000): 265–93.

———. "Kissinger, Ford, and Congress: The Very Bitter End in Vietnam." *Pacific Historical Review* 71, no. 3 (2002): 439–73.

———. "The Politics and Culture of Nonrecognition: The Carter Administration and Vietnam." *Journal of American–East Asian Relations* 4, no. 4 (1995): 397–412.

Johnson, Haynes. *Sleepwalking through History: America in the Reagan Years*. New York: Anchor Books, 1991.

Kammen, Michael. *Mystic Chords of Memory: The Transformation of Tradition in American Culture*. New York: Knopf, 1991.

Kazin, Michael. "The Grass-Roots Right: New Histories of U.S. Conservatism in the Twentieth Century." *American Historical Review* 97, no. 1 (1992): 136–55.

Keating, Susan K. *Prisoners of Hope: Exploiting the POW/MIA Myth in America*. New York: Random House, 1994.

Keegan, John. *The First World War*. New York: Alfred A. Knopf, 1999.

Keenan, Barbara Mullen. *Every Effort: One Woman's Courageous Search for Her Missing Husband: A True Story*. New York: St. Martin's Press, 1986.

Kennedy, David M. *Freedom from Fear: The American People in Depression and War, 1929–1945*. New York: Oxford University Press, 1999.

Kerry, John, and Vietnam Veterans against the War. *The New Soldier*. New York: Macmillan, 1971.

Kimball, Jeffrey. *Nixon's Vietnam War*. Lawrence: University Press of Kansas, 1998.

———. "The Stab-in-the-Back Legend and the Vietnam War." *Armed Forces and Society* 14, no. 3 (1988): 433–58.

———. *The Vietnam War Files: Uncovering the Secret History of Nixon-Era Strategy*. Lawrence: University Press of Kansas, 2004.

Kinney, Katherine. *Friendly Fire: American Images of the Vietnam War*. New York: Oxford University Press, 2000.

Kintz, Linda. *Between Jesus and the Market: The Emotions That Matter in Right-Wing America*. Durham, N.C.: Duke University Press, 1997.

Klatch, Rebecca. *Women of the Far Right*. Philadelphia: Temple University Press, 1987.

Knapp, Michael G., and Constance Potter. "Here Rests in Honored Glory: World War I Graves Registration." *Prologue* 23, no. 2 (1991): 190–93.

Koch, Jeffrey. "The Perot Candidacy and Attitudes toward Government and Politics." *Political Research Quarterly* 51, no. 1 (1998): 141–53.

Koenigsamen, Janet L. "Mobilization of a Conscience Constituency: VIVA and the POW/MIA Movement." Ph.D. diss., Kent State University, 1987.

Kraak, Charles F. *Family Efforts on Behalf of United States Prisoners of War and Missing in Action in Southeast Asia*. Carlisle Barracks, Pa.: Army War College, 1975.

Krowl, Michelle A. "'In the Spirit of Fraternity': The United States Government and the Burial of Confederate Dead at Arlington National Cemetery, 1864–1914." *Virginia Magazine of History and Biography* 111, no. 2 (2003): 151–86.

Kwon, Heonik. *Ghosts of War in Vietnam*. New York: Cambridge University Press, 2008.

Laderman, Gary. *The Sacred Remains: American Attitudes toward Death, 1799–1883*. New Haven, Conn.: Yale University Press, 1996.

Laqueur, Thomas W. "Memory and Naming in the Great War." In *Commemorations: The Politics of National Identity*, edited by John R. Gillis, 150–67. Princeton, N.J.: Princeton University Press, 1994.

Lassiter, Matthew D. *The Silent Majority: Suburban Politics in the Sunbelt South*. Princeton, N.J.: Princeton University Press, 2006.

Le Naour, Jean-Yves. *The Living Unknown Soldier: A Story of Grief and the Great War*. Translated by Penny Allen. New York: Metropolitan Books, 2002.

Lembcke, Jerry. *The Spitting Image: Myth, Memory, and the Legacy of Vietnam*. New York: New York University Press, 1998.

Lesinski, Jeanne M. *MIAs: A Reference Handbook*. Santa Barbara, Calif.: ABC-CLIO, 1998.

Linenthal, Edward T. *Sacred Ground: Americans and Their Battlefields*. Rev. ed. Urbana: University of Illinois Press, 1993.

———. *The Unfinished Bombing: Oklahoma City in American Memory*. New York: Oxford University Press, 2001.

Logevall, Fredrik. "Bringing in the 'Other Side': New Scholarship on the Vietnam Wars." *Journal of Cold War Studies* 3, no. 3 (2001): 77–93.

———. *Choosing War: The Lost Chance for Peace and the Escalation of War in Vietnam*. Berkeley: University of California Press, 1999.

Long, Robert Emmet, ed. *Vietnam Ten Years After*. The Reference Shelf, vol. 58, no. 2. New York: H. W. Wilson Company, 1986.

Lunch, William M., and Peter W. Sperlich. "American Public Opinion and the War in Vietnam." *Western Political Quarterly* 32, no. 1 (1979): 21–44.

Malarney, Shaun Kingsley. "'The Fatherland Remembers Your Sacrifice': Commemorating War Dead in North Vietnam." In *The Country of Memory: Remaking the Past in Late Socialist Vietnam*, edited by Hue-Tam Ho Tai, 46–76. Berkeley: University of California Press, 2001.

Mann, James. *Rise of the Vulcans: The History of Bush's War Cabinet*. New York: Penguin Books, 2004.

Mann, Robert. *A Grand Delusion: America's Descent into Vietnam*. New York: Basic Books, 2001.

Martini, Edwin. *Invisible Enemies: The American War on Vietnam, 1975–2000*. Amherst: University of Massachusetts Press, 2007.

Marvin, Carolyn, and David Ingle. *Blood Sacrifice and the Nation: Totem Ritual and the American Flag*. New York: Oxford University Press, 1999.

Mather, Paul D. *M.I.A.: Accounting for the Missing in Southeast Asia*. Washington, D.C.: National Defense University Press, 1994.

McAlister, Melani. "A Cultural History of the War without End." *Journal of American History* 89, no. 2 (2002): 439–55.

———. *Epic Encounters: Culture, Media, and U.S. Interests in the Middle East, 1945–2000*. Berkeley: University of California Press, 2001.

McCain, John S. "The Code of Conduct and the Vietnam Prisoners of War." Washington, D.C.: National War College, 1974.

McCain, John, and Mark Salter. *Faith of My Fathers: A Family Memoir*. New York: Random House, 1999.

———. *Worth the Fighting For: A Memoir*. New York: Random House, 2002.

McCann, James, Ronald Rapoport, and Walter Stone, "Heeding the Call: An Assessment of Mobilization into H. Ross Perot's 1992 Presidential Campaign." *American Journal of Political Science* 43, no. 1 (1999): 1–28.

McConnell, Malcolm, and Theodore Schweitzer III. *Inside Hanoi's Secret Archives: Solving the MIA Mystery*. New York: Simon & Schuster, 1995.

McCormick, Thomas J. *America's Half-Century: United States Foreign Policy in the Cold War*. Baltimore: Johns Hopkins University Press, 1989.

McCubbin, Hamilton I., Barbara B. Dahl, Philip J. Metres Jr., Edna J. Hunter, and John A. Plag, eds. *Family Separation and Reunion: Families of Prisoners of War and Servicemen Missing in Action*. San Diego: Naval Health Research Center, 1977.

McCubbin, Hamilton I., Edna J. Hunter, and Barbara B. Dahl. "Residuals of War: Families of Prisoners of War and Servicemen Missing in Action." *Journal of Social Issues* 31, no. 4 (1975): 95–109.

McCubbin, Hamilton I., Edna J. Hunter, and Philip J. Metres Jr. "Adaptation of the Family to the PW/MIA Experience: An Overview." In *Family Separation and Reunion: Families of Prisoners of War and Servicemen Missing in Action*, edited by Hamilton I. McCubbin et al., 21–47. San Diego: Naval Health Research Center, 1977.

McEnaney, Laura. "He-Men and Christian Mothers: The America First Movement and the Gendered Meanings of Patriotism and Isolationism." *Diplomatic History* 18, no. 1 (1994): 47–57.

McGirr, Lisa. "Piety and Property: Conservatism and Right-Wing Movements in the Twentieth Century." In *Perspectives on Modern America: Making Sense of the Twentieth Century*, edited by Harvard Sitkoff, 33–54. New York: Oxford University Press, 2001.

———. *Suburban Warriors: The Origins of the New American Right*. Princeton, N.J.: Princeton University Press, 2001.

McMahon, Robert J. "Contested Memory: The Vietnam War and American Society, 1975–2001." *Diplomatic History* 26, no. 2 (2002): 159–84.

———. *The Limits of Empire: The United States and Southeast Asia Since World War II*. New York: Columbia University Press, 1999.

Menétrey-Monchau, Cécile. *American-Vietnamese Relations in the Wake of War: Diplomacy after the Capture of Saigon*. Jefferson, N.C.: McFarland, 2006.

Metres, Philip J. Jr., Hamilton I. McCubbin, and Edna J. Hunter. "Families of Returned Prisoners of War: Some Impressions on Their Initial Reintegration." In *Family Separation and Reunion: Families of Prisoners of War and Servicemen Missing in Action*, edited by Hamilton I. McCubbin et al., 147–55. San Diego: Naval Health Research Center, 1977.

Michalowski, Raymond, and Jill Dubisch. *Run for the Wall: Remembering Vietnam on a Motorcycle Pilgrimage*. New Brunswick, N.J.: Rutgers University Press, 2001.

Moreau, Donna. *Waiting Wives: The Story of Schilling Manor, Home Front to the Vietnam War*. New York: Atria Books, 2005.

Morris, Richard, and Peter Ehrenhaus, eds. *Cultural Legacies of Vietnam: Uses of the Past in the Present*. Norwood, N.J.: Ablex, 1990.

Moser, Richard R. *The New Winter Soldier: GI and Veteran Dissent During the Vietnam Era*. New Brunswick, N.J.: Rutgers University Press, 1996.

Mosse, George. *Fallen Soldiers: Reshaping the Memory of the World Wars*. New York: Oxford University Press, 1990.

Neep, Wesley A. "Procedures Used by the U.S. Army to Ensure Proper Identification of the Vietnam War Dead and Their Acceptance by the Next-of-Kin." In *Personal Identification in Mass Disasters*, edited by T. D. Stewart, 5–9. Washington, D.C.: National Museum of Natural History, 1970.

Neff, John. *Honoring the Civil War Dead: Commemoration and the Problem of Reconciliation*. Lawrence: University Press of Kansas, 2005.

Nenninger, Timothy K. "United States Prisoners of War and the Red Army: Myths and Realities." *Journal of Military History* 66, no. 3 (2002): 761–81.

Neu, Charles E., ed. *After Vietnam: Legacies of a Lost War*. Baltimore: Johns Hopkins University Press, 2000.

Nickerson, Michelle. "Moral Mothers and Goldwater Girls." In *The Conservative Sixties*, edited by David Farber and Jeff Roche, 51–62. New York: Peter Lang Publishing, 2003.

Nicosia, Gerald. *Home to War: A History of the Vietnam Veterans' Movement*. New York: Crown Publishers, 2001.

Noonan, Peggy. *What I Saw at the Revolution: A Political Life in the Reagan Era*. New York: Random House, 1990.

Nudelman, Franny. *John Brown's Body: Slavery, Violence, & the Culture of War*. Chapel Hill: University of North Carolina Press, 2004.

O'Daniel, Larry. *Missing in Action: Trails of Deceit*. New Rochelle, N.Y.: Arlington House, 1979.

O'Neill, John E., and Jerome L. Corsi. *Unfit for Command: Swift Boat Veterans Speak Out against John Kerry*. Washington, D.C.: Regnery Publishing, 2004.

Paterson, Thomas G. "Historical Memory and Illusive Victories: Vietnam and Central America." *Diplomatic History* 12, no. 1 (1998): 1–18.

Patterson, James T. *Grand Expectations: The United States, 1945–1974*. New York: Oxford University Press, 1996.

———. *Restless Giant: The United States From Watergate to Bush v. Gore*. New York: Oxford University Press, 2005.

Pelton, Robert W. *Dead or Alive: Questions & Answers Regarding American POWs and MIAs*. Miami: J. Flores Publications, 1993.

Perlstein, Rick. *Nixonland: The Rise of a President and the Fracturing of America*. New York: Scribner, 2008.

Philpot, Tom. *Glory Denied: The Saga of Jim Thompson, America's Longest-Held Prisoner of War*. New York: W. W. Norton, 2001.

Piehler, G. Kurt. *Remembering War the American Way*. Washington, D.C.: Smithsonian Institution Press, 1995.

Porter, Gareth. *A Peace Denied: The United States, Vietnam, and the Paris Agreement*. Bloomington: Indiana University Press, 1975.

Posner, Gerald. *Citizen Perot: His Life & Times*. New York: Random House, 1996.

Quigley, Christine. *The Corpse: A History*. Jefferson, N.C.: McFarland & Company, 1996.

Randolph, Stephen P. *Powerful and Brutal Weapons: Nixon, Kissinger, and the Easter Offensive*. Cambridge: Harvard University Press, 2007.

Reagan, Ronald. *The Reagan Diaries*. New York: HarperCollins, 2007.

———. "Introduction." In *We Came Home*, edited by Barbara Powers Wyatt. Toluca Lake, Calif.: P.O.W. Publications, 1977.

Redfield, Marc. "Imagi-nation: The Imagined Community and the Aesthetics of Mourning." *Diacritics* 94, no. 4 (1999): 58–83.

Reed, David E. W. "U.S.-Vietnam Relations: The Domestic Context of Normalization." Ph.D. diss., University of South Carolina, 1996.

Reeves, Richard. *President Nixon: Alone in the White House*. New York: Simon & Schuster, 2001.

———. *President Reagan: The Triumph of Imagination*. New York: Simon & Schuster, 2005.

———. *The Reagan Detour*. New York: Simon & Schuster, 1985.

Ribuffo, Leo. "God and Contemporary Politics." *Journal of American History* 79, no. 4 (1993): 1515–33.

———. "Why Is There So Much Conservatism in the United States and Why Do So Few Historians Know Anything about It?" *American Historical Review* 99, no. 2 (1994): 438–49.

Roberts, Mary Louise. *Civilization without Sexes: Reconstructing Gender in Postwar France, 1917–1927*. Chicago: University of Chicago Press, 1994.

Robinson, Melissa B., and Maureen Dunn. *The Search for Canasta 404: Love, Loss, and the POW/MIA Movement*. Boston: Northeastern University Press, 2006.

Rochester, Stuart I., and Frederick Kiley. *Honor Bound: American Prisoners of War in Southeast Asia, 1961–1973*. Annapolis, Md.: Naval Institute Press, 1999.

Roeder, George H. Jr. *The Censored War: American Visual Experience during World War Two*. New Haven, Conn.: Yale University Press, 1993.

Rogin, Michael. "Healing the Vietnam Wound." *American Quarterly* 53, no. 1 (September 1999): 702–8.

———. "'Make My Day!': Spectacle as Amnesia in Imperial Politics." *Representations* no. 29 (1990): 99–123.

———. *Ronald Reagan, The Movie and Other Episodes in Political Demonology*. Berkeley: University of California Press, 1987.

Rowe, John Carlos, and Rick Berg. *The Vietnam War and American Culture*. New York: Columbia University Press, 1991.

Ryan, Maureen. "Pentagon Princesses and Wayward Sisters: Vietnam POW Wives in American Literature." *War, Literature and the Arts* 10, no. 2 (1998): 132–64.

Savage, Kirk. *Standing Soldiers, Kneeling Slaves: Race, War, and Monument in Nineteenth-Century America*. Princeton, N.J.: Princeton University Press, 1997.

Schaller, Michael. *Reckoning with Reagan: America and Its President in the 1980s*. New York: Oxford University Press, 1992.

———. *Right Turn: American Life in the Reagan-Bush Era; 1980–1992*. New York: Oxford University Press, 2007.

Schell, Jonathan. *The Military Half: An Account of Destruction in Quang Ngai and Quang Tin*. New York: Knopf, 1968.

———. *The Time of Illusion*. New York: Alfred A. Knopf, 1976.

Schneider, Gregory L. *Cadres for Conservatism: Young Americans for Freedom and the Rise of the Contemporary Right*. New York: New York University Press, 1999.

Schoenwald, Jonathan M. *A Time for Choosing: The Rise of Modern American Conservatism*. New York: Oxford University Press, 2003.

Schrecker, Ellen. *Many Are the Crimes: McCarthyism in America*. Princeton, N.J.: Princeton University Press, 1999.

Schudson, Michael. *Watergate in American Memory: How We Remember, Forget, and Reconstruct the Past*. New York: Basic Books, 1992.

Schulman, Bruce J. *The Seventies: The Great Shift in American Culture, Society, and Politics*. New York: Free Press, 2001.

Schulzinger, Robert D. *A Time for War: The United States And Vietnam, 1941–1975*. New York: Oxford University Press, 1997.

———. *A Time for Peace: The Legacy of the Vietnam War*. New York: Oxford University Press, 2006.

Searle, William J., ed. *Search and Clear: Critical Responses to Selected Literature and Films of the Vietnam War*. Bowling Green, Ohio: Bowling Green State University Popular Press, 1988.

Shafer, D. Michael, ed. *The Legacy: The Vietnam War in the American Imagination*. Boston: Beacon Press, 1990.

Sherman, Daniel. *The Construction of Memory in Interwar France*. Chicago: University of Chicago Press, 1999.

Sherry, Michael S. "Death, Mourning, and Memorial Culture." In *Columbia History of Post–World War II America*, edited by Mark C. Carnes, 155–77. New York: Columbia University Press, 2007.

———. *In the Shadow of War: The United States since the 1930's*. New Haven, Conn.: Yale University Press, 1995.

Shomon, Joseph James. *Crosses in the Wind*. New York: Stratford House, 1947.

Sledge, Michael. *Soldier Dead: How We Recover, Identify, Bury, and Honor Our Military Fallen*. New York: Columbia University Press, 2005.

Slotkin, Richard. *Gunfighter Nation: The Myth of the Frontier in Twentieth-Century America*. New York: Atheneum, 1992.

———. *Regeneration through Violence: The Mythology of the American Frontier, 1600–1860*. Middletown, Conn.: Wesleyan University Press, 1973.

Smith, George E. *P.O.W.: Two Years with the Vietcong*. Berkeley, Calif.: Ramparts Press, 1971.

Stahl, Pamela M., Maj. "The New Law on Department of Defense Personnel Missing as a Result of Hostile Action." *Military Law Review* 152 (Spring 1996): 75–177.

Steere, Edward. "Genesis of American Graves Registration, 1861–1870." *Military Affairs* 12, no. 3 (1948): 149–61.

Stern, Kenneth S. *A Force upon the Plain: The American Militia Movement and the Politics of Hate*. New York: Simon & Schuster, 1996.

Stern, Lewis M. *Imprisoned or Missing in Vietnam: Policies of the Vietnamese Government Concerning Captured and Unaccounted for United States Soldiers, 1969–1994*. Jefferson, N.C.: McFarland & Company, 1995.

Stockdale, James, and Sybil Stockdale. *In Love and War: The Story of a Family's Ordeal and Sacrifice during the Vietnam Years*. New York: Bantam, 1985.

Sturken, Marita. *Tangled Memories: The Vietnam War, The AIDS Epidemic, and the Politics of Remembering*. Berkeley: University of California Press, 1997.

Sutton, David L. "The Fullest Possible Accounting: The Myth of American POW/MIAs in Southeast Asia, 1973–1993." Ph.D. diss., University of Georgia, 1994.

Swerdlow, Amy. *Women Strike for Peace: Traditional Motherhood and Radical Politics in the 1960s*. Chicago: University of Chicago Press, 1993.

Tai, Hue-Tam Ho, ed. *The Country of Memory: Remaking the Past in Late Socialist Vietnam*. Berkeley: University of California Press, 2001.

Thelen, David, ed. *Memory and American History*. Bloomington: Indiana University Press, 1990.

Thompson, Wayne. *To Hanoi and Back: The United States Air Force and North Vietnam, 1966–1973*. Washington, D.C.: Smithsonian Institution Press, 2000.

Timberg, Robert. *The Nightingale's Song*. New York: Simon & Schuster, 1995.

Tumarkin, Nina. *The Living and the Dead: The Rise and Fall of the Cult of World War II in Russia*. New York: Basic Books, 1994.

Turner, Fred. *Echoes of Combat: The Vietnam War in American Memory*. New York: Anchor Books, 1996.

Vance, Jonathan F., ed. *Encyclopedia of Prisoners of War and Internment*. Santa Barbara, Calif.: ABC-CLIO, 2000.

Verdery, Katherine. *The Political Lives of Dead Bodies: Reburial and Postsocialist Change*. New York: Columbia University Press, 1999.

Viguerie, Richard A. *The New Right: We're Ready to Lead*. Falls Church, Va.: Viguerie Company, 1980.

Webster, Donovan. *Aftermath: The Remnants of War*. New York: Pantheon Books, 1996.

Westbrook, Robert B. "Fighting for the American Family: Private Interests and Political Obligation in World War II." In *The Power of Culture*, edited by Richard Wightman Fox and T. J. Jackson Lears, 195–222. Chicago: University of Chicago Press, 1993.

Wills, Garry. *Lincoln at Gettysburg: The Words That Remade America*. New York: Simon & Schuster, 1992.

———. *Reagan's America: Innocents at Home*. Rev. ed. New York: Penguin Books, 2000.

Winter, Jay. *Remembering War: The Great War between Memory and History in the Twentieth Century*. New Haven, Conn.: Yale University Press, 2006.

———. *Sites of Memory, Sites of Mourning: The Great War in European Cultural History*. New York: Cambridge University Press, 1995.

Winter, Jay, and Emmanuel Sivan. "Setting the Framework." In *War and Remembrance in the Twentieth Century*, edited by Jay Winter and Emmanuel Sivan, 6–39. New York: Cambridge University Press, 1999.

———. *War and Remembrance in the Twentieth Century*. New York: Cambridge University Press, 1999.

Wyatt, Barbara Powers, ed. *We Came Home*. Toluca Lake, Calif.: P.O.W. Publications, 1977.

Young, Marilyn B. *The Vietnam Wars, 1945–1990*. New York: HarperPerennial, 1991.

Zaretsky, Natasha. *No Direction Home: The American Family and the Fear of National Decline, 1968–1980*. Chapel Hill: University of North Carolina Press, 2007.

Zelizer, Barbie. "Reading the Past against the Grain: The Shape of Memory Studies." *Critical Studies in Mass Communication* 12, no. 2 (1995): 214–39.

Zinoman, Peter. *The Colonial Bastille: A History of Imprisonment in Vietnam, 1862–1940*. Berkeley: University of California Press, 2001.

ACKNOWLEDGMENTS

As this is my first book, it has been a lifetime in the making. Over my thirty-five years I have accumulated many debts, a few of which I gratefully acknowledge here. My most significant intellectual debts are owed to Michael Sherry, whose peerless work inspired this unorthodox study. Since I embarked on this project, he has read and commented on it in various forms numerous times, improving each iteration with incisive commentary and advice.

Others read this work as it progressed, some more than once, honing my thinking and writing along the way. Laura Hein and Nancy MacLean strengthened my analysis considerably in its early phases. I had the good fortune to run into Marilyn Young at the National Archives as a graduate student, and she has helped me in a multitude of ways ever since. Dirk Bönker and Jennifer Mittelstadt offered advice on revised chapters and provided encouragement. Robert McMahon and Paul Kramer read the revised manuscript and offered essential advice regarding final revisions, as did my editor Chuck Grench. Mark Bradley deserves a special word of thanks. Other than me, no one has devoted as much time and thought to this work, and it is a far better book thanks to his help.

Others contributed to this volume in more indirect ways. George Chauncey taught me my first vital lessons in how to be a historian. Alex Owen's seminar on women's and gender history taught me more than any course I have ever taken. Their influence informs much of what is here. Jim Merrell taught me how to write, though I fall far short of his lofty standard. Seth Jacobs gave advice whenever I asked. Ted Engelman went to great lengths to help track down illustrations. And Matthew Booker was a delight to work with during our years together in Harrelson 128, offering advice when I sought it and sustaining me with his friendship, moral support, and bottomless cups of black coffee. Jonathan Ocko made sure I had time and resources to devote to this book during my years at North Carolina State University.

Many of my historical subjects shared their time, insights, and materials with me. Ann Mills Griffiths, Paul Mather, Tom Holland, and Frank Sieverts sat for extended interviews and supplied me with valuable sources. Others too numerous to name deepened my understanding through phone calls, e-mail, and interviews. While their passion for the POW/MIA issue makes it likely that most of those who have helped me in this regard will disagree with much of my analysis, I am grateful to all of them for their assistance.

Archivists and librarians contributed mightily to my progress. Charles "Ed" Schamel and Bill Davis at the Center for Legislative Archives at the National Archives deserve special thanks for helping me navigate the records of the Senate Select Committee on POW/MIA Affairs and the House Select Committee on Missing Persons in Southeast Asia. Thanks also to Geir Gunderson of the Ford Presidential Library and Lisa Jones at the Reagan Presidential Library.

My research was funded by various sources. Initial support came from Northwestern University in the form of a Graduate Research Grant and a Dissertation Year Fellowship. The Gerald R. Ford Foundation paid for my research at the Ford Library. A Dirksen Congressional Center Congressional Research Award supported extended research at the Center for Legislative Archives. A fellowship at the Alice Berline Kaplan Center for the Humanities afforded me time to write. And a Scholarly Project Award through the College of Humanities and Social Sciences at North Carolina State funded research at the Reagan Library.

I am grateful to friends and family who helped me in so many ways. Brett Gadsden, Elizabeth Prevost, Amy Whipple, Christopher Tassava, and Erik Gellman shared in graduate school's triumphs and tragedies. John Sharp, Christie Sharp, and John Freymann provided food and shelter during my many trips to Washington, stretching my research dollars and keeping me company. Heather Krajewski and Robb Moore offered a welcomed stopover as I traveled back and forth, along with my most treasured friendship. Michele Karron, Barbara and David Karron, Geoffrey Collins, and Erikson Albrecht opened their homes to me as I conducted research at the Reagan Library, and Kirsten Albrecht and Marc Evans generously lent me their car to negotiate Los Angeles's freeways. Anne Sherman and Jeff Laufenberg, Eva Lu Bonn, Jiyeon Jeon, Nick Marsh, Natasha Trethewey, Kim and Nick Hammer, Blair Kelley, Thomas Ort, and others already mentioned made up a wonderful community of friends. Melissa Lehman and Elyse Cepull provided superb childcare, freeing my time to write. My sister, Amber, and my parents, Randy and Laura McCoy, deserve much of the credit for helping me get from there to here, as does the family I acquired along the way, particularly John and Pam Sharp. My children, Ellis and Finley, arrived as I wrote this book, bringing me great joy and giving me excellent reasons to finish it. Finally, I dedicate this work to my beautiful wife and best friend, Julie Ann. More than anything else, her love and support made this work and this life possible.

Abbott, Joan, 74

Abrams, Creighton, 57

Accounting effort for POWs/MIAs: and
Reagan, 2–3, 219–20, 232, 236, 237,
240, 243, 244, 248, 252–53, 254; and
George H. W. Bush, 2–3, 243, 261–62,
289; and Clinton, 3, 250, 283, 284,
285–89, 290; and POW/MIA families,
4, 5, 64, 93, 97–98, 140, 146, 148–49,
155, 157, 163, 166, 170, 171–72, 173,
176, 182, 183, 206, 215, 274, 287–88;
as reminder of loss, 5–6, 10, 117, 243;
challenges to legitimacy of, 6, 93–94,
97–98, 212, 213, 243, 247, 289–90;
and body recovery process, 8, 244,
246–47, 266; and U.S.-Vietnam relations, 10, 174, 183, 184–88, 189, 195,
198, 200, 251–52, 261, 265–66, 267,
274, 289–90, 351–52 (n. 193); and lists
of POWs, 37, 38, 91–99, 333 (n. 172);
and Shields, 83–84, 85, 92, 95, 332–33
(n. 170), 333 (n. 183); and Joint Casualty Resolution Center, 84–87; and
returned POWs' testimony, 85, 98–99;
and repatriation of remains, 86–87,
157, 185–86, 189, 190, 200, 220, 240–
41, 244–46, 252, 253, 258–59, 260,
261, 262, 274, 284, 285, 287, 288–89,
355 (n. 55), 356 (n. 103), 378 (n. 55),
383 (n. 143); and Paris Agreement violations, 87–91; and deaths in captivity,

94, 95, 97, 333 (n. 171); and discrepancy cases, 94, 179, 220, 257, 258, 274,
332 (n. 169); and unanticipated returnees, 94–95; and status determination process, 95, 140–46, 148; elastic
standard of, 139–40, 218; and Helms,
156; and Presidential MIA/POW Task
Force proposal, 163; and House Select
Committee on Missing Persons in
Southeast Asia, 165–71, 173, 175, 186,
211, 244, 255; and Veterans of Foreign
Wars, 173; and Woodcock Commission, 184–87; and Inter-Agency Group
on POW/MIA Affairs, 209; and Vessey, 257–58; casualties from, 289; and
George W. Bush, 292; institutionaliza-
tion of, 302–3

Ad Hoc Committee for POWs and MIAs,
51–54

Afghanistan, 206, 207, 304, 305

African Americans, 41, 119, 213. *See also*
Racial minorities

Agency for International Development,
267, 381 (n. 105)

Agnew, Spiro, 32, 39, 40, 50, 55

Agosto-Santos, Jose, 21

Albright, Scott, 97, 141, 149, 150–51, 342
(n. 23), 344 (n. 57), 345 (n. 63)

Alfond, Dolores, 287–88

Allen, Richard, 211, 216–17, 222, 223,
226, 234

Allred, Juanita, 126–27
Allred, Robert E., 127
Alvarez, Everett, 75
Alvarez, Tangee, 75
American Battle Monuments Commission, 120, 340 (n. 139)
American Defense Institute, 228
American Legion, 153, 168, 286
American Legion (magazine), 211, 214
Anderson, Benedict, 105
Antiwar activists: POW/MIA activism of, 4, 6, 15–16, 20–21, 23–24, 37, 56, 61; implication in victimization of POWs/MIAs, 5, 6, 7, 46; release of POWs to, 13, 15, 21, 22–23, 28, 31–32, 55; POWs as, 15, 28, 68, 77, 297, 389 (n. 30); inspection of prison camps, 22, 70; and Go Public campaign, 35; and POW/MIA families, 46, 47, 194; and challenges to POW testimony, 77; POWs' condemnation of, 79; Kerry as, 271, 296
Appeal for International Justice rally, 38–39, 56, 189
Appy, Christian, 43, 151, 382 (n. 126)
Arledge, Roone, 202
Arlington National Cemetery: Civil War Tomb of the Unknowns, 113; and Robert E. Lee, 114; Confederate Memorial, 115, 116; Tomb of the Unknown Soldier, 102, 122, 123, 237, 238; proposed memorial for Vietnam MIAs, 167, 173
Armitage, Richard, 220, 226, 234, 243, 263
Arnett, Peter, 71
Aspin, Les, 88, 137, 331 (n. 146), 341 (n. 1)
Asselin, Pierre, 89, 331 (n. 148)
Atkins, Chet, 261
Austria, 119–20, 337 (n. 73)
Ayers, William, 301

Bacevich, Andrew, 191, 192
Bailey, Jack, 231, 269, 270
Baker, James, 225, 261, 264, 265–66, 274
Baldwin, Hanson, 131

Barnes, Scott, 278
Barrows, Christine, 171
Bates, Carol, 58, 151, 183, 185, 193, 230, 323 (n. 265), 345 (n. 74)
Bayh, Birch, 212–13
Beattie, Keith, 155–56, 237, 248, 335 (n. 22), 346 (n. 91), 381 (n. 112)
Beers, Rand, 302
Behan, Katie, 115
Bennett, Charles, 54
Bennett, Harold, 18
Berger, Sandy, 386 (n. 183)
Berman, Larry, 88, 331 (n. 144)
Berrigan, Daniel, 21
Berrigan, Philip, 81
Biess, Frank, 159
Black, Jon, 21, 28
Black Hawk Down (film), 303
Blassie, Michael, 238, 239
Blight, David, 171
Bliss, Ron, 330 (n. 120), 360 (n. 127)
Borling, Lauren, 74
Borman, Frank, 48, 319 (n. 195)
Bosiljevac, Kay, 146, 148, 150, 152
Brace, Ernest, 75
Branch, Taylor, 53
Brigham, Robert, 48, 319 (n. 197), 322 (n. 255)
Brinkley, David, 70
Britain, and war dead, 102, 105–6, 118, 119, 120, 121, 122
Brooks, George, 150, 152, 170
Brooks, Gladys, 135, 168, 170, 205
Brown, Eva, 145
Brown, Frederick, 186
Brown, Hank, 270, 271, 275, 276
Brown, Harold, 188
Brown, Jim, 71
Brudno, Edward, 75
Brzezinski, Zbigniew, 184–88, 190, 197, 355 (n. 60)
Buckley, William F., 139
Bull, Steve, 35
Bunge, Sam, 66
Burch, J. Thomas, 293, 388 (n. 9)
Burer, Arthur, 72

Burer, Nancy, 72

Burgess, David, 345 (n. 68)

Bush, George H. W.: and accounting for POWs/MIAs, 2–3, 244, 252; and POW/MIA families, 2, 232, 233, 236, 243, 262, 279–81; and memory of Vietnam War, 8, 261, 262, 267, 273, 275; and Thorsness, 80; and Negroponte, 207; and Pakse excavation, 243; and U.S.-Vietnam relations, 252, 253, 257, 260, 261, 262, 265–66, 276, 289; and Perot Commission, 255, 256; and conservative movement, 263–64, 274, 280; and election of 1992, 276–77, 278, 279; and Inter-Agency Group on POW/MIA Affairs, 361 (n. 147); and POW/MIA records, 384 (n. 167)

Bush, George W.: and avoidance of Vietnam War service, 80, 295; and Negroponte, 207; and U.S.-Vietnam relations, 289, 291–92; and election of 2000, 292–93, 294, 388 (nn. 9, 11); and election of 2004, 295, 388 (n. 11); and Iraq War, 303–4

Butler, Phil, 301, 302

Butterfield, Alexander, 35

Bynum, Caroline Walker, 117, 248

Cambodia, 190–91, 207, 259, 261, 264–65, 267, 274, 355 (n. 56), 377–78 (n. 49)

Cannon, James, 254

Cannon, Lou, 217

Capen, Dick, 30

Captivity narratives: tradition of, 61, 77, 81, 328 (n. 88), 329 (n. 107); POW experience as captivity narrative, 77–80, 85, 93

Carlucci, Frank, 233, 257, 369 (n. 106)

Carpenter, Joe, 28

Carroll, James, 291, 292

Carson, Johnny, 222

Carter, Hodding, 202

Carter, Jimmy: and House Select Committee on Missing Persons in Southeast Asia, 143, 165, 172, 184; and

election of 1976, 177, 181–82; and POW/MIA families, 180, 181, 182–83, 184, 188, 190, 200, 206, 213; and crisis of confidence, 181, 182; and U.S.-Vietnam relations, 182, 184–87, 189, 190–91; and personal history with MIA status, 183; and Woodcock Commission, 184–86; and normalization with China, 190; and human rights, 199; and repatriation of remains, 200, 220, 358 (n. 103); and Iran hostage crisis, 202–3; and Negroponte, 207; and Griffiths, 211–12; and election of 1980, 212–13; and Beattie, 346 (n. 91)

Casanova, Gino, 256

Center for Prisoner of War Studies, 26, 74

Central Identification Laboratory in Hawaii, 189, 220, 240–43

Chafee, John, 287

Chanda, Nayan, 355 (n. 60)

Chapin, Dwight, 33, 34

Charney, Michael, 241–42

Cheney, Dick, 80, 232, 274, 275

Cherry, Fred, 41

Chicago Tribune, 16, 35, 37, 117, 360 (n. 134)

Childress, Richard, 225–26, 229, 232–34, 237–39, 255, 257, 258, 263, 279

China, relations with Vietnam, 190, 198, 259, 355 (n. 60), 377 (n. 49)

Christian church, and death, 104–5, 111, 117

Christopher, Warren, 289

Church, Frank, 212–13

Civil War: unrecovered/unidentified war dead from, 2, 108–9, 113, 334 (n. 2), 336 (n. 33); and relationship of war dead with nation-state, 8, 103; recovery of war dead in, 101, 108, 109–12, 113, 116–17, 120, 125; and South's memorialization of war dead, 103, 113–18; and embalming, 107, 110; and sectional reconciliation, 115; World War I memorials compared to, 118, 337 (n. 75)

Clark, Mark, 132

Clark, Wesley, 302

Clark, William, 225–26, 233

Clarke, Douglas, 95, 179, 345 (n. 68)

Clecak, Peter, 160

Clements, William, 99, 101, 102–3, 134–35, 334 (n. 1)

Clifford, Clark, 28, 54

Clinton, Bill: and accounting for POWs/MIAs, 3, 250, 283, 284, 285–89, 290; and avoidance of Vietnam War service, 80, 283, 290; and Negroponte, 207; and Inter-Agency Group on POW/MIA Affairs, 208; and POW/MIA families, 232, 236, 250, 291; visit to Vietnam, 250, 252; and U.S.-Vietnam relations, 252, 253, 257, 283–84, 285, 289, 291–92; and election of 1992, 276, 277, 279, 283; and election of 1996, 291; and Aspin, 341 (n. 1); and POW/MIA records, 384 (n. 167)

Coalition for Decency, 79

Cohen, William, 289

Cold War: risks of, 6; commitment to, 7; end of, 8; POW/MIA wives' support for, 29, 142; POWs/MIAs as icons of, 43–44; and World War II war dead, 128; and non-repatriation of Korean War POWs, 131, 340 (n. 135); intensification of, 140, 190–91; and U.S.-China relations, 190; and U.S.-Vietnam relations, 251–52, 264

Cole, Ken, 162

Cole, Paul, 129

College Republican National Committee, 231

Collins, J. Quincy, 80

Collins, Mrs. T. E., III, 48–49

Colson, Charles, 53, 295–96

Committee of Liaison with Families of Servicemen Detained in North Vietnam (COLIAFAM), 38, 39, 46, 55, 79, 318 (n. 183)

Commonweal (magazine), 139

Confederated Southern Memorial Association, 115

Congressional Medal of Honor, 42

Conservative movement: and Reagan, 7, 9, 29, 140, 174, 176, 212–13, 227, 263–64; resurgence of, 7, 9; and outrage over Vietnam War, 8, 140, 181, 191–92; and POW/MIA wives, 26, 28–29; and women's political mobilization, 26; and support for Vietnam War, 58; and returning veterans, 70–71; and POWs as candidates, 80; and Nixon, 140; and POW/MIA activism, 160, 181, 192–93; and distrust of government, 177, 192; and culture of appeasement, 191; and covert operations, 224–25; and George H. W. Bush, 264, 274, 280. See also Neoconservatives; Republican Party

Coppin, Gloria, 57–59, 146, 151, 323 (n. 265)

Corbitt, Phyllis, 169

Cordova, Eleanor, 154

Cormier, Eileen, 45, 74

Cotton, Norris, 89, 164

Cox, Archibald, 82

Crafts, Charlie, 21

Cullum, George, 110

Currall, Mary, 241

Curtin, Andrew, 110–11

Curtis, Carl, 58, 323 (n. 264)

Danielson, George, 201

Daschle, Tom, 80, 270, 271, 276, 382 (n. 122)

Daughters of the Confederacy, 115–16

Davis, Rennie, 28, 31–32, 37

Day, George "Bud," 42, 328 (n. 94)

Dean, John, 82

Death: of POWs/MIAs in captivity, 94, 95, 97, 333 (n. 171); presumptive findings of, 101, 102, 124–26, 131–32, 135, 140–46, 148, 150, 179–80, 189, 335 (n. 10); democracy of, 105, 112–13, 120; and submission to state, 156. See also War dead

Defense Intelligence Agency: and lists of POWs, 37, 90, 92, 332 (n. 163), 333 (nn. 171, 172); and Son Tay prison raid, 49; and Tran Vien Loc, 199, 201, 202, 206; and Inter-Agency Group on POW/MIA Affairs, 207, 209, 221; and MIA statistics, 209–11; staffing of, 220; and false POW/MIA information, 227–29

Defense Prisoner of War/Missing in Action Office (DPMO), 285, 302

Dellinger, David, 21, 31–32, 37, 38

Democratic National Convention (1972), 55

Democratic Party, 174, 177, 181–82, 257

Democratic Republic of Vietnam (DRV): use of POWs to pressure U.S. policymakers, 18–19, 21, 54, 56, 322 (n. 255); and release of POWs, 21, 31, 32; lists of POWs, 37, 38, 50, 94, 95, 98; and POW/MIA families, 34, 38, 40; and Joint Casualty Resolution Center, 86; and return of MIA remains, 86–87, 165; secret pledge for reconstruction of, 89–91, 164; and deaths in captivity, 97. *See also* Socialist Republic of Vietnam (SRV); U.S.-Vietnam relations; Vietnam; Vietnamese communists

Deng Xiaoping, 190, 355 (n. 60)

Dent, Harry, 33, 80

Denton, Jeremiah, 67, 68–69, 77, 79, 80, 213, 329 (n. 107)

Desperate Journey (film), 363 (n. 6)

DeWeldon, Felix, 128

Dirksen, Everett, 27

Diwan, Mushtaq Ahmed, 225

Dodge, Ron, 83, 94, 203, 220, 244, 330 (n. 120)

Dole, Bob, 38–39, 52, 53, 56–57, 88, 189, 291

Dole, Elizabeth, 232, 369 (n. 95)

Donahue, Jeff, 247, 263, 279

Dornan, Robert, 58, 197, 205, 356 (n. 83)

Dos Passos, John, 123

Douglass, Frederick, 115

Doumer, Paul, 121

Dowd, Maureen, 294

Downs, Frederick, Jr., 260–61

Draft evaders, 7, 138, 154–57, 160, 184

Dramesi, John, 301

Dudley, Jane, 40–41

Dunlop, Samuel, 373 (n. 165)

Dunn, Maureen, 154–55

Eagleburger, Lawrence, 236, 264, 275, 383 (n. 147)

Eastwood, Clint, 221–22, 223

Eberle, Bruce, 231

Edelman, Marian Wright, 184

Edwards, J. E., 116–17

Ehrlichman, John, 82

Eisenhower, Dwight, 132

Eisenstaedt, Alfred, 71–72

Eller Boyd, Cheryl, 154, 346 (n. 82)

Embargo Act, 106

Engelhardt, Tom, 35, 46, 76

Evangelicals, 213, 292

Evans, Daniel, 139

Evans, Maerose, 145, 148, 150

Evers, Charles, 81

Evert, Dan, 250

Evert, David, 250

Evert, Lawrence, 250, 252

Fairchild Hiller, 34

Families for Immediate Release, 51, 52, 53, 318 (n. 183)

Families of POWs/MIAs: lack of consensus among, 6, 51–54, 141–42, 143–46, 149–50; and military values, 8; and children, 26, 41, 312 (n. 57); and Nixon, 15, 30, 52–53, 97–98, 138, 180, 213; and Reagan, 29, 176, 179–81, 182, 193, 211–13, 215–20, 227, 230–34, 236–37, 239, 243, 248–49, 259–60, 389 (n. 50); official briefings for, 34, 53–54; and Appeal for International Justice, 38; and prisoner mail, 38; pay and allowances of, 42, 143–46; moral authority of, 43–44; war-weariness of, 46, 48–49, 54; and Vietnamization, 48, 50, 52; and troop withdrawals, 51–52, 54; and MIA families' separate concerns, 53, 91–92; and POW repatriation, 74, 75; and Pentagon's misleading information, 91–93; distrust of Vietnamese communists, 97–98, 193, 252; and presumptive findings of death, 102–3, 140, 141, 143–46, 148; and Korean War, 133–34; distrust of government officials, 136, 140; and accounting effort for POWs/MIAs, 140, 146, 148, 149; wives' interests contrasted with parents and siblings, 143–45; and VIVA, 146, 149, 151, 344 (n. 75); and memory of Vietnam War, 149, 152, 153, 154, 171, 193; and House Select Committee on Missing Persons in Southeast Asia, 169; Carter's identification with, 183; and Iran hostage families, 203, 205; and McCain, 293; and overlap between dissident groups, 321 (n. 240). *See also* National League of Families of American Prisoners and Missing in Southeast Asia

Families of war dead: and recovery and memorialization, 107, 110, 116, 117–18, 119, 120; and lack of remains, 126–27

Fanning, Kathryn, 241, 246

Fanning, Louis, 168, 349 (n. 151)

Farber, David, 43, 202

Faust, Drew Gilpin, 108, 112, 336 (n. 53)

Federalists, 106

FitzGerald, Frances, 180

527 groups, 295, 388 (n. 13)

Foley, Dermot, 97, 103, 140, 141–42, 143, 145, 150, 195, 197, 208, 356 (nn. 70, 80), 361 (n. 151)

Ford, Gerald: attempts at national reconciliation, 137–38, 139, 155, 171, 173, 177, 184; leniency toward draft evaders, 138, 154–56, 160; and POW/MIA families, 140–41, 159, 160–62, 176, 180, 182, 232, 236, 344 (n. 61); and House Select Committee on Missing Persons in Southeast Asia, 143, 165, 186; and Presidential MIA/POW Task Force proposal, 162–63, 165; and U.S.-Vietnam relations, 164, 174–75, 182; and Reagan, 173–74, 176, 181; and

criticism of his foreign policy, 173–75, 181–82; and election of 1976, 182; and Aspin, 331 (n. 146); and Beattie, 346 (n. 91)

Foreign Agents Registration Act, 38

Foster, Hilton, 282

Four-Part Joint Military Team (FPJMT), 85, 86, 91

France, 102, 105, 118–22, 200, 338 (nn. 87, 92)

Frank, Stephen, 58, 323 (n. 265)

Franklin, H. Bruce, 14, 94, 95, 158, 180, 333 (n. 175), 345 (n. 68), 374 (n. 180), 382 (n. 120), 387 (n. 212)

Frishman, Robert, 31, 34, 36, 37

Fulbright, William, 19–20, 49, 92

Fuller, James, 241, 243

Furue, Tadao, 242–43, 373 (nn. 165, 166)

Galanti, Paul, 72, 74, 297

Galanti, Phyllis, 74

Garwood, Ellen St. John, 225

Garwood, Robert, 3, 195–96, 356 (n. 79)

Gatwood, Robin, 171

Geneva Accords, 17

Geneva Convention, 18, 19, 28, 98

Germany: and World War I war dead, 118, 119–20, 337 (n. 73); World War II prison camps of, 127; and World War II war dead, 128; and World War II missing, 159, 168; American war dead repatriated from, 338 (n. 94)

Gettysburg, 108–12, 113, 116, 336 (n. 33)

Gigot, Paul, 214

Gill, George, 241

Gilman, Benjamin, 170, 197, 356 (n. 83)

Glenn, John, 287

Glenn, Lynn, 45–46

Gober, Herschel, 250–51

Gold Star Families for Peace, 305

Goldwater, Barry, 38, 39, 140

Good, Aaron, 110

Goodpaster, Andrew, 66

Go Public campaign: and public opinion of Vietnam War, 16, 29–30, 31, 40,

55–56; Sieverts on, 20; and Perot, 34, 37, 254; mail from, 35, 315 (n. 118); and POW treatment, 35–36; and POW homecoming, 66; Reagan's re-creation of, 217

Gordy, Dorothy, 183

Gordy, Tom, 183

Gore, Al, 80

Grant, Ulysses S., 109–10

Grassley, Charles, 267, 268, 269, 270, 272, 273, 275

Graves Registration Service, 101, 112, 116, 118–20, 126, 128–29, 132, 334 (n. 3)

Griffiths, Ann Mills: and accounting for POWs/MIAs, 6, 135, 219, 236, 242, 244, 274; on presumption of death, 146; and National League of Families, 149–50, 151, 190, 193, 230–32, 236, 237, 239, 259, 262–63, 279–80, 345 (n. 74), 367–68 (n. 81); and VIVA, 151, 345 (n. 73), 365 (n. 45); on draft evaders, 155; and Reagan, 193, 219, 227, 234, 262; Sybil Stockdale compared to, 193–94; and refugee reports on MIAs, 194–95, 196, 199; and Tran Vien Loc, 202; and Iran hostage crisis, 205; access to classified information, 206, 207, 208, 237, 360 (n. 138); and Inter-Agency Group on POW/MIA Affairs, 206–8, 211, 219, 225, 233–34, 258, 275, 282, 284, 369 (n. 104); and POW/MIA amalgamation, 211, 362 (n. 162); and Carter, 211–12; and Lao resistance elements, 225, 226; salary of, 231; and burial of Vietnam Unknown, 237, 238; and Perot, 254, 255–56, 273; and Vessey, 258; on interest sections, 259; and George H. W. Bush, 262, 279, 280; and Baker, 265–66; and Peck, 269; and Senate Select Committee on POW/MIA Affairs, 273–74, 275; death threats against, 282; and Clinton, 283, 284, 287; and Sampley, 294; and Vietnamese skulls, 358 (n. 106)

Gritz, James "Bo," 221–23, 254

Gruner, Elliot, 43, 69

Guy, Ted, 71, 75

Guyer, Tennyson, 197, 356 (n. 83)

Habib, Philip, 164

Hagel, Chuck, 294

Hagerman, Emma, 152, 169

Haig, Alexander, 50–51, 55, 62, 88, 314 (n. 105)

Halberstam, David, 264

Haldeman, H. R., 32, 33, 35–36, 52, 53, 62, 66, 82, 295

Halyburton, Porter, 41

Harding, Warren, 123

Harriman, W. Averell, 17, 19, 20, 22, 24, 27, 28

Harrison, Robert Pogue, 104

Hart, Anne, 146, 237, 241, 244, 245, 246

Hart, Tom, 245

Hatch, Orrin, 231

Havens, Charles, III, 39

Hawley, Thomas, 84

Hayden, Tom, 21

Hegdahl, Douglas, 31, 34, 36, 37

Helms, Jesse, 156, 266–68, 269, 270, 271, 272, 273, 380 (n. 96)

Hemingway, Ernest, 119

Hendon, Billy, 225, 270, 356 (n. 83), 375–76 (n. 18)

Hersh, Seymour, 40

Heston, Charlton, 57, 246

Hoa Lo prison, 22, 284

Ho Chi Minh, 17, 19, 20, 21

Hofstadter, Richard, 199, 381 (n. 109)

Holbrooke, Richard, 185, 186, 187

Holocaust, 102, 128, 170

Homecoming II Project, 247–48, 262

Honor Bound, 323 (n. 281)

Hopper, Earl, 148–51, 167, 195, 208, 218, 233, 236, 263, 345 (nn. 63, 74)

Hopper, Jr. v. Carter (1978), 356 (n. 70)

House Armed Services Committee, 34

House Select Committee on Missing Persons in Southeast Asia: and failure to resolve questions about MIAs, 2,

171–72, 177, 178, 271; and POW versus MIA status, 96; and presumptive findings of death, 142–43, 167, 188, 342–43 (n. 27); and Carter, 143, 165, 172, 184; and accounting effort for POWs/MIAs, 165–71, 173, 175, 186, 211, 244, 255; and Kissinger, 165, 175–76, 352 (n. 195); and release of Americans stranded in Vietnam, 165–66; and U.S.-Vietnam relations, 166, 167; and repatriation of remains, 167, 168; and disagreements within, 172–73, 177, 197; and Reagan, 173–75; and Garwood, 196; report on MIAs, 324 (n. 5)

House Subcommittee on East Asia and Pacific Affairs, 195, 197, 199–201, 207, 209, 212, 255

House Subcommittee on National Security Policy, 37

House Task Force on American Prisoners and Missing in Southeast Asia, 197, 202, 207, 356 (n. 83)

Howes, Craig, 69

Hughes, James, 52–53, 203

Hulbein, Sarge, 247

Hun Sen, 265

Hunt, Nelson Bunker, 225

Hurlburt, Burt, 225, 366 (n. 58)

Hurst, Steven, 187

Indochina War, 17

Ingle, David, 105, 156

Innes, Gail, 97

Inter-Agency Group on POW/MIA Affairs (IAG): and Griffiths, 206–8, 211, 219, 225, 233–34, 258, 275, 282, 284, 369 (n. 104); and POW/MIA families, 207–9, 211; public information campaign of, 209; and Negroponte, 207; and Reagan, 212, 225, 234, 259, 361 (n. 147); and Operation Lazarus, 221; and Childress, 225, 255, 257; Iran-Contra scandal compared to, 226; and repatriation of remains,

240–41; and Thach, 257, 258; and Hendon, 375–76 (n. 18)

Interdepartmental Prisoner of War Committee, 19

International Committee of the Red Cross (ICRC), 18, 21, 119

Iran-Contra affair, 223, 226, 227, 254, 366 (n. 58)

Iran hostage crisis, 179, 202–3, 205–6, 219, 227, 256, 303, 366 (n. 58)

Iraq Veterans against the War, 305

Iraq War, 303–5

Isaacs, Arnold, 15

Isham, Heyward, 30

Jackson, James, Jr., 21

James, Daniel "Chappie," 92

Japan, 128, 130, 276, 340 (n. 132), 383 (n. 147)

Jarriel, Tom, 243

Jefferson, Thomas, 106

Jeffords, Susan, 70

Jenkins, Harry, 71, 79

Jenkins, Philip, 159, 180, 309 (n. 22)

Jespersen, Christopher, 165

Jews, and Holocaust, 102, 128

Joe Hill Collective, 23

Johnson, Edward, 21

Johnson, Haynes, 202

Johnson, Lyndon: effect of partial bombing halt, 18; effect of air war on North Vietnam, 19; on Vietnamese war crimes trials, 20; and relations with POW/MIA wives, 27–28; avoidance of POW/MIA issue, 31, 62; Vietnamese communists' use of POWs/MIAs to influence, 61; death of, 65; and abuses of power, 247

Johnson, Sam, 80

Joint Casualty Resolution Center (JCRC): emphasis on MIAs, 84–85, 135; difficulties in operations of, 85–87, 289; and live-sighting reports, 197; staffing of, 220, 267; and cost of operations, 229, 260; and Cambodia,

265; and Americans accounted for, 355 (n. 55)

Joint Chiefs of Staff, 66, 88, 93, 199, 207, 232

Joint Economic Commission, 90

Joint Personnel Recovery Center (JPRC), 84, 85

Joint POW/MIA Accounting Command, 3, 6, 302–3, 308 (n. 10)

Joint Task Force–Full Accounting (JTF-FA), 285, 286, 288

Kanfer, Stefan, 70

Kassebaum, Nancy, 270, 271, 382 (n. 120)

Kavanaugh, Abel, 327 (n. 73)

Kay, Emmet, 160, 347 (n. 107)

Keegan, John, 338 (n. 92)

Kelman, Herbert, 81

Kemp, Jack, 231

Kennedy, Edward, 53, 55, 92, 163, 164, 165

Kennedy, Frank, 203

Kennedy, John F., 134

Kennedy, Robert F., 19

Kenny, Henry "Hank," 350 (n. 163)

Kerley, Ellis, 242, 246, 373 (n. 166)

Kerrey, Bob, 264–65, 267, 270, 271, 287, 289, 299, 380 (n. 86)

Kerry, John: as Senate Select Committee chairman, 1, 253, 270–72, 275, 276, 291, 295, 298; as adversary of POW/ MIA lobby, 5, 254, 294–95; as Vietnam veteran, 80, 272; and Sampley, 282; and U.S.-Vietnam relations, 284, 286, 289; and Clinton, 287, 289; and McCain, 291, 296; and election of 2004, 294–99

Khmer Rouge, 190, 264, 265

KIA/BNR status, 63, 93, 96–97, 135, 146, 173, 180, 209, 211, 231, 324 (n. 5), 334 (n. 192)

KIAs, statistics on, 63, 95, 324 (n. 3)

Kiba, Steve, 157–58

Kimball, Jeffrey, 15

Kingston, Robert, 85

Kinnard, Douglas, 24

Kissinger, Henry: and Senate Select Committee, 1, 2; and Vietnamization, 31; and POW/MIA families, 33–34, 50–51, 53, 54, 175–76, 314 (n. 105); and troop withdrawals tied to POW/ MIA release, 47, 48, 50, 54, 55; on Son Tay prison raid, 49; and Paris Agreement, 87, 89–90, 164, 176; and lists of POWs/MIAs, 93; and Presidential MIA/POW Task Force proposal, 161, 162; and economic sanctions on Vietnam, 164, 351 (n. 191); and House Select Committee on Missing Persons in Southeast Asia, 165, 175–76, 352 (n. 195); and criticism of, 173, 175, 176, 181; and accounting efforts for POWs/ MIAs, 174, 236; and memory of Vietnam War, 213

Klein, Herb, 33

Kleindienst, Richard, 82

Klemesrud, Judy, 44

Knapp, Helen, 143

Koenigsamen, Janet L., 330 (n. 120)

Kohl, Herb, 382 (n. 122)

Korean War: missing or identified Americans from, 2, 101, 132, 173, 287, 308 (n. 10), 340 (n. 139); and brainwashing, 66, 68; and Unknown Soldier remains, 102; recovery of war dead in, 128–32; and lists of POWs, 130, 131, 339 (n. 129); public opinion of, 130–31; accounting for POWs in, 131, 132–34, 350 (n. 163)

Kramer, Galand, 67

Krauthammer, Charles, 268

Kushner, Valerie, 26, 52, 55, 61

Kuwait, 266–67

Laird, Melvin: and Go Public campaign, 16; and briefing of POW/MIA wives, 30–31; on negotiations for release of POWs/MIAs, 32; and news conference of released POWs, 34; and Appeal for International Justice, 39; and

Son Tay prison raid, 49; relationship with POW/MIA families, 52, 53, 64, 135, 146; and POW/MIA Task Group, 66; and lists of POWs, 92; on POW/MIA status changes, 97

Lane, Thomas J., 133

Lansing, Robert, 120

Laos: repatriation of remains from, 3, 189, 260; POWs/MIAs in, 87, 89, 90, 94, 96, 98, 165, 333 (n. 184); and Operation Lazarus, 221–23, 278; and LeBoutillier, 225–26; and false POW/MIA information, 228–29; and Pakse excavation, 240–43, 245–46

Laqueur, Thomas, 113, 121

Larson, Charles, 286

Lassiter, David, 26

Lavelle, William, 66

Lawrence, David, 133

Lawson, Richard, 161, 162, 163, 207, 360 (n. 142)

League of Wives of American Prisoners in Vietnam, 25. *See also* National League of Families of American Prisoners and Missing in Southeast Asia

LeBoutillier, John, 225–26, 248, 266, 356 (n. 83)

Le Duan, 17

Le Duc Tho, 17, 50, 89, 90

Lee, Robert E., 114

Leenhouts, Fred, 222

Lelyveld, Joseph, 30, 188

Lembcke, Jerry, 70

Le Thi Anh, 198, 228

Liberalism: and abuses of power, 7; revolt against, 140, 192, 217, 224; and MIA issue, 174, 252, 351 (n. 187); and defeat in Vietnam War, 213, 217

Life (magazine), 21–22, 45, 74, 76, 203

Lifton, Robert Jay, 77, 81

Limbo (film), 45

Lincoln, Abraham, 111–12, 218

Lincoln, Felicia, 74

Lindland, Bobbe, 246

Lloyd, James, 169–70, 172

Lodge, Henry Cabot, 30

London Times, 122

Long, Donna, 3, 195, 289

Long, Steve, 75

Lord, Winston, 284, 285, 286

Low, James, 28

Lowenthal, David, 135

Luntz, Frank, 299

Lutyens, Edwin, 121

Lynch, Jessica, 303

MacArthur, Douglas, 129

MacDonald, J. Angus, 169, 172, 350 (n. 163)

MacLeish, Rod, 139

MacPhail, Don, 74–75

Mansfield, Mike, 38, 39, 184

Marsh, Jack, 140–41

Martini, Edwin, 15, 164–65

Marvin, Carolyn, 105, 156

Matheny, David, 21, 28

Mather, Paul, 260

Maynard, Robert, 72

McAlister, Melani, 203, 205

McCain, Carol, 74

McCain, Cindy Hensley, 74, 293, 327 (n. 63)

McCain, John: marriages of, 74, 327 (n. 63); POW experience of, 80–81, 96, 333 (n. 180); and Senate Select Committee on POW/MIA Affairs, 253, 270–73; and POW/MIA activism, 254, 270, 272, 282–83, 292, 293–94; and U.S.-Vietnam relations, 259, 267, 275, 284, 286, 289; and Kerry, 291, 296; and election of 2000, 292–94, 388 (n. 9); Sampley on, 292–94; temper of, 293–94; and election of 2008, 299–302, 304, 305, 329 (n. 106), 390 (n. 51); and POW/MIA records, 384 (n. 167)

McCarthy, Eugene, 20

McCloskey, Paul, 167, 169, 174–77, 351 (n. 191)

McClure, Claude, 13–14, 15, 18

McDaniel, Dorothy, 76

McDaniel, Red, 267, 269, 270

McDonald, David, 24

McDonald, Gregory, 237

McDonald v. McLucas (1973), 142, 143–44, 150, 356 (n. 70)

McFarlane, Robert "Bud," 217, 222, 232, 233–34, 239, 257

McGirr, Lisa, 26

McGovern, George, 20, 23, 55–57, 79–80, 212–13

McGovern-Hatfield amendment, 54–55

McKinley, William, 115

McMahon, Robert, 183

Meigs, Montgomery, 114

Memory of Vietnam War: and accounting for POWs/MIAs, 10, 243; scholarship on, 10–11, 103; and POW captivity narratives, 77–78, 80, 158; construction of, 139, 140, 152, 183–84; and POW/MIA families, 149, 152, 153, 154, 171, 193, 248; and Vietnamese communists, 165, 191; and House Select Committee on Missing Persons in Southeast Asia, 166, 171, 172–73, 176–77; and Reagan, 173–74, 217, 218, 248; and Carter, 184, 185, 186, 190; and conservative movement, 192; and Iran hostage crisis, 203, 205; and George H. W. Bush, 261, 262, 267, 275; and McCain, 273; and Swift Boat Veterans for Truth, 298, 299; and simulated imagery, 323 (n. 281)

Mexican War, 2, 101, 107–8

Meyer, Gail, 75, 76

MIA status: statistics on, 63, 102, 209, 210–11, 324 (nn. 3, 5), 362 (n. 162); and Nixon, 83–84, 97, 135; and uncertainty surrounding, 83–84, 95, 97–99, 156–57, 362 (n. 160); and identification of remains, 84, 85–86; and losses in enemy territory, 85; and losses over water, 85, 330 (n. 128); and pilots ejecting from aircraft, 95–96; and presumptive findings of death, 101, 102, 131–32, 135–36, 141–46, 148, 150, 173, 179–80, 188–89, 334 (n. 1), 335 (n. 10), 342–43 (n. 27)

Middle East, 191, 206, 227, 267

Military Families Speak Out, 305

Mills, E. C. "Bus," 150, 151, 152, 155, 157, 345 (n. 74)

Missing in Action (film), 309 (n. 16)

Missing Persons Act, 102, 124–25, 131–32, 141, 142, 143

Moakley, John "Joe," 172

Mobilization against the War, 32, 34, 37

Montgomery, G. V. "Sonny," 165, 167–72, 176–78, 184–86, 189, 197, 234, 271, 348 (n. 134)

Moorer, Thomas, 27–28

Morris, Stephen, 385 (n. 176)

Mosse, George, 80, 113, 337 (n. 75)

Mullen, Barbara, 39, 44, 52, 91, 318 (n. 183)

Mulligan, James, 77, 79

Mulligan, Louise, 26, 51, 53, 54, 141, 312 (n. 56)

Murder in the Air (film), 222

Murkowski, Frank, 287

Muskie, Edmund, 38, 39

Myers, Armand, 69

Nation (magazine), 20, 174, 351 (n. 187)

National cemeteries, 112–14, 116, 120, 121, 125, 337 (n. 58). *See also* Arlington National Cemetery

National Committee for a Sane Nuclear Policy, 20

National Forget-Me-Not Association, 244

National identity, 113, 116–17

National League of Families of American Prisoners and Missing in Southeast Asia: and George H. W. Bush, 2, 232, 233, 236, 243, 262, 279–81; and accounting for POWs/MIAs, 4, 5, 64, 93, 97–98, 155, 157, 163, 166, 170, 171–72, 173, 176, 182, 183, 206, 215, 274, 287–88; public standing of, 4, 43–44, 153–54, 177, 193, 283; women in leadership roles, 4; conspiracy theories and revenge fantasies of, 7, 8; and Nixon, 15, 29, 30, 34, 39–40, 53, 188–89, 215,

232; formation of, 24–25, 28; and
Reagan, 29, 176, 179–81, 182, 193,
211–12, 215–20, 227, 230–34, 236–
37, 239, 243, 248–49, 259–60, 378
(n. 50); and antiwar activists, 32, 46,
47; pressuring of Democratic Republic of Vietnam, 38, 40; and Appeal for
International Justice, 39, 56; mailing
list of, 39–40, 149, 262, 344 (n. 57);
finances of, 39–40, 197, 231; as non-
partisan, 39, 40; and Kissinger, 51, 53,
54, 175–76; and troop withdrawals, 51,
54; distrust of Nixon administration,
52–53, 97–99, 120; internal divisions
in, 53, 54, 141–42, 145, 149–53, 208,
262, 321 (n. 239), 345 (nn. 63, 79); and
Operation Homecoming, 64; and presumptive findings of death, 103, 150,
179, 180; and draft evaders, 138, 154–
57, 160; and Ford, 140–41, 159, 160–
62, 176, 180, 182, 232, 344 (n. 61);
men in leadership positions, 141, 150,
342 (n. 23), 344 (n. 61); membership
of, 149–54, 159, 177, 189–90, 197, 208,
230–31, 291, 321 (n. 283), 355 (n. 56),
367–68 (n. 81), 368 (n. 84); distrust
of federal authority, 150, 168, 177, 181,
193, 195, 208, 232, 262–63, 279–81;
and VIVA, 150–52, 197; as representative of families' opinions, 152, 153, 154,
193; and House Select Committee on
Missing Persons in Southeast Asia,
166, 167–71, 172, 180; and national
debate on Vietnam War, 175–76; and
Carter, 180, 181, 182–83, 184, 188, 190,
200, 213; and Woodcock Commission,
184–85; and Vietnamese refugees,
195, 196–202, 206; and Iran hostage
crisis, 205; and Inter-Agency Group
on POW/MIA Affairs, 207–9, 211; and
Clinton, 232, 236, 250, 291; opposition to Vietnam Unknown burial,
237–39; structure of, 342 (n. 23); and
Berger, 386 (n. 183)
National Liberation Front (NLF), 13, 18,
19, 21, 32, 41, 322 (n. 255). *See also*
Vietnamese communists
National Mobilization Committee to End
the War in Vietnam (the Mobe), 21, 28
National POW/MIA Recognition Day,
206, 239–40
National Review (magazine), 158, 199,
210, 214
National Security Council, 207, 225–26,
230, 233, 256, 257
National Vietnam Veterans Coalition,
281
Nation-state: and relationship with war
dead, 8–9, 105, 107–8, 111–12, 113,
114–15, 117, 119–23, 134, 135, 302, 335
(n. 22); and narratives of heroic sac-
rifice, 103, 105, 148, 166–67; POWs/
MIAs as betrayed by, 140; and POW/
MIA families, 142, 153–54
Neff, John, 114, 337 (n. 58)
Negroponte, John, 89, 206–7, 234, 331
(n. 148)
Nenninger, Timothy K., 339 (n. 119)
Neoconservatives, 181, 182, 191, 192–93,
213, 263
Newsweek (magazine), 59, 63, 72, 76, 86,
210, 269, 279
New Yorker (magazine), 15, 50, 285, 291
New York Times: on search for POW/MIA
remains, 3; on Sybil Stockdale, 30; on
Nixon, 33; on POW/MIA wives, 44;
on POWs, 45; on Son Tay raid, 49; on
POW repatriation, 63; on Operation
Homecoming, 67, 69; on Vietnam
veterans, 76; on Korean War, 130; on
Griffiths, 234; on George H. W. Bush,
281; on accounting effort for POWs/
MIAs, 285
New York Times Magazine, 30, 188, 202
Ngo Phi Hung, 195, 198, 357 (n. 89)
Ngo Vinh Long, 81
Nguyen Cao Ky, 18
Nguyen Co Thach, 190, 220, 229, 256–
60, 262, 265–66, 310–11 (n. 14)
Nguyen Huu Tho, 13, 17

Nguyen Khac Vien, 22
Nguyen Manh Cam, 265, 275, 289
Nguyen Minh Triet, 292
Nguyen Ngoc Loan, 311 (n. 18)
Nguyen Thi Binh, 17, 48, 50, 322 (n. 255)
Nguyen Van Linh, 257
Nguyen Van Thieu, 48, 50, 55, 87, 88
Nhan Dan, 19, 22, 163, 229
Nicaragua, 207
Nicaraguan Contras, 225
Nixon, Richard: and Paris Agreement,
    5, 87, 88, 89, 90, 164, 168, 176, 187,
    229; ascendancy of, 7, 35–36; pre-
    occupation with POWs/MIAs, 14–15,
    16, 20, 29–32, 33, 34–38, 40, 43, 47,
    49–50, 54, 55, 56, 60, 351 (n. 187);
    and POW/MIA families, 14–15, 30, 33,
    35, 52–53, 97–98, 138, 180, 213; and
    bombing of North Vietnam, 18, 56;
    election of 1968, 28–29, 313 (n. 75);
    Sybil Stockdale's support for, 28, 29;
    and Vietnamization, 30–31, 40, 48,
    50, 52; and "silent majority," 32, 33,
    34, 35, 58, 60, 192, 296; "stabbed-in-
    the-back" thesis of, 32, 213; attempts
    to shape public opinion, 33, 60–61;
    contempt for antiwar protesters, 39;
    and withdrawal of U.S. troops, 47–48,
    87–88, 100; negotiations for prisoner
    release, 48; and Son Tay prison raid,
    49; and Operation Homecoming, 63,
    64–65; and peace with honor, 63, 64;
    and POW repatriation, 66, 67, 68,
    69, 72, 82–83, 88; returning POWs'
    gratitude toward, 67; and Watergate,
    80, 82–83, 88, 175, 331 (n. 144); and
    MIAs, 83–84, 97, 135; resignation of,
    83, 89; and statistics on POWs/MIAs,
    92, 332 (n. 156); Ford's pardon of, 138;
    and conservative movement, 140; and
    benefits for POW/MIA families, 146;
    and criticism of his foreign policy, 173,
    175, 181–82; and abuses of power, 247;
    and Kerry, 295–96, 298. *See also* Go
    Public campaign

Nofziger, Lyn, 33
Nolan, McKinley, 196, 356 (n. 79)
Noonan, Peggy, 256, 263
North, Carol, 29
North, Oliver, 223, 226, 366 (n. 58)
North American Rockwell, 34
Nudelman, Franny, 113, 238
Nutter, G. Warren, 92

Obama, Barack, 300, 301, 302, 305
O'Grady, Scott, 303
Oksenberg, Michel, 184, 185, 187, 197
Ondarisk, Barbara, 49
O'Neill, John, 296–97
Operation Rescue, Inc., 231
Ortiz-Rivera, Luis, 21
Ottinger, Richard, 169–70, 172
Overly, Norris, 21, 28

Packwood, Bob, 157
Paley, Grace, 45, 46
Palin, Sarah, 301
Panama Canal, 173
Paris Agreement (1973): release of
    American POWs following, 3, 88; and
    aid to Vietnam, 5; release of American
    POWs preceding, 15; Article 8(b) of,
    84–85, 165, 187; and ceasefire viola-
    tions, 85, 86, 88–89, 164; Article 8(a)
    of, 87–88, 89, 90–91; Article 21 of,
    89–91, 163, 164, 165, 167, 187; secret
    concessions of, 89–91, 176, 187, 229;
    second anniversary of, 162; tenth
    anniversary of, 216
Paris Peace Talks: and release of Ameri-
    can POWs, 16, 48, 83; and communist
    strategy, 30, 37–38, 56, 91; and list of
    MIAs, 37–38; and U.S. withdrawal, 87
Parker, Barbara, 176
Pathet Lao, 221. *See also* Laos
Paulson, Allan, 225
Pearl Harbor attack, 123–24
Peck, Millard, 268–69
Pentagon: Sybil Stockdale's cooperation
    with, 24; and POW/MIA wives, 27, 47;

— • —

and National League of Families, 30, 40, 53–54, 91–93, 153; and released POWs/MIAs, 34; and lists of POWs, 37, 90, 92, 95; and compensation for POWs/MIAs, 42, 146; and POW Policy Committee, 66, 92; and POW repatriation policies, 66–68, 326 (n. 44); and Korean War POWs, 131; and presumptive findings of death, 141, 146, 179; ban on photographs of flag-draped coffins, 304, 305; release of POW/MIA records, 384 (n. 167). *See also* U.S. Defense Department

Perisho, Gordon, 150

Perisho, Nancy, 150

Perlstein, Rick, 310 (n. 5)

Perot, H. Ross: and Nixon, 34, 37, 315 (nn. 111, 118); and Appeal for International Justice, 38; and VIVA, 58; and election of 1992, 80, 276–78, 283; and North, 226–27, 366 (n. 58); and POW/MIA activism, 253, 254–57, 277–78; and Reagan, 256, 257, 376 (n. 27); and Armitage, 263; and simulated imagery of POWs/MIAs, 323 (n. 281)

Perot Commission on Americans Missing in Southeast Asia, 255–56, 273, 277

Perroots, Leonard, 254

Pershing, John J., 118

Persian Gulf War, 267, 269

Peterson, Pete, 80, 284, 287, 289

Pham Van Dong, 17, 90, 163–64, 189

Phan Hien, 165, 167, 175, 186–87

Philippine-American War, 103

Piehler, G. Kurt, 105

Pitzer, Daniel, 21

Platt, Nick, 207

Playboy (magazine), 71, 326 (n. 50)

Podhoretz, Norman, 191

Poindexter, John, 222, 255, 257

Politics of loss: forms of, 8; and nation-state's relationship to war dead, 9, 117; persistence of, 11, 294–95; and presumption of death, 146, 148; and betrayal, 154, 157, 159, 173–74, 177,

183, 218–19; and POW/MIA activism, 170, 181; and Reagan, 192, 213; and Senate Select Committee on POW/MIA Affairs, 272; and U.S.-Vietnam relations, 289; and Clinton's election, 291; and Kerry, 298

Poor, Enoch, 105–6

Porter, Gareth, 352 (n. 195)

POW captivity narratives, 77–80, 81, 85, 93, 329 (n. 107)

POW Code of Conduct, 28, 68, 134, 135, 158

Powell, Colin, 80, 232, 257, 289, 301

Powers, Iris, 145, 152

POW memoirs, 68

POW/MIA abandonment, belief in: effect on U.S. foreign policy, 1, 3, 5, 14; effect on U.S. politics, 1, 3–4, 6, 14, 302; accounting effort as evidence of, 6, 213–14, 246; and peace with honor claim, 63, 64; and Paris Agreement terms, 91; and distrust of Nixon, 97–99; and National League of Families, 157, 159, 177, 344 (n. 58); and Veterans of Foreign Wars, 173; and conservative movement, 192–93; and Reagan, 218–19; and Perot, 254, 278; and Persian Gulf War, 267; and McCain, 272, 301; effect on military culture, 303, 391 (n. 59)

POW/MIA activism: and Kissinger, 2, 5, 175–76; and Kerry, 5, 254, 294–95; politicians associated with, 6; as vehicle for dissent against war, 7, 15–16; focus on victimization, 10, 60, 117, 156, 158, 170, 177, 181, 192, 193, 213, 217, 290, 294; POW wives' involvement in, 26, 27; plasticity of, 40; and contest for moral supremacy, 78, 192–93; and Paris Agreement violations, 90; and living and dead categories, 91, 180, 209–10, 244, 245, 259, 262; and lists of POWs/MIAs, 93–94, 95; and discrepancy cases, 94, 179, 220, 332 (n. 169); and distrust of government officials, 135, 168–70, 177, 181, 247–48,

268–69, 281, 290; and accounting effort for POWs/MIAs, 139–40, 246, 247, 253–54, 287; National League of Families as representative of, 153; and domestic foes, 158–59; and conservative movement, 160, 181, 192–93; and Presidential MIA/POW Task Force proposal, 161–62; and House Select Committee on Missing Persons in Southeast Asia, 169, 172; and Reagan, 180, 215–18, 227–28; and repatriation of remains, 200; and Iran hostage crisis, 205; and false POW/MIA information, 227–28; and fundraising, 231, 282, 368 (n. 88); evolution of, 252; and Perot, 253, 254–57, 277–78; and McCain, 254, 270, 272, 282–83, 292, 293–94; "Until the last man comes home" as rallying cry for, 309 (n. 16)

POW/MIA bracelets, 57–60, 76, 83, 151, 174, 197, 205, 344 (n. 57)

POW/MIA wives: Sybil Stockdale's organizing of, 24–26, 202; and conservative movement, 26, 28–29; emotional archetype of, 26, 44–46; Louise Mulligan's organizing of, 26, 312 (n. 56); political mobilization of, 26–27, 141, 170, 295; as single parents, 26, 44; and military establishment, 27, 46–47; and Kissinger, 33–34, 50–51, 314 (n. 105); and Nixon, 33, 35, 37, 52; as Cold War feminine ideal, 44; critics of, 45; and POW repatriation, 70–72, 74–76, 91; independence of, 74, 75–76; leaving National League of Families, 141, 145–46; and presumptive findings of death, 141, 143–45, 148

POW propaganda: Vietnam's use of, 18, 21–24, 68, 78; Sybil Stockdale's reaction to, 24–25, 28, 46; Pentagon's sensitivity to, 66; and POW versus MIA status, 96. See also Go Public campaign

POW repatriation: and Garwood, 3, 195–96; and early release, 15, 22, 66, 68, 77, 203, 310 (n. 6); incidence

of divorce following, 26, 75–76, 327 (nn. 61, 66); and heroic status, 63, 66, 68, 77, 78–79, 81, 99, 294; and Operation Homecoming, 63–69, 71, 91, 94, 97, 99, 141, 271; controversy over, 65–68; and Nixon, 66, 67, 68, 69, 72, 82–83, 88; Pentagon's handling of, 66–68, 326 (n. 44); and misconduct, 68, 69; and peace with honor claim, 68, 88; and POWs' testimonials, 68, 76; and changes in American society, 69–72, 74–76; and gender identity, 70–72, 74; and suicide, 75, 327 (n. 73); and political office, 79–81; and Watergate, 82–83; and testimony on MIAs, 96, 98, 342 (n. 27)

POWs/MIAs: congressional hearings on, 2, 308 (n. 5); statistics on, 2–3, 17–18, 50, 91, 92–93, 308 (n. 6), 332 (n. 156); establishing accountability for loss, 4, 139; as victims, 6, 43, 61, 62, 158, 294, 318 (n. 173); white middle-class volunteers in population of, 6, 7–8, 41, 43, 81, 192–93; Nixon's preoccupation with, 14–15; mail of, 16, 22, 34, 38, 40, 70, 79, 93, 96; execution of, 18; lists of, 37, 38, 91–99; African Americans as, 41, 59; age of, 41; class consciousness of, 41–42, 44; officers as, 41, 44, 317 (n. 156); and rescue, 41, 317 (n. 154); and financial rewards, 42, 143–45; as Cold War icons, 42–43; missions of, 43, 45, 46; simulated imagery of, 60, 323 (n. 281); status changes of, 96–97, 101. See also Families of POWs/MIAs; MIA status

Presidential Commission on Americans Missing and Unaccounted for in Southeast Asia (1977). See Woodcock Commission

Presidential MIA/POW Task Force proposal, 161–63

Pressler, Larry, 259, 284, 287

Priest, Dana, 267

Prisoner of War (film), 217

Prison Ship Martyrs' Monument, 106–7

Provisional Revolutionary Government (PRG), 36, 48, 85, 86, 94, 95, 98
Public Advertiser, 106

Quayle, Dan, 190

Racial minorities, 81, 114–15, 116, 125. *See also* African Americans
Radio Hanoi, 163
Raines, Howell, 212
Rambo: First Blood Part II (film), 89
Randolph, Janet, 115–16
Ranger Creed, 303
Reader's Digest, 34
Reagan, Ronald: and accounting effort for POWs/MIAs, 2–3, 219–20, 232, 236, 237, 240, 243, 244, 248, 252–53, 254; and conservative movement, 7, 9, 29, 140, 174, 176, 212–13, 227, 263–64; and body recovery, 8, 244; and POW/MIA families, 29, 176, 179–81, 182, 193, 211–12, 215–20, 227, 230–34, 236–37, 239, 243, 248–49, 259–60, 389 (n. 50); and VIVA, 57, 58, 174, 180; and MIA issue, 173–74, 180–81, 192, 216–17, 220, 227, 234, 236–37, 239, 255, 259; and Veterans of Foreign Wars, 173, 212; and Ford, 174, 176, 181; and live-sighting reports, 198; and Iran hostage crisis, 203, 205, 219, 227; and Negroponte, 207; and Inter-Agency Group on POW/MIA Affairs, 212, 225, 234, 259, 361 (n. 147); rhetoric of, 212–13, 362 (n. 167); and election of 1984, 218, 237, 239; and critiques of U.S. foreign policy, 178, 223, 256; and Vietnam Unknown burial, 238–39; and Perot, 256, 277, 376 (n. 27); and ideology of unity, 346 (n. 91)
Reed, Ralph, 292
Rees, Richard, 86
Regan, Donald, 217
Reid, Harry, 270, 271
Remnick, David, 278
Republican Party, 8, 80, 176, 177, 263, 264. *See also* Conservative movement; Neoconservatives
Republic of Vietnam (RVN), 85
Reserve Officers Association, 39
Reston, James, 33, 88
Return with Honor (film), 330 (n. 120)
Revolutionary War, 105, 106, 107
Reynolds, Frank, 203
Richardson, Elliot, 32, 47, 66, 68, 82
Richmond Whig, 117
Ridge, Tom, 259
Ridgway, Matthew, 130
Risner, Kathleen, 47
Risner, Robinson "Robbie," 42, 67, 79
Robb, Chuck, 265, 271, 275, 287, 289
Roberts, Mary Louise, 70
Roberts, Steven, 69, 202, 203
Roeder, David, 205
Rogers, William, 54–55
Rogin, Michael, 223
Rolling Stone (magazine), 301
Roosevelt, Theodore, 120
Roraback, Kenneth, 18
Rosenthal, Joseph, 128
Rovere, Richard, 50
Rudloff, Stephen, 158–59
Rumble, Wesley, 31, 36, 37
Rusk, Dean, 19
Russell, Richard, 20
Russia, 120, 128, 338 (n. 94)

Safire, William, 34
St. Louis Post-Dispatch, 49
Salsig, Doyen, 47
Salter, Mark, 300–301
Sampley, Robin, 279
Sampley, Ted, 239, 282, 292–94, 296, 302, 379 (n. 74), 380 (n. 96)
San Diego Union, 28, 72, 74
Sauer, Norman, 373 (n. 165)
Saving Private Ryan (film), 303
Schell, Jonathan, 14, 78
Schieffer, Bob, 302
Schlesinger, James, 148, 150
Schuller, Robert, 194

428

Schulman, Bruce, 159

Schulzinger, Robert, 15, 252, 309 (n. 22), 378 (n. 50)

Scowcroft, Brent, 83, 97, 142–43, 162, 166, 263, 264, 271, 274

Secord, Richard, 226, 366 (n. 58)

Sellet, Alfonso, 173

Seminole Wars, 107

Senate Foreign Relations Committee, and Albright, 149

Senate Select Committee on POW/MIA Affairs: Kerry as chairman of, 1, 253, 270–72, 275, 276, 291, 295, 298; Kissinger's testimony before, 1, 2; and accountability, 4; and lists of POWs/MIAs, 93; Shields's testimony before, 95; and live-sighting reports, 197; and Inter-Agency Group on POW/MIA Affairs, 207–8, 225; on MIA statistics, 210; and false POW/MIA information, 227; and trust in government, 253, 270, 281, 384 (n. 167); and Smith, 269, 270, 271, 272, 273, 275, 281–82; and Helms, 269, 270, 271, 272, 273; and POW/MIA activism, 281, 282–83; and narratives of self-victimization, 290

September 11, 2001, terrorist attacks, 303

Shatner, William, 221–22, 223

Shealy, Rod, 294, 388 (n. 11)

Sheehan, Cindy, 305

Sheehan, Neil, 15, 200, 285

Sheer, Robert, 23

Shelton, Charles, 353 (n. 6)

Sherman, Daniel, 153–54, 338 (n. 92)

Sherwood, Carlton, 298

Shields, Roger: and families of POWs/MIAs, 53, 321 (n. 240); and POW repatriation, 66, 68–69; and accounting effort for POWs/MIAs, 83–84, 85, 92, 95, 332–33 (n. 170), 333 (n. 183); on POW/MIA status changes, 96–97, 334 (n. 1); on Presidential MIA/POW Task Force proposal, 161; and Vietnam Unknown burial, 238

Shultz, George, 220, 232

Shumaker, Lorraine, 72

Shumaker, Robert, 72

Shuman, Ned, 75

Sieverts, Frank: on war crimes trials, 20; and POW/MIA families, 30; on appeal of POWs/MIAs, 42; on lack of progress toward release of POWs, 47–48; and accounting effort for POWs/MIAs, 93, 96, 135; on Presidential MIA/POW Task Force proposal, 161–62; and Vietnamese refugees, 197–98

Sihanouk, Norodom, 265

Simpson, Alan, 287

Singlaub, John, 210–11, 226, 366 (n. 58)

Sivan, Emmanuel, 11, 152

60 Minutes (television show), 146, 148, 277, 279, 295

Slotkin, Richard, 81

Smith, Bernice, 148, 150

Smith, Bob, 268, 269, 270, 271, 272, 273, 275, 281–82, 287, 356 (n. 83), 382 (n. 122)

Smith, George, 13, 14, 15, 18

Smith, Terry, 222

Snow, Clyde C., 241

Socialist Republic of Vietnam, 140, 236, 257. See also Democratic Republic of Vietnam (DRV); Republic of Vietnam (RVN); Vietnam; Vietnamese communists

Social Security, 144–45

Solarz, Stephen, 234, 255, 256

Solomon, Richard, 267, 275

Solzhenitsyn, Aleksandr, 199

Son Tay prison raid, 49, 318 (n. 202)

Sophocles, Antigone, 104

Soviet Union, 190, 191, 207, 264, 265, 270, 274, 377 (n. 49)

Spanish-American War, 109, 115, 118, 120

Stanton, Edwin, 114

Steere, Edward, 336 (nn. 33, 53)

Stennis, John, 38, 39, 162

Sterba, James, 67

Steward, Mrs. William E., 81

Stichnoth, Ida Mae Reitz, 127, 339
(n. 119)
Stockdale, James, 22, 24, 27–28, 78, 80,
96, 278, 328 (nn. 92, 94)
Stockdale, Sybil: organizing POW/MIA
wives, 24–26, 202; reaction to POW
propaganda, 24–25, 28, 46; secret
communications with husband, 24,
27–28; roles of, 27; background of,
27; and Nixon, 29, 30–31, 34, 47, 313
(n. 76); and Appeal for International
Justice, 38; on antiwar activists,
46; and military establishment, 47;
on Son Tay prison raid, 49; meetings with Kissinger, 51, 54; Coppin
compared to, 57; and Reagan, 174;
Griffiths compared to, 193–94
Stolen Honor (film), 295, 297–98, 390
(n. 38)
Strobridge, Rodney, 238
Students for a Democratic Society
(SDS), 13, 21
Sullivan, Roger, 207
Support Our POW/MIAs, 151, 194, 197,
225, 226, 365 (n. 45)
Swift Boat Veterans for Truth, 295, 296–
99, 388 (n. 13)
Swindle, Orson, 278

Taft, William Howard, 106–7, 120
Tammany Society, 106, 107
Teague, Olin, 39
Tet Offensive, 21, 311 (n. 18)
Thanom Kittikachorn, 88
Thomas, Norman, 20
Thompson, Alyce, 75–76
Thompson, Fred, 28
Thompson, Jim, 71, 75–76, 96
Thoreau, Henry David, 107
Thorsness, Leo, 79–80
Tighe, Eugene, 199, 206, 207, 209–12,
228, 230, 254–55, 360 (n. 138)
Timberg, Robert, 227
Time (magazine): Middle Americans
as "Man of the Year," 35; and Risner,
42; on POW/MIA wives, 44; on war-

weariness, 46; on POW repatriation,
63, 64, 66, 70, 72, 74
Today (television show), 223, 269, 272
Tonkin Gulf attack, 78, 328 (n. 92)
Trang Den (magazine), 198
Tran Kim Phuong, 88
Tran Van Dong, 18
Tran Vien Loc, 199–202, 206, 209, 211,
212, 357 (nn. 96, 97), 358 (n. 109), 359
(n. 111)
Treaty of Versailles, 120
Treese, Robert, 59
Trinh Xuan Long, 267
Truman, Harry, 130–31
Truong Chinh, 17
Turkey, 120
20/20 (television show), 223, 241, 243,
247

Uniformed Services Savings Deposit
Program, 42, 144
United Nations, Vietnam's admission to,
189, 230
United Nations forces, and Korean War,
129, 132
USA Today, 269
U.S. Congress: and Go Public campaign,
35; condemnation of Vietnam's treatment of prisoners, 37; and benefits
for POW/MIA families, 42, 146; and
negotiations for prisoner release,
48; and accounting effort for POWs/
MIAs, 54, 86, 165–72; POW returnees
seeking office, 79; and reconstruction
aid, 90, 91, 164, 186, 187; and disposition of war dead, 106, 108, 125; and
death determination, 124–25, 131–32,
142–43, 145–46; and evacuation of
Americans from Vietnam, 137; and
Presidential MIA/POW Task Force
proposal, 162; Kissinger's contempt
for, 175; and Gritz, 223; and debate on
ending U.S. trade embargo, 286–87;
and statistics on POWs/MIAs, 332
(n. 156). See also House Select Committee on Missing Persons in South-

east Asia; Senate Select Committee on POW/MIA Affairs

U.S. Defense Department: and accounting effort for POWs/MIAs, 2, 3, 86, 99, 101, 332 (n. 163), 333 (n. 172); and POW homecoming, 66–67; and benefits for families of POWs/MIAs, 146; and Inter-Agency Group on POW/MIA Affairs, 207

U.S. foreign policy: effect of belief in POW/MIA abandonment on, 1, 3, 5, 14; and public diplomacy on behalf of POWs, 20; and return of POWs, 132; and Ford, 175, 181–82; and Kissinger, 175, 176, 181; and Nixon, 175, 181–82; and Carter, 179, 182, 184, 190; and live-sighting reports from Vietnamese refugees, 206; and Inter-Agency Group on POW/MIA Affairs, 207; and Reagan, 223, 256; and Republican Party, 264. *See also* U.S.-Vietnam relations

U.S. Justice Department, 32

U.S. News & World Report, 133

Usry, Tracy, 267–68, 269, 281

U.S. South: and memorialization of war dead, 103, 113–18; recovery of war dead, 113–14, 116–17, 120; and conservative movement, 213

U.S. State Department: and opposition to war crimes prosecutions, 19; and POW/MIA families, 30, 34; and lists of POWs, 92; and Korean War, 134; as culprit in alleged POW/MIA betrayal, 159, 213, and Woodcock Commission, 184–85; and status reviews, 188; and Inter-Agency Group on POW/MIA Affairs, 207, 209

U.S. Supreme Court, 142, 162

U.S.-Vietnam relations: and accounting effort for POWs/MIAs, 3, 10, 64, 140, 174, 183, 184–88, 189, 195, 198, 200, 251–52, 261, 265–66, 267, 274, 289–90, 351–52 (n. 193); and wounds of war, 5, 89, 164, 165, 167, 187, 229, 230, 258; and Dong, 163–64; U.S.

economic sanctions on Vietnam, 164–65; and House Select Committee on Missing Persons in Southeast Asia, 166, 167; and Carter, 182, 184–87, 189, 190–91; and Reagan, 220, 228, 236, 257, 258, 261; and Griffiths, 233–36, 258, 259, 262, 265, 274, 284; and Clinton, 252, 253, 257, 283–84, 285, 289, 291–92; and McCain, 259, 267, 275, 284, 289; and Thach, 310–11 (n. 14)

US War Crimes in North Vietnam, 19

Vallely, Thomas, 283

Van Atta, Michael, 244

Vance, Cyrus, 184, 185, 355 (n. 60)

Verdery, Katherine, 157

Versace, Humbert, 18

Vescelius, Milton, 241

Vessey, John W., Jr., 236, 244, 256–62, 265–66, 267, 273–75, 283–84, 286

Veterans Affairs Committee, 287

Veterans of Foreign Wars, 153, 163, 173, 174, 212, 238, 286, 351 (n. 178)

Viet Minh, 17

Vietnam: reconstruction aid denied to, 5, 164, 186, 229; statistics on missing Vietnamese, 102, 287, 387 (n. 212); evacuation of Americans from, 137, 163; and economic sanctions, 164–65, 175, 182, 230, 253, 258, 266, 274, 286–87, 288; relations with China, 190, 198, 259, 355 (n. 60), 377 (n. 49); and normalization of U.S. relations, 288–89. *See also* Democratic Republic of Vietnam (DRV); National Liberation Front (NLF); Republic of Vietnam (RVN); Socialist Republic of Vietnam (SRV); U.S.-Vietnam relations; Vietnamese communists

Vietnamese communists: use of American POWs in diplomacy, 5, 15, 20–23, 24, 30–32, 48–49, 50, 55, 61, 68, 163, 165, 200; and blame for disappearance of POWs/MIAs, 6, 7, 37, 97, 158; as participants in own history, 24; Sybil Stockdale's meeting with, 34;

and torture, 77, 78, 297; legitimacy of, 78; POW repatriation, 87–88; and lists of POWs, 91, 92–95; and POW/MIA families, 97–98, 193, 252; and accounting for POWs/MIAs, 163–64, 229–30, 265; and memory of Vietnam War, 165, 191; and POW/MIA information, 228–29. *See also* Democratic Republic of Vietnam (DRV); National Liberation Front (NLF); Socialist Republic of Vietnam; Vietnam

Vietnamese prisons, 22, 34, 35

Vietnam Independence, 17

Vietnamization, 30–31, 48, 50, 52

Vietnam Moratorium, 32, 34

Vietnam veterans: alienation of, 43, 66; protests against the war, 52; reaction to POWs' homecoming, 66; divorce rate among, 75, 327 (n. 71); and draft evaders, 184; and Garwood, 195; and Reagan, 218; as victims, 219, 294, 298; and Clinton, 283–84, 290; as presidential candidates, 302

Vietnam Veterans against Kerry, 296

Vietnam Veterans against the War, 153, 272, 295

Vietnam Veterans for a Just Peace, 296

Vietnam Veterans Memorial, 217, 256, 297

Vietnam Veterans of America, 286

Vietnam War: effect of defeat in, 3, 4–5, 7, 8, 9, 10, 11, 20, 60, 64, 117, 120, 133, 157, 168, 174, 175, 191, 192, 193, 203, 205, 212, 213, 217, 218, 222, 223, 227, 271, 290, 304; public attitudes toward, 4, 5, 9–10, 16, 27, 31, 32–33, 35, 37, 40, 43, 45, 50, 59–60, 62, 139, 167; U.S. withdrawal from, 4, 47–48, 54, 71, 87–88, 100; and draft evaders, 7, 138, 154–57; scholarship on, 9–10, 103, 309 (n. 22); and lists of POWs, 37, 38, 91–99, 332 (n. 163); air war of, 43, 45; troop withdrawals tied to POW/MIA release, 47, 48, 50, 51, 54; POWs/MIAs as rationale to end war, 54, 62; Nixon's ending of, 63, 100; returning

POWs as redemption for, 63, 64, 66, 81, 99; and wound metaphor, 63, 155–56, 167, 184, 185, 186, 187, 229, 248, 335 (n. 22); concerns about costs of, 64, 139; postwar debate over, 69, 99, 138–39, 155–56, 173, 175–76, 177; societal changes during, 69–72, 74–76; as ideological struggle, 78, 171; responsibility for, 78, 99, 140, 171–72, 184, 186, 218, 229; and U.S. war guilt, 91; and ideology of unity, 155–56, 269, 381 (n. 112); and inequities of draft, 156; Reagan's critique of, 173–74; Reagan's revisionism as noble cause, 180, 212, 213, 217–18, 219, 238, 239, 247, 248; and presumption of death, 335 (n. 10). *See also* Memory of Vietnam War

Virginian-Pilot, 52

VIVA (Victory in Vietnam Association; Voices in Vital America): and POW/MIA bracelets, 57–60, 76; and Reagan, 58, 174, 180; and accounting effort for POWs/MIAs, 83, 93, 94, 97, 136, 330 (n. 120); and Article 21 reconstruction aid, 91; and POW/MIA families, 146, 149, 151, 150–52, 197, 344 (n. 57); assets of, 151, 323 (n. 269), 345 (n. 73), 365 (n. 45); leadership of, 323 (n. 265)

Vo Nguyen Giap, 17

Vo Van Kiet, 257, 274

Vo Van Sung, 165, 167

Vu Hoang, 189

Wallace, George, 57

Wall Street Journal, 52, 266

Wall Street Journal/NBC News poll, 2

War Claims Act, 42

Ward, Marcus, 114

War dead: relationship with nation-state, 8–9, 105, 107–8, 111–12, 113, 114–15, 117, 121–23, 134, 135, 302; Civil War recovery of, 101, 108, 109–12, 116–17, 120, 125; memorialization of, 102, 103, 105, 107, 112–13; in South, 103, 113–18; and democracy of death, 105,

112–13, 120; rank of, 105–6, 112, 123; families of, 107, 110, 116, 117–18, 119, 120, 126–27; World War I recovery of, 118–23, 125, 337 (n. 73); and repatriation of remains, 120–21, 125; World War II recovery of, 123–28, 130; forensic identification of, 125, 339 (n. 110); and missing remains, 125–27; concurrent return of, 129–30; images of, 304

Warner, James, 298

Warner, Virginia, 389 (n. 33)

Warnke, Paul, 66

War of 1812, 107

Washington, George, 105, 106

Washington Post, 51, 67–68, 72, 83, 139, 169, 221, 260–61, 268

Watergate, 80, 82–83, 88, 175, 331 (n. 144)

Webb, Johnnie, 242

Webb, Ronald, 78–79

Weekly Standard (magazine), 298

Weinberger, Caspar, 221, 232, 237, 238, 244

Weiss, Cora, 38, 49

Welch, Raquel, 71

Westmoreland, William, 57

Weyrich, Paul, 293

White, Robert, 98

Whitman, Walt, 112, 113

Wicker, Tom, 63

Wilkerson, Larry, 301

Wills, David, 110–11

Wills, Garry, 111

Wilson, Bob, 38

Wilson, Woodrow, 123

Winter, Jay, 10–11, 152, 154, 170

Wolff, Lester, 200, 201, 202, 206, 212

Wolfowitz, Paul, 234

Womack, Sammie, 21

Women: political mobilization of, 26–27, 116–17, 141, 170, 295; women's liberation movement, 27, 71–73; and attitudes toward returning POWs, 81

Women Strike for Peace, 38

Woodcock, Leonard, 184–86, 187, 189

Woodcock Commission, 2, 184–86, 187, 188, 255

Woods, Paula, 46

World War I: missing Americans killed in, 2, 101, 102, 334 (n. 3); and democracy of death, 105, 113; Civil War memorials compared to, 118, 337 (n. 75); and graves registration units, 118, 119, 120, 334 (n. 3), 338 (n. 93); and identification discs, 118–19; and recovery of war dead, 118–23, 125, 337 (n. 73); and Unknown Soldier, 122–23; and private memorial associations, 337 (n. 73)

World War II: missing Americans killed in, 2, 101, 123–24, 132, 287, 308 (nn. 6, 10), 335 (n. 4); and Vietnamese rescue of American POWs, 17, 22; missing Germans killed in, 102; missing Japanese killed in, 102; missing Jews killed in Holocaust, 102, 128; missing Russians killed in, 102; and Unknown Soldier remains, 102, 128; and recovery of war dead, 123–28, 130; and lists of American casualties, 124; and graves registration units, 126; and sacrifice conceptualized in aggregate terms, 128, 339 (n. 122); POWs as justification for war, 130, 340 (n. 132)

Worrell, Elaine, 159

Wright, Guy, 168

Wyatt, Wendell, 54

Xuan Thuy, 17, 34, 50, 54, 55

Yorty, Samuel, 58, 322–23 (n. 264)

Yost, Charles, 184

Zablocki, Clement, 37, 38, 39, 98, 132, 133, 134, 340–41 (n. 144)

Zaretsky, Natasha, 15, 159, 192, 203, 309 (n. 22)

Ziegler, Ron, 33

Zinn, Howard, 21

Zogby, John, 304

Zuhoski, Patty, 44, 45, 46, 47

Zwenig, Frances, 275